EDB

Les Issues   aux
                              EDB
#03 Bourgogne France-Conté
        ISBN 2-913120-03-2

TheGreenGuide

Burgundy Jura

Cascade des Tufs, Petite source de la Cuisance near Arbois
© Mathieu Guy/Fotolia.com

MICHELIN

General Manager   Cynthia Clayton Ochterbeck

THEGREENGUIDE **BURGUNDY JURA**

Editorial Manager	Jonathan P. Gilbert
Editor	Jonathan P. Gilbert
Contributing Writers	Wink Lorch, Mike Pedley
Production Manager	Natasha G. George
Cartography	Stephane Anton, Thierry Lemasson
Photo Editor	Yoshimi Kanazawa
Proofreader	Nicky Gyopari
Interior Design	Chris Bell
Cover Design	Chris Bell, Christelle Le Déan
Layout	Michelin Apa Publications Ltd., John Heath
Cover Layout	Michelin Apa Publications Ltd.

Contact Us   The Green Guide
Michelin Maps and Guides
One Parkway South
Greenville, SC 29615, USA
www.michelintravel.com

Michelin Maps and Guides
Hannay House
39 Clarendon Road
Watford, Herts WD17 1JA, UK
℘01923 205240
www.ViaMichelin.com
travelpubsales@uk.michelin.com

Special Sales   For information regarding bulk sales,
customized editions and premium sales,
please contact our Customer Service
Departments:
USA   1-800-432-6277
UK   01923 205240
Canada 1-800-361-8236

Note to the reader Addresses, phone numbers, opening hours and prices published in this guide are accurate at the time of press. We welcome corrections and suggestions that may assist us in preparing the next edition. While every effort is made to ensure that all information printed in this guide is correct and up-to-date, Michelin Apa Publications Ltd. accepts no liability for any direct, indirect or consequential losses howsoever caused so far as such can be excluded by law.

HOW TO USE THIS GUIDE

PLANNING YOUR TRIP

The blue-tabbed PLANNING YOUR TRIP section gives you **ideas for your trip** and **practical information** to help you organise it. You'll find tours, a host of outdoor activities, a calendar of events, information on shopping, sightseeing, kids' activities and more.

INTRODUCTION

The orange-tabbed INTRODUCTION section explores Burgundy Jura's **Nature** and geology. The **History** section spans from prehistory to the 1100th anniversary of Cluny's Abbey. The **Art and Culture** section covers architecture, art, literature and music, while **The Region Today** delves into modern Burgundy Jura.

DISCOVERING

The green-tabbed DISCOVERING section features Principal Sights by region, featuring the most interesting local **Sights**, **Walking Tours**, nearby **Excursions**, and detailed **Driving Tours**. Admission prices shown are normally for a single adult.

ADDRESSES

We've selected the best hotels, restaurants, cafés, shops, nightlife and entertainment to fit all budgets. See the Legend on the cover flap for an explanation of the price categories. See the back of the guide for an index of hotels and restaurants.

Sidebars

Throughout the guide you will find blue, orange and green-coloured text boxes with lively anecdotes, detailed history and background information.

😊 A Bit of Advice 😊

Green advice boxes found in this guide contain practical tips and handy information relevant to the sight in the Discovering section.

STAR RATINGS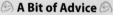

Michelin has given star ratings for more than 100 years. If you're pressed for time, we recommend you visit the ★★★ or ★★ sights first:

★★★	**Highly recommended**
★★	**Recommended**
★	**Interesting**

MAPS AND PLANS

- 🐾 Regional Driving Tours map.
- 🐾 Places to Stay map.
- 🐾 Principal Sights map.
- 🐾 Region maps.
- 🐾 Maps for major cities and villages.
- 🐾 Local tour maps.
- 🐾 Floorplans and illustrations.

All maps in this guide are oriented north, unless otherwise indicated by a directional arrow. The term "Local Map" refers to a map within the chapter or Tourism Region. A complete list of the maps found in the guide appears at the back of this book.

PLANNING
YOUR TRIP

INTRODUCTION
TO BURGUNDY
JURA

DISCOVERING
BURGUNDY
JURA

© Jean Pierre Lescourret/hemis.fr

CONTENTS

Welcome to Burgundy Jura

A heart-shaped wedge in the bosom of France, prosperous Burgundy is synonymous with robust food and heavenly wine. Powerful dukes left its vibrant green landscapes littered with a rich historical and cultural legacy. To the east, Franche-Comté is France off the beaten track, rising from sleepy farmland to scenic lakes and forest-cloaked Alpine peaks.

Burgundy

DIJON AND LA CÔTE (pp88–126)

Burgundy's A-list sights cluster in Dijon and Beaune. Dijon's ancient centre is a delight to discover on foot; wine capital Beaune's highlight is the superb Hôtel-Dieu with its famous polyptych of the Last Judgement. Between the two, the road signs along the N74 read like a roll-call of to-die-for wines beneath hillsides cascading with primped vineyards. Tasting sessions and cellar visits are a must.

SOUTHERN BURGUNDY (pp127–158)

The great Romanesque churches that sprang from Burgundy's monastic history are an essential facet of the region. Cluny's ruined abbey was once the greatest of them all – see it, then let off steam by exploring the car-free Voie Verte trail and the Mâconnais vineyards. In bucolic Bresse, the Louhans poultry market is a memorable spectacle.

BRIONNAIS AND CHAROLAIS (pp159–178)

Car touring is a good way to unlock the treasures of this region's rolling green pastures. Carnivores are in for a treat thanks to the renowned Charolais beef, while the golden Romanesque churches of the Brionnais country are food for the soul of culture vultures. The highlight is Charlieu abbey, an opportunity to see how Cluny once looked.

THE MORVAN (pp179–207)

The great outdoors beckons for sporty types in the Morvan's wild forests and lakes. But it's not all about hiking and biking: Vézelay's Romanesque basilica is a highlight of all France, and Rabelaisian food awaits in Saulieu.

THE NIVERNAIS AND PUISAYE (pp208–224)

The Loire has sculpted the character of the Nivernais region. Fine pottery and spun glass made lovely Nevers famous, while high-octane thrills are on offer at Magny-Cours racetrack. The moody forest country of the Puisaye was home to writer Colette; at Guédelon, see a medieval castle being built from scratch.

SENS AND THE AUXERROIS (pp225–248)

Auxerre and Sens on the River Yonne have the deeply-layered history you expect of ancient French towns, and a lively 21C buzz in their shopping streets. Elsewhere, the region offers Renaissance châteaux, the Burgundy canal and the Chablis vineyards.

FONTENAY AND THE AUXOIS (pp249–263)

The great abbey at Fontenay is the stand-out sight in this seductive region. Semur-en-Auxois is a classic French town made for aimless ambling before a visit to see Flavigny's aniseed sweets being made; and don't miss the unique portrait gallery at the Château de Bussy-Rabutin.

Franche-Comté Jura
PAYS DE DOLE AND BESANÇON
(pp266–298)

Dole never wanted to be French but Louis XIV won out and France can be proud of its fine old quarter. Lively Besançon ticks over nicely with its cathedral clocktower and Museum of Time, set dramatically in a coil of the River Doubs. The region's rivers and the Forêt de Chaux are made for outdoor pursuits; you can relax afterwards in a salt-water spa.

SAÔNE VALLEY *(pp299–312)*

The lazy Saône runs through gently rolling farmland east of the Burgundian heartlands, a landscape in complete contrast to the region's wooded mountains and lakes. From Gray to Vesoul is particularly scenic, with forest and riverside trails to hike and bike – or why not hop on a boat in Gray for a leisurely river cruise?

Ray-sur-Saône, Saône Valley

© Hervé Hughes/hemis.fr

MONTBÉLIARD, BELFORT AND BALLONS DES VOSGES *(pp313–332)*

Whether you're driving or hiking, the rounded summits and dramatic gorges of the Ballons des Vosges are unmissable. Vauban left his mark on pretty Belfort with his looming citadel, but Le Corbusier's curvy concrete chapel at Ronchamp will also stand the test of time. History has left Montbéliard with a distinct Germanic air, and the Peugeot motor museum.

PONTARLIER AND THE HAUT-DOUBS *(pp333–352)*

Once famous for its fiery absinthe, Pontarlier fosters healthier pursuits nowadays as a busy summer and winter resort for mountain sports. Hard by the Swiss border, hikers can test their mettle discovering trails around the plunging waterfalls and grottoes that litter the Doubs Valley.

LONS, ARBOIS AND THE LAKES
(pp353–381)

The Jura lake district, its forests and the Cascades du Hérisson waterfalls offer activities from hiking, biking and horse riding to every kind of watersport. For the less energetic, you can indulge in the unusual Jura wines from Arbois or Château-Chalon, with a piece of Comté cheese from Poligny.

HAUT JURA AND PAYS DE GEX
(pp382–400)

This region bordering Geneva and Lac Leman is where things start to look more like the Alps. The Monts Jura and Les Rousses offer winter sports of all kinds and summer hiking, while the views from some of the highest peaks in the Parc Naturel Régional du Haut-Jura provide the visual drama.

BUGEY *(pp401–415)*

Within easy striking distance of Lyon, the southern Jura's modest peaks such as Grand Colombier give sweeping views across the Alps. Necklaced by the Rhône, the Bugey offers great scenic drives, while pike from Nantua's lake find their way into *quenelles*, the local gastronomic speciality.

View of the Rhône and Lac de Bourget from the Grande Colombier, the Bugey

© Camille Moirenc/hemis.fr

When and Where to Go

WHEN TO GO

Burgundy enjoys a semi-continental climate with marked contrasts between the seasons. The air is sharp in spite of frequent periods of bright weather except in the south of the region where the Mediterranean influence can already be felt.

Other than at the height of summer, the mountainous Jura receives a fair amount of rain which is responsible for the lush pastures, rushing streams and rivers, and numerous cascades and waterfalls.

In **winter**, it can be very cold in Burgundy even when the sun is out. The Jura summits and plateaux are covered with snow and many resorts offer very good skiing conditions. When the weather turns extremely cold, it is even possible to skate on the many ponds and small lakes.

In **spring**, nights in Burgundy are fresh, even frosty, until late May. As for the Jura mountains, they are still white in late April, but when the snow starts to melt, the landscapes come to life with a multitude of cascading streams and rushing waterfalls.

Summer in Burgundy can be hot, although tempered by cool showers; glorious sunsets light up the façades of churches and old mansions. On the other hand, it is never too hot on the high plateaux and in the mountains of the Jura region; even down in the valleys, woods provide shade and keep the heat out.

Early **autumn** is the ideal season to enjoy Burgundian landscapes and gastronomy; the sun shines generously as the Morvan heights act as a screen against Atlantic weather. Later on fog invades river valleys and frost settles in the region's forests. In the Jura, deciduous trees put on warm golden hues which contrast with the dark green colour of fir trees; the inevitable heavy rainfall turns mountain streams into gushing torrents.

WEATHER FORECAST

Météo-France offers detailed information at national, regional and local level. This information is updated three times a day and is valid for five days. www.meteofrance.com.

THEMED TOURS

Travel itineraries on specific themes have been mapped out to help you discover the regional architectural heritage and the traditions which make up the cultural heritage of the region. You will find brochures in tourist offices, and the routes are generally well marked and easy to follow (signs along the roads).

Summer – walking along the vineyards in Mercurey, La Côte Chalonnaise

Alain Doire/Bourgogne Tourisme

Château de Sully – Route Historique des Ducs de Bourgogne

Alain Doire/Bourgogne Tourisme

HISTORIC ROUTES

The **Fédération nationale des Routes historiques** (*www.routes-historiques.com*) has created itineraries for the region that explore France's architectural heritage in a historical context. Brochures and maps are available from the local contacts listed, or from La Demeure Historique, Hôtel de Nesmond, 57 quai de la Tournelle, 75005 Paris. ℘01 55 42 60 00. www.demeure-historique.org.

Route Historique des Ducs de Bourgogne

Information is available from Château de Sully, 71360 Sully. ℘03 85 82 09 86. www.routedesducs.com, or from the Office de Tourisme de Pouilly-en-Auxois. ℘03 80 90 74 24. www.pouilly-auxois.com.

Route Historique des Monts et Merveilles de Franche-Comté

The route includes the châteaux of Arlay, Belvoir, Joux, Gy, Filain and the Saline royale d'Arc-et-Senans. Contact Christian Jouffroy, BP 233, 25204 Montbéliard. ℘03 81 91 45 12. www.chateaux-france.com.

TOURIST TRAINS

A number of charming old steam trains, often running off the beaten track, enable visitors to discover sites otherwise inaccessible.

Petit train de la Côte-d'Or (*Gare de Plombières-Canal, 21370 Plombières-lès-Dijon;* ℘03 80 45 88 51) runs along the Ouche and the Canal de Bourgogne. Departure from Lac Kir.

Train touristique des Lavières (*21120 Isle-sur-Tille;* ℘03 80 95 36 36), runs through the pine forest near Isle-sur-Tille.

Chemin de fer de la vallée de l'Ouche (*1 r. de la Gare, 21360 Bligny-sur-Ouche;* ℘06 30 01 48 29; *www.lepetittraindebligny.com*) takes steam or diesel trains along the old track between Dijon and Épinac, leaving from Bligny-sur-Ouche Station and running to Pont-d'Ouche; July and August: daily; early May to the end of September: Sundays and holidays.

Chemin de fer des Combes (*r. des Pyrénées, 71200 Le Creusot;* ℘03 85 55 26 23) offers a good view of Le Creusot and the Morvan heights; 10km/6mi journey through a wooded park; steam engine dating from 1917.

Chemin de fer touristique de Puisaye (*av. de la Gare, 89130 Toucy;* ℘03 86 44 05 58) runs small trucks and steam-powered tractors along the old track; railway museum open weekends and holidays from May to the last Sunday in September.

Coni'fer – Between Les Hôpitaux-Neufs and Fontaine Ronde (*description and information, see MÉTABIEF-MONT D'OR*).

11

View over Vézelay

© France Montgolfières SARL/Bourgogne Tourisme

Saint-Claude to Morez (*1 Grande-Rue, 39170 St-Lupicin;* ℘03 84 42 85 96) is an old 25km/15mi line running along part of the Bienne gorge, with unfolding beautiful landscapes. It is dotted with tunnels and various engineering structures. The journey is often combined with thematic visits.

FROM ABOVE

Weather permitting, there are various ways of getting a bird's-eye view of the Burgundy-Jura region, from microlights (ULMs, *ultra-legers motorisés*), light aircraft or hot-air balloons (*montgolfières*).
Microlights – École professionnelle Alizé, Route de Lons, 39130 Doucier. ℘03 84 25 71 93.
Light aircraft – Aéroclub de promotion de l'aviation comtoise, Aérodrome de la Vèze, 25660 La Vèze. ℘03 81 81 50 82.
Aéroclub de Gray – r. St-Adrien, 70100 Gray. ℘03 84 65 00 84.

Hot-Air Balloons

It is also possible to take a trip in a hot-air balloon (generally allow about half a day for 1hr–1hr 30min in the air). Balloons fly over the Côte de Beaune vineyards during fine weather; flights last from 1hr to 3hrs from April to November and take place either early in the morning or towards the end of the day to take advantage of the most favourable weather conditions.
Air Adventures – 21320 Commarin. ℘03 80 90 74 23.
Air Escargot – 71150 Remigny. ℘03 85 87 12 30. www.air-escargot.com.
France Montgolfières – ℘02 54 32 20 48. www.franceballoons.com.
Club aérostatique de Franche-Comté – 90150 Foussemagne. ℘03 84 90 20 20.

RIVER CRUISING

Three rivers – the Yonne, the Saône and its tributary the Seille – together with several canals or stretches of canal provide about 1 200km/1 931mi of navigable waterway for those who would like to visit Burgundy by boat. The Jura region offers its fair share of rivers (the Saône and the Doubs), canals (Canal de l'Est and Canal Rhin-Rhône) and lakes (Lac de Vouglans) – all in all, over 320km/200mi of waterways – to boating enthusiasts, who can either opt for a cruise or hire their own craft.

Houseboats

No licence is required to hire a boat but the helmsman must be an adult; a practical and theoretical lesson is given at the beginning of the hire period. To pilot such a boat successfully one must observe the speed limits and heed the advice of the rental company instructor, particularly when mooring or passing through locks. Canals are usually closed to navigation from mid-November to mid-March. Before leaving you are advised to obtain suitable maps and guides (*Collection Navicarte*, *Éditions du Breil,*or *Collection Vagnon*). The main embarkation ports are Digoin, St-Jean-de-Losne and Tournus (Burgundy), Gray, Joigny and Montbéliard.

The **Comité régional de tourisme de Bourgogne** (*see Know Before You Go*) publishes a brochure entitled *Tourisme fluvial en Bourgogne*, listing the names and addresses of all the boat-hire companies.

Groupement pour le tourisme fluvial (*6 r. de Chalezeule, 25000 Besançon; ℘03 81 88 71 38*) offers free brochures on request.

Boat Trips

These can last for 1hr, half a day or a day, in which case a meal is usually served aboard the vessel.

Les Bateaux du Saut du Doubs, Compagnie Droz-Bartholet, Les Terres Rouges, 25130 Villers-le-Lac. ℘03 81 68 13 25. www.sautdudoubs.fr. Trips to Besançon and the Saut du Doubs from Easter to 1 November.

CNFS – Vedettes panoramiques, BP 30, 25130 Villers-le-Lac. ℘03 81 68 05 34. www.vedettes-panoramiques. com. Cruises from Besançon and Villers-le-Lac with or without meal.

Le Vagabondo, departure from Quai Mavia, 70100 Gray. ℘06 07 42 75 54. www.bateauvagabondo.com. Guided trips along the Saône; also cruises with meal included.

Barge-Hotels

There are about a dozen of these in Burgundy; cruises lasting from two to seven days provide full board and offer a fine chance to discover and appreciate Burgundian gastronomy. Barges can accommodate 6 to 24 passengers and prices vary from 760€ to 2 300€ per person per week, including transfer from the airport, excursions, evening entertainment and wine-cellar visits.

TRADITIONS AND CULTURAL HERITAGE

These routes cover a selection of themes of regional interest from cheese and wine to art and famous figures of the past.

Route des Châteaux de Bourgogne du Sud

The itinerary includes, among others, the châteaux of Sully, Couches, Cormatin and La Ferté Abbey. Contact Maison de la Saône-et-Loire, 389 av. de Lattre-de-Tassigny, 71000 Mâcon. ℘03 85 21 02 20.

Exploring the region by houseboat

Alain Doire/Bourgogne Tourisme

Jura vineyards

© CRT Franche-Comté/Pierre Jouille

Route des Trésors de Puisaye
Contact the Maison de la Puisaye-Forterre. &03 86 74 19 27.
www.puisaye-forterre.com.

Route de Madame de Sévigné
From Châtillon-sur-Seine to Saulieu.
&03 80 92 18 87.

Route de la Bresse
Two signposted loops (200km/124mi) explore the landscape, traditions, heritage and gastronomy of the Bresse region. Free guidebook; enquire at the Fédération Départementale des Routes Touristiques, 34 r. Général-Delestraint, BP 78, 01002 Bourg-en-Bresse Cedex. &04 74 32 31 30. www.ain-tourisme.com. Other guides available: Route des Étangs de la Dombes, Route du Bugey.

Route des Vins du Jura
80km/50mi tour from Salins-les-Bains to St-Amour through the great vineyards of the Jura region; visit the wine museum in Arbois. Contact the Comité Interprofessionnel des Vins du Jura, Château Pécauld, BP 41, 39602 Arbois Cedex. &03 84 66 26 14. www.laroutedesvinsdejura.com.

Route des Retables
This route enables visitors to discover more than 80 splendid altarpieces

mostly made after the Reformation. Information is available from the SEM Destination 70, BP 57, 70001 Vesoul Cedex. &03 84 97 10 70. hautesaone retables.free.fr.

Routes du Comté
The famous Comté cheese represents one of the strongest traditions of the Jura region. Several itineraries have been mapped out to include visits to farms and maturing cellars as well as meetings with local people willing to share their knowledge and enthusiasm with visitors. Information from the Maison du Comté in Poligny. &03 84 37 23 51. www.lesroutesducomte.com.

Route Pasteur
In the footsteps of Louis Pasteur via Dole, Arbois and Salins-les-Bains. Contact:
Office de Tourisme de Dole, pl. Grévy, 39100 Dole. &03 84 72 11 22.
Office de Tourisme d'Arbois, Hôtel de Ville, 39600 Arbois. &03 84 66 55 50.
Office de Tourisme de Salins, pl. des Salines, 39110 Salins. &03 84 73 01 34.

A TASTE OF THE REGION

Several sites in the region (among them production facilities, fairs, markets, demonstrations) have been labelled *Sites Remarquables du Goût* (Noteworthy sites for taste).

In Burgundy, these include Beaune (vente des Hospices), Bourg-en-Bresse (Glorieuses), Chablis, Charolles, Flavigny (aniseed sweets), Louhans (poultry market), St-Christophe-en-Brionnais (beef market), Saulieu, Villargoix (Fête du Charolais) and Vougeot (Château du Clos de Vougeot). For more information on these and other sites, visit www.legout.com.

Anis de Flavigny

S. Sauvignier/MICHELIN

NATURE

The routes below focus on areas of exceptional natural beauty.

Route des Mille Étangs – 61km/38mi tour of the southern part of the Vosges: Melisey, Servance, Beulotte-St-Laurent, Faucogney, Écromagny… Contact the Parc Régional des Ballons des Vosges, Maison du Parc, 1 cour de l'Abbaye, 68140 Munster. ℘03 89 77 90 20. www.parc-ballons-vosges.fr.

Route des Sapins and Route des Lacs – ℭ see *ROUTE DES SAPINS* and *RÉGION DES LACS DU JURA* . Further information is available from the Office de Tourisme de Champagnole. ℘03 84 52 43 67.

LOCAL INDUSTRY AND HANDICRAFT

Burgundy and Jura have a wealth of traditional industries that perpetuate ancestral skills and contribute to technical innovation. The Chamber of Commerce and Industry in Dijon publishes a regularly updated guide to local indsuties in the Côte-d'Or département. Some interesting industrial sights covered in this guide include:

- ◆ The **Grande Forge de Buffon** near Montbard
- ◆ **La Mine et les Hommes** in Blanzy, near Le Creusot-Montceau
- ◆ The **Museum of Man and Industry** in Le Creusot
- ◆ The **underground quarry** in Aubigny
- ◆ The **Musée Nicéphore-Niépce** in Châlon-sur-Saône
- ◆ The **Musée Frédéric-Japy** in Beaucourt
- ◆ The **Forge-Musée** in Étueffont, near Belfort

Maturing of the Comté cheese

© CRT Franche-Comté/CIGC

- The **Écomusée du Pays de la Cerise** in Fougerolles
- The **Musée du Jouet** in Moirans-en-Montagne
- The **Taillanderie** in Nans-sous-Ste-Anne
- The **Musée de la Mine** in Ronchamp
- The **Salines** in Salins-les-Bains
- The **Forges de Syam**

COURSES IN LOCAL COOKING

The art of living well is also the art of eating well and Burgundy is, among other things, synonymous with fine food. The region boasts numerous renowned restaurants which form a sort of a triumphal path to Saulieu, the gourmet capital of Burgundy. But proceed carefully: each village possesses its little auberge, small establishments offering carefully prepared meals using the area's wealth of fresh products.

- **Maison Régionale des Arts de la Table**
  Lovers of fine cuisine will not want to miss this annual themed exhibition of gastronomy and the culinary arts, as well as a boutique and tearoom for tasting.
  15 r. St-Jacques, 21230 Arnay-le-Duc. &03 80 90 11 59.
  www.arnay-le-duc.com.

Cooking course at Château d'Ancy-le-Franc

© Château d'Ancy-le-Franc/Bourgogne Tourisme

- **Terroir de l'Yonne**
  Information and sales for regional products.
  7 pl. de l'Hôtel-de-Ville, 89000 Auxerre. &03 86 48 22 22.
  www.terroir-yonne.com.

If your favourite pastime involves pots and pans, why not spend a few days in a prestigious French kitchen for a holiday? These courses take place mainly in winter.

- **À la découverte de la truffe et des vins de Bourgogne**
  Saturday mornings from mid-September to mid-December: all about truffles with Chef Jean-Luc Barnabet and a truffle-grower, ending with a tasting session. Service Loisirs Accueil Yonne.
  1–2 quai de la République, 89000 Auxerre.
  &03 86 72 92 10.
  www.tourisme-yonne.com.
- **Visit Bourgogne (Charrecey)**
  Cooking lessons (1 to 5 days).
  M. Carpentier, &03 85 45 38 97.
- **ABC de la Cuisine (Joigny)**
  Contemporary cooking presented by Jean-Michel Lorain (course including accommodation); cost, programme and calendar on request.
  &03 86 62 09 70.
  www.cotesaintjacques.com.
- **Les Toques Nivernaises (Moulins-Engilbert)**
  Courses on a theme which can be chosen by the participants (from 6 to 12 persons).
  M. Jean-François Boschetti, Restaurant Le Bon Laboureur.
  &03 86 84 20 55.
- **Le cellier du Goût (La Charité-sur-Loire)**
  This association organises meals with a commentary, attended by famous chefs, as well as tasting sessions during the summer.
  &03 86 70 36 21.

What to See and Do

OUTDOOR FUN
NATURE PARKS

In this guide you will find information on three Regional Nature Parks; the Morvan in Burgundy, and the Haut Jura and Ballons des Vosges of the Franche Comté Jura.

Parc Naturel Régional du Morvan

🕭 *See p182.* With its forests, deep valleys, numerous waterways and lakes, the Morvan lends itself to a wide range of nature-friendly activities (rambling, themed walks, cycle tours, riding tours, sailing, swimming, white-water sports, rock-climbing…). For full information about the Regional Nature Parks and the leisure activities available, apply to the **Maison du Parc**, 58230 St-Brisson; 𝒞03 86 78 79 00; www.parcdumorvan.org.

Guided Hikes

Guides en Morvan, 71320 Charbonnat, guidesenmorvan@parcdumorvan.org.
Morvan Découverte
La Peurtantaine, École du Bourg, 71550 Anost.
𝒞03 85 82 77 74.
France Randonnée
9 r. des Portes-Mordelaises, 35000 Rennes.
𝒞02 99 67 42 21.
Association Morvan VTT,
Maison du Parc.
𝒞03 86 78 71 77.
Base de plein air,
Plan d'eau du Vallon, 71400 Autun.
𝒞03 85 86 95 80.

Riding Tours

Association pour la randonnée équestre en Morvan (**AREM**), same address as the Maison du Parc, www.morvanacheval.com; additional information available from the Maison du Parc.

ℹ Information and brochures outlining the sports and outdoor facilities available in the region can be obtained from the French Government Tourist Office, or from the organisations listed in this section.

On the Water

Base nautique des Settons,
58230 Montsauche-les-Settons.
𝒞03 86 84 51 98.
www.activital.ne.
Base Activital de loisirs,
Baye, 58110 Bazolles.
𝒞03 86 38 97 39.
White-water sports – AN rafting,
Auberge du lac, 58140 Plainefas.
𝒞03 86 22 65 28.
www.an-rafting.com.
Centre Sport nature de Chaumeçon,
58140 St-Martin-du-Puy.
𝒞03 86 22 61 35.
Ab Loisirs,
Route du camping.
89450 St-Père-sous-Vézelay.
𝒞03 86 33 38 38.

Rock-Climbing

Loisirs en Morvan,
105 r. des Mignottes, 89000 Auxerre.
𝒞03 86 49 55 50.

For other activities, apply to the Maison du Parc or send an email to: morvanloisirssportsnature@ parcdumorvan.org.

PARC NATUREL RÉGIONAL DU HAUT-JURA

🕭 *See p382.* You can find information about activities and nature trails in this regional park at the **Maison du Haut-Jura**, 39310 Lajoux. 𝒞03 84 34 12 30. www.parc.haut-jura.

PARC NATUREL RÉGIONAL DES BALLONS DES VOSGES

🕭 *See p393.* Permanent and temporary exhibitions are held in the **Maison du Parc**, which also provides information and welcomes visitors.

Maison du Parc,
1 cour de l'Abbaye, 68140 Munster.
𝄞03 89 77 90 34.
www.parc-ballons-vosges.fr.

CANOEING AND KAYAKING

This method of exploring local waterways need not be exclusively reserved
for seasoned canoeing experts.
Sometimes this sport can be a pleasant
way to discover secluded spots
inaccessible by any other means.
The main difference between a canoe
and a kayak is that the former is
propelled by a single-bladed paddle
and the latter by a double-bladed
paddle.
Besides the Morvan where streams
and small rivers offer exciting
possibilities to canoeists looking for
a challenge, the Yonne, the Canal
de Bourgogne, the Saône and the
Loire lend themselves to canoeing
trips and competitions organised by
the numerous sport centres of the
**Fédération française de canoë-
kayak** (*87 quai de la Marne, 94344
Joinville-le-Pont; 𝄞01 45 11 08 50;
www.ffcanoe.asso.fr).*
A guide entitled *Vacances en
canoë-kayak* is published annually
by the **Canoë-kayak magazine**
(*1 r. des Rivières, CP 421, 69338 Lyon
Cedex 9; 𝄞04 72 19 87 97; www.
canoekayakmagazine.com).*
🛈 For additional information, contact:

**Comité Régional de
Franche-Comté**
6 av. des Montboucons, 25000
Besançon. 𝄞03 81 48 29 19.
www.crck.org/franchecomte.

Comités Départementaux
Ain: Canoë-kayak 01, 01500
Ambronay. 𝄞04 74 39 14 17.
www.canoe-kayak01.com.
Doubs: Actions Loisirs Eaux Vives,
8 r. des Cantons, 25400 Audincourt.
𝄞03 81 30 62 14 or 06 10 16 38 29.
www.audincourt-ev-canoe.com.
Jura: 1 r. de Crissey, BP 302, 39104
Dole Cedex. 𝄞03 84 79 26 33
www.cdck39.org.

FISHING

Trout, perch, tench and pike abound
in the region's lakes, rivers and canals;
carp and bream are less commonly
found. Some of the rivers of the Jura
département are considered to be
among the best French rivers for
trout fishing.
Regulations – They differ according
to whether the water is classified as
first category (contains trout) or second
category (coarse fish). Generally
speaking, in the case of first category
rivers, the fishing season starts on the
second Saturday in March and ends
on the third Sunday in September.
For second category rivers, fishing
is authorised throughout the year.

Kayaking on the Doubs near Besançon

© steeve janvier/Fotolia.com

Stricter rules apply to fish needing special protection.

Anglers will need either to buy a special holiday fishing permit, valid for two weeks between June and September, or take out annual membership in an officially approved angling association. National regulations state that anglers must return to the water any fish they catch below the minimum permitted length (50cm/20in for pike, 40cm/16in for pike-perch, 23cm/9in for trout, 9cm/4in for crayfish).

Useful Addresses:

- **Maison nationale de l'eau et de la pêche**, 36 r. St-Laurent, 25290 Ornans. ✆03 81 57 14 49.
- **École française de pêche**, BP Courses year-round (1–15 days) for youths and adults. 25, 33112 St-Laurent-Médoc. ✆05 56 59 31 74. www.ecoledepeche.com.
- **Étang du Châtelet** (**Fédération départementale de la pêche**), Fly-fishing from March to October, daily except Tuesday. 7 quai de Mantoue, 58000 Nevers. ✆03 86 61 18 98.
- **Domaine de Tarperon**, rte. de St-Marc, 21510 Aignay-le-Duc. ✆03 80 93 83 74.
- **Château de Thenissey**, r. Pont, 21150 Thenissey. ✆03 80 35 85 55.
- **Au fil de l'eau**, 26 r. de Lyon, 89200 Avallon. ✆03 86 34 50 41.
- **Centre Pêche au Gros**, An introduction to fishing for the carnivorous sheath-fish (up to 3m/10ft long and 150kg/331lb in weight). 4 r. de la Liberté, 71000 Mâcon. ✆03 85 39 07 50. www.peche-au-silure.com.

Lakes and Reservoirs

They are the ideal setting for windsurfing, water-skiing, fishing, rambling and so on.

Burgundy has fewer lakes; however, the following are a selection from those suitable for watersports (mainly windsurfing and water-skiing): Lac de Bourdon (near St-Fargeau), Lac du Pont and Lac de Panthier (Côte-d'Or), Lac Kir (Dijon) and Lac de la Sorme (near Montceau-les-Mines).

Some sections of the Saône, the Yonne and even the Loire are also popular for watersports. Arc-sur-Tille has its own watersports centre, which seats up to 3 000 spectators and is used for competitions.

Further information is available from the **Fédération française de ski nautique**, 27 r. d'Athènes, 75009 Paris. ✆01 53 20 19 19. www.ffsn.fr.

HIKING

Short, medium and long-distance footpath *Topo-Guides* are published by the **Fédération Française de Randonnée Pédestre** (FFRP). These give detailed maps of the paths and offer valuable information to the rambler; they are on sale at the information centre: 64 r. du Dessous des Berges, 75013 Paris; ✆01 44 89 93 90; www.ffrandonnee.fr.

Several long-distance foot-paths *(sentiers de grande randonnée – GR – marked red and white)* cover the Jura:

- Two of them cross the region from north the south, **GR 5**, which skirts the Swiss border, and the **GR 59**, which follows the western edge of the region.
- Another two explore the Doubs area, **GR 590**, which runs through the Loue and Lison valleys starting from Ornans, and **GR 595**, which links GR 59 and GR 5 from Montfaucon (near Besançon) to Maison-du-Bois (near Pontarlier).
- **GR 559** crosses the Jura from Lons-le-Saunier to Les Rousses via Ilay and Bonlieu.
- **GR 9** crosses the Jura from St-Amour in the west to Les Rousses in the east then turns south.

There are a number of regional GR *(GR de pays – red and yellow markings)*; some of them link up with the main GR. The extensive network (6 000km/ 3 728mi) of footpaths crisscrossing Burgundy offers ramblers the possibility of visiting lesser known areas: the Loire islands with their remarkable fauna; Cîteaux or Vauluisant forests; the Puisaye countryside; the ochre-coloured villages of the Mâconnais area; or the vineyards of South Burgundy dotted with Romanesque churches.

Other Useful Addresses:

- **Comité régional de la randonnée pédestre de Bourgogne**, 2 r. des Corroyeurs, Boîte Y1, 21068 Dijon Cedex. ℘03 80 43 15 64. crrpbourgogne@wanadoo.fr.
- **Côte-d'Or**, 1 r. de Ferdinand Lesseps, BP 1601, 21035 Dijon Cedex. ℘03 80 63 64 60.
- **Nièvre**, 31 bis r. Roger Salengro, 58640 Varennes-Vauzelles. ℘03 86 59 09 44.
- **Saône-et-Loire**, Centre de loisirs, Vieille Route d'Ozenay, 71700 Tournus. ℘03 85 51 05 15.
- **Yonne**, Maison des Sports, 12 bd. Galliéni, 89000 Auxerre. ℘03 86 41 22 26. www.randopedestre89.com.

CYCLING

The **Fédération Française de Cyclo-tourisme** (*12 r. Louis-Bertrand, 94207 Ivry-sur-Seine Cedex; ℘01 56 20 88 88; www.ffct.org*) and its local committees recommend a number of cycling tours of various lengths.

The **Fédération Française de Cyclisme** (*5 r. de Rome, 93561 Rosny-sous-Bois; ℘01 49 35 69 00; www.ffc.fr*) publishes a guide which describes 36 000km/ 22 370mi of marked trails suitable for mountain biking.

The following organisations offer cycling holidays in Burgundy:

- **Bourgogne randonnée**, 7 av. du 8-Septembre, 21200 Beaune. ℘03 80 22 06 03. www.terroirs-b.com/br or www. bourgogne-randonnees.com.
- **Dili Voyages**, 10 av. de la République, 21200 Beaune. ℘03 80 24 24 82. dilivoyage@wanadoo.fr.
- **France randonnée**, 9 r. des Portes-Mordelaises, 35000 Rennes. ℘02 99 67 42 21. www.france-randonnee.fr.
- **Cycling for Softies** (*2/4 Birch Polygon, Manchester M14 5HX; ℘0161 248 8282; www.cycling-for-softies.co.uk*) offers three to 14-night bike tours in Burgundy. Stops along the way include famous wine cellars and châteaux, monuments, local markets and restaurants rated in the *Michelin Guide France*.

Burgundy has several mountain-bike (VTT) centres recognised by the Fédération française de Cyclisme:

Cycling in Ray-sur-Saône

© CRT Franche-Comté/Michel Joly

- **Morvan**, *see PARC NATUREL RÉGIONAL DU MORVAN*.
- **La Croix Messire Jean**, 71190 Uchon. ℘03 85 54 42 06. Alt 680m/2231ft. 230km/143mi of trails among rocks and ponds. Here you can learn to read maps and to find your bearings; the centre also organises night tours.
- **Centre VTT Les Granges**, 71960 Serrières; 226km/140mi of trails running across an undulating landscape of vineyards and châteaux. The centre also has a mountain-biking school.
- **Centre VTT de St-Saulge**, Syndicat d'initiative, 58330 St-Saulge. ℘03 86 58 25 74. 16 loops totalling 550km/342mi of trails through the Nièvre region.

The Jura is a mountainous region, so cycling itineraries should be designed according to the level of skill. Information and advice can be obtained from:
- **Ligue de cyclotourisme de Franche-Comté (FFCT)** 14 r. de la Pépinière, 70000 Vesoul. ℘03 84 76 75 53.
- **Comité régional de cyclisme de Franche-Comté** 3 av. des Montboucons, 25000 Besançon. ℘03 81 52 17 13. www.franchecomtecyclisme.fr.

There are excellent possibilities for downhill or cross-country mountain biking, the most famous site being Métabief where the world European and French championships take place. A highlight here for many is the 300km/186mi trail of the **Grande Traversée du Jura** (*see Cross-Country Skiing*).

HORSE RIDING

There are many riding centres in Burgundy and in the Jura. They offer courses, excursions, forest rides and riding holidays. In addition, a visit to the **Cluny stud farm**, one of the most renowned in France, is not to be missed (*Haras nationaux de Cluny, 2 r. Porte-des-Prés, 71250 Cluny*; ℘03 85 59 85 00; www.haras-nationaux.fr*).

Comité National de Tourisme Équestre
9 bd. Macdonald, 75019 Paris; ℘01 53 26 15 50; www.ffe.com. The Comité publishes an annual brochure entitled *Tourisme et loisirs équestres en France*. Information on riding in Burgundy and the Jura is available from the **Comités départementaux** (list of local centres, activities, accommodation, riding tours lasting from 2 to 8 days):
- **Côte-d'Or**: La Houblonnière, 21250 Pouilly-sur-Saône. ℘03 80 20 45 81.
- **Nièvre**: Marie-Pierre Lauprêtre, 58700 Nolay. ℘03 86 68 08 15.
- **Saône-et-Loire**: Pierre Jalabert, 71460 St-Gengoux-le-National. ℘03 85 50 77 80.
- **Yonne**: M. Bruneau, 89740 Cruzy-le-Châtel. ℘03 86 75 23 16. www.yonneacheval.com.
- **Doubs**: M. Patrick David, Les Attelages des deux lacs, 109 r. des Grangettes, 25160 Malpas. ℘03 81 69 64 09.
- **Jura**: Jean-Pierre Étienne, r. de la Fromagerie, 39150 Bief-des-Maisons. ℘06 48 95 83 49. j-p.etienne@hotmail.fr.
- **Haute-Saône**: Joël Monney, 5 r. de la Cornée, 70800 Anjeux. ℘03 84 49 43 00. joel.monney@wanadoo.fr.
- **Territoire de Belfort**: Pierre-Alain Steffen, 4ter r. des Rochers, 25490 Dampierre-les-Bois. ℘03 81 93 03 06. pat.steffen@hotmail.fr.

Other Regional Addresses:
- **Liberté (association)**: Mairie, 58800 Corbigny. ℘03 86 20 08 04. www.bourgogneacheval.com.
- **Ligue équestre de Bourgogne**: 6 r. du Palais, 21000 Dijon. ℘03 80 30 05 08.
- **Comité régionale de tourisme équestre de Franche-Comté**: 52 r. de Dole, 25000 Besançon. ℘03 81 80 11 16.

Mountain Safety

Choosing the right equipment for a rambling, cross-country ski or snow-shoe expedition is essential. If walking in the summer, choose flexible hiking shoes with non-slip soles, bring a rain jacket or poncho, an extra sweater, sun protection (hat, glasses and lotion), drinking water (1–2 litres per person), high energy snacks (chocolate, cereal bars, bananas), and a first aid kit. Of course, you'll need a good map (and a compass if you plan to leave the main trails). Plan your itinerary well, keeping in mind that while the average walking speed for an adult is 4kph/2.5mph, you will need time to eat and rest, and children will not keep up the same pace.

For winter expeditions, plan your itinerary carefully. Even if it is beautiful and sunny when you set out, take warm, waterproof clothing in case of a sudden storm or if you are surprised by nightfall. Always have some food and water with you. Do not leave the groomed trails unless you are with an experienced guide. Read the notices at trail entrances in regard to avalanche alerts and weather reports. Protect exposed skin from the sun with an effective lotion.

Always leave your itinerary and expected time of return with someone before setting out (innkeeper, fellow camper or friend).

If you are caught in an electrical storm, avoid high ground, and do not move along a ridge top; do not seek shelter under overhanging rocks, isolated trees in otherwise open areas, at the entrance to caves or other openings in the rocks, or in the proximity of metal fences or gates. Do not use a metallic survival blanket. If possible, position yourself at least 15m/16.5yd from the highest point around you (rock or tree); crouch with your knees up and without touching the rock face with your hands or any exposed part of your body.

◆ **Jura du Grand Huit**: 3 r. Louis-Rousseau, BP 458, 39006 Lons-le-Saunier Cedex. &03 84 87 08 88. www.jura-grand-huit.com.

BAROUCHE RIDES

Horse-drawn carriages make an interesting way to explore the countryside at a gentle pace, whether for a few hours or several days.
Ferme équestre de l'Étang Fourchu, Les Écarts de la Chapelle, 90100 Florimont. &03 84 29 61 59.
Association Picheval, 39230 Darbonnay, &03 84 85 53 00 (wagon rides from 1hr to several days).

GOLF

The popularity of golf, which took off in the early 1980s, is steadily increasing. In 1998, more than 260 000 golf players were officially registered in France, indulging in their favourite sport on around 500 golf links.
The map *Golfs, les Parcours Français,* published by Éditions Plein Sud and based on **Michelin map no 721**, provides useful information on the location, address and type of golf course open to players throughout the country.
Fédération Française de Golf, 68 r. Anatole-France, 92309 Levallois-Perret. &01 41 49 77 00. www.ffgolf.org. There are 19 golf courses in Burgundy's four *départements*; the website of the **Comité régional de tourisme** (*www.crt-bourgogne.fr*) provides all the relevant information: list of courses with detailed address, description, prices, accommodation and so on.

SKIING

Cross-Country Skiing

The Jura region is ideal for **cross-country skiing**, because of the variety of relief to be found here. There are more than 2 000km/1 245mi of clearly marked, well-groomed trails.
A big event for lovers of this strenuous, yet peaceful sport is the **Transjurassienne**, a 76km/47mi race

Transjurassienne

© Jeff Pachoud/AFP Creative/Photmonstop

from Lamoura to Mouthe. Since 1984, the course has been included in the Nordic World Cup series, a set of races held in different countries over the season. Contact Trans Organisation, Espace Lamartine, BP 20126, 39404 Morez; ☎03 84 33 45 13. A visit to the website (*www.transjurassienne.com*), with photographs and advice, will make you long to grab your poles and join this ski celebration.

Grande Traversée du Jura

Known as the GTJ to those in the know, this cross-country ski route of over 300km/124mi, with a main trail and five intermediate trails crossing through several French *départements*, along the contours of the Haut-Doubs and through evergreen forests. The national cross-country training school is at Prémanon, near Les Rousses. If you plan on skiing along this route, **Jura Randonnées** (*39370 Les Bouchoux;* ☎*03 84 42 73 17; www. jura-rando.com*), will help organise your tour (accommodation, transport of luggage, guides, maps etc).

🛈 For more information about courses and ski tours, contact:
Accueil Montagnard, *25240* Chapelle-des-Bois; ☎03 81 69 26 19; accueil.montagnard.free.fr.
To plan a ski adventure, contact the **Espace Nordique Jurassien**, BP 132, 390304 Champagnole

Cedex; ☎03 84 52 58 10; www. espacenordiquejurassien.com.

🛶 Alpine Skiing

The Jura cannot compete with the Alps in terms of snow cover, steepness of downhill runs and equipment, yet the three ski resorts of Les Rousses, Métabief-Mont d'Or and Monts-Jura are expanding owing to the quality of their equipment, including snow cannons, which make up for the irregularity of the snow cover.

Dog Sledging

Races are organised at La Pesse (Jura) and Les Fourgs (Doubs). Sledge racing began in 1979 with the creation of the first dog-sledging club and this sport has grown in popularity ever since. Four different breeds of dogs are used: Siberian huskies (the fastest), Alaskan malamutes (the strongest), wolf-like Eskimo dogs from Greenland and white Arctic Samoyeds. These breeds are better suited either for touring or racing and are trained accordingly. The driver, or musher, either stands at the back of a sledge pulled by a team of dogs or skis beside the team harnessed to a kind of Scandinavian sledge known as a *pulka*.

Parc du chien polaire

Le Cernois Veuillet, 25240 Chaux-Neuve. ☎03 81 69 20 20.

Dog sledging in Jura

© Patrick Frilet/hemis.fr

www.parcduchienpolaire.com. Sledge tours for beginners or specialists. You can visit the husky park, take sledge-driving treks (three or four dogs) and even sleep in tepees.

HANG-GLIDING AND PARAGLIDING

The Jura region is ideally suited to these airborne sports. Hang-gliding is the more complicated of the two, requiring a degree of technical understanding of aerodynamics. Beginners should only attempt it under properly qualified supervision.

École de vol libre du Poupet, 9 r. du Poupet, 39110 St-Thiébaud. ☎03 84 73 04 56. www.poupetvollibre.com.

Club des sports des Rousses (maiden flights on a paraglider for two), 495 r. Pasteur, 39220 Les Rousses. ☎03 84 60 35 14.

ROCK-CLIMBING

Burgundy offers valuable experience to would-be mountaineers at the following sites:

Saussois rocks (Yonne) and their overhangs: these overlook D 100 between Mailly-la-Ville and Châtel-Censoir;

Saffres (Côte-d'Or): 6km/3.7mi from Vitteaux, a rock-climbing school and site particularly sought after at weekends.

Other sites: Bouilland, Hauteroche and Vieux-Château (for experienced climbers), Chambolle-Musigny and Talant (for learning and practising);

Clamecy area (Nièvre): Surgy and Basseville rocks.

GO-KARTING

There is a karting track (1 110m/1 214yd long, forming two loops) for the over-12s beside the Nevers-Magny-Cours Grand-Prix race track.

Laffite Système Karting
Complexe Automobile de Pouilly-en-Auxois, 21320 Meilly-sur-Rouvres. ☎03 80 90 60 77. Quadbikes for guided forest trail rides.

NATURE AND THE ENVIRONMENT

Nature lovers will find a wealth of information about nature trails, hiking and outdoor activities, exhibitions concerning nature and the environment and ongoing projects in the brochure *La Bourgogne Loisirs nature* (available from tourist offices) and by contacting the following:

Maison de la nature des Vosges saônoises, Le Belmont, 70440 Haut-du-Them. ☎03 84 63 89 41. www.mnvs.fr.

**Maison départementale de
l'environnement**,
Étang de Malsaucy,
90350 Évette-Salbert.
✆03 84 29 18 12.
**DPIE Atelier de l'environnement
du Haut-Jura**,
1 Grande-Rue, 39170 St-Lupicin.
✆03 84 42 85 96.

SPAS [Spa]

The benefits of spa treatments,
known to the Romans and probably
the Gauls, were rediscovered in the
18–19C. At that time, taking the waters
was reserved for wealthy clients
with time to spare. Today, the French
national health system recognises the
therapeutic value of many cures, and
patients' stays are provided for, all or
in part, by the social security system.
Treatment takes up only part of the
day, so spas offer guests many other
sports and recreation activities.
Traditional treatment courses usually
last three weeks, but many resorts
offer shorter stays with specific
goals – stress relief, relaxation,
fitness, quitting smoking, weight
loss and more. Go to www.tourisme.
fr and search the category "Spas and
Fitness" for information (mostly in
French) on accommodation, short-
stay treatments, entertainment etc.
If you would like to arrange a spa
treatment, be sure to plan in advance.
Reservations may be scarce at
certain times of the year, and special
conditions, including a prior medical
examination, may apply.

- ◆ **Centre d'information thermale**
  – 1 r. Cels, 75014 Paris. ✆01 53 91
  05 75. www.france-thermale.org.
- ◆ **Bourbon-Lancy** – *quartier thermal*
  (slightly radioactive waters),
  5 pl. Aligre, 71140 Bourbon-Lancy.
  ✆03 85 89 18 84.
  www.bourbon-lancy.com.
- ◆ **Divonne-les-Bains** – Thermes
  de Divonne, av. des Thermes,
  01220 Divonne-les-Bains.
  ✆04 50 20 05 70 (fitness centre).
  www.valvital.fr.

- ◆ **Lons-le-Saunier** – Valvital Thermes
  de Lons-Le-Saunier – Parc des Bains.
  ✆03 84 24 20 34. www.valvital.fr.
- ◆ **Luxeuil-les-Bains** – Chaîne
  Thermale du Soleil – r. des
  Thermes. ✆03 84 40 44 22.
  www.luxeuil.fr.
- ◆ **Saint-Honoré-les-Bains** –
  Établissement thermal (the waters
  contain sulphur), BP 8, 58360
  St-Honoré-les-Bains.
  ✆03 86 30 73 27.
  www.saint-honore-les-bains.com.
- ◆ **Salins-les-Bains** – Les Thermes –
  (salt waters), pl. des Alliés, 39110,
  Salins-les-Bains. ✆03 84 73 04 63.
  www.thermes-salins.com.

ACTIVITIES FOR KIDS

Burgundy, the Franche Comté and
Jura abound in parks, zoos, museums,
attractions and leisure activities that
will appeal to children. These are
highlighted in the Discovering section,
by the 🛉🛉 symbol. The following is a
small selection:
Museums – The Heads of State
Limousines Museum in Montjalin, the
Motorbike Collection in Savigny-lès-
Beaune Castle, the Old Toys Collection
in the Musée Rural des Arts Populaires
in Laduz.
Buildings – The Briare Canal-bridge,
Le Creusot mining and industrial site,
the Guédelon medieval building site.
Parks and zoos – Parc de l'Auxois,
21350 Arnay-sous-Vitteaux; Parc
naturel de Boutissaint, 89520 Treigny;
Parc zoologique et d'attractions
Touroparc, 71570 Romanèche-Thorins.
Towns designated by the Ministry of
Culture as **Villes d'Art et d'Histoire**
organise discovery tours and cultural-
heritage workshops for children. Fun
books and specially designed tools
are provided, and the activities are
supervised by professionals such as
architects, stonemasons, storytellers,
actors. This programme, called **l'été
des 6-12 ans** (summer activities for 6-
to 12-year-olds), operates during
school holidays in Autun, Auxerre, Beaune,
Besançon, Chalon-sur-Saône, Dijon,
Joigny, Nevers and Paray-le-Monial.

Shopping

Most larger shops are open Mondays to Saturdays from 9am to 6.30pm or 7.30pm. Smaller, individual shops may close for lunch. Food shops – grocers, wine merchants and bakers – generally open from 7am to 6.30pm or 7.30pm; some open on Sunday mornings, many close between noon and 2pm and on Mondays. Some bakery and pastry shops close on Wednesdays. Hypermarkets usually open non-stop until 9pm or later. People travelling to the USA cannot import plant products or fresh food, including fruit, cheese and nuts, but tinned products or preserves are permitted.

RECOVERING VALUE ADDED TAX (VAT)

Value Added Tax in France is known as TVA and is set at 19.6% on almost every purchase. Non-European visitors who spend over 175€ (amount subject to change) in any one participating store can get the VAT refunded. Usually, you fill out a form at the store and present your passport. Upon leaving the country, you submit all forms to customs (they may want to see the goods, so try not to pack them in checked luggage). The refund is usually paid directly into your bank or credit card account, or it can be sent by mail. Big department stores may provide special services to help you; mention before you pay that you plan to seek a refund (no refund is possible for tax on services). If you visit two or more countries within the EU, you submit the forms on departure from the last EU country. The refund is good for visitors buying fashions, furniture or other expensive items, but remember, the minimum amount must be spent in a single shop on a single day.

MARKETS AND LOCAL SPECIALITIES

Markets – All towns and most villages hold traditional markets on at least one day of the week.

Monday mornings – Bresse chicken market in Louhans
Tuesday mornings – Cattle market in Moulins-Engilbert
Wednesday mornings – Cattle market in Charolles
Thursday mornings – Cattle market in St-Christophe-en-Brionnais
Friday mornings – Food market in Autun and Auxerre
Saturday mornings – Covered market in Beaune
Sunday mornings – Burgundy market in Chablis

Local Specialities – Burgundy has been synonymous with great **wine** since the 12C when the Citeaux Abbey monks developed the famous Clos Vougeot. Burgundy is not cheap, starting at around 12€ a bottle; grands crus around 23€; and special bottles can easily cost 75€, or even higher for collectibles. Good wine cellars abound in all the region's wine-growing towns and at specialists in Beaune (a famous wine sale is held during the second half of November, ℓ see Calendar of Events). To learn about wine and vineyards, try **L'Athenaeum**, 5 r. de l'Hôtel-Dieu, Beaune; ℘03 80 25 08 30; www.athenaeumfr.com. If you visit Arbois or Château-Chalon, the Jura region's unique vin jaune is a must.

Handicraft – **Nevers earthenware** is renowned worldwide and you will find a wide choice in the town's specialised shops. **Pottery** is big in the Puisaye and some workshops are open to visitors; enquire at the **Syndicat d'initiative intercommunal de la Puisaye nivernaise** (Square de Castellamonte, 58310 St-Amand-en-Puisaye; ℘03 86 39 63 15; www.ot-puisaye-nivernaise.fr. or) at the Association de potiers-créateurs de Puisaye (La Maison du Chanoine, Le Chaîneau, Treigny; ℘03 86 39 81 26). Jura handicrafts include: in St-Claude, craftsmen sell **pipes** beautifully carved from briar root; in Moirans-en-Montagne, high-quality wooden and plastic **toys**; **lace** is the speciality of Luxeuil and **clocks** abound in the Morteau area.

Calendar of Events

The list below is a selection of the many events which take place in this region. Visitors are advised to contact local tourist offices for fuller details of musical events, *son et lumière* shows, arts and crafts fairs etc., especially during July and August.

FESTIVALS

MARCH

Dijon, **Beaune**, **Auxerre**, **Nevers**, **Le Creusot**, **Mâcon**, **Montceau-les Mines**, **Quetigny** – Contemporary Dance Festival. www.art-danse.com.

WHITSUN WEEKEND

Belfort – International university student music festival. ℘03 84 54 24 43.

MAY – SEPTEMBER

Pontigny – Saison musicale des amis de Pontigny (music festival). ℘03 86 47 54 99.

MAY

Auxerre – Jazz in Auxerr. ℘03 86 94 08 12.

Semur-en-Auxois – Medieval festival. www.ville-semur-en-auxois.fr.

JUNE

Divonne-les-Bains – Chamber music festival. ℘04 50 40 34 16. www.domaine-de-divonne.com.

St-Claude – Haut-Jura music festival. ℘06 08 47 12 23. www.festival musiquehautjura.com.

Audincourt – Rencontres et Racines (music, crafts, food). ℘03 81 30 42 08.

Vauluisant – Festival de Vauluisan. www.vauluisant.com.

Le Creusot – Festival national de blues. ℘03 85 55 68 99. www.festival-du-blues.com.

Auxerre – Les Nuits métisses (world music).

JUNE – JULY

Belfort – Nuits d'été au Château (theatre, concerts). ℘03 84 55 90 90.

Dijon – L'Estivade. ℘03 80 74 53 33.

JUNE – SEPTEMBER

Tournus – Tournus Passion (various events). ℘03 85 27 00 20.

LATE JUNE – EARLY JULY

Sens – Festival "Quinte et sens" (music, theatre, dance). ℘03 86 65 19 49.

EARLY JULY

Selongey, **Seurre** – International bell-ringing festival. ℘03 80 21 15 92. www.selongey.com.

JULY

Beaune – International Baroque music festival. ℘03 80 22 97 20. www.festivalbeaune.com.

Belfort – Les Eurockéennes rock festival. ℘03 84 22 46 58.

Moirans-en-Montagne – Idéklic (International children's festival). ℘03 84 42 31 57.

International Baroque Music Festival, Beaune

Alain Doire/Bourgogne Tourisme

Tonnere and environs – Music festival. ℘03 86 54 45 26.

Saint-Bris-le-Vineux – Fête de peintres de vignes en caves. ℘03 86 53 31 79. www.saint-bris.com.

3rd WEEK IN JULY

Chalon-sur-Saône – "Chalon dans la rue" street artists festival. www.chalondanslarue.com.

2nd HALF OF JULY

Autun – Musique en Morvan (sacred choral music festival). www.musique-en-morvan.com.

Lormes – French song festival. ℘03 86 22 87 38.

JULY – AUGUST

Semur-en-Auxois and environs – Musicales en Auxois Festival. ℘03 80 96 20 24.

Château de Joux – Festival des Nuits de Joux (theatre). ℘03 81 46 48 33 (mid-July to mid-August).

Belfort – Wednesdays at the château. ℘03 84 28 08 28.

Nantua – Haut-Bugey international music festival. ℘04 74 75 24 94.

JULY – SEPTEMBER

Sens – International organ festival in the cathedral. ℘03 86 83 97 70.

JULY – NOVEMBER

Noyers, Cluny, Chablis, Mersault, Gevrey-Chambertin – Festival des Grands Crus de Bourgogne, Noyers-sur-Serein music festival. ℘03 80 34 38 40.

FIRST FORTNIGHT IN AUGUST

Besançon – Les Nuits de la citadelle (outdoor film festival). ℘03 81 87 83 33.

Trévillers – French country festival (American folk music). ℘03 81 44 45 39.

Semur-en-Auxois – Musicales en Auxois (nine concerts, various locations). ℘03 80 96 20 24.

Abbaye de Corbigny – Fêtes musicales de Corbigny. ℘03 86 20 27 90.

Saulieu – Cajun Nights. ℘06 08 53 88 75.

LATE AUGUST

Cluny – Jazz in Cluny. ℘03 85 59 04 04.

Vézelay – Rencontres musicales (vocal arts festival). ℘03 86 32 39 78. www.rencontresmusicales devezelay.com.

SEPTEMBER

Besançon – International music festival and young conductors competition. ℘03 81 25 05 85. www.festival-besancon.com.

Delle – Jazz festival. ℘03 84 36 68 50. www.delle-animation.com.

Various locations – "Musiques en voûtes" concert series in area churches. ℘03 80 67 11 22. www.musiquesenvoutes.com.

"Chalon dans la rue"

Alain Doire/Bourgogne Tourisme

Rencontres musicales, Vézelay

Alain Doire/Bourgogne Tourisme

MID-SEPTEMBER – MID-OCTOBER
Ambronay – Festival de l'Abbaye.
℘04 74 38 74 00.
LATE OCTOBER
Beaune – Cinema Festival.
℘03 80 24 50 24.
NOVEMBER
Auxerre –
International music and film
festival. ℘03 86 72 89 47.
www.festivalmusiquecinema.com.
**LATE NOVEMBER –
EARLY DECEMBER**
Belfort – Entrevues
(young filmmakers festival).
℘03 84 54 24 43.
www.festival-entrevues.com.

TRADITIONAL AND RELIGIOUS FEASTS, FAIRS AND PAGEANTS

JANUARY
Arlay, Champlitte – Feast of St Vincent,
patron of wine-growers, dating back
to 1719. ℘03 84 85 01 37 (Arlay).
LATE JANUARY – EARLY FEBRUARY
Villy – Feast of St Vincent procession
(location changes yearly; consult
www.cotedor-tourisme.com, or
www.tastevin-bourgogne.com).
LATE FEBRUARY – EARLY MARCH
Chalon-sur-Saône – Carnival: musical
parade and Grand Jour des Goniots;
parade and costume ball for
children; fun fair. Information:
www.carnavaldechalon.com.

MARCH – APRIL
Auxonne – Carnival. ℘03 80 37 34 46.
Vesoul – Carnival. ℘03 84 97 10 85.
Nuits-St-Georges – Wine auction sale.
℘03 80 62 11 77.
Tonnerre – Les Vinées tonnerroises.
℘03 86 55 14 48.
www.vignerons-tonnerrois.com.
Bassou – Festival de l'escargot.
℘03 86 73 23 73.
MAY – JUNE
Arlay – Medieval feast at the château.
Poligny – Les Épicuriennes
(Ascension weekend).
Dole – Pilgrimage to Notre-Dame-de-
Mont-Roland (2nd Sunday in May
and 2 August). ℘03 84 79 88 00.
Saulieu – Gourmet days.
℘03 80 64 00 21.
Besançon – Fair (week of Ascension).
℘03 81 41 08 09.
Mâcon – National Wine Fair. ℘03 85
21 07 07. www.leparcmacon.com.
3rd SUNDAY AFTER WHITSUN
Paray-le-Monial – Sacré-Cœur
pilgrimage. www.paray.org.
JUNE
Semur-en-Auxois – Fête de la Bague:
horse race whose origins date back
to 1639. ℘03 80 97 05 96.
Nozeroy – Medieval pageant.
℘03 84 51 19 15.
Le Russey – Fête des Gentianes.
℘03 81 43 72 35.
Levier – Fête des Sapins.

Fête de la Vielle, Anost

Alain Doire/Bourgogne Tourisme

Gex – Fête de l'Oiseau (bird festival): parade. ☏04 50 42 63 00.

St-Jean-de-Losne – Grand Pardon des mariniers (Blessing of river boats). ☏03 80 29 05 48.

Escolives-Ste-Camille – Cherry festival. ☏03 86 53 34 24.

JULY

Lons-le-Saunier – Fête de la St-Désiré (last Sun).

Haut-Jura – Fête du Haut-Jura, local crafts and products (location changes yearly). ☏03 84 41 27 81. www.parc-haut-jura.fr.

St-Saveur-en-Puisaye – Pottery fair. ☏03 86 45 69 12.

MID-JULY

Fondremand – Arts and crafts days. ☏03 84 78 98 89.

Pouilly-sur-Loire – Vintage fair (auction sale of great vintage wines). www.pouillysurloire.fr.

LATE JULY

Pontailler-sur-Saône – Fête de l'Oignon. ☏03 80 36 12 86.

AUGUST

Glux-en-Glenne – Fête des myrtilles (Bilberry Festival). ☏03 86 36 39 80.

Maîche – Fête du cheval (horse and cow competitions). ☏03 81 64 11 88.

St-Honoré-les-Bains – Fête des Fleurs (flower festival, 1st Sunday after 15 Aug). ☏03 86 30 71 70.

Cluny – Burgundy pottery market. ☏03 85 59 05 34.

Cluny – Harness and stallion show (last weekend).

15 AUGUST

Boutissaint – Festival of nature and wild animals. ☏03 86 74 07 08. www.boutissaint.com.

St Léger-sous-Beauvray – Accordion festival. ☏03 85 86 15 75.

2nd HALF OF AUGUST

Anost – Fête de la Vielle (Hurdy-gurdy Festival). ☏03 85 82 72 50. perso.wanadoo.fr/ugmm.

Saulieu – Fête du Charollais. ☏03 80 64 17 60.

Métabief-Mont d'Or – Descent of the cows.

1ST SUNDAY IN SEPTEMBER

Arbois – Fête du Biou (wine festival). ☏03 84 66 55 50.

EARLY SEPTEMBER

Alise-Ste-Reine – Pilgrimage and Ste-Reine mystery play. ☏03 80 96 86 55.

Ronchamp – Pilgrimage to Notre-Dame-du-Haut (8th). ☏03 84 20 65 13.

Belfort – Wine and fine food fair. ☏03 84 55 90 90.

2nd HALF OF SEPTEMBER

Arc-et-Senans – Fête des montgolfières (hot-air balloon event).

Books and Films

BOOKS
CLASSICS

Le Rouge et le Noir. Stendhal. (1830; trans. Roger Gard as The Red and the Black, Penguin Classics 2002).
This portrait of the foibles of French society, especially Franche-Comté, under the Second Restoration (1815–30) is based on a contemporary newspaper account of a crime of passion. In the book, Sorel is the ultimate opportunist, using seduction as a means to advance his career, but is undone by love and his final realisation of the vanity of worldly success.

The Complete Claudine. Colette. (trans. A. White, 2001). One of the best-loved writers of fiction from the region, Colette's *Claudine* series is full of verve and wit, and shows clearly her love of nature and her poetic childhood memories.

The Physiology of Taste, or Meditations on Transcendent Gastronomy. Jean Anthelme Brillat-Savarin. (1825, trans. MFK Fisher, Penguin Classics 1949).
Penned in the early 19C, the musings of this French judge who barely escaped death under the Reign of Terror go beyond the culinary to attain the far reaches of philosophy. This is a classic volume for lovers of fine food, good company and sensory pleasure.

The Art of Eating. MFK Fisher. (1954, reprinted 2004). One of Fisher's excellent books on the culinary arts, which includes notes from her studies in Dijon. Her award-winning prose has set a standard for food writers, as she discusses cooking with war rations, the social status of vegetables, and travelling to some wonderful places. If you love food, you will love her work, which is resonant with emotion, often surprising and joyful.

BIOGRAPHIES

A Life of Colette. Judith Thurman. (2000).
A beautifully written account of the fascinating life and work of the well-known author, who spent her childhood in Saint-Sauveur-en-Puisaye, in the Yonne.

Margaret of York: Duchess of Burgundy 1446–1503. Christine Weightman. (1993).
By both birth and marriage, Margaret played a pivotal role in the alliance between the dukes of Burgundy and the English crown. A patron of the arts, she was also remarkably independent and influential for a woman of her time. The book includes maps, genealogies and several other illustrations.

Alphonse de Lamartine: A Political Biography. William Fortescue. (1983).
Only a little of Lamartine's work has been translated into English, but this well-researched account of the author's career in politics gives a good insight into one part of his busy life.

GASTRONOMY

A Kitchen in Burgundy. Anne Willan. (2002). An evocative and readable book, elegantly interweaving tradtional and contemporary recipes with chapters on life in the 17C Chateau de Fey in Burgandy and its surroundings.

Burgundy Stars: A Year in the Life of a Great French Restaurant. W. Echikson. (1996). Worth tracking down is this 12-month account of Bernard Loiseau's famous restaurant in Saulieu, which is fascinating in its description of the frenetic pace and flurry in the kitchen and the elegance of one of the world's finest dining rooms.

WINE

Wines of Burgundy. Serena Sutcliffe. (2005). A comprehensive, up-to-date guide to the sought-after wines of Burgundy. An introductory section examines Burgundy's history and geography, as well as wine-growing, winemaking techniques,

Specialities of Burgundy

Office de tourisme de Dijon/Atelier Démoulin

and the classification system. Vintage reports are also included. The second section details Burgundy's key wine regions and the most prestigious properties, as well as the lesser-known names worth seeking out. There is also an A–Z listing of over 600 producers and their wines.

Côte d'Or: A Celebration of the Great Wines of Burgundy. Clive Coates. *(1997).* Another much-praised comprehensive book on Burgundy wine. This work seems to cover even the smallest vineyards, and takes a deeper look at 60 of the best domaines, all with wit and finely tuned British understatement.

The Great Domaines of Burgundy: A Guide to the Finest Wine Producers of the Côte d'Or. Remington Norman. *(second edition 1996).* Another good, all-encompassing book on the subject. Excellent maps and many pictures accompany the text, which concentrates on about 100 growers. Serious Burgundy lovers will lap up the historical accounts and descriptions of practices in the vineyards, as well as tasting notes on many vintages.

Burgundy and Its Wines: An Irresistible Portrait of Burgundy's Culture, History, Landscape and Wines. Nicholas Faith. *(2002).* A lavishly illustrated tome, with plenty of knowledgable advice about wines, for leisurely browsing before and after your trips.

FILMS

Burgundy and Jura sometimes catches the attention of the world's film-makers, but only a few titles a decade are worth mentioning.

Mondovino. (2004). An in-depth look into the wine business around the world, with Burgundy represented by a small family vineyard.

The Messenger: The Story of Joan of Arc. (1999). Milla Jovovich takes on the role of the French heroine in Luc Besson's update on the classic historical epic.

Wine auction of Hospices de Beaune

S. Sauvignier-MICHELIN

Know Before you Go

USEFUL WEBSITES

www.franceguide.com
The French Government Tourist Office/ *Maison de la France* site is packed with practical information and tips for those travelling to France. The home page has a number of links to more specific guidance, for American or Canadian travellers for example, or to the FGTO's London pages.

www.francekeys.com
This site has plenty of practical informa-tion for visiting France. It covers all the regions, with links to tourist offices and related sites. Very useful for planning the details of your tour in France.

www.visiteurope.com
The European Travel Commission provides useful information on travelling to and around 36 European countries, and includes links to some commercial booking services (such as vehicle hire), railway timetables, weather reports and more.

www.ambafrance-uk.org
The French Embassy in the UK provides useful information on France in general, pages about visiting the country, and links to other useful sites.

www.bourgogne.net
Use this site for general information about culture, accommodation, restaurants and tourism in Burgundy.

www.massifdujura.com
A good selection of interesting places to stay and things to do throughout the Jura region.

TOURIST OFFICES ABROAD

For information, brochures, maps and assistance in planning a trip to France, travellers should apply to the official French Tourist Office in their own country:

AUSTRALIA – NEW ZEALAND

- **Sydney**
  Level 13, 25 Bligh Street,
  Sydney, New South Wales 2000
  ✆ (02) 9231 5244
  info.au@franceguide.com

CANADA

- **Montreal**
  1800 Avenue McGill College,
  Suite 1010, Montreal H3A 2W9
  ✆ (514) 288 2026
  Fax (514) 845 4868
  canada@franceguide.com

EIRE

- **Dublin**
  30 Merrion Street, Dublin 4
  ✆ (01) 672 6172
  Fax (01) 679 0814
  info.ei@franceguide.com

SOUTH AFRICA

- **Johannesburg**
  P.O. Box 41022, 2024 Craig Hall
  ✆ (11) 523 8292
  info.za@franceguide.com

UNITED KINGDOM

- **London**
  178 Piccadilly, London W1J 9AL
  ✆ (09068) 244 123
  Fax (020) 7493 6594
  info.uk@franceguide.com

UNITED STATES

- **East Coast – New York**
  825 Third Avenue,
  29th Floor, New York, NY 10022
  ✆ (514) 288 1904
  info.us@franceguide.com

- **West Coast – Los Angeles**
  9454 Wilshire Boulevard,
  Suite 210, 90212 Beverly Hills, CA
  ✆ (514) 288 1904
  info.losangeles@franceguide.com

LOCAL AND REGIONAL TOURIST OFFICES

Visitors may also contact local tourist offices for more precise information, or to receive brochures and maps. The addresses and telephone numbers of tourist offices in the larger towns are listed after the symbol ⬛ in the town's description. The addresses given below are for the local tourist offices of the *départements* and *régions* covered in this guide.

Regional Offices
Address enquiries to:

* **Comité Régional du Tourisme de Franche-Comté** (Ain, Territoire de Belfort, Doubs, Haute-Saône, Jura), La City, 4 r. Gabriel-Plançon, 25044 Besançon Cedex. ℘0810 10 11 13. www.franche-comte.org.
* **Comité Régional du Tourisme de Bourgogne** (Côte-d'Or, Nièvre, Saône-et-Loire, Yonne), BP 1602, 21035 Dijon Cedex. ℘0 825 002 100. www.bourgogne-tourisme.com.

Département Offices
Address enquiries to the Comité Départemental du Tourisme (CDT), unless otherwise stated:

Ain – 34 r. du Général-Delestraint, BP 78, 01002 Bourg-en-Bresse Cedex. ℘04 74 32 31 30. www.ain-tourisme.com.

Côte-d'Or – 19 r. Ferdinand-de-Lesseps, BP 1601, 21035 Dijon Cedex. ℘03 80 63 69 49. www.cotedor-tourisme.com.

Doubs – 13 r. de la Préfecture, 25000 Besançon. ℘03 81 21 29 99. www.doubs.travel.

Jura – 8 r. Louis-Rousseau, BP 458, 39006 Lons-le-Saunier Cedex.

℘03 84 87 08 88. www.jura-tourism.com.

Nièvre – 3 av. Saint-Just, BP10318, 58003 Nevers Cedex. ℘03 86 36 39 80. www.nievre-tourisme.com.

Haute-Saône – SEM Destination 70, BP 57, 70001 Vesoul Cedex. ℘03 84 97 10 70. www.destination70.com.

Saône-et-Loire – 389 av. de Lattre-de-Tassigny, 71000 Mâcon. ℘03 85 21 02 20. www.bourgogne-du-sud.com.

Yonne – 1–2 quai de la République, 89000 Auxerre. ℘03 86 72 92 00. www.tourisme-yonne.com.

Maison du tourisme du Territoire de Belfort – 2 bis r. Clemenceau, 90000 Belfort. ℘03 84 55 90 90. www.ot-belfort.fr.

⬛ Tourist Information Centres
See the green orient panels in the Discovering section for the phone numbers and addresses of local tourist offices *(syndicats d'initiative)*. These offices provide information on craft courses and itineraries with special themes – wine tours, history tours, artistic tours.

Ten towns and areas, labelled *Villes et Pays d'Art et d'Histoire* by the Ministry of Culture, are mentioned in this guide (Autun, Auxerre, Beaune, Besançon, Chalon-sur-Saône, Dijon, Dole, Joigny, Nevers and Paray-le-Monial). They are particularly active in promoting their architectural and

Dole by the Doubs

© CRT Franche-Comté/Herbert Bertrand

cultural heritage and offer guided tours by highly qualified guides as well as activities for 6- to 12-year-olds. More information is available from local tourist offices and from www. vpah.culture.fr.

INTERNATIONAL VISITORS DOCUMENTS
PASSPORTS

Nationals of countries within the European Union entering France need only a national identity card. Nationals of other countries must be in possession of a valid national **passport**. In case of loss or theft, report to your embassy or consulate and the local police.

VISAS

No **entry visa** is required for Canadian, US or Australian citizens travelling as tourists and staying less than 90 days, except for students planning to study in France.
If you think you may need a visa, apply to your local French consulate. US citizens can obtain useful booklets on travelling abroad from the Government Printing Office, either by phone (*202 512 1800*) or online (*www.access.gpo.gov*).
General passport information is available by phone toll-free from the Federal Information Center (*800-688-9889*). US passport application forms can be downloaded from http://travel.state.gov.

EMBASSIES AND CONSULATES IN FRANCE

Australia Embassy, 4 r. Jean-Rey, 75015 Paris. *01 40 59 33 00. www.france.embassy.gov.au.
Canada Embassy, 35 avenue Montaigne, 75008 Paris. *01 44 43 29 00. www.amb-canada.fr.
Eire Embassy, 4 r. Rude, 75016 Paris. *01 44 17 67 00. www.embassyofireland.fr.
New Zealand Embassy, 7 ter r. Léonard-de-Vinci, 75016 Paris. *01 45 01 43 43. www.nzembassy.com.

South Africa Embassy, 59 quai d'Orsay, 75007 Paris. *01 53 59 23 23. www.afriquesud.net.
UK Embassy, 35 r. du Faubourg St-Honoré, 75008 Paris. *01 44 51 31 00. www.britishembassy.gov.uk. Consulate, 18 bis r. d'Anjou, 75008 Paris. *01 44 51 31 00.
USA Embassy, 2 avenue Gabriel, 75008 Paris. *01 43 12 22 22. www.amb-usa.fr. Consulate, 2 r. St-Florentin, 75001 Paris. *01 42 96 14 88. Consulate, 15 avenue d'Alsace, 67082 Strasbourg. *03 88 35 31 04.

CUSTOMS REGULATIONS

Apply to HM Revenue and Customs (UK) for a leaflet on customs regulations and the full range of duty-free allowances (*08450 109 000; www.hmrc.gov.uk). The US Customs Service offers a publication *Know Before You Go* for US citizens – for the office nearest you, consult the phone book or US Treasury (www.customs.ustreas.gov).
There are no customs formalities for bringing caravans into France for a stay of less than six months. No customs document is needed for pleasure boats and outboard motors for a stay of less than six months but the registration certificate should be kept on board.
Americans can bring home, tax-free, up to US$ 800 worth of goods (limited quantities of alcohol and tobacco products); Canadians up to CND$ 300; Australians up to AUS$ 400; and New Zealanders up to NZ$ 700.
Persons living in a member state of the European Union are not restricted with regard to purchasing goods for private use, but the recommended allowances for alcoholic beverages and tobacco are as shown below:

DUTY-FREE ALLOWANCES

Spirits (whisky, gin, vodka etc.) – 10 litres
Fortified Wines (vermouth, port etc.) – 20 litres

Vineyards of Crémant de Bourgogne

BIVB/Bourgogne Tourisme

Wine – (not more than 60 sparkling) – 90 litres
Beer – 110 litres
Cigarettes – 800
Cigarillos – 400
Cigars – 200
Smoking Tobacco –1 kg

HEALTH

First aid, medical advice and chemists' night-service rotas are available from chemists *(pharmacie)* identified by the green-cross sign. Clearly label all prescription drugs and carry a copy of the prescription. Comprehensive insurance coverage is advisable as you must pay for any medical treatment in French hospitals or clinics. **Nationals of non-EU countries** should check with their insurance companies about policy limitations. Reimbursement can then be negotiated with the insurance company according to the policy held.

- **British and Irish citizens** should apply to the Department of Health and Social Security before travelling for a European Health Insurance Card (EHIC), which entitles the holder to urgent treatment for accident or illness in EU countries. A refund of part of the costs of treatment can be obtained on application in person or by post to the local Social Security Offices *(Caisse Primaire d'Assurance Maladie)*.
- **Americans** can contact the International Association for Medical Assistance to Travelers,

which can also provide details of English-speaking doctors in different parts of France: ℘(716) 754-4883.

- **The American Hospital of Paris** is open 24hrs for emergencies as well as consultations, with English-speaking staff, at 63 bd. Victor-Hugo, 92200 Neuilly-sur-Seine. ℘01 46 41 25 25. Accredited by major insurance companies.
- **The British Hospital** is just outside Paris in Levallois-Perret, 3 r. Barbès. ℘01 46 39 22 22.

ACCESSIBILITY

Sights in this guide which are easily accessible to people of reduced mobility are marked by the symbol ♿. On TGV and Corail trains, operated by the national railway (SNCF), there are special wheelchair slots in 1st class carriages for holders of 2nd-class tickets.
On Eurostar and Thalys, special rates are available for accompanying adults. All airports are equipped for physically disabled passengers.
Find information for slow walkers, mature travellers and others with special needs at www.access-able.com. For information on museum access for the disabled consult http://museofile. culture.fr.
The **Michelin Guide France** and the **Michelin Camping France** indicate hotels and campsites with facilities suitable for physically handicapped people.

Getting There and Getting Around

BY AIR

Various international and other independent airlines fly to **Paris** (Roissy-Charles de Gaulle and Orly airports) and **Dijon** in the heart of Burgundy.

The Jura has only one regional airport, **Dole**, and therefore the international airports of **Mulhouse-Basle** to the north-east and **Geneva** to the south-east are useful alternatives. Check with your travel agent, however, before booking direct flights, as it is sometimes cheaper to travel via Paris. Air France (*0870 142 4343; www. airfrance.co.uk*), the national airline, links Paris to Dijon several times a day. Contact airline companies and travel agents for details of package tour flights with a rail or coach link-up as well as fly-drive schemes.

BY SEA
FROM THE UK OR IRELAND

For details of **cross-Channel services** from the UK and Ireland, and the rail shuttle via the Channel Tunnel (*Eurotunnel; *08705 35 35 35; www.eurotunnel.com*). Enquire at travel agencies or:
P & O Ferries, Channel House, Channel View Road, Dover CT17 9JT. *08705 980333. www.poferries.com.
Brittany Ferries, Millbay Docks, Plymouth, Devon PL1 3EW. *0870 9 076 103. www.brittany-ferries.co.uk.
Portsmouth Commercial Port (and ferry information), George Byng Way, Portsmouth PO2 8SP. *023 9229 7391. www.portsmouth-port.co.uk.
Irish Ferries, P.O. Box 19, Alexandra Road, Ferryport, Dublin 1. *08705 171717. www.irishferries.com.
Seafrance, Eastern Docks, Dover, Kent, CT16 1JA. *0871 663 2546. www.seafrance.com.
LD Lines, *0800 917 1201. www.ldlines.co.uk.

Norfolkline, *0871 574 7235 or +44 208 127 8303 (from outside UK).

BY RAIL

Eurostar runs via the Channel Tunnel between **London** (Kings Cross St-Pancras) and **Paris** (Gare du Nord) in 2hrs 15min (*bookings and information *08705 186 186 (UK); www.eurostar.com*). In Paris it links to the high-speed rail network (TGV) which covers most of France. There is fast inter-city service on the TGV from **Paris** (Gare de Lyon) to **Montbard** (*1hr 5min*), **Le Creusot** (*1hr 20min*), **Dijon** (*1hr 40min*), **Mâcon** (*1hr 40min*), **Bourg-en-Bresse** (*2hrs*), **Beaune** (*2hrs 5min*), **Dole** (*2hrs 5min*), **Châlon-sur-Saône** (*2hrs 20min*) and **Besançon** (*2hrs 30min*), with connections to other towns via the Trains Express Régionaux (TER).
Eurailpass, Flexipass, Eurailpass Youth, **EurailDrive Pass** and **Saver-pass** are five of the travel passes which may be purchased by residents of countries outside the European Union. In the US, contact your travel agent or **Rail Europe**, 44 S. Broadway, White Plains, NY 10601 (*914-682-2999 or 800-4-EURAIL; www.raileurope.com*) or **EuropRail International** (*1 888 667 9734; www.europrail.net*). If you are a European resident, you can buy an individual country pass, if you are not a resident of the country where you plan to use it. In the UK, contact EuropRail at; 179 Piccadilly, London W1J 9BA; *08705 848848. Information on timetables can be obtained on websites for these agencies and the **SNCF** (*www.sncf.fr*). At the SNCF site, you can book ahead, pay with a credit card, and receive your ticket in the mail at home.

There are numerous **discounts** available when you purchase your tickets in France, from 25–50% below the regular rate. These include discounts for using senior cards and youth cards (the cards, with a photograph, must be purchased), and lower rates for 2–9 people travelling together (no card required, advance purchase necessary).

There are a limited number of discount seats available during peak travel times, and the best discounts are available for travel during off-peak periods. Tickets bought in France must be validated *(composter)* by using the orange automatic date-stamping machines at the platform entrance (failure to do so may result in a fine).

BY COACH/BUS

Eurolines (**UK**), ℘08705 143219. **Eurolines** (**Paris**), 22 r. Malmaison, 93177 Bagnolet. ℘01 49 72 57 80. www.eurolines.com is the international website with information about travelling all over Europe by coach (bus).

BY CAR

The area covered in this guide is easily reached by main motorways and national roads. **Michelin map 726** indicates the main itineraries as well as alternate routes for avoiding heavy traffic during busy holiday periods, and gives estimated travel times. The latest Michelin route-planning service is available on the internet, **www.ViaMichelin.com**. Travellers can calculate a precise route using such options as shortest route, route avoiding toll roads or the Michelin-recommended route. In addition to tourist information (hotels, restaurants, attractions), you will find a magazine featuring articles with the up-to-the-minute reports on holiday destinations. The roads are very busy during the holiday period (particularly weekends in July and August) and to avoid traffic congestion it is advisable to follow the recommended secondary routes (signposted as *Bison Futé —itinéraires bis)*. The motorway network includes rest areas *(aires)* and petrol stations, usually with restaurant and shopping complexes attached, about every 40km/25mi, so that long-distance drivers have no excuse not to stop for a rest every now and then.

DOCUMENTS

Travellers from other European Union countries and North America can drive in France with a valid national or home-state **driving licence**. An **international driving licence** is useful because the information on it appears in nine languages (keep in mind that traffic officers are empowered to fine motorists). Permits are available from your local motoring organisations (or from the Post Office in the UK). For the vehicle, it is necessary to have the registration papers (logbook) and a nationality plate of the approved size. Certain motoring organisations (AAA, AA, RAC) offer accident **insurance** and breakdown service schemes for members. Check with your current insurance company in regard to coverage while abroad. If you plan to hire a car using your credit card, check with the company, which may provide liability insurance automatically (and thus save you having to pay the cost for optimum coverage).

ROAD REGULATIONS

The minimum driving age is 18. Traffic drives on the right. All passengers must wear **seat belts**. Children under the age of 10 must ride in the back seat. Headlights must be switched on in poor visibility and at night; use sidelights only when the vehicle is stationary. In the case of a **breakdown**, a red warning triangle or hazard warning lights are obligatory. In the absence of stop signs at intersections, cars must **yield to the right**. Traffic on main roads outside built-up areas (priority indicated by a yellow diamond sign) and on **roundabouts** has right of way. There are many roundabouts (traffic circles) located just on the edge of towns; they are designed to reduce the speed of the traffic entering the built-up area and you must slow down when you approach one and yield to the cars in the circle. Vehicles must stop when the lights turn red at road junctions and may filter to the right only when indicated by an amber arrow. The regulations on **drinking and driving** (limited to 0.50g/l) and **speeding** are strictly enforced – usually by an on-the-spot fine and/or confiscation of the vehicle.

SPEED LIMITS

Although liable to modification, these are as follows:

- toll motorways (**autoroutes**) 130kph/80mph (110kph/68mph when raining).
- dual carriageways and motorways without tolls 110kph/68mph (100kph/62mph when raining).
- other roads 90kph/56mph (80kph/50mph when raining) and in towns 50kph/31mph.
- outside lane on motorways during daylight, on level ground and with good visibility – minimum speed limit of 80kph/50mph.

PARKING REGULATIONS

In towns there are zones where parking is either restricted or subject to a fee; tickets should be obtained from the ticket machines (*horodateurs* – small change necessary) and displayed inside the windscreen on the driver's side; failure to display may result in a fine, or towing and impoundment. Other parking areas in town may require you to take a ticket when passing through a barrier. To exit, you must pay the parking fee (usually there is a machine located by the exit – *sortie*) and insert the paid-up card in another machine which will lift the exit gate.

TOLLS

In France, most motorways are subject to a toll (*péage*). You can pay in cash or with a credit card (Visa, Mastercard).

CAR RENTAL

Car rental agencies are at airports, railway stations and in all large towns in France. Automatic cars are available in larger cities by advance reservation only. Drivers must be over 21; between ages 21–25, drivers are required to pay an extra daily fee; some companies allow drivers under 23 only if the reservation has been made through a travel agent. It is relatively expensive

RENTAL CARS – CENTRAL RESERVATION IN FRANCE	
Avis	📞 08 20 05 05 05 www.avis.com
Europcar	📞 08 25 82 54 57 www.europcar.com
Budget France	📞 08 25 00 35 64 www.budget.com
Hertz France	📞 01 47 03 49 12 www.hertz.com
SIXT-Eurorent	📞 08 20 00 74 98 www.e-sixt.com
National-CITER	📞 01 45 22 77 91 www.citer.fr

to hire a car in France; Americans in particular will notice the difference and should book before leaving, take advantage of fly-drive offers, or see a travel agent. Online services will look for the best prices on car rental around the globe. Nova can be contacted at www.rentacar-worldwide.com or 📞0800 018 6682 (freephone UK) or 📞44 28 4272 8189 (calling from outside the UK). All of the firms listed below have internet sites for reservations and information.

MOTORHOME RENTAL

- **Worldwide Motorhome Rentals** Fully equipped camper vans for rent. 📞888- 519-8969 *US toll-free*. 📞530-389-8316 *outside the US*. www.mhrww.com.
- **Overseas Motorhome Tours Inc**. Organises escorted tours and rental of recreational vehicles. 📞800-322-2127 *US*. 📞1-310-543-2590 *outside the US*. www.omtinc.com.

PETROL

French service stations dispense:
- *sans plomb 98* (super unleaded 98)
- *sans plomb 95* (super unleaded 95)
- *diesel/gazole* (diesel)
- *GPL* (LPG).

Prices are listed on signboards on the motorways; it is usually cheaper to fill up after leaving the motorway; check the large hypermarkets on the outskirts of town.

Where to Stay and Eat

Hotel and restaurant listings fall within the description of each region.

WHERE TO STAY

Some of the maps in the following sections illustrate a selection of holiday destinations which are particularly recommended for the accommodation and leisure facilities they offer, and for their pleasant setting. They show **overnight stops**: fairly large towns worth visiting that have good accommodation facilities; as well as traditional destinations for a **short holiday**, which combine accommodation, charm and a peaceful setting. As for Dijon and Besançon, the influence they exert in the region and the wealth of monuments, museums and other sights to which they are home make them the ideal setting for at least a **weekend break**.

FINDING A HOTEL

The Green Guide is pleased to offer lists of selected hotels and restaurants for this region. See the Addresses in the DISCOVERING section for descriptions and prices of typical places to stay and eat with local flair. The legend at the back of the guide explains the symbols and abbreviations used in these sections. We have reported the prices and conditions as we observed them, but of course changes in management and other factors may mean that you will find some discrepancies. Please feel free to keep us informed of any major differences you encounter.

Use the **Map of places to stay** to identify recommended places for overnight stops. For an even greater selection, use The **Michelin Guide France**, with its famously reliable star-rating system and hundreds of establishments all over France. Book ahead to ensure that you get the accommodation you want, not only in tourist season but year-round, as many towns fill up during trade fairs, arts festivals and so on. Some places require a deposit or a reconfirmation. Reconfirming is especially important if you plan to arrive after 6pm.

For a selection of reasonably priced small hotels, see Michelin's publication **1 000 Charming Hotels and Guest-houses**; the guide covers all of France, with individual chapters on Burgundy and Franche-Comté.

For further assistance, **Loisirs Accueil** is a booking service that has offices in some French *départements* – for further information, contact the tourist offices listed above or the **Fédération nationale des services de réservation Loisirs-Accueil** (*280 bd. St-Germain, 75007 Paris; ℘01 44 11 10 44; www.resinfrance.com or www.loisirsaccueilfrance.com*).

A guide to good-value, family-run hotels, **Logis et Auberges de France**, is available from the French Tourist Office, as are lists of other kinds of accommodation such as hotel-châteaux, bed-and-breakfasts etc. **Relais et châteaux** provides information on booking in luxury hotels with character (℘00800 2000 00 02 (from UK); 800 735 2478 (from US); www.relaischateaux.com).

ECONOMY CHAIN HOTELS

These can be useful, as they are inexpensive (less than 38€ for a double room) and generally near a main road. Breakfast is available, but there may not be a restaurant; rooms are small, with a television and bathroom. Central reservation numbers:

- ◆ **Akena** ℘01 69 84 85 17
- ◆ **B&B** ℘0892 782 929
- ◆ **Etap Hôtel** ℘0892 688 900
- ◆ **Villages Hôtel** ℘03 80 60 92 70

The following hotel chains offer slightly more expensive accommodations, with a few more amenties and services.

- ◆ **Campanile** ℘01 64 62 46 46
- ◆ **Kyriad** ℘0825 003 003
- ◆ **Ibis** ℘0825 882 222

Reserve online at www.etaphotel.com or www.ibishotel.com.

GÎTES, RENTING A COTTAGE, BED & BREAKFAST

The **Maison des Gîtes de France** gives information on self-catering accommodation in the Burgundy-Jura region (and the rest of France). Gîtes usually comprise a cottage or apartment, or B&B accommodation (*chambres d'hôtes*) at a sensible price. Contact the Gîtes de France office in Paris (*59 r. St-Lazare, 75439 Paris Cedex 09; ℘01 49 70 75 75*), or their representative in the UK, **Brittany Ferries** (*see Address under Getting There and Getting Around*). The website, **www.gites-de-france.fr**, has a good English version, where you can order catalogues for different regions with photographs of the properties. Local tourist offices may also have lists of properties and B&Bs.

The **Fédération des Stations Vertes de Vacances et Villages de Neige** (*BP 71698, 21016 Dijon Cedex; ℘03 80 54 10 50; www.stationsvertes.com*) is an association which promotes 854 rural localities across France, chosen for their natural appeal, the quality of their environment, accommodation and leisure activities.

For **farm holidays**, three guides – *Guide des fermes-auberges, Bienvenue à la ferme* and *Vacances et week-ends à la ferme* – list farms with guest facilities which have been vetted for quality and meet official standards. For more information, apply to local tourist offices (*see Know Before You Go*).

HOSTELS, CAMPING

To obtain an International Youth Hostel Federation card (no age requirement; senior card also available) contact the IYHF in your own country. An online booking service (*www.hihostels.com*), lets you reserve rooms up to six months ahead. The two main youth hostel associations (*auberges de jeunesse*) in France are:

- **Ligue Française pour les Auberges de la Jeunesse**
  67 r. Vergniaud, Bâtiment K, 75013 Paris. ℘01 44 16 78 78. www.auberges-de-jeunesse.com.

- **Fédération Unie des Auberges de Jeunesse**
  27 r. Pajol, 75018 Paris. ℘01 44 89 87 27. www.fuaj.org.

There are numerous officially graded camp sites with varying standards of facilities throughout the Burgundy-Jura region.

The **Michelin Camping France** guide lists a selection of camp sites. The area is very popular with campers in the summer months, so it is wise to reserve in advance.

ACCOMMODATION FOR RAMBLERS

For rambling, ski or bike touring, mountaineering, canoeing etc., the useful guide *Gîtes d'étapes, refuges* by A. and S. Mouraret is published by Rando Éditions La Cadole (*74 R. A. Perdreaux, 78140 Vélizy; ℘01 34 65 11 89; www.gites-refuges.com*).

WHERE TO EAT

Consult the Addresses in the Discovering section for listings of selected places to eat in each area. The key on the cover flap explains the symbols and abbreviations used in the Addresses sections.

For an even greater choice, use the **Michelin Guide France**, with its famously reliable star-rating system and hundreds of establishments all over France. If you would like to dine in a highly rated restaurant from the *Michelin Guide*, be sure to book ahead. In the countryside, lunch is usually served between noon and 2pm and dinner between 7.30–10pm. It is not always easy to find something between those times, other than a sandwich in a café, or hot dishes may be available in a *brasserie*.

French restaurants and cafés include a service charge. Tipping is not necessary, but French people often leave the small change from their bill, or about 5% for the waiter in a nice restaurant.

For more on local specialities, see Gastronomy in the INTRODUCTION section.

Useful Words and Phrases

Sights

	Translation
Abbey	Abbaye
Belfry	Beffroi
Chapel	Chapelle
Castle	Château
Cemetery	Cimetière
Cloisters	Cloître
Courtyard	Cour
Convent	Couvent
Lock (Canal)	Écluse
Church	Église
Fountain	Fontaine
Covered Market	Halle
Garden	Jardin
Town Hall	Mairie
House	Maison
Market	Marché
Monastery	Monastère
Windmill	Moulin
Museum	Musée
Park	Parc
Square	Place
Bridge	Pont
Port/Harbour	Port
Gateway	Porte
Quay	Quai
Ramparts	Remparts
Street	Rue
Statue	Statue
Tower	Tour

Natural Sites

	Translation
Chasm	Abîme
Swallow-Hole	Aven
Dam	Barrage
Viewpoint	Belvédère
Waterfall	Cascade
Pass	Col
Ledge	Corniche
Coast, Hillside	Côte
Forest	Forêt
Cave	Grotte
Lake	Lac
Beach	Plage
River	Rivière
Stream	Ruisseau
Beacon	Signal
Spring	Source
Valley	Vallée

On the Road

	Translation
Car Park	Parking
Driving Licence	Permis De Conduire
East	Est
Garage (For Repairs)	Garage
Left	Gauche
Motorway/Highway	Autoroute
North	Nord
Parking Meter	Horodateur
Petrol/Gas	Essence
Petrol/Gas Station	Station Essence
Right	Droite
South	Sud
Toll	Péage
Traffic Lights	Feu Tricolore
Tyre	Pneu
West	Ouest
Wheel Clamp	Sabot
Zebra Crossing	Passage Clouté

Time

	Translation
Today	Aujourd'hui
Tomorrow	Demain
Yesterday	Hier
Winter	Hiver
Spring	Printemps
Summer	Été
Autumn/Fall	Automne
Week	Semaine
Monday	Lundi
Tuesday	Mardi
Wednesday	Mercredi
Thursday	Jeudi
Friday	Vendredi
Saturday	Samedi
Sunday	Dimanche

Numbers

	Translation
0	zéro
1	un
2	deux
3	trois
4	quatre
5	cinq
6	six
7	sept
8	huit
9	neuf
10	dix
11	onze
12	douze
13	treize
14	quatorze
15	quinze
16	seize
17	dix-sept
18	dix-huit
19	dix-neuf
20	vingt
30	trente
40	quarante
50	cinquante
60	soixante
70	soixante-dix
80	quatre-vingt
90	quatre-vingt-dix
100	cent
1000	mille

Shopping

	Translation
Bank	Banque
Baker's	Boulangerie
Big	Grand
Butcher's	Boucherie
Chemist's	Pharmacie
Closed	Fermé
Cough Mixture	Sirop Pour La Toux
Cough Sweets	Cachets Pour La Gorge
Entrance	Entrée
Exit	Sortie
Fishmonger's	Poissonnerie
Grocer's	Épicerie
Newsagent, Bookshop	Librairie
Open	Ouvert
Post Office	Poste
Push	Pousser
Pull	Tirer
Shop	Magasin
Small	Petit
Stamps	Timbres

Food and Drink

	Translation
Beef	Bœuf
Beer	Bière
Butter	Beurre
Bread	Pain
Breakfast	Petit-Déjeuner
Cheese	Fromage
Chicken	Poulet
Dessert	Dessert
Dinner	Dîner
Fish	Poisson
Fork	Fourchette
Fruit	Fruits
Glass	Verre
Ice Cream	Glace
Ice Cubes	Glaçons
Ham	Jambon
Knife	Couteau
Lamb	Agneau
Lunch	Déjeuner
Lettuce Salad	Salade
Meat	Viande
Mineral Water	Eau Minérale
Mixed Salad	Salade Composée
Orange Juice	Jus D'orange
Plate	Assiette
Pork	Porc
Restaurant	Restaurant
Red Wine	Vin Rouge
Salt	Sel
Spoon	Cuillère
Sugar	Sucre
Vegetables	Légumes
Water	De L'eau
White Wine	Vin Blanc
Yoghurt	Yaourt

Personal Documents and Travel

	Translation
Airport	Aéroport
Credit Card	Carte De Crédit
Customs	Douane
Passport	Passeport
Platform	Voie
Railway Station	Gare
Shuttle	Navette
Suitcase	Valise
Train/Plane Ticket	Billet De Train/D'avion
Wallet	Portefeuille

Clothing

	Translation
Coat	Manteau
Jumper	Pull
Raincoat	Imperméable
Shirt	Chemise
Shoes	Chaussures
Socks	Chaussettes
Stockings	Bas
Suit	Costume
Tights	Collants
Trousers	Pantalon

Useful Phrases

	Translation
Goodbye	Au Revoir
Hello/Good Morning	Bonjour
How	Comment
Excuse Me	Excusez-Moi
Thank You	Merci
Yes/No	Oui/Non
I Am Sorry	Pardon
Why	Pourquoi
When	Quand
Please	S'il Vous Plaît

Do you speak English? Parlez-vous anglais?

I don't understand Je ne comprends pas

Talk slowly Parlez lentement

Where's...? Où est...?

When does the... leave?
A quelle heure part...?

When does the... arrive?
A quelle heure arrive...?

When does the museum open?
A quelle heure ouvre le musée?

When is breakfast served? A quelle heure sert-on le petit-déjeuner?

What does it cost? Combien cela coûte?

Where can I buy a newspaper in English?
Où puis-je acheter un journal en anglais?

Where is the nearest petrol/gas station?
Où se trouve la station essence la plus proche?

Where can I change traveller's cheques?
Où puis-je échanger des traveller's cheques?

Where are the toilets? Où sont les toilettes?

Do you accept credit cards? Acceptez-vous les cartes de crédit?

Basic Information

DISCOUNTS

Significant discounts are available for senior citizens, students, under 25s and teachers for public transport; museums; monuments; and some leisure activities such as films (at certain times of day). Bring student or senior cards with you, and bring along some extra passport-size photos for discount travel cards.

The **International Student Travel Confederation** (*www.istc.org*), global administrator of the International Student and Teacher Identity Cards, is an association of student travel organisations around the world. ISTC members collectively negotiate benefits with airlines, governments, and providers of other goods and services for the student and teacher community, both in their own country and around the world. The non-profit association sells international ID cards for students, under-25s and teachers. The ISTC is also active in a network of international education and work exchange programmes.

ELECTRICITY

The electric current is 220 volts. Circular two-pin plugs are the rule. Adapters and converters should be bought before you leave home; they are on sale in most airports. If you have a rechargeable device (video camera, laptop, battery re-charger), read the instructions carefully: in some cases you must use a voltage converter as plug adaptor, or risk ruining your appliance.

EMERGENCIES

EMERGENCY NUMBERS
Police: ☎17
Ambulance: ☎15 (SAMU / Paramedics)
Fire (Pompiers): ☎18

PUBLIC HOLIDAYS

Museums and other monuments may be closed or may vary their hours of admission on certain public holidays (*see chart below*). National museums and art galleries are closed on Tuesdays; municipal museums are generally closed on Mondays. In addition to the usual school holidays at Christmas and in the spring and summer, there are long mid-term breaks (10 days to a fortnight) in February and early November.

PUBLIC HOLIDAYS	
1 January	New Year's Day (*Jour de l'An*)
April (no fixed dates)	Easter Day and Easter Monday (*Pâques*)
1 May	May Day (*Fête du Travail*)
8 May	VE Day (*Fête de la Libération*)
Thu 40 days after Easter	Ascension Day (*Ascension*)
7th Sun–Mon after Easter	Whit Sunday and Monday (*Pentecôte*)
14 July	France's National Day (*Fête de la Bastille*)
15 August	Assumption (*Assomption*)
1 November	All Saints Day (*Toussaint*)
11 November	Armistice Day (*Fête de la Victoire*)
25 December	Christmas Day (*Noël*)

MAIL/POST

Post offices open Mondays to Fridays, 8am–7pm, Saturdays, 8am–noon. Smaller branch post offices often close at lunchtime between noon and 2pm and in the afternoon at 4pm.

Postage via airmail to:
- **UK:** letter (20g) 0.60€
- **North America:** letter (20g) 0.85€
- **Australia and NZ:** letter (20g) 0.85€

Stamps are also available from newsagents and tobacconists. Stamp collectors should ask for *timbres de collection* in any post office.

Poste Restante (General Delivery) mail should be addressed as follows: Name, *Poste Restante*, *Poste Centrale*, post code of the département followed by town name, France. **The Michelin Guide France** gives local post codes.

American Express ✆ 01 47 77 72 00	
Visa ✆ 08 36 69 08 80	
MasterCard/Eurocard ✆ 01 45 67 84 84	
Diners Club ✆ 01 49 06 17 50	

MONEY
CURRENCY

There are no restrictions on the amount of currency visitors can take into France. Visitors carrying a lot of cash are advised to complete a currency declaration form on arrival, because there are restrictions on currency export.

NOTES AND COINS

Since 17 February 2002, the **euro** has been the only currency accepted as a means of payment in France, as in the 15 other Eurozone countries participating in the monetary union. It is divided into 100 cents or centimes. Since June 2002, it has only been possible to exchange old French franc currency at the Banque de France.

BANKS

Although business hours vary from branch to branch, banks are usually open from 9am to noon and 2pm to 5pm and are closed either on Mondays or Saturdays. Banks close early on the day before a bank holiday. A passport is necessary as identification when cashing travellers cheques in banks. Commission charges vary and hotels usually charge more than banks for cashing cheques.

Debit and Credit Cards

One of the most economical ways to use your money in France is by using **ATM machines** to get cash directly from your bank account (with a debit card) or to use your credit card to get a cash advance. Be sure to remember your PIN number; you will need it to use cash dispensers and to pay with your card in shops, restaurants, etc. Pin numbers have four digits in France; enquire with the issuing company or bank if the code you usually use is longer. Visa is the most widely accepted credit card, followed by Mastercard; other cards, credit and debit (Diners Club, Plus, Cirrus, etc.) are also accepted in some cash machines. American Express is more often accepted in premium establishments. Most places post signs indicating which card they accept; if you don't see such a sign and want to pay with a card, ask before ordering or making a selection. Cards are widely accepted in shops, hypermarkets, hotels and restaurants, at tollbooths and in petrol stations.

Before you leave home, check with the bank that issued your card for emergency replacement procedures. Carry your card number and emergency phone numbers separate from your wallet and handbag; leave a copy of this information with someone you can easily reach. If your card is lost or stolen while you are in France, call one of the 24-hour hotlines listed in the box: These numbers are also listed at most ATM machines.

You must report any loss or theft of credit cards or travellers cheques to the local police who will issue you with a certificate (useful proof to show the issuing company).

TELEPHONES

Most public phones in France use pre-paid phone cards *(télécartes)*, rather than coins. Some telephone booths accept credit cards (Visa, Mastercard/ Eurocard). *Télécartes* (50 or 120 units) can be bought in post offices, branches of France Télécom, *bureaux de tabac* (cafés that sell cigarettes) and newsagents and can be used to make calls in France and abroad. Calls can be received at phone boxes where the blue bell sign is shown; the phone will not ring, so keep your eye on the little message screen.

NATIONAL CALLS

French telephone numbers have 10 digits. Paris and Paris region numbers begin with 01; 02 in northwest France; 03 in northeast France; 04 in southeast France and Corsica; 05 in southwest France. Numbers beginning with 08 are special rate numbers, available only when dialling within France.

INTERNATIONAL CALLS

International Dialling Codes (00 + code)			
Australia	☎61	**NZ**	☎64
Canada	☎1	**UK**	☎44
Eire	☎353	**USA**	☎1

To call France from abroad, dial the country code (33) + 9-digit number (omit the initial 0). When calling abroad from France dial 00, then dial the country code followed by the area code and number of your correspondent.

◆ **International information**: US/Canada: ☎00 33 12 11
◆ **International operator**: ☎00 33 12 + country code
◆ **Local directory assistance**: ☎12

MINITEL

France Télécom's system has directory enquiries, travel and entertainment reservations, and other services. Small computer terminals can be found in some post offices, hotels and France Télécom agencies, and in many French homes. 3614 PAGES E is the code for **directory assistance in English** (turn on the unit, dial 3614, hit the *connexion* button when you get the tone, type in "PAGES E", and follow the instructions.

MOBILE PHONES

In France mobile phone numbers start with 06. Two-watt (lighter, shorter reach) and eight-watt models are on the market, using the Orange (France

Télécom) or SFR networks. *Mobicartes* are prepaid phone cards that fit into mobile units. Mobile phone rentals (delivery or airport pickup provided):

◆ **A.L.T. Rent A Phone** ☎01 48 00 06 06
◆ **Rent a Cell Express** ☎01 53 93 78 00
◆ **Ellinas Phone Rental** ☎01 47 20 70 00

TIME

France is 1hr ahead of Greenwich Mean Time (GMT). France goes on daylight-saving time from the last Sunday in March to the last Sunday in October.

WHEN IT IS **NOON IN FRANCE**, IT IS	
3am	in Los Angeles
6am	in New York
11am	in Dublin
11am	in London
7pm	in Perth
9pm	in Sydney
11pm	in Auckland

PRICES AND TIPS

Since a service charge is automatically included in the price of meals and accommodation in France, any additional tipping is up to the visitor, generally small change, and generally not more than 5%. Taxi drivers and hairdressers are usually tipped 10–15%.

As a rule, the cost of staying in a hotel, eating in a restaurant or buying goods and services is significantly lower in the French regions than in Paris.

Cafés have very different prices, depending on where they are located. The price of a drink or a coffee is cheaper if you stand at the counter *(comptoir)* than if you sit down *(salle)* and sometimes it is even more expensive if you sit outdoors *(terrace)*.

CONVERSION TABLES

Weights and Measures

EU	US	UK	
1 kilogram (kg)	2.2 pounds (lb)	2.2 pounds	To convert
6.35 kilograms	14 pounds	1 stone (st)	kilograms
0.45 kilograms	16 ounces (oz)	16 ounces	to pounds,
1 metric ton (tn)	1.1 tons	1.1 tons	multiply by 2.2
1 litre (l)	2.11 pints (pt)	1.76 pints	To convert litres
3.79 litres	1 gallon (gal)	0.83 gallon	to gallons, multiply
4.55 litres	1.20 gallon	1 gallon	by 0.26 (US)
			or 0.22 (UK)
1 hectare (ha)	2.47 acres	2.47 acres	To convert
1 sq kilometre (km²)	0.38 sq. miles (sq mi)	0.38 sq. miles	hectares to acres, multiply by 2.4
1 centimetre (cm)	0.39 inches (in)	0.39 inches	To convert metres
1 metre (m)	3.28 feet (ft) or 39.37 inches or 1.09 yards (yd)		to feet, multiply by 3.28; for
1 kilometre (km)	0.62 miles (mi)	0.62 miles	kilometres to miles, multiply by 0.6

Clothing

Women	EU	US	UK
	35	4	2½
	36	5	3½
	37	6	4½
Shoes	38	7	5½
	39	8	6½
	40	9	7½
	41	10	8½
	36	6	8
	38	8	10
Dresses	40	10	12
& suits	42	12	14
	44	14	16
	46	16	18
	36	6	30
	38	8	32
Blouses &	40	10	34
sweaters	42	12	36
	44	14	38
	46	16	40

Men	EU	US	UK
	40	7½	7
	41	8½	8
	42	9½	9
Shoes	43	10½	10
	44	11½	11
	45	12½	12
	46	13½	13
	46	36	36
	48	38	38
Suits	50	40	40
	52	42	42
	54	44	44
	56	46	48
	37	14½	14½
	38	15	15
Shirts	39	15½	15½
	40	15¾	15¾
	41	16	16
	42	16½	16½

Sizes often vary depending on the designer. These equivalents are given for guidance only.

Speed

KPH	10	30	50	70	80	90	100	110	120	130
MPH	6	19	31	43	50	56	62	68	75	81

Temperature

Celsius (°C)	0°	5°	10°	15°	20°	25°	30°	40°	60°	80°	100°
Fahrenheit (°F)	32°	41°	50°	59°	68°	77°	86°	104°	140°	176°	212°

To convert Celsius into Fahrenheit, multiply °C by 9, divide by 5, and add 32.
To convert Fahrenheit into Celsius, subtract 32 from °F, multiply by 5, and divide by 9.
NB: Conversion factors on this page are approximate.

Hôtel Dieu, Beaune
© Jean-Jacques Cordier/
Fotolia.com

The Region Today

ECONOMY

France's largely prosperous postwar period has seen farming and industry slowly being replaced as main wealth generators by service businesses. This shift has been accompanied by a movement of people away from the urbanised north and north-east of the country towards parts of the south and west. Burgundy and Jura remain sparsely populated, although the northernmost parts of Burgundy have seen a rise in the number of inhabitants caused by new arrivals from the Paris region.

Both regions remain largely agricultural, with beef and dairy cattle, cereal crops, fruit, timber and wine among the main crops. Many people work in the service industries and there is a healthy tourist trade. Otherwise, people work in various industries, from pharmaceuticals and metallurgy to clocks and toy-making.

France's postwar economic growth has brought about a substantial rise in living standards. The working week is fixed at 35 hours and income tax and indirect taxes are relatively high, helping to pay for a generous welfare system.

Recent years, however, have seen growing worries over unemployment and sluggish economic growth. On 6 May 2007, centre-right Nicolas Sarkozy defeated his Socialist rival Segolene Royal in the presidential elections with promises of reforms to boost the economy, such as incentives to encourage overtime and social security reforms.

GASTRONOMY IN BURGUNDY

Burgundy's reputation as a gastronomic paradise has been established for a long time. Dijon has been a city of fine food since Gallo-Roman times. In the 6C, Gregory of Tours praised the quality of Burgundian wines, and King Charles VI lauded the gastronomic delights of Dijon, both good wines and local dishes. The historic États Généraux de Bourgogne and the gastronomic fair at Dijon perpetuate this tradition of good food and wine in the region.

The raw materials – Burgundy is home to first-class beef cattle in the regions of Auxois, Bazois and Charollais, as well as some of the tastiest game in France. It produces incomparable vegetables, many varieties of fish (white fish from the Saône and Loire and trout and crayfish from the rivers of the Morvan), delicious mushrooms *(cèpes, girolles, morilles* and *mousserons)*, snails and mouth-watering fruit (cherries from the Auxerre region, for example). And of course, Dijon is forever associated with the **mustards** produced there.

Burgundian cuisine is both rich and substantial, reflecting the Burgundian temperament and robust appetite; people here expect both quality and quantity at the table. Wine, the glory of the province, naturally plays an important part: the *meurette* sauces made from wine thickened with butter and flour with flavourings and spices added are the pride of Burgundian cuisine. These sauces work well with fish – carp, tench and eel – brains, poached eggs and **bœuf bourguignon** (Burgundian beef casserole). Cream is used in many dishes: **jambon à la crème** (cooked ham in a cream sauce) and **champignons à la crème** (mushrooms in a cream sauce). **Saupiquet** is a spicy wine and cream sauce that dates back to the 15C.

Burgundian specialities – Beyond the long-simmering *bœuf bourguignon,* the cuisine of this region is renowned for **escargots** (snails cooked in their shells with garlic, butter and parsley), **jambon persillé** (ham seasoned with parsley), **andouillette** (small sausages made from chitterlings), **coq au vin** (chicken in a wine sauce), **pauchouse** (stew of various fish cooked in white wine) and **poulet en sauce** (chicken cooked in a cream and white wine sauce). In the Nivernais and Morvan regions, home-cured ham and sausage, ham and eggs, calf's head *(sansiot)*, eggs cooked in wine *(en meurette)*, roast veal and pullet fried with bacon and pearl onions *(jau au sang)* figure among the traditional dishes.

Perhaps the greatest moment in the meal comes with the **cheese** course. A good vintage wine enhances the experience of eating **Soumaintrain**, **Saint-Florentin**, **Époisses**, **Bouton-de-culotte**, or **Citeaux**, all produced locally. A traditional preparation that honours a great vintage is **gougère**, cheese pastry.

IN JURA

Poultry and freshwater fish go particularly well with Jura wines, and **coq au vin jaune** or **truite au vin jaune** are classic local specialities.

Game is abundant and there are many traditional recipes for hare, wild boar, venison, woodcock etc. Wild hare in white wine sauce, venison casserole with cream and roast thrush flambéed in Marc d'Arbois are just a few dishes.

Potée is made with a variety of vegetables cooked slowly in a casserole with Morteau sausage, a speciality of this region, as is sausage from Montbéliard. Local *charcuterie*, such as Jésus from Morteau and the many smoked hams (Luxeuil-les-Bains), is also appreciated. For centuries, pork and bacon were the only meat eaten in the mountain regions. Pigs were therefore very important on the farms, and careful calculation went into the diet on which they were fattened. On pig-killing day, an occasion for great celebration in the family, a pig feast was prepared consisting of black pudding *(boudin)*, sausages made from tripe *(andouilles)*, head-cheese *(fromage de tête)*, chops and various other bits. In Jura, there are as many types of fish as there are rivers and lakes for them to thrive in: char and trout from the Loue; carp and pike from the Doubs; tench and perch from the Ain. In the lakes there are fish from the salmon family (Coregonidae), white fish and small fry. *Meurette* sauces and *pauchouse* stew are as popular here for fish dishes as they are in Burgundy.

Mushrooms from the forests – *morilles*, *chanterelles* and *cèpes* – add their delicate flavour to aromatic sauces.

The local cheeses are excellent: **Comté**, with its hazelnut flavour, can be used to make a fondue. Try a mild and delicate **Emmenthal**, rich and creamy **Morbier**, or **Mont d'Or**, a subtly flavoured cheese made from milk from cows that have been kept on mountain pastures. **Gex Septmoncel** is a blue cheese with a delicate parsley flavour; **Cancoillotte**, a soft fermented cheese, is one of the region's oldest specialities.

To top off your meal in style, all the local vineyards produce good-quality **marc** spirits, but the **kirsch** from the Loue Valley (Mouthier-Haute-Pierre, Ornans) is particularly well regarded. Pontarlier, generally acknowledged as the capital of absinthe, produces an apéritif based on green aniseed, **Pontarlier Anis**. Liqueurs made from gentian and pine in the Haut-Jura plateaux are also popular.

WINEMAKING IN BURGUNDY

Burgundy wines are so well known that the name itself is synonymous with the deep red colour of some of the great vintages; yet the fine white wines are certainly not to be neglected!

The history of Burgundy wine – The cultivation of vines was introduced to the region by the Romans and spread rapidly. Wine from Burgundy was quick to win accolades, a historical fact confirmed by the names of certain vineyards (Vosne-Romanée) which recall the popularity of the wines with the Roman prefects of the province of Maxima Sequanorum.

In the 12C, Cistercian monks built up the vineyards, in particular the famous Clos-Vougeot. In the 15C the dukes of Burgundy took to styling themselves "lords of the best wines in Christendom" and supplying their wine to royalty. Louis XIV is known to have contributed to the fame of Côte de Nuits, whereas Madame de Pompadour favoured Romanée Conti and Napoleon preferred Chambertin.

In the 18C the first commercial warehouses opened at Beaune, Nuits-St-Georges and Dijon, sending representatives all over France and Europe to find new markets for Burgundy wines.

One of the enemies of the vine is a small aphid from America, phylloxera,

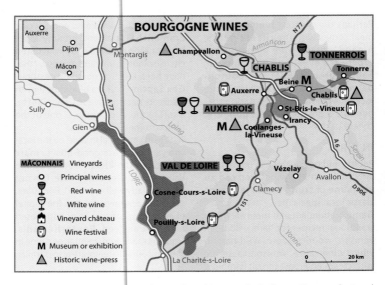

BOURGOGNE WINES

MÂCONNAIS Vineyards
- ○ Principal wines
- ♀ Red wine
- ♀ White wine
- 🏠 Vineyard château
- 📷 Wine festival
- **M** Museum or exhibition
- △ Historic wine-press

0   20 km

which made its appearance in the Gard *département* in 1863. In 1878, it was found at Meursault and within a short time it had completely ravaged the Burgundy vineyards. Luckily disaster was checked by grafting French vines onto resistant American root stock, enabling the slow restoration of the Burgundy vineyards.

Distribution of vineyards – There are 25 000ha/62 500 acres of vineyards producing officially registered vintages in the Yonne, Nièvre, Côte-d'Or, Saône-et-Loire and Rhône *départements*. Average annual production of high-quality wines is about 1 400 000hl/36 400 000 gal.

In the Yonne, the region of **Chablis** produces some excellent crisp, dry white wines, and the hillsides of the Auxerrois some pleasant rosés and reds (**Irancy, Coulanges-la-Vineuse**).

Well-known wines such as **Pouilly-Fumé** come from Pouilly-sur-Loire in Nièvre. In the **Côte-d'Or** highly reputed vineyards stretch from Dijon to Santenay. The **Côte de Nuits** produces almost exclusively top vintage reds, some of the most famous of which are **Gevrey-Chambertin**, **Vougeot**, **Vosne-Romanée** and **Nuits-St-Georges**. The **Côte de Beaune** wines include reds such as **Volnay**, **Savigny-lès-Beaune** and **Pommard** and whites such as

Meursault, Puligny-Montrachet and **Chassagne-Montrachet**.

In Saône-et-Loire, the Mercurey region (Côte Chalonnaise) produces high quality reds (**Givry, Rully**) and whites (**Rully-Montagny**), whereas the Mâconnais is justly proud of its **Pouilly-Fuissé**, widely considered one of the best white wines in France.

Grape varieties – All the great red Burgundy wines are made from the **Pinot Noir**, the aristocrat of grapes. It was already highly prized at the time of the Great Dukes. The Pinot Noir is native to Burgundy but has been successfully grown elsewhere. The juice of the Pinot Noir grape is colourless, and a special vinification process produces Champagne.

The **Chardonnay** grape is to white wines what the Pinot Noir is to red. It makes all the great white wines of the Côte d'Or (Montrachet-Meursault), the famous vintages of the Côte Chalonnaise (Rully), of the Mâconnais where it grows best (Pouilly-Fuissé) and the wines of Chablis (where it is known as the Beaunois grape).

Other grape varieties include the **Aligoté**, which has been cultivated for centuries in Burgundy, as it grows in the areas where the Pinot Noir and Chardonnay grapes do not thrive, and

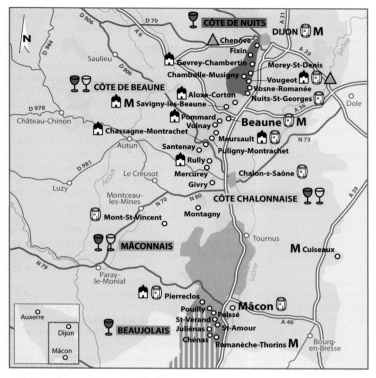

which produces white wines which are popular, even if they do not have quite the same reputation for character and quality as those from the more famous vineyards. These are the wines that are combined with blackcurrant liqueur *(cassis)* to make the popular French apéritif known as Kir after the man who is credited with its invention, a mayor of Dijon, Canon Kir.

Soil – The soil type plays an important role in allowing the particular characteristics of the vines to develop. Vines grow best in dry, stony soils, which are well drained and easily warmed by the sun. Limestone soils produce wines with rich bouquets and a high alcohol content, which can be aged for many years (Côte de Nuits, Côte de Beaune), whereas mixed soils of silicas, limestone and clay yield lighter wines (Chablis).

Climate – The prevailing climate in Burgundy is temperate, but frosts do occur and must be taken into consideration. Burgundy vineyards are usually laid out in terraces on the hillsides at altitudes of between 200–500m/656–1 640ft. They seem to thrive best when facing between south and east (south-west for Pouilly-sur-Loire). In each village, the vineyards are divided into *climats*, as determined by the soil content and exposure of the plot. The name of an individual vineyard with excellent conditions for producing fine wine, often known as a *clos*, may be added to the name of the village on the label. Some of the *climats* have earned such a reputation over the years that their name alone suffices to identify them: Chambertin, Musigny, Clos de Vougeot and Richebourg.

Millésime and aging – When selecting a Burgundy wine, it is important to take into account the year in which it was bottled, as the weather conditions have a big impact on quality. Although they do not enjoy the exceptional longevity of the famous *vin jaune du Jura*, Burgundy wines mature well. Generally, they are best kept for five to seven years, but some white wines can age eight to ten years and exceptional reds can be stored for up to 15 years. Wines mature best in a dark, well-ventilated area at a constant cool temperature and about 70 percent humidity.

Serving Burgundy wines

Certain dishes enhance the pleasure of drinking Burgundy wines:

– with oysters, shellfish, fish: Chablis, Meursault, Pouilly-Fuissé, Mâcon, or other dry white wines, chilled.

– with fowl, veal, pork and light dishes: Côte de Beaune, Mercurey, Beaujolais or other light red wines served at the storage temperature.

– with game, red meat, wild mushrooms and cheese: Chambertin, Côte de Nuits, Pommard and other hearty reds served at room temperature.

Beaujolais wine

The Beaujolais vineyards cover an area 60km/37mi long and 12km/7.5mi wide from the Mâcon escarpment to the north to the Azergues Valley to the south. This area occupies about 22 500ha/55 595 acres and yields an average of 1 250 000hl/27 375 000 gallons of wine a year. The majority of these (99 percent) are red, exclusively from the Gamay grape. There are three categories of Beaujolais wine, starting with the *crus*, the best vintages, followed by **Beaujolais Villages** and **Beaujolais supérieurs**.

The 10 leading *crus* are **Moulin-à-Vent,** an elegant wine with lots of substance, which can be kept for 5–10 years, closely followed by **Morgon** with its fine bouquet, which has often been described as the "Beaujolais most like a Burgundy". Firm and fruity **Juliénas**, well-rounded **Chénas**, classy **Fleurie** and **Côte de Brouilly** all have a keen following, whereas the fresh and lively **Saint-Amour**, **Chiroubles** (which the French consider to be a feminine wine), **Brouilly** and **Régnié-Durette** (the baby of the *crus*, having been promoted in 1988) are best enjoyed young.

Fruity Beaujolais-Villages is at its best after about a year in the bottle. Beaujolais or Beaujolais *supérieurs* do not age

well and are best served slightly chilled (unlike most red wines).

IN JURA

The vineyards of the Franche-Comté extend south-west of Salins, along a narrow strip of land 5km/3mi wide, covering the limestone and mixed clay and limestone slopes of the western edge of Jura.

Four vintages are produced from these vineyards: **Arbois**, the most famous, **Château-Chalon**, **Étoile** and those of the **Côtes du Jura** appellation, which includes local wines such as Poligny and Arlay. A Jura wine festival is held each September in Arbois.

The grape varieties cultivated in Jura include Trousseau for red wines, Poulsard for rosé, Chardonnay for white wines and Savagnin, used to create the celebrated *vin jaune du Jura*.

Red wines are produced in small quantities and are fresh and fruity when young, developing a subtle, characteristic bouquet with age. The most famous **rosé wines** come from Arbois and Pupillin. These lively but not overpowering wines have a pleasant fruity flavour. Local **white wines**, mainly from the Arbois and Étoile regions, are dry, yet supple, and fairly heady. Not only do these wines accompany local dishes, they are also excellent apéritif wines. The region also produces **sparkling wines**, both white (Étoile, Arbois and Côtes du Jura) and rosé (Arbois and Côtes du Jura).

Vin jaune is a speciality of the Jura region (Château-Chalon and Arbois), made from the Savagnin grape. The wine is left to age in barrels for 6–10 years, where it begins to oxidise and acquires its characteristic deep yellow colour and distinctive bouquet beneath a film of yeasts (similar to the production of sherry). A good vintage can be kept for over a century. It is relatively rare and expensive, with a strong flavour.

Vin de paille, straw wine, also particular to the Jura region, is made from almost over-ripe grapes dried on a bed of straw for a couple of months before being pressed. This produces a strong, sweet dessert wine.

Macvin is another Jura dessert wine, made from grape must blended with Franche-Comté eau-de-vie, and can reach up to 16–20 percent alcohol content. It is usually drunk chilled as an apéritif.

Red and rosé **Bugey wines** are light and fruity, but the white Bugey wines are the best. Particularly good examples are Roussette and Seyssel, followed by rarer wines such as Virieu or Montagnieu. This region also produces some sparkling wines, **Seyssel** and **Cerdon**.

Wine Country

The art of drinking wine – To identify and describe the qualities or defects of a particular wine, both wine buffs and wine experts use an extremely wide yet precise vocabulary. Assessing a wine involves three successive stages, each associated with a particular sense and a certain number of technical terms:

The eye – General impression: crystalline (good clarity), limpid (perfectly transparent, no particles in suspension), still (no bubbles), sparkling (effervescent wine) or *mousseux* (lots of fine, Champagne-type bubbles).

Colour and hues – a wine is said to have a nice robe when the colour is sharp and clean; the main terms used to describe the different hues are pale red, ruby, onionskin, garnet (red wine), salmon, amber, partridge-eye pink (rosé wine), and golden-green, golden-yellow and straw (white wine).

The nose – Pleasant smells: floral, fruity, balsamic, spicy, flinty.
Unpleasant smells: corked, woody, hydrogen sulphide, cask.

The mouth – Once it has passed the visual and olfactory tests, the wine undergoes a final test in the mouth. It can be described as agreeable (pleasant), aggressive (unpleasant, with a high acidity), full-flavoured (rich and well-balanced), structured (well-constructed, with a high alcohol content), heady (intoxicating), fleshy (producing a strong impact on taste buds), fruity (flavour evoking the freshness and natural taste of grapes), easy to drink, jolly (inducing merriness), round (supple, mellow), lively (light, fresh, with a lowish alcohol content) etc.

Quality control – French wines fall into various official categories indicating the area of production and therefore the probable quality of the wine.
AOC *(appellation d'origine contrôlée)* denotes a wine produced in a strictly delimited area, stated on the label, made with the grape varieties specified for that wine in accordance with local traditional methodology. VDQS *(vin délimité de qualité supérieure)* is also produced in a legally controlled area, slightly less highly rated than AOC. *Vin de pays* denotes the highest ranking table wine after AOC and VDQS.

Wine cellar visits – The **Bureau interprofessionnel des vins de Bourgogne (BIVB)**, *(12 bd. Bretonnière, BP 150, 21024 Beaune Cedex; ✆03 80 25 04 80; www.vins-bourgogne.fr)*, provides information and publishes brochures about wines including a repertory of wine cellars selling bottled wine with the names of the different estates, cooperatives and wine-producers/merchants.

Wine-tasting courses lasting from two hours to several days are organised by the **École des vins de Bourgogne** *(BIVB; ✆03 80 25 04 95)*.

In addition, 250 wine-producers/merchants, cooperatives and municipal cellars have formed an association known as the **De Vignes en Caves**. Members display a sign at the entrance of their estate and a list of all members with their location is offered to visitors in tourist information centres.

Wine Museums

These are described in the guide:
- **Beaune**
  Musée du Vin de Bourgogne
- **Chenôve**
  Cuverie des Ducs de Bourgogne
- **Vougeot**
  Château du Clos de Vougeot
- **Reulle-Vergy** Musée des Arts et Traditions des Hautes-Côtes
- **Cuiseaux** Maison de la Vigne et du Vigneron
- **Romanèche-Thorins**
  Hameau du Vin

Office de tourisme de Dijon/Atelier Démoulin

KIR

Kir is a friendly little before-dinner drink made of cool white wine and a touch of cassis, a blackcurrant liqueur and a Dijon speciality. Its rosy colour and sweet aroma make you feel better just looking at it. Start with champagne and it becomes a *kir royal*, or innovate with other flavoured liqueurs (peach, blackberry). While the origins of the concoction itself are lost in time, the name is that of Dijon's mayor (from 1945 until his death in 1968), who tirelessly served this drink to his guests at the town hall.

- **Coulanges-la-Vineuse** Musée de la Vigne et du Vieux Pressoir

Internet
Many wine-makers maintain websites and sell their wine via the Internet; others have chosen to be included on the portal of their merchants.

- **www.bourgogne.net**
  This portal includes numerous informative websites on the themes of economy, tourism, wine, wine-growing estates etc. and is a good introduction to the region.

- **www.frenchwines.com**
  Linked to the previous portal, this website offers a repertory of French wines with maps, a list of wine-growing villages, of events concerning wine, of wine-growers and merchants, an explanation of the *appellations* system and a vintage table with ratings.
- **www.louisjadot.com**
  The geographical specificity of this wine-growing estate is explained in detail. Wide list of appellations.
- **www.louislatour.com**
  Map of the various plots of land which make up this estate and the wines produced are described with tasting tips.

Beaune Wine Auction Sale
Find out all about this famous wine auction sale (the world's most important charity sale) on the website at www.hospices-de-beaune.com.

Buying Wine Online:
- **www.denisperret.fr**
- **www.vins-du-beaujolais.com**
  This elaborate website includes a great number of wine-growers and is one of the best for buying wine.
- **www.vintime.com**
  This site offers a wide selection of great Burgundy wines; the company is also renowned for its collection of old vintages.

Wine and Music
Each summer, the Festival Musical des Grands Crus de Bourgogne offers a programme linking wine tastings with musical performances. Several concerts a piano competition, and a programme of flute music are among the offerings located in intriguing locations: the cellars of the Château de Meursault, the Château du Clos-Vougeot, the Église de Noyers, the Farinier de Cluny, the Collégiale de Chablis and the Proche Chapelle de Préhy. Courses in music and enology are also offered. Contact ☎03 80 34 38 40.

History

PREHISTORY

BC   Bone fragments found at Solutré show there were humans there between 18 000 and 15 000 BC.

ANTIQUITY

6C   During the Gaulish period Burgundy is inhabited by the **Aedui**; their capital is Bibracte.

4C   The **Sequani**, from the Haute Seine, settle in Franche-Comté. They build fortified camps, including Vesontio (Besançon).

58   Under threat from the **Helvetii**, the Aedui ask for help from Caesar. The Sequani also request his help, this time against the Germanic threat. Caesar drives out the Helvetii and the Germanic tribes... but stays on in Gaul himself.

52   Gaul rises up against **Caesar**. The Sequani and the Aedui join forces, but are forced to concede victory to Caesar at the decisive battle of Alésia.

51   End of the Gaulish War.

AD   Roman civilisation spreads throughout Gaul.

1–3C   **Autun**, city of Augustus, becomes capital of north-east Gaul and supplants Bibracte.

313   **Edict of Milan**: the Emperor Constantine grants freedom of worship to Christians.

Late 4C   Christianity gradually spreads into Burgundy. The Roman Empire finally collapses.

BURGUNDY

5C   Burgundians, **natives of the Baltic coast**, settle in the Saône plain. They give their name to their new homeland: Burgundia (which evolved in French into Bourgogne).

534   The **Franks** seize the Burgundian kingdom.

800   **Charlemagne** becomes Emperor of the West.

814   The death of Charlemagne plunges the Empire into a period of instability. The sons of Emperor Louis the Pious dispute his legacy.

841   **Charles the Bald** defeats his brother Lothar at Fontanet (Fontenoy-en-Puisaye).

843   **Treaty of Verdun**: Charlemagne's empire is divided between the three sons of Louis the Pious. Frankish Burgundy reverts to Charles the Bald. It is separated by the Saône from imperial Burgundy, Lothar's territory, the north of which becomes the County of Burgundy (or Comté).

Late 9C   Frankish Burgundy becomes a duchy and takes in Langres, Troyes, Sens, Nevers and Mâcon.

THE DUCHY OF BURGUNDY

987–996   Reign of **Hugues Capet**.

996–1031   Reign of **Robert II the Pious**.

1002–1016   The King of France occupies the Duchy of Burgundy.

1032   The Germanic Emperor becomes suzerain of the Comté. But both his power and that of the count decline as the great feudal landowners gain influence, headed by the Chalons. **Henri I**, son of Robert II the Pious, to whom Burgundy returns, hands it over as a fief to his brother Robert I the Old (a Burgundian branch of the Capet family which survived until 1361). Under the Capetian dukes, Burgundy is one of the bastions of Christianity; **Cluny**, then Cîteaux and Clairvaux reach the height of their influence.

1095   **First Crusade**.

1270   Death of **St Louis** at the siege of Tunis.

1295   **Philip the Fair** buys the Comté as an apanage for his son Philip

Philip the Bold

© Christophe Boisvieux/hemis.fr

the Long and his descendants. This is the beginning of a period of peace and prosperity.

1337–1453 Hundred Years War.

1349 The Comté is devastated by the **Black Plague**; this is *l'année de la grande mort* (the year of widespread death).

1353 Switzerland frees itself from imperial domination.

1361 Duke Philippe de Rouvres dies young without issue, bringing the line of the Capet dukes to an end. The Duchy of Burgundy passes to the King of France, John the Good, who was regent during the duke's minority.

1366 The name **Franche-Comté** appears for the first time, on an official decree proclaiming the value the inhabitants attach to their rights, as had been done in the Franche-Montagnes of the Swiss Jura.

THE COMTÉ RETURNS TO BURGUNDIAN RULE

1384–1477 Philip the Bold (son of the King of France, John the Good), who had already been given the duchy in apanage, marries the heiress to the Comté and takes possession of the whole of Burgundy. He is the first of the dynasty of the "great dukes of Burgundy", whose power came to exceed that of the kings of France.

He is succeeded by John the Fearless, Philip the Good and Charles the Bold. In the Comté, these rulers keep a tight rein on the feudal lords, enforce the authority of Parliament and the State bodies and become patrons of art and literature.

1429 Orléans is saved by **Joan of Arc**.

1453 Constantinople falls to the Turks.

1461–1483 Reign of **Louis XI**.

THE GRAND DUKES OF BURGUNDY

Under this branch of the House of Valois, Burgundy reached the height of its power, where it remained for over a century (1364–1477).

PHILIP THE BOLD (1364–1404)

While scarcely more than a child, Philip fought bravely beside his father, King John II of France, at the battle of Poitiers (1356). He earned the nickname "the Bold" when, although wounded and a prisoner, he landed a well-aimed blow on an English lord who had insulted the French King.

By the time he became Duke of Burgundy (1364), Philip was a superb knight, who loved sport and women, and who devoted himself heart and soul to his duchy and the interests of his House. His marriage in 1369 to Margaret of Flanders, the richest heiress in Europe, made him the most powerful prince in Christendom. He lived in great splendour and kept a large and magnificent household in the palace he had built, where he employed painters and sculptors from Flanders.

Philip founded the Chartreuse de Champmol in Dijon as a mausoleum for himself and his descendants. The finest marble from Liège and alabaster from Genoa were provided for the tomb which was designed in 1384 by the sculptor **Jean de Marville**. On his death, the decoration was entrusted to **Claus Sluter**. Philip the Bold spent so much money that, when he died in 1404, his sons had to pledge the ducal silver to pay for his funeral.

John the Fearless (1404–19) – John succeeded his father, Philip the Bold. Although puny to look at, he was brave, intelligent and ambitious.

No sooner had he become Duke of Burgundy than he started a quarrel with the royal council against his cousin, Louis d'Orléans, brother of the mad king, Charles VI, and in 1407 had his rival assassinated. John took control of Paris, where he was opposed by the Orleanist faction which controlled the king. When the Orleanist leader, the poet Charles d'Orléans, was captured at Agincourt (1415) and taken to England, where he was a prisoner for 25 years, his father-in-law, Count Bernard VII of Armagnac, took over his leadership.

During the struggle between the Armagnacs and the Burgundians, in which the French were drawn into fighting each other, John the Fearless, realising the potential harm of the struggle for French interests, sought to negotiate an agreement with the dauphin, the future king, Charles VII. He agreed to meet him on 11 September 1419 on the bridge at Montereau, but was murdered there.

PHILIP THE GOOD (1419–67)

Filled with desire for vengeance, Philip the Good, son of John the Fearless, allied himself with the English and in 1430 handed them Joan of Arc, whom he had captured at Compiègne, for the enormous sum of 10 000 livres. A few years later, however, Philip came to an understanding with Charles VII at the Treaty of Arras, which enabled him, once again, to enlarge his territory. Dijon became the capital of a powerful state which included a large part of Holland, most of Belgium, Luxembourg, Flanders, Artois, Hainaut, Picardy and all the land between the Loire and Jura.

Philip, who had an even greater taste for magnificence than his predecessors, lived like a king. Five great officers of state, the Marshal of Burgundy, the Admiral of Flanders, the Chamberlain, the Master of the Horse and the Chancellor, were part of the Duke's immediate entourage, in a court that was among the most sumptuous in Europe.

On the day of his marriage with Isabella of Portugal, 14 January 1429, Philip founded the sovereign Order of the Golden Fleece (▣ see DIJON) in honour of God, the Virgin Mary and St Andrew. The Order originally had 31 members, all of whom swore allegiance to the Grand Master, Philip the Good and his successors. They met at least once every three years and were lavishly dressed: a long scarlet cloak, trimmed with squirrel fur, hung from the shoulders over a robe of the same colour, also trimmed with squirrel fur. The ducal motto, *Aultre n'auray* (not for others), stood out against a background of firestones, quartz, sparkling stones and fleeces. The neck chain of the Order was made of sparkling firestones and quartz. The headquarters of the Order was the ducal Holy Chapel at Dijon, destroyed during the Revolution. The Order is now one of the most prestigious and exclusive.

CHARLES THE BOLD (1467–77)

He was the last, and possibly the most famous, member of the House of Valois and the dukes of Burgundy. Tall, vigorous and strongly built, Charles loved violent exercise, and in particular hunting. However, he was also a cultured man and spent much of his time in study. Above all he was passionately interested in history. As his father had the same name as Philip of Macedonia, Charles dreamed of becoming a second Alexander and was constantly waging

Charles the Bold

The Art Archive/Musée du Château de Versailles/Gianni Dagli Orti war in an effort to undermine Louis XI, who in turn did everything possible to break up the Burgundian state. Charles was killed during the siege of Nancy.

RETURN TO THE FRENCH CROWN

1477 On the death of Charles the Bold, **Louis XI** invades the Comté, annexing Burgundy and the Burgundian towns in Picardy to the royal territory. Mary of Burgundy, the daughter of the dead duke, deprived of a large part of her inheritance marries Maximilian of Habsburg who thus acquires the rest of the old duchy. Their union produces Philip the Handsome whose son, the future emperor, **Charles V**, will continue the struggle against the Kingdom of France ruled by François I.

1519 The Comté enjoys a period of prosperity under Charles V. He includes people from the Comté, such as the Granvelles, in his immediate circle.

1556–98 Emperor Charles V bequeaths the Comté to his son, **Philip II**, King of Spain, who proves to be far less sympathetic a ruler to the people of the Comté.

1589–1610 Reign of **Henri IV**.

1598 On the death of Philip II, the Comté passes to his daughter **Isabelle**, who marries the Archduke of Austria. The province of the Comté belongs to the archdukes until it is seized by the French in 1678.

THE FRENCH CONQUEST

In order to understand the resistance to French rule of a French-speaking country, one must remember that, finding itself on the borders of the Holy Empire, Austria and Spain, the Comté had become used to directing its own affairs. The independent people of the Comté regarded the rule of a Richelieu or a Louis XIV with trepidation.

1601 Henri IV acquires the territories of Bresse, Bugey, Valromey and the Gex region from the Duke of Savoy, in return for some Italian territory of his.

1609 After 50 years of struggle against the Spanish, the Netherlands wins its independence.

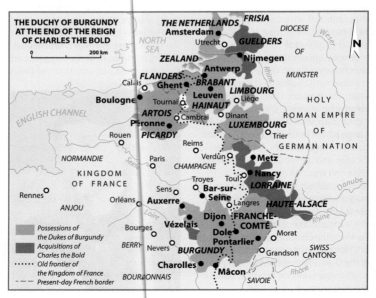

1610	Beginning of the reign of **Louis XIII**, who dies in 1643.
1618	Start of the **Thirty Years War** between Austria and France allied with Sweden. The war ends in 1648 with the **Treaty of Westphalia**.
1635	Richelieu gives the order to invade the Comté which gave refuge to his enemy, Gaston d'Orléans. The Ten Years War brings the country to ruin.
1643–1715	Reign of **Louis XIV**.
1648	**Mazarin** withdraws French forces from the Comté and restores it to its neutral status.
1668	Louis XIV reclaims the Comté as part of the dowry of his wife **Marie-Thérèse**, daughter of the late King of Spain. However, he is forced to abandon it and return it to Spain.
1674	Louis XIV, at war with Spain, makes a fresh attempt to take control of the province, and this time is successful. His conquest is ratified by the **Peace of Nimègue** (1678). Besançon takes over from Dole as capital. From now on, the history of the Comté follows that of the rest of France.

FROM REVOLUTION TO MODERN TIMES

1715–74	Reign of **Louis XV**.
1789	Fall of the **Bastille**.
1793	The Montbéliard region is annexed to France.
1804	Consecration of **Napoleon I** as Emperor of France.
1815	The battle of **Waterloo**. Heroic defence of Belfort by Lecourbe.
1822	Invention of photography by Nicéphore Niepce at St-Loup-de-Varenne.
1870	Colonel Denfert-Rochereau resists attack by 40 000 Germans during the **siege of Belfort**.
1871	General Bourbaki is defeated at Héricourt, having won victory at Villersexel, and has to fall back to Besançon.

1878	Vines devastated by the **phylloxera** aphid.
Late 19C–	As industrialisation gains pace,
early 20C	the Jura region is transformed. Great industrial dynasties such as **Peugeot** and Japy are born, compensating for the decline in the clockmaking industry.
1914	Joffre gives his famous order of 6 September at Châtillon-sur-Seine.
1940	Occupation of Jura by the **Germans**, who use the region to block the retreat of French forces trying to reach central France along the Swiss border.
1940–44	The **Resistance movement** is active in Burgundy: Châtillonnais forests are used as a hideout.
14 September 1944	**Leclerc**'s division joins the army of De Lattre de Tassigny near Châtillon-sur-Seine.
November 1944	The **Allied conquest** of the northern part of the Doubs *département* completes the liberation of Jura.
1948	Génissiat reservoir is filled with water.
1970	A6-A7 motorway from Paris to Marseille opens up the west of Burgundy (Auxerre, Beaune and Mâcon).
1981	High-speed rail service (**TGV**) links Paris-Le Creusot-Mâcon-Lyon and Paris-Dijon-Besançon.
1986	Setting up of the **Haut-Jura** regional nature park.
1992	Fabrice Guy, native of Pontarlier, wins the Olympic gold medal for Nordic combined.
2001	After an 85-year prohibition, production of **absinthe** is again allowed in Pontarlier.
2007	Tricentenary of the death of Burgundy-born Sebastien le Prestre de Vauban, Louis XIV's influential military engineer.
2010	1100th Anniversary of the foundation of Cluny's abbey.

Religious Architecture

RELIGIOUS ORDERS

After the fall of Charlemagne's empire, the Church used its considerable influence to resume a leading role in society; there was a renewal of fervour for the monastic life throughout Europe, but especially in Burgundy.

St Benedict and his Rule – In 529 Benedict, who was born in Italy, moved to Monte Cassino where he worked out his Constitution, soon to be adopted by many monasteries. His advice was moderate: fasting, silence and abstinence were recommended, but mortification was strongly condemned. Relations with the outside world were to be avoided, and Benedictine communities were to be self-sufficient through their own work.

The rise of Cluny – In 910 the founding of a monastery in the Mâcon region by the Duke of Aquitaine marked the start of an important religious reform associated with the name of Cluny. The spirit of the Benedictine Rule was marked by the observance of the three cardinal rules of obedience, chastity and fasting, but there was a much heavier emphasis on prayer, which almost eliminated the time for manual labour and other work. Another innovation was that Cluny was directly attached to the Holy See in Rome, effectively making it autonomous. The Order grew rapidly; by the 12C there were 1 450 monasteries throughout Europe.

Cîteaux and St Bernard – When a young French nobleman from near Dijon spoke out about the lazy ways and luxury among the monks of Cluny, he could not have known that it was the start of a new Order. St Bernard, having entered the monastic life at Cîteaux, embarked on a new and more austere interpretation of Benedictine Rule: plain woollen tunics, frugal meals, the simplest of beds, early rising and hard physical work.

Like St Bernard, the Cistercians had an impact on society that went beyond issues of faith. Well organised and hardworking, the monks were able to bring prosperity to the harshest and most isolated places by clearing and draining land and setting up irrigation systems.

The contemporary order – After the turmoil and physical destruction of the Revolution, monastic life has found a place in the modern world. Today there are about 3 000 Trappist Cistercians (the name is derived from the abbey of Notre-Dame-de-la-Trappe, reformed in the 17C), in 92 establishments worldwide, 15 of which are in France.

IN BURGUNDY

Burgundy has a rich artistic tradition. Since Antiquity, the region has been a crossroads where a wide variety of peoples and influences have met. The treasure found near Vix shows that strong currents were active in the region of Châtillon-sur-Seine in about the 6C BC. In the 15C, on the initiative of the Great Dukes, artists from Paris and Flanders settled in Dijon, which became an important artistic centre.

This penetration of foreign influences, and the enduring qualities of Roman civilisation, combined with the expression of the Burgundian temperament, led to a blossoming of regional art that holds a special place in French artistic history.

Pre-Romanesque – The Carolingian epoch (8–9C) saw architectural revival in Burgundy in particular. The religious buildings were simple. Part of the former crypt of the cathedral of **St-Bénigne** at Dijon and the crypts of **Flavigny-sur-Ozerain** and **St-Germain** of Auxerre are among the oldest examples.

Romanesque – Numerous towns, wealthy abbeys and abundant building material were favourable conditions in which the Romanesque School of Burgundy flourished, showing an extraordinary vitality in the 11C and 12C, not only in architecture, but in sculpture and painting (*see below*). The school's influence spread far beyond Burgundy's borders.

In the year 1000, the desire to build was given fresh impetus by the end of inva-

Ecclesiastical architecture

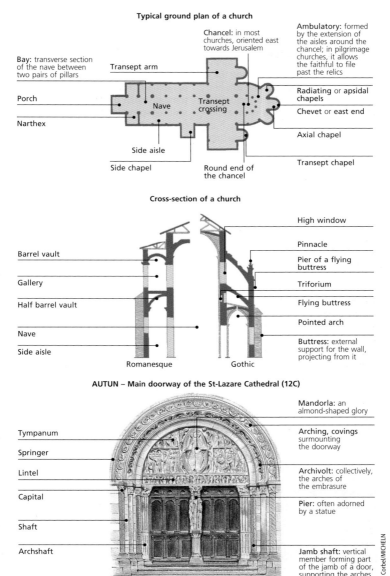

Typical ground plan of a church

Chancel: in most churches, oriented east towards Jerusalem

Ambulatory: formed by the extension of the aisles around the chancel; in pilgrimage churches, it allows the faithful to file past the relics

Bay: transverse section of the nave between two pairs of pillars

Transept arm

Radiating or apsidal chapels

Porch

Nave

Transept crossing

Chevet or east end

Narthex

Axial chapel

Side aisle

Side chapel

Round end of the chancel

Transept chapel

Cross-section of a church

High window

Barrel vault

Pinnacle

Pier of a flying buttress

Gallery

Triforium

Half barrel vault

Flying buttress

Pointed arch

Nave

Side aisle

Buttress: external support for the wall, projecting from it

Romanesque

Gothic

AUTUN – Main doorway of the St-Lazare Cathedral (12C)

Mandorla: an almond-shaped glory

Tympanum

Arching, covings surmounting the doorway

Springer

Lintel

Archivolt: collectively, the arches of the embrasure

Capital

Pier: often adorned by a statue

Shaft

Archshaft

Jamb shaft: vertical member forming part of the jamb of a door, supporting the arches

R. Corbel/MICHELIN

sions, the strengthening of royal power and new building techniques.
Early Burgundian Romanesque churches – Among the great builders of this period, Abbot Guglielmo **da Vol-** **piano**, of Italian origin and related to some of the greatest families of his time, built a new basilica in Dijon on the site of the tomb of St Bénigne. The building, begun in 1001, was consecrated in 1018.

Though this abbey was destroyed by fire in the 12C, the church of **St-Vorles** in Châtillon-sur-Seine – much modified in the first years of the 11C – provides an example of the features of Romanesque art at this time: slipshod building methods with badly placed flat stones; thick pillars; crude decoration of mural niches; and cornices with Lombard arcades.

The most striking example of the architecture of this time is the church of **St-Philibert in Tournus**. The narthex and the upper storey of the narthex, built at the beginning of the 11C, are the oldest extant parts to date. The most striking aspect of this solid, powerful architecture is its sober, almost austere style.

Cluny and its school – Although in the beginning Romanesque art owed much to foreign influences, the following period witnessed the triumphant emergence of a new style from Cluny, which was to spread throughout Burgundy.

In 1247 an Italian visitor noted that "Cluny is the noblest Burgundian monastery of the Benedictine Black Monk order. The buildings are so extensive that the Pope with his cardinals and entire retinue and the king and his court may be accommodated together, without upsetting the monks' routine or putting them out of their cells".

The extent and exceptional size of the remains of the abbey, which was started by St Hugh in 1088 and completed about 1130 (& see CLUNY), are still impressive

and allow one to recognise the general characteristics of the School of Cluny. Burgundian architects avoided semicircular vaulting and substituted broken-barrel vaulting which was far more efficient at withstanding the strains and stresses of the building. This style of vaulting consists of each bay having a transverse arch; the use of broken arches reduces stress and thereby the weight on the walls, thus making it possible to raise the vaulting to a far greater height. The pillars are flanked by fluted pilasters in the Antique style; a false triforium of alternating bays and pilasters, surmounted by a clerestory, runs above the narrow arches. This arrangement of three storeys rising to a pointed vault is found in many churches in the region.

The priory church of **Paray-le-Monial** is a smaller replica of the great abbey church at Cluny. At **Semur-en-Brionnais**, home of the family of St Hugh, the church is almost as high as Cluny. On the interior of the west front, the gallery is similar to one in St-Michel in Cluny.

Vézelay and its influence – The Cluny School was repudiated by a whole family of churches, the purest example of which is the basilica of **Ste-Madeleine in Vézelay**, although there are others that display characteristics even further removed from Cluny. Built at the beginning of the 12C, Vézelay constitutes the synthesis of true Burgundian Romanesque architecture. The essential difference between this church and earlier Romanesque buildings is that the nave has groined vaulting whereas up to that time only the side aisles had this feature, their small size mitigating the risk of the vaulting subsiding as a result of lateral pressure.

This design, originally without the support of flying buttresses which were added in the Gothic period, required the incorporation of iron bars to prevent the walls of the nave from bulging outwards.

Clerestory windows placed directly above the main arches opened onto the axis of each bay, shedding light into the nave. Columns projecting slightly

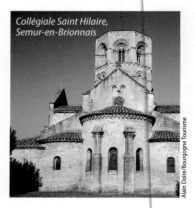

Collégiale Saint Hilaire, Semur-en-Brionnais

Alain Doire/Bourgogne Tourisme

VÉZELAY – Nave of the Ste-Madeleine Basilica

High window

Pier: a kind of pilaster supporting the column

Wall arch or **stringer:** lateral arch of a vault

Cornice with frieze

Abacus

Groined vaulting: two ribs meet at a right angle

Archstone (here, dark and light cut stone blocks alternate)

Historiated capital decorated with scenes or characters

Triumphant arch: a large arcade separating the central nave from the transept or the chancel

Triforium: a gallery and passageway hollowed from the thickness of the wall. At the end of the Gothic period, this feature became purely decorative

Engaged half-columns: set around the four faces of a cruciform pillar

Transverse arch: reinforces the vault

Cross-ribbed vault

Chancel

R. Corbel/MICHELIN

TOURNUS – St-Philibert Abbey Church (11-12C)

The fortress-like appearance of the front wall, which was a defensive feature of the abbey, is one of the first examples of Romanesque art in Burgundy, dating to around the year 1000.

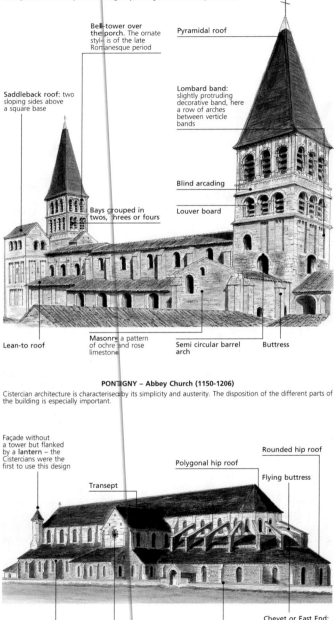

Bell-tower over the porch. The ornate style is of the late Romanesque period

Pyramidal roof

Saddleback roof: two sloping sides above a square base

Lombard band: slightly protruding decorative band, here a row of arches between verticle bands

Blind arcading

Bays grouped in twos, threes or fours

Louver board

Lean-to roof

Masonry a pattern of ochre and rose limestone

Semi circular barrel arch

Buttress

PONTIGNY – Abbey Church (1150-1206)

Cistercian architecture is characterised by its simplicity and austerity. The disposition of the different parts of the building is especially important.

Façade without a tower but flanked by a lantern – the Cistercians were the first to use this design

Rounded hip roof

Polygonal hip roof

Flying buttress

Transept

Side aisle

Round quatrefoil window

Buttress

Chevet or East End: the far end of the chancel (outside). Inside the church, this is the **apse**

R. Corbel/MICHELIN

from the walls replace the rectangular pilasters of Cluny style. The vaulting is supported by semicircular transverse arches.

The church in **Anzy-le-Duc** appears to have served as a model for the building in Vézelay; it is probable that Renaud **de Semur**, who came from the Brionnais region, wished to rebel against the all-powerful influence of Cluny and took as his model the church in Anzy-le-Duc, which at that time was the most perfect piece of architecture of the region. There is no shortage of points of comparison: the elevation of the storeys is the same; both have a solitary window above the main arches; both share the same style of semicircular vaulting and cruciform pillars flanked by engaged columns. This style, created in Anzy-le-Duc and perfected in Vézelay, has been copied in **St-Lazare in Avallon** and **St-Philibert in Dijon**.

Fontenay and the Cistercian School – Cistercian architecture first appeared in Burgundy in the first half of the 12C (Cistercium was the Latin name for the town of Cîteaux). It is characterised by a spirit of simplicity in keeping with the teaching of **St Bernard**. He objected bitterly to the luxury displayed in some monastic churches, opposing the theories of some of the great builders of the 11C and 12C with extraordinary passion. His argument against the belief of abbots such as St Hugh, Peter the Venerable and Suger, who believed that nothing could be too rich for the glory of God, was expressed for example in the letter he wrote to William, Abbot of St-Thierry, in which he asks, "Why this excessive height in the churches, this enormous length, this unnecessary width, these sumptuous ornaments and curious paintings that draw the eye and distract attention and meditation?… We the monks, who have forsaken ordinary life and renounced worldly wealth and ostentation for the love of Christ… in whom do we hope to awaken devotion with these ornaments?"

There is nonetheless a certain grandeur even in the sobriety and austerity that he advocated. The uncluttered style and severe appearance reflected the principles of Cistercian rule, which regarded everything that was not indispensable to the development and spread of the monastic way of life as harmful.

The Cistercians almost always insisted on the identical plan of construction for all the buildings of their order and themselves directed the work on new abbeys. The abbey of Fontenay is a good example of the standard plan (*see photograph*). This design is found throughout Europe from Sicily to Sweden. Every new monastery was another link with France, and craftsmen followed the monks. It was the turn of the Burgundian Cistercian monasteries to spearhead the expansion of monasticism.

In **Cistercian churches**, the blind nave is covered by broken-barrel vaulting, as at Cluny; the side aisles are generally arched with transverse barrel vaulting, and their great height enables them to take the thrust of the nave. This is found in many 12C Burgundian churches.

The transept, also of broken-barrel vaulting, juts far out and has two square chapels opening into each transept arm. The choir, of broken-barrel vaulting, is square and not very deep. It ends in a flat chevet lit through two tiers of three windows. Five windows are placed above the chancel arch, and each bay of the side aisles is also lit through a window. The fact that most Cistercian churches have no belfry is evidence of St Bernard's desire to adhere to poverty, humility and simplicity. Living far from their fellow men, the religious communities did not wish to attract the faithful from far and wide. Belfries, which drew attention to the existence of a church by their silhouette and shape, were thus banned.

By avoiding all decoration, be it painting or sculpture, and by eliminating every kind of superfluous ornamentation (such as stained-glass windows, or illuminated paving stones), Cistercian art achieved a remarkable purity of execution.

Gothic – In the mid-12C, perhaps even earlier, pointed vaulting appeared in Burgundy, heralding a new development in architecture. The Gothic style originated around Paris (Ile-de-France), and seeped into Burgundy, to be adapted according to circumstances and trends.

Period of transition – In 1140, the gallery of the narthex at Vézelay was given pointed vaulting. The Cistercians were among the first to adopt this style of architecture and used it at Pontigny in about 1150. The choir of **Ste-Madeleine at Vézelay**, the work of Abbot Gérard **d'Arcy**, was started in the last years of the 12C; the flying buttresses were not added until the 13C. It was in the 13C that a Burgundian Gothic style emerged in religious buildings.

First half of the 13C – The church of **Notre-Dame in Dijon**, built between 1230 and 1251, is the most perfect and best-known example of this style. Its characteristics are found in many religious buildings of the period in Burgundy; beyond the transept, the fairly deep choir is flanked by apsidal chapels (there are generally two) and ends with a high apse. The use of sexpartite vaulting permitted the replacing of the uniformly sized pillars with alternating thick and thin pillars. A triforium runs above the great arches; at the clerestory level, the nave wall is set back slightly allowing for a gallery above that of the triforium. In the external decoration, the presence of a cornice goes round the choir, the nave, the apse, or the belfry and is a typically Burgundian mode of decoration.

Of the buildings constructed in this style, the most important are: **Auxerre Cathedral**, the collegiate church of **St-Martin in Clamecy** and the church of **Notre-Dame** in **Semur-en-Auxois**. In the latter, the absence of a triforium further enhances the effect of dizzying height created by the narrow nave.

End of the 13C – Architecture now became much lighter and developed a boldness, seeming to defy gravity.

The choir of the church of **St-Thibault** in Auxois is in such a style, with its keystone at a height of 27m/89ft. The five-sided, four-storey apse is amazingly light. Below the highest windows is a clerestory composed of three tiers reaching to the ground: the top tier is a gallery, the middle one is composed of pairs of radiant windows and the bottom tier consists of blind arcades.

The church of **St-Père** shares similarities with Notre-Dame in Dijon, but it differs in its height, being of two storeys with a gallery in front of the windows.

14C – The Flamboyant Gothic style, characterised by the pointed, S-shaped ogee arch, appeared; the number of ribs multiplied and the capitals were reduced to a simple decorative role or were even dispensed with completely.

Renaissance – Under Italian influence, Burgundian art took a new turn in the 16C with a revival of Antique styles.

In architecture the transition from Gothic to Italian art met with some resistance. The church of **St-Michel in Dijon** shows evidence of this: the nave (started at the dawn of the 16C) imitates Gothic art, but the façade (built between 1537 and 1570) embodies the Renaissance style, with two towers split into four storeys, on which Ionic and Corinthian orders are superimposed alternately, three semicircular doorways and the porch with its richly sculpted coffered vaulting all reflecting a strong Italian influence.

IN JURA

The religious architectural heritage of Franche-Comté owes much to its monastic communities during the Middle Ages, who played a vital role in developing this rugged, primitive country. By the Merovingian period, two abbeys were already making waves throughout the region: Luxeuil in the north and Condat (later St-Claude) in the south. The former rapidly became an intellectual centre exerting an influence on the whole of Gaul, whereas the latter devoted its energies to spreading the Christian message and to the enormous task of clearing space in the forests of Jura.

Sadly, the anarchy which greeted the end of Carolingian rule sounded a death knell for both these abbeys. In the 10C, the Benedictines faced the task of winning back territory in Burgundy. They were followed by the Cluny order, which soon dominated the province. However, in the 12C the Cluny order itself gave way to the many Cistercian communities which were springing up. At the same time, communities were set up by the Premonstratensians, the Augustinians and the Carthusians who all set about clearing the forest and draining the soil, thus attracting their share of local residents, who set up communities round their abbeys. The churches, now used as parish churches, were originally monastery churches usually built according to the rules of the religious order which was to use them: thus, the Benedictine order introduced a primitive architectural style influenced by early Italian basilicas; the Cluny order preferred Burgundian style churches; and the Cistercians built churches with a flat chevet, like that at Cîteaux, and generally paved the way for Gothic art.

Romanesque – There is no Romanesque art specific to Franche-Comté; the primitive churches built there during the Romanesque period were inspired by Burgundian and Lombard architecture. They generally have a basilical floor plan with a transept hardly wider than the nave itself. The chancel ends in a semicircular apse, flanked by two apsidal chapels opening into the transept, or it ends in a flat chevet (as in the church at Courtefontaine). Large arcades are supported by heavy pillars, which can be square, round or octagonal, with no capitals. The buildings and pillars are often made of small quarry stones. The nave and side aisles were originally covered by a timber roof, later replaced by ogival vaulting. The roofs over the side aisles are sometimes groined vaulting. The apse and apsidal chapels are closed off by half domes. The roof above the transept crossing is either a dome or a bell tower, which never features as part of the façade.

The Jura churches are understated, with sparse decoration to underline their austerity. The churches of **St-Hymetière** and **St-Lupicin** (early 12C), **Boussières**, the crypt of **St-Denis at Lons-le-Saunier** are the best preserved examples. The cathedral of **St-Jean at**

St-Hymetière

G. Magnin/MICHELIN

Besançon is almost the only remaining trace of Rhenish Carolingian influence in Franche-Comté; it has an apse at either end of its nave. Inside, square sturdy pillars alternate with round slender ones, creating a regular division of space.

Gothic – Romanesque art continued to exert its influence in Franche-Comté for some time. Even at the end of the 13C, which marked the culmination of the great boom in Gothic art elsewhere, there were still many Romanesque features evident in buildings in Franche-Comté which had adopted the new style. The most typical and best-preserved example of this period of transition is the church of St-Anatoile at Salins. This has a semicircular arched doorway, large pointed arches in the nave and a triforium with Romanesque arcades. This long-lasting preference for semicircular arches is what makes the churches of Franche-Comté distinctive. The Gothic style did not really take over here until the mid-15C, when Flamboyant Gothic features were adopted. It did not reach its apogee until the next century, even surviving into the middle of the 17C, when the Renaissance style was starting to decline in other parts of France.

Flamboyant Gothic churches in Franche-Comté typically have three tall blind naves separated by elegant pointed arches supported on round pillars. The ribs from the vaulting and the moulding from the arches run down these pillars. The church is topped by an enormous bell tower. Large windows shed light

Chapelle de Ronchamp by Le Corbusier

© CRT Franche-Comté/Sandrine Baverel

into the deep, five-sided choir (St-Claude Cathedral, Poligny Collegiate Church), which is flanked by two chapels. These open onto the transept, which is a little wider than the nave. However, vaulting is generally uncluttered and only seigneurial chapels, such as the Chalon family chapel at Mièges, are ornate.

Renaissance – The Italian Renaissance had little effect on the religious buildings of Franche-Comté, which adhered to Flamboyant Gothic until quite late on. Once the new style began to creep in, it is seen mostly in church annexes, such as chapels (Pesmes) or entrance doorways (Collège de l'Arc at Dole).

Classical to modern periods – Classical art was slow to catch on in Franche-Comté; it began to appear from 1674 onwards, when churches destroyed in the Ten Years War (1633–43) and the campaigns of Louis XIV were re-built. The small, run-down churches which had survived from the Middle Ages, coupled with a huge rise in population from the mid-18C, may explain the boom in construction before the Revolution.

The most typical feature from this period is the way the porch is incorporated in a bell tower, which is topped by an imperial style pointed dome, formed of four reversed curve sides covered with glazed tiles. There are three common layouts: a church with a single nave, with or without a transept; a church with a centralised floor plan, either octagonal or in the shape of a Greek cross; or a hall-church with three naves of equal height, generally without a transept. The naves are covered by pointed vaulting, and buttressed outside to counter the outward pressure which might make the walls bulge at the top. The interior is often white, with columns, pillars and ribs, picked out in grey; frontons, pilasters and columns enliven the façade.

In the late 18C and early 19C, the simple, almost austere neo-Classical style took over. As in the Antique temples, straight lines replace curves, and side aisles with ceilings replace the side naves with pointed vaulting of the hall-churches. The central nave is covered with a barrel vault. After 1850, the neo-Gothic style revived pointed arches.

In the **contemporary** period, Jura is proud to have been the setting for a revival of religious art. Since the 1950s and 1960s, important projects have been undertaken, for example, at Audincourt, Ronchamp and Dole. A desire to emphasize the spirituality of such places is often clear in the powerful movement of the line of the building and in the way the decorative effects of light are used. Many artists, such as Manessier, Gabriel Saury, Bazaine, Le Moal and Fernand Léger, have contributed in the same spirit, giving a new or renewed vitality to religious buildings with their stained-glass windows, sculptures, mosaics or tapestries.

Civil and Military Architecture

IN BURGUNDY

Gallo-Roman art – The Romans were responsible for many monuments in Burgundy. To this day the town of **Autun**, built by order of Emperor Augustus to replace Bibracte, capital of the Aedui tribe, recalls Roman civilization with its monumental gateways and vast theatre. Excavations at **Alésia**, the possible site of the camp where Vercingetorix made his last stand in 52 BC, have led to the discovery of a complete town built a little later, including paved streets, the foundations of temples and a forum, and many dwellings. Other excavations out at the source of the Seine have revealed the ruins of a temple and a number of bronze statuettes and wooden sculptures. Pottery dating from Gallo-Roman times as well as examples of gold and silver work of great value were found more than 50 years ago at **Vertault**, not far from **Châtillon-sur-Seine**.

At **Dijon**, the remains of an entrenched camp (Castrum Divionense), built about AD 273, have been uncovered. Excavations at **Fontaines-Salées** near St-Père-sous-Vézelay have revealed very extensive Gallo-Roman baths.

Gothic – Fine mansions and houses built by wealthy merchants in the 15C have survived in Dijon and some other towns, such as **Flavigny-sur-Ozerain** and **Châteauneuf**. Part of the palace of the dukes of Burgundy in Dijon, the synodal palace in **Sens** and the hospital in **Beaune** all date from this period. Among the fortified castles of the 13C, those of Châteauneuf, built by Philippe Pot the Seneschal of Burgundy, Posanges and the ducal palace at Nevers are particularly interesting.

Renaissance – There was no blossoming of Renaissance châteaux in Burgundy. However, towns such as **Ancy-le-Franc**, **Tanlay** and **Sully** boast some magnificent mansions.

Classical – The reunion of Burgundy with the crown of France marked the end of the duchy's political independence, but its artistic expression survived. Classical art, initially imitated from Paris and later Versailles, is to be seen in **Dijon** in the layout of the **Place Royale**, the alterations to the old **Palais des Ducs** and in the building of the new Palais des Ducs. Many fine mansions were built by the families of parliamentarians who were in favour at Court at the time and who held high positions.

Although retaining the characteristics of the Renaissance period, the Hôtel de Vogüé (built 1607–14) features the new design where the living quarters are set

Château de Commarin

© Manfred Mehlig/Mauritius/Photononstop

back behind a courtyard with access to the street only through the coach gateway, with the opposite façade of the house opening onto the gardens.

Among the numerous châteaux built in the 17C and 18C, those of **Bussy-Rabutin**, **Commarin**, **Grancey**, **Beaumont-sur-Vingeanne**, **Menou** and **Talmay** deserve a special mention. The sculptors – **Dubois** in the 17C and **Bouchardon** and **Attiret** in the 18C – were very influential, as were painters and draughtsmen such as Greuze and François Devosge and above all **Mignard**, master painter at the court of Louis XIV.

Burgundy prides itself on its contribution to the musical world, **Jean-Philippe Rameau**, born in Dijon at the end of the 17C. He was a contemporary of Bach and Handel and ranks as one of the great French classical composers. Besides many pieces for the harpsichord, he composed some operas, of which one, *Les Indes Galantes*, is still included in the contemporary repertoire.

19C and 20C – In architecture, **Gustave Eiffel** (1832–1923), an engineer from Dijon, specialised in metal construction: bridges, viaducts etc. The mention of his name conjures up the tower he erected in Paris for the universal exhibition in 1889; its structure is based on a web of girders.

IN JURA

The architectural heritage of Franche-Comté reflects its turbulent history. The region was regularly subjected to the ravages of war and invasion, and it spent most of its rare periods of peace rebuilding its ruins. For this reason, there are relatively few real architectural masterpieces. However, the restrained style of the buildings has its own charm. During the **Gallo-Roman** period, Sequania was wealthy, but little trace of this glorious past remains after the invasions of the 9C and 10C. The Roman triumphal arch which the inhabitants of **Besançon** call Porte Noir (the black gate), the Roman road at Boujailles, the remains of a theatre at Mandeure near Montbéliard are about all that is left from this period.

The Middle Ages – After the Carolingian invasions and the subsequent disintegration of Carolingian rule, power devolved into the hands of local lords. These felt the need to protect themselves and their property, and turned to the Scandinavians for a design of fairly crude castle: the **keep** or **castle mound** (11C).

This consisted of an earth mound surrounded by a moat, and surmounted by a square wooden tower, which was later replaced by a stone tower.

At the same time, **stone fortresses** (Pesmes, Champlitte) made their appearance, generally on existing hills. The surrounding fortified wall – a stone embankment with a moat around its outer edge – enclosed the living quarters and outbuildings, whereas the keep remained the stronghold. This kind of fortress reached its apogee in the late 12C and the 13C.

At this point, a new kind of seigneurial dwelling evolved with the rise of the middle-ranking class of knights: the **fortified house** (especially after 1250). This would be located just outside the village near a stream or river, and be constructed on a man-made platform surrounded by a water-filled moat. The residential wings and outbuildings are arranged around a central courtyard.

Fortresses did not fare well during the 14C and 15C, as first the Hundred Years War, then the guns of Louis XI's troops wreaked devastation. However, the Château du Pin (15C), which is very well preserved, is an interesting example of medieval military architecture.

At the end of the Gothic period, town houses began to feature much more prominently, and were decorated with mullioned windows surmounted by ogee arches.

Renaissance – The return of peace and prosperity to Franche-Comté during the 16C was marked by numerous castles being modified to reflect the new style, while at the same time having their defences reinforced to withstand the new metal cannon balls, which were much more destructive than the old stone ones. But the aristocracy tended to

Military architecture

CLÉRON – Castle (14C)

This old feudal castle stands on the banks of the River Loue, which makes an excellent natural moat.

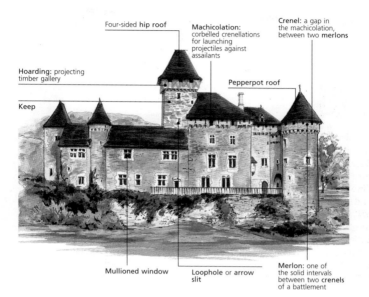

Four-sided **hip roof**

Machicolation: corbelled crenellations for launching projectiles against assailants

Crenel: a gap in the machicolation, between two **merlons**

Hoarding: projecting timber gallery

Pepperpot roof

Keep

Mullioned window

Loophole or **arrow slit**

Merlon: one of the solid intervals between two **crenels** of a battlement

BESANÇON – The citadel

An impressive sight: the fortifications hang 118m/387ft above the River Doubs. Vauban designed the citadel in the 17C.

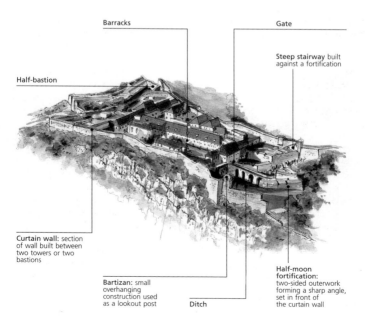

Barracks

Gate

Steep stairway built against a fortification

Half-bastion

Curtain wall: section of wall built between two towers or two bastions

Bartizan: small overhanging construction used as a lookout post

Ditch

Half-moon fortification: two-sided outerwork forming a sharp angle, set in front of the curtain wall

R. Corbel/MICHELIN

Civil architecture

NEVERS – Palais Ducal (16C)

The former home of the Dukes of Nevers was a precursor to the famous châteaux of the Loire Valley. Note the Renaissance harmony of the structure, and the great towers revealing medieval influence.

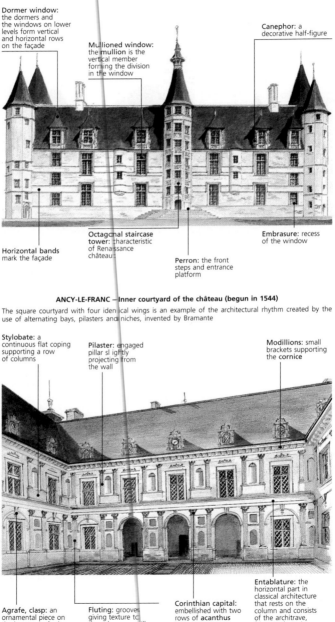

Dormer window: the dormers and the windows on lower levels form vertical and horizontal rows on the façade

Mullioned window: the mullion is the vertical member forming the division in the window

Canephor: a decorative half-figure

Octagonal staircase tower: characteristic of Renaissance châteaux

Embrasure: recess of the window

Horizontal bands mark the façade

Perron: the front steps and entrance platform

ANCY-LE-FRANC – Inner courtyard of the château (begun in 1544)

The square courtyard with four identical wings is an example of the architectural rhythm created by the use of alternating bays, pilasters and niches, invented by Bramante

Stylobate: a continuous flat coping supporting a row of columns

Pilaster: engaged pillar slightly projecting from the wall

Modillions: small brackets supporting the cornice

Agrafe, clasp: an ornamental piece on the keystone of a bay

Fluting: grooves giving texture to the columns or pillars

Corinthian capital: embellished with two rows of acanthus leaves

Entablature: the horizontal part in classical architecture that rests on the column and consists of the architrave, frieze and cornice

R. Corbel/MICHELIN

The Rooftops of Burgundy

The colourful rooftops of the Hôtel-Dieu in Beaune and the Hôtel de Vogüe in Dijon are classic images of Burgundy. **Glazed polychrome tiles**, laid out in geometrical designs, may have arrived in Burgundy from Central Europe via Flanders. The patterns carry symbolic messages, signifying status or reputation.

Finials in glazed earthenware, ornate weathervanes and crockets are all decorative features of the pinnacles and crests of the distinctive roofs of Burgundy, especially in the Côte d'Or region. Upland, the broad, slanted roofs are covered in flat dark-brown tiles known as **tuiles de Bourgogne**, much used on Cistercian abbeys. The tiles called **laves** are by-products of quarrying. An upper layer was removed from the surface of building stones. Roofers used these leftover pieces, interspersed with small rocks (as in the church at Ozenay in the Mâconnais region) as an aerated and frost-proof covering. The weight (600–800kg/1 320–1 760lb per m²) of the tiles required a heavy-duty framework. In the Morvan, thatch has slowly replaced tile and slate.

The area around Tournus is a transitional zone where flat tiles are used on the main house, and rounded tiles, **tuile canal**, on the outbuildings or porch roof. Rounded tiles are more prevalent in the southern reaches of Burgundy; the pitch of the roofs decreases (less than 35°) and framing is different. In Beaujolais, the style already shows Mediterranean influence.

prefer their mansions in town where Renaissance art really came into its own. Unlike religious architecture, civil architecture drew very little inspiration from Gothic art, while it was wide open to the graceful, attractive lines and forms which arrived from Italy. Emperor Charles V's Chancellor, Perrenot de Granvelle, set the example by building himself a mansion in Besançon in 1534. On the façades of Franch-Comté, different styles were superimposed on columns (Hôtel de Ville at Gray), moulded bands were added between storeys, ogee arches above windows gave way to simpler geometric forms. On the ground floor, the basket-handle arch was used for doorways or open arcades, introducing a regular movement clearly Spanish in inspiration (the interior courtyard of the Palais Granvelle at Besançon). Architectural renewal was apparent in floral decoration.

The decorative artist and architect **Hugues Sambin** (1518–1601), born near Gray, left a magnificent example of his energetic artistic creativity on the polychrome façade of the Palais de Justice at Besançon (1581), his finest piece of work in Jura.

Classical – In the 17C, Franche-Comté was crushed by the Ten Years War. It was not until after 1674, when the province was incorporated into France, that a new architectural impetus came to life. The strategic position of the region compelled the French to consider implementing a comprehensive project of fortification without further ado. The task was entrusted to **Vauban**, who paid particular attention to the defence of the points along the routes leading to Switzerland. Although part of it has been destroyed, Vauban's monumental work has left an indelible impression on parts of the Jura countryside. The royal architect's greatest achievement is to have developed the concept of bastion layout (adopted during the 16C) to its maximum potential. This idea had been developed before Vauban, but he not only refined it to its definitive form but was able to adapt it to suit the terrain of any site, whether it be a fortified town wall (Belfort, Besançon) or an isolated fortress (Fort St-André near Salins-les-Bains).

Civil architecture flourished in its turn in the 18C, which was a richly productive period for art in Franche-Comté.

SYAM – Palladian Villa

One of the forge masters, Mr. Jobez, had this villa built in 1818. He drew inspiration from the Italian villas designed by Palladio (16C)

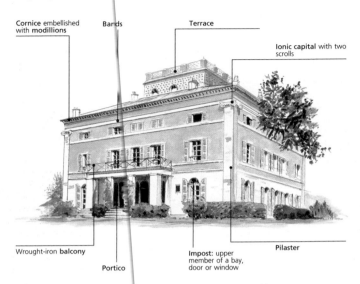

Cornice embellished with modillions

Bards

Terrace

Ionic capital with two scrolls

Wrought-iron balcony

Portico

Impost: upper member of a bay, door or window

Pilaster

VOUGLANS – Dam

Flooding part of the Ain Valley, the Vouglans Dam forms France's third largest reservoir.

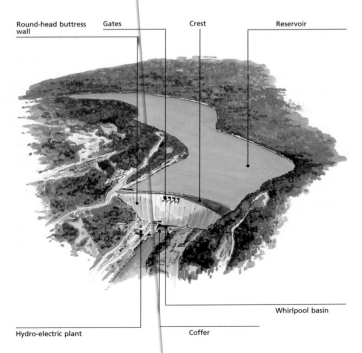

Round-head buttress wall

Gates

Crest

Reservoir

Hydro-electric plant

Coffer

Whirlpool basin

R.Corbel/MICHELN

The most original work of this period is the royal salt works at Arc-et-Senans, designed as an ideal town by visionary architect Ledoux (🛈 see ARC-ET-SENANS). Châteaux (typically on a horseshoe layout, as at Moncley), private houses and civil buildings display perfectly symmetrical façades, pierced with large windows surmounted by triangular or rounded pediments.

Another characteristic of these monuments, which some consider to be on a level of perfection with the Louis XVI style, is their traditional high roof.

Bresse farmhouse in Saint-Trivier-de-Courtes

Ph. Gajic/MICHELIN

19C and 20C – In the region of Franche-Comté, military architecture continued to evolve throughout the 19C and 20C. In the 19C, a number of fortresses were built (including the large fort at Les Rousses) to improve sites vulnerable to gun warfare. Most of these constructions have survived. The invention of the torpedo shell in 1885, then of the double-action fuse meant that forts were abandoned in favour of semi-underground concrete bunkers.

During the Second World War, the French High Command even went so far as to build 30 or so blockhouses to protect Swiss neutrality. Modern architecture has produced some great works of civil engineering in the region; in the 19C, impressive viaducts (Morez) were built to span some of the Jura gorges. Since the war, engineers have been concerned mainly with constructing dams; the Génissiat dam (1948) on the Rhône and the Vouglans dam (1968) in the Ain Valley are two impressive examples.

RURAL ARCHITECTURE

The wine-growers of Burgundy have large, comfortable houses; the vats and storerooms are on the ground floor, with living quarters on the first floor reached by a covered outside staircase. Often the houses are built into the hillside. The storage rooms may be partly underground, but are protected from fluctuations in temperature by thick stone walls.

The farmhouses of the **Bresse plain** look much as they always have, although cob walls and thatched roofs have gradually given way to bricks and tiles. The houses are low, with a wide overhanging roof for drying maize. Inside, there is the traditional stove room. A few 17C and 18C houses have a **Saracen chimney**, high on the roof like a belfry.

In **Jura**, besides the traditional **chalets** (wooden buildings on a stone foundation), there are **mountain houses** which consist of living quarters, stable and barn under the same roof. They are compact, built close to the ground to shut out the wind. The thick stone walls have tiny windows; those on the sides exposed to wind and snow are protected by wooden slats known as *tavaillons*. Roofing materials are the tiles typical of Jura or, more commonly, steel sheeting. The living quarters occupy the ground floor: the *houteau*, or kitchen, in which there is almost always a huge fireplace, and the *poêle*, a big heated room used as a bedroom or a dining room. The stable next door is joined to the house. The barn is on the first floor and has an opening through which fodder can be thrown down into the stable below.

The typical dwelling of the plateaux shares traits with that of the mountains, not least having man and beast under the same roof. However, they are taller, with a rectangular roof with edges that slope steeply downwards, covered in typical Jura tiles. Walls divide the ground floor lengthways to separate the living quarters from the stable. The main rooms are as above, but the first floor is often also given over to bedrooms.

Painting and Sculpture

IN BURGUNDY

Pre-Romanesque – During this period, sculpture was clumsily executed: the crypt of **Flavigny-sur-Ozerain**, all that remains of an 8C basilica, contains four shafts of columns, of which three appear to be Roman and the fourth Carolingian. The capitals are of great interest: they carry a decoration of fairly crudely executed flat foliage. Two of the capitals in the crypt of the cathedral of St-Bénigne at Dijon are decorated on each face by a man with his arms raised in prayer.

During the same period, frescoes and glazed surfaces were used to decorate the walls of religious buildings. In 1927, frescoes of the stoning of St Stephen (among other scenes) were discovered in the crypt of St-Germain in Auxerre.

Romanesque sculpture – The Cluny School of Sculpture is the most significant in the Romanesque period.

Artists revealed a new interest in nature in the variety of vegetation and keenly observed poses of the human figures they carved on the capitals in the choir (only rare examples survive). The influence of Cluny's sculpture was at first apparent in the church of **Ste-Madeleine at Vézelay** – both in the carved capitals and in the tympanum of the doorway in the narthex, which shows Christ sending out his Apostles before his ascension into heaven. This sculpture (1120) has much in common with the doorway of the church of St-Lazare in Autun.

The two doorways of the church of St-Lazare in **Avallon**, which date from the mid-12C, reveal a desire for a new style: luxuriant decoration including wreathed columns, an expression of the Baroque tendency of Burgundian Romanesque art, is depicted side by side with a column statue which recalls Chartres. The gravity of the round bosses on the tomb of St Lazarus in **Autun** (1170–84) already point ahead to the Gothic style.

The Brionnais, where there is an unusual profusion of sculpted doorways, seems to have been the oldest centre for Romanesque sculpture in Burgundy. From the mid-11C to the great projects of **Cluny** this region produced a slightly crude and gauche style.

After working in Cluny, the Brionnais artists had a new grace to their work. These trends appeared beside traditional elements, and evolved towards a mannerist decorative style (tympanum of St-Julien-de-Jonzy).

Romanesque painting – The crypt of the cathedral in **Auxerre** contains some 11C frescoes depicting Christ on horseback. At Anzy-le-Duc, restoration work in the choir in the mid-19C uncovered a large collection of murals with different characteristics from those at Auxerre: subdued, dull tints with dark outlines on a background of parallel bands.

Another style (blue backgrounds) appears at Cluny and at **Berzé-la-Ville**, in the chapel of the Château des Moines, where one can see a fine collection of Romanesque mural paintings. These frescoes, uncovered at the end of the 19C, were painted in the early years of the 12C. The use of glossy, bright paints is the distinctive feature of this innovative technique. As Berzé-la-Ville was one of the residences of the abbots of Cluny, it appears certain that these frescoes were painted by the same artists employed in the building of the great abbey.

Doorway, Église St-Lazare, Avallon

Alain Doire/Bourgogne Tourisme

Fresco in the crypt of the Auxerre Cathedral museum

S. Sauvignier/MICHELIN

Gothic sculpture – Gothic sculpture conceded nothing in terms of quality to Romanesque art.

13C – The influence of the Paris and Champagne regions is evident in the composition and presentation of subjects, but the Burgundian temperament shows itself in the interpretation of some scenes, where local artists have given free rein to their fantasy and earthy realism. Much of the statuary of this period was destroyed or damaged during the Revolution; some examples survive in Vézelay, St-Père, Semur-en-Auxois, St-Thibault, Notre-Dame in Dijon and Auxerre.

At **St-Père** the sculpted decoration of the gable on the west front is repeated in a floral decoration on the capitals. It is probable that the gable of the Vézelay basilica was inspired by St-Père, but the statutes in St-Père are of a much finer workmanship than those in Vézelay.

The tympanum of the Porte des Bleds in **Semur-en-Auxois** depicts the legend of St Thomas: the figures are heavy and the draperies lack grace – characteristics of the Burgundian style. This style was modified at the end of the 13C: the bas-relief sculptures on the base of the doorways on the western side of Auxerre Cathedral are of a delicacy and grace never achieved before.

14C – The advent of the Great Dukes of Burgundy in 1364 coincided with a period of political expansion and the spread of artistic influence.

In 1377, Philip the Bold began the construction of the **Chartreuse de Champmol** at the gates of Dijon. The Duke spared no expense in the decoration of this monastery, bringing in a large number of artists from elsewhere. A new trend in sculpture emerged: statues ceased to be part of pillars and doorways; facial expressions were treated with realism, and the artist, searching for authentic representation first and foremost, did not hesitate to portray ugliness or suffering.

15C – The tomb of Philip the Bold has given rise to many imitations: the mausoleum of John the Fearless and Margaret of Bavaria is a faithful replica; the tomb of Philippe Pot, Seneschal of Burgundy, shows more originality, since it is the mourners who support the flagstone bearing the recumbent figure.

Sculpture now turned to a different style from that of the 13C; proportions were more harmonious and the draperies simpler. The Virgin Mary in the Musée Rolin at **Autun** is a good example of this particular Burgundian style.

Gothic painting – The Valois dukes surrounded themselves with painters and illuminators whom they brought from Paris or from their possessions in Flanders. In Dijon, **Jean Malouel**, Jean de Beaumetz and **André Bellechose**, natives of the north, created an artistic style remarkable for its richness of colour and detail of design, a synthesis of Flemish and Burgundian styles.

Among the best-known works, the polyptych in the Hôtel-Dieu at Beaune by Roger van der Weyden and the paintings in the Dijon museum are of great interest.

During the Gothic period, frescoes came into favour again. Apart from the frescoes in the church of Notre-Dame in Beaune by Pierre Spicre, a painter of Dijon, the curious Dance of Death in the little church at La Ferté-Loupière is also noteworthy. Pierre Spicre created the designs for the remarkably bright tapestries in the church of Notre-Dame at Beaune.

The tapestries in the Hôtel-Dieu at Beaune, commissioned by Chancellor Nicolas Rolin in the 15C, are among the most beautiful of this period.

Renaissance sculpture – While Burgundian Renaissance architecture was characterised by the triumph of horizontal lines and semicircular arches, sculpture of this style used the antique form of medallions and busts in high relief, and gradually replaced sacred subjects with the profane.

In the second half of the 15C, ornamental decoration such as that conceived by **Hugues Sambin**, artist of the gateway of the Palais de Justice in Dijon and probably also of a large number of mansions, was much in vogue in the city.

In the 16C, decorative woodwork – door panels, coffered ceilings, church stalls – was prevalent. The 26 stalls in the church of Montréal, carved in 1522, are a work of local inspiration in which the Burgundian spirit is plain for all to see.

Classical to modern – The transition from the 18C to the 19C is marked by **Girodet**, the famous citizen of Montargis. Proud'hon and Rude, both pupils of **Devosges** and attached to the academic tradition, were producing paintings and sculpture at the beginning of the 19C; the work of the former is characterised by muted tones and dreamy, sensual figures; that of the latter recalls his Neoclassical debut, and the force of his subsequent expression of his romantic temperament in the Marseillaise on the Arc de Triomphe in Paris.

They were followed by Cabet, Jouffroy, and the contemporary sculptor François **Pompon**, all of whom contributed to the artistic reputation of Burgundy.

IN JURA

Jura cannot pride itself on having been home to a regional school of painting or sculpture. However, despite having been under the influence mainly of Burgundian and Flemish artists, local artists produced numerous works of art which reflect their talent. Unlike painting, sculpture was overlooked by local artists as a way of expressing their ideas during the Romanesque period.

Romanesque painting – The art of painting underwent significant development during the 12C and 13C, while sculpture was making little progress. During the Romanesque and Gothic periods, artists turned to frescoes in particular to decorate the interiors of churches.

Gothic sculpture – During the 13C, craftsmen produced emotive wooden statues in a naïve style, mainly Virgins. It was not until the 14C that a real surge of creativity burst onto the scene, inspired by Burgundian art and in particular the work of **Claus Sluter**. The production and decoration of religious furniture also developed during this period; the magnificent choir stalls at St-Claude (15C) and the ones at Montbenoît (16C) are some interesting examples.

Gothic painting – In the 14C and 15C, the art of painting altarpieces spread at the same time as the fresco technique. Painters of altarpieces were primarily in-spired by Flemish artists. Unfortunately, in the 16C, the initial impetus of the primitive artists of Franche-Comté petered out. **Jacques Prévost**, trained in Italy, was the only artist to produce works of any quality (triptych at Pesmes). The aristocracy and merchant classes took advantage of their travels abroad to buy Flemish and Italian paintings, some of which are still part of the artistic heritage of Jura (church at Baumes-les-Messieurs, cathedral and Musée des Beaux-Arts at Besançon).

Renaissance sculpture – In the 16C, sculptural forms became less tortured, and Italian sculptors were brought in to work on projects in Franche-Comté. The Gothic tradition was dropped as artists such as **Claude Arnoux**, known as Lullier (altarpiece of the Chapelle d'Andelot in the church at Pesmes), and **Denis le Rupt** (pulpit and organ loft in Notre-Dame at Dole) adopted the new style.

Classical to modern sculpture – During the Classical period, religious statuary became bogged down in academism. Only furniture showed signs of the originality and good taste of the local artists (Fauconnet woodwork at

Detail of The Funeral at Ornans (1850) by Gustave Courbet

© Imagestate/Tips Images

Goux-les-Usiers). Later, some sculptors achieved a certain degree of fame, such as Clésinger, Luc Bretonand Perraud (1819–1876), who were inspired by the Romantic movement to produce sensitive works.

At the end of the century, **Bartholdi** immortalised the resistance of the city of Belfort in 1870, by sculpting an enormous lion out of rock.

Classical to modern painting – From the 17C, French art became less regionalised. Famous artists from Jura include **Jacques Courtois** (1621–1676), who specialised in painting battle scenes, **Donat Nonotte** (1708–1785), a portrait painter from Besançon, and above all **Courbet** (1819–1877), an ardent defender of realism.

TRADITIONAL CRAFTS

The Comtoise Clock – Cabinetmakers craft the traditional long-case clocks known in France as *horloges comtoises*. The early models were usually made of oak wood, and embellished with ornaments and moulding. Beginning in 1850, pine wood became the material of choice and simple painted motifs were used to decorate the case. Enamel artists worked to create stylised clock faces.

Smaller and smaller – The first French watch was made towards the end of the 15C, and there were many models by the second half of the 16C. At the courts of Henri II and Henri III, women would wear watches as pendants and men had them set into the handles of their daggers as decoration. These timepieces only had one hand, the hour hand.

In 1694, the Dumont brothers, master watchmakers, brought out the first watches manufactured in Besançon, entirely handmade. In 1767, Frédéric Japy of the Beaucourt village mechanically manufactured some rough models of watches, using machines he had invented. This was an immediate success, and his production was soon turning out 3 000–3 500 watches per month. In 1793, a Swiss watchmaker, Mégevand, and 80 master watchmakers immigrated to Besançon. The *Convention* (national assembly) took them under its wing and advanced them some money to enable them to set up a factory and a national school of clock and watchmaking. They were to take in 200 apprentices per year, funded by the *Convention*.

A matter of time – From then on, sales grew rapidly. In 1835, 80 000 watches were made in Besançon and 240 000 in 1878. The industry spread to many Jura towns.

Today, clock and watchmaking are of little economic importance, yet a certain reputation for craftsmanship has been maintained. Morez and Morbier still make grandfather clocks, as they have since the 17C.

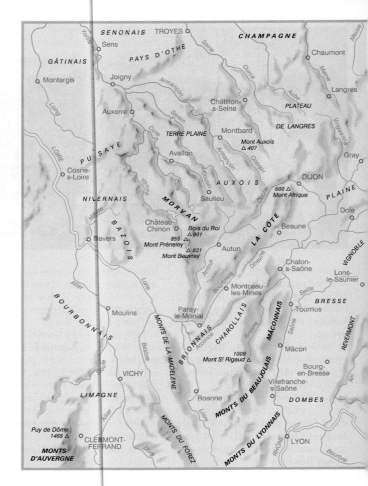

Nature

LANDSCAPES
POLITICAL DIVISIONS

France, exclusive of its overseas territories, is divided into administrative units: *96 départements* and *22 régions,* including **Bourgogne** and **Franche-Comté**. The région of Burgundy includes the *départements* of **Côte-d'Or**, **Nièvre**, **Saône-et-Loire** and **Yonne**; Franche-Comté encompasses **Doubs**, **Jura** and **Haute-Saône**. Jura is also the name of the 250km/155mi-long mountain range running from the Rhine to the Rhone. Perhaps because the mountains cover most of the region, Jura is generally used to refer to the whole region of Franche-Comté, except for administrative or historical purposes.

The region of Burgundy has several distinct geographical areas, which are commonly referred to as **Basse Bourgogne** (the Auxerre and Chablis areas), the **Arrière-Côte** and Côte, and the ancient granite massifs known as the **Morvan**, the **Charollais** and the **Mâconnais** to the south.

The Jura mountains reach a width of 61km/38mi; the tallest peak is the Crêt de la Neige (1 717m/5 633ft). The relief, while modest in height, is striking, characterised by long parallel ridges and valleys along a northeast-southwest axis

that converge at each end. This pattern of folds steps down to an undulating plateau in the west, which rises around Montbéliard to meet the Vosges.

FORMATION OF THE LAND

Primary Era – This is believed to have begun about 600 million years ago. Modern France was entirely under water, until the movement of the earth's crust known as the **Hercynian fold** took place, which created a number of high mountain ranges.

The seas that covered the Paris and Rhône basins were linked by a strait which corresponds to the "threshold of Burgundy". Erosion wore down the highest parts of the Morvan to their rocky base, while the warm, humid climate produced lush vegetation, eventually buried under layers of alluvial deposits and pressurised into coal between the Morvan and Beaujolais massifs.

Secondary Era – This began about 200 million years ago. The Hercynian base subsided and the seas flooded the Paris basin and Jura region, covering even the highest land. They deposited strata of sedimentary rocks – marl (chalk mixed with impermeable clay) and limestone (formed from fossilised shells and fish skeletons) – on the granite seabed. The formation of such sedimentary rock strata was so prolific in Jura in

Jura mountain landscape

© David Mathieu/Fotolia.com

particular that geologists named the middle period of the Secondary Era, which lasted about 45 million years, the Jurassic period.

Tertiary Era – This began about 60 million years ago. The parallel rock strata of the Jura region, sloping gently down to the Swiss plain, were still covered with water (the lakes of **Biel, Neuchâtel** and **Geneva** still remain). Then came the great Alpine folding movement, and the land was once again forced upwards and the seas pushed back.

The pressure during this Alpine-building period folded the Jura rock strata along a northeast-south west axis into parallel ridges and valleys, curving in a giant crescent between the **Vosges** and the **Massif Central** and sloping down towards the River Saône, where all the rivers drained into the great lake of Bresse (which later vanished). Nearer the Alps, the thick layers of sedimentary rock folded under pressure, giving rise to the Jura mountains. The layers of the western edge, not so thick, split along the faults formed by the movements of the earth's crust into a series of stepped plateaus. Not far from the slopes overlooking the **Saône Valley**, salt deposits were formed (later to become a local resource).

Quaternary Era – This began about 2 million years ago. Erosion continued to shape the region into its present appearance: ancient massifs (Morvan, Beaujolais); limestone plateaux (La Côte, l'Arrière Côte); sedimentary basins (Bazois, Terre-Plaine, Auxois); valleys (surrounding the Jura); and low-lying plains (Saône Valley).

The era was marked by two significant events: the appearance of man, and the coming of the Ice Age with its glaciers, which invaded the valleys from the Alps. As the glaciers receded, they left in their wake a huge amount of debris, including glacial moraine, which blocked the drainage of water in many places, giving rise to the Jurassic lakes.

THE REGIONS OF BURGUNDY

From the Auxois to the Beaujolais regions, from the River Saône to the River Loire, the varied regions that make up Burgundy have preserved their own appearance, economy and way of life.

The historical links which united them in the 15C have proved strong enough, however, for several common characteristics to be apparent to this day. Administrative divisions, modern economic demands and the attraction of Paris notwithstanding, the ties holding together the constituents of this province, of which Dijon is capital in more than name, remain unbroken.

The Alluvial Plains – The **Sénonais**, **Gâtinais** and **Puisaye** plains are situated on the northern borders of Burgundy. These are well-watered, fertile lands, rich in alluvial deposits, where the lakes and forests provide a rich catch for hunters and anglers alike. The Sénonais is furthest to the north; agriculture there is varied and productive. The Gâtinais extends from Gien (in the Loire Valley) to just north of Montargis, and is mostly limited to dairy farming. Similar in landscape, the Puisaye, produces fodder crops among abundant woodlands.

The Nivernais – This region of plateaux and hills, essentially a crossroads, stretches away to the west of the Morvan Massif and slopes gently down to the Loire Valley. To the west of Château-Chinon are the verdant slopes of **Bazois**: cereal and fodder crops on the hillsides, rich pasture for stock-breeding below. To the north, the hilly region of **Clamecy** and **Donzy** (peaks up to 450m/1 476ft high) is watered by a dense network of rivers, and used for stock-breeding and crop farming.

From Nevers to Bonny the River Loire marks the boundary between the Nivernais and the Berry region. Stock-breeding pasture alternates with wooded spurs. **Pouilly** lies at the heart of a well-reputed vineyard stretching over the hills above the Loire Valley.

The Morvan – after the great Alpine thrust, the edges of the Morvan granite massif were broken up; the softer limestone strata bordering the massif were

Maison du tourisme du Parc du Morvan

Parc naturel régional du Morvan

eroded, scouring out a hollow on three sides. This depression is surrounded by limestone plateaux towering at its outer edges. The Morvan is known for its dense tree cover, river network and patchwork of fields bounded by hedges. Long isolated, the Morvan is now sought out for its unspoiled landscapes.

The Auxois – To the east of the Morvan lies the Auxois region, a rich and fertile land of hard blue limestone, crisscrossed by many rivers, given over to pasture for stock-breeding. Rocky outcrops are home to fortified towns, such as Semur, Flavigny-sur-Ozerain and Mont-St-Jean, or by ancient *oppidums* from Roman times, such as Alésia on Mont Auxois.

The Charolais and Brionnais – These regions of sweeping hillsides and plateaux, with superb rich pasturage, are the home of Charolais cattle.

The Autun basin – During the Primary Era, this was a vast lake, which was gradually filled in with the coal-bearing deposits and bituminous schists.

The Dijonnais – The region around Dijon is an area of limestone plateaux, isolated outcrops, rich pastureland, wide alluvial plains and steep hillsides covered with vineyards.

The Côte – This is the edge of the last slope of the mountains (La Côte d'Or) overlooking the Saône plain. This escarpment was formed by the cracks which

appeared as the Saône's alluvial plain subsided. The Arrière-Côte plateau is given over to crops and pasture, and the eastern slope is covered with vines.

The Mâconnais – This is where the mountain range formed by the Côte d'Or extends southwards. The steep faces of the escarpment are turned towards the interior, whereas along the Côte d'Or they overlook the valley of the Saône. This is a region of vine-covered hillsides and pastureland; cereal crops, beets, vegetables and poultry are also raised.

The Saône Valley – Major communications routes run through this valley which stretches along the foot of limestone cliffs. Civil engineering works have opened the river to navigation year-round. The alluvial plains of the Saône, often flooded in winter, are covered with rich pastures and arable land. In addition to wheat, beet and potato crops, there are now market gardens and fields of maize, tobacco and oilseed.

The Bresse – The Bresse plain, composed of clay and marl soil, stretches from the Saône to the foothills of the Jura, the Revermont. Numerous streams cut across the rolling countryside, which is dotted with copses. In France, the name is indissociable from the *Poulet de Bresse,* the delicious chickens raised here.

Vineyards of Vosne-Romarée, Côte d'Or
© Jean Pierre Lescourret/hemis.fr

The handsome city of Dijon has been the capital of Burgundy since the 11C, a rich history that is reflected in its streets of medieval timbered buildings propped against grand 17C and 18C townhouses, and the glorious Palace of the Dukes. But Dijon is not a city resting on its cultural laurels: this is a regional powerhouse of industry and transport, with a go-getting attitude and a lively student buzz. For gourmets, superb food and some of the world's finest wines are never far away in this gastronomic paradise. Head south from here and en-route to Beaune and Santenay you will find the Côte d'Or, which produces some of the world's finest Pinot Noir and Chardonnay wines.

Highlights

Discovering Dijon

Dijon is a city made for exploring on foot, or if you're feeling adventurous, try a guided Segway tour – a whizz around town on these space-age scooters can be organised at the Tourism Office. Trip planning is easy: a visit to the Musée des Beaux-Arts in the Dukes' Palace to see the tombs of Philip the Bold and John the Fearless is unmissable. The Dukes of Burgundy gave the province its Golden Age in the 14C and 15C, when it was one of the most powerful states in Europe. Afterwards, the warren of little streets around the Palais des Ducs is bursting with a fascinating mix of historic buildings. Rue des Forges was once the main street, with its magnificent mansions built by Dijon's first bankers and wealthy merchants. François I called Dijon the "city of a hundred steeples"; well, there aren't quite that many these days, but top of the spires is the much-loved Jacquemart clock atop the 13C Gothic Notre-Dame church.

Dijon may have been officially recognised as a "City of Art and History" in 2008, but this is not a place that is living in the past. Whenever you visit, there will be a programme of events and exhibitions, notably the Gastronomic festival held each year in autumn. And on the subject of gastronomy, don't forget to load up with foodie treats to take home: shop in the magnificent 19C ironwork market hall, an Aladdin's cave of Burgundian delights, then call into opulent Mulot et Petitjean to pick up gingerbread, and the Boutique Amora-Maille for a pot of mustard.

Discovering Beaune

Beaune may not hum with the life force of Dijon, but from a visitor's point of view it is equally enticing. Beaune has one of Burgundy's highlights, in the spectacular shape of the Hôtel-Dieu. Its kaleidoscopic glazed tile roof alone is a wondrous sight – and that's before you have seen the splendid interior and Rogier van der Weyden's remarkable *Last Judgement* polyptych.

Moreover, this is the wine capital of Burgundy, and therefore – some might say – the world. Wine is the lifeblood of Beaune. Each year, once the grape harvest is picked, crushed and quietly turning into another knockout vintage, the vinous calendar ends in great splendour and ceremony during the Hospices de Beaune charitable wine auctions.

Taste a selection of great Burgundies at Marché aux Vins or Athenaeum, then primed with a better eye for what makes Burgundy a Premier League wine region, set off on a trip to discover where the A-list bottles come from. Between Dijon and Beaune, neatly combed vineyards cascade down the hillsides to the villages of the Côte d'Or, where the road signs read like a wine-lover's wish list.

Dijon for Foodies

Famed pain d'épices

Perched at the head of the Côte d'Or, and with the finest Burgundian produce readily to hand, Dijon is a gourmet's delight. For an overview of the local goodies on offer, start early at the cavernous glass and ironwork market hall when it's in full swing: it houses cheese stalls, Bresse poultry specialists, charcutiers and excellent butchers – it's up to you whether you tackle breakfast before or after viewing their displays of ox tongues and calves feet. Within easy strolling distance of the *Halles* you will find plenty more addresses to stock up on splendid local delicacies.

On Pl. Bossuet, the timbered façade of Mulot et Petitjean opens onto an interior as deliciously extravagant as their renowned *pain d'épices* gingerbread, bejewelled with crystallised fruit. At 32 rue de la Liberté, mustard-maker Maille sets out its products in an 18C boutique with the look of an apothecary's dispensary, while Auger at no. 61 is a glitzy Aladdin's cave of top-drawer Burgundian wares, particularly of the alcoholic variety, such as Boudier's pukka crème de cassis de Dijon, fiery marc de Bourgogne, and fruit liqueurs made from raspberries, cherries and blackberries. Crèmerie Porcheret on rue Bannelier is a mecca for cheese aficionados, with its sagging époisses, and mould-furred cakes of goat's cheese jostling for nasal pole position; there might also be sheep's milk butter, a curiosity worth tasting.

The well-heeled Dijonnais like their sweet treats too, so Dijon is home to splendid chocolatiers. Fabrice Gillotte at 21 rue du Bourg is a master of his art; his chocolates are little works of art that local fans queue out in the street for. Chocoholics should also try Guy Carbillet's chocolate shops where the artisans lay out tray after tray of hand-made creations. Finally, put your feet up with a cup of one of the dozens of speciality teas and coffees on offer amid the 19C splendour of the Comptoir des Colonies salon de thé on place François-Rude.

Market Hall

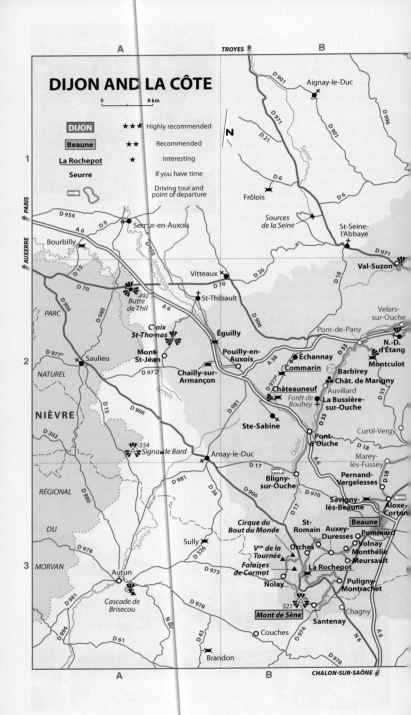

DIJON AND LA CÔTE

0   8 km

DIJON   ★★★   Highly recommended

Beaune   ★★   Recommended

La Rochepot   ★   Interesting

Seurre   If you have time

Driving tour and
point of departure

TROYES

N

PARIS

AUXERRE

Aignay-le-Duc

Frôlois

Sources
de la Seine

St-Seine-
l'Abbaye

D 954

D 9

A 6

Semur-en-Auxois

Bourbilly

D 15

D 70

D 906

D 880

PARC

Butte
de Thil

Croix
St-Thomas

Mont-
St-Jean

Saulieu

NATUREL

Chailly-sur-
Armançon

D 977

Vitteaux

St-Thibault

Éguilly

Pouilly-en-
Auxois

D 26

D 70

Val-Suzon

Velars-
sur-Ouche

Pont-de-Pany

N.-D.
d'Étang

Montculot

Échannay

Commarin

Barbirey

Chât. de Marigny

Auvillard

Châteauneuf

Forêt de
Bouhey

La Bussière-
sur-Ouche

NIÈVRE

D 302

Signal de Bard

Arnay-le-Duc

Ste-Sabine

Pont-
d'Ouche

Curtil-Vergy

Marey-
lès-Fussey

Bligny-
sur-Ouche

Pernand-
Vergelesses

Savigny-
lès-Beaune

Aloxe-
Corton

RÉGIONAL

DU

MORVAN

Autun

Cascade de
Brisecou

Sully

Cirque du
Bout du Monde

V^on de la
Tournée

Falaises
de Cormot

Nolay

St-
Romain

Orches

Auxey-
Duresses

La Rochepot

Beaune

Pommard

Volnay

Monthélie

Meursault

Puligny-
Montrachet

Mont de Sène

Santenay

Chagny

Couches

Brandon

CHALON-SUR-SAÔNE

90

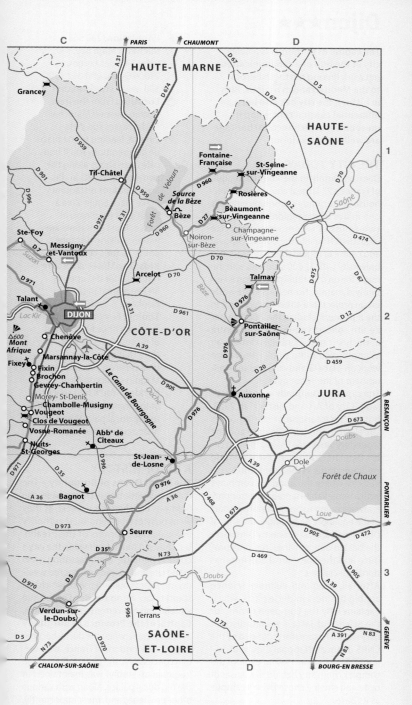

Dijon★★★

The capital of Burgundy is a lively city at the hub of a communications network linking northern Europe to the Mediterranean regions. Rich in history, the city has also been an influential cultural centre and its museums and architectural heritage are well worth exploring.

THE CITY TODAY

Dijon sits firmly in the Premier League of France's 25 largest cities. The power-house of Burgundy's economy employs one in five of the region's population, two-thirds of whom work in service industries. Home to the Court of Appeal and centre of regional administration, a university with 32 000 students, and the huge Toison d'Or retail park, Dijon is certainly dynamic. Numerous large-scale urban projects are either underway or in the pipeline, including the 7 000-seater Zenith concert venue, a media centre in the heart of the Grésilles district, an olympic swimming pool, renovation work on place Grandville, and redevelopment of the Junot quarter.

The capital of Burgundy won the accolade "City of Art and History" in 2008, but has no intention of resting on its laurels: together with Beaune and the legendary vineyards linking the two cities, Dijon hopes to gain UNESCO World Heritage status in the near future.

In a city where the good life combines with a remarkable heritage, gastronomy is always going to be an important part of the equation. Accordingly, the annual Dijon Festival of Gastronomy celebrates the best in dining, wines, regional produce and the finest local and international specialities.

After all, food and culinary science are big business in these parts, which explains why the European Centre for the Science of Taste – a multi-disciplinary research laboratory founded by the CNRS (France's National Centre of Scientific Research) in 1997 to explore the complex chemistry behind the senses of taste and smell – chose Dijon's campus as its base.

▶ **Population:** 236 953
⚅ **Michelin Map:** 320: K-6.
▤ **Info:** 34 r. des Forges, 21000 Dijon. ℘0 892 700 558. www.visitdijon.com.
▶ **Location:** From the train station, avenue Maréchal Foch crosses rue de la Liberté, leading to the place de la Libération. You'll find cafés and shops along the pedestrian streets in this area. Outdoor restaurants make Place Emile-Zola a great spot for dining al fresco. Most museums are within walking distance of the historic centre.
👪 **Kids:** The Musée d'Histoire Naturelle for its superbly lifelike animal habitat displays.
⚆ **Timing:** Buy tickets from the Tourism Office for the Well of Moses (Puits de Moïse). Note that many museums close on Tue; Musée Magnin closes on Mon.
🅿 **Parking:** You'll find spaces at the train station, adjacent to the ducal palace, and near many public squares.

A BIT OF HISTORY

The Great Dukes of Burgundy – The dukes spent little time in Dijon (Charles the Bold was only here for a week), as they were busy establishing their authority in recalcitrant corners of their realm, but they did much to develop the city's cultural heritage. Manufacturing grew in the city and as trade prospered wealthy merchants built mansions which still stand today along rue des Forges, rue Vauban and rue Verrerie, among others.

Capital of the Province of Burgundy – Change came when the duchy became part of the kingdom of France, with certain concessions: the *États de Bourgogne* (regional assembly) was maintained in the old ducal palace, along with various other privileges and, most importantly,

Palais des Ducs and Place de la Libération

Alain Doire/Bourgogne Tourisme

the Burgundy Parliament was transferred from Beaune to Dijon. The King visited Saint-Bénigne in 1479 and solemnly swore to preserve "the freedoms, liberties, protections, rights and privileges" previously enjoyed by the duchy. All the same, he did build a fortress, repair the fortifications and appoint a governor.

A provincial town comes of age – As an administrative centre, seat of the princes of Condé, Dijon underwent significant urban development in the 17C and 18C. Jules Hardouin-Mansart (the architect who designed the Versailles Palace) and later his brother-in-law Robert de Cotte rebuilt the ducal palace as the splendid Palais des États de Bourgogne on a monumental esplanade then known as the place Royale. Local officials and parliamentarians built many of the fine houses that give Dijon its character. The University was founded in 1723, the Academy in 1725 and, in 1731, Dijon became the Episcopal See. From 1851 onwards, the construction of the railway from Paris through Dijon and to the Mediterranean brought new life and new people; the population doubled between 1850 and 1892, as the industrial era took hold.

PALACE OF THE DUKES AND STATES OF BURGUNDY★★
℘03 20 74 52 09. http://mba.dijon.fr. During restoration work the site will not close completely, but displays will be altered and the way in which visits take place will be reorganised. Closed since 2008, the Salle d'Armes (Arms Room) and Galerie de Bellegarde are due to re-open in 2012. The ducal tombs will be inaccessible from late 2009 until late 2013, and the statues of the mourners will be displayed in the USA. Enter the courtyard to look through the railings.

Cour d'honneur
The old Logis du Roi (King's House), a handsome ensemble marked by strong horizontal lines and terminating in two wings at right angles, is dominated by the tall medieval tower of Philippe-le-Bon. The ducal palace houses, to the left, the departments of the town hall and, to the right, the famous Museum of Fine Art.

Tour Philippe-le-Bon
◷*Open daily Apr–Nov 9am–noon, 1.45–5.30pm. Rest of the year Wed 1.30–3.30pm, Sat–Sun 9–11am, 1.30–3.30pm. ◌5€. ℘03 80 74 52 09.*
The tower (46m/151ft high) was built by Philip the Good in the 15C. From the terrace at the top (316 steps), there is a fine **view**★ over the town, the valleys of the Ouche and the Saône and the first foothills of the Jura mountains.

▷ *The vaulted passageway to the left leads to the Flore courtyard.*

Cour de Flore
The buildings surrounding the courtyard were finished just before the Revolution in 1789. In the north-east corner is the

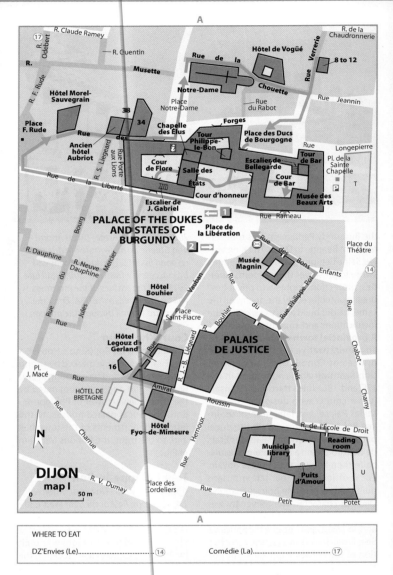

Chapelle des Élus; its interior décor and the doors date from the period of Louis XV. Mass was celebrated in the chapel during the sittings of the States of Burgundy.

Under the porch which gives access to rue de la Liberté (former rue Condé) a magnificent staircase, designed in 1735 by Jacques Gabriel, father of the architect who designed the Petit Trianon at Versailles, leads to

the **Salle des États** (⊶ *not open to the public*).

▶ *Return to the main courtyard, walk across it and through the vaulted passageway leading to the Cour de Bar.*

Cour de Bar

The **tower**, built by Philip the Bold in the 14C, preserves the name of an illustrious prisoner who was kept there by Philip the Good: René d'Anjou, Duke of Bar and Lorraine, Count of Provence, who was known as King René. The charming 17C **Bellegarde staircase**, which goes round the tower, leads to the north gallery of the same period. Note the statue of the sculptor **Claus Sluter** by Bouchard.

MUSÉE DES BEAUX-ARTS★★

🕐 *Open daily except Tue May–Oct 9.30am–6pm; Nov–Apr daily except Tue 10am–5pm.* 🕐 *Closed 1 Jan, 25 Dec.* ♿ ✆ *03 80 74 52 70. www.mba.dijon.fr.*
The huge fine arts museum created in 1799 is in the former ducal palace.

Ducal kitchens
Ph. Gajic/MICHELIN

Ground floor

On the left, at the far end of the rooms devoted to temporary exhibitions, are the **ducal kitchens**, built in 1435. The six huge chimneys were scarcely sufficient for the preparation of feasts worthy of the Burgundian court.

The **chapter-house** of the former 14C ducal chapel *(ground floor of the Tour de Bar)* illustrates the evolution of religious sculpture – an art form held in high regard in Burgundy – from the 14C to the 17C. The works of art include 15C stained-glass windows, reliquaries, 16C silver gilt altarpiece together with a St Robert's cross (11C) and a cup belonging to St Bernard. On the grand staircase is a statue of the Maréchal de Saxe by **François Rude** (1784–1855).

On the landing is the old door of the Dijon law courts, carved by Hugues Sambin (16C), and some fine medieval and Renaissance pieces of religious gold- and silver-ware and carved ivory.

First floor

This floor houses Italian painting from the 14C to the 16C, with particularly good examples of the Primitive schools of Florence (Taddeo Gaddi) and Siena (Pietro Lorenzetti) and of the Florentine Renaissance. Two galleries contain paintings by 15C and 16C German and Swiss masters, including the Master of the Darmstadt Passion (1425), Conrad Witz *(Emperor Augustus and the Tibur Sibyl)*.

Of the next three galleries *(overlooking the courtyard)*, the first two are devoted to Renaissance art: furniture, medals, enamels and paintings *(Lady dressing, Fontainebleau School)*; the third is hung with 17C Burgundian paintings.

The wing overlooking rue Rameau is devoted to French painting, starting with 17C works by painters under Louis XIV: Philippe de Champaigne *(Presentation in the Temple)*, Le Sueur, Le Brun and François Perrier. Note also the *Portrait of a Painter* by P Mignard and the *Holy Family Resting* by Sébastien Bourdon. Artists from the late 17C and 18C are represented in two galleries, in particular Burgundian painters such as JF Gilles, known as Colson (*Rest*, 1759) and JB Lallemand (Dijon 1716–Paris 1803), creator of landscapes and genre scenes. A large gallery displays paintings by Nattier *(Portrait of Marie Leszczynska)*, Van Loo *(St George and the Dragon)* and others.

The **Salle des Statues**, in the corner of the west wing, which contains copies of ancient works and 19C pieces including *Hebe and the Eagle of Jupiter* by Rude, has a view of place de la Libération.

The adjacent **Salon Condé** is decorated with woodwork and stucco of the Louis XVI period. It displays 18C French art: furniture, terracottas and paintings as well as sculptures by Coysevox (bust of Louis XIV) and Caffieri.

The **Prince's Staircase**, which is built against the Gothic façade of the old

The Prestigious Order of the Golden Fleece

In 1404, Philip the Bold created the Order of the Golden Tree, which John the Fearless and Philip the Good perpetuated and enhanced.

It was this second Philip who, at the time of his marriage to Isabella of Portugal in Bruges in 1429, first wore the insignia of the **Golden Fleece**: a chain encircling his neck, from which hung a sheepskin. The symbolism of the Order relates to Jason of Greek mythology as well as Gideon in the Old Testament.

There were two reasons for creating the Order: first, to draw Burgundy closer to the Church by keeping the spirit of the Crusades and chivalry alive, and second, to strengthen the duchy's position in regard to the English crown, the Holy Roman Empire and the Kingdom of France.

The Order was based in the chapel of the ducal palace in Dijon, where the young Count of Charollais, who was later to become Charles the Bold, was knighted in 1433.

The marriage of his only daughter, Marie de Bourgogne, in 1477, to Archduke Maximilian of Austria, brought the Hapsburgs into the Order.

The Order of the Golden Fleece still carries great prestige and implies a commitment to a disciplined life. It is not hereditary, and the official insignia must be returned by the heirs upon a knight's death.

Dukes' Palace, leads down to the **Salle d'Armes** (Arms Room) on the ground floor, which exhibits weapons and armour from the 13–18C and cutlery and knives dating from the 16–18C.

The **Salle du Maître du Flémalle**, which contains 14–15C Flemish and Burgundian painting, including the famous *Nativity*★★ by the **Master of Flémalle** and several works of art from the Chartreuse de Champmol, provides an excellent introduction to the Salle des Gardes.

The **Salle des Gardes**★★★ overlooking place des Ducs is the most famous gallery in the museum. It was built by Philip the Good and used as the setting for the Joyous Entry of Charles the Bold in 1474; it had to be restored in the early 16C after a fire. It houses treasures from the Chartreuse de Champmol (&see p104), the necropolis of the dukes of Valois.

From 1385 to 1410 three men – Jean de Marville, Claus Sluter and his nephew, Claus de Werve – worked successively on the **tomb of Philip the Bold**★★★. The magnificent recumbent figure, watched

Ph. Gajic/MICHELIN

Procession of mourners at the tomb of Philip the Bold, Musée des Beaux-Arts over by two angels, rests on a black marble slab surrounded by alabaster arches forming a cloister to shelter the procession of mourners composed of 41 very realistic statuettes. The funeral procession consists of clergymen, Carthusians, relatives, friends and officials of the Prince, all hooded or dressed in mourning.

The **tomb of John the Fearless and Margaret of Bavaria**★★★, dating from between 1443 and 1470, is in a similar, although more Flamboyant style.

The two altarpieces in gilt wood commissioned by Philip the Bold for the Chartreuse de Champmol are very richly decorated. They were carved between 1390 and 1399 by Jacques de Baerze and painted and gilded by Melchior Broederlam. Only the **Crucifixion altarpiece** ★★★ near the tomb of Philip the Bold has retained Broederlam's famous paintings on the reverse side of the wings: the *Annunciation*, the *Visitation*, the *Presentation in the Temple* and the *Flight into Egypt*.

At the other end is the **altarpiece of the Saints and Martyrs**★★★. In the centre, note an early-16C **altarpiece of the Passion**★★ from an Antwerp workshop. Above the central altarpiece, between two 16C wall hangings from Tournai, hangs a tapestry dedicated to Notre-Dame-de-Bon-Espoir, protector of the city since the raising of the siege of Dijon by the Swiss on 11 September 1513.

A niche contains a handsome portrait of Philip the Good wearing the collar of the Order of the Golden Fleece, painted by the Rogier Van der Weyden workshop (c. 1455). A staircase leads to the tribune, from which there is a good **view**★.

The **Galerie de Bellegarde** contains some good examples of 17C and 18C Italian and Flemish painting, in particular *Moses in the Bullrushes* by Veronese and *Adam and Eve* by Guido Reni; there is an unusual panoramic landscape of the *Château de Mariemont* and its grounds by Velvet Brueghel, and a *Virgin and Child* with St Francis of Assisi by Rubens. Next comes a gallery devoted to 19C French sculpture and displaying works by Rude, Canova, Carpeaux and Mercié.

Second and third floors

These are devoted to modern and contemporary art. Works by the great animal sculptor **François Pompon** (1855–1933) are displayed in an old gallery in the Tour de Bar *(signposted)*.

The other galleries contain paintings, drawings, graphics and sculptures dating from the 16C to the present. Particularly famous names include Georges de la Tour *(Le Souffleur à la lampe)*, Géricault, Delacroix, Victor Hugo (imaginary landscapes in wash), Daumier, Courbet, Gustave Moreau and various painters from the Barbizon School (Daubigny, Rousseau, Diaz de la Peña etc), Rodin, Maillol, Bourdelle and others.

The Impressionists and Post-Impressionists are represented by works by Manet (*Portrait of Méry Laurent* in pastel), Monet, Boudin, Sisley and Vuillard.

A remarkable collection of African sculpture and masks (Mali, Cameroon, Congo) gives an insight into the art forms which inspired Cubist painters and sculptors. Among the rich collection of contemporary painting and sculpture note in particular works by artists in or linked with the Paris School and abstract artists of the 1950s to 1970s: Arpad Szenes and Vieira da Silva, his wife, Lapicque, De Staël (Footballer), Bertholle, Manessier, Messagier, Mathieu and Wols; also several lovely sculptures by Hajdu.

⬥ WALKING TOURS

PALAIS DES DUCS AREA★★
Map I. Allow 3hrs.

The old district around the palace of the dukes of Burgundy is charming. As you stroll along the streets, many of which are for pedestrians only, you will come across beautiful old stone mansions and half-timbered 15–16C houses.

Place de la Libération

This is the former place Royale. In the 17C, when the town was at the height of its parliamentary power, it felt itself to be a capital and decided to transform the ducal palace, which had stood empty since the death of Charles the Bold, and to re-arrange its approaches. Plans for

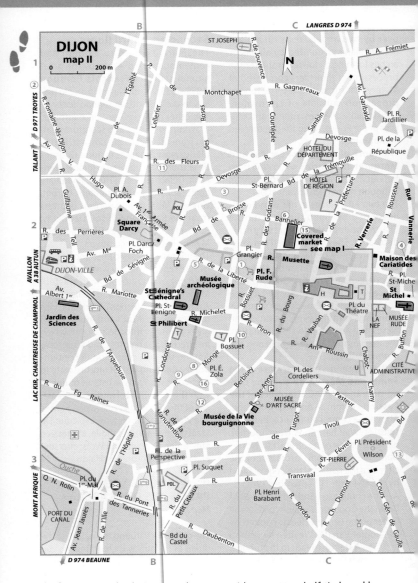

DIJON
map II

0   200 m

the fine semicircular design were drawn up by Jules Hardouin-Mansart, the architect of Versailles, and were carried out by one of his pupils from 1686 to 1701; the arcades of place de la Libération, surmounted by a stone balustrade, enhance the main courtyard.

Place François-Rude

At the heart of the pedestrian zone is this irregularly shaped, lively square,

with one or two half-timbered houses overlooking it. When the statue by the fountain (the Bareuzai) was erected in 1904, it provoked some raised eyebrows, but the grape-treading winegrower, clad only in verdigris, has since been accepted as part of the scenery and is even looked on with affection by many.

Further on, on the corner of rue des Godrans and rue Bossuet, a depart-

Rue Stéphen Liégeard with a view to Ancien Hôtel Aubriot

© Christophe Boisvieux/hemis.fr

ment store now occupies the site of the former Maison du Miroir but the locals still agree to meet "on Miroir corner"!

Rue des Forges★

This is one of the most characteristic old streets of the town. Note the 15C façade of the **Hôtel Morel-Sauvegrain** at nos. 52, 54 and 56. At no. 40 the **Ancien Hôtel Aubriot** has a Classical doorway, which contrasts with the elegant 13C arcaded façade of the mansion built by the first bankers of Dijon. This was the birthplace of Hugues Aubriot, provost of Paris under Charles V. He was responsible for building the Bastille, several of

Ph. Gajic/MICHELIN

Jacquemart and Family

The clock has quite a history. The name of Jacquemart, describing the figure of the man who strikes the bell of the clock with a hammer, first appeared in 1500. The people of Dijon were very fond of him and in 1610 considered that his continued celibacy must be weighing very heavily on the poor man. So he was given a female companion.

In 1714 the poet Aimé Piron took pity on this brave couple, who seemed to have undertaken a vow of chastity. They were given a son, Jacquelinet, whose hammer strikes the little bell on the half-hours; in 1881, a daughter was added, Jacquelinette, who strikes the quarter-hours.

the bridges over the Seine (notably the St-Michel Bridge), and the first vaulted sewers. Opposite, at no. 8 rue Stephen-Liégeard, note the Renaissance façade of the Maison Chissere.

Further along, at no. 38, note the Renaissance façade of **Maison Milsand**, lavishly decorated in the style of Hugues Sambin. Finally, in the inner courtyard of no. 34, is the **Hôtel Chambellan**, a 15C house built by a rich family of drapers. It has a very fine spiral staircase; the central column rises to a flamboyant palm-tree vault supported by the statue of a wine-grower carrying a basket.

Église Notre-Dame★

This church is a good example of 13C Gothic architecture in Burgundy. With only a restricted space in which to work, the master mason showed astonishing technical prowess. The façade is original. Above the great porch with its three bays, closed in laterally as is the porch at Autun, two delicately arcaded galleries are underscored by three tiers of **gargoyles**. Two graceful bell-turrets top the towers hidden by the façade: that on the right carries the **Jacquemart clock** brought from Courtrai by Philip the Bold in 1382 after his victory over the Flemish (see box above).

Interior – The overall effect is harmonious; the triforium of small tapering columns is of great delicacy. Note the height of the transept crossing beneath the lantern tower. The boldly conceived choir, ending with a polygonal chevet, is sober and graceful.

The stained-glass windows of the north transept date from the 13C. The 15C fresco has been restored. The chapel situated to the right of the choir houses the statue of Notre-Dame-de-Bon-Espoir (Our Lady of Good Hope). This 11C Virgin has been the object of particular veneration since the Swiss raised the siege of the town on 11 September 1513; the tapestry given at that time as a votive offering is now to be found in the fine arts museum. After Dijon had been liberated without damage from the German occupation on 11 September 1944, a second tapestry, made by Gobelins, commemorating the town's two liberations, was given as a new votive offering to Notre-Dame-de-Bon-Espoir. It can be seen in the south arm of the transept. Rue Musette offers an overall view of the west front and leads to the market.

Quartier Notre-Dame

Rue Musette gives a good view over the façade of the church and leads to the market. Local merchants have congregated in this quarter since the Middle Ages, but the covered market hall was not built in the former Jacobin church until the time of the Revolution. The local council decided to build the new market hall in 1868, but work did not begin until 1873 and was finished in 1875. The metal-frame architecture was inspired by the grand Parisian Halles market and today still houses a bustling market several times each week.

Rue de la Chouette provides a good view of the east end of the church. On one of the buttresses (15C), there is a statue of the owl who gives the street its name. Legend has it that the wise bird will grant the wishes of visitors who stroke it with their left hand.

Hôtel de Vogüé

This early-17C mansion with its colourful tiled roof was one of the early meeting places of the representatives of the province. A portico richly decorated in the Renaissance style opens to a courtyard. The mansion is now occupied by the offices of the city architect and the department of cultural affairs. In July, the main courtyard is the venue of the Estivade, a dance, theatre and singing festival.

Rue Verrerie

Nos. 8, 10 and 12 form an attractive group of half-timbered houses. Some of the beams have been richly carved. At no. 28, the **Maison des Cariatides**, (1603), has 12 caryatids on its façade. No. 66 rue Vannerie is a Renaissance house with ornamental windows flanking a watchtower by Hugues Sambin.

Place des Ducs-de-Bourgogne

From this little square, one can imagine what the palace must have looked like at the time of the dukes. The handsome Gothic façade is that of the Salle des Gardes, dominated by Philip the Good's tower.

AROUND THE PALAIS DE JUSTICE

Map I. Leave from place de la Libération by way of rue Vauban heading south.

Rue Vauban

No. 12 rue Vauban, the **Hôtel Bouhier**, has a Classical façade adorned with pilasters and pediments, overlooking the inner courtyard. Take rue Jean-Baptiste-Liégeard to the left to skirt the mansion of **Hôtel Legouz de Gerland**, with its Renaissance façade pinpointed

by four watch-turrets. The Classical inner façade may be seen from no. 21 rue Vauban. At the corner of rue Vauban and rue Amiral-Roussin is a half-timbered house (**no 16**), which once belonged to a carpenter. This craftsman embellished his shutters with linenfold panelling and some of the beams with scenes of his craft. The house almost opposite, at no 29, has an elegant courtyard screened off by a curved balustrade. Note the fine door of no 27.

Hôtel Fyot-de-Mimeure

The façade in the inner courtyard of no. 23 rue Amiral-Roussin is in the style of Hugues Sambin (16C).

Municipal Library

🕐*Open Tue, Thu, Fri 9.30–12.30, 1.30–6.30pm, Wed and Sat 9.30am–6.30pm.*
🖉*03 80 44 94 14. www.bm-dijon.fr.*
Enter by no. 3 rue de l'École-de-Droit.
The 17C chapel of the former college of Les Godrans, founded in the 16C by a rich Dijon family, has been transformed into a reading room. Among its 300 000 or more items, the Bibliothèque Municipale contains precious illuminated manuscripts, including some executed at Cîteaux in the first 30 years of the 12C.

Palais de Justice (Law Courts)

The gabled façade of the former Burgundian Parliament is in the Renaissance style and has a covered porch supported by columns. The door is a copy of a work by Sambin (the original is in the Musée des Beaux-Arts). The huge Lobby (Salle des Pas-Perdus) is covered by a **vaulted ceiling**★ in the shape of an up-turned boat. The ceiling of the Chambre Dorée, seat of the Court of Appeal, is adorned with the arms of François I (1522).

Musée Magnin★

🕐*Open Tue–Sun 10am–noon, 2–6pm.*
🕐*Closed 1 Jan and 25 Dec.* ✆*3.50€.*
🖉*03 80 67 07 15. www.musee-magnin.fr.*
The museum is in an elegant 17C mansion, the home of art lovers Maurice Magnin (a magistrate) and his sister Jeanne, herself a painter and art critic. Their collection covers lesser-known

painters, and reveals hidden talents. The more than 1 500 paintings also include works by great masters. On the ground floor are Flemish and Dutch paintings of the 16C and 17C. Italian painting has a place of honour with paintings by Cariani, Di Benvenuto, Allori, Cerano, Strozzi and Tiepolo. On the first floor, French paintings from the late 16C through 19C are on display, including works by Claude Vignon, Le Sueur, Bourdon, Girodet, Géricault, Gros and others.

The furnishings from the early 18C through the Second Empire were clearly chosen with as much care as the works of art, creating an intimate atmosphere.

AROUND SAINT-BÉNIGNE
Map II.

St-Bénigne's Cathedral

The ancient abbey church, the Cathédrale St-Bénigne is on the site of an earlier Romanesque building, and is pure Burgundian-Gothic in style.

The **west front** of is supported by massive buttresses flanked by two great towers with conical roofs of multicoloured tiles. Within the porch, which is surmounted by a delicately pierced gallery, is the old 12C Romanesque doorway in the centre of the Gothic façade. The transept crossing is marked by a tall spire (93m/305ft) in the Flamboyant style.

The **interior** is quite austere; its lines are unadorned: plain capitals, simply moulded arcades in the triforium, little columns extending unbroken from the vault to the floor in the crossing and to the tops of massive round pillars in the nave. Since St-Bénigne lost its own works of art during the Revolution, it has provided a home for tombstones and pieces of sculpture from other churches in Dijon. The organ (1743) is by Riepp. The only remaining traces of the Romanesque **crypt**★ (⏲open 9am–6pm, 1€ donation) consist of part of the transept with four apsidal chapels on the east side and a trench in the middle containing the remains of a sarcophagus which was probably used for the burial of

St Benignus, the first Burgundian martyr who died in the 3C; there is a pilgrimage to his tomb on 20 November.

The sarcophagus faces a broad opening in the lower storey of the **rotunda**★★ which echoes the highly symbolic architecture of the tomb of Christ in Jerusalem built in the 4C; only eight rotundas of this type are known in the world. Three circles of columns radiate from the centre; some have retained their original capitals decorated with palm leaves, interlacing, monstrous animals or praying figures, rare examples of pre-Romanesque sculpture. The eastern end of the rotunda opens into a 6C chapel which may be a *cella* (sanctuary).

Musée Archéologique★

⏲*Open daily except Tue 9am–12.30pm, 1.30–6pm.* ⏲*Closed Mon (Oct–May), 1 Jan, 1 and 8 May, 14 Jul, 1 and 11 Nov, 25 Dec.* ℘*03 80 48 83 70. www.dijon.fr.* The museum is in the eastern wing of what used to be the cloisters of St-Bénigne. Galleries on the lower level hold Gallo-Roman sculptures, including a bronze statue of the **goddess Sequana**★ found during the excavation of the sanctuary at the source of the River Seine.

The 13C Gothic monk's dormitory on the next floor is devoted to medieval sculpture from the region of Dijon, such as a head of Christ, made by Claus Sluter for the Chartreuse de Champmol. From St-Bénigne, two Romanesque tympana frame the **Christ on the cross**★★ (1410) attributed to Claus de Werve.

The top storey is home to a varied collection of items from different periods, from Paleolithic times to the Merovingian Era. Included in the collection are a **gold bracelet** which weighs 1.3kg/3lb found in **La Rochepot** (9C BC), and the **Blanot Treasure**★, a hoard of objects from the late Bronze Age (belt buckle, leggings, necklace and bracelet). In the last room, among some typical stone renderings of Gallo-Roman deities, notice the frieze from Alésia, representing mother-goddesses, and a marble portrait of a woman found in Alise-Ste-Reine.

Église Saint-Philibert

Built in the 14C and reworked in the 15C, the church is currently disused. You can still appreciate the flowery Romanesque relief of the western entrance.

Square Darcy

Named after the engineer who brought drinking water to Dijon in 1839 and helped set up the PLM (Paris-Lyon-Mediterranean) railway line. In pride of place is a replica attributed to Henri Martinet of the famous White Bear statue by the burgundian sculptor Pompon (*see SAULIEU*). Pools, waterfalls, bowls and balustraded terraces are laid out in a delightfully verdant composition made up of floral banks and plant essences.

Jardin des Sciences★

1 av. Albert-Premier and 14 r. Jehan-de-Marville. ⏰Open daily May–Sept 9am–12.30pm, 2–6pm, Sat and holidays 2–6pm, Sun 2–7pm ; rest of year : 9am–noon, 2–6pm, Sat and Sun and holidays 2–6pm. ⏰Closed Mar, 1 Jan, 1 and 8 May, 14 Jul, 11 Nov, 25 Dec. ✎Free entry. ✆03 80 48 82 00.

Muséum de la ville de Dijon★ – Founded in 1836 by Léonard Nodot, a Dijonnais with a passion for nature, the museum is housed in the old cross-bowmen's barracks built in 1608. On the ground floor an interactive display of the last 300 million years, plus some fine rock and fossil specimens, deals with Burgundy's geological history. Look for surprising exotica such as the glyptodon – a sort of giant south-American armadillo which appeared in the tertiary era. The incredible diversity of the animal world is revealed on the first floor by an impressively life-like series of dioramas: animal figures placed in minutely reconstructed habitats illustrate not only the principal ecosystems of the Côte-d'Or, but also the tundra, prairie, desert, savanna, tropical forest, etc. found around the world. Don't leave without a look at the mind-boggling variety of insects and the superb butterfly collection in the entomology room, and check out the temporary exhibitions in the Pavillon du Raines.

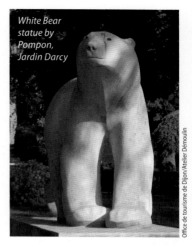

White Bear statue by Pompon, Jardin Darcy

Office de tourisme de Dijon/Atelier Démoulin

Jardin de l'Arquebuse★ – This park owes its name to the company of *harquebusiers*, who occupied the site in the 16C. All the western part is taken up by the botanical gardens (3 500 different species), which were founded in the 18C and joined to the Promenade de l'Arquebuse. In addition there is an arboretum, tropical glasshouses and a vivarium. Magnificent trees surround the colourful flower beds.

ADDITIONAL SIGHTS

Église St-Michel★

This Flamboyant Gothic church was consecrated in December 1529, although its façade was eventually completed in the full Renaissance style (the four-storey framing towers were finished in the 17C). The façade, on which the three classical orders are superimposed, is the most curious part of the building. The porch, which juts far out, is pierced by three doorways: a long frieze of ornamental foliage and grotesque decorations runs along the upper part of the porch for its whole length. Under it, in medallions, are busts of the prophets Daniel, Baruch, Isaiah and Ezekiel, as well as of David with his harp and Moses with the Tablets of the Law. The right doorway dates from 1537 and is the oldest of the three. The interior is Gothic in style. Note the height of the choir, which like St-Bénigne lacks an ambulatory, the 18C woodwork, and four paintings by Franz Kraus (18C German): *Adoration of the Shepherds* and The Flight into Egypt (deteriorated) in the north transept; *Adoration of the Magi* and *Presentation in the Temple* in the chapel of the Saint-Sacrament, which also has a fine Flamboyant altar. The far north chapel contains a fragment of a 15C Entombment.

Chartreuse de Champmol★

🕒*Open daily 9.30am–12.30pm, 1.30–5pm. Follow signs to the Puits de Moïse.* This former monastery was largely destroyed in the Revolution; a psychiatric hospital now occupies the site. The first dukes of Burgundy were buried at Cîteaux, but Philip the Bold wanted an almost royal burial place for himself and his heirs and in 1383 he founded the charter house, which was consecrated five years later by the Bishop of Troyes. The best artists of the period contributed to the magnificent undertaking but nothing remains except the tombs of the dukes, the retables preserved in the Musée des Beaux-Arts, and two works by Claus Sluter (late 14C), the sculptor from Haarlem who became the leader of the Burgundian-Flemish School of Art: the **chapel doorway★** and the **Well of Moses★★ (Puits de Moïse)**.

The well *(walk round the buildings to reach the courtyard)* is actually the base of a polychrome Calvary made between 1395 and 1405 to decorate the font in the great cloisters (the painting is barely visible). It is named after the figure of Moses, probably the most impressive of the six huge and strikingly lifelike statues which surround the hexagonal base; the other five figures are the prophets *(going round to the right from Moses)* David, Jeremiah, Zachariah, Daniel and Isaiah. The angels beneath the cornice are the work of Claus de Werve, Sluter's nephew; each one expresses his suffering before the Calvary.

The doorway, which is now inside the chapel, consists of five statues sculpted by Claus Sluter between 1389 and 1394. Duke Philip the Bold and Margaret of Flanders, his wife, are depicted kneeling, watched by their patron saints (St John the Baptist and St Catherine), on each side of the Virgin Mary and Child who are portrayed on the central pier.

Musée de la Vie bourguignonne★

🕒*Open May–Sept daily except Tue 9am–6pm; Oct–Apr daily except Tue 9am–noon, 2–6pm.* 🗪*Guided tour (1hr) Sun 3pm and 4pm.* 🕒*Closed 1 Jan, 1 and 8 May, 14 Jul, 1 and 11 Nov, 25 Dec.* ♿ 𝒫*03 80 44 12 69. www.dijon.fr.* This museum of local history uses furnishings, household items, clothing and other souvenirs of times past to bring to life the daily habits, ceremonies and traditions of Burgundy at the end of the 19C. On the upper floor, a whole street has been re-created, complete with a beauty salon whose tools of the trade look more like instruments of torture.

Musée Amora

🕒*Open year round.* 🗪*Guided tours mid-May–mid-Sept daily except Sun and public holidays 3pm and 4pm; rest of the year times vary. Enquire at the tourist office.* 𝒫*03 80 44 11 41.* This museum, created by the Amora mustard company, recounts the history of the condiment, its origins, and every aspect of its production. Dijon has become the "Mustard Capital of the World", although mustard is not farmed in France.

Puits de Moïse, Chartreuse de Champmol

Ph. Gajic/MICHELIN

🚗 DRIVING TOUR

Suzon Valley

◔ *See the Region map BC1-2. 40km circuit. Allow around 1hr 30min.*

▷ *Leave Dijon to the north via D 974, the follow the D 107A and D 996.*

In **Messigny-et-Vantoux** is a late 17C château designed by architect Jules Hardouin-Mansart. As you leave the village, turn left onto the D 7. The Suzon, a tributary of the River Ouche, passes between sylvan hillsides, spilling out from its narrow valley into the pretty Ste-Foy basin; its rock-scattered slopes reach all the way to Val-Suzon.

ADDRESSES

⌂ STAY

⊜⊜ **B & B Hôtels** – *5 r. du Château.* ☏*0 892 707 506. www.hotel-bb.com.* ♿ *55 rooms.* ☲ *6 €.* If you don't mind the rather formulaic character of chain hotels, you'll have a happy stay in this town-centre hotel. Priced very keenly, all 55 rooms come with functional contemporary style and air-con.

⊜⊜ **Hostellerie le Sauvage** – *64 r. Monge.* ☏*03 80 41 31 21. www.hotelle sauvage.com.* ▣ *22 rooms.* ☲ *6.50 €.* This 15C coaching inn has a prime spot, just a ten minute walk from the Ducal Palace and smack in the middle of a lively quarter with a great café and restaurant scene. Peace is assured inside the cobbled courtyard, and pleasant bedrooms.

⊜⊜ **Hôtel Montigny** – *8 r. Montigny.* ☏*03 80 30 96 86. www.hotelmontigny. com. Closed 18 Dec–2 Jan. Wi-Fi. 28 rooms.* ☲ *8 €.* Efficiently run hotel near the town centre with secure parking. Rooms, although rather functional, are spotlessly kept and well soundproofed.

⊜⊜ **Hôtel Victor Hugo** – *23 r. Fleurs.* ☏*03 80 43 63 45. www.hotelvictorhugo-dijon.com. Wi-Fi. 23 rooms.* ☲ *6 €.* A friendly place with bright, smartly decorated and well-kept rooms. Bag one over the courtyard for more space.

⊜⊜⊜ **Hôtel Wilson** – *1 r. de Longvic.* ☏*03 80 66 82 50. www.wilson-hotel.com. Wi-Fi. 27 rooms.* ☲ *12 €.* This former post house has retained its traditional charm and charisma. You immediately feel at home in the cosy atmosphere of its bright rooms that come prettily decorated with light wood furniture and exposed beams.

⊜⊜⊜ **Hôtel Du Nord** – *Pl. Darcy.* ☏*03 80 50 80 50. www.hotel-nord.fr. Closed 17 Dec–2 Jan. 27 rooms.* ☲ *12 €.* Right on the bustle of Dijon's central shopping square, this hotel has serviceable, well-soundproofed rooms.

NEAR DIJON

⊜⊜⊜ **Hôtel Le Relais de la Sans-Fond** – *33 rte de Dijon, 21600 Chevigny, 16km/10mi south.* ☏*03 80 36 61 35. sansfond@aol.com. Closed 15 Dec–5 Jan.* ▣*. Wi-Fi. 17 rooms.* ☲ *8 €, half-board possible.* ✕*.* A simple and well-kept family inn with airy, uncluttered rooms. Traditional cuisine served in contemporary dining rooms or on the garden terrace.

♨ EAT

⊜ **Le Chabrot** – *36 r. Monge.* ☏*03 80 30 69 61.* If you're after traditional tastes and a laid-back ambience, this bistro is right up your street. Choose your wine from the racks along the walls to go with classic Burgundian dishes. Add in switched-on service, and an agreeable soundtrack, and you have a winning formula.

⊜ **La Comédie** – *3 pl. du Théâtre.* ☏*03 80 67 11 62. www.la-comedie.com. Dinner menu 14 €.* This bistro appeal to those seeking traditional flavors and atmosphere. You can choose your wine from the the wine racks lining the walls. Good service and good food accompanied by a little music.

⊜ **Le Dôme** – *16 bis r. Quentin.* ☏*03 80 30 58 92.* This modern restaurant is near the market hall. The mouth-watering menu deals in traditional and contemporary cooking, with a good showing of Burgundian specialities.

⊜ **L'Émile Brochettes** – *16 pl. Émile-Zola.* ☏*03 80 49 81 04. Closed 25 Dec–1 Jan.* This quirky cavern-style restaurant looking onto lovely place Émile Zola celebrates the kebab in all of its savoury and sweet forms. Must-try dishes include a shark steak kebab.

La Mère Folle –102 r. Berbisey. *03 80 50 19 76. Closed Mon. Dinner set menu available.* This small, town-centre restaurant offers regional specialities such as snails, eggs *en meurette* (baked in red wine) and *sandre* (pikeperch) *au Chablis*. Convivial atmosphere, good service and 1930s-style décor.

Le Bistrot des Halles – 10 r. Bannelier. *03 80 49 94 15. bistrotdeshalles@club-internet.fr. Closed 25 Dec–2Jan, Sun and Mon.* A typical bistro a stone's throw from the covered market. Choose one of the dishes chalked up on a slate and enjoy the warm and friendly ambience.

Le Bento – 29 r. de la Chaudron-nerie. *03 80 67 11 50. Lunch set menu 16 €. Sun brunch noon–6pm.* Japanese food fans should try this place – the chef invents new sushi, sashimi and maki dishes every day. The nutella pancake makis are to die for.

La Dame d'Aquitaine – 23 pl. Bossuet. *03 80 30 45 65. www.ladame daquitaine.fr. Closed for lunch 20 Jul–20 Aug, Mon lunch and Sun. Lunch set menu 22 €.* In the town centre, a paved courtyard and a long flight of steps descend to a superb 13C vaulted dining hall. The décor is medieval, with tapestries and stained glass. Regional cuisine.

Le DZ'Envies – 12 r. Odebert. *03 80 50 09 26. www.dzenvies.com.* This recently opened contemporary gastronomic bistro on the market square reworks French cuisine with Japanese and North African touches.

ON THE TOWN

Theatres and Opera – Full programme of plays and comedy at the Théâtre du Sablier (R. Berbisey), the Théâtre du Parvis-St-Jean (Pl. Bossuet), the Bistrot de la Scène (R. D'Auxonne). In May the city hosts the Rencontres Internationales du Théâtre. For classical music, opera and dance, visit the Auditorium and the Opéra de Dijon (Pl. du Théâtre).

L'Agora Café – 10 pl. de la Libération. *03 80 30 99 42. Open Tue–Sat 11.30am–2am.* Piano-bar in a former 16C convent chapel with a laid-back vibe.

Le Caveau de la Porte Guillaume – pl. Darcy. *03 80 50 80 50. www.hotel-nord.fr. Open daily 7am–2am. Closed 20 Dec–5 Jan.* Quaff regional delights by the glass or the bottle.

TAKING A BREAK

Comptoir des Colonies – 12 pl. François-Rude. *03 80 30 28 22. Open Mon–Sat 8am–7.30pm.* Colonial-style tea shop, with a large sunny terrace.

Maison Millière – 10 r. de la Chouette. *03 80 30 99 99. www.maison-milliere.fr. Open Tue–Sun 10am–7pm.* Pleasant tearoom in a former 15C fabric shop.

La Causerie des Mondes – 16 r. Vauban. *03 80 49 96 59. Open 11am–7pm, Sundays Oct–Mar 3–7pm. Closed Mon.* Asian-themed décor and mood music, make for an exotic take on the tearoom.

Mulot et Petitjean – 13 pl. Bossuet. *03 80 30 07 10. www.mulotpetitjean.fr. Open Mon 2–7pm, Tue–Sat 9am-noon, 2–7pm.* This Dijon institution, founded in 1796, specialises in gingerbread.

SHOPPING

Marché des Halles – centre of town. Tue, Thu and Fri mornings, and Sat.

Nicot Yves – 48 r. Jean-Jacques-Rousseau. *03 80 73 29 88. nicotvins@ infonie.fr. Open Mon–Fri 8am–12.30pm, 3–8pm, Sat 8am–8pm, Sun 8am–12.30pm.* M Nicot has a passion for Burgundy's wines. Try the wine tasting course.

Auger – 16 and 61 r. de la Liberté. *03 80 30 26 28. Open Sun–Tue 10am–noon, 2–pm, Wed–Sat 9am–7pm.* One of Dijon's last producers of traditional gingerbread - in business since the 14C.

Boutique Amora-Maille – 32 r. de la Liberté. *03 80 30 41 02. Open Mon–Sat 9am–7pm.* Specialist in the mustards and vinegars of Dijon since 1777.

L'Escargotière de Marsannay-le-Bois – rte d'Épagny, 21380 Marsannay-le-Bois. *03 80 35 76 15. sylvainmansuy@ wanadoo.fr. Open 10am–8pm.* Learn how snails are raised, harvested and prepared – then try before you buy.

Côte d'Or★★

The celebrated vineyards of the Côte d'Or (Golden Hillside) stretch from Dijon to Santenay (60km/37mi). Each place bears the name of a famous wine, making it a desirable destination for both connoisseurs and gourmets alike.

BURGUNDY'S FINE WINES
Natural conditions

The Côte is formed by the eastern edge of the region known as La Montagne, whose rectangular shape is cut by transverse combes in the same way as the blind valleys of the Jura vineyards.

The vineyards cover about 8 000ha/19 768 acres in the Côte-d'Or and 10 000ha/24 711 acres in the Saône-et-Loire and are planted with first-quality vines (Pinot Noir for red, Chardonnay for white). They are set in terraces overlooking the plain of the Saône at an altitude varying from 200m to 300m/686ft to 984ft.

The vineyards are planted on the south and east-facing limestone slopes, exposed to the morning sun – the best – and sheltered from cold winds. This position makes the grapes extremely sweet, which in turn gives the wine a high alcohol content. In addition, the slopes facilitate drainage; vines like dry soil and the slope is therefore an important factor in the quality of the grape. The finest wines generally come from grapes grown halfway up the slopes.

South of the Dijon vineyards the Côte d'Or is divided into two parts, the **Côte de Nuits** and the **Côte de Beaune**. The wines of both are well known; those of Nuits for their robustness; those of Beaune for their delicacy. The former extends from the village of Fixin to the southern limits of the Côte d'Or; its most famous wines are Chambertin, Musigny, Clos-Vougeot and Romanée-Conti.

The Côte de Beaune stretches from north of Aloxe-Corton to Santenay and produces great smooth reds such as Corton, Volnay, Pommard and Beaune and rich and fruity whites such as Meursault and Montrachet.

Michelin Map:
320: I-6 to J-8.

Info: Nuits-St-Georges Tourism. ℘03 80 62 11 17. www.ot-nuits-st-georges.fr.

Location: Anchored by Dijon and Santenay, the wine route runs mostly north–south, paralleling the A 6 and passing through Beaune.

🚗 DRIVING TOURS

1 CÔTE DE NUITS★★

Leave Dijon on D 122, known as the Route des Grands Crus.

The Côte de Nuits road follows foothills covered with vines and passes through villages with world-famous names.

Chenôve

The Clos du Roi and Clos du Chapitre recall the former owners of these vineyards, the dukes of Burgundy and the canons of Autun. The dukes' wine cellar, **Cuverie des ducs de Bourgogne** (♿ ⏱ *open Jul–Sept 2–7pm; rest of the year by appointment; ℘03 80 51 55 00*) contains two magnificent 13C presses.

Marsannay-la-Côte

Part of the Côte de Nuits, Marsannay produces popular rosé wines, obtained from the black Pinot grapes.

Fixin

This village produces wines that some consider among the best of the Côte de Nuits appellation. The small **Musée Noisot** (⏱ *open mid-Apr to mid-Oct Sat–Sun 2–6pm;* 🔹*4.50€;* ℘*03 80 52 45 52*) houses mementoes of Napoleon's campaigns.

The 10C church in nearby **Fixey** is thought to be the oldest in the area.

Brochon

Brochon, which is on the edge of the Côte de Nuits, produces excellent wines.

The **château** was built in 1900 by the poet Stephen Liégeard who coined the phrase Côte d'Azur for the Provençal coast. The name has stuck long after the poet has faded into obscurity, together with his poem which was honoured by the French Academy.

Gevrey-Chambertin

This village is typical of the wine-growing community immortalised by the Burgundian writer **Gaston Roupnel** (1872–1946). It is situated at the open end of the gorge, Combe de Lavaux, and surrounded by vineyards. The older part lies grouped around the church and château whereas the Baraques district crossed by N 74 is altogether busier.

The famous Côte de Nuits, renowned for its great red wines, starts to the north. In the upper village is this square-towered fortress **château** (○*open Jun–Sept;* *guided tours (1hr) 10am–noon, 2–6pm;* ⚫*6€;* ℰ*03 80 34 35 77; www. chateau-de-gevrey-chambertin.com*), lacking its portcullis; it was built in the 10C by the lords of Vergy.

Chambolle-Musigny

The road from Chambolle-Musigny to Curley *(north-west)* passes through a gorge, Combe Ambin, to a charming beauty spot: a small chapel stands at the foot of a rocky promontory overlooking the junction of two wooded ravines.

Vougeot

Vougeot red wines are highly valued. The walled vineyard of Clos-Vougeot (50ha/124 acres), owned by the abbey of Cîteaux from the 12C up to the French Revolution, is one of the most famous of La Côte. Since 1944 the **Château du Clos de Vougeot**★ (&○*open daily year round;* *guided tours (45min) Apr–Sept, 9am–6.30pm, rest of year 9–11.30am, 2–5.30pm;* ○*closed 1 Jan, and 24–25 and 31 Dec;* ⚫*3.90€;* ℰ*03 80 34 36 77; www.tastevin-bourgogne.com*) has been owned by the **Confrérie des Chevaliers du Tastevin** (Brotherhood of the Knights of the Tastevin).

Ten years earlier in 1934 a small group of Burgundians met in a cellar in Nuits-St-

Georges and decided to form a society whose aim was to promote the wines of France in general and, in particular, of Burgundy. The brotherhood was born and its renown spread throughout Europe and America. The château was built in the Renaissance and restored in the 19C. The rooms visited include the Grand Cellier (12C cellar) where the *disnées* (banquets) and the ceremonies of the Order are held, the 12C cellar containing four huge winepresses, the 16C kitchen with its huge chimney and the monks' dormitory with a spectacular 14C roof.

Vosne-Romanée

2km/1.25mi N of Nuits-St-Georges.
These vineyards produce only red wines of the highest quality. Among the various sections (*climats*) of this vineyard, Romanée-Conti and De Richebourg have a worldwide reputation.

Nuits-St-Georges

This attractive little town is surrounded by the vineyards to which it has given its name. The fame of the wines of Nuits goes back to Louis XIV. When the royal doctor advised him to take some glasses of Nuits and Romanée with each meal as a tonic, the whole court wanted to taste it. The vast **church of St-Symphorien** was built at the end of the 13C although it is pure Romanesque in style. The flat chevet is pierced by a large rose window and three windows flanked by small columns and sculptures.

A massive belfry surmounts the transept crossing. In addition, there are two fine 17C edifices: the **belfry** of the former town hall and the St-Laurent hospital. The **museum** (○*open May–Oct daily except Tue 10am–noon, 2–6pm;* ⚫*2.30€;* ℰ*03 80 62 01 37*), in the cellars of an old wine business, shows items found in the Gallo-Roman settlement excavated at Les Bolards near Nuits-St-Georges.

② CÔTE DE BEAUNE

& *See Region map.*

65km/40mi from Pernand-Vergelesses to Puligny-Montrachet. Allow around 1hr

30min. Head for Aloxe-Corton, 2km/1.2mi south of Pernand-Vergelesses, via the D 18 and D 115D.

With its vast acreages of white wine production, the Côte de Beaune stands out from the Côte de Nuits. Pernand-Vergelesses, the adopted home of Jacques Copeau (1879–1949) who founded the Vieux-Colombier theatre, offers a superb vista over the vineyards.

Aloxe-Corton

This village (pronounced *Alosse*), the northernmost village of the Côte de Beaune, is of ancient origin. Emperor Charlemagne owned vineyards here and Corton-Charlemagne, "a white wine of great character", recalls this fact. However, red wines are produced almost exclusively at Aloxe-Corton, the firmest and most forward wines of the Côte de Beaune. The bouquet improves with age and the wine remains full-bodied and robust.

To reach Pommard, you can go via the 14C castle at Savigny-lès-Beaune, and then through Beaune itself via the D18, N74 and D973.

Pommard

3km/2mi SW of Beaune on N 74 and D 973.
The large village of Pommard takes its name from an ancient temple dedicated to Pomona, the goddess of fruits and gardens. These vineyards of the Côte de Beaune produce red wines that were greatly appreciated by Ronsard, Henri IV, Louis XV and Victor Hugo.

Volnay

1km/0.5mi SW of Pommard on D 973.
Volnay reds have a delicate bouquet and silky taste. When he acquired the Duchy of Burgundy in 1477, Louis XI had the whole production of Volnay taken to his château at Plessis-les-Tours.

Meursault

2km/1.25mi SE of Auxey.
This little town, dominated by the beautiful Gothic stone spire of its church, produces high-quality red and white wines. It owes its name to a valley that clearly divides the Côte de Meursault from the Côte de Beaune. This valley, known as the Rat's Leap (*Saut du Rat* – in Latin *Muris Saltus*), is said to have given the present name of Meursault. Its white wines, with those of Puligny and Chassagne-Montrachet, are considered the best in the world.
The *Paulée de Meursault*, the final day of a yearly celebration of the grape known as **Les Trois Glorieuses**, is a well-known local fête. At the end of the banquet, to which each guest brings bottles of his own wine, a literary prize is awarded. The happy laureate receives 100 bottles of Meursault.

Continue west to Auxey-Duresses by way of Monthélie, which produces excellent red premiers crus.

Auxey-Duresses

This village is set in a deep *combe* leading to La Rochepot and its château. The vineyards of Auxey-Duresses produce fine red and white wines which, before the law on nomenclature, were sold as Volnay and Pommard. The church, with its fine 16C triptych, is worth a visit.

Saint-Romain

This township is made up of two distinct parts: St-Romain-le-Haut perched high on a limestone spur, surrounded by a semicircle of cliffs, with the ruins of its 12C–13C castle *(archaeological site, short visitor trail marked out)* on the southern edge. Right at the top stands the terraced 15C church, tastefully restored; it contains 2C fonts and a pulpit dating from 1619. Lower down in St-Romain-le-Bas, the **town hall (**open 8.30am–5.30pm; weekends on request; ℘03 80 21 28 50) contains displays on local archaeology and ethnology.

N of St-Romain turn left on D 171 to Orches and La Rochepot.

As the road approaches **Orches**, in its attractive rocky site, there is a fine **view**★ of St-Romain, Auxey, Meursault and the Saône Valley.

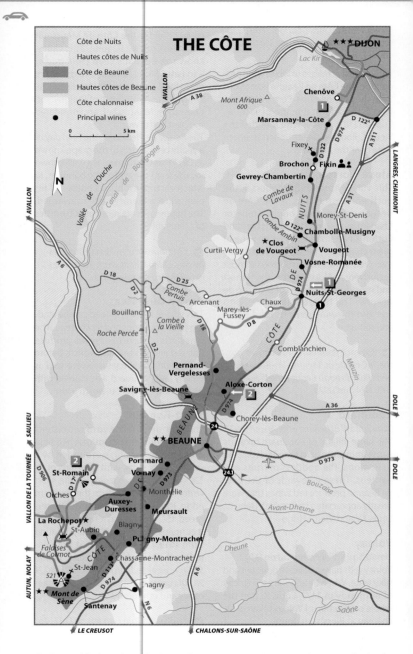

THE CÔTE

- Côte de Nuits
- Hautes côtes de Nuits
- Côte de Beaune
- Hautes côtes de Beaune
- Côte chalonnaise
- Principal wines

0   5 km

★★★ DIJON

Lac Kir

Chenôve

Marsannay-la-Côte

Fixey

Brochon   Fixin

Gevrey-Chambertin

Morey-St-Denis

Chambolle-Musigny

Clos de Vougeot   Vougeot

Curtil-Vergy   Vosne-Romanée

Nuits-St-Georges

Arcenant   Chaux

Bouilland   Marey-lès-Fussey

Roche Percée

Comblanchien

Pernand-Vergelesses

Savigny-lès-Beaune   Aloxe-Corton

Chorey-lès-Beaune

★★ BEAUNE

Pommard

St-Romain   Volnay

Orches   Monthélie

Auxey-Duresses   Meursault

La Rochepot★   Blagny

St-Aubin   Puligny-Montrachet

Falaises de Cormot   Chassagne-Montrachet

St-Jean   Chagny

★★ Mont de Sène

Santenay

LE CREUSOT   CHALONS-SUR-SAÔNE

Beyond Orches, drive 4km/2.5mi S.

La Rochepot★

The village sits at the foot of a rocky promontory on which stands the restored feudal castle. It was the birthplace of Philippe Pot (1428–1494), famous statesman and London ambassador of the dukes of Burgundy. His tomb is now in the Louvre Museum.

Château de la Rochepot

© Christophe Boisvieux/hemis.fr

◠ *From La Rochepot take D 973 NE skirting the château.*

The road follows a narrow valley and prior to Melin crosses a series of limestone escarpments worn by erosion.

♣♦ Vallon de la Tournée
⚐ *5km/3mi. Allow 30min.*
Climbing through woods, the left-hand trail leads to a cave where the Cosanne river cascades over pink granite rocks. The other path traverses meadows to the "End of the World" *cirque*, where a waterfall plummets 28m/30yd. Twitchers might spot peregrine falcons and white-bellied martins.

◠ *Pass through Vauchignon.*

Nolay
24 r. de la République, 21340 Nolay.
◷*Open Apr–Oct 10am–12.30pm, 2–6.30pm; Jan–Feb daily except Mon 10am–1pm, 2–5pm.* ◷*Closed Sun and holidays, 24 Dec–3 Jan.* ℘*03 80 21 80 73. www.nolay.com.*
In the delightful medieval town of Nolay, postcard-pretty timbered houses sit in a patchwork of hillsides and vineyards watered by the Cosanne. On fine days, rock climbers drop by for a refreshing glass of fruity Nolay with a slice of red berry tart after testing their mettle on the surrounding limestone cliffs.
Old market hall – come on Mon morning for the market. Built in the 14C, the

beefy timbers are roofed over with heavy limestone slabs known as "laves".
Église Saint-Martin – Built in the 15C, the church was burnt down in the Wars of Religion, and rebuilt in the 17C. Inside the strange stone belfry is a 16C painted wood automaton.

Mont de Sène★★
The Mont de Sène is also known as the **Montagne des Trois-Croix** after the three crosses on the summit. The **panorama**★★ from the top reveals (north) the vineyards of the Côte beyond La Rochepot (east), the Saône Valley, the Jura and the Alps (south) and Mont St-Vincent and the Morvan (west).

Santenay
The three localities that go to make up Santenay – Santenay-le-Bas, Santenay-le-Haut and St-Jean – are spread along the banks of the River Dheune. Santenay derives its reputation not only from its vast vineyards but also from the local mineral water. The church of **St-Jean** is at the foot of a semicircle of cliffs; a wooden porch protects the round-headed doorway.

Puligny-Montrachet
The white wines of Puligny-Montrachet, like those of Meursault, are excellent. The red wines of this old walled vineyard are full-bodied and have subtle qualities of taste and bouquet.

Burgundy's Legendary Vineyards

The lie of the land

The Côte runs along the east-facing slopes of the "mountain", dominating the plains of the Saône at an altitude varying from 200–300m (219–328yd), and slashed by cross-cut combes in a similar layout to the blind valleys of the Jura vineyards. Only the east- and south-facing slopes of the combes are planted with vines– around 8 000 hectares of first-quality grapes; the north-facing slopes are often densely wooded. While the hilltops are crowned with scrubland or thickets, the vineyards carpet the limestone slopes, basking in the morning sunlight and well protected from cold winds. This exposure to sunlight is what determines the production of sugar in the grapes and the final alcohol content of the wine. The slopes also ensure that rain runs off, keeping the soil well drained and nicely dry – just how the vines like it – to produce top-class wines.

Burgundy's fine wines – the "grands crus"

For much of its length, the D 974 marks the dividing line between the "noble" grape varieties and the rest, with the grands crus generally planted mid-way up the slopes. Pinot Noir is the king of Burgundy grapes: it is used to make red wines, whereas the great white wines are made from the Chardonnay grape. After the devastation of the phylloxera blight in the 19C, the vineyards were entirely replanted with resistant vines grafted from North American stock. But it's an ill wind that blows no good. Paradoxically, the pesky parasites brought beneficial changes in their wake: small producers were able to buy back land from the big boys, and a reduction in the quantity of wine produced led to much-improved quality. The Côte d'Or divides into two main areas: the superstars are the Côte de Nuits and the Côte de Beaune. The wines of the Côte de Nuits are prized for their robustness, while those of the Côte de Beaune are admired for their delicacy.

The Côte de Nuits

The Côte de Nuits extends from Fixin to Corgoloin. Its vineyards cover around 3 740 hectares and produce 104 950 hectolitres annually – that's 14 million bottles, give or take. The vineyards are planted on limestone slopes rich in calcium from fossils. This is red wine country whose most famous crus, running from north to south, are Chambertin, Musigny, Clos-Vougeot et Romanée-Conti. Rich and beefy, these wines need 8 to 10 years to develop the incomparable body and character of the best Burgundy. To the south, the Hautes-Côtes de Nuits vineyards produce uncomplicated wines on the west-facing slopes of the Côte.

The Côte de Beaune

The Côte de Beaune stretches over 5 950 hectares from north of Aloxe-Corton to Santenay, producing not only top-notch white wines, but also superb reds. On the upper slopes, the vineyards grow in limestone-rich soil, which changes its character to brown marly earth mingling with pebbles and clay as it washes down towards the lower reaches. The bottom line is an annual production of some 214 335 hectolitres, equating to 28 million bottles. Its most prestigious crus are, in the red corner, Corton, Volnay, Pommard and Beaune; in the white camp are Meursault and Montrachet. The reds are muscular and fruity – rather like the whites, which deliver a fabulously rich intensity on the nose and palate.

Beaune★★

Right at the heart of the Burgundian vineyards lies Beaune, a name synonymous with good wine; a visit to this ancient city, which boasts a splendid architectural heritage and some fine museums, is not complete without a tour of the vineyards of La Côte.

A BIT OF HISTORY

Birth of a town – First a Gaulish centre and then an outpost of Rome, Beaune was the seat of the dukes of Burgundy to the 14C. After the death of Charles the Bold, last Duke of Burgundy, in 1477, the town refused Louis XI's efforts to annex it and gave in only after a five-week siege.

Wine auction at the Hospices de Beaune – This is the main event of the year and draws a large crowd. The Hospices de Beaune (this name includes the Hôtel-Dieu, the Hospice de la Charité and the hospital) acquired a very fine vineyard (58ha/143 acres) between Aloxe-Corton and Meursault through Chancellor Rolin. The wines from this vineyard have won international acclaim. The proceeds of the auction sales, **Les Trois Glorieuses**, known as the "greatest charity sale in the world", go to the modernisation of the medical facilities and maintenance of the Hôtel-Dieu.

HÔTEL-DIEU★★★

Open 26 Mar–20 Nov 9am–6.30pm; rest of year 9–11.30am, 2–5.30pm. ₷6.50€. ₰03 80 24 45 00. www.hospices-de-beaune.com.

The Hôtel-Dieu in Beaune, a marvel of Burgundian-Flemish art, was founded as a hospital by Chancellor Nicolas Rolin in 1443. The building with its medieval décor has survived intact and was used as a general hospital until 1971. Today it is a very successful tourist attraction.

Exterior

Street façade – The main decorative elements of this sober façade with its tall and steeply pitched slate roof are the dormer windows, the weather vanes, the delicate pinnacles and lacework cresting of lead. The roof line is broken by the bell turret surmounted by a slim Gothic spire 30m/98ft high.

The delicate roof above the porch is composed of three slate gables terminating in worked pinnacles. Each weather vane bears a different coat of arms. On the panelled door, note the ironwork grille and the door knocker, a magnificent piece of sculpted wrought-iron work.

Courtyard – The wings to the left and rear have magnificent roofs of coloured glazed tiles (recently restored) in geometric patterns. These roofs are punctuated by turrets and a double row of dormer windows, surmounted by weather vanes adorned with heraldic bearings and small spires of worked lead.

Interior

Grand'Salle or Chambre des Pauvres ★★★ – This immense hall (72m/236ft long, 14m/46ft wide, 16m/52ft high), used as the poor ward, has a magnificent timber roof in the shape of an upturned keel which is painted throughout; the ends of the tie-beams disappear into the gaping mouths of monsters' heads.

In earlier times on feast days the 28 four-poster beds were covered with fine tapestry bedspreads, now displayed in the Salle du Polyptyque. Even without

---

▶ **Population:** 22 012
◔ **Michelin Map:** 320: I-7
▮ **Info:** rue de l'Hôtel-Dieu, 21200 Beaune. ₰03 80 26 21 30. www.beaune-tourisme.fr.
◖ **Location:** Traffic moves anticlockwise along the one-way boulevard *(peripherique)* encircling the historic centre. Restaurants, cafés and shops offering regional specialities cluster around place de la Halle, the city's heart.

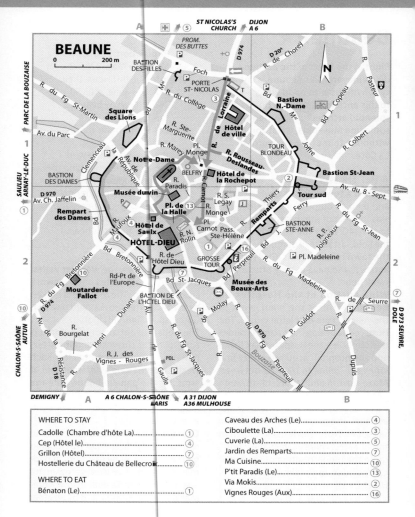

BEAUNE

0   200 m

the tapestries, the double row of beds with their red and white bedclothes, hangings and testers makes a striking impression. At the end of the room stands an arresting, larger-than life-size polychrome wooden statue (15C) of **Christ seated and bound**★ carved from a single piece of oak.

The Flamboyant style screen separating the Grand'Salle from the chapel was reconstructed in the 19C together with the large stained-glass window. The chapel exhibits a copper funerary plaque in memory of Guigone de Salins, wife of Nicolas Rolin and co-founder of

the Hôtel-Dieu. The Clermont-Tonnerre collection of sacred art is displayed here.

Salle Ste-Anne – The linen room, visible through the windows, was originally a small bedroom reserved for the nobility. The work of the nursing nuns is illustrated by life-size models dressed in the habits worn by the staff until 1961.

Salle St-Hugues – This ward, taken out of use in 1982, has been partly refurbished with its 17C décor; the beds are those in use from the end of the 19C. The frescoes, by Isaac Moillon, depict St Hugues, as bishop and Carthusian monk, and the nine miracles of Christ.

Grand'Salle, Hôtel-Dieu

Ph. Gajic/MICHELIN

Salle St-Nicolas – This ward now houses a permanent exhibition on the history of the Hôtel-Dieu and the healing of the body and mind which it offered to the poor and sick. A glass slab in the centre reveals the Bouzaise stream flowing beneath the hospital to carry away waste.

Cuisine – *Son et lumière presentation every 15min.* In the kitchen, an old-fashioned scene has been set up round the huge Gothic fireplace with its double hearth and automatic spit, which dates from 1698.

Pharmacie – The first room of the pharmacy contains pewter vessels displayed on a handsome 18C dresser; the second, which is panelled, contains a collection of 18C Nevers porcelain and a huge bronze mortar.

Salle St-Louis – The walls are hung with early-16C tapestries from Tournai depicting the parable of the Prodigal Son and a 16C series illustrating Jacob's story.

Salle du Polyptyque – This room was designed to exhibit the famous polyptych of the Last Judgement by Rogier van der Weyden. This masterpiece of Flemish art, commissioned by Nicolas Rolin to grace the altar in the Grand Salle and completed between 1445 and 1448, was extensively restored in the 19C and sawn in two so that both faces could be displayed simultaneously. A mobile magnifying glass enables viewers to study the smallest detail on the highly expressive faces of the subjects.

In the central panel Christ presides at the Last Judgement; he is enthroned on a rainbow amid golden clouds; four angels carrying the instruments of the Passion stand at his sides in the flanking panels. St Michael weighs souls, while angels sound their trumpets on either side of him. The Virgin Mary and St John the Baptist appeal to the Saviour for mercy. Behind them, the Apostles and a few important people (including the donors) intercede on behalf of humankind.

The reverse side of the polyptych is on the wall to the right. In the past, this was opened only on Sundays and feast days. Portraits of Nicolas Rolin and his wife are accompanied by monochromes of St Sebastian and St Anthony, the first patrons of the Hôtel-Dieu, and the Annunciation. On the wall to the left hangs a beautiful early-16C *mille-fleurs* tapestry depicting the legend of St Eligius.

The tapestries hanging opposite the Last Judgment belonged to Guigone de Salins; against the deep rose-coloured background, scattered with turtle doves, are the arms of the founder of the hospital, an interlaced G and N and the motto *Seulle* (you alone) expressing Nicolas Rolin's faithful attachment to his wife. In the centre is St Anthony the hermit, patron saint of Guigone de Salins.

✧✦WALKING TOURS
TOWN CENTRE

Enter the town centre through Porte St-Nicolas, a triumphal arch erected during the reign of Louis XV. Among the many old houses, those at nos. 18, 20, 22 and 24 **Rue de Lorraine** form a fine 16C ensemble. The town hall (**Hôtel de ville**) is in a 17C former Ursuline convent. The right wing houses two museums. At no. 10 **rue Rousseau-Deslandes** there is a house with its first floor decorated with trefoiled arcades.

Hôtel de la Rochepot★

○—Not open to the public.

This 16C building has an admirable Gothic façade. In place Monge is a 14C belfry and a statue of **Gaspard Monge** (1746–1818), a local shopkeeper's son who became a famous mathematician. No. 4 **place Carnot** is a 16C house with attractive sculptures.

Place de la Halle

The Hôtel-Dieu with its fine slate roof overlooks the square. Avenue de la République and rue d'Enfer lead to the former mansion of the dukes of Burgundy, dating from the 15C and 16C, now the museum of Burgundy wine. No. 13 **place Fleury** is the **Hôtel de Saulx**, a mansion with a quaint tower and an interior courtyard. The Maison des Vins (tastings) is on rue Rolin, beyond the Hôtel-Dieu.

Musée du Vin★

🕐Open Apr–Nov daily 9.30am–6pm; Dec–Mar daily except Tue 9.30am–5pm. 🕐Closed 1 Jan and 25 Dec. ☜3.50€. 📞03 80 22 08 19.

The museum is in the former mansion of the dukes of Burgundy, dating mainly from the 15C and 16C. The history of Burgundian vineyards and vine cultivation is explained in a comprehensive exhibit on the ground floor. Note the 16C polychrome statue known as the *Virgin Mary with a Bunch of Grapes* or *Notre-Dame de Beaune*. The large first-floor room decorated with two huge Aubusson tapestries is the headquarters of the Ambassade des Vins de France.

Collégiale Notre-Dame★

The daughter house of Cluny, begun about 1120, was considerably influenced by the church of St-Lazare in Autun; it is a fine example of Burgundian Romanesque art despite successive additions.

Exterior – The façade is concealed by a wide 14C porch with three naves. The sculpted decoration was destroyed during the Revolution, but the 15C carved door panels have survived.

Walk clockwise round the church to get the best view of the chevet. Three different phases of construction – the pure Romanesque of the ambulatory and apsidal chapels, the 13C refurbishment of the chancel and the 14C flying buttresses – can be detected in the handsome proportions of the whole. The crossing tower, which is formed of Romanesque arcades surmounted by pointed bays, is capped by a dome and a 16C lantern.

Interior – The lofty nave of broken-barrel vaulting is flanked by narrow aisles with groined vaulting. A triforium, composed of open and blind bays, goes round the building, which is strongly reminiscent of Autun with its decoration of arcades and small fluted columns. Besides the decoration of the small columns in the transept, it is worth noting the sculptures on certain capitals in the nave representing Noah's Ark, the Stoning of St Stephen and a Tree of Jesse and the Renaissance chapel with the fine coffered ceiling off the south aisle.

Tapestries★★ – In the choir behind the high altar are some magnificent tapestries which mark the transition from medieval to Renaissance art. Five richly coloured panels, worked in wool and silk, trace the whole life of the Virgin Mary in a series of charming scenes. They were commissioned in 1474 and offered to the church in 1500 by Canon Hugues le Coq.

At no. 2 **rue E.-Fraysse**, the Maison du Colombier is a Renaissance house which can be seen from the square in front of the church of Notre-Dame.

Vineyards of Savigny-lès-Beaune

© Jean-Baptiste Rabouan/hemis.fr

THE RAMPARTS★

You can do this tour on foot or by car. Follow the outer boulevards anti-clockwise around the ramparts from Bastion St-Jean, starting at Boulevard Joffre.

The relatively well-preserved ramparts form an almost continuous wall walk (2km/1mi). They were built between the end of the 15C and the middle of the 16C, and are adorned with a few surviving towers and eight rustic bastions of various shapes – the double one, originally a castle, is known as the **Bastion St-Jean**. The encircling moat is now occupied by gardens, tennis courts etc. The north tower of the Bastion St-Jean has gargoyles and a niche occupied by a Virgin and Child. Pass the Blondeau Tower to get to the **Bastion Notre-Dame**, with a charming turret covering the spur. The line of the ramparts is broken by the 18C Porte St-Nicolas at the end of rue Lorraine. Next come the Bastion des Filles, spoilt by the addition of an ugly new roof, and the now filled-in Bastion St-Martin forming a triangular terrace (**square des Lions**) overlooking a shaded garden.

The route now takes you past the Bastion des Dames, the **Rempart des Dames** and the now-abandoned Bastion of l'Hôtel-Dieu. The 15C Grosse Tour on the Rempart Madeleine is followed by the Bastion Ste-Anne with a turret overlooking the moat. The tour ends in front of the castle's **south tower**.

EXCURSIONS
Château de Savigny-lès-Beaune★
⊙ *5km/3mi NW.*

⊙ *Open Apr–Oct daily 9am–6.30pm; rest of the year 9am–noon, 2–5.30pm.* ⊗*8€.* ℰ*03 80 21 55 03.* *www. chateau-savigny.com.*

This village, known for its quality wines, has a 14C castle with some interesting collections on display. The smaller 17C château is now home to a wine-tasting and sales room and an exhibit of **Arbath endurance cars**. Visitors to the park will see 60 **jet fighter planes**, including Mirages (I to V), MIG 21 US (1962), Sikorsky helicopters and more.

The château was built by Jean de Frolois, Maréchal de Bourgogne, and restored by the Bouhier family in the 17C. An upper floor has been set aside for the **motorcycle collection**★, including over 500 models from around the world, which gives an overview of changes in mechanics and design over the 20C.

Montagne de Beaune
⊙ *5km/3mi NW along D 970.*

Seen from the orientation table near the war monument (about 600m/656yd south of the statue of Notre Dame-de-la-Libération), a lovely view extends over the brown-tiled roofs of the town to the vineyards beyond, and the Mâconnais hills to the south. Come in the afternoon when the light is at its best!

ADDRESSES

▲ STAY

◉◉ **Chambre d'hôte La Cadolle** – Grande-Rue, 21200 Bouze-les-Beaune. 6km/3.7mi northwest of Beaune on D970. ℘03 80 26 08 99. www.lacadolle.com. Closed Dec and Jan. ▣ 🛏 3 rooms. ⊡. This delightfully renovated stone house offers three rooms with original wood parquet flooring. Those on the first floor open onto their own little balconies, while the third has a more cosy character. All in all, a nice little set-up run by welcoming owners.

◉◉ **Hôtel Grillon** – 21 rte Seurre. ℘03 80 22 44 25. www.hotel-grillon.fr. Closed 1–7 Dec and all Feb. Wi-Fi. 21 rooms. ⊡ 10 €. A spruce little bolthole tucked away in a walled garden, with attractive personal touches in the bedrooms. There's a lounge-bar in the cellar, and a flowery alfresco terrace for summery breakfasts.

◉◉ **Hôtel Le Parc** – 13 r. du Golf, 21200 Levernois. 6km/3.7mi southeast of Beaune on D970. ℘03 80 24 63 00. www.hotelleparc.fr. Closed 31 Jan–13 Mar. ▣ Wi-Fi. 17 rooms. ⊡ 8 €. Charming hotel clad with Virginia creeper and bursting with flowers in summer. The two buildings are separated by a patio. The grounds at the back look out over fields.

◉◉◉ **Hostellerie du Château de Bellecroix** – 20 chemin de Bellecroix, 71150 Chagny. 18km/11mi southeast of Beaune on D974 then N6. ℘03 85 87 13 86. www.chateau-bellecroix.com. Closed 15 Dec–13 Feb and Wed (except Jun–Sept). 19 rooms. ⊡ 16 €, half-board available. ✕. The two towers of this 18C château stand amid wooded parkland. Nearby lie the turrets of a former 12C Knights Templar building of the Order of Malta. Bedrooms come with antique furniture.

◉◉◉◉ **Hôtel Le Cep** – 27 r. Maufoux. ℘03 80 22 35 48. www.hotel-cep-beaune.com. Wi-Fi. 49 rooms. ⊡ 22 €. Ravishing 16C house in the old quarter. Cosily old-fashioned bedrooms are named after famous vintages from the Côte-d'Or. Breakfast is served in the vaulted cellar or in the courtyard with its pretty Renaissance arcades.

⍭ EAT

◉ **Aux Vignes Rouges** – 4 bd Jules-Ferry. ℘03 80 24 71 28. www.auxvignes-rouges.com. Closed Mar and Wed. Lunch menu 12 €. Two dining rooms in a stone vaulted cellar done out with a natural look are the setting for regional cuisine built on fresh local produce.

◉◉ **Le Bénaton** – 25 r. fg Bretonnière. ℘03 80 22 00 26. www.lebenaton.com. Closed 1–7 Jul, 5–15 Dec, Feb holidays, Sat lunch Apr–Nov, Thu lunch Apr–Nov and Wed. Small, tranquil restaurant with a covered terrace for warm days. Delicious meals made with fresh seasonal produce are great value for money.

◉◉ **Caveau des Arches** – 10 bd Perpreuil. ℘03 80 22 10 37. www.caveau-des-arches.com. Closed 18 Jul–19 Aug, 20 Dec–19 Jan, Sun and Mon. Set lunch menu 15 €. Savour fine classic Burgundy cooking in the cosy vaulted dining rooms of this restaurant on the ramparts.

◉◉ **La Ciboulette** – 69 r. de Lorraine. ℘03 80 24 70 72. laurent.male@orange.fr. Closed 2–20 Aug, 1–25 Feb, Mon and Tue. Two cheerful dining rooms furnished with green rattan and wood panelling. Appetising menu of traditional dishes given a Bourguignon spin.

◉◉ **La Cuverie** – 5 r. Chanoine-Donin, 21420 Savigny-lès-Beaune. ℘03 80 21 50 03. Closed 20 Dec–20 Jan, Tue and Wed. This 18C stone wine cellar with bourguignon furniture and a snazzy collection of cafetières is just the job for traditional dining featuring local produce.

◉◉ **Le Jardin des Remparts** – 10 r. Hôtel-Dieu. ℘03 80 24 79 41. www.le-jardin-des-remparts.com. Closed Dec, Sun and Mon except public holidays. ▣. Comfy dining rooms and a delightful garden terrace in this 1930s house up against the ramparts. Contemporary cooking using top-class materials.

◉◉ **Ma Cuisine** – passage Ste-Hélène. ℘03 80 22 30 22. macuisine@wanadoo.fr. Closed Aug, Wed, Sat and Sun. Located along a tiny street, this small dining room sports the colours of Provence. Regional bottles on the wine list.

◎◉ **Via Mokis** – *1 r. Eugène Spüller.* ☏*03 80 26 80 80. www.viamokis.com. Closed 23 Dec–2 Jan. Set lunch 15 €. 5 rooms. ☞ 15 €.* Masterfully creative cooking served on small plates, or *mokis* in a trendy bistro setting. Good choice of wines by the glass. Spacious, individual, modern rooms and there's a basement spa.

◎◉◉ **Le P'tit Paradis** – *25 r. Paradis.* ☏*03 80 24 91 00. leptitparadis@orange.fr. Closed 2 weeks in Aug, 2 weeks in Dec, 2 weeks in Apr, Sun and Mon.* Dining room and terrace by a flower garden. Modern cuisine with regional flair and wines from boutique producers.

🍴 TAKING A BREAK

Bouché – *1 pl. Monge.* ☏*03 80 22 10 35. Open Tue–Sun 8am–8pm, Sun 8am–1pm and 3–8pm.* Inside this pretty tearoom are lovely gift boxes to fill with tantalising house specialities – chocolate "snails", candied chestnuts and fruits. At table, you're spoilt for choice with 20 or so speciality sweets.

Palais des gourmets – *14 pl. Carnot.* ☏*03 80 22 13 39. Open daily 7am–7.30pm (7pm Oct–Apr and closed Tue).* This delightful patisserie–tea room serves many local delicacies, including *cassissines* (blackcurrant jelly flavoured with blackcurrant liqueur).

🍸 ON THE TOWN

Le Bistrot Bourguignon – *8 r. Monge.* ☏*03 80 22 23 24. www.restaurant-le bistrotbourguignon.com. Open Tue–Sat 11am–3pm, 6–11pm. Closed mid-Feb to mid-Mar.* Relax on the terrace or sink into a comfy armchair in this old house as you sip a glass of wine to the mellow strains of classic jazz.

🍷 WINE LOVERS' PARADISE

L'Athenaeum de la Vigne et du Vin – *5 r. de l'Hôtel-Dieu.* ☏*03 80 25 08 30. www.athenaeumfr.com. Open daily 10am–7pm. Closed 25 Dec and 1 Jan.* This bookshop has a reputation as the best on oenology, Burgundy and gastronomy. Also wine-related items from corkscrews to cellarman's knives.

Cave Patriarche Père & Fils – *5–7 r. du Collège.* ☏*03 80 24 53 79. www.patriarche.com. Open daily 9.30–11.30am, 2–5.30pm (Nov–Mar Sat–Sun 5pm). Closed 24, 25, 31 Dec and 1 Jan.* Burgundy's largest cellars are housed in a former convent dating from the 14C. Guided tours and tasting sessions.

Caves de La Reine Pédauque – *Porte St-Nicolas.* ☏*03 80 22 23 11. www.reine-pedauque.com. Open end of Nov–Mar daily 10am–noon, 2–5pm; Apr–Nov daily 9.30am–12.30pm, 2–7pm. Closed Christmas and Jan.* After exploring the 18C vaulted cellars, go for a wine tasting around an imposing, round, marble table.

La Cave des Cordeliers – *6 r. de l'Hôtel-Dieu.* ☏*03 80 25 08 85. Open daily Oct–Apr 10.30–11.30am, 2–5.30pm; May–Sept 9.30am–noon, 2–6pm. Closed 25 Dec and 1 Jan.* The Couvent des Cordeliers, built in 1242, provides a splendid backdrop to these wine cellars, which you can visit before tasting six fine wines.

Le Comptoir Viticole – *1 r. Samuel Legay.* ☏*03 80 22 15 73. www.comptoir viticole.com. Open daily 8am–noon (9am Mon), 2–7pm. Closed Sun and public holidays.* Wine buff heaven in a shop selling all manner of wine-making kit.

Marché aux Vins – *2 r. Nicolas Rolin.* ☏*03 80 25 08 20. www.marcheauxvins. com. Open Jul–Aug daily 9.30am–5.45pm, rest of the year daily 9.30–11.45am, 2–5.45pm. Closed 25 Dec and 1 Jan.* Wine market in Beaune's oldest church offering 18 wines of between 3 and 15 years of age.

Vins de Bourgogne Denis-Perret – *40 r. Carnot.* ☏*03 80 22 35 47. www.denisperret.fr. Open May–Oct Mon–Sat 9am–7pm, Sun 9am–noon; rest of the year Mon–Sat 9am–noon, 2–7pm.* Five wine-growers and a group of landowners have teamed up to offer you some of the most prestigious names from the Burgundy region.

Pouilly-en-Auxois area

The small town of Pouilly-en-Auxois lies at the foot of Mont de Pouilly, at the exit of the tunnel through which the Canal de Bourgogne flows from the Rhône basin to the Seine basin. It is the ideal starting point for excursions in the surrounding area.

▶ **Population:** 1 502
  Michelin Map: 320: H-6.
  Info: Le Colombier, 21320 Pouilly-En-Auxois. 03 80 90 74 24. www.pouilly-auxois.com.

A BIT OF GEOGRAPHY

Watershed line – All the water streaming down the southern slopes of Mont Pouilly runs to the Mediterranean sea, while the run-off from the northern slopes heads for the River Seine and the North sea; the water flow from the western slopes ends up in the River Loire. Thus the relatively low Mont Pouilly (alt 559m/1 834ft) marks the watershed line between three main river basins: the Rhône, the Seine and the Loire.

EXCURSIONS

St-Thibault
◉ *17km/10.6mi NW.*
The village is named after St Theobald, whose relics were presented to the local priory in the 13C. The **church**★ (◉*open mid-Mar to mid-Nov 9.30am–6pm; visit of chapel of St Gilles by request; 03 80 64 66 07 or 03 80 64 62 63)* has a graceful five-sided **choir**★ and a main **doorway**★ which is considered among the most beautiful examples of 13C Burgundian architecture. Also of note are the altar **furnishings**★, including two carved wooden retables representing episodes from the life of St Theobald. The oldest part of the church is St Giles' Chapel.

Châteauneuf-en-Auxois★
◉ *12km/7.5mi SE.*
This old fortified market town, in a picturesque **spot**★, is famous for its fortress, which commanded the road from Dijon to Autun and the surrounding plain. Another château open to visitors lies nearby.

The **château**★ (◉*open daily except Mon 10am–12.30pm, 2–7pm (mid-May to mid-Sept), rest of year until 6pm; closed 1 Jan, 1 May, 11 Nov, 25 Dec; 5€; 03 80 49 21 89)* was built in the 12C by the lord of Chaudenay, whose own ruined castle is on an attractive site in Chaudenay-le-Château *(6km/3.5mi S)*. It was enlarged and refurbished at the end of the 15C in the Flamboyant Gothic style. The impressive structure, enclosed by thick walls flanked by massive towers, is separated from the village by a moat. There used to be two fortified gates; now a single drawbridge, flanked by

Canal de Bourgogne, Châteauneuf in the background

S. Sauvignier/MICHELIN

huge round towers, gives access to the courtyard and the two main buildings. Although partially ruined, the **guest pavilion** has retained its handsome ogee-mullioned windows. The **grand logis** in the other wing with its high dormer windows has been restored: the impressive guard-room has a huge chimney with a coat of arms. The chapel (1481) has been carefully restored to show off the frescoes and the replica of Philippe Pot's tomb (the original is in the Louvre). The rooms upstairs were decorated in the 17C and 18C. Next to the Charles I of Vienna (1597–1659) room, in the keep, is a room which has kept its original brick partition (15C). From the round room, there is a view over the Morvan foothills and the Burgundy Canal.

The vast guard-room, the chapel (1481) and several rooms decorated in the 17C and 18C are open to visitors. From the circular chamber there is a panoramic view of the Morvan plain.

Château de Commarin★

◐ 8km/5mi N of Châteauneuf along D 977bis.

◷ Open Apr–Nov daily. ◑ Guided tours (30min) 10am–noon, 2–6pm. ◉6.50€. ℘03 80 49 23 67. www.commarin.com.

This graceful 14C castle remodelled in the 17C and 18C, contains some fine 16C **tapestries★** with incredibly well-preserved colours.

◄◓ DRIVING TOUR

Ouche Valley

68km/42mi from Bligny-sur-Ouche to Dijon. Allow 1hr 30min.

The River Ouche snakes through a landscape of cliffs, meadows and wooded hillsides known as Swiss Burgundy. Highlights along the way include the ancient abbey church at la Bussiere-sur-Ouche, the magnificent gardens of Barbirey and the 18C Château de Mont-culot. Finish with a stroll to the chapel of Notre-Dame de l'Etang.

ADDRESSES

▨ STAY

◷◷ **Chambre d'Hôte Mme Bagatelle** – r. des Moutons, 21320 Châteauneuf-en-Auxois. ℘03 80 49 21 00. www.chezbagatelle.fr. Closed Feb school holidays. ◴ Reservations required. 4 rooms. Attractively restored sheepfold in the heart of a small village. Comfy rooms with stone walls, beams and wooden furnishings. Two mezzanine rooms are perfect for families. Not to be missed.

◷◷ **Chambre d'Hôte Péniche Lady A** – Canal de Bourgogne, 21320 Vandenesse-en-Auxois. 7km/4.3mi SE of Pouilly-en-Auxois by D 970 and D 18. ℘03 80 49 26 96. www.peniche-lady-a.com. Closed Dec–Jan. ◴ 3 rooms. Meals◷◷. Three small bright cabins on a barge anchored on the quays of the Canal de Bourgogne. The deck has pretty views of Châteauneuf, its castle and the rolling countryside.

◷◷◷◷ **Hostellerie du Château Ste-Sabine** – 21320 Ste-Sabine. 8km/5mi SE of Pouilly by N 81, D 977bis then D 970. ℘03 80 49 22 01. www.hostellerie-sainte-sabine.com. Closed 3 Jan–25 Feb. 30 rooms. ◻10€. Restaurant ◷◷. This superb 17C château sits in a vast estate. Rooms are a marvel of simplicity and sobriety. Fine vista of the lake. Summer pool. Animals roam freely on the property.

◉ EAT

◷◷ **Le Grill du Castel** – 21320 Châteauneuf-en-Auxois. ℘03 80 49 26 82. ◴. Although there's no blazing fire in the hearth during the summer heat, the grill turns out tasty grilled meats (with local mustards) all year long.

▷ SHOPPING

Maison de Pays de l'Auxois Sud – Le Seuil. ℘03 80 90 75 86. Open winter Mon–Fri 10am–noon, 1.30–6pm, Sat 10am –6pm, Sun 3–6pm; summer daily 10am –7pm, Sun 3–7pm. Closed 25 Dec and 1 Jan. The clue is in the name: this shop features the wonderful products of the Auxois region, from gingerbread and terrines to wines and liqueurs and local artisans' work.

Til-Châtel

The town sits at the confluence of the Ignon and the Tille in verdant countryside watered by the river's numerous tributaries. Famous for its church dedicated to Saint Florent who was martyred by Barbarians in the 3C, it has a core of fine old buildings.

VISIT

Église Saint-Florent

This 12C Romanesque church is entered through a handsome portal on the tympanum, a majestic Christ is surrounded by the symbols of the four evangelists. The lateral doorway is similarly inspired but more sparsely decorated.

Inside, the eye is drawn to the capitals of the nave, the dome above the transept and the vaulted apse. The church conceals a rich heritage: an ancient wooden statue of Christ being mocked dating from the 12C, a 17C Italian calvary scene, the 16C tomb of St Honoré and the reliquary in naive-style painted wood, baptismal fonts from the 9C and five carved tombstones. The 12C altar is built on an enormous stone said to be the one taken from the bridge where St Florent was decapitated.

EXCURSION

Château de Grancey

26 km/16mi northwest on the D 959. Guided tours (45min) Jul and Aug 3pm and 4pm, closed Sun, 14 Jul and 15 Aug. 1.50 €. 03 80 75 63 45.
This pocket-sized "Burgundian Versailles" was built between the 17C and 18C on an elevated terrace above a fine estate on an eye-catching site. It sits beside the remains of a château dating from the 12 and 15C (moats, drawbridge and huge manorial chapel).

ADDRESSES

STAY / EAT

Hôtel Le Bourguignon – *R. Porte-de-Bessey, 21310 Bèze. 03 80 75 34 51. www.lebourguignon.com. Closed 20 Oct*

▶ **Population:** 957

Info: Tourist Office of the Pays des Trois Rivières – Pl. de la République – 21120 Is-sur-Tille. 03 80 95 24 03. www.covati.fr. Open Jun–Aug 9am–noon, 2–6pm, Sun and public holidays 9am–noon; Apr–May and Sept–Oct daily, except Sun and Mon 9am–noon, 2pm–6pm; rest of year: daily except Sun and Mon 9am–noon. Closed 1 Jan, Easter Sun and Mon, 1 May, 14 Jul, 15 Aug, 25 Dec.

Location: Til-Châtel lies 21km/13mi north-east of Dijon on D 974; you can also take exit 5 off the A31 motorway – Fontaine-Française is 20km/12mi east.

Kids: All aboard the Lavières tourist train for a fun family trip through the pine forest.

Timing: Make time for a walk in the grounds of the Château de Grancey.

Don't Miss: Wonder at the majestic figure of Christ on the portal of Église St-Florent.

–10 Nov. 25 rooms. 8 €. *Restaurant*. Rooms in a modern vein in a recently-built wooden house. Exposed beams and a fireplace in the rustic dining room inside a building with a Renaissance façade. When it's time for an apéritif, go for a kir!

SPORT AND LEISURE

Lavières Tourist Train – *03 80 95 36 36. www.e-monsite.fr/cfti. Open daily from mid-Jun–mid-Sept, Sun and public holidays 3–7pm (runs every 20min).* This dinky tourist train takes you on a 1.4km/0.9mi trip through the pine forests near Is-sur-Tille.

Fontaine-Française

Near to Franche-Comté, Fontaine-Française was once a powerful fief at the heart of an enclave connected closely to the French crown. This tranquil spot boasts a superb 18C château.

CHÂTEAU

Guided tours (40min) Jul–mid-Sept daily except Mar 10am–noon, 2–6pm. 5€. 03 80 75 80 40.

Built in the 18C above the ruins of an 11C feudal castle, this classically elegant stately home once hosted famous writers such as Voltaire and Madame de Staël. Inside is a fine collection of furniture, notably a set of armchairs decorated with St Cyr embroidery scenes of Aesop's Fables, and Gobelin tapestries. The French-style estate is planted with handsome linden trees and has as its centrepiece the glorious Pagosse lake, which mirrors the château.

🚗 DRIVING TOUR

36km/22mi. Around 3hrs. 5km/3mi east on D 960. See Region map.

Saint-Seine-sur-Vingeanne

The village's 17C **château** has two round towers and a **church** with a Romanesque three-storey belfry. Note the splendid 19C stained glass in the chancel and a painted 16C stone Christ figure to the right of the altar.

Château de Rosières

Open 9am–7pm. 4€ (under 18s free). 03 80 75 96 24. www.chateau derosieres.com.

The massive keep and one of the towers date from the 15C.

Château de Beaumont-sur-Vingeanne

Guided tours (20min) Jul and Sept daily (not Sun), 2.30–6.30pm. 4€. 03 80 47 70 04.

- ▶ **Population:** 931
- 🕭 **Michelin Map:** Fontenois Carte générale C2 – Carte Michelin Départements 320 M4 – Côte-d'Or (21).
- ▷ **Location:** On the D 960, 35km from Dijon, near the Marne to Saône canal.
- **Kids:** Take a boat trip on the mysterious subterranean pools in the Bèze grottoes.
- 👁 **Don't Miss:** Take a guided trip around the château, then set off to explore the pretty villages on the driving tour.

This small-but-perfectly-formed château was built in 1724 by Abbot Claude Jolyot, the King's chaplain, who came for a bit of peace and quiet away from Versailles. It is a rare example of a French "folly" set in six hectares of gardens.

Bèze

This small town merits a stop for its ruins of a 9C tower, the "Tour des Francs", Gothic arcades in the former monastic college, and the Église St-Rémi, whose belfry dates from the 13C. The famous Canon Kir once lived in the spa building.

The Source of the Bèze – When the waters are in flood this splendid source spouts 18 000 litres a second. The water is drinkable, and trout swim in it. Lovely walks along the river banks.

Grottes de Bèze – *Guided tours (30min) May–Sept 10am–noon, 1.30–6pm; Apr and Oct: weekend and public holidays 1.30–6pm. 4.50€ (ch. 2.15€). 03 80 75 31 33.*

The passages of the River Tille have carved out an impressive underground channel and linked cave system. Take a boat ride for 300m/984ft through a bewitching subterranean world – the gin-clear lake is 18m/59ft deep, and there are rock formations in the shape of cannon shells and Mexican hats.

Saône Valley★

The mighty River Saône starts its journey at Vioménil, at an altitude of 395m/1 296ft in the Lorraine Plateau and Vosges area. It enters Burgundy near Pontailler and joins up with the Rhône as it flows out of Lyon. Its mild gradient and orderly flow make for a gentle, user-friendly waterway, navigable along most of its length.

A BIT OF HISTORY

Landscapes of the Saône – The lazy waters of the River Saône amble through a wide plain between the Massif central and the Jura. Each winter, the river floods its valley, depositing fertile silt in the neighbouring meadows, giving a helping hand to the "Pacuiers" and market gardeners around Auxonne. The Ouche and Tilles valleys were once marshland, but are now given over to industrial-scale production of tobacco and sugar beet. After Seurre, the Saône passes near to the Côte, but is kept at bay by the scattered woodland of the Cîteaux and Gergy forests.

A trade route – Commerce developed very quickly after the Roman age. Lyon was linked to Trèves by the Via Agrippa passing through Mâcon, Tournus, Chalon-sur-Saône and Langres. The river was also put to use and Chalon-sur-Saône soon became an important river port and warehousing centre. Wine was one of the imports from Italy: shards of around 24 000 amphora have been found in the river bed at Chalon-sur-Saône. In the 13 and 14C, the trade fairs held in Chalon-sur-Saône were important events for international business: the cloth manufacturers of Dijon, Châtillon and Beaune rubbed shoulders with their competitors from Flanders and Italian merchants.

The Saône was linked to the Loire by a canal in 1793, then to the Seine in 1832, to the Rhine in 1833, and the Marne in 1907. Further expansion was planned to allow convoys of up to 4 000 tonnes between Fos-sur-Mer and Auxonne, but the project was abandoned and traffic of this size can only travel as far as Mâcon.

Michelin Map:
General Map C3/4; Department maps 320 K/M-5/8 Côte-d'Or (21), Saône-et-Loire (71).

Location: The Saône flows from north to south, via Chalon-sur-Saône, Tournus et Mâcon.

Kids: Learn about the art of flour milling and bread baking at la Maison du blé et du pain, an offshoot of the Ecomuseum of Bresse bourguignonne, at Verdun-sur-le-Doubs.

Don't Miss: Explore the small fortified villages along the river: Auxonne, Verdun-sur-le-Doubs, St-Jean-de-Losne. Tuck into a "pôchouse" à Verdun-sur-le-Doubs: this fish stew is a real treat! To walk off this hearty meal, take a short stroll along the banks of the Saône.

For now, the Saône is quite happy with its cruise ship business.

ABBAYE DE CÎTEAUX

14km/9mi E of Nuits-St-Georges. *Open May–Oct.* *Guided tours (2hrs) Jul to Aug daily except Mon 9.45am–6.30pm, Sun noon–6.30pm. Rest of the year 9.45am–12.45pm, 2.15–6pm, Sun 2.15–6pm. 7.50€. 03 80 61 32 58. www.citeaux-abbaye. com. It is important to remember that this is not just a historical site, but also a working religious community. Expect your two-hour guided tour to reflect this.* Cîteaux, like Cluny, is an important centre in western Christendom. It was here, among the cistels, or reeds, that Robert, Abbot of Molesme, founded the Order of Cistercians in 1098, an off-shoot of Cluny, which under the great driving force of St Bernard (who joined the community in 1112 and later became abbot), spread its influence throughout the world. The abbey of La Trappe, which was attached to Cîteaux in 1147 and reformed in 1664, has given its name to several monasteries which joined the Strict Observance. In 1892, the Order was officially divided into two branches: Cistercian monks who may devote themselves to a pastoral or intellectual life, such as teaching; and the more numerous Trappist monks who follow a strictly contemplative vocation, as here.

During the Revolution, Cîteaux nearly perished in its entirety. The monks were expelled and did not return until 1898. The church containing the tombs of the first dukes of Burgundy and of Philippe Pot *(now in the Louvre, Paris)* was completely destroyed.

All that remains are relics of the library, faced with 15C enamelled bricks, which incorporates six arches of a Gothic cloister and a vaulted room on the first floor; a handsome 18C building still used by the 35 or so monks; and a late-17C building beside the river.

A new church was built and inaugurated in 1998 to commemorate the 900th anniversary of the abbey's foundation.

🚗 DRIVING TOURS

FROM TALMAY TO VERDUN-SUR-LE-DOUBS

76km/47mi. Allow 3hrs.

Château de Talmay★

🔊 *Guided tours (45min) Jul–Aug daily except Mar 3–6pm (last entry 15min before closing).* ⬡7 €. ℘03 80 36 13 64.
All that remains of the feudal castle destroyed in 1760 is the square 13C keep. The splendid classic château that now stands in its place sits among French-style gardens. Each floor of the tower is furnished in style – carved Renaissance ceilings, a library, and a lounge with Louis XIV panelling.

Pontailler-sur-Saône

Provides a great view from Mont Ardoux across the Saône plains and the Jura peaks away to the east.

Auxonne (🔊 *see entry*)

Saint-Jean-de-Losne

A true crossroads of the waterways, the old boating capital sits at the start of the canal de Bourgogne, and near to that of the Rhône and Rhine canal.

This old stronghold was the scene in 1636 of a siege against Austrian forces in the days when the Saône formed the border between France and the Holy Roman Empire. The garrison of a few hundred men held out against General Gallas and his 60 000 soldiers, forcing them to retreat.

This astonishing victory against the Empire is celebrated in a stained glass window in the **church**. In the oldest house in town (15C) is the **Maison des mariniers**, which has an exhibition about boats.

Seurre

This bustling small town sits near to the confluence of the two arms of the Saône, best seen from the end of rue de Beauraing. Seurre's 17C **hôpital** (hospice) is a smaller version of the Grand-Salle of the hôtel-Dieu in Beaune. Also worth a look is the 14C Église St-Martin, as well as numerous timbered houses and at 13 rue Bossuet, the house now shared by the Tourism Office and the écomusée de la Saône.

Verdun-sur-le-Doubs

This pretty little settlement sits at the confluence of the unhurried Saône and the tempestuous Doubs in a landscape of meadows and crumbling stone walls. The local speciality is **pôchouse verdunoise**, a stew of freshwater fish including pike, perch, eel and tench.

👥 **Maison du blé et du pain** – 🕐*Open mid-May–end Sept 2–7pm; Oct–mid-May 2–6pm;* 🕐*closed 25 Dec–1 Jan. 3 € (children 7–18 yrs 1.50 €);* ℘03 85 76 27 16; www.ecomusee-de-la-bresse.com. This outpost of the Écomusée de la Bresse Bourguignonne (🔊 *see p141*) is a reminder that Verdun-sur-le-Doubs lies on the grain growing plain of the Saône Valley. Learn all about the origins and evolution of wheat cultivation as well as flour milling and breadmaking (display of bread, models of tools and machines, and various activities).

FROM VERDUN-SUR-LE-DOUBS TO MÂCON

90km/56mi. Allow 2hrs 30min.
The Saône broadens out after Verdun-sur-le-Doubs, and just before Chalon, the D 5 crosses the Canal du Centre, which links to the Loire via the Dheune Valley and Bourbince Valley. In this last loop of the river before Chalon you'll find the sport and recreational park as well as the St-Nicolas rose garden.

Chalon-sur-Saône★
(see entry)

The old lock at Gigny

At the lock keeper's house *(now a café-restaurant in season)*, you have a splendid vantage point over the Saône. Since Chalon, the river has settled into its broad and majestic north–south axis, where it stays until it meets the confluence with the Rhône.
On the left bank (the Empire side, as the old-timers knew it, as opposed the Kingdom's side) are vast expanses of flood meadows where large numbers of cattle are raised.

If you're up for a walk, wander at will along the old towpath where rows of poplars run alongside *péniches* (large canal barges) and summer season pleasure boats

Tournus★ *(see entry)*

South of Tournus, the Seille flows into the left bank of the Saône in the little village of **La Truchère** (there is a charming lock on the southern arm of the mouth of the Seille, with restaurants and boat hire). Various small roads lead off the N6 towards the ancient "ports" of Farges and Uchizy (access to the water is easy from these villages built on raised terraces 2–3km/1.2–1.9mi from the river). This is a good place to fish from the pleasant banks of the Saône. In the "ports" on the riverside are clusters of houses with the odd little auberge where you can tuck into traditional fried fish and frogs legs.

Le Villars

Commemorative plaques by the entrance to the church inform you that the pianist **Alfred Cortot** (1877–1962) and the engineer **Gabriel Voisin** (1880–1973) once lived in the village. The latter was, together with his brother, the first industrial aircraft manufacturer in France. **Anatole France** sets the epilogue of his Voltairean satirical novel *Rôtisserie de la reine Pédauque* here.
The **church** is a strange building dating from the 11C and 12C. It has two naves – one was blocked off for the sole use of the nuns in an adjacent priory, and is entered through a vast porch.

Farges-lès-Mâcon

This village boasts an 11C Romanesque **church**. It is modest in size, but has plenty of interest inside, thanks to the splendid columns of the nave which resemble those in the church of St-Philibert in Tournus. *Free entry or ask at Town Hall, 8am–6pm; ℘03 85 40 51 00.*

Uchizy

The monks of Tournus built the **church** here at the end of the 11C. It is crowned by a soaring five-storey bell tower; the last level is a later addition.
At **Fleurville**, the river is joined by the Ressouze after it has come through Pont-de-Vaux, in Bresse.
Fans of Romanesque churches should make a stop at **St-Albain** to delight in the harmonious proportions of its church.
Just before you arrive in Mâcon, keep an eye open for the quarries in ochre-coloured cliffs at **St-Martin-Belle-Roche**.

South Burgundy seems a land apart from the rest of the region. The Saône valley broadens out into pastoral plains where cattle and chickens seem to be just as valued as the grape; even the curvy red roof tiles speak of southern France. That said, there's still plenty to keep wine lovers happy – top wines of the Côte Chalonnaise can't quite compete with their illustrious northern relatives, but there are some great tastings to be had. Nor does the region lack in culture: Cluny once had the greatest Romanesque church in Europe, Tournus is one of France's most venerable monastic centres, and Romantic poet Alphonse de Lamartine penned an ode or two in these parts.

Cultural Southern Burgundy

Culture vultures will find plenty to feed their appetites in the south of Burgundy. You might need to use a bit of imagination in Cluny, though, thanks to the post-Revolutionary orgy of vandalism that left the one-time "Light of the World" to be ransacked. Could this sleepy little backwater of Burgundy really have been the high point of medieval monasticism? As you will learn on fascinating tours, the abbey was once 180m/590ft long, the largest church in Christendom until St Peter's in Rome took the title. Its influence left the region around Cluny peppered with Romanesque churches worth tracking down on a driving tour. You should also call in at Tournus: bracketed by the motorway and river, its old town sits beneath the austere fortress-like Église St-Philibert.

The excellent network of car-free trails for cycling and walking known as the Voie Verte has opened up more options for families to get out of the car and explore the area in different ways – why not cycle through idyllic countryside from Cluny to see the splendid Louis XIII interiors of the Château de Cormatin, calling in at Romanesque churches along the way? Fans of the romantic poetry of Alphonse de Lamartine could follow in his footsteps on a fascinating driving tour through landscapes that inspired him and places where he once stayed. Retail therapy comes courtesy of Chalon-sur-Saône in the old streets around the cathedral.

Rural Southern Burgundy

Ask any Frenchman where the best, tastiest chickens come from and he won't hesitate to say Bresse, where the birds

Highlights

1. The old centre of **Chalon-sur-Saône** (p130)
2. Bresse poultry at **Louhans** livestock market (p141)
3. Touring the **Mâconnais** vineyards (p142)
4. **Cluny**'s splendidly ruined abbey (p153)
5. Exploring by bike on the **Voie Verte** (p158)

come with blue legs and white feathers. The Plains of Bresse are a rural idyll with a character all their own, feeling neither wholly a part of Burgundy, nor part of the rugged Jura to the east.

Make sure to visit Louhans – its lovely arcaded high street is good to browse any day of the week, but the town takes on a medieval feel when the poultry market is in full swing and country folk haggle over ducks, geese and chickens. Spread all around Louhans, the outposts of the Écomusée de la Bresse Bourguignonne offer insights into the region's traditions and handicrafts.

And no trip to any region of Burgundy is complete without checking out its vineyards. Once you're south of the Côte d'Or, the wines are less sophisticated country cousins of the A-listers, but the vineyard landscapes are just as charming. In the Mâconnais, you can neatly combine tasting the wines of the top appelation, the tongue-twisting Pouilly-Fuissé, with a leg-stretching climb to the top of the landmark Roche de Solutré.

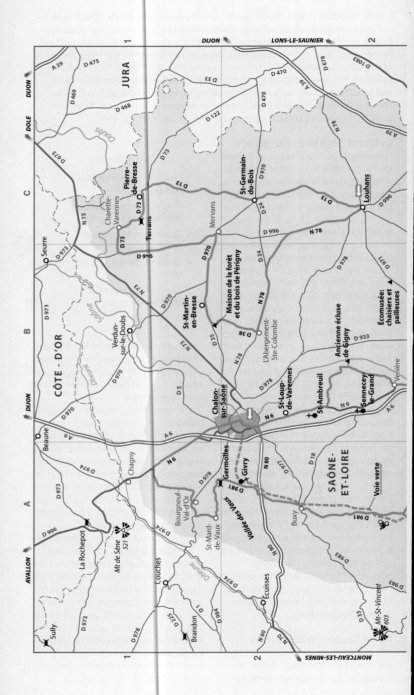

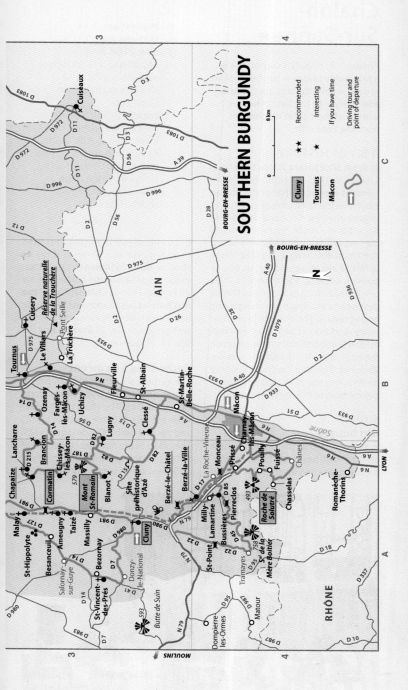

SOUTHERN BURGUNDY

Recommended ★★

Interesting ★

Driving tour and point of departure

Cluny

Tournus

Mâcon

0   8 km

N

AIN

RHÔNE

BOURG-EN-BRESSE

BOURG-EN-BRESSE

LYON

MOULINS

Cuiseaux

Cuisery
Réserve naturelle
de la Trouchère
Pont Seille
Le Villars
La Truchère
Tournus
Ozenay
Farges-
lès-Mâcon
Uchizy
Fleurville
St-Albain
St-Martin-
Belle-Roche
Lancharre
Brancion
Chissey-
lès-Mâcon
Lugny
Clessé
Chapaize
Cormatin
Mont
St-Romain
Blanot
Site
préhistorique
d'Azé
Berzé-la-Ville
Berzé-le-Châtel
Mâcon
Charnay-
lès-Mâcon
Prissé
Pouilly
Fuissé
Chânes
Romanèche-
Thorins
Chasselas
Monceau
La Roche-Vineuse
Malay
St-Hippolyte
Besanceuil
Salornay-
sur-Guye
Amougny
Taizé
Massilly
Bezornay
Donzy-
le-National
St-Vincent-
des-Prés
Butte de Suin
Cluny
Milly-
Lamartine
Pierreclos
Bussières
St-Point
Tramayes
Dompierre-
les-Ormes
Matour
Roche de
Solutré
St de la
Mère Boitier
579
593
493
758

Sône

Sône

Chalon-Sur-Saône ★

Chalon is Burgundy's second town, a prosperous place in the heart of an area of arable farming, stock raising and vineyards; the best wines are worthy of their great neighbours from the Côte d'Or.

A BIT OF HISTORY

Joseph Nicéphore Niépce, born in Chalon in 1765, devoted himself to scientific research. After perfecting an engine on the same principles as the jet engine (the Pyreolophore), along with his brother Claude, he then devoted his time to lithography and in 1816 succeeded in obtaining a negative image with the aid of a camera obscura, or pinhole camera, and then a positive one in 1822. In 1826 Nicéphore Niépce developed a process of photoengraving: **heliogravure**. The inventor of photography died in Chalon in 1833. A statue in Quai Gambetta and a monument on the edge of the N 6 road at St–Loup-de-Varennes *(7km/4mi S of Chalon)*, where his discovery was perfected, perpetuate the memory of this great inventor.

SIGHTS

Old houses

In the streets near the cathedral there are fine half-timbered façades overlooking place St-Vincent (note also at

▸ **Population:** 75 447
 Michelin Map: 320: J-9.
 Info: 29 bd. de la République, 71100 Chalon-sur-Saône. ✆03 85 48 37 97. www.chalon-sur-saone.net.
 Location: Chalon is on the banks of the Saône where it meets the Canal du Centre. To the north are the Côte de Beaune and Côte de Nuits vineyards; to the south, those of the Mâconnais and the Beaujolais.

the corner of rue St-Vincent the statue of a saint), rue aux Fèvres and rue de l'Évêché. **Rue St-Vincent** forms a picturesque crossroads at the junction of rue du Pont and rue du Châtelet. No. 37 **rue du Châtelet** has a handsome 17C façade with low-relief sculptures, medallions and gargoyles. No. 39 **Grande Rue** is a fine 14C house (restored).

Cathédrale St-Vincent

The cathedral of the old bishopric of Chalon (suppressed 1790) is not uniform in appearance. The oldest parts date from the late 11C; the chancel is 13C; and the neo-Gothic façade is from 1825. The pillars in the nave are composed of fluted pilasters and engaged columns. A 15C font and a Flamboyant vault adorn

Café in front of Cathédrale St-Vincent

© Ludovic Maisant/hemis.fr

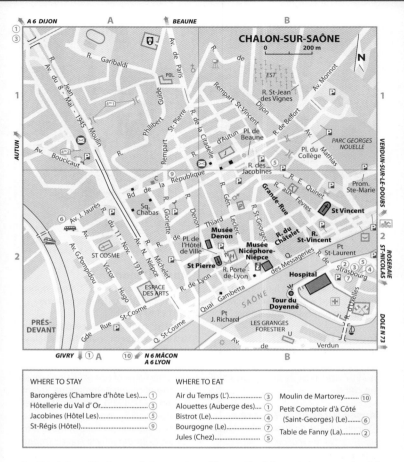

WHERE TO STAY		WHERE TO EAT		
Barongères (Chambre d'hôte Les)..... ①		Air du Temps (L')................... ③	Moulin de Martorey.......... ⑩	
Hôtellerie du Val d'Or............................ ③		Alouettes (Auberge des).... ①	Petit Comptoir d'à Côté	
Jacobines (Hôtel Les)............................ ⑤		Bistrot (Le)............................ ④	(Saint-Georges) (Le)......... ⑥	
St-Régis (Hôtel).. ⑨		Bourgogne (Le)..................... ⑦	Table de Fanny (La)........... ②	
		Jules (Chez)............................ ⑤		

the third chapel in the north transept. The north apsidal chapel contains a large contemporary tabernacle in bronze gilt (1986). A finely sculpted canopy adorns the chancel, and a triptych of the Crucifixion (1608) the apse.

The 15C sacristy was divided horizontally in the 16C, and the lower chamber covered with a vault supported by a central pillar. The ante-chapel is vaulted with five pendant keystones and lit through a stained-glass window of the woman with the 12 stars of the Apocalypse.

The south transept opens into the chapel of Notre-Dame-de-Pitié (15C Pietà and Renaissance tapestry) and into the 15C cloisters (restored) which contain four wooden statues. The well in the cloister garth has also been restored.

The south aisle contains many burial stones; some chapels are closed off by stone screens (claustra); the last chapel contains a 16C polychrome Pietà.

L'Ancien Hôpital St-Laurent (Hospital)

🕑 *Open year round.* 👓 *Guided tours (1hr 30min) Apr–Sept Wed–Fri 3pm; Oct–Mar Wed 3pm.* 🕑 *Closed public holidays.* 👓 *3€.* ✆ *03 85 44 65 87. www.ch-chalon71.fr.*

The Flemish-style building on an island in the River Saône was started in the 16C. The first floor, the nuns' quarters, comprises several panelled rooms, including the infirmary which contains four curtained beds. The buildings were extended in the 17C, and in the 18C certain rooms were decorated with magnificent **wood**

131

Durville Room, Musée Nicéphore-Niépce

© Patrice Josserand/Musée Nicéphore Niépce

panelling★. The nuns' refectory and the kitchen passage, which is furnished with dressers lined with pewter and copper vessels, are particularly interesting.

Tour du Doyenné

The 15C deanery tower originally stood near the cathedral. It was dismantled in 1907 and rebuilt at the point of the island.

Musée Nicéphore-Niépce★

○*Open Jul–Aug daily except Tue 10am –6pm; rest of the year daily except Tue 9.30–11.45am, 2–5.45pm.* ○*Closed public holidays.* ◉*3.10€.* ✆*03 85 48 41 98. www.museeniepce.com.*

This museum is in the 18C Hôtel des Messageries on the banks of the Saône. The rich collection includes photographs and photographic equipment, and some of the earliest cameras ever made, used by Joseph Nicéphore Niépce, and his first **heliographs**. There are also works by well-known contemporaries of Niépce in the world of photography, including Daguerre, his associate in 1829.

Note in particular Niépce's first camera (1816), the machinery for producing **daguerreotypes**, the first colour and relief photographs and the famous 19C cameras: Chevalier's Grand Photographe (c. 1850), the Bertsch cameras (1860) and the Damoizeau cyclographs (1890).

Musée Denon★

○*Open daily except Tue 9.30am–noon, 2–5.30pm.* ○*Closed public holidays.* ✆*03 85 94 74 41.*

The 18C building, once part of an Ursuline convent, had the Neoclassical façade added to it when it was converted to house the museum which bears the name of one of Chalon's most illustrious citizens, Dominique Vivant **Denon** (1747–1825), a diplomat under the Ancien Régime, who was also a famous engraver and one of the first to introduce lithography to France. During Napoleon's campaign in Egypt he pioneered Egyptology and became artistic adviser to the Emperor, Grand Purveyor and Director of French Museums (including the Louvre), which he endowed with works of art.

The museum displays an important collection of 17C–19C paintings. The Italian School is represented by three large canvases by Giordano, as well as works by Bassano *(Plan of Venice, Adoration of the Shepherds)*, Solimena and Caravaggio. The golden age of Dutch painting (17C) is represented by Hans Bollongier *(Bouquet of Tulips)* and De Heem (still-life paintings). 19C French painting is represented by Géricault *(Portrait of a Black Man)* and the pre-Impressionist landscape painter Raffort, a native of Chalon.

Local history is illustrated by examples of domestic traditions, the life of the Saône boatmen and a collection of local furniture. Also on display is a collection of wood carvings dating from before the Revolution.

The ground floor is devoted to fine archaeological collections: prehistoric flint implements from Volgu (Digoin-Gueugnon region – the largest and most beautiful Stone Age relics discovered, dating from the Solutré period), many antique and medieval metal artefacts, a magnificent Gallo-Roman group in stone of a lion bringing down a gladiator. There are also Gallo-Roman and medieval lapidary collections.

🚗 DRIVING TOURS

LA CÔTE CHALONNAISE
See Region map. 70km/43.5mi. Allow 3hrs. Leave Chalon SE via N 80, then D 981.

The Cote Chalonnaise produces some well-reputed crus such as Mercurey, Givry, Montagny and Rully. Highlights along the way include the small 18C town of Givry; its church is a many-domed masterpiece by Gauthey.

The Château de Germolles has a staggering history dating from the 13C and some incredibly rare murals from the period.

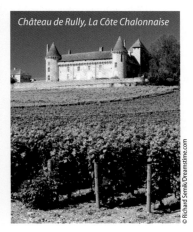

Château de Rully, La Côte Chalonnaise

© Richard Semik/Dreamstime.com

In the Valley des Vaux are villages of houses where the producers' cellars adjoin their houses. Finish in the wine-producing village of Rully where there is a medieval castle with a 12C keep.

FROM VERDUN-SUR-LE-DOUBS to MÂCON
90km/56mi – around 2hrs 30min.
The Saône broadens out after Verdun-sur-le-Doubs, and just before Chalon, the D 5 crosses the Canal du Centre, which links to the Loire via the Dheune Valley and Bourbince Valley. In this last loop of the river before Chalon you'll find the sport and recreational park as well as the St-Nicolas rose garden.

Chalon-sur-Saône★
See entry.

The old lock at Gigny
At the lock keeper's house *(now a café-restaurant in season)*, you have a splendid vantage point over the Saône. Since Chalon, the river has settled into its broad and majestic north–south axis, where it stays until it meets the confluence with the Rhône.

On the left bank (the Empire side, as the old-timers knew it, as opposed to the Kingdom's side) are vast expanses of flood meadows where large numbers of cattle are raised.

🐾 If you're up for a walk, wander along the old towpath where rows of poplars run alongside *péniches* (large canal barges) and summer season pleasure boats.

Tournus★
South of Tournus, the Seille flows into the left bank of the Saône in the little village of **La Truchère** (there is a charming lock on the southern arm of the mouth of the Seille, with restaurants and boat hire).

Various small roads lead off the N6 towards the ancient "ports" of Farges and Uchizy (access to the water is easy from these villages built on raised terraces 2–3km/1.2–1.9mi from the river). This is a good place to fish from the pleasant banks of the Saône. In the "ports" on the riverside are clusters of houses with the odd little auberge where you can tuck into traditional fried fish and frogs legs.

Le Villars

Commemorative plaques by the entrance to the church inform you that the pianist **Alfred Cortot** (1877–1962) and engineer **Gabriel Voisin** (1880–1973) once lived in the village. The latter was, together with his brother, the first industrial aircraft manufacturer in France. **Anatole France** sets the epilogue of his Voltairean satirical novel *Rôtisserie de la reine Pédauque* here.

The **church** is a strange building dating from the 11C and 12C. It has two naves – one was blocked off for the sole use of the nuns in an adjacent priory – and is entered through a vast porch.

Farges-lès-Mâcon

This village boasts an 11C **Romanesque church**. It is modest in size, but has plenty of interest inside, thanks to the splendid columns of the nave which resemble those in the church of St-Philibert in Tournus. *Free entry or ask at Town Hall, 8am–6pm, ℘03 85 40 51 00.*

Uchizy

The monks of Tournus built the **church** at the end of the 11C. It is crowned by a soaring five-storey bell tower; the last level is a later addition.

At **Fleurville**, the river is joined by the Ressouze after it has come through Pont-de-Vaux, in Bresse.

Fans of Romanesque churches should make a stop at **St-Albain** to delight in the harmonious proportions of its church.

Just before you arrive in Mâcon, keep an eye open for the quarries in ochre-coloured cliffs at **St-Martin-Belle-Roche**. Stop at the lock keeper's house in Gigny for a superb **view**★★★ over the Saone.

ADDRESSES

☞ STAY

➾ **Hôtel Les Jacobines** – *10 r. des Jacobines. ℘03 85 48 12 24. www.hotel-lesjacobines.com. Closed 1 week in winter and 2 weeks in Aug. 23 rooms. ⊐ 6€.* Rooms here are a touch small and basic, but it's good to find a bargain-priced town centre hotel.

➾➾ **Chambre d'hôte les Barongères** – *3 r. du Boubouhard, 71150 Farges-lès-Chalon. 10km/6mi north on N 6. ℘03 85 41 90 47. www.les barongeres.com. ♿ ⊞ ⋈ 3 rooms. ⊐.* This renovated house in a tranquil village has small, simply-furnished rooms with good bathrooms opening onto the lawn. Shaded terraces and a pool complete the peaceful scene.

➾➾➾ **Hôtellerie du Val d'Or** – *140 Grande-Rue, 71640 Mercurey. 13km/8mi northwest on D 978. ℘03 85 45 13 70. www.le-valdor.com. Closed 22–27 Aug, 20 Dec–17 Jan, lunch and Mon in Mar. Wi-Fi. 12 rooms. ⊐ 11€, half-board available.* The old coaching inn of this wine-producing village in the Côte chalonnaise has a dozen rooms, plus a rustic dining room with a fireplace and exposed beams.

➾➾➾➾ **Hôtel St-Régis** – *22 bd de la République. ℘03 85 90 95 60. www.saint-regis-chalon.com. Wi-Fi. 36 rooms. ⊐16€, half-board available, ✕ set lunch menu 23€.* Country charm in the town centre. The well-kept rooms are suffused with light. Relax in a leather armchair in the wood-panelled lounge-bar. Bright, airy dining room.

☞/EAT

➾ **Le Petit Comptoir d'à Côté** – *℘03 85 90 80 52. www.le-saintgeorges.fr. ♿. Set lunch menu 13€. 50 rooms. ⊐11€.* Art Deco-inspired brasserie smartly done out in leather and wood serving traditional dishes. The hotel has 70s-style rooms or ultra-modern junior suites.

➾➾ **Le Bourgogne** – *28 r. Strasbourg. ℘03 85 48 89 18. www.restau-lebourgogne-chalon.fr. Closed 26 Apr–4 May, 4–20 Jul, 8–16 Nov, 25–30 Dec, Sat lunch, Sun eve* and Mon. Set lunch menu 15€. Candlelight and Louis XIII-style furniture, fireplaces and exposed beams all lend an air of comfort. Go for Burgundy escargots and tournedos de Charolais.

◎◎ **L'Air du Temps** – 7 r. de Strasbourg, Île St Laurent. ℘03 85 93 39 01. lair.du. temps.71@orange.fr. Closed Sun and Mon. L'Air du Temps means fashionable, and this friendly bistro certainly lives up to its name, both in the décor of its two dining rooms as well as on the sensibly priced menu of local produce.

◎◎ **Chez Jules** – 11 r. de Strasbourg. ℘03 85 48 08 34. Closed 26 Jul–16 Aug, Feb holidays, Sat lunch and Sun. Set lunch menu 15€. Simple, rustic dining room on the île St-Laurent. On the plate, you'll find traditional, daily-changing specials and a huge choice of puddings.

◎◎ **La Table de Fanny** – 21 r. de Strasbourg. ℘03 85 48 23 11. Closed 5–20 Sept, 24 Dec–4 Jan, Mon and Sat lunch, and Sun. Set lunch menu 20€. Playful menu descriptions and an inventive spirit at the stoves are the key at this trendy address.

◎◎ **Auberge des Alouettes** – 1 rte de Givry, 71880 Châtenoy-le-Royal. 4km/2.5mi west. ℘03 85 48 32 15. aubergedesalouettes@orange.fr. Closed 21 Jul–11 Aug, 5–19 Jan, Sun and Tue eve and Wed. This welcoming restaurant on the road to Givry has two rustic dining rooms and a fine fireplace. Traditional cooking at affordable prices.

◎◎ **L'Auberge des Gourmets** – Pl. de l'Église, 71700 Le Villars. 32km/20mi south on N6 and A6. ℘03 85 32 58 80. www.aubergedesgourmets.fr. Closed 2–9 Jun, 3–12 Nov, 23–26 Dec, 9 Jan–2 Feb, Sun and Tue eve and Wed, except hols. ⓖ P. A pleasant little auberge with a renovated façade, and a convivial dining room decorated with exhibitions of art. On the menu is traditional cooking with personality.

◎◎◎ **Le Bistrot** – 31 r. de Strasbourg. ℘03 85 93 22 01. Closed 1–15 Aug, 6–21 Feb, Sat and Sun. ⓖ. Wood panelling, old posters, faded postcards and enamelled advertising plaques decorate this typical bistro. Traditional cuisine with a regional feel.

◎◎◎ **Moulin de Martorey** – 71100 St-Rémy. 3km/2mi southwest. ℘03 85 48 12 98. www.moulindemartorey.net. Closed 8–18 Aug, 4–15 Jan, Sun eve, Tue lunch and Mon except holidays. P. Peaceful 19C flour mill overlooking a canal. Charming rustic interior arranged around the antique machinery. Cuisine with a personal touch.

🍴 TAKING A BREAK

Place St-Vincent – Pl. St-Vincent. Lined with colourful half-timbered houses, this square brings together most of the town's cafés, pubs and wine bars.

Aux Colonies des Arômes – 67 Grande -Rue. ℘03 85 93 99 40. Open Mon 2.30–6.30pm, Tue–Fri 8.30am–7pm, Sat 9am–noon, 2–7pm. Closed 2 weeks in Jan. Sip scented tea or one of the many brands of coffee in this luminous tea shop with elegant blue and white décor.

Paddy Brophy's – 4 bd. de la République. ℘03 85 93 15 19. Open Mon–Sat 11–1am, Sun 5pm–1am. Closed 3 weeks in Aug. Most of this cheery pub's décor came from Ireland, including the huge fresco and the welcome stone in Gaelic.

🛒 SHOPPING

La Maison des Vins de la Côte Chalonnaise – 2 prom. Ste-Marie. ℘03 85 41 64 00. Open Mon–Sat 9am–7pm. Closed public holidays. The Maison des Vins organises tastings of around 100 vintages, among the best in the region.

Le Cellier Saint-Vincent – 14 pl. St-Vincent. ℘03 85 48 78 25. Open Tue–Sat 9am–noon, 2–7pm; Sun 9am–12.30pm. Closed public holidays and Mon. The owner designed the ash barrels where wines and liqueurs are matured, as well as the "Les Impitoyables" tasting glasses.

Légendes gourmandes – 4 pl. St-Vincent. ℘03 85 48 05 64. Open Tue–Sat 9.30am–12.30pm, 2.30–7pm; Sun 9.30am–12.30pm. Vinegars, caramels, liqueurs, syrups and terrines all sit cheek -by-jowl with homemade marc de Bourgogne.

Tournus★

This small town on the right bank of the Saône, between Chalon and Mâcon, is one of the oldest and most important monastic centres in France owing to the architectural beauty and harmonious proportions of the church and the 10C convent buildings.

A BIT OF HISTORY

Monastic centre – When St Valerian, a Christian from Asia Minor, escaped from persecution in Lyon in 177, he travelled to Tournus to convert the people but was martyred on a hillside above the Saône; a sanctuary was built beside his tomb. In the Merovingian period it was converted into an abbey and dedicated first to St Valerian, and later St Philibert. A Hungarian invasion in 937 checked the prosperity of the abbey which was destroyed by fire and rebuilt. In about 945 the monastery was abandoned by the monks, but in 949 Abbot Stephen, formerly prior of St Philibert, was ordered to return to Tournus with a group of monks. The reconstruction which he set in motion was completed in the 12C; it produced one of the most beautiful parts of the church.

Over the centuries the building underwent damage, repair and modification;

- **Population:** 5 941
- **Michelin Map:** 320: J-10 Local map see Le Mâconnais.
- **Info:** 2 pl. de l'Abbaye, 71700 Tournus. ℘03 85 27 00 20. www.tournugeois.fr.
- **Location:** Tournus sits on the unofficial boundary between northern France and the Midi, about halfway between Chalon-sur-Sâone and Mâcon.

in 1562 it was sacked by the Huguenots. The abbey became a collegiate church in 1627 and in 1790 a parish church, avoiding irrevocable damage in the Revolution.

ABBEY★★
Église St-Philibert

Enter the church by the doorway to the right of the main façade.

The façade, dating from the 10C and 11C and built of beautifully cut stone, has almost the appearance of a castle keep with the dark loophole slits emphasising the warm colour of the stone. The crenellated parapet with machicolations linking the two towers accentuates the military appearance of the building. Both this gallery and the porch are the work of Questel in the 19C.

The right tower is topped by a saddle-back roof; the other was heightened at the end of the 11C by the addition of a two-storey belfry surmounted by a tall spire.

Chapelle St-Michel (a) – The chapel occupies the upper room in the narthex which was built before the nave *(access via a spiral staircase).* In plan, it is identical with the ground floor but the astonishing height of the central section and the amount of light give it an entirely different feel. The great arched bay opening into the organ loft was once the entrance to a small oven-vaulted apsidal

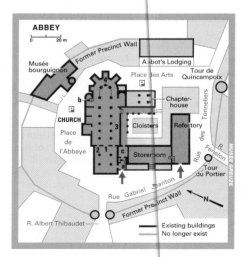

chapel which was suppressed when the organ loft was built in 1629. The ancient sculpture on the capitals and the blocks which they support have survived from the Carolingian period.

Narthex – This is the place of transition from the outer world to the house of God, where reflection and preparation for prayer are encouraged by the half-light. Its rugged and simple architecture achieves a singular grandeur. Four enormous circular abacus pillars divide it into a nave and two aisles, each of three bays. One bay of the vault is painted in a black and white chequered pattern, the arms of Digoine, an old and powerful Mâcon family. On the wall above the entrance to the nave is a 14C fresco of Christ in Majesty (**1**); the end wall of the north aisle carries another 14C fresco portraying the Crucifixion (**2**). The round tombstones are peculiar to this region.

The nave – The nave, which dates from the beginning of the 11C, is now devoid of decoration. Magnificently tall cylindrical pillars made from the rose-coloured stone of Préty (a small place near Tournus) are surmounted by ordinary flat capitals, like those in the narthex; they divide the five bays of the nave from the aisles.

A most unusual feature is the central vault which consists of five transverse barrel vaults resting on transverse arches with alternating white and pink arch stones; great columns surmounted by slim columns support the arches, which obscure the clerestory, through which light enters the nave.

The side chapels in the north aisle date from the 14C and 15C.

A 15C niche in the south aisle contains a 12C statue-reliquary of the Virgin (**3**), Notre-Dame-de-la-Brune, which shows the artistic influence of the Auvergne. The statue, which is made of painted cedar wood (re-gilded in the 19C) retains an aura of calm and majestic beauty.

Transept and choir – Built at the start of the 12C, the transept and choir contrast strongly with the rest of the building in the whiteness of the stonework; they show the rapid evolution of Romanesque art.

Mosaics in the ambulatory, Église St-Philibert
© Franck Guiziou/hemis.fr

In the transept the contrast can be seen between the spaciousness of the nave and the narrowness of the choir which the architect restricted to the dimensions of the existing crypt.

The oven-vaulted apse is supported by six columns with capitals, surmounted by semicircular windows framed by delicately sculpted decoration. The barrel-vaulted ambulatory built at the beginning of the 11C has three radiating chapels and two oriented chapels; the axial chapel contains the shrine of St Philibert (**4**). The modern stained-glass windows blend well with the rest.

Crypt★ – *Access by steps in the north transept.* The crypt with its thick walls was built by Abbot Stephen at the end of the 10C and restored by Questel in the 19C. The height (3.5m/12ft) is quite exceptional. The central part, flanked by two rows of slender columns (some have a typical archaic bulge) with delightful foliated capitals, is surrounded by an ambulatory with radiating chapels. The 12C fresco, decorating the chapel on the right and representing a Virgin and Child and a Christ in Majesty, is the best preserved in the church.

CONVENTUAL BUILDINGS

To reach the cloisters one passes through the old alms room (**b**) or warming room (13C) adjoining the south wall

of the narthex. It contains a lapidary collection including the column-statues
and capitals from the north tower as well
as a few sculptures from the cloisters.

Cloisters – Only the north gallery
remains; at the end, a 13C doorway leads
into the aisle of the church. The buildings on the south side now house both
the public and abbey libraries (many illuminated medieval manuscripts). They
are dominated by the square Prieuré
Tower.

Chapter-house – Rebuilt by Abbot
Bérard following a fire in 1239 and
now houses temporary exhibitions.
The pointed vaulting is visible through
Romanesque apertures overlooking the
cloisters. Leave by place des Arts. Admire
the east end with its five chapels and the
12C belfry over the transept crossing.

Abbot's Lodging – This is a charming
late-15C building. In rue des Tonneliers
stands the Quincampoix Tower which
was built after the Hungarian invasion in
937; it was part of the wall of enclosure
of the old abbey as was the neighbouring tower, called the Tour du Portier.

Refectory – This magnificent 12C
chamber has no transverse arches but
is vaulted with slightly broken barrel
vaulting. When the abbey was secularised in 1627 the hall was used for tennis
matches and was called the Ballon (ball).
It is now used for temporary exhibitions.

Storeroom – The storeroom, also 12C,
has broken barrel vaulting resting on
transverse arches. It is lit by two small
windows set high up. The vast cellars
below are now occupied by various
craftsmen.

AROUND TOWN
Musée Bourguignon

⊙*Open Apr–Oct Wed–Sun 10am–1pm,
2–5pm.* ⊛*2.50€.* ℘*03 85 51 29 68.*
Wax models in Burgundian costume re-
create scenes from daily life of past centuries. The scenes include the interior of
a Bresse farm, a local Tournus interior
with various regional costumes, the
large room of the Burgundian spinners,
collections of headdresses, and in the
basement, a Burgundian cellar.

Hôtel-Dieu★

⊙*Open Apr–Oct daily except Tue 10am
–1pm, 2–6pm.* ⊛*4€.* ℔ ℘*03 85 51 23 50.*
After three centuries of providing health
care to the poor, this historic hospital
closed in 1982. The traditional curtained
beds in oak wood are still lined up in
three vast rooms set around the chapel:
one for men, one for women and one
for soldiers.

The **apothecary**★ displays typical 17C
Nevers ceramic jars used to store pow-
ders and herbs.

ADDRESSES

⊯STAY

◹◹**Le Terminus** – *21 av. Gambetta.*
℘*03 85 51 05 54. www.hotel-terminus-
tournus.com. Closed Thu lunch and Wed
18/50€. 11 rooms.* Modern
rooms in an early 20C building a short
hop from the station. Deliciously retro
breakfast room. Contemporary cooking.

⊮/EAT

◹◹**Aux Terrasses** – *18 av. 23-Janvier.*
℘*03 85 51 01 74. www.aux-terrasses.com.
Closed 31 May–7 Jun, 15–29 Nov, 3–25 Jan,
Sun eve, Tue lunch and Mon. 18 rooms*
◹◹. ⊠ *12€.* This well-known
restaurant serves carefully prepared
traditional dishes, some at extremely
reasonable prices, in a pretty dining
room.

⊨ SHOPPING

La Cave des vignerons de Mancey –
N 6. ℘*03 85 51 00 83. www.cave-mancey.
com. Open daily 8am–noon, 2–6pm.*
Cooperative association showcasing
wines from some 80 regional wine-
growers. The selection is diverse and
of high quality. Try the Essentielles,
including remarkable Mâcon-Villages,
Mâcon-Mancey and Burgundy Pinot
Noir.

Louhans★

and La Bresse Bourguignonne

Louhans is a picturesque market town at the heart of rich countryside famed for its butter, eggs and Bresse poultry. The Bresse region is the southernmost part of Burgundy; it is a pastoral landscape of babbling brooks and ancient hedgerows, old windmills and timber-framed farmhouses. The differing influences of Burgundy and of the Mediterranean divide the region in two. The northern part is known as *Bresse bourguignonne* and the southern as *Bresse savoyarde.*

▶ **Population:** 6 420

Michelin Map: 320: L-10. 328: D-2 to E-3.

Info: Place St-Jean, 71500 Louhans. ℰ03 85 75 05 02. www.bresse-bourguignonne.com.

Don't Miss: The Monday morning market in Louhans, especially the larger ones in the 1st and 3rd weeks of the month, for a staggering array of local produce and lots of atmosphere. Poultry from the Bresse region is world renowned, so be sure to sample this regional delicacy while you're here.

TOWN

Grande Rue★

The arches of the old houses with wood or stone pillars, date from the late Middle Ages.

Hôtel-Dieu

🕘*Open daily except Tue.* ➦*Guided tours (1hr) mid-Jun–mid-Sept 10.30am, 2.30pm, 4pm and 5.30pm. Rest of the year 2.30pm and 4pm.* 🕘*Closed 1 Jan, 1 May and 25 Dec.* ➾*4€.* ℰ*03 85 75 54 32.*
A wrought-iron screen divides the two public rooms of the 17C–18C hospital Each curtained bed bears a plaque indicating for whom it was intended. The **pharmacy** has a beautiful collection of hand-blown glass and Hispano-Moorish lustreware.

Church

Restored with stone and brick and roofed with glazed tiles. On the left is a belfry-porch and large chapel with turreted pavilions (14C).

L'Atelier d'un journal

🕘*Open mid-May to Sept daily 3–7pm, rest of year Mon–Fri 2–6pm.* ➾*3€.* ♿ ℰ*03 85 76 27 16. www.ecomusee-de-la-bresse.com.*
Visit the old premises of *l'Indépendant*, a Bresse newspaper abandoned in 1984 after 100 years of publication. The old machines are still in place.

Poultry market, Louhans

Alain Doire/Bourgogne Tourisme

EXCURSIONS

Cuiseaux

▸ *21km/13mi southeast of Louhans via D 996 and D 972.*
This former fortified town on the border between Burgundy and Franche-Comté is in a peaceful agricultural landscape. There are traces of the 12C fortifications, which originally included 36 towers.

Rancy

▸ *12km/8mi SW by D 971.*

Chair-making had become a vital part of the local economy in Rancy and Bantanges by the end of the 19C.

Visit **Chaisiers et pailleuses de Rancy** (*on the outskirts of Rancy;* ⏰open mid-May–Sept: daily except Tue 3–7pm; ≤3€; ☏03 85 76 27 16; www.ecomusee-de-la-bresse.com), France's second largest producer of cane chairs, to see how they are made.

🚗 DRIVING TOUR

1 LA BRESSE BOURGUIGNONNE ★

⏱See Region map and La Bresse map. 138km/86mi round tour.

The proximity of the powerful Duchy of Burgundy long overshadowed the modest Bresse. These lands along the Saône were often the subject of dispute and acted as a border until the southern part of the Bresse and Franche-Comté were united to France in the 17C.

Left without effective local administration, the region slowly built its own identity through the excellence of its agricultural output and the eventual emergence of a bourgeois class that took the management of business and government in hand.

St-Germain-du-Bois
Maison de l'Agriculture (⏰open mid-May to end-Sept daily except Tue 2–6pm; ≤3€; ♿ ☏03 85 76 27 16; www.ecomu-

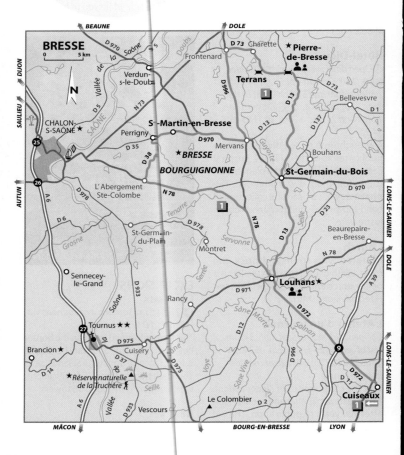

see-de-la-bresse.com) – This museum of rural life includes a collection of farm implements from the 19C to today, and exhibitions on local products.

Pierre-de-Bresse★

The Château de Pierre-de-Bresse is a handsome 17C building. The left wing houses the **Écomusée de la Bresse bourguignonne** (○*open all year daily 10am–noon, 2–6pm, except Oct–mid-May Sat 2–6pm;* ○*closed 25 Dec–1 Jan;* ☜*6€;* ☏*03 85 76 27 16; www.ecomusee-de-la-bresse.com).* The exhibits cover the environment, history, traditional way of life and present economic situation in Burgundian Bresse. It has branches at Louhans, Rancy, St-Germain-du-Bois, St-Martin-en-Bresse, Verdun-sur-le-Doubs and Cuiseaux.

Château de Terrans

The design of the château, begun in 1765, is plain. An attractive wrought-iron gate closes off the courtyard, beyond which the elegant façade rises.

Saint-Martin-en-Bresse

At St-Martin-en Bresse, continue along the D 35 to the hamlet of Perrigny.
👥 **Maison de la forêt et du bois de Perrigny** (○*open from mid-May–end-Sept 2pm–6pm;* ○*closed Mar;* ☜*3€;* ☏*03 85 76 27 16; www.ecomusee-de-la-bresse.com)* – Amid the Bresse woodlands, this exhibit looks at the different trees in the region and related trades and crafts.

ADDRESSES

🛏 STAY

⊖⊖ **Hôtel Le Moulin de Bourgchâteau** – *R. Guidon, rte de Chalon.* ☏*03 85 75 37 12. www.bourgchateau.com.* ▣ *Wi-Fi. 19 rooms.* ⊡ *9€, half board available,* ✗ *set lunch menu 21€.*
This 18C grain mill on the Seille is now a characterful hôtel-restaurant. The mill machinery, beams and stone walls add charm to go with traditional dishes, some with a nod to the Italian origins of the owners.

⊖⊖ **Hostellerie du Cheval Rouge** – *5 r. d'Alsace.* ☏*03 85 75 21 42. www.hotel-chevalrouge.com. Closed 22 Dec–19 Jan, Sun eve from Dec to Mar and Mon Wi-Fi. 20 rooms.* ⊡ *9€, half board available.*
This old coaching inn on a busy street has well-priced rooms. Go for the more modern ones in the annexe for extra comfort and character.

🍴 EAT

⊖⊖ **Le Comptoir** – *9 Grande Rue, 01340 Montrevel-en-Bresse. 66km/41mi to the south.* ☏*04 74 25 45 53. www.restaurant-lea.com. Closed 25 Jun–9 Jul, 17 Dec–7 Jan, Sun and Tue eve and Wed.* ♿. If you're after

an authentic traditional café, look no further than le Comptoir's classic banquettes, posters, mirrors, and mouthwatering bistro cooking.

⊖⊖ **L'Ancienne Auberge** – *Pl. du Marché, 01540 Vonnas. 75km/47mi southeast.* ☏*04 74 50 90 50. www.georges blanc.com. Closed Jan. Set lunch menu 20€.* The retro décor, including old photos and posters, in this bistro pays homage to the auberge (a former lemonade factory) opened by the Blanc family in the late 19C. Regional cuisine.

⊖⊖ **Hôtel de la Place** – *51 pl. de la Mairie, 01310 Polliat. 66km/41mi south.* ☏*04 74 30 40 19. hoteldelaplacepolliat@ orange.fr. Closed 24 Jul–14 Aug, 2–15 Jan, Sun eve and Mon.* ▣ *Set lunch menu 18€. 7 rooms.* ⊡ *8.50€, half board available.*
A bright, cheery décor with rustic and wrought-iron furniture is the setting for tasty and generous local cooking, served with a smile. Refurbished rooms.

🛍 SHOPPING

Marché aux volailles de Bresse – *Pl. de la Charité, Grande-Rue.* ☏*03 85 76 75 10. www.louhans-chateaurenaud.fr. Mon 8am–noon.* The poultry market is recognised as a "Site remarquable du goût" (Site of exceptional taste).

Le Mâconnais★★

The delightful and varied landscape of the Mâconnais is a joy to explore, especially for wine lovers. It is at the point where the north becomes the south, with a milder climate than that of northern Burgundy, and houses with low-pitched roofs covered with rounded red tiles known as Roman or Provençal.

A BIT OF HISTORY

A blessed crop – The monks of Cluny planted the first vines in the Mâconnais many centuries ago, of which the Chardonnay, the Pinot and the Gamay are the best known. The whites are made from Chardonnay, the great white grape of Burgundy and Champagne. The most celebrated is Pouilly-Fuissé.

This wine has a beautiful green-gold colour; when young it is fruity but with age acquires a bouquet. Pouilly-Loché, Saint-Vérand, Pouilly-Vinzelles, Mâcon-Lugny and Mâcon-Viré, members of the same family as Pouilly-Fuissé, are also well known. The other white wines are sold under the names of White Burgundy, White Mâcon and Mâcon-Villages.

As for the reds, without pretending to equal the great wines, they are excellent value. Fairly full-bodied and fruity, they are generally produced from Gamay, a red grape with white juice.

🚗 DRIVING TOURS

1 AMONG THE VINES

See Region map and Le Mâconnais map. 79km/49mi – 3hrs 30min.

This drive passes through a picturesque region of fine views and wide panoramas, dotted with Romanesque churches (signposted itinerary).

Tournus★ *See TOURNUS.*
Leave Tournus along D 14.

The road climbs, providing views over Tournus, the Saône Valley and the Bresse region. Southwest of the Beaufer Pass

- **Michelin Map:**
  320: H-10 to I-12.
- **Info:** 6 r. Dufour, 71000 Mâcon. ℘03 85 38 09 99. www.route-vins.com.
- **Location:** The region is bounded by the Saône River to the east, and the Grosne River valley to the west. The cities of Mâcon and Tournus serve as south and north anchors.
- **Don't Miss:** The frescoes in the Chapelle des Moines at Berzé-la-Ville, a fine example of Cluniac art.

the countryside has many valleys with boxwood and conifers.

Ozenay

Set in a little valley, Ozenay has an impressive 13C fortified farm (castel) and a rustic 12C church.

Continue along D 14 to Brancion.

Brancion★

www.brancion.fr. Walk through the gateway in the 14C ramparts, where you will find the imposing ruins of a fortress, narrow streets lined with medieval-style houses, the 15C covered market (halles) and the church. Vehicles are not allowed into town, so leave them in the car park outside the walls.

The old feudal market town of Brancion is perched on a spur overlooking two deep ravines, forming a picturesque and most unusual sight.

The feudal **château** (*open Apr–Sept 10am–12.30pm, 1–6.30pm; Oct–mid-Dec weekends 10am–4pm; 5€; ℘03 85 51 14 38; www.chateau-de-brancion. fr*) dates to the beginning of the 10C. It was enlarged in the 14C by Duke Philip the Bold, who added a wing to lodge the dukes of Burgundy. In the 16C it was assaulted by Catholic League militants, and finally ruined by D'Ornano's troops. The keep has been restored. From the viewing platform (*87 steps*) there is a

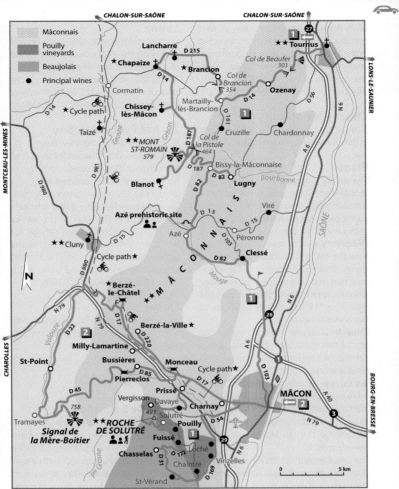

good **view**★ of the town and its church, the Grosne Valley and, to the west and northwest, the mountains of Charollais and the Morvan.

Lancharre

Within the hamlet is the ruined convent of an order of female clerics established in the 11C by the lords of Brancion. The former **convent church** presents a melancholy sight in its dereliction; it comprises two adjacent buildings from the 12C and 14C that make up the apse and the transept, above which rises a square belfry indented with large ogival recesses. The cemetery has taken the place of the ruined nave, whose remains amount to just a wall and a bay up against the chancel.

Worthy of note inside are: the vaulted arches of the huge apse and absidioles, in the chancel; the triumphal arch supported by two elegant columns with sculpted heads; the cupola that supports the bell tower; and ten tombstones dating from the 13C and 14C engraved with figures of ladies and knights.

Chapaize★

On the River Bisançon, to the west of the magnificent forest of Chapaize, this little village is dominated by the high belfry of its **Romanesque church**★, all that remains of a Benedictine priory founded in the 11C. There are clear Lombard influences in the architecture; Italian stone-masons almost certainly worked on it. The interior has a stark beauty.

Chissey-lès-Mâcon

This 12C church has an elegant bell tower in the Cluny style, and an unusual history.

Blanot

The pretty village of Blanot lies at the foot of Mont St-Romain. Its old houses – surrounded by dry-stone walls – and the slate-covered church and neighbouring priory make it a charming spot.

Old priory★ – The main building dates from the 14C and is fortified in the Cluny style. It's lovely dry-stone façade is punctuated on the left by a the entrance to a passageway and a tower, and on the right by a 15C round tower, the site of three Merovingian tombs.

Church – This late 11C building retains an openwork frieze in the apse, and a curious bell tower. Inside, the vaulted choir is worth a look.

Caves – *North of Blanot, take the D446 towards Fougnières. 500m/545yd after this hamlet, turn left (guided tours (50min) May–Aug noon–7pm; 5.50€; 03 85 50 04 00; www.blanot.fr).*

The caves are 80m/260ft deep in places. Over time, the roof has collapsed, creating a forest of massive rocks. Between the hamlet of Vivier and Mont St-Ronan (1km/0.6mi with steep staircases), the tour takes in 21 rooms. At the end, visitors are shown a collection of flints and animal bones found in the caves since 1988, which date from the Mousterian period (approximately 100 000–40 000 years ago).

Mont Saint-Romain★

From the top of the tower, an orientation table points out places of interest in the magnificent **panorama**★★: to the east on the Saône plain, and beyond to Bresse, the Jura et the Alpes; to the south lie the Mâconnais and Beaujolais; to the west is the Charolais.

Lugny

Lugny produces an excellent white wine and is on the Mâconnais Wine Route *(Route des Vins du Mâconnais)*.

Beside the ruins of a fortress stands the **church** which has a 16C stone altarpiece portraying Jesus with the 12 Apostles.

Azé Prehistoric Site

8.5km/5.3mi SW of Lugny via Bissy. Open Apr–Oct. Guided tours (1hr 30min) daily 10am–noon, 2–7pm (Oct Sun only). 6€ (children 4€). 03 85 33 32 23. www.grottes-aze.com.

The **museum** has over 2 000 artefacts found locally. The first of the **caves** (208m/682ft long) was a refuge for bears, prehistoric man, the Aedui, the Gallo-Romans and so on; the second cave has an underground river which can be followed (800m/2 625ft).

Clessé

This wine-growers' village (cooperative) has a late-11C **church** with a spire clad with varnished tiles.

Mâcon

See MÂCON.

Roche de Solutré★★

This superb limestone escarpment with a distinctive profile can be seen from miles away. There is a footpath to the top *(45min there and back)*, with views to the Alps in clear weather. At the foot of the rock is the **Musée départemental de Préhistoire** (*open Apr–Sept 10am–6pm; Jan–Mar and Oct–Nov daily except Tue 10am–noon, 2–5pm; closed Dec–Jan, 1 May; 3.50€; 03 85 35 85 24)*, devoted to the prehistoric archaeology of the south Mâconnais, including the important hunting grounds at Solutré.

Pouilly

This hamlet gives its name to various wines: Pouilly-Fuissé, Pouilly-Loché and Pouilly-Vinzelles. These wines are highly appreciated and go well with certain Burgundian specialities. Beyond this village the patterns of the vineyards spread over the gentle curves of the hillsides.

Roche de Solutré and Pouilly-Fuissé vineyards in autumn

© Bertrand Rieger/ hemis.fr

Fuissé

This is one of the communes (Chaintré, Fuissé, Solutré, Pouilly and Vergisson) producing Pouilly-Fuissé, classed as one of the world's great white wines.

Chasselas

3.5km/2mi W of Fuissé.
This village has developed a vine that produces a well-known dessert grape. In the background appear the valley of the Saône, the Bresse countryside and the Jura mountains.

② LAMARTINE HERITAGE TRAIL

See region and Le Mâconnais map.
70km/44mi – about 3hrs. Head west out of Mâcon on D 17 for 9km/5.6mi.

This countryside inspired the poet and statesman Alphonse de Lamartine.

Château de Monceau

Park, garden and chapel open daily.
This château (now a home for the elderly) was one of Lamartine's favourites, where he lived the life of a vineyard owner and wrote his *Histoire des Girondins*.

Milly-Lamartine

An ironwork grille stands before the **Maison d'Enfance de Lamartine** (*open year round; guided tours (1hr) at 3pm and 4.30pm; enquire for* days on which tours run. Closed Tue; *7€; 03 85 37 70 33*) where the poet spent his holidays as a child, free to enjoy the beautiful countryside nearby. It was at Milly that Lamartine composed his first meditation, *L'Isolement*.

Berzé-la-Ville★

Towards the end of his life St Hugh of Cluny lived in the Château des Moines, a country house near the priory in Berzé owned by the abbey of Cluny.
The 12C Romanesque **Chapelle des Moines** (*open Jul–Aug 9am–12.30pm, 1.30–6pm; May, Jun, Sept 9am–noon, 2–6pm; Mar–Apr, Oct–Nov 10am–noon, 2–5.30pm; 3€; 03 85 38 81 18*), built at first floor level in an earlier (11C) build-

© Bertrand Rieger/ hemis.fr

Frescoes, Chapelle des Moines, Berzé-la-Ville

ing, was decorated with Romanesque **frescoes**★★; only those in the chancel are well preserved. The clear Byzantine influence is probably due to the fact that the Cluniac artists who worked here were directed by Benedictine painters from Monte Cassino in Latium, where the eastern Roman Empire's influence lasted to the 11C.

Château de Berzé-le-Châtel★
Open Jun–Sept. Guided tour (45min) Jul–Aug 2–6pm; Jun and Sept daily except Thu 2–6pm. 4.50€. 03 85 36 60 83.
This feudal castle was once the principal seat of the most important barony in the Mâconnais. It protected the southern approaches to Cluny from its attractive site on the vineyard-covered slopes.

Saint-Point
The church, in the style of Cluny, has a fresco of Christ in Majesty in the apse. To the left of the church, a small door opens on to the park of the **château**★ (open Apr–Oct; guided tours (45min) at 11am, 3, 4, 5, 6pm; 7€; 03 85 50 50 30; www.chateaulamartine.com), which was given to Lamartine on his marriage in 1820. The study, bedroom and salon are much as they were when Lamartine used to invite many famous guests there.
South of St-Point beside the road (D 22) lies an artificial lake which is used as a leisure and water-sports centre.

Signal de la Mère-Boitier
A steep road leads up to a car park. 15min round trip on foot.
The signal station (758m/2 487ft) is the highest point of the Mâconnais region, with a fine **panorama** of the Butte de Suin to the north-west, St-Cyr mountain to the west and the Bresse and Jura to the east.

Château de Pierreclos
Open Apr–Nov daily 10am–6pm, Fri and Sat 10am–4pm; rest of the year Mon–Thu 10am-noon, 2–5pm, Fri and Sat closes 4pm. 6.50€. 03 85 35 73 73. www.chateaudepierreclos.com.

Dating from the 12C to the 17C, the château has had a hard life: razed several times during the Wars of Religion, it was finally saved from destruction in 1986. It is associated with Mlle de Milly, depicted as the character Laurence in Lamartine's epic poem *Jocelyn*, and with Nina de Pierreclos, her sister-in-law and the poet's lover.
Inside, note the elegant **spiral stairway**, the Renaissance chimney-piece in the guard-room, the kitchen's 12C fireplace, and the bakery, which made bread for the whole village.

Bussières
Abbot Dumont, Lamartine's first teacher and friend immortalised in his epic work *Jocelyn*, is buried in the apse of the little church. From the Monsard spur (reached via Grand-Bussières), you can enjoy a view over the entire area you have just covered.

ADDRESSES

STAY
Hôtel Montagne de **Brancion** – At Col de Brancion. 03 85 51 12 40. www.brancion.com. Closed early Nov to mid-Mar. 19 rooms. 16€. Restaurant. This hotel dominating the vineyards on the Mâconnais heights is a haven of peace. The bright bedrooms are decorated with bamboo and wooden furniture painted white. The radiant dining room opens out on to the garden with its pool.

EAT
Ferme-Auberge de Malo – In the locality of Malo, 71240 Étrigny. 9km/5.6mi N of Brancion by D 159 then a minor road. 03 85 92 21 47. www.aubergemalo.com. Closed 10 Nov–1 Apr. Reservation required. This pretty medieval farmhouse offers traditional cuisine made with home-grown produce and poultry reared on the property. Delicious home-made charcuterie.

Mâcon

Mâcon spreads along the west bank of the Saône between the river and the Mâconnais heights with their slopes covered in vineyards. The round roof tiles mark it as a southern town. Its lively atmosphere is due partly to the busy waterfront, the marina and, not least, to the national French wine fair (♦ *see Calendar of Events*) held here every year.

▶ **Population:** 33 865
ⓘ **Michelin Map:**
320: I-12. Local map see Le Mâconnais.
🅱 **Info:** 1 pl. St-Pierre, 71000 Mâcon. ℘03 85 21 07 07. www.visitezle maconnais.com.
🅰 **Don't Miss:** The quai Lamartine is lined with pavement cafés; from here, walk to the Pont St-Laurent from which there is a pretty view of the town.

A BIT OF HISTORY

The Prince of French Romanticism – Alphonse de Lamartine (♦ *see MÂCON-NAIS*) was born in Mâcon in 1790 and took an interest in literature and religious issues from an early age. In 1816, he met a great love of his life, Julie Charles, but her premature death drove him to write the melancholy ode *Le Lac*. His *Méditations poétiques*, in which the poet extols Julie under the name of Elvira, were published in 1820, and it was these that won Lamartine fame.

SIGHTS

Musée des Ursulines★

ⓞ*Open daily except Mon 10am–noon, 2–6pm, Sun and public holidays 2–6pm.*
ⓞ*Closed 1 Jan, 1 May, 14 Jul, 1 Nov, 25 Dec.* ⊜*3.40€.* ℘*03 85 39 90 38.*
The museum, housed in a 17C Ursuline convent, contains sections on prehistory, Gallo-Roman and medieval archaeology, regional ethnography, painting and ceramics.

Among the displays are articles from excavations at Solutré and other regional sites, such as tools, weapons and ceramics from the Paleolithic period to the Iron Age. Other rooms are given over to the Gallo-Roman period (statuettes, tools, funerary urns from the Mâcon necropolis), medieval artefacts (Merovingian weapons and sepulchres) and sculpture from the 12C to the 17C. Further galleries are devoted to 17C and 18C furniture, French and foreign glazed earthenware and painting: 16C Flemish works; Fontainebleau School; 17C and 18C French and Northern schools (Le Brun, De Champaigne, Greuze); 19C Romanticism (Corot), academics and

View of Mâcon with the Saône

Alain Doire/Bourgogne Tourisme

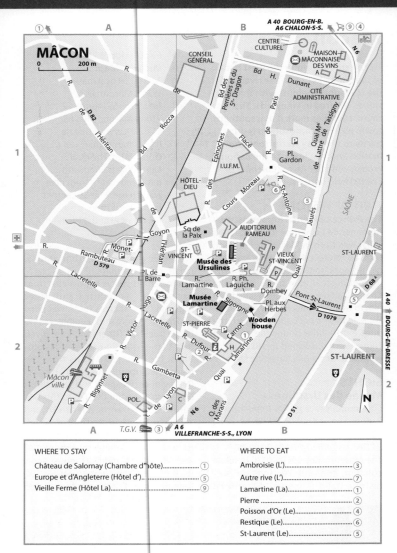

MÂCON

0   200 m

WHERE TO STAY

Château de Salornay (Chambre d'hôte)	①
Europe et d'Angleterre (Hôtel d')	⑤
Vieille Ferme (Hôtel La)	⑨

WHERE TO EAT

Ambroisie (L')	③
Autre rive (L')	⑦
Lamartine (La)	①
Pierre	②
Poisson d'Or (Le)	④
Restique (Le)	⑥
St-Laurent (Le)	⑤

Symbolists (Busière); 20C post-Cubist canvases (Gleizes, Cahn) and contemporary works (Bill, Honegger, Boussard).

Musée Lamartine

🕐 Open daily except Mon 10am–noon, 2–6pm, Sun and public holidays 2–6pm. 🕐 Closed 1 Jan, 1 May, 14 Jul, 1 Nov, 25 Dec. ⊚ 3.40€. ✆ 03 85 39 90 38.
The museum dedicated to the man is in the Hôtel Senecé (18C), an elegant, Régence-style mansion. It contains paintings, tapestries and furniture of the period. A collection of documents recalls the life and work of Lamartine.

Wooden House

22 r. Dombey (now a tea shop).
This pretty Renaissance house, decorated with finely sculpted columns sits at the junction with Place aux Herbes. Look for the grotesque carvings of fantastic animals and characters, some of them rather cheeky, which decorate the eaves.

The Prince of French Romanticism

"Love, prayer and song – that is my life"

Born in 1790 in Mâcon, **Alphonse de Lamartine** spent a happy childhood in Milly. Aged 21, while on his first trip to Italy, he fell in love with a Napolitan girl named **Antoniella**, who later appears in his work as the fictional character Graziella. Whilst taking the cure at Aix-les-Bains in 1816, the young man then fell hopelessly in love with **Julie**, the wife of Dr Jacques Charles. This unconditional love, which he called the "inexpressible joy of loving", together with his illness and the absence of Julie (who died several months later) inspired him to write *Le Lac*, an ode to Lake Bourget.

The *Méditations poétiques* published in 1820 were the start of his fame. Married to an English wife, **Mary Ann Birch**, and building a career as a diplomat, Lamartine entered into an intense period of creativity: *The Death of Socrates, the Nouvelles Méditations poétiques*, and the *Last Canto of Childe Harolde's Pilgrimage* followed in succession, and on 5 November 1829, he was elected to the Académie Française.

From 1831 to 1833, he travelled in the Orient in an attempt to rediscover the faith which had been weakened by his philosophical doubts. The trip took him as far as Nazareth and Jerusalem, and it was during this "pilgrimage" that his 10-year-old daughter **Julia**, who he had left with her mother in Beirut, died of consumption. This painful tragedy is the subject of his poem *Gethsémani*. Deeply affected and questioning the religious principles that had guided him thus far, he published *Jocelyn* in 1836, which was received rapturously.

"Poetry should be for the people"

While in charge of the Florence embassy in October 1827, Lamartine resigned his diplomatic post as he felt no loyalty for the new king Louis-Philippe and preferred to stay free in order to engage in politics. His first post was MP for Bergues in the north, before being elected to represent Mâcon in 1837, where he was re-elected in 1842 and 1846. He fought for "the interests of the working class, the proletarian masses who are so often trampled by our blind laws". He published his ideas in the newspaper *Le Bien public,* which he launched in Mâcon in September 1842. Together with his *Histoire des Girondins*, an evocation of the revolutionary period published in 1847, he received great acclaim. In 1848, after the dismissal of Guizot and the king's abdication, Lamartine stood opposed to another regency, and contributed to the foundation of the Republic, which was proclaimed on 27th February.

As a member of the short-lived provisional government, he held the Foreign Affairs portfolio until the closure of National Workshops and the June riots marked the beginning of the end of his prominence. The result of the President of the Republic's universal suffrage elections on 20th December was beyond question: Louis-Napoleon Bonaparte won easily with 5 million votes against Lamartine's modest showing of 18 000 votes.

His political career ended as the Second Empire began, while constant financial problems forced him to undertake what he referred to as "literary hard labour". His wife's death in 1863 cast a shadow over his latter years. The poet passed away on 28th February 1869 in Paris. He was to be buried in the Panthéon, but his wishes were respected and he lies in St-Point (see p146), near to his family.

EXCURSIONS
Romanèche-Thorins
◐ *15km/9.5mi S Via N 6.*
This, and the neighbouring village of Chénas, is the home of arguably the most famous of the Beaujolais crus, Moulin-à-Vent: a powerful, full-bodied wine suitable for laying down.

♿👤 **Le Hameau Dubœuf**★★ *(La Gare;* ♿*;* 🕐 *open 10am–6.30pm;* 🕐 *closed 25 Dec;* ⊜*18 €, under 16s free;* 📞*03 85 35 22 22; www.hameauduboeuf.com)* – This extensive site in the Romanèche-Thorins railway station is first and foremost a big-budget promotional display for the Beaujolais producer Dubœuf, but it also opens a window onto the world of the vineyard. Begin the tour of the **Hameau Dubœuf** in the grand hall of the reconstructed 1900-era station. A maze of rooms takes in the history of the vineyards, the wine maker's tools, the flavours of the wines and their links with the land, the stages of wine-making (see the impressive Mâconnais grape press from 1708), barrels, corks, glass and labels. Modern museum interpretation paints a picture; lovely artefacts, along with a mechanical theatre and short films, including a 3D musical comedy starring Paul Bocuse and Bernard Pivot. Naturally, the tour ends with a tasting (**salle du limonaire**★.)

Hameau Dubœf

Opposite the Hameau Dubœuf, the close links between wine and the railways in the 19C and 20C are explained in the **station**. The handsome **imperial carriage** used by Napoleon III to greet the crowds is inside, as well as a collection of electric trains running through model towns and landscapes, and an exhibition on the TGV.

Next stop, is the **Jardin en Beaujolais** *(*🚂*take the little train as it's not all that close)*, to learn about the aromas typical of Beaujolais wines by means of themed flower beds (floral, vegetable, woody, nutty, fruity, spicy). Centre stage in the 5 000sq m/5 980yd gardens is the Georges Dubœuf **vinification centre**, where you learn more about wine-making.

Musée Guillon du Compagnonnage *(*🕐*open Jun–Sept 10am–6pm, Oct–May 2–6pm;* ⊜*3.50€;* 📞*03 85 35 22 02)* – This small museum has exhibits from the days of travelling craftsman; there are some fine examples of their work.

♿👤**Touroparc**★ – ♿ 🕐 *Open daily 9.30am–7pm;* ⊜*15.50€;* 📞*03 85 35 51 53; www.touroparc.com.* This 10ha/25-acre zoo and breeding centre houses 800 animals from all over the world. Many roam free in the park, which also has a monorail, swimming pools with water slides, a picnic area and bars.

ADDRESSES

🛏**STAY**

⊜⊜ **Hôtel d' Europe et d'Angleterre** – *92–109 quai Jean-Jaurès.* 📞*03 85 38 27 94. www.hotel-european gleterre-macon.com.* 🅿 *29 rooms.* ⊐ *7€.* Renovation work is under way, but several rooms still retain the splendour that made them famous in the days when Queen Victoria and Marcel Pagnol stayed there. Ample comfort at a keen price.

⊜⊜ **Hôtel La Vieille Ferme** – *Bd Gén.-de-Gaulle, 71000 Sancé.* 📞*03 85 21 95 15. www.hotel-restaurant-lavieilleferme.com. Closed 20 Dec–10 Jan.* ♿🅿 *24 rooms.* ⊐*7€. Set lunch menu 12€.* A rustic bolthole on the banks of the Saône.

Plain, functional rooms in a motel-style building. The *vieille ferme* (old farm) houses a homely restaurant with a fireplace, exposed timbers and stone walls opening onto a lovely terrace.

⊜⊜ **Chambre d'hôte Château de Salornay** – *1024 rte de Salornay, 71870 Hurigny. 6km/3.7mi west of Mâcon on D82 then secondary road. ℰ03 85 34 25 73. chateaudesalornay71@orange.fr.* 🅿 *5 rooms. ⌕.* Delightful 11C château sporting towers and sturdy walls topped by a walkway. Huge rooms, one of which is in the keep, are kitted out plushly with antiques. Two characterful gîtes also available.

⊖/EAT

⊜ **La Lamartine** – *259 quai Lamartine. ℰ03 85 35 16 63. r.lelamartine@orange.fr. Set lunch menu 13€.* Brasserie buzz in a venue that has been around since 1804. Among the house specialities are *moules frites*, veal sweetbreads and frogs' legs.

⊜ **Le Restique** – *56 r. St-Antoine. ℰ03 85 38 38 76. Closed 24 Dec–4 Jan, Sun, Mon and Tue eve. ⇗ Set lunch menu 12.50€.* Two well-priced menus from land and sea are the attraction in this rustic-style restaurant. Wooden floors and furniture make for a fuss-free interior to match the down-to-earth welcome.

⊜⊜ **L'Ambroisie** – *103 r. Marcel-Paul. ℰ03 85 38 12 21. www.lambroisie.fr. Closed 12–19 Apr, 1–15 Aug, 13–22 Feb, Mon and Tue eve and Sun. Set lunch menu 15€.* This friendly little bistro with a fresco, stone walls and veranda extension is worth a detour for its trendy cooking and professional service.

⊜⊜ **L'Autre Rive** – *143 quai Bouchacourt, 01750 St-Laurent-sur-Saône. 1.5km/1mi east. ℰ03 85 39 01 02. www.lautrerive.fr. Closed 24–29 Dec, Sun eve and Mon. Set lunch menu 17€.* Nothing is lacking in this restaurant on the "other bank": a cosy veranda, an agreeable terrace facing the Saône and a menu that brings together Bresse chicken and the flavours of the sea.

⊜⊜ **Le Poisson d'Or** – *port de plaisance. ℰ03 85 38 00 88. www.lepoissondor.com. Closed 24 Mar–2 Apr, 19 Oct–12 Nov, Mar*

and Wed. ♿ 🅿. This restaurant beside the Saône puts a new spin on local cooking and summery fried fish. The dining room perches above the river and the waterfront terrace.

⊜⊜ **Le Saint-Laurent** – *1 quai Bouchacourt, 01750 St-Laurent-sur-Saône. 1.5km/1mi east. ℰ03 85 39 29 19. www.georgesblanc.com.* Cross the St-Laurent bridge to reach this retro brasserie made famous when Mitterrand et Gorbachev dropped in. Enjoy well-cooked dishes and a view over Mâcon from the terrace.

⊜⊜ **Pierre** – *7 r. Dufour. ℰ03 85 38 14 23. www.restaurant-pierre.com. Closed 5–27 Jul, Feb holidays, Sun eve, Tue lunch and Mon. Set lunch menu 20€.* Stone walls, bare beams and a fireplace make for an elegant setting and cosy ambience in this restaurant. The kitchen brings together classicism, terroir and modern trends with aplomb.

🚋 TAKING A BREAK

Le Petit Monde des Douceurs – *268 r. Carnot. ℰ03 85 39 17 90. Open Mon–Sat 9.30am–7pm.* On cold days take refuge in this pleasant tearoom over a cup of hot chocolate flavoured with caramel, orange or hazelnut and a pastry.

🛍 SHOPPING

Maison des Vins – *484 av. de Lattre-de-Tassigny. ℰ03 85 22 91 11. www.maison-des-vins.com. Open daily 11.30am–6.30pm.* An exhibition, shop and wine tastings led by connoisseurs.

Cave de Chaintré – *rte. de Juliénas. 71570 Chaintré. ℰ03 85 35 61 61. www.cavedechaintre.com. Open Mon–Fri 8am–noon and 2–6pm, Sat 8am–noon.* This cellar focuses on Chardonnay varietals (Pouilly-Fuissé, Saint-Véran, Beaujolais, Mâcon), with a few reds.

Château du moulin-à-vent – *71570 Romanèche-Thorins. 15km/9.5mi S via N 6. ℰ03 85 35 50 68. chateaudumoulinavent@wanadoo.fr. Open Mon–Fri 9am–noon, 2–6pm, weekends and public holidays by appointment.* The most celebrated of Beaujolais wines, made to be kept and aged. Tastings for old vintages available.

Cluny★★

Cluny is synonymous with the religious order that exercised such an immense influence on the religious, intellectual, political and artistic life of western Europe in medieval times. Until the Revolution, every century left its architectural mark here. From 1798 to 1823, this centre of civilisation was ransacked, but one can still get an idea of the majesty of the basilica from what remains. The town itself also has plenty of sights for the visitor.

▶ **Population:** 4 585
- **Michelin Map:** 320: H-11. Local map see Mâconnais.
- **Info:** 6 r. Mercière, 71250 Cluny. ℘03 85 59 05 34. www.cluny-tourisme.com.
- **Location:** A climb to the top of the Tour des Fromages will give you the best view of the town and its historic structures.
- **Timing:** If you're here between late July and late August, don't miss the Grandes Heures de Cluny, a series of classical concerts in the abbey's former Flour Store followed by wine tastings in the cellars.

A BIT OF HISTORY

The rise – Cluny's influence grew rapidly from the moment it was founded in the 10C, particularly through the establishment of numerous daughter abbeys. "You are the light of the world" said Pope Urban II (himself from Cluny, as were many other popes) to **St Hugh** in 1098. When St Hugh died in 1109, having begun the construction of the magnificent abbey church which **Peter the Venerable**, abbot from 1122 to 1156, was to finish, he left the abbey in a state of great prosperity. In 1155 there were 460 monks resident in the abbey alone, and young men from all over Europe flocked here.

The decline – Rich and powerful, the monks of Cluny slipped gradually into a worldly way of life that was strongly condemned by **St Bernard**. The 14C saw the decline of Cluny's power, and by the 16C it was reduced to a quarry for spoils. It was devastated during the Wars of Religion and the library was sacked.

Destruction – In 1790 the abbey was closed. Its desecration began at the height of the Revolution. In September 1793, the local authority gave the order for the tombs to be demolished and sold for building. In 1798 the buildings were sold to a property speculator who

Ancienne Abbaye

Alain Doire/Bourgogne Tourisme

knocked down the nave and sold off the abbey church bit by bit until by 1823 all that was left was what we see today.

ANCIENNE ABBAYE★★

🕐 *Open May–Aug 9.30am–6.30pm; Sept–Apr 9.30am–noon, 1.30–5pm.*
🕐 *Closed 1 Jan, 1 May, 1 and 11 Nov, 25 Dec.* ✆ *7€ combined ticket from the Musée d'Art et d'Archéologie.*
📞 *03 85 59 15 93.*

Most of the abbey church of St Peter and St Paul, called Cluny III, was built between 1088 and 1130 when the Cluniac Order was at its most powerful. It was the largest Christian church (177m/581ft long) until the reconstruction of St Peter's in Rome (186m/610ft long). It consisted of a narthex, a nave and four aisles, two transepts, five belfries, two towers, 301 windows and 225 decorated stalls. The painted apsidal vault rested on a marble colonnade. Sadly, only the south transepts are still standing.

Narthex – The site of the narthex is now bisected by rue Kenneth-J.-Conant. During excavations in 1949 the base of the south end of the façade was uncovered, together with the footings of the doorway which was flanked by square Barabans towers (only the foundations survive). The south aisle of the narthex was uncovered later, revealing a wall with pilasters attached to semi-columns.

The long Gothic façade (restored) in place de l'Abbaye is named after Pope Gelasius who died at Cluny in 1119 (abbey entrance).

Cloisters – The 18C monastic buildings form a harmonious group enclosing the vast; two great flights of stone steps with wrought-iron railings occupy two corners.

Galilee Passage – The 11C passage, which was used by the great Benedictine processions, linked the Galilee (a covered porch) of Cluny II with the south aisle of the great church of Cluny III.

Traces of the church of St Peter and St Paul – From the size of the south transepts it is possible to work out the size of the whole basilica. Its height (30m/98ft under the barrel vaulting, 32m/105ft under the dome) is excep-

tional in Romanesque architecture. The church consisted of three bays; the central one, topped by an octagonal cupola on squinches, supports the handsome **Clocher de l'Eau-Bénite★★** (Holy Water Belfry). St-Étienne (St-Stephen's Chapel) is Romanesque; St-Martial's Chapel dates from the 14C. The right arm of the smaller transept contains the Bourbon Chapel with its late-15C Gothic architecture and a Romanesque apse.

Monastic buildings – The buildings, which house the School of Arts and Crafts, were nicknamed Little Versailles owing to the elegant Classical east façade.

Flour Store – The storehouse (54m/177ft long) was built in the late 13C; in the 18C it was truncated (by about 20m/65ft) to reveal the south end of the façade of the cloister building overlooking the gardens. The low storeroom with its two ranges of ogive vaulting houses sculptures including a doorway with recessed arches from Pope Gelasius' palace.

The **high chamber**, with its beautiful oak roof, makes an dramatic setting for pieces of sculpture from the abbey. The fine **capitals★** and column shafts saved from the ruins of the abbey church are exhibited by means of a scale model of the chancel: the eight capitals on their columns are set in a semicircle round the old Pyrenean marble altar consecrated by Urban II in 1095. They are the first examples of the Burgundian Romanesque sculpture which was to blossom in Vézelay, Autun and Saulieu. The two models, of the great doorway and of the apse of the basilica, were designed by Professor Conant, the archaeologist who directed the excavations from 1928 to 1950.

Art and Archaeology Museum★ – Models in the entrance hall and, upstairs, an audio-visual reconstruction of Cluny III allow visitors to appreciate the greatness of the abbey. Two basement rooms contain stone fragments of the monument: part of the frieze of the narthex and arcading from the choir screen. Upstairs, sculptures and architectural elements from various façades give an insight into the decoration of medieval

Cluny at the end of the 18C.

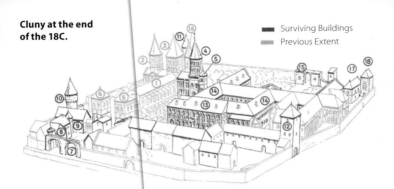

■ Surviving Buildings
■ Previous Extent

(**1**) Abbatiale Saint-Pierre-et-Saint-Paul; (**2**) Clocher des Bisans; (**3**) Clocher du Chœur; (**4**) Clocher de l'Eau-Bénite; (**5**) Clocher de l'Horloge; (**6**) Les Barabans; (**7**) Portes d'Honneur; (**8**) Palais de Jean de Bourbon; (**9**) Palais de Jacques d'Amboise; (**10**) Tour Fabry; (**11**) Tour Ronde; (**12**) Tour des Fromages; (**13**) Façade du pape Gélase; (**14**) Bâtiments claustraux; (**15**) Porte des Jardins; (**16**) Clocher des Lampes; (**17**) Farinier; (**18**) Tour du Moulin.

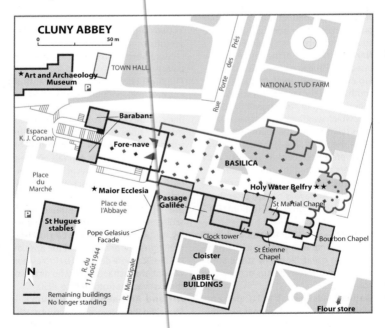

houses (harvest frieze, capital decorated with a shoemaker, lintel carved with a tournament scene).

OLD TOWN

Tour Fabry and Tour Ronde – The Fabry Tower (1347) with its pepper-pot roof and the older Ronde Tower

are visible from the garden near the town hall.

Hôtel de Ville – The town hall now occupies the building erected for Cluny's abbots at the end of the 15C and beginning of the 16C. The garden front has an original decoration in the Italian Renaissance style.

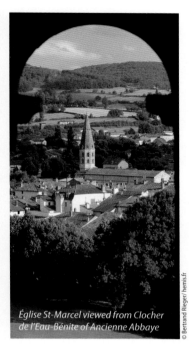

Église St-Marcel viewed from Clocher de l'Eau-Bénite of Ancienne Abbaye

© Bertrand Rieger / hemis.fr

Romanesque houses – Cluny has several fine Romanesque dwellings: note in particular a 12C house at no. 25 rue de la République and the 13C mint (restored) at no. 6 rue d'Avril.

Tour des Fromages – ⏱ *Open May–Sept daily 9.30am–7pm; rest of the year times vary;* ⏱ *closed 1 May, 1 and 11 Nov;* 2€; 📞 *03 85 59 05 34.* From the top (120 steps) of the curiously named 11C Cheese tower there is a good view of the abbey, Clocher d'Eau-Bénite, flour store and adjoining mill tower, belfry of St-Marcel and Notre-Dame.

Église Notre-Dame – The square in front of the church has an 18C fountain and old houses. The church, built shortly after 1100, was enlarged in the Gothic period. The 13C doorway is badly weathered. The interior is a good example of Cluniac architecture.

Église St-Marcel (⏱ *open Jun–Sept 8am–7pm;* 📞 *03 85 59 07 18*) – This church has a fine octagonal Romanesque belfry of three storeys, topped by a graceful 15C polygonal brick spire (42m/138ft high).

🚗 DRIVING TOUR

ÉGLISES DU CLUNISOIS (CLUNY CHURCHES)

🕐 *See Region map. Allow 1hr. Leave Cluny heading north on D 981.*

Taizé – Perched on the hills of the Grosne, Taizé sees the arrival each summer of tens of thousands of young people who come to pray in a spirit of brotherhood. The monastic community, visited by Pope Jean-Paul II in 1986, consists of a hundred or so monks from a variety of Christian churches spread throughout 20 countries, whose aim is to reconcile separated communities and divided Christians. Prayers are held three times daily in the Church of Reconciliation, a modern structure built in 1962 (enlarged in 1990). The venerable parish church is a 12C Romanesque affair, austere inside, and lit by tiny stained-glass windows.

Ameugny – Built in attractive local red limestone, the sturdy 12C church has a nave with three vaulted bays and, above the transept, a dome holds up the heavy square bell tower.

Malay – Seen from the cemetery, the 12C Romanesque church of this parish of Cluny presents a harmonious ensemble of chancel, transept and apse and a solid, square bell tower.

St Hippolyte – The partially-ruined priory church crowns the promontory where the hamlet lies. Next door to the former convent (now a farm) the mighty belfry is visible from afar. Explore what remains of the honey stone walls of the nave and the chancel structure, enjoying the sweeping views across the Guye Valley.

Nearby is the curious yellow stone village of Besanceuil; its knot of houses nestles at the foot of a wooded spine together with a 14C castle and a fine 11C Romanesque chapel.

Bezornay – This pretty hamlet perched on a hillcrest was a dependency of Cluny in the Middle Ages, as shown by its ruined walls, defensive tower and chapel.

Finish with a look around the tiny 11C Romanesque church in **Saint-Vincent-des-Prés.**

ADDRESSES

⚫STAY

⚫⚫ **Chambre d'hôte La Courtine** – *Pont de la Levée. Leave Cluny east on D15 (rte d'Azé) immediately after the bridge.* ☎*03 85 59 05 10. www.lacourtine.net.* **P** ⚫ *5 rooms.* ⚫. Virginia creepers and wisteria curtain the façade of this former farm by the River Grosne. In a smart Scandinavian style interior, some of the cosy bedrooms overlook the river. Home-made jam for breakfast.

⚫⚫ **Chambre d'hôte La Maison des Gardes** – *18 av. Charles-de-Gaulle.* ☎*03 85 59 19 46. www.lamaisondesgardes.com.* ⚫ *5 rooms.* ⚫. This old guard's house right by the abbey has 3 rooms in the main building, and 2 more, including a suite, in the annexe. Pieces of old furniture complete a deliciously simple look. Breakfast is taken in the garden or by the lounge fireplace.

⚫⚫⚫ **Hôtel de Bourgogne** – *Pl. de l'Abbaye.* ☎*03 85 59 00 58. www.hotel-cluny.com. Closed 1 Dec–11 Feb.* ⚫ *Wi-Fi. 14 rooms.* ⚫ *11€, half board available. Set lunch menu 17€.* Lamartine used to stay in this characterful mansion opposite the Benedictine abbey. Pleasant lounge and individually styled bedrooms. The restaurant has a chequerboard floor, pale walls, Louis XVI seats, a stone fireplace and traditional menu.

View of the town

Alain Doire/Bourgogne Tourisme

⚫/EAT

⚫⚫ **La Brasserie du Nord** – *Pl. du Marché.* ☎*03 85 59 09 96. Closed 5 Dec–15 Jan.* ⚫. Completely reworked with a plush brasserie look, this restaurant will win you over with its gorgeous terrace on the place de l'Abbaye. Better still, it is keenly priced, even at weekends, and stays open late in the evening – a rare occurrence in Cluny.

⚫⚫ **Hostellerie d'Héloïse** – *pont de l'Étang.* ☎*03 85 59 05 65. www.hostelleriedheloise.com. Closed mid-Dec until mid-Feb.* ⚫ *Set lunch menu 18€. 13 rooms.* ⚫ *8.50€.* A family-run set up on the edge of town prized for its sincere welcome and its skilled traditional cooking. Colonial-style grand dining room and veranda. If you're intending to stay, bag one of the refurbished bedrooms.

⚫SHOPPING

Dentelle Cluny – *Aymé de Réa, 15 r. Lamartine.* ☎*03 85 59 31 78. brunoindiana@aol.com. Open Apr–Sept daily 9am–8pm.* A young craftsman has set up his lacemaking studio in a small medieval building. He designs original pieces inspired by traditional motifs, including the legendary Cluny stitch.

Le Cellier de l'Abbaye – *13 r. Municipale.* ☎*03 85 59 04 00. Open Tue–Sat 9.30am–12.30pm, 2.30–7pm; Sun 10am–12.30pm (open Mon 14 Jul–15 Aug). Closed Feb.* A total of 250 Burgundy wines, 90 whiskies and a wide choice of local liqueurs are on offer in this superb store made of 13C stone.

Château de l'Aubespin – *71220, St-André-le-Désert.* ☎*03 85 59 49 48. Open daily from 9am.* This family business produces gourmet delicacies, from fruit liqueurs to jams, in a medieval chateau.

⚫ TAKING A BREAK

Au Péché Mignon – *23–25 r. Lamartine.* ☎*03 85 59 11 21. www.chocolateriegermain.fr. Open daily 7.30am–8pm. Closed 2 weeks in Jan.* This patisserie-tea room sells a mouthwatering selection of cakes and delicacies of all kinds, such as perle d'or (almond paste with griotte cherries) and tomato jam.

Château de Cormatin★★

Cormatin was built in the aftermath of the Wars of Religion between 1605 and 1616 by the Governor of Chalon, Antoine du Blé d'Huxelles.

CHÂTEAU

⏲ *Open Apr–Nov.* 🔊*Guided tours (1hr) Jul–Aug 10am–6.30pm. Rest of the year times vary. Grounds open.* 🎫*9€.*

The north wing contains a magnificent grand **staircase**★★ (1610); the straight flights of steps, flanked by balustrades, open directly on to the central well. It is the oldest and largest staircase of this kind (25m/82ft high).

The sumptuous Louis XIII décor in this wing is the work of Marquess Jacques du Blé and his wife Claude Phélypeaux, who were close friends of Marie de Medici and the literary salon of the Précieuses. They intended their summer house to reflect the sophistication of Parisian fashion, so they used the artists and craftsmen who had worked for the Queen at the Luxembourg Palace. The gilt, paintings and sculptures which cover the walls and ceilings are proof of an informed mannerism; each painting has an allegorical meaning reaffirmed in the symbolism of the decorative motifs and the colours used for the panelling.

The **ante-chamber of the Marchioness**★ (daughter and sister of government ministers), which was created in the middle of the Protestant revolt (1627–28), is in homage to Louis XIII who is represented above the chimney-piece: the red panelling (colour of authority) celebrates the activities and virtues of the king. The **Marchioness' room**★★ has a magnificent French ceiling in gold and blue, symbol of fidelity; the great painting of Venus and Vulcan, a work of the second Fontainebleau School, symbolises love and the baskets of fruit and flowers on the woodwork represent plenty. One of the oldest heavenly ceilings, made fashionable by Marie de Medici, adorns the **Cabi-**

⏱ **Michelin Map:** 320: I-10. Local map see Mâconnais.

🛈 **Info:** Chateau de Cormatin, 71460 Cormatin. ✆03 85 50 16 55. www.chateaude cormatin.com.

▷ **Location:** 13km/8mi north of Cluny.

👁 **Don't Miss:** The understated exterior, probably designed by Jacques II Androuet du Cerceau, architect to Henri IV.

Château de Cormatin

© Christophe Boisvieux/hemis.fr

net des Curiosités★★ The sumptuous Baroque décor in Jacques du Blé's tiny study, the **Cabinet de Ste-Cécile**★★★, is dominated by blue lapis-lazuli and rich gilding; the figure of St Cecilia accompanied by the cardinal virtues represents moral harmony.

GARDENS★★

The lovely view of the park from the aviary reveals its typical 17C symbolism: the flower beds represent paradise, with the fountain of life in the centre. Within a triangle, the apple tree recalls the forbidden fruit and paradise lost; the labyrinth symbolises mankind's errant ways. From the borders inward, the seven walkways culminate in seventh heaven at the highest point.

La Voie Verte★

The Voie Verte (Green Trail) is a vast, ever-expanding network of cycle paths, part of an ambitious pan-European initiative that is intended to run for 2 400km/1 490mi, linking Nantes to Budapest. Its 600km/373mi of waymarked paths follows disused railways, vineyard trails and canal towpaths. Cyclists, rollerskaters and walkers will appreciate the gentle gradients and lack of traffic on the "Tour de Bourgogne" through the region's four departments. These three tours put a new spin on southern Burgundy, but there's nothing to stop you making up your own itineraries – that's the whole point of the Voie Verte!

CYCLE TOURS
 See Region map.

Charnay-Lès-Mâcon to Cluny
 See Region map. 23km/14mi round-trip.
The Voie Verte starts in Charnay-lès-Mâcon, with its landmark octagonal bell tower above the Romanesque church of St Madeleine. After a flat start, the trail crosses a more dramatic landscape. To the left a superb view sweeps across a series of crystalline rocky escarpments, among which you can spot the famous Roche de Solutré (see p144). Coming up on the right are the neatly combed vineyards of the Mâconnais. Prissé makes a good pitstop – if you're feeling fit, you could make a 21km/13mi diversion into the Lamartine Valley to follow in the footsteps of the poet. Soon you're passing through the Bois Clair tunnel (home to bats) on a section of the old railway, before the path winds its way to Cluny.

Cluny to Cormatin
 See Region map.
14km/9mi round-trip.
Don't miss the centre of Cluny, as it is just 800m/31.5in from the Voie Verte. Visit the abbey, its museum and take in the view from the Tour des Fromages.

 Michelin Map: General map C4 – Michelin départements 320 H/I-9/12 Saône-et-Loire (71).

 Info: Tourism Office of Charnay-lès-Mâcon – Rte de Davayé, 71850 Charnay-lès-Mâcon. 03 85 21 07 14. www.visiterlemaconnais.com. See info for opening times. Closed Nov–Feb.

 Location: The three cycle routes covered in this section run from Charnay-lès-Mâcon to Châlon-sur-Saône, around 75km/47mi in total. Part of the route follows the very first stretch of the Voie Verte along the former railway track from Buxy to Cluny.

 Kids: The Voie Verte offers families a safe environment away from traffic – great for fun days out by bike, rollerskates or on foot. The children get to travel in a new way, and it's good exercise to boot!

Continue past fields of horses and cattle, and through copses of the Cluny forest to Massilly where a 10km/6mi loop links the Romanesque churches of Bray, Chissey-lès-Mâcon, Ameugny and Taizé. The opulent Louis XIII interiors of the château in Cormatin are a fine reason to pause here.

Cormatin to Chalon-sur-Saône
 See Region map. 38km/24mi round-trip.
After Cormatin, have a good look at the Romanesque church in **Malay** (see p155). then push on 5km/3mi to the medieval heart of **St-Gengoux-le-National**. Carry on through Etiveau and its vineyards, and stop off to admire the ancient winemakers' houses in the old centre of **Buxy**. Make a last stop in **Givry** (see p133) before finishing the tour in **Châlon-sur-Saône**.

BRIONNAIS AND CHAROLAIS

In the Brionnais and Charolais regions of the southwestern corner of Burgundy, the all-powerful vineyards give way to a rolling landscape of golden villages and verdant pastures freckled with muscular white Charolais cattle. Great, then, for dining on top-class *steak-frites*, and pretty impressive too for its architectural heritage, and a fair sprinkling of venerable churches and castles. This is an area best explored by easy driving tours through idyllic rural countryside where every sleepy village seems to hide a Romanesque church or the ruins of an abbey – part of the legacy of the great abbey of Cluny when it was at the peak of its power.

The Brionnais

This tranquil corner of Burgundy to the west of the vineyards is bracketed by the River Loire and the foothills of Beaujolais. Charlieu is a top sight – it has its own splendid Benedictine abbey, whose fate was to mirror that of its illustrious sister in Cluny: largely demolished after the Revolution, its evocative ruins are still well worth visiting.

The influence of the once-powerful abbey at Cluny over the whole area can still be seen in the Romanesque churches around Charlieu.

Absolutely the best way to see these 12C treasures and a brace of fine châteaux is to take the driving tour on a route that passes through the honey-hued Brionnais towns and villages – the churches at Anzy-le-Duc and Semur-en-Brionnais are the stars of the show. Try to do it in the afternoon, when the warm golden limestone churches glow in the setting sun. And don't miss the Leblanc oil mill in Iguérande, where the most sublime oils from hazelnuts, pistachios and sesame seeds are pressed the old way. Chocoholics should schedule in a pilgrimage to La Clayette, where the masterful work of chocolatier Bernard Dufoux is available in his temple to the art of making divine confectionery. If you're travelling with children, the vintage car museum in the lakeside château should go down well, as will feeding the sheep at the Plassard woollen mill in Varennes-sur-Dun.

Afterwards, the splendid Château de Drée shows how the other half lived, and a trip out to the Montagne de Dun has views over the whole area from a panoramic location just made for a picnic.

Highlights

1. The splendid Basilica of Sacré-Coeur in **Paray-le-Monial** (p162)
2. Chocolate heaven Chez Bernard Dufoux in **La Clayette** (p165)
3. **Charlieu**'s atmospheric Benedictine abbey (p167)
4. A tour of Romanesque churches of the **Brionnais** (p171)
5. Thermal spas, golf, art and hiking around **Bourbon-Lancy** (p175)

Around Charolles

In a glorious spot by the waters of the Bourbince, the basilica of Sacré-Coeur is a Romanesque gem that gives an idea – albeit on a smaller scale – of what the abbey church of Cluny once looked like. But unlike Cluny, Paray-le-Monial has gained in importance and is a major centre of Christianity and pilgrimage, dedicated to the cult of the Sacred Heart of Jesus.

Heading northwest of Paray-le-Monial, you could take the cure in the splendid old spa town of Bourbon-Lancy, where the quirky bell tower is rung by a figure who sticks out his tongue. The children can let off steam in the park around Breuil lake. Exploring the area nearby, you will find splendid Flemish tryptychs tucked away in a simple village church in Ternant, and 18C Aubusson tapestries in the town hall at Luzy.

Make sure to spend time relaxing in the old streets and flowery squares of Charolles, while the white cattle named after the town munch away in lush pastures, growing beefy for a date at one of the huge livestock markets.

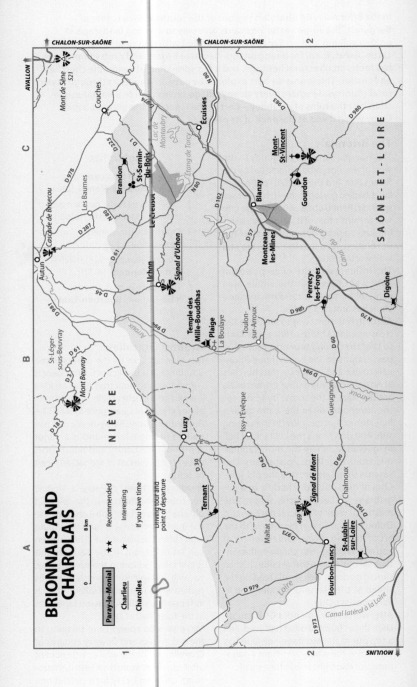

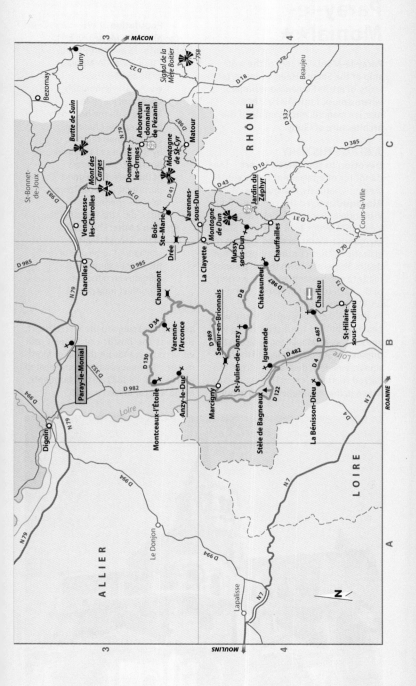

MÂCON

Cluny

Bezornay

Butte de Suin

St-Bonnet-de-Joux

Vendenesse-les-Charolles

Mont des Carges

Dompierre-les-Ormes

Arboretum domanial de Pézanin

Signal de la Mère Boitier 758

D 22

D 79

N 79

D 18

RHÔNE

Beaujeu

D 337

D 385

Matour

D 987

Montagne de St-Cyr

Bois-Ste-Marie

Drée

Varennes-sous-Dun

D 41

D 43

Jardin du Zéphyr

D 10

C

Cours-la-Ville

D 31

D 70

Charolles

D 985

D 983

D 985

La Clayette

Montagne de Dun

Mussy-sous-Dun

Chauffailles

Châteauneuf

Charlieu

St-Hilaire-sous-Charlieu

D 987

D 8

D 989

D 4

D 482

D 487

D 13

B

Chaumont

Varenne-l'Arconce

Semur-en-Brionnais

St-Julien-de-Jonzy

Iguerande

D 34

D 130

Paray-le-Monial

D 352

Anzy-le-Duc

Marcigny

Stèle de Bagneaux

D 122

La Bénisson-Dieu

D 982

Montceaux-l'Étoile

Loire

Digoin

D 994

N 79

ROANNE

N 7

A

LOIRE

ALLIER

Le Donjon

D 994

N 79

N 7

Lapalisse

MOULINS

Z

3

4

3

4

Paray-le-Monial★★

Paray-le-Monial, cradle of the worship of the Sacred Heart of Jesus, is a city of art: its Romanesque basilica, where a music festival is held in summer, is a magnificent example of the architecture of Cluny.

A BIT OF HISTORY

Devotion to the Sacred Heart – The daughter of a royal notary in Verosvres-en-Charollais, **Marguerite-Marie Alacoque** entered the convent of the Visitation at Paray-le-Monial as a novice in 1671. From 1673 onwards, Sister Marguerite-Marie received a series of visitations that continued up to her death. She wrote down the revelations made to her, thus initiating the worship of the Sacred Heart in France. She died on 17 October 1690.

In 1864, Sister Marguerite-Marie was beatified. In 1873, the first great pilgrimage in Paray-le-Monial took place in the presence of 30 000 people, and the decision was made to dedicate France to the Sacred Heart of Jesus. This event was linked to the vow made in 1870 to build

▶ **Population:** 9 191
Michelin Map: 320: E-11.
Info: 25 av. Jean-Paul-II, 71600 Paray-le-Monial. ℘03 85 81 10 92. www.paraylemonial.fr.
Location: Paray-le-Monial is on the boundary between the Charollais and Brionnais regions, by the banks of the River Bourbince, a tributary of the Loire. For a good introduction to the town, take the guided tour offered by the tourist office.
Don't Miss: The Basilica of the Sacred Heart, considered to be one of the finest examples of religious architecture from the Cluny period.

a church dedicated to the Sacred Heart; this was the basilica of Sacré-Cœur which now stands on the hill of Montmartre. Pilgrimages have been repeated each year since 1873. Sister Marguerite-Marie was canonised in 1920.

Basilique du Sacré Cœur

© Daniel Thierry/Photononstop

Many religious orders have communities at Paray-le-Monial which has become one of the great centres of Christianity.

SIGHTS

Basilique du Sacré-Cœur★★

On the right bank of the Bourbince stands the church; it was originally dedicated to the Virgin Mary but in 1875 it was raised to the level of a basilica and consecrated to the Sacred Heart.

The church was built without interruption between 1092 and 1109 under the direction of St Hugues, Abbot of Cluny, and restored in the 19C and 20C; it is a model on a smaller scale of the famous Benedictine abbey at Cluny. Only the architectural style is similar; the builders eschewed decorative splendour in favour of abstract beauty, which is conducive to contemplation. The rare sculptures make use of the geometric motifs found in Islamic art, probably discovered by St Hugues during visits to Spain.

Exterior – Two buttressed square towers surmount the narthex, with four storeys of windows. The right-hand tower, built in the early 11C, has plain decoration; the other later one is more richly decorated. The octagonal tower over the transept crossing was restored in 1856. Enter the basilica by the north arm of the transept; the beautiful Romanesque doorway is decorated with floral and geometric designs.

Interior – One is struck by the height of the building (22m/72ft in the main nave) and the simplicity of its decoration, characteristic of the art of Cluny. Huysmans (French novelist, 1848–1907) saw the symbol of the Trinity in the three naves, three bays supporting above the great arches three arcades surmounted by three windows. The choir and its ambulatory with three small apses – the Gallery of the Angels – make an elegant ensemble. The capitals of the delicate columns are a typical example of 12C Burgundian art. The oven-vaulted apse is decorated with a 14C fresco, representing a benedictory Christ in Majesty, which was brought to light only in 1935.

Musée Eucharistique du Hiéron

🕒Open Tue–Sun Jul–Aug 11am–6pm; 21 Mar–30 Jun and Sept–Dec 10am–noon, 2–6pM. 🕒Closed 1 Jan, 25 Dec–mid-Mar. ⸚4€. 🖉03 85 81 79 72. www.musee-hieron.com.

This museum of sacred art houses a varied collection: 13C to 18C Italian art including works from the schools of Florence (Donatello, Bramante), Venice, Rome and Bologna; a few works from Flanders and Germany (engravings by Lucas of Leyden and Dürer); and some from France, particularly a very beautiful 12C **tympanum**★ from the Brionnais priory at Anzy-le-Duc. In the turmoil of 1791 the doorway was taken to Château d'Arcy and then given to the museum.

Espace Saint-Jean

In the former house of the pages of Cardinal de Bouillon, this welcome centre for pilgrims has a film introduction to Paray-le-Monial, as well as several objects of convent life dating from the time of St Marguerite-Marie.

Parc des Chapelains

🕒Open mid-Jan–end Dec 9am–noon, 2–6pm; Sun 2–6pm. ♿ www.sanctuaires-paray.com.

It is in this large park, containing Stations of the Cross, that the great pilgrimage services take place. A diorama in the park depicts the life of St Marguerite-Marie.

Chapelle des Apparitions

🕒Open 6.30am–9pm. ♿

It was in this little chapel that St Marguerite-Marie had her main revelations. The silver-gilt reliquary in the right-hand chapel holds the saint's relics.

EXCURSIONS

Digoin

▶ 11km/6.8mi W.

This peaceful town, on the east bank of the Loire at the junction of two canals, is popular with anglers, ramblers and boaters. The early-19C **canal-bridge** was built 50 years before the Briare Bridge.

Château de Digoine

▶ *15km/9.4mi N on D 974.*
🕐 *Open Jul–Aug daily 2–7pm; May–Jun and Sept–Oct weekends and public holidays only.* ⊜*7€ (park 3.50€).* 𝒸*06 75 04 83 68. www.chateaude digoine.com.*

The main entrance to the château, built in the 18C on the site of a defensive castle, is fronted by a courtyard with a wrought-iron gate. On each side, two pavilions form the wings of the main building. The large park has a lake and there are three marked footpaths to guide you around.

ADDRESSES

🛏 STAY

⊜⊜**Grand Hôtel de la Basilique** – *18 r. de la Visitation.* 𝒸*03 85 81 11 13. www.hotelbasilique.com. Open 27 Mar– 30 Oct. 54 rooms.* ⊊ *7€, half board available.* ✕ *Set lunch menu 12–15€.*
The same family has run this place for five generations. Meals are served in a pleasant dining room with a traditional country décor. Several simple rooms, some with a view of the basilica.

⊜⊜**Hôtel Terminus** – *27 av. de la Gare.* 𝒸*03 85 81 59 31. www.terminus-paray.fr. Closed All Saints' Day and Sun.* 📶 *W-Fi. 16 rooms.* ⊊ *8€, half board available.* ✕.
A classic turn-of-the-century railway hotel, well-renovated and unmissable with its candy pink façade. Period foyer and comfortable bedrooms with smart bathrooms. Traditional cuisine, served alfresco on fine days on a terrace shaded by linden trees.

🍴 EAT

⊜⊜**La Poste et Hôtel La Reconce** – *71600 Poisson. 8km/5mi S of Paray-le-Monial on D 34.* 𝒸*03 85 81 10 72. Closed 1–15 Nov, Tue lunch and Mon from Jul to Sept. Set lunch menu 16 €. 7 rooms.* ⊊ *12€.* Traditional cooking based on local produce with a modern slant is the deal in this handsome Charolais building. Terrace shaded by plane trees. Quiet rooms are nicely decked out.

⊜⊜**Auberge de Vigny** – *71160 Digoin. 13km/8mi W of Paray-le-Monial.* 𝒸*03 85 81 10 13. Closed 9–30 Oct, 2–20 Jan, Sun evening from Nov to Mar, Mon and Tue.* 🚻📶. *Set lunch menu 16€.*
Contemporary cooking in an old classroom that oozes good cheer. The mistress here is an excellent pastry chef! Sunny garden terrace.

Charolles

Bygone capital of the counts of Charolais, the appealing little town of Charolles draws its charm from the rivers and canals winding through the old streets and the flower-decked squares, which invite relaxation. The distinctive white **Charolais cattle** raised on the rich pasture lands in this area are valued for their tasty beef. Regional cattle markets take place several times a year; hundreds of hardy animals are offered for sale by local breeders, valued for their ancestral know-how.

TOWN

The town is proud of the 14C vestiges of its castle: two towers known as the

▶ **Population:** 2 829
⏱ **Michelin Map:** 320: F-11.
ℹ **Info:** Ancien Couvent des Clarisses, 24 r. Baudinot, 71120 Charolles. 𝒸03 85 24 05 95. www.charolles.fr.
▶ **Location:** Paray-le-Monial lies between Digoin and Charolles, 71km/44mi E of Moulins and 66km/41mi W of Mâcon.
⊛ **Don't Miss:** Pilgrims flock to Paray-le-Monial in Jul and Aug, as well as the festival of St Marguerite-Marie on 16 Oct. Be sure to book hotels ahead.

Tour du Téméraire and Tour des Diamants, the latter now serving as the town hall. There is a nice **view** of the landscape from the terrace gardens. The tourist office is at the bottom of rue Baudinot, in a former Poor Clare's convent house, once home to St Marguerite-Marie Ala-coque (&see PARAY-LE-MONIAL).

Le Prieuré Sainte-Madeleine

Under the authority of the abbot at Cluny, this building welcomed pilgrims on their way to Santiago de Compost-ela. Note the collection of capitals and the remarkable carved beams of the chapter-house.

The priory also houses a **museum** (open Jun–Sept daily except Tue 2–6pm; rest of the year by appointment; 3€; 03 85 24 24 74) where you can see a collection of **earthenware**★ using the typical bright motifs of Charolles – flowers, butterflies, dragonflies – and, in particular, works by the region's seminal ceramics artist, Hippolyte Prost (1844–1892).

Maison du Charolais

Open daily 10am–6pm.
Closed late Dec, 1 May and 1 Nov.
4.60€. 03 85 88 04 00.
www.institut-charolais.com.
This attraction provides a wealth of information about the distinctive white **Charolais cattle** raised on the rich pas-ture lands in this area, which are highly valued for their meat.

EXCURSIONS
Mont des Carges★

12km/8mi E.
From the esplanade, with its monuments to the underground fighters of Beaubery and the Charolais battalion, an almost circular **view**★★ takes in the Loire country to the west, all the Charolais and Brionnais regions to the south and the mountains of Beaujolais to the east.

ADDRESSES

LIFE ON THE FARM

Ferme-Auberge de Lavaux – *71800 Châtenay. 8.5km/5.3mi E of La Clayette by D 987 then D 300. 03 85 28 08 48. Closed 1 Nov to Easter and Tue. Reserva-tions required. Meals.* This tastefully restored 19C farmhouse with old-fash-ioned turrets has a dining room under the eaves and a covered terrace. There is a charming room in the square tower, with antique furniture and a private balcony giving onto the courtyard.

Chambre d'Hôte M. et Mme Desmurs – *La Saigne, 71800 Varennes-sous-Dun. 4km/2.5mi E of La Clayette by D 987 then a minor road. 03 85 28 12 79. michelealaindesmurswanadoo.fr. 3 rooms. Meals.* This converted farmhouse is deep in the countryside. Two rooms are furnished in old-fash-ioned style and one suite has been set up under the eaves. You may want to choose the third room, quite charming with its stone walls and tiled floor. Warm, friendly welcome. Charolais cows are reared in the grounds.

Ferme-Auberge des Collines – *In the hamlet of Amanzé. 9km/5.6mi NW of Clayette by D 989 then D 279. 03 85 70 66 34. www.fermeaubergedescollines. com. Closed 1 Nov to Easter. Reserva-tions required. Meals.* The pretty square tower of this farmhouse testifies to its long-history. The sturdy beams, tiled floors and stone walls make for a strong rustic atmosphere. Peaceful rooms look out onto the fields or the flowery garden. Charolais cows and pigs are reared in the grounds. Home-grown vegetables.

SHOPPING

Les Chocolats Bernard-Dufoux – *32 r. Centrale 7180 La Clayette. 19k/11.8mi S of Charolles via the D 985. 03 85 28 08 10. www.chocolatsdufoux.com. Open daily 9am–7.30pm.* Widely regarded as being one of France's finest chocolatiers, Dufoux puts 40 years of experience into the creation of such delicacies as the golden palette of chocolates, and special spiced chocolate. He also gives lessons.

La Clayette

Renowned for its horse races and shows, La Clayette (pronounced La Claite) perches above the Genette Valley, its imposing fortified château rising above the gorgeous plane tree-shaded lake. Don't miss the sumptuous interiors of nearby Château de Drée. Nature, history and tradition are thick on the ground in the surrounding area.

TOWN

The town marks the border between the royal lands of the Mâconnais and the Duchy of Burgundy. Its coat of arms displays a horse, the symbol of an ancient tradition – it is said that **Henry IV**'s white horse was bred here. The **château** dates from the 14C – but was extensively altered in the 18C and 19C; huge carp swim in its moats.

EXCURSIONS
Varennes-sous-Dun

Learn all about wool weaving at the **Musée de la Filature** (*06 70 01 58 44; www.musee-filature.com; 5.80€ (under 16s 4.80€) in a 17C mill, and meet 25 breeds of sheep in the **moutonthèque**. Children can have fun feeding them.

Château de Drée★

*03 85 26 84 80. www.chateau-de-dree.com. 10€ (under 7s free).
The 17C château in Curbigny sports a profusion of trompe-l'œil painting, both inside and out. The façade is a splendid sight with its portico of ionic columns supporting a balcony and coat of arms. Inside, the rooms display a stunning collection of Louis XIV, XV and XVI **furniture**★★, Savonnerie carpets and opulent fabrics (the owners are a mill-owning family from the north). Note the Directoire-style dining room and the delightful Louis XV corner salon. But you will also find some of the château's more unexpected places equally fascinating, such as the bathroom, the stables and tack rooms, the kennels, the ice house, the lamp man's room, the dovecote and the prison.

- **Population:** 2 070
- **Michelin Map:** 320 12 F – Saône-et-Loire (71).
- **Info:** 3 rte de Charolles, 71800 La Clayette. *03 85 28 16 35. www.laclayette.fr.
- **Location:** La Clayette lies on D 985, between Charolles and Charlieu.
- **Kids:** Superb car collections in the museums of La Clayette and Chauffailles; feed the sheep at Plassard Woollen Mill in Varennes-sous-Dun.
- **Timing:** Go in June or July to see the rose gardens of Château de Drée and Jardin du Zéphyr in bloom.

A restored 10-hectare estate encloses gorgeous French **gardens** with rose gardens, fountains, topiary and elegant terraces (*Easter egg hunts take place here*).

Montagne de Dun

Take the road towards Chauffailles and head up to the 721m/2 365ft summit. Seen from the esplanade, the **panorama**★ sweeping over the surrounding area is spectacular.

Automusée du Beaujolais

*03 85 84 60 30. www.automusee.fr. .
The permanent collection runs to around 100 cars dating from 1900 to 1975. Most of the cars on display are for sale, which means there is always something new to see in the changing collection.

Jardin du Zéphyr★

In Anglure-sous-Dun, 14km/8.5mi SE on D 987. *03 85 26 06 47. http://lejardin-duzephyr.free.fr. 5€ (under 16s free).
The smell of roses leads the way up the rocky path. Once inside, you can feast on the sight and perfume of a profusion of tastefully chosen roses, perennials and shrubs, and enjoy basking in views of the surrounding hillsides.

Charlieu★

and the Churches and Château of the Brionnais

Pretty Charlieu was a bustling market town on the road linking the Saône and Loire valleys in Gallo-Roman times. These days it is a centre for the millinery and silk industries. However, it is Charlieu's archaeological treasures in particular that have won the town its renown.

BENEDICTINE ABBEY★

🕒 *Open Jul–Aug daily except Mon 10am–noon, 1–7pm. Rest of the year daily except Mon 10am–12.30pm, 2–6.30pm (5.30pm in winter).*
🕒 *Closed Jan and 25 Dec.*
🎫 *4.30€.* ✆ *04 77 60 09 97.*

The abbey was founded c. 872, attached to Cluny c. 930, converted into a priory c. 1040 and then fortified on the orders of Philippe Auguste, its protector. The architects and artists from Cluny collaborated here with particularly happy results to rebuild the 11C church and add on the 12C narthex. Excavations show that a small 9C church was replaced by a 10C church, which was replaced in turn by an 11C abbey church, on a slightly different axis. This church had a nave with four bays and aisles either side, a transept with transept chapels and an ambulatory with radiating chapels

▶ **Population:** 3 624
♿ **Michelin Map:** 320: F-13.
🛈 **Info:** Maison de Pays, pl. Saint-Philibert, 42190 Charlieu. ✆04 77 60 12 42. www.ville-charlieu.fr.
▷ **Location:** Charlieu lies 20km N of Roanne on D482. In July and August, the tourist office offers tours of the Old Town; otherwise pick up a leaflet from them and follow the arrows set into the pavements.
◉ **Don't Miss:** Charlieu's Benedictine abbey, or Anzy-le-Duc and its church, among the loveliest in the area, on the Brionnais driving tour.

opening off it. The abbey was not to escape the ravages of the Revolution, however; the Benedictine priory, which at the time still housed two monks, was secularised in March 1789. The abbey buildings and the church of St-Fortunat, one of the finest of Cluny's daughters, were largely demolished. All that remains of the church are the narthex and the first bay, in which the capitals bear a resemblance to those of the

Cloister and the chapterhouse, Benedictine Abbey

© Christian Guy/hemis.fr

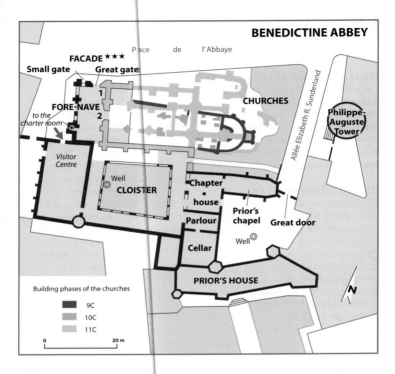

BENEDICTINE ABBEY

Place de l'Abbaye

FACADE ★★★
Small gate   Great gate

FORE-NAVE
to the charter room

Visitor Centre

Well
CLOISTER

CHURCHES

Allée Elizabeth R. Sunderland

Philippe-Auguste Tower

Chapter house
Prior's chapel   Great door
Parlour
Cellar   Well

PRIOR'S HOUSE

Building phases of the churches
  9C
  10C
  11C

0   20 m

N

Brionnais. The warm golden glow of the stone of the abbey buildings adds to the charm of the scene.

There is a good view of the two doorways, which are the abbey's best feature, from place de l'Abbaye.

Façade★★★

The north façade of the narthex is entered through a **great doorway**, dating from the 12C, which is decorated with some wonderful sculpture work. Christ in Majesty is depicted on the tympanum in a mandorla, supported by two angels and surrounded by the symbols of the four Evangelists. On the lintel, the Virgin Mary appears with two attendant angels and the 12 disciples. The arch mouldings and the columns which frame the doorway are decorated with geometrical and floral motifs. The abbey owed this luxuriant plant-like decoration, of Eastern inspiration, to the Crusades. The inside of the left doorpost bears a representation of Lust, depicted as a woman grappling with frightful reptilian monsters.

The **small gate**, to the right of the great gate, also dates from the 12C. The Wedding at Cana is depicted on its tympanum, the Transfiguration of Christ on its archivolt and an Old Testament sacrifice on the lintel.

As you enter, you will see to your left the foundations of the various churches which have stood on this site. They can be seen more clearly from the Salle du Chartrier.

Cloisters

These were built in the 15C to replace the previous ones, which were Romanesque. The east gallery contains six huge arches supported on twin colonnettes, whose capitals are richly decorated with sculpted acanthus leaves, birds and geometrical motifs.

Chapter-house

This dates from the early 16C and features pointed arches supported on a round stone pillar, into which a lectern has been carved.

Prior's chapel

This dates from the late 15C. The old terracotta floor tiling has been reconstructed based on the original. Above the chapel is a bell turret with a timber roof. The next two rooms form the **Musée Armand-Charnay**.

Parlour

This lovely vaulted room dating from the early 16C houses a **lapidary museum** in which, next to old capitals from the priory, note two bas-relief sculptures: a 10C Carolingian one depicting Daniel in the Lions' Den and a 12C one depicting the Annunciation amid interlaced arches.

Cellar

The cellar, beneath two semicircular vaults, houses a museum of sacred art including a lovely collection of polychrome wood statues from the 15C to the 18C. Note in particular a Virgin Mary with Bird, from the church in Aiguilly (near Roanne), and a Virgin with Child, both Gothic dating from the 15C.

Narthex

This rectangular building, 17m/56ft long and about 10m/33ft wide, comprises two rooms, one above the other, with ribbed vaulting.

One of these contains a **Gallo-Roman sarcophagus** (**1**) which was found in the crypt of the Carolingian church. The east wall of the narthex is the former west front of the 11C church of St-Fortunat, consecrated in 1094, comprising: a doorway (**2**), on the tympanum framed by three well-defined arch mouldings, Christ is depicted in Majesty in a mandorla held by two angels; two twin windows with arch mouldings, and above, a pair of figures facing each other.

Charter room
(Salle du Chartrier)

A spiral staircase leads up to this room, which is also known as the Salle des Archives. It contains an exhibition on the history of the abbey.

The great window to the east has two small blind arcades either side of it, and beautiful arch mouldings above it which are supported on engaged columns with capitals decorated with foliage. From here there is a good view of the site of the previous churches – the outline of each of their foundations shows up in the grass. The view also takes in the Philippe-Auguste tower, the prior's lodging (*not open to the public*) and the rooftops of the town.

Before leaving the abbey, have a quick look down into the courtyard of the prior's lodging.

Philippe-Auguste Tower

This imposing tower of ochre-coloured stone, was built c. 1180 on the orders of Philippe-Auguste, who considered the fortified town of Charlieu to be of great use to the French crown. It was part of the abbey's fortifications.

WALKING TOUR

Follow the route marked on the town plan (see p170).

Strolling through the streets near place St-Philibert, you will come across numerous picturesque houses dating from the 13C to the 18C. On the corner of place St-Philibert and rue Grenette stands a 13C stone house which has twin windows with colonnettes as mullions on its upper floor.

Église St-Philibert

This 13C church, which has no transept, has a layout typical of 13C Burgundian architecture: a nave with five bays, side aisles and a rectangular chancel. It houses some beautiful works of art, such as a 15C pulpit hewn from a single block of stone and 15C and 16C stalls with pretty painted panels. One chapel contains a 16C Madonna (Notre-Dame-de-Charlieu). In the chapel of Ste-Anne on the south side of the chancel there is a 15C polychrome stone altarpiece depicting the Visitation and the Nativity.

The chapel of St-Crépin on the north side of the chancel contains a 17C Pietà and a statuette of St-Crispin, patron saint of shoemakers and saddlers.

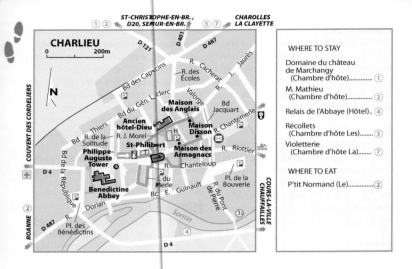

ST-CHRISTOPHE-EN-BR.,
D20, SEMUR-EN-BR.

CHAROLLES
LA CLAYETTE

WHERE TO STAY

Domaine du château
de Marchangy
(Chambre d'hôte).............. ①

M. Mathieu
(Chambre d'hôte).............. ②

Relais de l'Abbaye (Hôtel).. ④

Récollets
(Chambre d'hôte Les)........ ③

Violetterie
(Chambre d'hôte La)........ ⑦

WHERE TO EAT

P'tit Normand (Le)..............②

Ancien Hôtel-Dieu

The 18C hospital has a beautiful façade overlooking rue Jean-Morel and consists of two huge rooms for the sick, separated by a chapel in which there is a handsome 17C gilded wood altar. The building now houses two museums.

The **Musée de la Soierie**★ (open Jul–Aug daily except Mon 10am–1pm, 2–7pm; rest of the year 2–6pm; closed Jan; 4.30€; 04 77 60 28 84; www.amisdesartscharlieu.com) documents the history of the silk industry in Charlieu. The large room on the left houses the statue of Notre-Dame-de-Septembre, patron of the powerful weavers' guild, in whose honour there is an annual procession (2nd Sunday in September). The exhibition includes samples of local silk production (sumptuous clothing, one-off creations commissioned by aristocratic families etc.) and impressive old looms, giving a good overview of the technical developments in weaving from the 18C on. All the equipment on display is in working order, and from time to time there is a **demonstration**★. On the first floor there is a display of materials and designer clothes as well as a video on silk weaving techniques.

The Hôtel-Dieu, where for three centuries the sisters of the Order of St Martha cared for the sick, closed its doors in 1981 and reopened as a museum. The **Musée**

Hospitalier (as for the Musée de la Soierie) is a faithful representation of a small provincial hospital from the end of the 19C through the 1950s. The apothecary is fitted with 18C woodwork to accommodate medicinal herbs, flacons with ground-glass stoppers and ceramic urns. Past the operating and treatment rooms, the wooden linen press, the work of regional craftsmen, has room for 850 sheets. The wealth of bedding was due to the infrequency of wash days, which only came around twice a year. One of the two large wards has been recreated with its rows of curtained beds.

◗ Continue along rue Jean-Morel and stop outside no 32.

The **Maison des Anglais** dating from the 16C, has mullioned windows on its upper storey with Gothic niches in between them. Two watch-turrets frame the façade.

◗ Turn right onto rue André-Farinet.

No. 29: 13C stone house; no. 27: 15C half-timbered house, the **Maison Disson**; on the corner opposite, no. 22: old 14C salt warehouse.

◗ Turn right again onto rue Charles-de-Gaulle.

At no. 9, the 13C–14C **Maison des Armagnacs** has two twin windows surmounted by trefoil arches. That on the left is decorated with a floral motif, and that on the right with a human face. The upper storey is half-timbered and overhangs the street.

▷ *Take rue Michon and then rue Chanteloup, a shopping street, to reach rue du Merle.*

On the corners of rue du Merle and rue des Moulins (no. 11), and of rue des Moulins and place St-Philibert, stand old half-timbered houses.

FURTHER OUT
Couvent des Cordeliers★

⊙*Open Jul–Aug daily except Mon 10am–noon, 1–7pm. Rest of the year times vary.* ⊙*Closed Dec–Jan.* ⊸4€. ✆04 77 60 07 42.

This Franciscan monastery was founded in the 13C in St-Nizier-sous-Charlieu. Its unprotected site outside the town walls meant that it suffered quite a lot of damage both during the Hundred Years War and at the hands of roving bands of mercenaries. The monastery buildings have recently undergone restoration.

The **Gothic cloisters**, of pale gold stone, were sold to the United States and were to be taken down and rebuilt there, but luckily they were rescued at the last minute by the French State, which managed to buy them back in 1910. The arcades (late 14C–15C) are decorated with a fascinating variety of plant motifs. The capitals along the north arcade depict vices and virtues in an amusing series of figures and animals; one capital portrays the expressive face of a monk, another has the dance of death as its theme. The west arcade is adorned with a frieze of oak leaves with snails, rabbits and caterpillars on the capitals.

The single-nave church (late 14C), with no transept, has three side chapels on its south side (late 15C–early 16C) and has been partially restored. Originally, it was entirely decorated with paintings, but only a few mural paintings now remain in the chancel.

🚗 DRIVING TOUR

CHURCHES AND CHÂTEAUX OF THE BRIONNAIS★★

Allow one day. Drive W out of Charlieu along D 487 then D 4.

This part of south Burgundy, with Semur-en-Brionnais at its heart, is a tranquil corner with an impressive architectural heritage. The rolling countryside, dotted with churches and castles, is given over mainly to cattle rearing. At the peak of its power, the great abbey at Cluny (♦ *see CLUNY*) had a great impact on the religious architecture of the Brionnais, and there are still about a dozen Romanesque churches in the area well worth seeing. Part of their beauty is down to the local materials. The medieval stonemasons found the yellowish, fine-grained limestone of the region relatively easy to work but at the same time very durable, making it ideal for decorative sculpture on façades and doorways. It gives the churches a lovely warm colour, which looks particularly striking in the rays of the setting sun.

La Bénisson-Dieu

The village **church** and the imposing 15C square bell tower in front of it are all that remains of the abbey founded in the 12C by disciples of St Bernard, which became a convent in the 17C. The early-Gothic nave is roofed with superb glazed tiles forming diamond motifs.

▷ *Drive back towards the Loire, cross the river and turn left onto D 482.*

Iguerande

The 12C church is at the top of a steep hill overlooking the Loire and offering an interesting view of the Loire Valley, the Forez to the left and the Madeleine hills to the right. The nave and the chancel contain some unusual capitals; note, in particular, the musician-cyclop at the top of the first pillar on the left.

Marcigny

This picturesque town close to the Loire, on the edge of the Brionnais region, has some 16C timber-framed houses (round the church) and a mansion dating from 1735 (between place du Cours and place Reverchon).

The 15C tower, **Tour du Moulin** (◎open Jul–Aug 10am–12.30pm, 2–5pm; rest of year times vary; ⊜3.50€; ℘03 85 25 37 05), once part of a Benedictine priory, has unusual walls decorated with stone cannon-balls. It houses a museum of local history, with everything from sculptures to chemist's jars in Nevers faience.

▷ *Follow D 10 towards Charolles.*

Anzy-le-Duc★

This hillside village in the Arconce Valley possesses one of the most beautiful Romanesque churches in the area.

The harmonious **church**★ in golden stone was probably built in the early 11C. Its fine doorway is now in the Musée du Hiéron in Paray-le-Monial. There is a magnificent Romanesque belfry, a polygonal tower with three storeys of bays. The nave is roofed with groined vaulting and lit through the clerestory windows. The capitals have been well preserved; those in the nave represent biblical and allegorical scenes. The frescoes of the apse,

Detail of the capital of the Romanesque church, Anzy-le-Duc

© Franck Guiziou/hemis.fr

now in poor condition, portray the lives of St John the Baptist and Hugues d'Anzy. Those in the choir show the Ascension of Christ.

☺*If you have time, make a short detour N along D 174 then drive directly to Varenne along D 130.*

Montceaux-l'Étoile

The doorway of the church features a tympanum and lintel carved out of one block of stone, illustrating the Ascension as at Anzy-le-Duc and St-Julien-de-Jonzy. The arching framing the tympanum rests on columns decorated with capitals.

▷ *In Bornat, turn right onto D 34.*

Varenne-l'Arconce

The **church** looks rather massive owing to its projecting transept and square tower. Its decoration was limited by the use of hard sandstone as building material. Note the elegant tympanum surmounting the south doorway and depicting the Agnus Dei.

Château de Chaumont

5km/3mi SE along D 158 (near Oyé).
The Renaissance façade is flanked by a round tower, the other façade in the Gothic style is modern.

▷ *Head towards Semur via St-Chris-tophe-en-Brionnais, famous for its cattle markets held on Thursday mornings.*

Semur-en-Brionnais★

The small town is on a promontory covered with vines and fruit trees. The château, the Romanesque church, the former priory and 18C court room (now the *mairie*, or town hall) make an attractive ensemble in pinkish stone.

The **Église St-Hilaire**★ (☛guided tours by request; ℘03 85 25 13 57) in the Cluniac style, has an elegant octagonal belfry decorated with a double band of twin Romanesque arcades; the upper band is framed by a series of recessed arches.

The west doorway is richly decorated. The lintel depicts a scene from the life

DIGOIN PARAY-LE-MONIAL MÂCON

Montceaux-l'Étoile
Bornat D 20
Anzy-le-Duc
Varenne-l'Arconce Chaumont
Chaumont Drée
Oyé
St-Christophe
Marcigny St-Laurent La Clayette
Artaix Semur-en-Brionnais
St-Julien-de-Jonzy Montagne de Dun
Jardin du Zéphyr
Stèle de Bagneaux Châteauneuf
Melay Iguerande Chauffailles
La Bénisson-Dieu Charlieu Sornin

BRIONNAIS
0 6 km
N

ROANNE

of St Hilary of Poitiers: condemned by a council of bishops, he sets off into exile, a begging bag on his shoulder; on the road he meets an angel who returns him to his place among the bishops; meanwhile the devil makes off with the soul of the Council President.

The nave is attractive; at the west end the triforium, which consists of an arcade with twin arch stones, forms a bowed gallery which is supported by an impressive corbel springing from the keystone of the west door. The gallery may be an imitation of the chapel of St-Michel above the west door of Cluny abbey church.

The 9C rectangular keep of the **Château St-Hugues** (◔ open mid-May–mid-Sept 10am–noon, 2–7pm, Sun and public holidays 2–7pm; rest of the year times vary; ◌3€; ℘03 85 25 13 57; www.semur-en-brionnais-vp.fr) was the birthplace of the famous abbot St Hugh of Cluny. The two round towers served as a prison in the 18C.

▷ *Follow D 9 for 5km.*

St-Julien-de-Jonzy

From its position on top of one of the highest hills in the area, the village offers a fine panorama of the Brionnais and Beaujolais rolling countryside.

The present church has retained the square bell tower and lovely carved **doorway**★ of its 12C Romanesque predecessor. The tympanum and lintel are carved out of a single block of sandstone. The former shows the Last Supper; all the heads except two were damaged in 1793.

▷ *Drive E along D 8.*

Châteauneuf

The church, standing out against its wooded setting, was one of the last Romanesque buildings erected in Burgundy; the west front is massive, the south doorway has an interesting lintel featuring a naïve representation of the 12 Apostles. Inside, note the clerestory windows in the nave with their slender columns decorated with capitals and, surmounting the transept, the dome on squinches with its octagonal base and arcaded gallery.

▷ *Return to Charlieu along D 987.*

ADDRESSES

🏠 STAY

➿➿ **Hôtel Relais de l'Abbaye** – *415 rte du Beaujolais. ℘04 77 60 00 88. www.relais-abbaye.fr.* 🅿 *Wi-Fi. 27 rooms.* 😋 *10 €, half board available.* ✕ *Set lunch menu 15 €.* This recently renovated hostelry welcomes visitors to its well-kept rooms. Sizeable garden with playground for children. Traditional French cuisine in the large, contemporary dining room with a fireplace for cold nights.

➿➿ **Chambre d'hôte M. Mathieu** – *71600 Sermaize-du-Bas. Take D 34, then D 458 to Poisson towards St-Julien-de-Civry. ℘03 85 81 06 10. Open 15 Mar–11 Nov.* 🅿 🚳 *5 rooms.* 😋*.* An old yellow stone hunting lodge with smart rooms reached through a round tower; the family furniture adds personal touches, and the welcome is friendly.

➿➿ **Chambre d'hôte La Violetterie** – *71740 St-Maurice-lès-Châteauneuf. 10km/6.2mi NE on D 987 (direction La Clayette). ℘03 85 26 26 60. Closed 11 Nov–Easter.* 🅿 🚳 *3 rooms.* 😋 ✕*.* This 19C mansion is charming with its perron and its gate fronting the courtyard. The bedrooms are light and open onto the garden. The large dining hall-lounge features wainscoting and a fine fireplace. Charming hospitality.

➿➿➿ **Chambres d'hôte Les Récollets** – *4 pl. du Champ-de-Foire, 71110 Marcigny, 22km/13.5mi NW on D 487, D 482 and D 982. ℘03 85 25 05 16. www.lesrecollets.com.* 🅿 🚳 *5 rooms.* 😋*.* Renovation is still under way, but the attraction of this 17C former convent is clear as you are greeted in a relaxing atmosphere. The kitchen and dining room have retained their old world charm, while the bedrooms are good-sized and prettily decorated. Swimming pool. Wine and cookery-themed weekends.

➿➿➿ **Chambre d'hôte Domaine du château de Marchangy** – *Château de Marchangy, 42190 St-Pierre-la-Noaille. 5.5km/3.4mi NW on D 227, then secondary road. ℘04 77 69 96 76. www.marchangy.com.* 🅿 🚳 *3 rooms.* 😋*.* Set in lush parkland, this 18C château features a series of outbuildings, stables, a farmhouse and a courtyard. The calm, cosy and spacious rooms all have canopied beds. Relax on the terrace or by the pool and enjoy the view of the surrounding vineyards.

🍴 EAT

➿ **Le P'tit Normand** – *8 r. Chanteloup. ℘04 77 60 38 29. Closed Sun eve and Mon. Set lunch menu 10.50 €.* Expect the warmest of welcomes in this charming little restaurant on the semi-pedestrianised strip in Charlieu. On the menu are good value, hearty fixed-price menus; the home-made rabbit terrine comes particularly recommended. Smartly intimate interior.

➿➿ **La Colline du Colombier** – *71340 Iguerande. 3.5km/2mi SW on D 9 and secondary road. ℘03 85 84 07 24. www.troisgros.com. Closed mid-Nov to end-Feb, Thu from Sept to June, and Wed.* ♿ 🅿 *Set lunch menu 25 €.* This former farm in the middle of countryside above the Loire has been made over in a rustic-chic style with exposed stone and beams. Fine cooking with local accents.

➿➿ **Le Moulin de Rongefer** – *300 chemin de Rongefer, 42190 St-Nizier-sous-Charlieu. ℘04 77 60 01 57. lemoulinderongefer.fr. Closed 16 Aug–10 Sept, 15 Jan–5 Feb, Sun and Tue eve, and Wed* 🅿*.* Arrows guide you to this former mill on the bank of the Sornin River. The comfortable rustic dining room opens out to a lovely flower-decked terrace.

🛍 SHOPPING

BRIONNAIS

Leblanc – *71340 Iguerande. ℘03 85 84 07 83. Open daily 9am–7pm.* On the shelves of this boutique you'll find hazelnut oil, pistachios, pine nuts, toasted sesame seeds and a selection of fine vinegars as well as mustards ground by hand on site. Take a look at the mustard mill, used by the family since 1878.

Bourbon-Lancy★

Built on a hillside at the gateway to the Loire Valley and the Bourbonnais Plains, Bourbon-Lancy is both a venerable old town and a well-reputed spa resort with a casino and golf course. The Route of Southern Burgundy Châteaux passes close by, at the Château de St-Aubin. To the north, Ternant pulls in art lovers, while Luzy is a magnet for hikers.

OLD TOWN

Near the town hall, the bell tower (late 14C) sits atop a fortified gateway, now known as the **tour de l'Horloge**★. Have a look at the "bredin", a mechanical figure who sounds the hours by sticking his tongue out.

In Rue de l'Horloge, pause to admire a richly decorated 16C **wooden house**★ with a single-angled column, sculpted capitals, bracketed windows and glazed medallions. Continue along Rue Notre-Dame and cast an eye over the garden of the collegiate church. Pass beneath the porch of the Guy de Salin mansion and turn right onto the ramparts (complete circuit 4km/2.5mi) to see the two guards' turrets.

Straight ahead the view opens to reveal a fine **panorama**. The path passes beneath an acacia grove before you climb to the left towards the Sacré-Cœur church, near the town hall.

Bourbon-Expo

Guided tour (1hr) by request Jul–Aug 3pm–6pm. Closed Mar. 2 € (children free). 03 85 89 23 23.

This museum looks back over the agricultural machinery made by the Puzenat factory (1874–1956), which revolutionised farmwork at the start of the 20th century. Z-shaped harrows, harvesting and threshing machines, haymaking rakes before they were fitted with hefty motors. Another room deals with woodworking and its tools of the trade.

▶ **Population:** 5 502

Michelin Map: Map B4 – Michelin Departements Map 320 C10 – Saône-et-Loire (71).

Info: Pl. d'Aligre – 71140 Bourbon-Lancy. 03 85 89 18 27. www.bourbon-lancy.com.

Location: Bourbon-Lancy lies downhill from Digoin on D 979.

Kids: Exploring the area around Luzy using the local walking trails.

Timing: Turn up on time to see the "bredin" ring in the hours with his tongue. And for a spot of relaxation, make time for a trip to the new Celtô fitness centre.

Don't Miss: Visit the old town and its quirky Tour de l'Horloge, then nose around the classy interiors of the Château de St-Aubin on the banks of the Loire. Admire the Aubusson tapestries telling the story of Esther in Luzy town hall, then check out the superb Flemish triptychs in the church at Ternant.

Saint-Nazaire church and museum

Open Jul–Aug 3pm–6pm.
Guided tour(1hr) by advance request. Closed Mar. 2 € (children free). 03 85 89 18 27.

This Romanesque-style edifice with a panelled ceiling and basilica floorplan augmented by a transept, was a dependency of the cluniac priory founded by Ancel de Bourbon. Its museum was set up in 1901 to house local antiquities (such as the Gallo-Roman Venus figures discovered in 1984), stone artefacts from local churches, as well as 19C paintings and sculptures – notably those by Puvis de Chavannes.

THERMAL QUARTER
Hospice d'Aligre
In the chapel is an attractive carved pulpit, which was a present from Louis XIV to Miss Élisabeth d'Aligre, the abbess of St-Cyr in 1687. To the left of the chapel on the landing of the grand staircase is a silver statue of her offspring, the marchioness d'Aligre (1776–1843), the hospital's benefactress.

Thermal Spa
The hot springs rise in the courtyard of the baths at a temperature of 56–60 °C, supplying over 400 000 l/88 000 gallons daily. In use since Roman times, they are beneficial for treating circulatory and rheumatic conditions (arthritis).

EXCURSIONS
Château de Saint-Aubin★
◗ 7km/4.3mi S on D 979.
🕔Open 2pm–6pm. 🚫Closed Sat. ☜9 € (under 18s 6 €). ℘03 85 53 95 20. www.chateaudestaubin.com.
Dominating the Loire, the elegant honey-hued Neoclassical pile was built in the 1770s by the architect Verniquet as a hunting lodge for the president of the Aix-en-Provence parliament. The furniture and decoration throughout the interior is refined.
Enjoy the portraits of the Saint-Mauris family (15C–19C), and finish on the chaises longues by the kennels at the foot of a vast kitchen garden.

Signal de Mont★
◗ 8km/5mi N on D 60.
🔁 15min round trip. From the viewpoint, the **panorama**★ spans the Loire Valley, Morvan hills, the Uchon signal point, the Charolais, the Bourbonnais mountain, and on a clear day, the Auvergne peaks.

Ternant★
◗ 19km/12mi NE on D 973 then D 223.
A must for art lovers in the Nivernais and Morvan, the modest village church of Ternant houses two magnificent Flemish triptychs.
Church Triptychs★★ The 15C works in carved wood are richly painted and gilded. They were gifted to the church by Baron Philippe de Ternant, chamberlain to the Burgundian Duke Philippe le Bon, and his son Charles.
The **grand triptych** depicts the Passion of Christ: the central panel shows his death; beneath, the Virgin faints and is supported by St John; in the foreground, the donor Charles de Ternant and his wife Jeanne are shown kneeling. In the left-hand panel, the Pietà scene shows the Virgin Mary surrounded by St John, Mary Magdalen and the holy women. On the right, Christ is entombed.
The older **small triptych** is a work of sublime delicacy dedicated to the Virgin. The Dormition scene in the centre of the carved panel shows an angel carrying off her soul, represented as a young girl praying. Above this, the Assumption scene shows Mary carried to heaven on a crescent moon borne by an angel – the only such image in existence.

Luzy
◗ 28km/17.3mi NE on D 973.
Pl. Chanzy, 58170 Luzy. ℘03 86 30 02 65. 🕔Open 25 Apr–10 Sept daily except Sun. 🚫Closed 1 and 8 May, Ascension Day, Whit Sun and Mon, 14 Jul, 15 Aug. www.mairie-luzy.fr.
An important town in the Middle Ages, Luzy flourished again when the circular keep of the barons' tower appeared in the 14C. Nowadays it is a pleasant spot astride the river Alène on the southern edge of the Morvan region. A network of walking trails makes a great way to explore the area.
Tapisseries de l'hôtel de ville (🕔open 9am–noon, 1.30pm–5pm, Sat 9am–11.30am, closed Sun; ☜ free entry; ℘03 86 30 02 34; ♿) is an astonishing collection of 18C Aubusson tapestries that tell the story of **Esther**, who freed the Hebrews exiled in Persia, an episode which inspired one of Racine's works. The two main compositions and six panels of individual characters are realised in beautifully fresh colours.

Le Creusot-Montceau

Created in 1970, the conurbation of Le Creusot-Montceau is an interesting place to learn more about France's industrial heritage, thanks to its wealth of mines, foundries, factories, workshops and workers' settlements.

A BIT OF HISTORY

Development of industry – Although iron ore was mined in the Middle Ages in the region of Couches, the discovery of vast coal deposits at Épinac, Le Creusot and Blanzy in the 17C marked the real origin of the industrial development of the whole area. Industrial exploitation really began in 1769 and by 1782, The Royal Foundry of Montcenis consisted of a foundry and blast-furnaces.

City of steel – In 1836 **Joseph-Eugène Schneider**, forge-master at Bazeilles, and his brother, **Adolphe Schneider**, set themselves up at Le Creusot, at that time a little township of 3 000 inhabitants. The rapid expansion of the Schneider works was to contribute to the wealth of the town, which from that date increased its population tenfold.

LE CREUSOT

Château de la Verrerie★

The crystal manufactory which supplied Marie-Antoinette , and later home of the Schneider family, now houses the tourist office and various exhibits on the region's industrial heritage.

In front of the **château** stand two huge conical glass-firing ovens. They were converted in 1905, one into a **miniature theatre** and the other into a chapel now used for temporary exhibitions.

The **Écomusée** (◔ open Jul–Sept, Mon–Fri 10am–noon, 1–6pm; weekends 2.30–6.30pm; rest of year times vary; ◔ closed 1 Jan, 25 Dec; ⚫6€; ℘03 85 73 92 00; www.ecomusee-creusot -monceau.com) covers the history of Le Creusot and the life of the Schneiders, among other things, through displays of everything from crystal to tools.

▶ **Population:** 92 000
ⓖ **Michelin Map:** 320: G-9.
ⓘ **Info:** Château de la Verrerie, 71200 Le Creusot. ℘03 85 55 02 46. www.le-creusot.fr.
◐ **Location:** The Le Creusot basin, on the northeast edge of the Massif Central, is a natural depression containing the towns of Montceau-les-Mines, Blanzy, Montchanin and Le Creusot.

Crystals on display, Écomusée Creusot Montceau, Château de la Verrerie

Document Écomusée Creusot Montceau/cliché Daniel Busseuil

EXCURSIONS

Promenade des Crêtes

◐ Follow rue Jean-Jaurès, rue de Longwy, D 28 (towards Marmagne) and a sharp right-hand turn to join this scenic road.

The switch-back road overlooks the Le Creusot basin. A clearing in the woods (viewing table) provides an overall view of the town and its surroundings. Further on another viewpoint reveals the extent of the old Schneider works and the central position, in this context, of the Château de la Verrerie.

Blanzy

At the **Musée de la Mine** (ⓖ ◔open Jul–Aug daily except Tue 2–5pm; Mar–Jun and 1 Sept–11 Nov Sat–Sun 2–5pm;

∞5€; ☎03 85 68 22 85; www.ecomusee-creusot-monceau.com), a 22m/72ft-high head frame marks the location of the former St-Claude mine shaft, which was worked from 1857 to 1881, and has now been refitted with its original equipment: light maintenance, machinery in working order (for operating lifts and pumping water). Former miners show visitors round galleries where extracting and pit-propping techniques are illustrated (15min audio-visual presentation).

Écuisses

In Écuisses, the **Musée du Canal** (🕓 open May–Sept daily 10am–noon, 2–6pm (Sun 2–7pm); rest of year 2–6pm; ∞3.10€; ☎03 85 78 97 04) is an annexe of the Écomusée. Housed in an 18C lock-keeper's house and in a barge, *L'Armançon*, tells the history of inland water transport and *bargees*. Boat trips are organised in summer.

Mont-St-Vincent★

▶ *12km/7.5mi SE of Montceau–les-Mines.* The Charollais village stands on a bluff, on the watershed between the Loire and the Saône. It is one of the highest peaks (603m/1 987ft) in the Saône-et-Loire. The **church**, built at the end of the 11C, was once a priory of Cluny Abbey.

Above the doorway is a carved tympanum, now badly damaged, showing Christ in Majesty between two figures, believed to be St Peter and St Paul. There is transverse barrel vaulting, similar to that in St-Philibert in Tournus, in the nave and groined vaulting in the aisles.

Gourdon

▶ *9km/5.6mi S of Montceau-les-Mines on D 980.*

A narrow road climbs steeply to Gourdon, where a sweeping **panorama**★ opens onto the town, the Blanzy basin, Montcenis, Le Creusot, and the more distant Morvan hills. This little hill village has an 11C Romanesque **church**, with a blind triforium, high windows and an engaging collection of capitals. Restoration has work brought 12C frescoes whose central theme is the vision of the Apocalypse.

ADDRESSES

🛏 STAY

⊜⊜ **La Petite Verrerie** – *4 r. J. Guesde.* ☎03 85 73 97 97. www.hotelfp-lecreusot.com. Closed 23 Dec–3 Jan. 43 rooms. ⊑11.50€. Restaurant⊜⊜. Formerly a factory pharmacy, then an employee club and finally, in its latest incarnation, a spacious hotel imbued with the history of the city. Newly renovated rooms.

⊜⊜ **Hôtel Le Moulin Rouge** – *71670 Le Breuil. 3km/1.9mi E of Le Creusot by D 290.* ☎03 85 55 14 11. www.le-moulin-rouge.com. Closed 20 Dec–10 Jan, Fri evenings, Sat lunchtime and Sun evenings. 31 rooms. ⊑9€. Restaurant⊜⊜. This hotel located near a farmhouse is a haven of peace. Large, comfortable rooms decorated in the classical tradition. Meals are served in two dining rooms, one of which has a fireplace. Have a nap in the garden or down by the pool.

🍴 EAT

⊜⊜ **Moulin de Galuzot** – *In Galuzot, 71230 St-Vallier. 5km/3.1mi SW of Montceau-les-Mines by N 70 and D 974.* ☎03 85 57 18 85. Closed 20 Jul–14 Aug, Tue evenings, Sun evenings and Wed. A typical country inn on the banks of the Bourbince Canal. Meals are served in two dining rooms on a raised platform: one with a colourful setting and old-fashioned chairs, the second with a more rustic touch. Traditional fare.

⊜⊜ **Le France** – *7 pl. Beaubernard, 71300 Montceau-les-Mines.* ☎03 85 67 95 30. www.jeromebrochot.com. Closed 6–20 Jan and 29 Jul–19 Aug, Sat lunch, Sun evening and Mon. Tucked away from the bustling town centre, this friendly restaurant is run by a charming young couple. Lovingly prepared dishes are served in an elegant dining room with fireplace. The smallish rooms are light and very quiet.

Countryside, crusades, churches, châteaux and pilgrimages to Compostela all play their part in the story of the Morvan. The Celtic word meaning "Black Mountain" is an apt enough description for the densely wooded hills rising from lush plains and farmland. If you want to immerse yourself in the great outdoors as an antidote to over-indulgence at Burgundy's rich table, the Morvan's vast network of marked trails for walking, riding and biking, and lakes and rivers for water sports are just the job. Culture hounds are in for a treat too – Vézelay's Romanesque basilica is a place of great beauty, and Avallon, Autun and Saulieu are all unmissable sights of history and culture.

The Great Outdoors

Pack your hiking boots and make for the information centre in the Maison du Parc – the HQ of the Morvan National Park – your first port of call for maps and leaflets about the spider's web of marked trails that run through the park's splendid forests. Whether you're into walking, mountain biking, horse riding or canoeing, there's something for everyone here.

There's also one of the five branches of the Écomusée du Morvan here, a splendid set of sites that explains every aspect of the traditions of this unique area. Not surprisingly, this vast forest was a stronghold of the French Resistance in World War II, a moving subject that is also dealt with in a fascinating display.

If water sports are more your thing, head for the Base Nautique at the Lac des Settons, a huge reservoir that is a playground for sailing, canoeing, windsurfing and other water-based fun. Now that the timber felled from the forests travels by truck rather than floats out to Paris by river and lake, the Rivers Yonne, Cousin and Cute provide further leisure opportunities.

Even if your level of fitness isn't up to taking on the more demanding long-distance trails, you can enjoy easy short strolls, or take driving tours, including the forest track to the Haut-Folin, the highest peak of the Morvan at 901m/2956ft.

Cultural Morvan

You want history? Vézelay has it in spades: follow the footsteps of medieval pilgrims to this hilltop village and explore one of France's true gems. The relics of Mary Magdalene are said to be housed in the golden Romanesque

Highlights

1 Immerse yourself in the forest trails of the **Morvan** (p182)

2 **Vézelay**'s sublime Romanesque basilica (p192)

3 Stroll around splendid fortified **Avallon** (p197)

4 Make a foodie pilgrimage to **Saulieu** to sample gastronomic delights (p199)

5 Autun's cathedral and Roman remains (p203)

basilica that bears her name. As you wonder at its magnificent sculptures, reflect that it was from this very spot that St Bernard preached the Second Crusade, Richard the Lionheart set off on the Third Crusade, and countless pilgrims have started out on the long pilgrimage to Santiago de Compostela in Spain.

You can also travel back in time by taking a stroll through the walled stronghold of Avallon, and imagine medieval life in a picturesque Burgundian town.

Autun, or Augustodunum to the Romans, when it was one of the most important Gallo-Roman cities, has a pair of splendid town gateways and the remains of the largest theatre in Gaul, not to mention the wonderful 12C St-Lazare cathedral, and amazing medieval art in the Musée Rolin.

If it was good enough for Rabelais, foodies should push the boat out on a culinary pilgrimage to the fine restaurants of Saulieu; with its three Michelin stars, things don't get much better than the legendary Relais Bernard Loiseau.

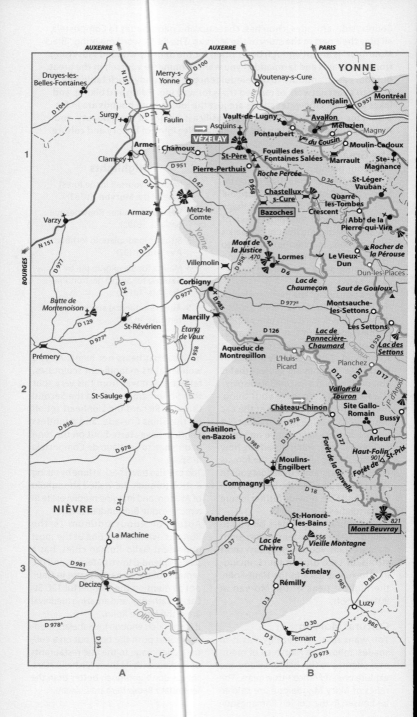

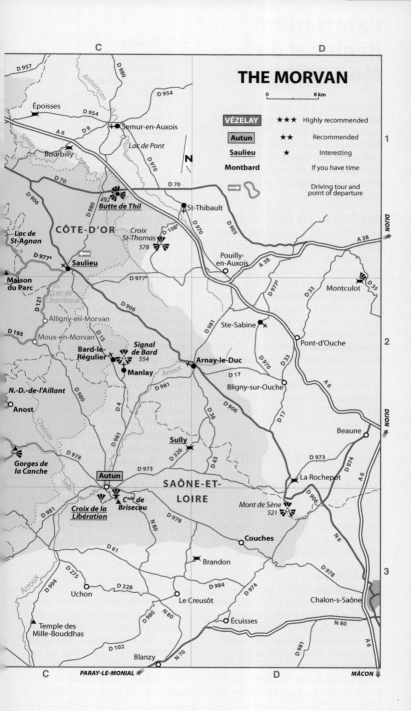

THE MORVAN

0 ——— 8 km

VÉZELAY	★★★	Highly recommended
Autun	★★	Recommended
Saulieu	★	Interesting
Montbard		If you have time
		Driving tour and point of departure

D 957
D 980
D 954
Armançon
Époisses
D 954
D 9
Semur-en-Auxois
A 6
Lac de Pont
Bourbilly
Seine
D 970
N
D 70
D 70
D 906
492
Butte de Thil
D 880
St-Thibault
CÔTE-D'OR
Croix
St-Thomas
578
D 108⁶
D 970
D 905
A 38
Pouilly-
en-Auxois
A 38
DIJON
_Lac de
St-Agnan_
D 977⁸
Saulieu
D 977⁸
D 977⁸
D 33
Montculot
D 35
■ **Maison
du Parc**
D 121
_Lac de
Chamboux_
D 906
D 981
Ste-Sabine ✕
Pont-d'Ouche
Alligny-en-Morvan
D 193
Moux-en-Morvan
D 15
_Signal
de Bard_
554
Arnay-le-Duc
D 970
D 33
**Bard-le-
Régulier**
Manlay
Arroux
D 17
Bligny-sur-Ouche
A 6
DIJON
N.-D.-de-l'Aillant
D 980
D 981
D 981
D 36
D 906
D 17
Beaune
◆ **Anost**
Chaloire
_Gorges de
la Canche_
D 978
D 981
Sully
D 326
D 43
D 973
Autun
D 973
SAÔNE-ET-
Saône
C°ᵈᵉ _de
Brisecou_
LOIRE
Mont de Sène
521
La Rochepot
D 906
_Croix de la
Libération_
D 981
D 978
N 80
Couches
A 6
N 6
D 61
Brandon
D 978
D 275
D 994
Uchon
D 228
D 984
D 974
Chalon-s-Saône
Arroux
Le Creusôt
▲ **Temple des
Mille-Bouddhas**
D 980
N 80
Écuisses
N 80
A 6
D 102
Blanzy
N 70
D 981
C **PARAY-LE-MONIAL** **D** **MÂCON**

Parc Naturel Régional du Morvan

The Morvan – from the Celtic for black mountain – is a distinct natural region between the Nivernais and Burgundy, distinguished by its vast and sombre forests. It receives an ever-growing number of visitors who are attracted by the dramatic unspoilt scenery.

- **Michelin Map:** 319: G-8 to H-10.
- **Info:** Maison du Parc, Parc naturel régional du Morvan, 58230 Saint-Brisson. ℘03 86 78 79 00. www.parcdumorvan.org.
- **Location:** The Morvan (70km/44mi long, 50km/31mi wide) stretches from Avallon to St-Léger-sous-Beuvray and from Corbigny to Saulieu. There are no main roads through the area.

PARC NATUREL RÉGIONAL

Most of the Morvan region was desi-gnated a Regional Nature Park in 1970, helping to attract visitors interested in activities such as hiking, canoeing, cycling, riding or fishing. The park's headquarters at St-Brisson, set in 40ha/99-acre grounds, are not only home to an information centre, but also an abo-retum, herbarium and one branch of the ♣♣**Ecomusée du Morvan** (○open Apr–mid-Nov; May–Sept daily except Tue (Jul–Aug daily), 10am–1pm, 2–6pm; rest of the year 5pm; ◯3€, children 1.50€), the Maison des Hommes et des Paysa-ges, about life in the Morvan from ear-liest times to the present.

🚗 DRIVING TOURS

1 AROUND VÉZELAY
73km/45mi – allow one day.

This route enters the Morvan from the north as far as Lormes, returning via the Chaumeçon and Crescent lakes.

Saint-Père★
The village of St-Père, at the foot of the hill of Vézelay on the banks of the River Cure, has a beautiful Gothic church.
Église Notre-Dame★ – The church, begun in about 1200 and completed in 1455, shows all the stages in the deve-lopment of the Gothic style between the 13C and 15C. In the 16C it became the parish church in place of the church of St-Pierre (from which the name St-Père

is derived) which burned down in 1567 in the Wars of Religion. The porch added at the end of the 13C and restored by Viollet-le-Duc (1814–1879) has three doorways. The central one, which has a trefoiled archway, depicts the Last Jud-gement. Rebuilt in the 15C the choir is encircled by an ambulatory with five radiating chapels.

The vaulting of the nave has painted bosses and corbels carved in the form of expressive faces. In a chapel on the south side of the choir is a 10C stone altar which probably belonged to the original church. As you leave, note the curious painted baptismal font from the Carolingian period.

Musée Archéologique Régional
○Open Jul–Aug 10am–12.30pm, 2.30–6.30pm; Apr, Jun and Sept 10am–12.30pm, 1.30–6.30pm. ◯4€. ℘03 86 33 37 31.
This archaeological museum contains objects excavated at Fontaines-Salées, in particular sections of a water conduit made from tree trunks hollowed out by fire to carry mineral water from a spring; it dates from the Hallstatt period (First Iron Age). Also on display are a 4C Gallo-Roman weighing device, enamelled bronze fibulae in the form of sea hor-ses or wild ducks, Merovingian weapons and jewellery found in the tombs at Vaudonjon near Vézelay, and Gratteloup near Pierre-Perthuis. The medieval room

Morvan landscape

Ph. Gajic/MICHELIN

contains sculpture from the 12C to the 16C from the Vézelay region.

▶ *Drive S out of St-Père.*

The road follows the upper valley of the River Cure through a wooded gorge.

Fouilles des Fontaines-Salées

1.5km/1mi. ⏱*Open Apr–mid-Nov 10am –12.30pm, 1.30–6.30pm.* ⬟*4€.* ℘*03 86 33 37 36.*

These excavations have unearthed Gallo-Roman baths, built on to what was once a Gaulish sanctuary within a vast precinct dedicated to the gods of the springs. These saline springs, which were used in the Iron Age, by the Romans and again in the Middle Ages, were filled in by the salt tax authorities in the 17C. Nineteen wooden casings dating from the first millennium BC have been preserved by the water's high mineral content. A stone duct from the Roman period gives access to the waters of a spring which is once again being used for treating arthritic complaints.

▶ *4km/2.5mi along D 958.*

Pierre-Perthuis★

This tiny village in its picturesque **site**★ is named after a rocky spur, **Roche Per-cée**, which can be seen from the modern bridge spanning the Cure.

▶ *Continue S towards Lormes.*

Château de Bazoches★

⏱*Open Jul–Aug 9.30am–6pm; 25 Mar –30 Jun and 1 Sept–11 Nov 9.30am– noon, 2.15–6pm (Oct–5 Nov 5pm).* ⬟*7.50€.* ℘*03 86 22 10 22. www.chateau-bazoches.com.*

This 12C château was once the favoured dwelling of the famous military engineer and marshal of France, **Vauban** (1633–1707). Visitors are reminded that he was an author as well, and mementoes recall his family life and work habits. The Grand Gallery built by Vauban was used as a design and drafting office; parts of it have been set up to look as they must have when the engineer was at work there. Vauban would have easily recognised his own **room**★, with its well-crafted bed and six armchairs (17C). On the ground floor, more memorabilia is exhibited in his wife's room; she lived here until her death in 1705.

Vauban's tomb is in the church in Bazoches (12C–16C), whereas his heart has been laid to rest in the cenotaph erected in his memory in the Invalides, in Paris.

▶ *Continue towards Lormes via Mont de la Justice.*

Mont de la Justice★

The summit (470m/1 542ft) affords a fine **panorama**★ encompassing Vézelay (N), the Yonne Valley and Montenoison hill (W), the Bazois region (SW) and the Morvan ridge (SE).

Beech trees in Mont Beuvray

© Christophe Boisvieux/hemis.fr

Le Massif du Morvan

A Bit of Geography

A Land of Water and Forest

Seen from the north the Morvan appears as a vast, slightly undulating plateau, which rises slowly towards the south. The northern section (maximum altitude 600m/2 000ft) descends in terraces to the Paris basin; this is Le Bas Morvan (Lower Morvan). The southern section, Le Haut Morvan (Upper Morvan), south of Montsauche, contains the higher peaks, including the Massif du-Bois-du Roi or Haut-Folin (901m/2 956ft).

The Morvan forest

This land without vineyards or fertile pastures was once spurned. Why bother, when the neighbouring Bazois and Auxois plains offered rich land for raising animals and growing crops? It is a different story nowadays: thanks to extensive acreages of conifers planted since the Second World War, the forest is now a source of local wealth, transformed by modern forestry exploitation. These tracts of woodland represent a major investment for the region's future.

The forest – the largest in Burgundy, covering 45 percent of the Morvan region – is the dominant characteristic of the massif. Plantations of beeches and oaks are gradually giving way to more profitable fir trees in a process of replanting that many oppose due to the risks of environmental imbalance; the soil is already acidic. The kings of the Morvan forest are now Douglas firs – also known as Oregon pines – whose salmon-pink trunks soar to a height of

Morvan forest

Maison du tourisme du Parc du Morvan

Landscape near Ouroux-en-Morvan

© Christophe Boisvieux/hemis.fr

50m/164ft. Its properties have made it the tree of choice for reforestation in France. Forestry management has been revolutionised by mechanisation: gone are the days when rafts of logs floated down the rivers towards Paris (see CLAMECY), instead, lorries transport the timber to nearby factories to be put to use in carpentry, or more likely, to be turned into charcoal. So the forest is simultaneously a source of income for its owners, a vast leisure area for locals and visitors seeking a taste of nature, and an essential link in the ecological chain.

The Morvan also provides an essential element of Christmas for many French families: two million Christmas trees are grown here on a thousand hectares of land. Spruce trees take about six years to grow to the right size to thrill the children.

The Waters of the Morvan

The Morvan is subject to heavy rain and snowfall because of its geographical location and altitude; it rains or snows for 180 days in an average year on the peaks. As the ground is composed of non-porous rock covered with a layer of granitic gravel (a sort of coarse sand), the rivers – Yonne, Cure, Cousin and their tributaries – can quickly become turbulent, particularly when the spring thaw turns streams into raging torrents. Various reservoirs – at Pannecière-Chaumard, les Settons, Crescent and Chaumeçon – help to absorb the flow during the flood period and preserve resources when water levels drop; the St-Agnan lake is an important reservoir of drinking water.

Tourism in the Morvan

With its exceptional heritage, the Morvan's tourism strategy aims to reconcile sports and leisure activities with learning about the land. The lac des Settons, for example, draws in many thousand of holidaymakers each year for its excellent water sports facilities, while a network of 3 500km/2 175mi of walking trails criss-crosses the Morvan National Park, allowing hikers of all abilities to explore the natural world. In winter, cross-country skiers head for the slopes of Haut-Folin, the Morvan's highest point. Elsewhere, visitors can learn all about local traditions, arts and crafts by visiting the various themed outposts of the Écomusée du Morvan spread around the area. In the Morvan, a walk through nature can neatly lead on to a trip back in time.

▷ *Continue to Lormes.*

Lormes

This small town is an ideal departure point for trips to the nearby reservoirs. Rue du Panorama leads up to the lookout point by the cemetery, from where there is a **panorama**★ of the wooded heights of the Morvan (to the southeast), and the farmland of the Bazois and Nivernais regions dotted with little villages and woods (to the southwest).

▷ *D 6 towards Dun-les-Places.*

Lac de Chaumeçon

The twisting road runs across undulating woodland dotted with rocks then across pastoral open country. Drive over the dyke and turn immediately left; a short section of road (840m/875yd) leads to D 235. The road overlooks the Chaumeçon reservoir hemmed in by wooded heights.

Beyond Vaussegrois, the road plunges towards the lake shore and follows it closely before running over the crest of the dam towering 42m/138ft above the gorge of the River Chalaux.

▷ *Continue to Plainefas and turn right towards Chalaux.*

Barrage du Crescent

Built between 1930 and 1933 this dam retains the accumulated waters of the Cure and the Chalaux. It has a maximum height of 37m/122ft and a total length of 330m/1 083ft. The reservoir is used by the Bois-de-Cure power station to generate electricity and to help to regulate the flow of the Seine.

▷ *Take D 944 towards Avallon.*

Château de Chastellux-sur-Cure

This château was altered in the 13C and restored in 1825 and has been the seat of the Chastellux family for over 1 000 years. The best view of the château is from the viaduct which carries D 944 across the Cure. The building clings to a rocky slope amid much greenery.

▷ *Return to Vézelay along D 20 and D 36.*

② AROUND SAULIEU
80km/50mi – allow one day.

The route affords charming views over Les Settons reservoir and the upper valley of the Cure and includes visits to a remote abbey and the Musée Vauban. From Saulieu, head W on the D 977. The road runs across a plateau dotted with woods and ponds, then through a forested area.

Lac de Saint-Agnan

From the village, the road runs across the southern end of the lake, the granite-built dam being at the other end.

▷ *At Les Michaux, follow a minor road on the left towards St-Léger-en-Vauban.*

Abbaye de la Pierre-qui-Vire

◷ *Open Jul–mid-Sept 10.15am–12.15pm, 3–5.30pm (Mon closes 5pm); rest of year times vary.* ◷ *Closed Jan.* ⊜ *Free (2€, exhibition).* ⌖ ☎ *03 86 33 19 20. www.abbaye-pierrequivire.asso.fr.*

This monastery is in a wild and lonely part of the Morvan, on a hilly bank of the Trinquelin, the local name for the River Cousin, flowing at the foot of granite rocks in the middle of thick woods. In 1850 **Father Muard** laid the foundations of his monastery on land donated by the Chastellux family. It took its name of Pierre-Qui-Vire (the Rocking Stone) from a druidic monument, an enormous block of granite, placed on another rock, which rocks with a push of the hand. Father Muard's death in 1854 did not stop the development of the community, which joined the Benedictine Order in 1859. On the contrary, it grew so fast that the buildings put up between 1850 and 1953 were not big enough to accommodate the 85 monks and many guests. An architectural competition was launched in 1988; the winning project, completed in 1995, unified the group of buildings which had gone up over time. Other parts of the abbey, including the cloisters, have been restored but are closed to tourists.

Although the rules of monastic enclosure forbid tours of the monastery, the **salle d'exposition** is always open to visitors interested in the life of the monks and their work *(audio-visual presentation on the life of the monastery)*. The church is open for **services** *(&🕐mass at 9.15am, Sun and public holidays 10am, vespers at 6pm (Mon 5.30pm); 🎧03 86 33 19 20)* and one can visit the **druidic stone** *(pierre plate)* which is outside the monastery walls.

Saint-Léger-Vauban

Sébastien le Prestre, who under the name of the **Marquis de Vauban** became one of the outstanding figures of the Grand Siècle (as the 17C is known in France), was born in 1633 in this little village which was then called St-Léger-de-Foucheret. The **Église St-Léger** where Vauban was baptised was originally built to a cruciform plan in the Renaissance period; it was transformed in the 19C and boasts some interesting modern additions by the sculptor Marc Hénard: carved wooden panels in the south door; the sculptures and stained-glass window in the chapel of Notre-Dame-du-Bien-Mourir (1625), left of the chancel; the beautiful blue and pink ceramic **tiles**★ (1973) which surround the high altar and depict the planets, animals, tools and so on round the triangle of the Holy Trinity.

Maison Vauban – &🕐*Open 1 Apr–11 Nov 10am–1pm, 2.30–6.30pm. ⚭5€. 🎧03 86 32 26 30. www.vaubanecomusee. org.* In a small room information panels and an audio-visual presentation (20min) retrace the life and work of this great Frenchman.

▷ *Return to Dun-les-Places, then take D 236 S for 6km/3.7mi and turn left onto D 977B.*

Quarré-les-Tombes

This village owes its name to the numerous limestone sarcophagi dating from the 7C to the 10C found near the church. It is thought there must have been a sanctuary to St George in Quarré, near which knights and other people of rank were buried.

▷ *Follow D 10 towards Saulieu, then 3.5km/2.2mi past the path leading to La Roche des Fées (rock-climbing site), take the forest track towards Dun. Turn right just before Vieux-Dun onto a forest track and drive 1.6km/1mi to a signposted parking area 200m/218yd from Rocher de la Pérouse.*

🚶 A steep footpath climbs to the rocky summit *(30min round trip on foot)*. From the top there is an interesting **view** over the isolated Cure Valley and the rounded summits of the massif.

▷ *Return to the road leading to Dun-les-Places then continue S on D 236.*

Saut de Gouloux

6km/3.7mi NE then 15min round trip on foot. Access by a path (right) from the first bend in the road after the bridge over the Cure.

🚶 Just upstream from its confluence with the Cure, the Caillot flows over an attractive waterfall.

▷ *Go left back onto D 977B (6km/3.7mi).*

Montsauche-les-Settons

This village is the highest resort (650m/2 133ft) in the massif, at the centre of the Parc Naturel du Morvan, and was rebuilt after almost total destruction in 1944.

▷ *Continue south on D 193.*

Lac des Settons★

S of Montsauche along D 193.
The reservoir was created originally to aid logging on the River Cure but is now used to regulate the flow of the Yonne.

▷ *After crossing the River Cure, the road follows the north shore of the reservoir, offering pretty views over the lake and its wooded islands, and leads to the charming resort of Les Settons.*

The reservoir of Les Settons, covering an area of 359ha/887 acres (alt 573m/1 880ft) is a peaceful place, surrounded by fir and larch woods, where wildfowl congregate in the autumn. Footpaths and a lakeside road provide easy access for walking, fishing and water sports.

▶ *The road continues through forests and across a plateau, dotted with woods and ponds, before reaching Saulieu via Moux, Alligny and Chamboux Lake.*

3 AROUND MONT BEUVRAY
84km/52mi, allow one day.

This drive crosses several forested massifs and offers far-reaching views. Leave Château-Chinon by D 27 going south. A view opens out towards the west of a landscape of meadows, arable fields and woods. The road then rises steeply before entering the **Forêt de la Gravelle**. It follows the ridge between the basins of the Seine and the Loire.
At one point near the summit (766m/2 513ft) there is a view to the right of bleak broom-covered moorland. The road then leaves the forest.
Another good view opens out southwards over a small dam nestling at the bottom of a green hollow dominated by the wooded crests which mark the limit of the Morvan.

▶ *The road leads (18km/11mi) to D 18; turn left to Mont Beuvray.*

Mont Beuvray★★
Start with a guided tour of the excavations to help make sense of what remains and hear all about the archaeologists' latest finds. You can always return later on your own.
A Gaulish tribe known as the Aedui established their capital in a fortified settlement *(oppidum)* on one of the highest points of the Haut-Morvan, and named it Bibracte. Dating from the early 2C BC, it was protected by a double line of fortifications – Bibracte was probably a term meaning "twice fortified" – of wood, earth and stone. Extensive excavations have focused attention on the site and led to the opening of a museum offering an insight into Celtic history.

Dumnorix, Celtic chieftain

A. de Valroger/MICHELIN

A historic site – Of the 200ha/494 acres, about 40 were built up and may have housed as many as 10 000 people. Strategically placed at the crossroads of trade routes linking the Mediterranean to Celtic Europe, Bibracte was also a political, religious and crafts centre.
In the early Christian era, Bibracte sank in importance as Augustodunum (presently Autun) grew. However, it remained a centre for trade up to the 16C.
Musée de la Civilisation Celtique★ – The museum (○*open Mar–Nov daily 10am–6pm (Jul–Aug 7pm);* ≈*5.75€;* &. ℘*03 85 86 52 35; www.bibracte.fr*) displays artefacts from ancient Bibracte: amphorae, ceramic vases, bronze dishes, tools, weapons, jewellery and sculpture. Video films, computer terminals, maps, photos taken during excavations, models, dioramas etc. provide a wealth of information about the daily life of the Celts arranged thematically (economy, religion, funeral traditions, wars…). The ticket includes use of an audioguide to the displays.
Oppidum de Bibracte (○*open Jul–Aug 10am–7pm; mid-Mar–end Jun, Sept–mid-Nov 10am–6pm;* ⤳*guided tours (1 1/2hrs) on request;* ≈*9.50€ site and museum;* ℘*03 85 86 52 35; www.bibracte. fr*) – The first excavations took place in the late 19C, but it was not until 1984 that an international effort got underway to explore the area in depth. Today,

Vauban: The Most Decent Man of His Century

Sébastien le Prestre was left a penniless orphan early in life. At the age of 17, while in revolt against the court, he joined the army of the Prince of Condé, and was taken prisoner by the royal forces.

Thereafter, he entered the service of Louis XIV. As a military engineer, from the youthful age of 22, he worked on 300 ancient fortified places and built 33 new ones; he successfully directed 53 sieges, justifying the saying: "A town defended by Vauban is an impregnable town: a town besieged by Vauban is a captured town". Appointed Brigadier General of the royal armies and then Commissioner General of fortifications, he was made a Field Marshal in 1704. He was extremely inventive in thinking up tactics for breaking into fortresses and designed a number of weapons and other instruments of war which were revolutionary for his period. He also systematically fortified the north and east borders of France with a belt of fortresses entirely new in conception (Verdun, Metz, Strasbourg, Neuf-Brisach).

Saint-Simon (1675–1755), a writer not known for his kind remarks, wrote of Vauban: "A man of medium height, rather squat, who had a very warlike air, but at the same time an appearance that was loutish and coarse, not to say brutal and ferocious. Nothing could be further from the truth; never was there a gentler man, more compassionate, more obliging, more respectful, more courteous, and most sparing in the use of men's lives, a man of great worth capable of giving himself in the service of others..."

The last years of Vauban's life were unhappy. Deeply affected by the misery of the common people, he sent his *Projet d'une dîme royale* (Plan for a Royal Tithe) to the king, in which he proposed ways of bettering the living conditions of the lower classes. The work was banned and Vauban, relegated virtually to disgrace by Louis XIV, died of grief on 30 March 1707.

In 1808 Vauban's heart was placed in the Invalides in Paris by Napoleon I; the rest of his body lies in the church in **Bazoches** *(20km/12mi SW of Avallon)*, near the château which was largely reconstructed by his efforts.

Château de Bazoches

© Christophe Boisvieux/hemis.fr

The Gaulish Wars

It was in Bibracte, in 52 BC, that the king of the Arverni, Vercingetorix, was chosen to lead the combined Gaulish forces in their fight against the Romans. The Aedui, originally allies of the Romans, changed sides after Caesar's defeat at Gergovia in the Auvergne. This only delayed Caesar's victory at Alesia where Vercingetorix waited in vain for reinforcements (⊘ see ALISE-STE-REINE).

The following winter, Caesar began writing his *Commentaries on the Gaulish Wars*, in which he reveals his talent as a historian as well as his huge personal ambition.

the site (135ha/333 acres) offers a look at the organisation of the ancient city: the craftsmen's quarter, the network of streets, a section of the ramparts and one of the monumental gateways (Porte de Rebout) have been partially restored. **Panorama**★★ – From the platform with its orientation table, amid gnarled beech trees, there is a magnificent view over Autun, the Uchon beacon (⊘ see Le CREUSOT-MONTCEAU) and Mont St-Vincent. On a clear day, you can see as far as the Jura range and even Mont Blanc.

▶ *Take D 274 right round and back to D 18 then drive N to Glux-en-Glenne and the Forêt de St-Prix via D 300 and D 500 (✿very steep). The Bois-du-Roi forest track leads close to Haut-Folin.*

Haut-Folin

The Haut-Folin (901m/2 956ft), the highest peak in the Morvan, is crowned by a telecommunications mast. The slopes of this peak have been developed for skiing by the French Alpine Club.

The Bois-du-Roi forest track continues through the **Forêt de St-Prix**, a magnificent stand of spruce and fir trees with immense trunks and joins D 179 at La Croisette.

Gorges de la Canche
4km/2.5mi NE.

The road follows the gorge along the side of a hill in a wild landscape of rocks and trees. There is a fine viewpoint in a bend to the right (partly screened by trees).

▶ *Turn left onto D 978 towards Château-Chinon then right 1km/0.6mi further onto D 388 to Anost.*

Anost

🚶In a pleasantly picturesque site, Anost is the hub of various walks on waymarked forest trails, and also offers open-air swimming by the bridge at Bussy.

Bussy itself was once the hub of a transport system of itinerant ox-drawn carts, known as *galvache*, that was prevalent in the haut Morvan until the World War I. 1 May was the day of departure when the *galvachers* bade farewell to their homeland.

👥**Maison des Galvachers** (✆03 85 82 73 26 (town hall); www.anost.com; ✆for opening times call 03 85 82 78 16 (library); ⊜entry 2 € (6–12yrs 1.50 €), free 1st Sun of the month) – This branch of the Écomusée du Morvan tells the story of the Morvan hauliers who set off to work from May to November, sometimes travelling as far as the Belgian Ardennes Interesting exhibitions show how they unloaded timber and transported their loads.

Notre-Dame-de-l'Aillant
15min on foot, NE of Anost.

Climb above Joux to the level of the statue of the Virgin for a semi-circular **panorama**★ of the Anost basin and beyond the hill to the depression around Autun.

Cross the Anost forest on the D 2 (note the 16ha/40-acre wild boar reserve after 1km/0.6mi) as far as Planchez, then take the twisting D 37 towards Château-Chinon. After 9km/5.6mi, enjoy the view on the left of the village of **Corancy**, plastered against a hillside. After a bridge over the Yonne, return to the capital of the Morvan.

ADDRESSES

🛏STAY

🛏 **Camping La Plage des Settons** – *58230 Les Settons. ℰ03 86 84 51 99. www. settons-camping.com. Open May–15 Sept. 68 sites. Reservations recommended.* At this peaceful lakeside site the lazy can rest on the beach while the more energetic use the nearby tennis court. Playing area for children.

🛏🛏 **Chambre d'Hôte L'Eau Vive** – *71990 St-Prix. 4.5km/2.8mi NW of St-Léger by D 179. ℰ03 85 82 59 34. Closed Nov– Mar and 15–30 Jun.🍽 4 rooms. Meals 🛏🛏.* A stone's throw from Mont Beuvray, this house is the perfect starting point for long, bracing walks. The drawing room and the bedrooms are pleasantly decorated with holiday mementoes. *Table d'hôte* meals are served in the dining room with exposed beams, blue pottery and old farming tools on the walls.

🛏🛏 **Chambre d'Hôte du Moulin de Bousson** – *By the lake. 71190 St-Didier-sur-Arroux. ℰ03 85 82 35 07. www.bousson.fr. Closed 15 Nov–15 Mar. ♿🅿🍽 3 rooms.* The traces of its past life are well preserved in this delightfully restored old mill. In the first-floor bedrooms, rustic character, courtesy of wooden floors and beams, mixes with a hint of the exotic. Soothing pastoral views over the lake and a genuine smiling welcome await.

🛏🛏 **Chambre d'Hôte Le Château** – *58120 Chaumard. ℰ03 86 78 03 33. Closed 28 Dec–10 Mar.🍽 6 rooms. Meals🛏🛏.* With its 2ha/5-acre park, this large 18C house is a haven of comfort and tranquillity. In summer, have breakfast on the terrace facing Pannessière Lake. Two self-catering *gîtes* are available. Riding enthusiasts are welcome.

🍴EAT

🍴 **L'Auberge Ensoleillée** – *58230 Dun- les-Places. ℰ03 86 84 62 76. Closed 25 Dec. Reservations needed.* On Wednesdays you can sample famed regional dishes such as *tête de veau* (boiled calf's head – it's better than it sounds), *œufs en meurette* (poached eggs served in red wine sauce with lardoons) and *crapiaux* (thick pancakes cooked with pork fat). The accommodation is unpretentious.

🍴🍴 **Le Morvan** – *89630 Quarré- les-Tombes. ℰ03 86 32 29 29. www.le- morvan.fr. Closed 4–12 Oct, 22 Dec–24 Feb.* This family restaurant offers lovingly prepared regional specialities at reasonable prices. Meals are served in the restored traditional dining room. A few rooms are available.

🛒SHOPPING

Ferme de l'Abbaye de la Pierre- qui-Vire – *1 Huis-Saint-Benoît, 89630 St-Léger-Vauban. ℰ03 86 33 03 73. www.abbaye-pierrequivire.asso.fr. Open Mon–Sat 10.45am–noon and 3–5.30pm (Mon 5pm), Sun 11.30am–12.15pm and 3–5pm.* La Pierre-que-Vire is a soft, cow's milk cheese, for sale in a shop near the monastery of the same name, as well as in the monastery shop. Group visits of the farm can be arranged.

🏃ACTIVITIES

Base Nautique des Settons – *Open May–Sept daily 9am–7pm; Oct– Apr Mon–Fri 9am–noon, 2–6pm. Closed public holidays Oct–Apr, 25 Dec–1 Jan. ℰ03 86 84 51 98. www.activital.net.* The Settons sports centre is near the lake at an altitude of 600m/1 969ft. It offers facilities for water sports (sailing, canoeing, water-skiing, wake-board) and outdoor activities (hiking, cycling).

Hiking – Whether you are a hardened walker or just looking for a simple stroll, the Morvan offers 3 500km/2 175mi of marked trails. For a list of the various regional guides covering the Morvan region visit the websites of the Fédération française de randonnée pédestre (**www.ffrandonnee.fr**) and the Parc naturel régional du Morvan (**www.parcdumorvan.org**).

Mountain Biking – The Morvan has a huge network of over 2 300km/1 430mi of marked trails designed for mountain biking. All levels of expertise and fitness are catered for. For more information, contact the **Association Vélo Morvan Nature, Maison du Parc** – 58230 St-Brisson; ℰ03 86 78 71 77; velo.morvan.nature@gmail.com.

Vézelay★★★

In a beautiful setting on a hill over-looking the Cure Valley on the edge of the Morvan, Vézelay with its old houses and ramparts is one of the treasures of Burgundy and France.

A BIT OF HISTORY

The call of St Bernard – Vézelay's abbey, founded in the middle of the 9C, was at the height of its glory when St Bernard preached the Second Crusade there on 31 March 1146. For a century the church had sheltered the relics of Mary Magdalene, and Vézelay was one of the great places of pilgrimage and the start of one of four routes that led pilgrims and merchants across France to Santiago de Compostela in Spain.

St Bernard launched his vibrant call for the Crusade in the presence of King Louis VII of France and his family as well as a crowd of powerful barons. His call was received with great enthusiasm by all those present.

Although the Third Crusade, undertaken in 1190, was not preached at Vézelay, it was there that King Philippe-Auguste of France and King Richard the Lionheart of England met before their departure.

BASILIQUE SAINTE-MARIE-MADELEINE★★★

⏱ *Open 8am–noon, 1.30–5pm.*
💬 *Guided tours on request.*
📞 *03 86 33 39 50. vezelay.cef.fr.*

▶ **Population:** 478
♿ **Michelin Map:** 319: F-7. Local map see LE MORVAN.
🛈 **Info:** 12 r. St-Étienne, 89450 Vézelay. 📞03 86 33 23 69. www.vezelay tourisme.com.
◖ **Location:** The 11C basilica, heart of Vézelay, overlooks the town from its tall hill. The Promenade des Fossés and the Grande-Rue both lead from the place du Champ-de-Foire at the lower end of town to the basilica.

The monastery founded in the 9C was dedicated to Mary Magdalene. The miracles that happened at her tomb soon drew so great a number of penitents and pilgrims that it became necessary to enlarge the Carolingian church (1096–1104); in 1120 a fire broke out on the eve of 22 July, day of the great pilgrimage, destroying the whole nave and engulfing more than 1 000 pilgrims.

The work of rebuilding was immediately begun, the nave was soon finished and, about 1150, the pre-nave or narthex was added. In 1215 the Romanesque-Gothic choir and transept were completed.

After the discovery at the end of the 13C of other relics of Mary Magdalene at St-Maximin in Provence, pilgrimages

View of Vézelay with Basilique Sainte-Marie-Madeleine

J. Damase/MICHELIN

became fewer and the fairs and market lost much of their importance. The religious struggles caused the decline of the abbey, which was transformed into a collegiate church in 1538, pillaged by Huguenots in 1569 and finally partially razed during the French Revolution.

In the 19C **Prosper Mérimée** (novelist, 1803–1870), in his capacity as Inspector of Historical Monuments, drew the attention of the public works' authorities to the building, which was on the point of collapsing. In 1840 Viollet-le-Duc, who was then less than 30 years old, undertook the work, which he finally finished in 1859.

Exterior
Façade
This was reconstructed by Viollet-le-Duc according to plans contained in the ancient documents. Rebuilt about 1150 in pure Romanesque style it was given a vast Gothic gable in the 13C, with five narrow bays decorated with statues. The upper part forms a tympanum decorated with arcades framing the statues of Christ Crowned, accompanied by the Virgin Mary, Mary Magdalene and two angels.

The tower on the right – Tour Saint-Michel – was surmounted by a storey of tall twin bays in the 13C; the octagonal wooden spire was destroyed by lightning in 1819. The other tower remained unfinished.

Three Romanesque doorways open into the narthex; the tympanum of the central doorway on the outside was remade in 1856 by Viollet-le-Duc, who took the mutilated original tympanum as his inspiration: the archivolt, decorated with plant designs, is authentic, but the rest of the arches and the capitals are modern.

Tour of the exterior
Walk round the building counterclockwise to appreciate its length and the flying buttresses which support it. This side of the church is dominated by the 13C tower of St-Antoine (30m/98ft high) which rises above the junction of the nave and the transept; the two storeys

of round-headed bays were originally intended to be surmounted by a stone spire.

The chapter-house, built at the end of the 12C, abuts the south transept. The gallery of the cloisters was entirely rebuilt by Viollet-le-Duc.

Château Terrace
Access by rue du Château. From this terrace, shaded by handsome trees, situated behind the church on the site of the old Abbot's Palace, there is a fine **panorama**★ *(viewing table)* of the valley of the River Cure and the northern part of the Morvan.

Continue round the basilica past the attractive houses built by the canons of the chapter in the 18C.

Interior
Enter the basilica by the door on the south side of the narthex.

Narthex
This pre-nave, consecrated in 1132 by Pope Innocent II, is later than the nave and the interior façade. Unlike the rib-vaulted church, the Romanesque narthex is roofed with pointed arches and ogival vaulting.

The narthex is so large it seems like a church in its own right. The nave is divided into three bays flanked by aisles surmounted by galleries. The four cruciform pillars of engaged columns decorated with historiated capitals are extremely graceful. The capitals portray scenes from both the Old and New Testaments.

Three doorways in the narthex open into the nave and the aisles of the church. When the central door is open, there is a marvellous perspective along the full length of the nave and choir.

Tympanum of the central doorway★★★
This is a masterpiece of Burgundian-Romanesque art, ranking with that of St-Lazare at Autun. At the centre of the composition a mandorla surrounds an immense figure of Christ Enthroned (**1**) extending his hands to his Apostles (**2**)

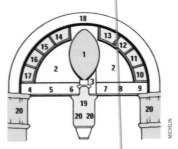

Tympanum of the central doorway

MICHELIN

assembled round him; the Holy Ghost is shown radiating from the stigmata to touch the head of each of the Twelve. All around, on the arch stones and the lintel, are crowded the converts to be received at the feet of Christ by St Peter and St Paul (**3**), symbols of the universal Church. People of every sort are called: on the lintel are *(left)* archers (**4**), fishermen (**5**), farmers (**6**), and *(right)* distant and legendary people – giants (**7**), pygmies climbing a ladder to mount a horse (**8**), men with huge ears – one with a feather-covered body (**9**). The arch stones show Armenians wearing clogs (**10**), Byzantines perhaps (**11**), Phrygians (**12**) and Ethiopians (**13**); immediately next to Christ are men with dogs' heads, the cynocephalics converted by St Thomas in India (**14**). The next two panels show the miracles that accompanied the divine word preached by the Apostles: two lepers show their regenerated limbs (**15**) and two paralytics their healthy

arms (**16**). Lastly two Evangelists record all that they have seen (**17**).

The large-scale composition seeks to demonstrate that the word of God is intended for the whole world. The signs of the zodiac which alternate with the labours of the months on the outer arch stone (**18**) introduce the notion of time: the Apostles' mission must also be transmitted from generation to generation. On the central pier John the Baptist (**19**) carrying the paschal lamb (unfortunately missing) is shown at the feet of Christ as if supporting Him and introducing Him to His rightful place in the centre. Below Him and on the flanking piers are more Apostles (**20**).

The power of the Holy Ghost which fills the 12 Apostles is symbolised by a strong wind which ruffles the garments and sways the bodies. The linear skill, which is the dominant feature of this masterly work, suggests that in the principal scene the sculptor was following the work of a calligrapher, whereas in the medallions, showing the signs of the zodiac and the months of the year, he felt free to carve humorous interpretations of his contemporaries at work.

Tympana of the side doors

Two recessed arches with ornamental foliage and rosettes frame the historiated tympana on the side doors.

The one on the right represents the Childhood of Christ: on the lintel are the Annunciation, the Visitation and

Tympanum of the central doorway, Basilique Sainte-Marie-Madeleine

© Sylvain Sonnet/hemis.fr

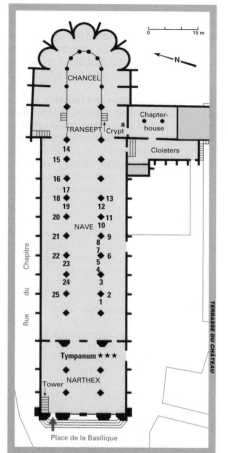

Right side

1) *A duel.*
2) *Lust and Despair.*
3) *Legend of St Hubert.*
4) *Sign of the Zodiac: Libra.*
5) *The mystical mill.*
6) *The death of Dives and Lazarus.*
7) *Lamach kills Cain.*
8) *The four winds of the year.*
9) *David astride a lion.*
10) *St Martin avoids a tree about to fall on him.*
11) *Daniel subdues the lions.*
12) *An angel wrestling with Jacob.*
13) *Isaac blessing Jacob.*

Left side

14) *St Peter delivered from prison.*
15) *Adam and Eve.*
16) *Legend of St Anthony.*
17) *The execution of Agag.*
18) *Legend of St Eugenia.*
19) *Death of St Paul the hermit.*
20) *Moses and the Golden Calf.*
21) *Death of Absalom.*
22) *David and Goliath.*
23) *Killing of the Egyptian by Moses.*
24) *Judith and Holophernes.*
25) *Calumny and Greed.*

the Nativity; on the tympanum is the Adoration of the Magi. The one on the left represents the apparitions of Christ after His Resurrection; on the tympanum is the apparition to the Apostles; on the lintel is the apparition to the disciples at Emmaus.

Nave

Rebuilt between 1120 and 1135, this Romanesque nave is noteworthy for its huge size (62m/203ft long), the use of different coloured limestone, the lighting and the fine series of capitals.

The nave is much higher than the side aisles and is divided into 10 bays of groined vaulting separated by transverse arches with alternating light and dark stones. These do much to mitigate the severity of the lines.

The great semicircular arches, surmounted by windows, rest on cruciform pillars ornamented with four engaged columns decorated with capitals. A graceful decoration of convex quarter-section mouldings, rosettes and pleated ribbons goes round the arches, the main arches and the string course that runs between the windows and the arches.

The capitals★★★

As they are more beautiful than those in the narthex they deserve to be examined in detail (&see plan).

The sculptors – five different hands have been detected in the work – must have had an astonishing knowledge of composition and movement.

Transept and choir

Built in 1096, when the Carolingian church was enlarged, the Romanesque transept and choir were demolished at the end of the 12C and replaced by this beautiful Gothic ensemble completed in 1215. The relics of Mary Magdalene (**a**), preserved in the base of a column surmounted by a modern statue, are in the south transept. A vast ambulatory, with radiating chapels, surrounds the choir.

Crypt

The Carolingian crypt was completely altered in the second half of the 12C. It used to contain Mary Magdalene's tomb and still houses part of her relics. The painting on the vaulting is 13C.

Chapter-house and cloisters

Built at the end of the 12C, shortly before the choir of the basilica, the chapter-house has pointed vaulting. It was completely restored by Viollet-le-Duc. The cloisters were razed during the French Revolution; Viollet-le-Duc rebuilt one gallery in Romanesque style.

ADDRESSES

🛏 STAY

🍽🛏 **Hotel Compostelle** – *Pl du Champ de Foire. ℘03 86 33 28 63. www.lecompostellevezelay.com. Closed 1–23 Dec and 3 Jan–20 Feb. Wi-Fi. 18 rooms. ⇱ 10€.* Small family-run hotel with basic garden or balcony rooms looking over the valley. Breakfast room with a view.

🍽🛏 **Hôtel La Palombière** – *Pl du Champ-de-Foire. ℘03 86 33 28 50. www.lapalombierevezelay.com. Closed Jan–Feb. 10 rooms. ⇱12€.* This characterful creeper-clad 18C mansion has cosy rooms a with satin bedspreads, old-style bathrooms and Louis XIII, Louis XV and Empire furniture.

🍽🛏🛏 **Hotel de la Poste et du Lion d'Or** – *Pl du Champ de Foire. ℘03 86 33 21 23. www.laposte-liondor.com. Closed 3 Jan–25 Feb. Wi-Fi. 38 rooms. ⇱26€. Set lunch menu 18€.* This plush old coaching inn has been welcoming travellers for over 200 years. Comfortable classic rooms; those with views over the countryside are in demand. Reworked regional dishes in the restaurant.

🍽🛏🛏 **Hôtel Crispol** – *rte. d'Avallon, 89450 Fontette. 5km/3mi E of Vézelay on D 957. ℘03 86 33 26 25. www.crispol.com. Closed Jan, Feb, and Mon from Nov–Apr. ♿ 🅿 12 rooms. ⇱9€. ✗.* Stone house at the edge of the village with Vézelay hill as a backdrop. The annexe has vast rooms decorated with artworks by the lady owner. Light and airy dining room whose window bays frame a lovely view of the basilica.

🍴 EAT

🍽🍽 **Le Bougainville** – *28 rue St-Étienne. ℘03 86 33 27 57. lebougainvillevezelay@wanadoo.fr. Open mid-Feb–mid-Nov, closed Tue, Wed, and Mon (in low season).* Retro-style family-run restaurant in an old house on the street leading to the basilica serving local dishes with wine to match.

🍽🍽 **Le St-Étienne** – *39 rue St-Étienne. ℘03 86 33 27 34. www.le-saint-etienne.fr. Closed 10 Jan–28 Feb, Wed and Thu.* This 18C building on the high street climbing to the basilica has a warm, fresh décor with painted beams and up-to-date cooking.

🍽🍽🍽 **L'Entre-Vignes** – *89450 St-Père. ℘03 86 33 39 10. www.marc-meneau-esperance.org. Closed mid-Jan–Feb, Mon, Tue and Wed lunch. ♿🅿 Set lunch menu 57€.* Warm, cheery bistrot with an inviting traditional menu. Sunday brunch.

🍽🍽🍽 **L'Espérance** – *89450 St-Père. ℘03 86 33 39 10. www.marcmeneau.org. Closed mid-Jan–Mar. 19 rooms. ⇱25€.* Conservatory restaurant serving creative cooking based on the classics; superb choice of Burgundies. Elegant contemporary rooms in the mansion house have private terraces.

Avallon★

This pretty town, on a rocky outcrop high above the Cousin Valley, retains an old fortified town centre. It is the ideal starting point of excursions into the surrounding Morvan region.

A BIT OF HISTORY

A powerful stronghold – Avallon was one of the key cities of Burgundy during the Middle Ages. In 1432, Jacques d'Espailly, known as Forte-Épice seized several castles of lower Burgundy. Protected by their fortifications, the people of Avallon felt safe, yet Forte-Épice took the guard by surprise, climbed the walls and seized the town. The Duke of Burgundy hurried back, made a breach in the city walls with a bombard and launched an attack, yet his troops were forced to withdraw. Infuriated by this delay, he immediately called on knights and cross-bowmen whereupon Forte-Épice disappeared through one of the posterns opening onto the riverside, abandoning his men.

☙WALKING TOUR
FORTIFIED TOWN★

Start from the bastion of the Porte Auxerroise to the north. Allow 2hrs.

Tour of the ramparts

From the hospital, an early-18C building, follow rue Fontaine-Neuve overlooked by the Tour des Vaudois; next comes the Bastion de la Côte Gally towering over a ravine. Continue along rue du Fort Mac-Mahon to the Bastion de la Petite-Porte, past the Tour du Chapitre (1454) and the Tour Gaujard.

From the **Promenade de la Petite Porte**, a terrace shaded by lime trees, there is a lovely view of the Cousin Valley 100m/109yd below, of several manor houses and of the Morvan heights in the distance.

▷ *Continue eastwards round the ramparts.*

This section of wall overlooks another ravine and runs past the well-preserved

▶ **Population:** 7 366
⌖ **Michelin Map:** 319: G-7.
▤ **Info:** 6 r. Bocquillot, 89200 Avallon. ℘03 86 34 14 19. www.avallonais-tourisme.com.
◔ **Location:** The old town is bounded by ancient ramparts and circular bastions, so there's no danger of getting lost.

Tour de l'Escharguet and the Tour Beurdelaine, the oldest tower built in 1404 and reinforced in 1590 by a bastion. Adjacent is the pretty 15C **Clock Tower**.

Église St-Lazare

Built on the site of several previous sanctuaries, the church has two interesting **doorways**★ on the façade. Note in particular the richly carved archivolt of the main doorway.

The carvings on the tympanum and lintel of the small doorway have been badly damaged but it is possible to see the Adoration, the Three Kings riding and visiting Herod then the Resurrection and the Descent in limbo. The archivolt is decorated with flower motifs.

To the right is the old Église St-Pierre which now houses temporary exhibitions. The interior is on different levels, the chancel being 3m/10ft lower than the west doorway. In the south aisle there are 17C statues in polychrome wood, a 15C Virgin with St Ann and a 14C stone statue of St Michael slaying the dragon.

The chapel to the right of the chancel is profusely decorated with trompe-l'œil paintings dating from the 18C.

Do not miss the splendid 15C organ loft. Nearby, in rue Bocquillot, there is a **salt storehouse**, a former 15C winepress with its recess and mullioned windows.

Musée de l'Avallonnais

◔*Open Jul–Sept daily except Tue 2–6pm. Rest of year, weekends and public holidays 2–6pm.* ◔*Closed Tue. ℘03 86 34 03 19.*

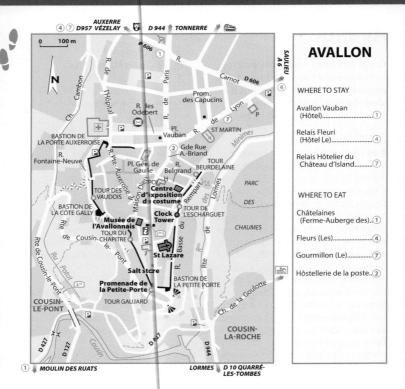

The local museum, founded in 1862, contains an eclectic collection of exhibits, including a number of Gallo-Roman artefacts (a mosaic thought to be of Venus) and an exceptionally fine collection of Roman and medieval coins. In the Fine Arts section, local artists are well represented; note also the famous 58-plate Expressionist series of the **Miserere**★ by Georges Rouault (1949).

EXCURSIONS

👥 Château de Montjalin

◆ 7km/4.3mi E on D 957. ◆ Open 1 Apr –11 Nov 9am–7pm. ◆ 6€ (children 3€). 🚶 ✆ 03 86 37 46 42. www.voitures presidentielles.com.

The outbuildings of this elegant 18C castle house the Musée des Voitures de chefs d'État. Among the 30 or so official cars, note De Gaulle's Citroen DS 19 with its bullet holes, Pope Paul VI's Popemobile and the extravagant Cadillac of the Emir of Abu Dhabi.

Ste-Magnance

◆ 19km/9.3mi SE towards Saulieu (N 6). The Gothic church of this small village was erected in 1514. The chancel and the apse are covered with Flamboyant vaulting. Inside, note the unusual **tomb**★ of St Magnance from the 12C; the low-relief carvings depict the legend of St Magnance and the miracles she performed.

🚗 DRIVING TOUR

Vallée du Cousin★

The D 427 follows the River Cousin through verdant countryside; the route is dotted with castles and pretty watermills. Highlights along the way include the painted mural of the 15C church at Vault-de-Lugny, and a Romanesque church at Pontaubert. At Ruats, old mills have been turned into residences. The rivers Vaux and Cousin join at Méluzien before the bridge at Moulin-Cadoux and the 18C château at Marrault.

ADDRESSES

🛏️STAY

⊜🖥️ **Hôtel Avallon Vauban** – *53 r. de Paris. ℰ03 86 34 36 99. www.avallon vaubanhotel.com. Wi-Fi. 26 rooms. ⊡ 8.50 €.* Located near a busy intersection, this pretty building opens on to a vast, shaded park. There are cool colours and cherrywood furniture in the guest rooms (those at the back are quieter).

⊜🖥️🖥️ **Hôtel Le Relais Fleuri** – *La Cerce. ℰ03 86 34 02 85. www.relais-fleuri.com. 🅿 Wi-Fi. 48 rooms. ⊡ 14 €. ✕.* Functional motel-style rooms in a 4ha/10-acre park with a tennis court and heated pool. An elegant rustic dining room serves reworked regional cuisine.

⊜🖥️🖥️ **Relais hôtelier du Château d'Island** – *89200 Island. 7km/4.3mi SW of Avallon on D 957 then D 53. ℰ03 86 34 22 03. http://disland.free.fr. Closed 4 Jan–1 Mar and 15 Nov–23 Dec. 🅿 5 rooms. ⊡ 11 €.* Choose between a bedroom and a suite in this 15C and 18C château nestling in a lovely park. Beams, antiques and fireplaces await. Franco-Vietnamese cuisine.

🍽️/EAT

⊜ **Ferme-auberge des Châtelaines** – *Les Châtelaines. 3km/1.2mi S of Avallon on D 127 then secondary road. ℰ03 86 34 16 37. Closed mid-Nov–mid-May and Mon–Wed from 1 Jul–1 Sept. 🅿 📺* *Set lunch menu 12 €.* Pigs, rabbits and lambs are raised on this farm near the Cousin Valley. Delicious views of Avallon to go with tasty cheese pies and cakes served in the rustic-style dining room.

⊜ **Le Gourmillon** – *8 r. de Lyon. ℰ03 86 31 62 01. www.legourmillon. com. Closed 11–24 Jan, Thu eve out of season and Sun eve. Set lunch menu 11 €.* Nice little family-run place in the town centre. Fresh, country-style dining room with local cooking.

⊜🖥️ **Hostellerie de la Poste** – *13 pl. Vauban. ℰ03 86 34 16 16. www.hostelleriedelaposte.com. 30 rooms. ⊡ 13 €.* Classic cuisine served in the former stables of a handsome old Burgundian coaching house built in 1707. Among others, Napoleon I and Kennedy have stayed here. Pretty rooms.

⊜🖥️ **Les Fleurs** – *69 rte de Vézelay - 89200 Pontaubert. 4km/2.5mi W of Avallon on D 957. ℰ03 86 34 13 81. www. hotel-lesfleurs.com. Closed 18 Dec–3 Feb. 🅿 7 rooms. ⊡ 8 €.* Friendly family-run auberge serving traditional local dishes in a classic setting or on the garden terrace. Renovated rooms.

Saulieu★

Saulieu has a long-standing gastronomic renown with a string of fine restaurants. Art lovers will find interest in the basilica of St-Andoche and in the works of François Pompon, a sculptor who was born at Saulieu in 1855.

A BIT OF HISTORY

A gastronomic centre – The gastronomic reputation of Saulieu goes back to the 17C. In 1651 the Burgundian states decided to restore the old Paris-Lyon road, which passed along the eastern

▸ **Population:** 2 616
🏛️ **Michelin Map:** 320: F-6 Local map see LE MORVAN.
🏢 **Info:** 24 r. d'Argentine, 21210 Saulieu. ℰ03 80 64 00 21. www.saulieu.fr.
◗ **Location:** Saulieu is pleasantly situated on the boundaries of the Morvan and the Auxois, making it a convenient base for a variety of excursions.

edge of the Morvan, to the importance that it had before the Middle Ages. Saulieu set about increasing its prosperity by developing local industry and fairs. The town became a post house on the route and obliged itself to treat travellers well. Rabelais had already praised Saulieu and its excellent meals.
Madame de Sévigné stopped in the town on her way to Vichy on 26 August 1677, and she avowed later that for the first time in her life she was a little tipsy.

SIGHTS
Basilique St-Andoche
Open Apr–Nov Tue–Sat 9am–noon, 2–6.30pm, Sun 2–6.30pm. Rest of the year Mon–Sat 9am–noon, 2–4.30pm. 03 80 64 00 21.

The church, which dates from the early 12C, was influenced by St-Lazare in Autun of which it was a sister house. The main point of interest is the series of historiated or decorated **capitals**★★, inspired by those in Autun. After its restoration, the tomb of St Andoche was placed in the last chapel in the right aisle. In the north aisle is a handsome tombstone and Pietà, presented, it is

said, by Madame de Sévigné as a penance for over-indulgence.

Musée Municipal François-Pompon
Open Apr–Sept daily except Tue 10am-12.30, 2–6pm (Apr–Sept 6pm), Sun and public holidays 10.30am–noon, 2.30–5pm. Rest of year times vary.
Closed Jan–Feb, 1 May and 25 Dec. 3€. 03 80 64 19 51.

On the ground floor of this new museum are Gallo-Roman tombstones, religious statuary, milestones and so on. The first floor is devoted to sculptor **François Pompon**, born in Saulieu in 1855. A student of Rodin, he is best known for his representations of animals; **le Taureau**★ (The Bull), one of his greatest works, was erected on a square at the town's northern entrance in 1948.

EXCURSION
Butte de Thil★
18km/11mi N along D 980.

The hill, visible from afar, is crowned with the ruins of a former 14C collegiate church and a medieval castle (9C–14C) dismantled by Richelieu.

ADDRESSES

STAY
La Vieille Auberge – *15 r. Grillot. 03 80 64 13 74. Closed 4–29 Jan, 29 Jun –9 Jul, Tue evenings and Wed except 14 Jul–31 Aug.* This country inn on the edge of Saulieu offers a good choice of reasonably priced menus combining traditional cuisine with a regional touch. Functional guest rooms.

La Guinguette – *Moulin de la Serrée, 58230 Alligny-en-Morvan. 7km/ 4.3mi S of Saulieu by D 26. 03 86 76 15 79. Open Sat evenings and Sun lunch Easter–Oct and daily Jul–Aug.* This welcoming cabin is the delight of Sunday afternoon strollers. Fish farm on the property. Trout and salmon can be eaten on the premises or bought to be taken away. Fishing rods available.

Hôtel le Relais Bernard Loiseau – *2 r. d'Argentine. 03 80 90 53 53. www.bernard-loiseau. 18€. Restaurant.* Illustrious chef Bernard Loiseau's team offers palate-pleasing meals to the gourmet diners who come from afar to this temple of gastronomy. Refined atmosphere and smart setting in a former coaching inn.

SHOPPING
La Fouchale – *4 pl. de la République. 03 80 64 02 23. Open Tue–Sat 9am– 12.30pm, 3–7pm; Easter to Oct Sun 10am– 12.30pm.* An astonishing variety of cheeses and dairy produce: magnificent Époisses and Saint-Marcellins, yoghurts, crème fraîche, plus local wines.

Poulizac – *4 r. des Fours. 03 80 64 18 52. Open Tue–Sat 8.30am–12.30pm and 3–7pm.* After 30 years of baking, M. Poulizac truly knows his bread. Don't miss the country bread with dried figs!

Autun★★

The city of Autun is flanked by wooded hills overlooking the valley of the Arroux and the vast plain that extends westwards. The cathedral, the museums and the Roman remains bear witness to the city's past greatness.

A BIT OF HISTORY

The Rome of the Gauls – Autun, from Augustodunum, was founded by Emperor Augustus with the aim both of honouring the Aedui, the local tribe, and of making them beholden to Rome. The splendour of the new town, which was known as the sister and rival of Rome, soon eclipsed the contemporary Gaulish settlement at Bibracte. The city's location on the great commercial and military road between Lyon and Boulogne brought it prosperity. All that remains of the fortified enclosure and the numerous public monuments are two gates and traces of the largest Roman theatre in Gaul.

The century of the Rolin family – In the Middle Ages Autun became prosperous again, largely because of two men: Nicolas Rolin and one of his sons. Born in Autun in 1376, **Nicolas Rolin** became one of the most celebrated lawyers of his time. He attracted the attention of the Duke of Burgundy, Philip the Good, who made him Chancellor. Despite rising to such heights, he never forgot his native town, helping to restore its fortunes. A son, **Cardinal Rolin**, who became Bishop of Autun, made the town a great religious centre. The completion of the cathedral of St-Lazare, the ramparts to the south of the town and many private mansions date from this time.

☙❧WALKING TOUR
UPPER TOWN
Start from place du Champ-de-Mars (parking area, tourist office).

Lycée Bonaparte
This was once a Jesuit college, built in 1709, and it provides a noble focal point for place du Champ-de-Mars. The

- ▶ **Population:** 15 069
- **Michelin Map:** 320: F-8.
- **Info:** 13 rue du Gen-Demetz, 71400 Autun. ℘03 85 86 80 38. www.autun.com.
- **Location:** The cathedral and several museums are close to Place du Champ de Mars. There are excellent shops in the pedestrian streets near the square, along Avenue Charles de Gaulle, Rue Guerin and by the cathedral.
- ○ **Timing:** If you visit in August, stop at the cathedral in the evening for "Nocturnes de la cathédrale", a free cultural series featuring art, music and poetry.
- **Don't Miss:** The ruins of the Roman theatre, the largest in Gaul.

wrought-iron **grille**, dating from 1772, is adorned with gilded motifs of medallions, globes, astrolabes and lyres. On the left, the 17C **church of Notre-Dame** was once the college chapel. Notable pupils included the Bonaparte brothers, Napoleon, Joseph and Lucien.

Walk along rue St-Saulge, admiring the 17C Hôtel de Morey at no. 24; continue along rue Chauchien and note the façades decorated with wrought-iron balconies.

▷ *Continue along rue des Bancs.*

Musée Rolin★
○*Open Apr–Sept daily except Tue 9.30am–noon, 1.30–6pm. Rest of the year daily except Tue 10am–noon, 2–5pm, Sun 10am–12pm, 2–5pm.* ○*Closed 1 Jan, 1 May, 14 Jul, 1 and 11 Nov, 25 Dec.* ⊛4€. ℘03 85 52 09 76. The 20 rooms contain many noteworthy exhibits. Two rooms (8 and 9) are devoted to masterpieces of Roman **statuary**★★, mostly by the two great sculp-

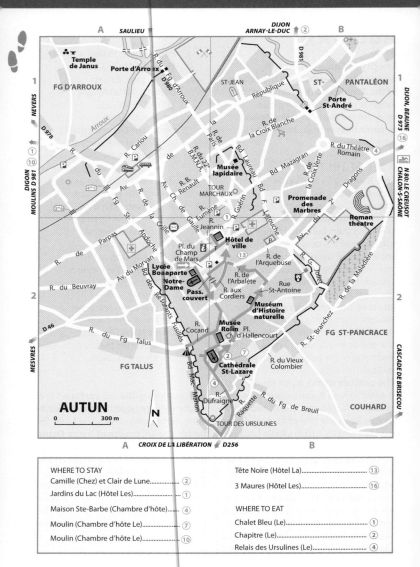

AUTUN

0 ___ 300 m

N

tors of the Burgundian School, Gislebertus and Martin, a monk. Gislebertus' **Temptation of Eve**★★ expresses sensuality through the curves of the body and the plants; the carving adorned the lintel of the north door of the cathedral before 1766. Martin created part of the **tomb of St Lazarus**, which took the form of a miniature church and stood behind the altarpiece in the chancel of the cathedral until it was destroyed during the changes made by the canons in 1766. The surviving figures from the main group, which depicted the Resurrection of Lazarus, are the slim and poignant figures of St Andrew and Lazarus' sisters, Martha (who is holding her nose) and Mary. The rest of the work is represented by a few fragments supplemented by a sketch.

The first floor houses 14C and 15C sculptures from the Autun workshops and works by French and Flemish Primitive painters. The room devoted to the Rolin family contains the famous 15C painting of the **Nativity**★★ by the Master of Moulins.

15C Burgundian statuary is represented by the **Virgin**★★ of Autun in polychrome stone and a St Catherine attributed to the Spanish sculptor Juan de la Huerta who worked in the region during the reign of Philip the Good.

◐ *Rue Cocand leads to the ramparts.*

Ramparts

The walk round the ramparts begins at boulevard des Résistants Fusillés to the west of town. Follow the ramparts south as far as the Tour des Ursulines, a 12C keep.

◐ *Return towards the cathedral on rue du Faubourg St-Blaise, then stroll past the timbered houses in rue Dufraigne into rue Notre-Dame, admiring n° 12 the hôtel de Millery) and in impasse du Jeu-de-Paume, the hôtel Mac-Mahon.*

Cathédrale St-Lazare★★

In the 12C the Bishop of Autun decided to supplement the existing cathedral (destroyed in the 18C) with a new church, to house the relics of St Lazarus, in the hope of creating a place of pilgrimage to rival the Basilique Ste-Madeleine in Vézelay. Construction took place from 1120 to 1146, and the cathedral was consecrated in 1130 by Pope Innocent II.

The exterior of the cathedral no longer looks particularly Romanesque because of later modifications. The belfry was destroyed by fire in 1469, and when it was rebuilt later that century, a Gothic spire was added. The upper part of the choir and the chapels in the right aisle date from the same period. Those in the left aisle are 16C. The two towers flanking the main front, which resemble those at Paray-le-Monial, were added in the 19C.

The building was seriously damaged during the French Revolution; the cathedral canons demolished the rood screen, the tympanum of the north doorway and the tomb of St Lazarus which stood behind the high altar *(what remains can be seen in the Musée Rolin).*

Tympanum of the central doorway★★★ – The tympanum (1130-35), one of the masterpieces of Romanesque sculpture, bears the signature of its creator, **Gislebertus**, beneath the feet of Christ. Nothing is known about him, except that his work suggests he was trained in Vézelay, and perhaps also in Cluny. Unlike his contemporaries, he did not conform to the Cluniac tradition, but produced his own distinctive style. The composition of the central tympanum

Cathédrale St-Lazare

© Franck Guizou/hemis.fr

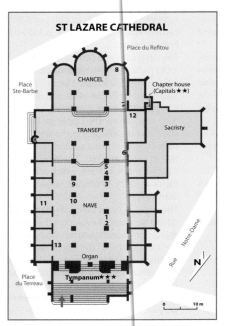

ST LAZARE CATHEDRAL

Place du Refitou

Place Ste-Barbe

CHANCEL

Chapter house (Capitals ★ ★)

TRANSEPT

Sacristy

NAVE

Organ

Place du Terreau

Tympanum ★ ★ ★

Rue Notre-Dame

N

0   10 m

3) *The stoning of St Stephen.*

4) *Symbolic representation of Samson pulling down the temple.*

5) *The loading of the Ark, with Noah supervising from an upper window.*

6) *16C sacristy door.*

7) *Statues of Pierre Jeannin, who died in 1623, President of the Burgundian Parliament and a minister of Henri IV, with his wife.*

8) *The relics of St Lazarus are placed under the high altar.*

9) *Jesus appearing to Mary Magdalene against a background of curled foliage.*

10) *The second temptation of Christ. Oddly enough the devil is the only figure placed high up on the roof.*

11) *A 16C stained-glass window representing the Tree of Jesse in the burial chapel of the bishops of Autun.*

1) *and* 2) *Simon the Sorcerer tries to ascend to Heaven watched by St Paul and St Peter with his key. Simon falls head first under Peter's approving eye. The devil (visible from the main nave) is beautifully portrayed.*

12) *Painting by Ingres (1834) representing the martyrdom of St Symphorian, by the Porte St-André.*

13) *The Nativity. St Joseph meditating in a strange, arched chair.*

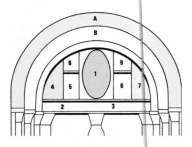

is a masterly solution of the problems posed by the decoration of such a large area. The theme is the Last Judgement, despite its apparent complexity, the design is highly structured.

At the centre, dominating the composition, is the tall figure of Christ in Majesty (1) surrounded by a mandorla supported by four angels. Below are the dead rising from their graves, summoned by four angels blowing trumpets (4, 7, 8, 9); in the centre of the lintel, an angel is separating the blessed (2) from the damned (3). At the left hand of Christ, the Archangel Michael confronts Satan, who is trying to upset the weighing of souls by pressing on the beams of the scales (6). Behind him yawns the mouth of Hell, which is squeezed to the extreme right of the tympanum (7), whereas Heaven occupies the whole of the upper register with *(right)* two Apostles or Enoch, the patriarch, and Eli, the prophet, transported straight to Heaven (9) and *(left)* Mary (8) in the heavenly Jerusalem (4) and the Apostles (5) attending the weighing of souls. St Peter, with the key on his shoulder, lends a hand to one of the blessed, while a soul tries to escape by clinging to the robe of an angel.

The whole composition is crowned by three orders of rounded arches. The outer order (**A**) represents the passing of time, the labours of the months alternating with the signs of the zodiac in the medallions; in the centre, between Cancer and Gemini, is a small crouching figure representing the year. The middle order (**B**) bears a serpentine garland of leaves and flowers. The inner order, destroyed in 1766 when the tympanum was plastered over, showed the elders of the Apocalypse.

Interior – The pillars and vaulting date from the first half of the 12C. The Cluniac Romanesque style survives in spite of much alteration: three rows of elevation (large pointed arches, false triforium and high windows), massive cruciform pillars divided by fluted pilasters, broken-barrel vaulting with transverse ribs in the nave and rib vaulting in the aisles.

The chancel conforms to the early Christian design of an apse flanked by two apsidal chapels. The over-vaulting disappeared in the 15C when the tall windows were put in by Cardinal Rolin (the glass in the pointed windows is from the 19C, in the Romanesque ones from 1939).

The use of fluted pilasters surmounted by foliated capitals, found throughout the upper gallery, gives a sense of unity to the interior of the cathedral; the majestic effect is enlivened by the carved capitals (*binoculars are useful here*).

Chapter-house – The chapter-house was built in the early 16C, using some fine **capitals**★★ made of heavily grained stone containing mica, which originally capped the pillars in the chancel.

Belfry – The belfry (80m/262ft high) was built by Bishop Jean Rolin in 1462. From the top (230 steps) there is a good **view**★ of the old roofs of the town, the bishops' palace and the hills of the Morvan.

Passage couvert
This mid-19C covered passageway opens onto place du Champ-de-Mars through an imposing Classical doorway.

Follow rue De-Lattre-de-Tassigny, lined with 18C private mansions.

Hôtel de Ville
The town hall has a **library** with a rich collection of **manuscripts**★ and incunabula, shown in summer exhibitions. Finally, walk along rue Jeannin behind the town hall, and enter one of the gardens through a porte-cochère.

GALLO-ROMAN TOWN
Roman Theatre
These ruins were once the largest theatre in Gaul (capacity: 12 000).

Porte St-André★
This gate is where the roads from Langres and Besançon meet. It is the sole survivor of four original gates in the Gallo-Roman fortifications, which were reinforced with 54 semicircular towers.

Porte d'Arroux
This gateway was the Roman Porta Senonica, leading towards Sens and the Via Agrippa which ran from Lyon to Boulogne. The upper arcading dates from the time of Emperor Constantine.

EXCURSIONS
Croix de la Libération★
6km/4mi S.
The snaking road climbs to give fine views of the cathedral and the old town; 50m/55yd beyond the entrance to Montjeu Castle, a steep path on the right leads to the granite cross put up in 1945 to commemorate the liberation of Autun; from here, there is a good **view**★ of Autun.

Château de Sully★
15km/9.3mi NE along the road to Nolay. Open Apr–Nov. Guided tours (1hr) Jul–Aug 10am–7pm, rest of year 10am–6pm. 7.50€. ℘03 85 82 09 86. www.chateaudesully.com.
This Renaissance mansion in a vast park is similar in its layout and decoration to Ancy-le-Franc. It was begun early in the 16C by Jean de Saulx, who had already acquired the land at Sully, and continued by his son, the Maréchal de Tavannes.

ADDRESSES

🛏 STAY

Hôtel Clair de Lune – 1 pl. Édouard-Herriot, 21230 Arnay-le-Duc. 29km/18mi NE of Autun on D 981. &03 80 90 01 38. www.chez-camille.fr. 13 rooms. ⌑ 5 €, half board available. ✗. The 13 functional yet comfy rooms in the annex of Hôtel Chez Camille offer a tempting alternative to its older sibling.

Hôtel Les Jardins du Lac – 1 r. Louis-Aragon. &03 85 86 25 25. 20 rooms. ⌑ 7 €, half board available. ✗. Set lunch menu 17.50 €. In an ideal spot between the golf course and the leisure park, this hotel offers well-equipped, unfussy rooms, much as you might expect from a chain hotel.

Chambre d'hôte Maison Sainte-Barbe – 7 pl. Ste-Barbe. &03 85 86 24 77. www.maisonsaintebarbe.com. 4 rooms. ⌑. Dating from the 15C–18C, the former canons' lodge by the cathedral has spacious bedrooms with individual décor, a pleasant breakfast room kitted out with old furniture, and a walled garden.

Chambre d'hôte La Ferme de la Chassagne – La Chassagne, 71190 Laizy. 14km/8.5mi SW of Autun on D 981, then right onto the lane to La Boulaye. &03 85 82 39 47. Closed 1 Nov–1 Mar. 4 rooms. ⌑. ✗. The restored building oozes the charm of an old-world farm with its chunky exposed beams and old furniture. Décor in the bedrooms is simple but very pleasant. Table d'hôte menu based around home-grown ingredients.

Chambre d'hôte Le Cottage du Château – R. Le-Petit-Charron, 21360 Chaudenay-le-Château. 15km/9.3mi W on D 17 and D 115B. &03 80 20 00 43. www.chambres-hotes-bourgogne.com. Closed 5–25 Jan. 5 rooms. ⌑. At the forest's edge, this house and its former sheep pen hold five spacious rooms done out with impeccably-chosen furniture and fabrics. Breakfast in the flowery garden on sunny days.

Hôtel La Tête Noire – 3 r. Arquebuse. &03 85 86 59 99. www.hoteltetenoire.fr. Closed 20 Dec–26 Jan. Wi-Fi. 31 rooms. ⌑ 10 €. ✗. Set lunch menu 15 €. Smartly-decorated rooms done out with rustic painted wood furniture in a charming property. Traditional dishes are served in the pleasant dining room.

Chambre d'hôte Le Moulin – Le Bois du Caveau, 71320 La Boulaye. 33km/20.5mi SE of Autun on D 981 and D 994. &03 85 79 58 43. www.chambres-hotes-la-boulaye.com. 3 rooms. ⌑ ✗. Behind the imposing façade of this 19C former mill are spacious rooms spread around the whole house. Enormous dining room and lounge with mezzanine.

Hôtel Chez Camille – 1 pl. édouard-Herriot, 21230 Arnay-le-Duc. 29km/18mi NE of Autun on D 981. &03 80 90 01 38. www.chez-camille.fr. Wi-Fi. 11 rooms. ⌑ 9 €, half board available. Rather cosy, individually styled rooms. Some come with a small lounge; those on the second floor have exposed beams.

🍽 EAT

Le Relais des Ursulines – 2 r. Dufraigne. &03 85 52 26 22. www.lerelaisdesursulines.com. Closed Sat noon and Sun. Set lunch menu 12 €. Half bistro, half restaurant, this place sports a winning décor involving oriental *objets* and a mechanical piano. On the menu are pizzas, wood-oven grills and regional specialities.

Le Chalet Bleu – 3 r. Jeannin. &03 85 86 27 30. www.lechaletbleu.com. A glass frontage opens into a dining room with frescos of fantasy gardens and landscapes. The menu unites tradition and terroir, with themed dining on Friday evenings.

Le Chapitre – 11 pl. du Terreau. &03 85 52 04 01. www.lechapitre71.com. Closed 20–27 Dec, 15–28 Feb, Sun eve and Mon. Set lunch menu 15 €. Hard by the cathedral, this dinky restaurant delights with tasty up-to-date cooking in a romantic candlelit ambience with wrought-iron furniture.

Château-Chinon★

The little town of Château-Chinon, in the heart of the Morvan regional park, occupies a **picturesque site**★ on the ridge that separates the Loire and Seine basins on the eastern edge of the Nivernais. Its easily defended hilltop position made this place successively a Gallic settlement, a Roman camp and a feudal castle, which gave its name to the town. More recently, a certain François Mitterand was mayor for 22 years before becoming President.

TOWN

The "seven years" in the name of the **Musée du Septennat**★ (⏱open Jul–Aug 10am–1pm, 2–7pm; rest of the year times vary; ⏱closed 26 Dec; ∞2€; ✆03 86 85 19 23; www.cg58.fr) refer to the President's term of office in France (now only five years), and the displays include presidential memorabilia and gifts given to former mayor **François Mitterrand** (1916–1996) during his 14-year tenure which began in 1981. The 18C building used to be a Poor Clare's convent.

Visitors will see photographs of world leaders and international events, medals and honorific decorations. The collection includes a surprising range of art.

The town's **calvary** (15min on foot there and back from square Aligre; 609m/1 998ft) is built on the site of the fortified Gallic settlement and the ruins of the fortress.

There is a fine **panorama**★ (viewing table) of Château-Chinon's slate roofs, and further off the wooded crests of the Morvan. The two summits of the Haut-Folin (901m/2 956ft) and the Mont Préneley (855m/2 805ft) are to the south-east.

A road (starting in faubourg de Paris and returning via rue du Château) encircles the hill halfway up. Through the trees there are glimpses of the Yonne gorge on one side and countryside on the other.

▶ **Population:** 2 196
⏱ **Michelin Map:** 319: G-9.
   Local map see LE MORVAN.
▤ **Info:** 6 Bd de la République,
   58120 Château-Chinon.
   ✆03 86 85 06 58. www.ot-chateauchinon.com.
◖ **Location:** Château-Chinon is located 36.5km/23mi northwest of Autun.

🚗 DRIVING TOURS

ALONG THE YONNE

70km/43mi. Allow 2hrs 30min.
⏱See Region map. Drive N out of Château-Chinon then bear right onto D 37 and left onto D 12 to Lac de Pannecière-Chaumard.
The largest of the Morvan lakes, the lac de Pannecière-Chaumard, stretches almost 7.5km/4.5mi amid wooded hills – a setting that is wilder than that of the Lac des Settons. The dam holds in over 80 million cubic metres of water. For a fine view of the lake, call at Ouroux-en-Morvan; return to the dam and make your way on the D 126 past the magnificent Montreuillon aqueduct and the 15C church in Marcilly to Corbigny and the Abbaye St-Leonard; it was rebuilt just before the Revolution with harmonious symmetrical façades.

Ongoing restoration work has brought to light its superb Louis XV staircase. The contemporary art centre puts on a year-round programme of dance, theatre etc.

DELL OF TOURON

30km/18.5mi. Allow 1hr 30min.
⏱See Region map.
Take the D 978 to Arleuf where the west-facing houseshave tiled gables to protect against the rains. Head north, and near to Bardiau you'll see the ruins of a 700-seat Gallo-Roman theatre before the route crosses the Dell of Touron. The wooded rump of the Haut-Folin is visible to the south. The D500 then runs through rolling green country to Château-Chinon.

The Nivernais Loire marks the watery boundary between Burgundy and the rolling agricultural plains of the Berry, and defines the history and character of the Burgundian towns along its banks. In Nevers and La Charité-sur-Loire you are a long way from the vineyard-carpeted slopes of the heartland: amazingly, Burgundy plays second fiddle in the wine world here, as the best appellations are on the wrong side of the river in Sancerre and Pouilly-sur-Loire. This is a gently seductive region that comes to life when you tour its wooded hills and meadows, calling at splendid châteaux and pulling on the walking boots to discover lakes hidden deep in silent forests.

Highlights

1 Discover fine pottery and spun glassware in **Nevers** (p210)

2 White-knuckle thrills at **Magny-Cours** racetrack (p213)

3 Splendid priory church in **La Charité-sur-Loire** (p215)

4 Renaissance romance in the **Château de St-Fargeau** (p221)

5 Do things the medieval way in the castle at **Guédelon** (p223)

The Nivernais

The Burgundian riverside towns look their best when seen from the west bank of the Loire: Nevers is the main town, famous since the 16C for its porcelain and spun glass, after Luigi de Gonzaga took over the Nivernais duchy and imported Italian artists; there's a good pottery collection in the town museum. Although Nevers has no sights of major significance, it's a lovely place to wander, calling at its huge basilica (10C–16C) before indulging in a bit of retail therapy in the shopping streets and tasting the goodies from its celebrated pâtisseries and confectioners; try the *négus*, a soft caramel with a candy coat.

Outside town, budding Formula 1 champions can experience the high-octane buzz of the Magny-Cours racetrack, then move on to discover the lovely villages and ancient churches in the countryside between the Loire and Allier. If you fancy a bit of a hike, explore the secretive trails of the Forêt du Perray.

La Charité-sur-Loire was once an important river port, when the Loire was the main "road" to Paris. Standing proud above the town, the 12C Notre-Dame

priory church hints at its glory days when it was the second largest in France after Cluny.

Fans of the great outdoors should pack a picnic and strike out to the east of La Charité to hit the trails of the beautiful Forêt des Bertranges, or head for Prémery on the River Nièvre. Around here are lakes, such as the Étang de Vaux, for water sports, and a network of walking trails that are ideal for spotting wildlife.

The Puisaye region

The flat expanses of marshy woodland and pastures that make up the Puisaye are made for explorations on foot or by bike. Try the cyclo-rail route from Villiers-St-Benoît for a quirky take on pedalling your way along the old railway track.

The Bourdon lake and Parc Naturel de Boutissaint near St Fargeau offer further scope for outdoor activities.

On a more cultural note, the Puisaye's main town, St-Fargeau, has a romantic Renaissance château where Louis XIV's cousin, known as La Grande Demoiselle, was exiled.

In Guédelon, a trip back to the Middle Ages beckons at the Chantier Médiéval, a fascinating contemporary project to build a medieval castle using authentic 13C building methods and materials. You can see the real thing at the Château de Ratilly.

Visit St-Amand-en-Puisaye to see the area's famous stoneware in potters' studios and the Musée du Grès.

A must for literary types is a pilgrimage to the house in St Sauveur-en-Puisaye where the writer Colette was born; there's also a Colettte trail, and the Musée Colette in the town's château.

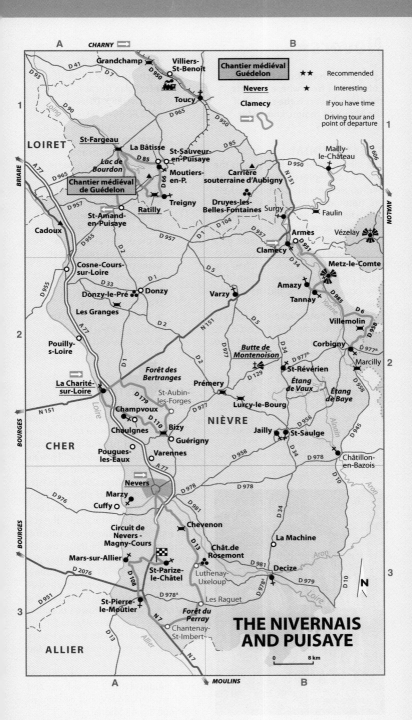

THE NIVERNAIS
AND PUISAYE

Nevers★

Lying in terraces above the River Loire not far from where it meets the Allier, Nevers is the capital of the Nivernais region, known for its fine pottery.

THE CITY TODAY

The silhouette of the cathedral is the town's centrepiece, rising from the bluff above the Loire. It symbolises Nevers' status as a town of art and history with a fine heritage to explore, despite being badly damaged by bombardment in 1944. There is plenty to explore on a stroll around the Old Town, in addition to the cathedral are fine churches, the ducal palace, handsome 17C and 18C townhouse mansions, and the potters' quarter.

On a lighter note, make sure to treat yourself to the delights in the excellent pastry shops and confectioners who make the renowned *négus* – candy-covered chocolate caramels.

Outside the town, petrol-heads can try their hand at the wheel of a fast car on a white-knuckle spin around the Magny-Cours racetrack. For a more leisurely experience, pack a picnic and walk the paths along the River Loire, or take in the town from a different perspective on a boat trip.

Nave, Cathédrale Saint-Cyr-et-Ste-Julitte

© Camille Moirenc/hemis.fr

▶ **Population:** 100 556

◔ **Michelin Map:** 319: B-10.

▣ **Info:** Palais Ducal, r. Sabatier, 58000 Nevers. ℘03 86 68 46 00. www.nevers-tourisme.com.

▷ **Location:** Nevers is 173km/ 107 SE of Orléans and 123km/76mi SE of Auxerre.

✦ **Don't Miss:** There is an excellent view of the old town, dominated by the tower of the cathedral and the graceful silhouette of the ducal palace, from the sandstone bridge that spans the River Loire. The best shopping is along rue St-Étienne, rue François-Mitterrand and rue St-Martin, or at the market on place Carnot on Tuesday, Wednesday and Saturday.

A BIT OF HISTORY

Pottery and spun glass – Luigi di Gonzaga, the Duke of Mantua's third son who became Duke of Nevers in 1565, brought artists and artisans from Italy. He introduced artistic earthenware in Nevers between 1575 and 1585. The three Italian brothers Conrade, master potters in white and other colours, taught their art to a group of local artisans. Little by little, the shape, the colours and the decorative motifs, which at first reproduced only the Italian models and methods, evolved into a very distinctive local style. At the same time, he developed the glass industry as well as the art of enamelling, which became very fashionable. The town's products – spun glass was generally used in the composition of religious scenes – were sent by boat on the Loire to Orléans and Angers.

By about 1650 the pottery industry was at its height with 12 workshops and 1 800 workers. Today, four workshops continue this traditional craft.

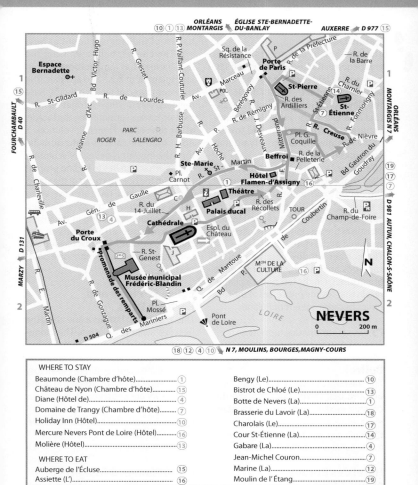

WHERE TO STAY		
Beaumonde (Chambre d'hôte)	①	
Château de Nyon (Chambre d'hôte)	⑮	
Diane (Hôtel de)	④	
Domaine de Trangy (Chambre d'hôte)	⑦	
Holiday Inn (Hôtel)	⑩	
Mercure Nevers Pont de Loire (Hôtel)	⑯	
Molière (Hôtel)	⑬	
WHERE TO EAT		
Auberge de l'Écluse	⑮	
Assiette (L')	⑯	

Bengy (Le)	⑩
Bistrot de Chloé (Le)	⑬
Botte de Nevers (La)	①
Brasserie du Lavoir (La)	⑱
Charolais (Le)	⑰
Cour St-Étienne (La)	⑭
Gabare (La)	④
Jean-Michel Couron	⑦
Marine (La)	⑫
Moulin de l'Étang	⑲

🔍 WALKING TOUR
Start from the Porte du Croux.

Cathédrale Saint-Cyr-et-Ste-Julitte★★

This vast basilica displays all the architectural styles from the 10C to the 16C. The plan is characterised by two apses at opposite ends of the nave: Romanesque to the west and Gothic to the east. This arrangement, common in the Carolingian period and found in some cathedrals on the banks of the Rhine, is rare in France. The exterior bristles with buttresses, pillars, flying buttresses and pinnacles; the square tower (52m/171ft high) standing against the south arm of the transept, is flanked by polygonal buttresses.

Inside, the most striking feature is the sheer size of the 13C nave with its triforium and clerestory and the choir encircled by the ambulatory. The Romanesque apse, raised by 13 steps and with oven vaulting, is decorated with a 12C fresco representing Christ surrounded by the symbols of the Evangelists. The stained-glass windows are the work of five contemporary artists. In 1944, allied bombing damaged the Gothic apse and at the same time revealed a 6C baptistery *(open to visitors)*.

Palais Ducal★

The former home of the dukes of Nevers was begun in the second half of the 15C by Jean de Clamecy, Count of Nevers. It was completed at the end of the 16C by the Clèves and Gonzagas and is a beautiful example of early civil Renaissance architecture. The great round towers at the rear give on to a courtyard that overlooks rue des Ouches.

The ochre façade is surmounted by a slate roof and flanked by twin turrets; the canted tower in the centre rising to a small belfry contains the grand staircase; a graceful effect is created by the placing of the windows which follow the spiralling of the stairs.

The dormer windows are flanked by caryatids and the chimneys resemble organ pipes. On the left turret a plaque recalls that several princesses of the Nivernais became queens of Poland.

Pass place Mancini, turn left on rue François-Mitterrand.

Beffroi

The vast 15C belfry, dominated by a pointed bell tower, once housed the covered markets and council chamber.

Right on place Guy-Coquille; then rue du Fer to rue de Nièvre; turn left.

Hôtel des Bordes et Rue Creuse

At the top of rue Creuse, the Hôtel des Bordes (17C) was, at the time of its construction, at the edge of the city. The widow of Jean Sobieski, King of Poland, visited here. Along rue Creuse, note the monumental structure of the Mutuelle de la Nievre (19C) and the Hotel Marmigny (15–16C).

At the corner of rue des Francs-Bourgeois, turn right.

Église Saint-Étienne★

This beautiful Romanesque church, which once belonged to a priory of Cluny, has a remarkable purity of style. It was built from 1063 to 1097 at the behest of Guillaume I, Count of Nevers. The chevet, best seen from rue du Charnier, has a magnificent tiered arrangement of apse and apsidals. The transept tower, of which only the base remains, was destroyed together with the two towers surmounting the façade, at the time of the French Revolution. Apart from the capitals in the ambulatory, the interior is devoid of sculpture but its attraction lies in its fine proportions and the golden colour of the stone. The six bays of the nave are covered by barrel vaulting with transverse arches; there is groined vaulting in the aisles. A Romanesque altar stands in the chancel (restored). The row of windows beneath the vault is of impressive boldness.

Église St-Pierre and Porte de Paris

This 17C church houses a fine altar; the frescoes await restoration. The monumental portal dates from 1676.

The triumphal Porte de Paris was built in the 18C to commemorate the victory of Fontenoy; verses by Voltaire in praise of Louis XV are engraved on it.

Retrace your steps to get back to rue François-Mitterrand, the turn right on place St-Sébastien.

Hôtel Flamen d'Assigny

Note at number 1 one of the loveliest hôtels particuliers in Nevers (18C), with its rococo-style facade.

Continue along rue St-Martin.

Chapelle Ste-Marie

This is the former chapel, now deconsecrated, of the 7th convent of the Visitandines founded in France. The façade, of Louis XIII style, is covered with Italian-type ornamentation: niches, entablatures, columns and pilasters.

Rue St-Martin (Maison du Prieur at no 5), rue du 14-Juillet and rue de la Porte-du-Croux lead back to the Porte du Croux.

Porte du Croux

Ph. Gajic/MICHELIN

Porte du Croux★

This handsome square tower gateway, built in 1393, is one of the last remnants of the town's fortifications. It houses the Musée Archéologique du Nivernais (*open by request only*) which has Greek, Roman and Romanesque sculptures.

○ *Follow the rampart walk.*

Promenade des Remparts

A well-conserved section of the town walls, built by Pierre de Courtenay in the 12C, stretches from the Porte du Croux southwards to the Loire. Several of the original towers (Tours du Hâvre, St-Révérien and Gogin) are still standing. From quai des Mariniers, there is a fine view of the Pont de Loire.

Musée Municipal Frédéric-Blandin

○ *Closed for restoration work. Re-opening scheduled for mid-2011. For information call* ℘*03 86 68 44 60.* The museum, in an old abbey, has a fine collection of **Nevers pottery**★, as well delicate enamels and spun glass.

○ *Return to the crossroads and turn right onto rue des Jacobins.*

🚗 DRIVING TOUR

Pays d'entre Loire et Allier

82km/51m circuit. Allow 4hrs.
See Region map. South out of Nevers; join D7.

Nevers-Magny-Cours Racetrack (*group visits only*) – Inaugurated in 1961, this legendary racetrack is the venue for prestigious events, such as the French Motorcycle Grand Prix. On race days it can hold up to 110 000 spectators. Courses in racing driving and go-karting can be organised on the Club track.

Saint-Parize-le Châtel – Near to the racetrack, this delightful village was already flourishing in the Gallo-Roman era, thanks to its mineral water springs. In the crypt of the church are splendid 12C capitals.

Mars-sur-Allier – In the 12C, the little Romanesque church sitting on a small square was a priory of Cluny. Its tympanum show Christ in glory, amid the symbols of the four evangelists and several apostles.

Saint-Pierre-le-Moûtier – This ancient seat of a Royal bailliwick is a market town with tranquil little squares. As well as vestiges of the 15C defensive walls and some fine old houses, the church merits a visit. Standing foursquare on the market square, it once belonged to a Benedictine priory linked to St-Martin d'Autun. The dilapidated tympanum above the north door is worth a look, as are the capitals in the nave.

Forêt du Perray – 2 200 hectares of forest and lakes make for fine walking country. At its heart is the Rond-du-Perray, a vast clearing from which trails radiate outwards.

Continue to **Luthenay-Uxeloup**, where the 13C **Château de Rozemont** is visible across the valley.

Chevenon – Built in the 14C by Guillaume de Chevenon, Charles V's "Captain of the castles and towers of Vincennes", this robust baronial residence with four solid round towers dominates the valley.

ADDRESSES

⌂ STAY

Hôtel Molière – *25 r. Molière.* 𝒫*03 86 57 29 96. www.hotel-moliere-nevers.com. Wi-Fi. 18 rooms.* ⊑ *7 €.* A warm welcome awaits at this simple, spotlessly-kept, business-like hotel in a residential area. Rustic and contemporary rooms.

Chambre d'hôte Domaine de Trangy – *8 rte de Trangy, 58000 St-Eloi on D176.* 𝒫*03 86 37 11 27. http://chambreshotestrangy.free.fr.* ⊑ ⊳ *4 rooms.* ⊑×. At the heart of the Burgundian Loire Valley, this fine 18C house offers four charming country-style rooms. Pleasant garden with century-old trees and swimming pool.

Hôtel Mercure Nevers Pont de Loire – *Quai de Médine.* 𝒫*03 86 93 93 86. www.accor-hotels.com.* ⊑ *59 rooms.* ⊑ *12 €.* Despite the charm-free architecture and stripped-out décor, this hotel is top-of-the-range in Nevers. On the plus side, it is both beside the Loire and near the town centre. Bag a room with a view over the Loire.

Hôtel De Diane – *38 r. du Midi.* 𝒫*03 86 57 28 10. www.bestwesterndiane-nevers.com. Closed 20 Dec–4 Jan. Wi-Fi. 30 rooms.* ⊑ *12 €, half board available.* × *Set lunch menu 16 €.* This old residence by the station has airy rooms updated and furnished with care. The breakfast room is in a 14C tower. Classic cuisine is served in a formal restaurant, ⊑⊑.

Chambre d'hôte Château de Nyon – *58130 Nyon. 15km/10mi NE of Nevers on D 977, D 26 then D 104.* 𝒫*03 86 58 61 12. chateaudenyon@gmail.com.* ⊳ *3 rooms.* ⊑. Divine little 18C Burgundian château with stylish rooms set in verdant meadows and delightful grounds with mature trees. Two small houses can be hired on a weekly basis.

Chambre d'hôte Beaumonde – *18 Le Margat, 58400 Chaulgnes. 7km/4.5mi N Pougues-les-Eaux on D 138 then D 267.* 𝒫*03 86 37 86 16. www.beaumondebedandbreakfast.iowners.net. Closed15 Nov–28 Feb.* ⊑⊳ *4 rooms.* ⊑ ×. There's plenty of 1960s character in this house set in 7 ha/17-acres of grounds, plus a swimming pool, fitness centre and fireside reading room. The tastefully decorated rooms have a touch of class. The Australian owner is happy to offer you a taste of her country's specialities.

Hôtel Holiday Inn – *Ferme du domaine de Bardonnay, 58470 Magny-Cours. 12km/7.5mi S of Nevers on D 907.* 𝒫*03 86 21 22 33. www.holidayinn-nevers.com.* ⌲⊑ *Wi-Fi. 70 rooms.* ⊑ *18 €.* × *Set lunch menu 13 €.* Modern hotel close to the Magny-Cours racing circuit. Reception is in an old farmhouse adjoining the main building. Large, bright rooms, and the restaurant is built around the poolside terrace.

⊗ EAT

Le Bistrot de Chloé – *25 av. du Général-de-Gaulle.* 𝒫*03 86 36 72 70. www.le-bistrot-de-chloe.com.* Town-centre location, young and dynamic vibe and suitably modern repertoire.

L'Assiette – *7bis r. F. Gambon.* 𝒫*03 86 36 24 99. pelissou.nadege@orange.fr. Closed 15–30 Aug, evenings Mon–Wed and Sun. Set lunch menu 13 €.* A charming place with an original concept: themed dishes follow a starter, main course and cheese format, based on fresh produce, and are served in a modern blue and chocolate brown setting.

La Marine – *10 quai de la Jonction.* 𝒫*03 86 37 58 61. nomail@voila.fr. Closed Sun (except in summer) and Mon.* ⊳. This bistro by the Jonction marina on the lateral Loire canal is known for its fresh fried Loire whitebait, its goat's cheese *bavarois* and winter season Morvan rösti. Seen at its best on fine days out on the terrace.

La Cour Saint-Étienne – *33 r. St-Étienne.* 𝒫*03 86 36 74 57. www.restaurant-la-cour.com.* The chef of this charming restaurant makes good use of fresh ingredients from the local market to create dishes such as Nivernais goat cheese cannelloni, and knuckles of veal with raisins.

La Botte de Nevers – *R. du Petit Château.* 📞*03 86 61 16 93. labottedenevers@wanadoo.fr. Closed Sun eve, Tue lunch and Mon. Set lunch menu 17 €.* This restaurant close to the Palais Ducal has a traditional décor: tapestries, sturdy beams, stone walls and imposing fireplace. Traditional cooking.

Jean-Michel Couron – *21 r. St-Étienne.* 📞*03 86 61 19 28. www.jm-couron.com. Closed 12 Jul–3 Aug, 20 Feb–8 Mar, Sun eve, Tue lunch and Mon.* Reservations required. This discreet restaurant has three dining rooms, one of which is crowned by the arches of a former chapel. The inventive cuisine is very popular among gourmets.

La Gabare – *171 rte de Lyon, 58000 Challuy. 3km/2mi S of Nevers on D 907.* 📞*03 86 37 54 23. www.restaurant-lagabare.fr. Closed 20 Jul–19 Aug, Sun and Wed.* 🅿️. This restaurant has old-fashioned charm with its exposed beams and fireplace. Simple, unpretentious cuisine with fresh ingredients.

La Brasserie du Lavoir – *Le bourg. 18150 Apremont-sur-Allier. 16km/10mi SW of Nevers.* 📞*02 48 80 25 76.* 📠. Extremely pleasant restaurant in the lovely village of Apremont. Good for fried whitebait and river fish.

Le Bengy – *25 rte de Paris, 58640 Varennes-Vauzelles. 4.5km/2.8mi on D 907.* 📞*03 86 38 02 84. www.le-bengy-restaurant.com. Closed 1–24 Aug, 1–4 Jan, 20 Feb–8 Mar, Sun and Mon.* Hues of beige and chocolate, contemporary lines, leather, wrought iron and verdant plants set a rather Japanese tone in this, well-frequented restaurant. Up-to-date cooking.

Auberge de l'écluse – *12 levée de la Loire, Givry. 18320 Cours-les-Barres, 13km/8mi W of Nevers on D 40 and D 12.* 📞*03 86 90 97 28. www.auberge-ecluse.com.* Riverside terraces overlooking the Loire and traditional regional cuisine: fish and Charolais meat.

Le Charolais – *33 bis rte Moulins, 58300 Decize. 35km/22mi SE of Nevers on D 978 and D 981.* 📞*03 86 25 22 27. rapiau.franck@neuf.fr. Closed 1–9 Jan, 1 week in Feb, Tue from 10 Oct until 15 Jun, Sun eve and Mon.* The chef here cooks up modern dishes in a suitably modern setting. When weather permits, food is grilled on open fires and cooked *à la plancha* (griddled) on the terrace.

Moulin de l'Étang – *64 rte de l'Étang, 58160 Sauvigny-les-Bois. 9.5km/6mi E of Nevers on D 978 and D 18.* 📞*03 86 37 10 17. www.moulindeletang.fr. Closed 1–20 Aug, Feb holidays, Sun and Wed eve and Mon.* 🅿️. This former dairy on the outskirts of the village and near to the lake is home to a modern dining room with an old clock as its centrepiece. Contemporary menu.

🏃 ACTIVITIES

Karting de Nevers/Magny-Cours – *Technopôle, 58470 Magny-Cours.* 📞*03 86 21 26 18. Open until dusk.* Try the excitement of motor racing by jumping into a go-kart or something more sophisticated, or go for a spin with an experienced racing driver.

🛒 SHOPPING

Au Négus – *96 r. François-Mitterrand.* 📞*03 86 61 06 85. Open Mon–Sat 9am–noon, 2–7pm. Closed public holidays except Easter and Christmas mornings.* This shop is named after the *négus*, a delicious sweet made with soft caramel coated with crystallised sugar.

Édé – *75 r. François-Mitterrand.* 📞*03 86 61 02 97. Open Tue–Sat 8.45am–12.15pm and 2–7pm, Sun 8.45am–12.15pm.* The famed *Nougatine de Nevers* was created in this shop, established in 1840. Other sweet temptations include chocolates flavoured with orange, rum or jasmine.

🍴 TAKING A BREAK

Au Bistro Gourmand – *sq. de la Résistance.* 📞*03 86 61 45 09. www.au-bistro-gourmand.com. Open noon–2.30pm and 7pm–midnight. Closed Sun evening and Mon.* This smart café's unusual décor includes colourful clowns' portraits on the walls. Jazz concerts twice a month.

La Charité-sur-Loire★

La Charité, which is dominated by the belfries of its handsome church, rises in terraces from the majestic sweep of the Loire. La Charité was a busy port in the days when the river was active with traffic.

▸ **Population:** 5 362
◔ **Michelin Map:** 319: B-8.
▣ **Info:** 5 pl. Ste-Croix, 58400 La Charité-sur-Loire. ✆03 86 70 15 06. www.lacharitesurloire-tourisme.com.
◉ **Don't Miss:** There is a good view of the town from the picturesque 16C stone bridge over the Loire.

A BIT OF HISTORY

The Charity of the Good Fathers – The founding early in the 8C of a convent and church marked the start of a period of prosperity which was interrupted by Arab invasions and attendant destruction. By the 11C, when the present church was built, the reorganised abbey began to attract travellers and pilgrims. The hospitality of the monks became so widely known that the poor came in droves to ask for the good fathers' charity (charité) and the town acquired a new name.

TOWN

Église prieurale Notre-Dame★★

Despite the damage it has incurred over the centuries (a few bays, the transept and the chancel are all that remain), this **priory church** is still one of the most remarkable examples of Romanesque architecture in Burgundy.

Eldest daughter of Cluny – The church and its attendant Benedictine priory, a daughter house of Cluny, were built during the second half of the 11C. The church was consecrated in 1107 by Pope Paschal II. Its outline and decoration were modified in the first half of the 12C. After Cluny the priory church of La Charité was the largest church in France; it consisted of a nave and four aisles (122m/399ft long, 37m/120ft wide, 27m/89ft high under the dome). It could hold a congregation of 5 000, carried the honorary title Eldest daughter of Cluny and had at least 50 daughter houses.

Exterior – The façade, which was separated from the rest of the church by a fire in 1559, is in place des Pêcheurs. Originally, two towers framed the central doorway; only one (left), the 12C **Tour Ste-Croix**, has survived.

The steps of the Romanesque central doorway, of which very little is left and which was replaced by a Gothic construction in the 16C, lead to place Ste-Croix, on the site of six bays of the nave destroyed in the fire of 1559.

Houses have been built into the former north aisle, which was used as a parish church from the 12C–18C. The arcades of the false triforium are still visible.

Interior – The present church consists of the first four bays of the original nave, the transept and the chancel. The transept and the chancel constitute a magnificent Romanesque ensemble.

The transept crossing is surmounted by an octagonal dome on squinches. The arms of the transept have three bays and two apsidal chapels dating from the 11C; this is the oldest part of the church. In the south transept, the second Romanesque **tympanum**★ of the Tour Ste-Croix is visible, representing the Transfiguration with the Adoration of the Magi and the Presentation in the Temple.

A bestiary of eight motifs accentuates the false triforium; its five-lobed arcades, of Arabic inspiration, are supported by ornamented pilasters. There are good modern stained-glass windows by Max Ingrand.

Old Priory

The vast ensemble formed by the old priory is gradually being restored: note in particular the 14C chapter-house, the 18C cloisters, the refectory, the prior's drawing room and dining room.

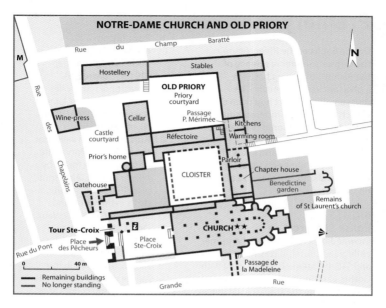

NOTRE-DAME CHURCH AND OLD PRIORY

Les Quartiers

Little remains of the Fishermen's Quarter except for a few fine houses and the salt warehouse on Quai Clemenceau. In the Merchants' Quarter, the 13C Maison de la Revenderie on the place des Pêcheurs is where the abbey once sold its produce. The Bourgeois Quarter is notable for its grand 16–19C houses along the prestigious Grande-Rue. The Quartier des Guêtrots is named for the 18 and 19C wine producers who wore gaiters (*guêtres* in French). Their houses lining rue Ste-Anne, rue St-Jacques and rue des Halles once sat among vineyards.

DRIVING TOUR

FORÊT DES BERTRANGES
45km/28mi. See Region map.

Lying 5km/3.1mi east of the Loire, the Forêt des Bertranges is a vast and beautiful 10 000 ha/24 500-acre expanse of oak, beech, pine and larch trees. Around the area are the ruins of iron-making workshops, an important local industry from the 14C to 19C thanks to abundant ore and the river at La Charité-sur-Loire. Taking the Rond-de-la-Réserve forest road, you will find a lovely picnic spot at Fontaine de la Vache. Pick up the switchback D 179 to St-Aubin-les-Forges, then the D 117 to Bizy, where a château beside a lake comes into view. Continue on the D 8, then D 110, enjoying fine forest views as far as Chaulgnes. Next comes Champvoux, where you can explore an interesting 13C church, before returning on the D 907 along the Loire to La Charité.

ADDRESSES

STAY

Relais de Pouilly – *58150 Pouilly-sur-Loire. 03 86 39 03 00. www.relaisdepouilly.com. 24 rooms. 8.50€. Restaurant* . Near the new motorway, but restful thanks to double glazing. A lush setting for cosy rooms decorated with bamboo furniture.

EAT

Le Moulin aux Crêpes – *26 r. des Hôtelleries. 03 86 70 00 55.* . Simple, quiet and welcoming are the watchwords for this small *creperie*. Regulars turn up for the short but well-rounded menu.

Prémery

On the banks of the River Nièvre, the former summer residence of the Bishops of Nevers basks in a pleasant verdant setting. Its museum, just a short hop from the church and an old timbered house, is home to an exceptional collection of ancient stoneware pottery. With its hiking trails and lakes, the area around Prémery is ideal for fishing, walking and messing about on the water.

SIGHTS

Église St Marcel

Crowned by a huge belfry, the former collegiate church dates from the 13 and 14C. Its interior is resplendent with Gothic vaulting and a double row of windows along the apse. The 15C pietà was sculpted by a disciple of the famous Claus Sluter (& see DIJON). The remains of Canon Nicolas Appeleine lie in the church, a man considered so holy that the ailing Louis XI sent for his robe – and although he got better, the taxes on the citizens of Prémery were not lifted out of gratitude as they had hoped!

The Château

The summer residence of the Bishops of Nevers retained its medieval fortified porch (14C), although the bulk of the building was reworked in the 16C.

Musée du Grès Ancien

Open Jul–Aug weekends 2.30pm–6.30pm. 03 86 68 10 32.

Presented in a modern and attractive manner, this significant private collection numbers 1 250 items and represents the culmination of 25 years of passionate research. Three floors of exhibits present everyday utilitarian pieces from the Puisaye and Berry regions, including rare blue pottery from the 16C and 17C, as well as 250 superb works from the School of Carriès (1884–1914), which developed during the Art Nouveau period and was clearly influenced by Japanese art.

▶ **Population:** 2 201

Michelin Map: Map A3 – Michelin regional map 319 C8 – Nièvre (58).

Location: Prémery lies along the Nevers-Clamecy-Auxerre axis 29km/18mi NE of Nevers.

Kids: The sylvan valleys of the Nivernais-Morvan are great for family forays by bike or on foot. Also, spot wildlife from observation posts in the woodland around the Étang de Vaux.

Don't Miss: The pure lines of the ceramic pieces made by the Carriès school, displayed in the Musée du Grès Ancien; the Romanesque church of St-Révérien; the panorama over the Morvan seen from the top of the Butte de Montenoison.

EXCURSIONS

Gardens of Château de Lurcy-le-Bourg – The French gardens of this 17C manor house were added in the 18C (*open Aug–Sept 2.30pm–8pm; 03 86 68 16 83*).

Butte de Montenoison – On the summit of a beacon hill (one of the highest points of the Nivernais at 417m/1 368ft) are the ruins of a 13C castle. A vast panorama over the Morvan hills opens out from the orientation table.

Saint-Révérien – One of the region's most interesting Romanesque churches, although a fire in 1723 destroyed all but its chancel and apse.

Saint-Saulge – According to local lore, its church was built by fairies, who couldn't be bothered to finish the job.

Clamecy

The old town, with its narrow winding streets, is perched on a spur overlooking the confluence of the Yonne and Beuvron. It remains "the town of beautiful reflections and graceful hills" described by Romain Rolland (1866–1944), the French writer and philosopher, who is buried in the Nivernais not far from his native town.

A BIT OF HISTORY

Log floating – This method of moving timber, which goes back to the 16C, brought wealth to the river port of Clamecy for nearly 300 years. The logs, cut in the forests of the Upper Morvan, were piled along the banks of the rivers and marked with their owners' signs. On an agreed day, the dams holding back the rivers were opened and the logs thrown into the flood which carried them to Clamecy.

There, a dam stopped the wood, the timbermen dragged the logs from the water and piled them up by mark. From here, immense rafts of wood, called *trains*, were sent down the Yonne and the Seine towards Paris, where the wood was used for heating. The building of the Nivernais Canal ended this; the last *train* of wood left Clamecy in 1923.

TOWN

Église St-Martin★ was built between the end of the 12C and the beginning of the 16C. Episodes in the life of St Martin are illustrated on the arches over the door (damaged during the Revolution). The interior reveals the rectangular plan and the square ambulatory characteristic of Burgundian churches. The rood screen was built by Viollet-le-Duc to counteract the bowing of certain pillars in the chancel.

EXCURSIONS
Druyes-les-Belles-Fontaines
⊙ *18km/11.2mi NW.*
The hilltop ruins of the 12C **feudal castle** (⊙*open Jul–Aug daily 3–6pm; Easter–end Jun and Sept, Sat and Sun*

- **Population:** 4 424
- **Michelin Map:** 319: E-7.
- **Info:** r. du Grand-Marché, 58500 Clamecy. ✆03 86 27 02 51. www.vaux-yonne.com.
- **Location:** The Bethlehem Bridge, on which there is a statue in memory of the loggers, provides a good overall view of the town and its quays.

3–6pm; ∞4€; ⎣ ✆03 86 41 51 71; www. chateau-de-druyes.com) are best seen from the south, along D 148 or D 104. From the road to Courson-les-Carrières, a 14C fortified gate gives access to the rocky outcrop occupied by the old village and the castle ruins.

Carrière souterraine d'Aubigny
⊙ *6km/3.7mi N of Druyes along D 148.*
⊙*Open Jul–Aug 10am–6.30pm (Sun from 2.30pm. Apr–Jun and Sept–Oct 10am–noon, 2.30–6.30pm (Sun from 2.30pm). ∞6€. ⎣ ✆03 86 52 38 79. www.carriereaubigny.com.*
This underground quarry dates from Roman times. The limestone was first used for sacred funeral items, later for castles and, in the 19C in Paris, for buildings such as the Hôtel de Ville and the Opera. Exhibits explain the formation and uses of this 150-million-year-old mineral, and display various tools.

🚗 DRIVING TOUR

Vallée de l'Yonne from Clamecy to Corbigny
38km/24mi along D 951 and D 985; allow 2hrs 30min.
The road runs alongside the river and the Canal du Nivernais overlooked by wooded hills. The itinerary is dotted with pleasant riverside villages such as Armes, and hilltop ones such as Metz-le-Comte and Tannay offering wide views of the Yonne Valley.

Cosne-Cours-sur-Loire

Situated on the right bank of the Loire where the Nohain Valley opens out, this small hub of trades and industry is linked by a suspension bridge to a wooded island. The wild coils of the Loire and the vineyards of the coteau du Giennois offer plenty of scope for outdoor types to enjoy pleasant walks.

- **Population:** 11 300
- **Michelin Map:** General map A2 – Michelin Departements map 319 A7 – Nièvre (58).
- **Location:** Cosne-Cours-sur-Loire lies 19km/11.8mi SW of St-Amand-en-Puisaye and 17km/10.5mi west of Donzy.
- **Don't Miss:** The Musée de la Loire's fishing and boating displays; country houses in the Musée Paysan de Cadoux in La Celle-sur-Loire.
- **Kids:** For great family days out, try a cyclo-rail trip from Cosne to Sancerre, or explore the Loire Valley by boat.

A BIT OF HISTORY

A coveted arsenal – In the 18C, Cosne was known for its **forges** (in operation since 1666; *see Decize*) and its manufacture of cannons, muskets and ship's anchors. With the coal and timber resources of the nearby Nivernais, and the rivers Nohain and Loire to transport its products to the Atlantic ports, the town was in an ideal position to prosper. **Jacques Masson**, owner of the forges at **Guérigny** (*see Nevers*), acquired those in Cosne in 1738, and **Babaud de La Chaussade** bought the lot seven years later. Under his ownership they went through such a phenomenal boom period that Louis XVI bought them in 1781 for the astronomical sum of £2 500 000. Unfortunately, the near-bankruptcy of the state, followed hotly by the Revolution meant that the Baron never saw his cash and died almost penniless. Transfered to Guérigny in 1872, the "nationalised" forges continued in production, serving the navy until 1971. Nowadays, the **Forges de la Chaussade** (quai Maréchal-Joffre; &03 86 28 11 85; no entry) house interesting industrial relics, including waterways, and fine ironwork buildings facing the Loire.

VISIT

Cosne grew from the Gallo-Roman town of Condate; relics from the site are on display in the Maison des Chapelains.

Église Saint-Agnan

A Romanesque portal and apse survive in this Cluniac priory church. Don't miss the decorated capitals.

Behind the church, on the riverside promenade des Marronniers the 17C gateway and a huge anchor evoke the past grandeur of the Royal Forges.

Musée de la Loire

Pl de la Résistance. &03 86 26 71 02. Housed in a former convent building along the Nohain, the museum houses displays covering fishing, boating and the commercial activities of the Loire. On the upper floor is a rich collection of modernist art by the likes of Chagall, Utrillo, Dufy and Derain. Finish with a walk around place de la Pêcherie, where the bargees houses are a reminder of days gone by.

EXCURSION
Donzy

17 km/10.6mi E on D 33.
At the confluence of the rivers Nohain and Talvanne, this cluster of timbered houses with Renaissance façades was a powerful barony in the Middle Ages. Try its speciality almond sweets, have a look at the Moulin de Maupertuis, one of 57 mills that once lined the Nohain, then walk 1km to the ruined Cluniac priory at Donzy-le-Pré to see its 12C tympanum, a masterpiece of Romanesque sculpture.

La Puisaye

The Puisaye region has a reputation for being monotonous and even austere. The uniformity is however only superficial and the visitor will find a variety of scenery: forests dotted with ponds, wooded hills and meadows graced with the silhouettes of many châteaux *(Ratilly, St-Fargeau, St-Sauveur and St-Amand).*

⚐ **Michelin Map:** 319: B-5.

▯ **Info:** pl. de la République, 89170 St-Fargeau. ℘03 86 74 10 07. www.tourisme.ccpf.fr.

◖ **Location:** The books of Colette *(◔ see below)* are rich in poetic descriptions of this area, her birthplace.

A BIT OF HISTORY
Pottery in the Puisaye

The soil of the Puisaye contains uncrushed flint coated with white or red clays which were used in the Middle Ages by the potters of St-Amand, Treigny, St-Vérain and Myennes.

It was in the 17C that the pottery trade really began to develop; the fine pieces of pottery, known as the *Bleu de St-Verain* (Blue of St Verain), were followed in the next century by utility products. Pottery making is now concentrated in **St-Amand-en-Puisaye**, where there is a training centre, and where, on the outskirts of the town, several potters' shops produce first-rate stoneware. Moutiers, near St-Sauveur, is known for the earthenware and stoneware produced at La Batisse. At the Château de Ratilly *(◔ see below)* those interested in ceramic art can observe the different stages of the potter's craft: casting, moulding and throwing on the wheel.

🚗 DRIVING TOURS

Heart of the Puisaye
36km/22mi circuit. Allow 2hrs.
◔ See Region map.

Saint-Amand-en-Puisaye
The capital of Puisaye pottery is packed with studios and shops selling ceramics. Track down Jean Cacheleux, who is one of the finest artists in town.

Saint-Fargeau★
Don't miss the amazing Spectacles Historiques which take place on Friday and Saturday evenings in summer at the château: 600 actors, 60 horsemen, lights and sounds all help bring the past to gloriously entertaining life.

Saint-Fargeau, chief town of the Puisaye, has a fine château filled with memories of Anne-Marie-Louise d'Orléans, cousin of Louis XIV, better known under the name of Mademoiselle de Montpensier or La Grande Mademoiselle, a supporter of the Fronde, a rising of the aristocracy and Parliament from 1648 to 1653.

Château★ *(◔ ◷ open mid-Mar–mid-Nov 10am–noon, 2–7pm; ⊜9€; ℘03 86 74 05 67; www.chateau-de-st-fargeau. com)* – The château is on the site of a fortress erected at the end of the 10C. The present building was begun in the Renaissance period and was built in several stages. However, it is La Grande Mademoiselle who can claim the honour of completely changing the appearance of the buildings. Mademoiselle de Montpensier was exiled to St-Fargeau for several years on the orders of Louis XIV as punishment for her attitude during the uprising of the Fronde. When she arrived in 1652 she had "to wade through knee-high grass in the courtyard" and found a dilapidated building. To make her place of exile more comfortable, she called in Le Vau, the king's architect, who laid out the inner courtyard and completely refurbished the interior of the château.

In 1681, Mlle de Montpensier made a gift of St-Fargeau to the Duc de Lauzun, whom she married in a secret ceremony. In 1715 the property was bought by Le Pelletier des Forts. His great-grandson, Louis-Michel Le Pelletier de St-Fargeau, became deputy to the National Convention in 1793 and voted for the death of

Colette

Sidonie Gabrielle, daughter of Jules Colette, was born in St-Sauveur-en-Puysaye on 28 January 1873 and spent her first 19 years there. During her marriage to Henry Gauthier-Villars, she wrote the four novels in the Claudine series, which her husband, under his pen name of Willy, took credit (and cash)

© Lebrecht Music & Arts/Corbis

for. Blazing the trail of independent womanhood, she obtained a divorce and took to the stage (inspiration for *La Vagabonde*). After a failed second marriage, she finally found happiness with author Maurice Goudeket, whom she married in 1935. They set up house, with Colette's legendary cats, in an apartment overlooking the elegant Palais Royal gardens in Paris, where she died, much admired and honoured, in 1954.

Colette's novels, concerned with the pleasures and pain of love, are rich in sensory evocation of the natural environment in her native Burgundy. She brought a great sensitivity to her descriptions of the animal world (*The Cat, Creatures Comfort*) and childhood (*My Mother's House, Sido*). Her masterpieces also include post-World War I works steeped in the troubling ambivalence of those times (*Chéri* and *The Last of Chéri*); *Gigi* (1944) was adapted for stage and screen, and became a popular musical comedy.

Louis XVI. He was assassinated on the eve of the king's execution and was the revolutionaries first martyr.

Within the feudal enclosure is a huge, elegant courtyard bordered by five ranges of buildings (the most recent on the right of the entrance dates from 1735). A semicircular stair in the corner between the two main wings leads to the entrance rotunda. The chapel is housed in one of the towers: on the left is the portrait gallery which led into the apartments of the *Grande Mademoiselle* until they were burned in 1752; on the right is the 17C guardroom. A grand stair leads to the rooms on the first floor. The tour of the attic lets visitors see the vast roof area and handsome timberwork.

In the English-style park (118ha/292 acres) with its charming groves there is a large lake, fed by the River Bourdon. At the ♠♠ **Ferme du Château** (◑*open Apr–Jun and Sept 10am–noon and 2–5pm weekend, public and school holidays (Jul–Aug daily 10am–noon and 2–6pm);* ◈*6€ (children 4€);* ℘*03 86 74 03 76; www.ferme-du-chateau.com)* some of the buildings have been refurbished to house an exhibit on rural life and trades 100 years ago and plenty of farmyard animals to pet.

The former town hall is now a small museum, the **Musée de l'Aventure du Son**★, devoted to the history of ways of reproducing music and to their inventors: Cros, Edison, Bell, Lioret, Pathé, Berliner etc. Early music boxes, a German calliope from 1910 with a vertical disc, an automatic orchestra dating from 1925, a Limonaire carrousel organ and more, make up this charming collection. The set of phonographs, some portable, shows models in fanciful shapes. Demonstrations are provided (◑*open May–Sept daily 10am–noon, 2–6pm; Mar–Apr and Oct daily except Tue 2–6pm;* ◈*5.50€;* ℘*03 86 74 13 06; www.aventureduson.fr).*

▷ *From the castle, drive 3km/1.7mi SE along D 185.*

Lac de Bourdon

This 220ha/544-acre reservoir feeds the Briare Canal and offers leisure activities (boat trips, sailing, fishing, swimming).

👥 Parc Naturel de Boutissaint★

🕐*Open Feb to mid-Nov 8am–8pm (last entrance 6.30pm).* 🚗*8€ (children 5€).* 📞*03 86 74 07 08. www.boutissaint.com.*
Created in 1968, this park of 400ha/988 acres of pastures, ponds and woods is home to over 400 large animals (deer, bison, wild boars, moufflons) and a multitude of smaller ones (squirrels, rabbits, weasels, stoats) as well as birds. Visitors can walk, ride or cycle along 100km/62mi of waymarked trails. Picnics are allowed.

▷ *A little further on, turn left onto D 955 towards St-Sauveur-en-Puisaye.*

👥 Chantier Médiéval de Guédelon★★

🕐*Open Jul–Aug 10am–7pm (last admission 1hr before closing). Rest of the year not Wed, times vary.* 🕐*Closed Nov to mid-Mar.* 🚗*9€ (children 7€).* 📞*02 38 31 64 66. www.guedelon.fr.*
Learn more about the medieval way of life at this unusual site in a disused quarry. In 1998, the owner of St-Fargeau and the association of master builders of the Puisaye region decided to build a medieval castle using only the means available in the 13C; the project is due to last 25 years. Pottery made on the premises are on sale. There is also a workshop which introduces visitors to the art of illuminating manuscripts.

▷ *Continue along D 955 towards St-Amand-en-Puisaye; left on D 185.*

Château de Ratilly★

🕐*Open mid-Jun to mid-Sept 10am–6pm. Rest of the year call for information.* 🚗*4€.* 📞*03 86 74 79 54. www.chateauderatilly.fr.*
The first sight of this large 13C castle, surrounded by magnificent trees, will charm visitors. Massive towers and high walls of an austere appearance overlook the dry moat surrounding the castle, which is built in fine ochre-coloured stone that time has mellowed.
The left wing now houses a stoneware workshop *(courses available)*. Both the workshop and the showroom, with its small exhibition on the original Puisaye stoneware, are open to the public. Other premises have been refurbished to house temporary art exhibitions.

▷ *Drive back down towards the village.*

Treigny

This village boasts an unusually vast 15C Flamboyant-Gothic church. Note the massive buttresses supporting the edifice and the two crucifix inside; the one in the aisle is the work of a 16C leper.

▷ *Follow D 66 to Moutiers.*

Moutiers-en-Puisaye

The parish church once belonged to a priory dependent on the Abbaye d'Auxerre. Note the 13C carvings decorating the narthex and, in the nave, the medieval frescoes dating from two successive periods: 12C frescoes on the north wall (Annunciation, Nativity, Christ surrounded by angels), on the west wall (large figures) and on part of the south wall; Gothic frescoes (c. 1300) on the remainder of the south wall depicting a procession (top), scenes from Genesis (centre) and the story of John-the-Baptist and Noah's Ark (bottom).

Saint-Sauveur-en-Puisaye

On Colette's namesake street, a red-marble medallion on the façade of her former home simply states, *Ici Colette est née* (Colette was born here).
Housed in one of the pavilions of the Château de St-Sauveur, close to the unusual 12C ironstone-built Tour Sarrasine, the **Musée Colette**★ *(♿🕐open mid-Mar–end Oct daily except Tue 10am–6pm; 🚗5€; 📞03 86 45 61 95)* contains a collection of photographs, objects, furniture, manuscripts and books illustrating Colette's life and career. There is also a recording of some of her writings. Her drawing room and bedroom in Paris, where she spent the last years of her life,

have been reconstructed with her own furniture. The visit ends in the library.

▶ *Return to St-Fargeau via D 85.*

Vallée de l'Ouanne
25km/15.5mi circuit.
👃*See Region map.*

▶ *Follow the D 950 along the route of the tourist train of Puisaye-Forterre.*

Toucy
The historic centre of the Puisaye region until the 14C, Toucy is dominated by its fortress-like church, built partially from the ruins of the baronial castle. In the lower town, a bust celebrates Pierre Larousse, a local lad whose name lives on in his famous French dictionary.

▶ *Take the tourist train to Villiers-Saint-Benoît.*

Villiers-Saint-Benoît
A magnificent 15C fresco of a supernatural conversation between tricks of living and dead characters makes the church here a special place.
Housed in a grand 18C house, the **Musée d'Art et d'Histoire de Puisaye** (℘03 86 45 73 05) houses reconstructed interiors from Puisaye houses, pottery, and superb Burgundian sculptures from the 12C to 16C.

Grandchamp
The unusually long château, was reworked several times from the Renaissance to the Second Empire; its brick façades are a masterpiece.

Charny
A plaque in this village commemorates the terrible events of 14 July 1944, when all the men and women suspected of helping the Resistance were herded into the school. Forty five were arrested, of whom 14 were tortured and deported to Germany.

ADDRESSES

🛌STAY

⊖ **Domain des Sapins** – *89520 St-Sauveur-en-Puisaye.* ℘*03 86 45 50 32. www.domaine-des-sapins.com.* 🅿 ⇄ *3 rooms.* ⌂. 2km/1.2mi from the village where Colette was born, this mid-19C family home lies at the heart of an old pine arboretum. The owner is a keen local historian who passes on fascinating tips about the area. Comfy, spacious rooms with period furniture.

⊖ **Chambre d'hôte La Bruère** – *La Bruère, 89130 Fontaines. 9km/6mi SW of Toucy on D 955, rte de St-Sauveur.* ℘*03 86 74 30 83.* 🅿 ⇄ *5 rooms.* ⌂ ✕. This farmhouse is perfect for relaxing in the country. Spacious rooms are in the former granary. The chef uses fresh, home-grown organic ingredients.

⊖⊖⊜ **Hôtel Les Grands Chênes** – *Les Berthes-Bailly, 89170 Saint-Fargeau. 4.5 km/3mi S on D 18.* ℘*03 86 74 04 05. www.hoteldepuisaye.com. Closed 20 Dec–4 Jan and 6–22 Feb.* 📶. Wi-Fi. *13 rooms.* ⌂ *8 €.* This classy bolthole has loads of character and colourful bedrooms. Near to the Guédelon medieval site.

🍽/EAT

⊖ **Café Restaurant du Bal** – *7 r. du Prof. Lian, 89520 Treigny.* ℘*03 86 74 66 18. www.gite-puisaye.com.* 👃🅿 *Set lunch menu 9.80 €. 2 rooms.* ⌂ *6 €.* This café-restaurant with stone walls and exposed beams is the hub of the hamlet. Enjoy traditional dishes in the air-con dining room, or order take-away. *Tête de veau* is the speciality.

⊖ **La Mare aux fées** – *1 pl. Lucien-Gaubert, 89130 Mézilles. 11km/7mi NE of St-Fargeau on D 965.* ℘*03 86 45 40 43. www.restaurant-mareauxfees.fr. Closed Feb, Mon and Tue eve and Wed.* 🅿 *Set lunch menu 13 €.* Behind the ivy-clad façade, two rustic dining rooms have beams, stone walls and tiled floors, Warm welcome and generous helpings of traditional food.

⊖⊖⊜ **Ferme-auberge Les Perriaux** – *89350 Champignelles.* ℘*03 86 45 13 22. www.lafermedesperriaux.com.* 👃🅿. Terrine, foie gras and cider are made in-house at this 16C farm. Rustic setting with fireplace, and pleasantly arranged upstairs guest room.

Heading south, you know you've arrived in Burgundy when the fecund Auxerrois landscape spreads before you in a patchwork of bright yellow mustard fields and emerald vineyards. Sens and Auxerre are the northern gateways to Burgundy: both sit pleasantly beside the Yonne, and both can trace their origins back to Roman times; two millennia of history have left magnificent cathedrals, fine museums and there's a lively buzz in the shopping streets. Elsewhere, you can explore a rich legacy of Renaissance châteaux in Tanlay and Ancy-le-Franc, and the abbey at Pontigny where Thomas à Becket took refuge. For wine lovers, one word will do: Chablis!

A tale of Two Cities

Take in the silhouette of Auxerrre from the east bank of the Yonne: above the tree-lined quays, a trio of magnificent churches soars from the hill. That should whet the appetite for strolling through the town's cobbled streets of timbered houses; tick off the sights – the Gothic Tour de l'Horloge with its astronomical clock, the Carolingian crypt of the Abbaye St-Germain with its 9C frescoes, and the superb 13C stained glass windows in the St-Étienne cathedral. And when you're all cultured out, the town's shops offer plenty of diversions – try Monsieur Soufflard's splendid array of local cheeses.

Sens is not such a looker as Auxerre, but its trump card is the Cathédrale St-Étienne, the first of the great French Gothic cathedrals. After feasting on its beautiful medieval stained glass windows, one of which tells the story of the murder of Thomas à Becket, and the Flamboyant decoration, you can boggle at the wealth of precious items tucked away in the Treasury. Sens is an inviting town simply to amble around; check out the shops and cafés of Grande Rue and place de la République. A short way south, Villeneuve-sur-Yonne is a good place to head for a swim in the river.

Around the Auxerrois

The Burgundy Canal is a brilliant way to explore this part of the region. You could access it from Joigny where wonderful medieval houses cluster around two 15C churches.

A medieval gem, Noyers is a seductive place when illuminated in the evening, and a great place for music lovers during its summer season of Rencontres Musicales.

Highlights

1 France's first great Gothic cathedral in **Sens** (p228)

2 A magical candlelit visit to **Pontigny Abbey** (p233)

3 Superb frescoes in Auxerre's **St Germain Abbey** (p235)

4 Medieval romance in the streets of **Noyers** (p247)

5 Renaissance splendour at the **Château d'Ancy-le-Franc** (p248)

At Pontigny, the abbey where Thomas à Becket was exiled has survived in a rather better state than its grand sister at Cîteaux; try to catch a classical concert there, or pay a candlelit evening visit.

On a hill above a sea of vineyards, the lovely market town of Tonnerre's Hôtel-Dieu hospice and the lovely sepulchre within are some of Burgundy's finest treasures. Tonnerre is a good jumping-off point for the châteaux at Tanlay and Ancy-le-Franc – both are unmissable If you have a taste for Renaissance splendour.

Driving tours are also a high point of the region: the Cure Valley is a splendid route south from Auxerre to Vézelay passing limestone cliffs riddled with caves, while the Yonne Valley takes you through vineyards and cherry orchards, past dramatic cliffs, fortified villages and ancient churches.

And what would a trip to Burgundy be without wine? Chablis is not only a lovely small town with a medieval feel, but also the epicentre of its own prestigious appellation.

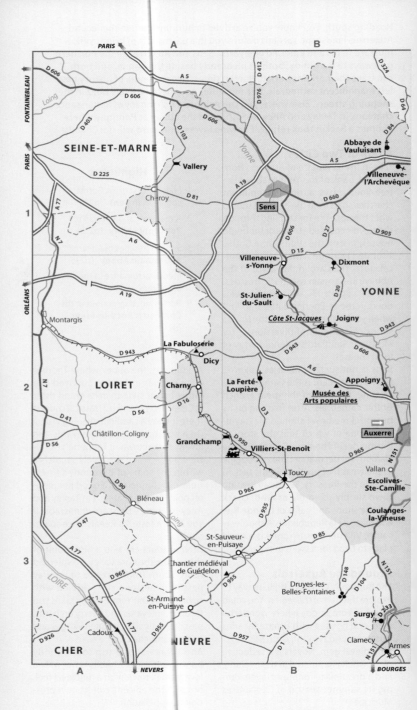

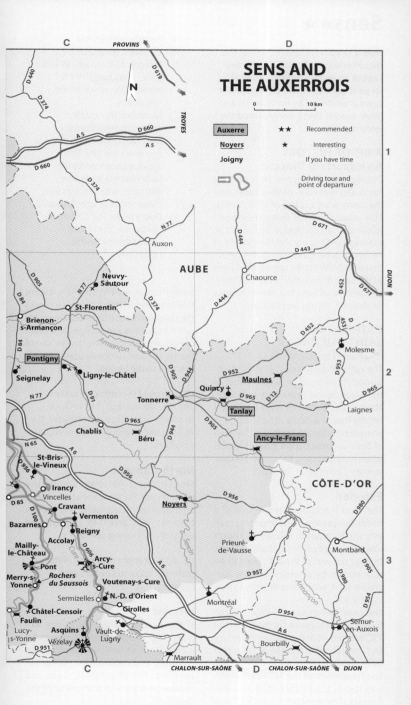

SENS AND THE AUXERROIS

Auxerre	★★	Recommended
Noyers	★	Interesting
Joigny		If you have time
		Driving tour and point of departure

0   10 km

AUBE

CÔTE-D'OR

PROVINS

TROYES

DIJON

CHALON-SUR-SAÔNE   CHALON-SUR-SAÔNE DIJON

Auxon
Chaource
Molesme
Neuvy-Sautour
St-Florentin
Brienon-s-Armançon
Pontigny
Seignelay
Ligny-le-Châtel
Tonnerre
Quincy
Maulnes
Tanlay
Laignes
Chablis
Béru
Ancy-le-Franc
St-Bris-le-Vineux
Irancy
Vincelles
Cravant
Vermenton
Reigny
Noyers
Bazarnes
Accolay
Mailly-le-Château
Pont
Arcy-s-Cure
Prieuré-de-Vausse
Montbard
Merry-s-Yonne
Rochers du Saussois
Voutenay-s-Cure
N.-D. d'Orient
Sermizelles
Girolles
Montréal
Semur-en-Auxois
Châtel-Censoir
Faulin
Lucy-s-Yonne
Asquins
Vézelay
Vault-de-Lugny
Bourbilly
Marrault

Sens★★

Now a simple sub-prefecture in the département of Yonne, Sens is the seat of an archbishopric, proof of its past grandeur. The attractive old town is encircled by boulevards and promenades that have replaced the ancient ramparts.

A BIT OF HISTORY
An Important Diocese

During the residence in Sens of Pope Alexander III in 1163–64 the city became the temporary capital of Christianity. The church council that condemned Abélard was also held at Sens and the marriage of St Louis and Marguerite of Provence was celebrated in the cathedral in 1234. With the elevation of Paris to the rank of an archbishopric in 1622, the diocese of Sens lost the bishoprics of Meaux, Chartres and Orléans.

CATHÉDRALE SAINT-ÉTIENNE★★

Guided tours. ℘03 86 64 46 22.
The cathedral, started c. 1130 by Archbishop Henri Sanglier, was the first of the great Gothic cathedrals in France. Many other buildings have borrowed largely from the design (the layout, the alternating pillars, the triforium; William of Sens, architect, used it as his model when reconstructing the chancel of Canterbury Cathedral (1175–92).

Exterior

The west front, despite the loss of a tower, has preserved its imposing majesty and harmony of balance. The north tower (*tour de plomb* or Lead Tower), built at the end of the 12C, used to be surmounted by a timbered belfry covered in lead, which was destroyed during the 19C.

The south tower (*tour de pierre* or Stone Tower), which collapsed at the end of the 13C, was rebuilt in the following century and completed in the 16C. It is topped by a graceful campanile.

The tympanum of the 12C north doorway recalls the history of St John the Baptist. The central doorway has a

▶ **Population:** 25 844
 Michelin Map: 319: C-2.
 Info: pl. Jean-Jaurès, 89100 Sens. ℘03 86 65 19 49. www.office-de-tourisme -sens.com.
 Location: If possible, approach Sens from the west for scenic views as you enter the city. There are nice shops along the pedestrian Grande-Rue, and cafés with terraces line the place de la République.
 Don't Miss: The Cathédrale St-Étienne, the first of France's great Gothic cathedrals.

beautiful statue of St Stephen, dating from the end of the 12C, which marks the transition period between the sculptures of Chartres and Bourges and those of Paris and Amiens. The tympanum of the right-hand doorway (early 14C) is devoted to the Virgin.

 Go round the cathedral to the N and take the passage (14C St-Denis doorway) to the Maison de l'Œuvre, the 16C chapter library. Carry on to impasse Abraham.

North transept

From impasse Abraham admire the magnificent Flamboyant-style façade built by Martin Chambiges and his son between 1500 and 1513. The sculpted decoration is very graceful.

 Go back to the west front of the cathedral and enter by the south doorway.

Interior

The nave is impressive for its size and unity; it is divided from the aisles by magnificent arches surmounted by a triforium and roofed with sexpartite vaulting. The alternating stout and slender pillars are characteristic of the Early Gothic style.

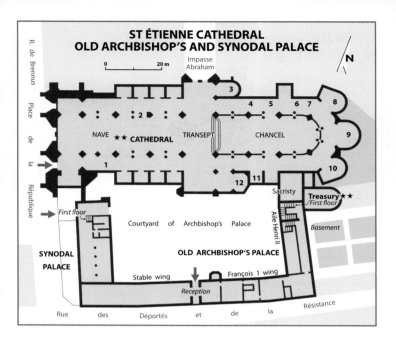

ST ÉTIENNE CATHEDRAL OLD ARCHBISHOP'S AND SYNODAL PALACE

The **stained-glass windows**★★, dating from the 12C to the 17C, are magnificent. In the third bay of the south aisle is a window (**1**) by Jean Cousin, dating from 1530. On the north side of the nave is a Renaissance retable and a monument (**2**) given by Archbishop de Salazar in memory of his parents.

The stained-glass windows of the south transept (1500–02) were made in Troyes – those portraying the Tree of Jesse and Legend of St Nicholas are outstanding; the rose window represents the Last Judgement. Those in the north transept were made between 1516 and 1517 by Jean Hympe and his son, glaziers from Sens; the rose window represents Paradise.

The choir is enclosed by handsome bronze screens (1762) bearing the arms of the Cardinal de Luynes. The large high altar is 18C by Servandoni and the stained glass of the clerestory dates from the 13C.

Both St John's Chapel, which contains a fine 13C calvary (**3**), and the blind arcade round the ambulatory are part of the original building. The oldest stained glass, dating from the late 12C, is in the four windows overlooking the ambulatory: the story of Thomas à Becket (**4**), the story of St Eustache (**5**) and the parables of the Prodigal Son (**6**) and the Good Samaritan (**7**). The tomb (**8**) of the dauphin, father of Louis XVI, by Guillaume Coustou is placed in the next chapel. The 13C apsidal chapel has stained-glass windows (**9**) of the same period. In the chapel of the Sacré-Cœur (**10**) one of the windows is attributed to Jean Cousin. In summer, a 13C staircase leads up to the cathedral **treasury**★★ (🔒 *in winter, go via the museum, as the staircase is closed*). In the chapel beyond the sacristy is a Renaissance retable (**11**). The Lady Chapel contains a 14C seated statue of the Virgin (**12**) above the altar.

◗ *Leave by the south transept.*

South transept

This was built by Martin Chambiges, master mason, who had worked at both Beauvais and Troyes. It is a fine example of the Flamboyant style (1490–1500); the Moses doorway is quite remarkable.

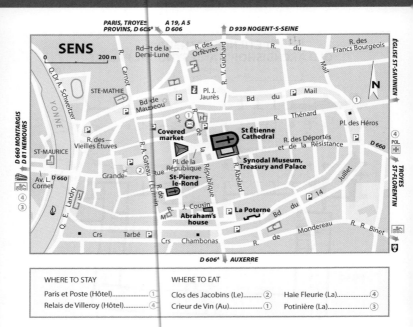

WHERE TO STAY		WHERE TO EAT	
Paris et Poste (Hôtel)....................①		Clos des Jacobins (Le)..........②	Haie Fleurie (La)....................④
Relais de Villeroy (Hôtel)...............④		Crieur de Vin (Au)...................①	Potinière (La)........................③

MUSEUM, TREASURY AND PALAIS SYNODAL★

⊙Open Wed, Sat, Sun 10am–noon, 2–6pm; Mon, Thu, Fri 2–6pm. ⊙Closed Tue, 1 Jan and 25 Dec. ⊚4.20€ ℘03 86 83 88 90.

The Musées de Sens are housed in the **Old Archbishop's Palace** (15C–18C) and the Synodal Palace which stand on the south side of the cathedral.

François I and Henri II wings – These 16C galleries are devoted to the history of Sens and the Sens district. The first rooms display prehistoric and protohistoric articles: Paleolithic stone tools, Neolithic house and burials (7 500 to 2 500 BC), Bronze Age objects (2 500 to 750 BC) including the treasure of Villethierry (jeweller's stock), many Iron Age weapons and ornaments.

The basement contains pieces of **Gallo-Roman stonework**★ reused in the building of the town walls of Sens: architectural pieces, sculptures, tombstones. Excavations under the courtyard have revealed the foundations of a 4C bathhouse and a collection of bone combs. Sculpture from the 18C is displayed on the first floor: reliefs from the Porte Dauphine erected in memory of the dauphin, Louis XV's son, and of the dauphin's wife, as well as parts of a rood screen removed from the cathedral in the 19C.

Cathedral treasury (Trésor)★★ (access via the museum) – One of France's richest treasure houses, containing a magnificent collection of materials and liturgical vestments: the shroud of St Victor, a 13C white silk mitre embroidered with gold thread, St Thomas à Becket's alb; handsome 15C high warp tapestries (Adoration of the Magi and Coronation of the Virgin); ivories (5C and 6C pyx, the 7C liturgical comb of St Lupus, an 11C Byzantine coffret and a 12C Islamic one) as well as gold plate (late-12C ciborium).

Synodal Palace – A beautiful 13C palace restored by Viollet-le-Duc. The great vaulted chamber on the ground floor was the seat of the ecclesiastical tribunal (officialité). In the 13C two bays served as a prison and there are still traces of graffiti on the walls. The magnificent hall on the first floor was where the bishops deliberated. The archaeological collection and the collections of the adjoining treasury (Lemoine paintings, tapestries) will be rearranged once the rooms of the new museum are ready.

ADDITIONAL SIGHTS
Covered Market
The ironwork and pink brick of the marché couvert opposite the cathedral is typical of the late 19C. The pitched roof is ornamented with pinnacle turrets.

Around St-Pierre-le-Rond
Beside the **church** is the bell tower (1728) and a building which in 1927 was faced with the 13C façade of the Sens charity hospital (Hôtel-Dieu).
At the corner of rue de la République and rue Jean-Cousin, stands a 16C

house, **Abraham's House**. The carved corner post is decorated with a Tree of Jesse. The house next door, at no. 50 rue Jean-Cousin, known as the House of the Pillar (Maison du Pilier) (16C), has a curious porch.
Further along, at no. 8, the 16C Maison Jean-Cousin has a garden façade overlooking rue Jossey. The pedestrian shopping street, Grande Rue, has numerous half-timbered houses.

La Poterne
Traces of the Gallo-Roman walls are visible on boulevard du 14-Juillet.

ADDRESSES

☆ STAY

◯ **Hôtel Relais de Villeroy** – rte de Nemours, 89100 Villeroy. 9km/6mi SE on D 81. ℘03 86 88 81 77. www.relais-de -villeroy.com. 🖪 8 rooms. ⊇ 9 €. ✕.
Cute house typical of the region with comfy little rooms. Take a seat on the veranda for dishes rooted in tradition.

◯◯🗎 **Hôtel de Paris et de la Poste** – 97 r. de la République. ℘03 86 65 17 43. www.hotel-paris-poste.com. Wi-Fi. 26 rooms. ⊇ 14 €. Half board available.
✕. Traditional provincial hostelry; the largest, most modern rooms open onto a pretty patio. The restaurant serves up reworked classics in an inviting setting.

⑨/ EAT

◯ **Au Crieur de Vin** – 1 r. Alsace-Lorraine. ℘03 86 65 92 80. Closed 7–22 Jun, 9–23 Aug, 20 Dec–4 Jan, Tue lunch, Sun and Mon. ⌲. Traditional dishes like tête de veau (boiled calf's head) and roasts are the specialities here, along with wines from the Yonne area.

◯ **Le Clos des Jacobins** – 49 Gde-Rue. ℘03 86 95 29 70. www.restaurantles jacobins.com. Closed 29 Apr–6 May, 15 Jul–5 Aug, 23 Dec–5 Jan, Sun and Tue eve and Wed. Set lunch menu 22 €.
A complete makeover has given this restaurant a contemporary look in tones of beige and chocolate to suit its modern food.

◯ **La Haie Fleurie** – 30 rte de Coutenay, 89100 Subligny. 7km/4.5mi E of Sens on D 660. ℘03 86 88 84 44. Closed 26–31 Jul, Sun and Wed eve, and Thu. 🖪. Set lunch menu 17 €. Country inn in a hamlet with a genial rustic-chic dining room serving traditional cuisine.

◯◯🗎 **La Potinière** – 51 r. Cécile de Marsangy on D 660. ℘03 86 65 31 08. www.restaurant-lapotiniere.fr. Closed Sun eve and Mon. ⓺. A mooring jetty brings waterborne diners to the shaded terrace on the Yonne. Light and trendy dining room with up-to-date cuisine.

⑨ ON THE TOWN

Brasserie des champs – In the Parc d'Activité Les Prunelliers, 89100 St-Martin-du-Tertre. ℘03 86 65 19 89. Four types of beer to sample at a small artisan brewery near Sens – a summer blanche, aromatic blondes or caramel-tinged amber.

⤳ SHOPPING

Marché – Sens market days are Mon and Fri mornings (town centre) and Wed and Sun mornings (Champs-Plaisants).

À la Renommée des Bons Fromages G. Parret – 37 Grande-Rue. ℘03 86 65 11 54. Open Mon 7.30am–3pm, Fri–Sat 8am–12.30pm. Small dairy offering local cheeses: Époisses, Chaource, Soumaintrain, and an interesting choice of wines from the cellar.

Joigny

Joigny (whose townsfolk are known as Joviniens) is a busy, picturesque little town at the gateway to Burgundy on the borders of the forest of Othe. It is built in terraces on the side of a hill, the Côte St-Jacques, overlooking the River Yonne.

▶ **Population:** 10 605

◔ **Michelin Map:** 319: D-4.

▤ **Info:** quai H. Ragobert, 89300. ℘03 86 62 11 05. www.tourisme-joigny.fr.

◑ **Location:** From the Yonne bridge, which has six 18C arches, there is a pretty view of the river, the quays, the shady promenades and the town.

A BIT OF HISTORY
The Revolt of the Maillotins
In 1438 the people of Joigny rebelled against the lord of the manor, Count Guy de la Trémoille. They attacked his castle and killed the Count with blows from their mauls or mallets, tools used by wine-growers of those days. Since then the Joviniens have been known as Maillotins (Maul-bearers) and the maul figures in the town's coat of arms.

SIGHTS
Saint-Thibault
This church, built in both the Gothic and Renaissance styles between 1490 and 1529, is dominated by a 17C square tower crowned by a delicate belfry. Above the door is an equestrian statue of St Theobald (1530) by the sculptor who settled in Spain and took the name Juan de Juni (Jean de Joigny). Inside the church, the chancel slants to the left; this asymmetry is emphasised by the chancel vaulting.

Église Saint-Jean
A belfry porch precedes the west front of this church which lacks transepts but has a pentagonal chevet. The Renaissance-style coffered ceiling has carved medallions framed by decorated ribs. In the south aisle is the 13C recumbent figure of the Comtesse de Joigny. The tomb is lavishly sculptured and includes the figures of the countess' children. The Louis XV woodwork and the furnishings of the sacristy came from Vézelay.

Old houses
In the narrow streets around St-Thibault and St-Jean are half-timbered houses dating from the 15C and 16C. Most were badly damaged, in the bombardments of 1940 and a gas explosion in 1981, but have been restored. The best-known is the one on the corner, called the *Arbre de Jessé* (Tree of Jesse).

EXCURSIONS
Côte Saint-Jacques★
◑ *1.5km/1mi N.*
The road climbs in hairpin bends round the Côte St-Jacques. From a right-hand bend there is a semicircular **panorama**★ over the town and valley of the Yonne.

♟♟Musée Rural des Arts Populaires de Laduz★
◑ *15km/10mi S on D 955.* ◷*Open Jul–Aug daily 2.30–6pm; Easter–Jun and Sept weekends only 2.30–5.30pm; Nov–Mar Wed 2–5pm.* ◉*6€ (under 14 3€).* ℘*03 86 73 70 08. www.artpopulaire-laduz.com.*
This folk museum recalls rural working life before 1914; the tools and products of about 50 craftsmen are on display together with a large collection of old toys and carved figures.

La Ferté-Loupière
◑ *8km/11mi SW.*
This fortified market town is home to a 12C and 15C **church** with remarkable 15C–16C **mural paintings**★★ depicting the parable of the three living and three dead men and a Dance of Death. The latter represents 42 figures from all walks of life and is thus an interesting historical document as well as a moral lesson. On the larger pillars, look for the archangel St Michael Slaying the Dragon and an Annunciation.

Pontigny★

This little village on the edge of the River Serein is celebrated for its former abbey, the second daughter house of Cîteaux, founded in 1114. Whereas Cîteaux is now in ruins, the abbey of Pontigny has preserved its church intact.

A BIT OF HISTORY

The foundation – At the beginning of the year 1114 twelve monks with the Abbot Hugues de Mâcon at their head were sent from Cîteaux by St Stephen to found a monastery on the banks of the Serein, in a large clearing at a place known as Pontigny. The abbey was situated on the boundaries of three bishoprics (Auxerre, Sens and Langres) and three provinces (counties of Auxerre, Tonnerre and Champagne) and thus from its beginning benefited from the protection and the generosity of six different masters. Thibault the Great, Count of Champagne, was the abbey's most generous benefactor: in 1150 he gave the abbot the means to build a larger church than that existing at the time (the chapel of St Thomas), which had become too small for the monks. He enclosed the abbey buildings with a wall (4m/13ft high) sections of which still remain.

A refuge for archbishops – During the Middle Ages Pontigny served as a refuge for ecclesiastics fleeing from persecution in England; three archbishops of Canterbury found asylum here. Thomas à Becket, Primate of England, came to Pontigny in 1164 after incurring the wrath of Henry II. He returned to his country in 1170 but was murdered in his cathedral two years later.

Stephen Langton took refuge at Pontigny from 1208 to 1213 because of a disagreement with King John.

Edmund Rich, St Edmund of Abingdon, lived in Pontigny in saintly exile for several years until his death in 1240, when he was buried in the abbey church. He was canonised in 1246 and is venerated throughout the region (known locally as St Edme).

▶ **Population:** 748.
◉ **Michelin Map:** 319: F-4.
▤ **Info:** 22 r. Paul-Desjardins, 89230 Pontigny.
ℹ 03 86 47 47 03.
www.ot-pontigny.com.
◷ Abbey open summer 9am–7pm, winter 10am–5pm. ⚑ Guided tours by request. ℹ 03 86 47 54 99.
http://abbayedepontigny.eu.
◔ **Location:** As you approach the village from the north along the RN 77, the vast abbey church seems to loom out of the poplars that line the River Serein.
◉ **Don't Miss:** The classical concerts held here in summer and, even more magical, the occasional candlelit evening visits.

The decades of Pontigny – Abandoned during the French Revolution, the abbey served as a quarry for the nearby villages up to 1840. The ruins were then bought back by the Archbishop of Sens and given to the Congregation of Missionary Fathers founded by Father Muard (ℹ see Le MORVAN Excursion, Abbaye de la Pierre-qui-Vire) who restored the church and other buildings. At the start of the 20C, the fathers were expelled and the property was bought by the philosopher, Paul Desjardins (1859–1940), who organised the famous Décades, bringing together eminent personalities of the period including Thomas Mann, André Gide, TS Eliot and François Mauriac, who had lengthy literary conversations in the celebrated avenue of arbours.

ABBAYE★

Opposite the War Memorial in the village, an 18C entrance flanked by small pavilions, opens into a shady avenue leading past the conventual buildings to the abbey church.

Built in the second half of the 12C in the transitional Gothic style by Thibault, Count of Champagne, this church is austere, in conformity with Cistercian rule. Of notable size (108m/354ft long inside, 117m/384ft with the porch, and 52m/171ft wide at the transept), it almost rivals Notre-Dame in Paris.

Church Exterior – The porch, festooned with arcades standing on consoles and small columns, takes up the whole width of the façade. Closed at the sides, it is pierced by twin, double-semicircular bays and a central doorway with a low arch. The façade, decorated with a tall lancet window and two blind arcades, ends in a pointed gable with a small oculus. The sides of the church are typically bare; no belfry breaks the long line of the roof. The transept and the aisles are of a great simplicity; flat-sided buttresses and flying buttresses support the chevet and the north side.

Church Interior – The long, two-storey nave has seven bays; it is the earliest Cistercian nave with pointed vaulting to have survived to the present day. The perspective is interrupted by the wooden screen of the monks' choir. The squat side aisles of groined vaulting contrast with the more unrestricted nave. Lit at either end by a rose window, the transept has six rectangular chapels opening on to each of its arms.

The choir, rebuilt at the end of the 12C, is very graceful with its ambulatory and 11 apsidal chapels. The crocketed capitals of the monolithic columns are more elaborate than those of the nave where rudimentary water-lily leaves constitute the main decorative element.

At the end of the choir under a baldaquin is the 18C shrine of St Edmund; the earlier Renaissance wooden shrine, is kept in one of the apsidal chapels.

The beautiful **stalls**★, the transept grille and the organ case date from the end of the 17C. The organ loft, which is heavily ornamented, the choir parclose and the altar date from the end of the 18C.

Monastery buildings – All that is left of the 12C Cistercian buildings is the wing of the lay brothers' building; the rubblestone and delicate Tonnerre stone harmonise well in the façade, which is supported by buttresses. Of the other buildings, only the southern gallery of the cloisters, rebuilt in the 17C, remains today (*access via the church*).

Auxerre★★
and the Yonne, Cure and Auxerrois

Auxerre (pronounced Oh-ssair, the capital of Lower Burgundy (Basse Bourgogne), is on a hillside beside the River Yonne, at the start of the Nivernais canal. The town's fine monuments are highlighted in summer by a son et lumière show near the cathedral, while the shady boulevards, steep streets and old houses contribute to its overall interest. From the bridges and the right bank of the river, there are fine views of the town.

A BIT OF HISTORY

The Romans built Autessiodurum on the road from Lyon to Boulogne, near a simple Gaulish village, and from the 1C it thrived. By the Middle Ages, Auxerre

▶ **Population:** 10 605

◉ **Michelin Map:** 319: E-5.

▣ **Info:** 1 quai de la République, 89000 Auxerre. ℘03 86 52 06 19. www.ot-auxerre.fr.

▶ **Location:** Boulevard du 11 November encircles the historic downtown area, where most of the sights are located. For a self-guided walking tour of the old town, follow the markings painted on the ground (enquire at the tourist office).

☺ **Don't Miss:** St Germain Abbey, home to some of the oldest frescoes in France.

was a spiritual centre, and was declared a Holy City by the Pope in the 12C. Two great figures in history have visited Auxerre. In 1429 **Joan of Arc** passed through twice; and on 17 March 1815, **Napoleon** arrived on his return from Elba.

WALKING TOUR

See town plan. Start from quai de la Marine.

Quartier de la Marine

This part of town with its narrow streets was once home to the boatmen. Take rue de la Marine to see the remains of the north-east tower of the Gallo-Roman fortified wall. Walk across pretty **place St-Nicolas**, overlooking quai de la Marine. The square is named after the patron saint of boatmen. Rue du Mont-Brenn leads to the place du Coche-d'Eau. At no. 3, a 16C house hosts temporary exhibitions as part of the **Musée du Coche-d'Eau**.

Ancienne Abbaye St-Germain★★

Open year round. Guided tours of the crypt (45min; last tour departs 1hr before closing) May–Sept daily except Tue 10am–6.30pm; rest of year daily except Tue 10am–noon, 2–6pm. Closed 1 Jan, 1 and 8 May, 1 and 11 Nov, 25 Dec; 4.80€. 03 86 18 05 50.

This Benedictine abbey was built in the 6C by Queen Clotilda, wife of Clovis, on the site of an oratory where St Germanus, the 5C Bishop of Auxerre, was buried. In the time of Charles the Bald the abbey had a famous school; St Patrick, who converted the Irish, was a student.
Abbey church – The upper part of the church was built from the 13C–15C and is Gothic in style; it replaced a Carolingian Romanesque church. The 10-sided Lady Chapel, dating from 1277, is linked to the ambulatory by a passageway and overlies two semi-underground chapels (*see below*) from the same period. In 1811, bays were demolished at the west end of the church isolating the 12C Romanesque **bell tower** (51m/167ft high).

Auxerre on the banks of the River Yonne

S. Sauvignier/MICHELIN

Crypt★★ – The crypt forms a semi-underground church consisting of a nave and two aisles; the barrel vaulting dates from the Carolingian period. The confessional, raised on three steps in the centre of the crypt, provides a fine view of the Carolingian, Romanesque and Gothic vaulting; four Gallo-Roman columns, with composite capitals, support two millennial oak beams. The ambulatory is decorated with red and ochre **frescoes**★ which date from 850 and are among the oldest in France.
The axial chapel, dedicated to St Maxime, was rebuilt in the 13C on the site of the rotunda of the Carolingian crypt. The vaulted roof is divided by ribs into 10 panels. Below is the Chapelle St-Clément, which can be reached via a narrow staircase (*to the right on leaving the Chapelle Ste-Maxime*). The steeply sloping ground means that only part of the chapels are underground, so there are good views of the valley from some windows.
Musée St-Germain – This museum is in the old conventual buildings of the abbey, including the abbot's residence rebuilt at the beginning of the 18C (*entrance to abbey and museum*), 14C cellars, 12C chapter-house (the latter's façade was found behind the cloisters – *restoration work in progress*) and sacristy. There is an archaeological collection in the monks' dormitory.

Return along rue du Dr-Labosse to rue Cochois. Along the way, note the préfecture in the former Bishops' Palace, and maison Defert.

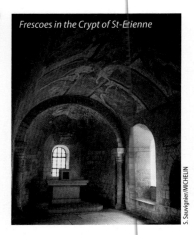

Frescoes in the Crypt of St-Étienne

S. Sauvignier/MICHELIN

Cathédrale Saint-Étienne★★

🕐 *Open 7.30am–6pm.* 🔊 *Tour of the treasury and crypt available from Easter to All Saints Day daily 9am–6pm (Sun 2–6pm); rest of the year daily except Sun 10am–5pm. ✆03 86 52 21 29.*

The fine Gothic cathedral was built between the 13C and 16C to replace the existing Romanesque one. The building was practically finished by 1515.

West front – The Flamboyant style façade has four storeys of arcades surmounted by gables. The sculptures on the doorways (13C–14C) were mutilated in the 16C during the Wars of Religion, and the soft limestone has weathered badly. Among the scenes are the Last Judgement (lintel) and Christ between the Virgin Mary and St John (*tympanum*). The sculptures framing the north door trace the lives of the Virgin Mary, St Joachim and St Anne. The Coronation of the Virgin is on the tympanum. The sculptures round the south door are 13C. The tympanum, divided into three, and the recessed arches are dedicated to the childhood of Christ and the life of John the Baptist. The more interesting of the side entrances is the 14C south door, which is dedicated to St Stephen; the north is dedicated to St Germanus.

Interior – The nave, built in the 14C, was vaulted in the 15C. The choir and the ambulatory date from the beginning of the 13C. In 1215, the cathedral's Romanesque choir was pulled down; ris-

ing above the 11C crypt is the beautiful piece of architecture built to replace it, completed in 1234.

The ambulatory is lit by a magnificent array of **stained-glass windows**★★ composed of 13C medallions in which blue and red are the dominant colours. They represent scenes from Genesis, the stories of David, of Joseph and of the Prodigal Son and many saintly legends.

Romanesque crypt★ – The crypt, the only remaining part of the 11C Romanesque cathedral, has 11–13C frescoes.

Treasury★ – The many interesting exhibits include a collection of 12C–13C chased enamels, manuscripts, 15C–16C books of hours and miniatures.

▷ *Walk towards the town centre via place St-Étienne, then rue Maison-fort on the left running into rue Joubert.*

Town centre

There are many interesting old houses here, mostly 16C with half-timbering. **Rue Fécauderie** intersecting with rue Joubert has two half-timbered houses with a sculpted corner post; it leads to **place de l'Hôtel-de-Ville**; note nos. 4, 6, 16, 17 and 18.

Tour de l'Horloge (Clock Tower)

This tower, also called the Tour Gaillarde, was built in the C15. The astrological clock (17C) has faces showing the movement of the sun and moon.

A vaulted passageway beside the clock tower leads to place du Maréchal-Leclerc. Continue along **rue de l'Horloge**: no. 6 (sculpted corner post) and the four houses opposite; then along **rue de la Draperie**: note the houses occupied by a bank and a jeweller's. It leads to **place Charles-Surugue** which has interesting houses at nos. 3, 4, 5 and 18.

Pass beneath the clocktower. At no 6, note the sculpted corner post and four terraced houses opposite. Go left into **rue de la Draperie**, which opens into **place Charles-Surugue**, where its fountain has a figure of Cadet Roussel. Have a look at the timbered houses

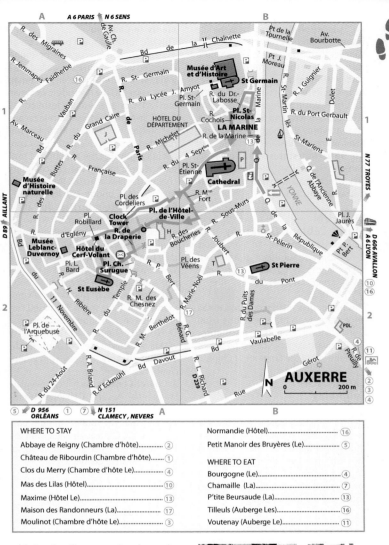

A 6 PARIS · N 6 SENS

A · B

R. des Migraines
R. de Ch. de Gaulle
R. Jemmapes Faidherbe
Vauban
Av. Marceau
Bd
Buttes
Grand Caire
R. du Paris
R. St- Germain
R. du Lycée J. Amyot
HÔTEL DU DÉPARTEMENT
Française
R. des
R. Michelet
R. du 4 Septbre

Musée d'Art et d'Histoire
St Germain
R. du Dr- Labosse
R. Cochois
Pl. St- Nicolas
LA MARINE
R. de la Marine
Pt de la Tournelle
Pt J. Moreau
Av. Bourbotte
R. J. Guignier
Dolet
St- Martin lès
R. du Port Gerbault
YONNE
Q. de l'Ancienne Abbaye
St-Mariens

Pl. St- Germain

1 · 1

N 77 TROYES

Musée d'Histoire naturelle
Pl. des Cordeliers
Pl. Robillard
d'Eglény
Clock Tower
R. de la Draperie
Hôtel du Cerf-Volant
Pl. L. Bard
Musée Leblanc- Duvernoy
Pl. Ch. Surugue
St Eusèbe
Pl. de l'Arquebuse
R. du 24 Août
R. A. Briand
R. d'Eckmühl
11 Novembre
Ribière
R. M. des Chesnez
Temple
R. Marie-Noël
Bert
Bd Berthelot
R. M. Davout
R. G. Bénard
R. L. Richard D 239
Rue

Pl. St- Étienne
Cathedral
R. M on Fort
Pl. de l'Hôtel- de-Ville
R. des Boucheries
Pl. des Véens
R. Sous-Murs
Joubert
St-Pélerin
R. R. du Puits des Dames
Vaulabelle
Gérot
N AUXERRE
0 · 200 m

St-Mariens
Pl. J. Jaurès
D 606 AVALLON · A 6 LYON
de la République
P. P. Bert
St Pierre
du Pont
POL.
R. de Preuilly

2 · 2

5 · D 956 ORLÉANS
1 · 7 · N 151 CLAMECY, NEVERS

A · B

and the Art Nouveau sketch on the post office (1909). Follow it along rue René-Schaeffer as far as the church of **St-Eusèbe**, which is all that remains of an old priory. The church has a 12C tower decorated with multifoil arches. The stone spire dates from the 15C. Inside, note the rib vaulting in the high hexagonal drum above the Renaissance chancel, the beautiful axial chapel and the 16C stained-glass windows. Take rue Diderot to arrive at the town's oldest house, from the 14C and 15C, at

Astronomical clock, Tour de l'Horloge

© Gräfenhain Günter/Sime/Photononstop

no. 5 **place Robillard**, known as the Kite House (14C and 15C). Its lovely weather vane recalls the days when it was a musical instrument shop. *Return towards the cathedral across place des Cordeliers.*

Note the Renaissance mansion, Hôtel de Crole, with dormer windows and sculpted cornice at no 67 **rue de Paris**. Head towards the footbridge over the River Yonne via rue des Boucheries and rue **Sous-Murs**; this street owes its name to the walls of the Gallo-Roman city which ran alongside it; note the houses at nos. 14 and 19.

MUSEUM
Musée Leblanc-Duvernoy

🕐 *Open May–Sept Wed–Fri 10am–noon, 2–6pm; Sat and Sun 10am–6.30pm; rest of year times vary.* 🕐 *Closed 1 Jan, 1 and 8 May, 1 and 11 Nov, 25 Dec.* ⊛ *2.40€.* 🖉 *03 86 18 05 50.*

This museum is mainly devoted to faience ware, with many exhibits from French or local ceramists, It also houses 18C Beauvais tapestries depicting scenes from the life of the Emperor of China.

EXCURSION
Seignelay

📀 *10km/6mi N.*

Charming hillside town. Note the 17C covered market on place Colbert and the church of St-Martial. All that remains of the castle destroyed during the Revolution is a section of the curtain wall, a tower restored in the 19C, a 17C gatehouse and the former park.

🚗 DRIVING TOURS

Vallée de l'Yonne
🕐 *See Region map. 59km/38mi along D 163 and D 100. Allow 4hrs.*

Between Auxerre and Cravant, at the confluence of the Rivers Yonne and Cure, the road runs through a wide valley overlooked by low hills planted with vines and cherry trees. Upriver from Cravant, the valley becomes narrower and the river flows faster.

Mailly-le-Château
This old fortified town perches on an escarpment above a curve in the Yonne. A shaded terrace above the walls gives a lovely view over the river and Nivernais canal, as well as the riverside lower town and its 15C bridge. Visit the fortified 13C Église St-Adrien, whose Gothic façade has statues of Countess Mathilde surrounded by serfs, celebrating her contribution towards the abolition of serfdom. Have a look at the 12C cemetery chapel, then leave across the Yonne on the lovely 15C bridge with its chapel.

Réserve naturelle du Bois du Parc
♿ *No access for persons of restricted mobility. Free pamphlet available from tourism offices.* 🌼 *Floral displays are at their best in May and June.*

Wooden walkways anchored to the hillside start off steeply for a stroll through cliffside gardens of plants more commonly seen in the south. Fossilised corals can be seen in another section.

The D 100 continues south to the pretty village of Merry at the foot of the **Rochers du Saussois**, a rocky wall where climbers train.

At **Châtel-Censoir**, the hilltop collégiale St-Potentien has an 11C chancel, Renaissance portals and bas-reliefs from the 15C and 16C. The route continues past the huge 15C Château de Faulin and the 16C church of St Martin in the village of Surgy to finish in Clamecy.

Vallée de la Cure
♿ *See Region map. 54km/33mi. Allow 4hrs 30min.*

The River Cure flows into the Yonne at **Cravant**, where you can walk along the former moat. The village has timbered houses and a 13C church with a Renaissance chancel and spire. Beyond Cravant, the road runs close to the river through a hilly landscape of woodlands and vineyards, through Accolay, known for its glazed pottery, to Vermenton, a pretty river port on the banks of the Cure. On the outskirts is the **Abbaye de Reigny**. Founded in 1128, it was home to 300 monks at its peak in the

Middle Ages, and despite damage in the Hundred Years War and the Revolution, it has a fine 14C Cistercian refectory. At **Arcy-sur-Cure** admire the fine classical façade of the Château d'Arcy, and stop at the Manoir de Chastenay.

Upriver from Arcy-sur-Cure, the limestone cliffs towering above the west bank are riddled with caves; the **Grande Grotte**★ is the only one open to visitors, and is the second-oldest painted cave in the world (after Chauvet in the Ardèche). Inside are fantastic formations of stalagmites and stalactites. From there, take a pleasant walk along the Cure beneath cliffs honeycombed with caves.

Continue through Voutenay-sur-Cure to Sermizelles, where the energetic can climb to the hilltop chapel of Notre-Dame-d'Orient for a view over the Cure Valley. Stop at **Asquins**, whose church of St-Jacques-le-Majeur is the start of the Vézelay pilgrimage route to Compostela, before finishing in Vézelay.

Auxerrois
See Region map. 40km/24mi.
Allow 2hrs 30min.

This excursion around Auxerre is particularly good when the cherry trees blossom in April. The landscape is an undulating patchwork of vineyards and orchards.

In **Saint-Bris-le Vineux** you will find a 13C Gothic church with Renaissance vaulting and stained glass amid its ancient houses. Don't miss a visit to the **Caves de Bailly**, which supplied the stones for the square of Notre-Dame in Paris, and now have 3 hectares of cellars full of fizzy Crémant de Bourgogne, which you can, of course, taste and buy. Pursuing a vinous theme, call at **Irancy**, which produces the best reds and rosés of the Auxerre region. At **Escolives-Sainte-Camille** the charming Romanesque church once held the relics of the eponymous saint in its crypt.

At **Coulanges-la-Vineuse**, the name is an obvious clue to the ancient wine-producing traditions of this hill village.

Its Musée du Vieux Pressoir et de la Vigne displays the vigneron's tools of the trade, and a medieval wine press.

ADDRESSES

STAY

A few kilometres from Seignelay, take exit 19 off the motorway to a cluster of hotels and restaurants. They may be well-known and unexciting chain establishments, but they offer perfectly good services at a good range of prices.

La Maison des Randonneurs – *5 r. Germain-Bénard. ☎03 86 41 43 22. www.maison-rando.fr. 8 rooms. 5 €.* The local council has turned this solid old house into a hostel. The rather spartan rooms have from 4 to 8 bunks, but you can't fault the location, smack in the town centre next to a lovely wooded park.

Gîte de séjour municipal – *1 r. Hérisson, 58500 Surgy. 38km/24mi S on N 151 and D 144. ☎03 86 27 97 89. www.domaine-de-surgy.com. Closed Nov–Mar. 7 rooms. 4.50 €, half- and full board available.* Set in 6 000sq m/65 000sq ft of grounds, this handsome 18C building has been recently restored. It offers 35 beds.

Chambre d'hôte Le Clos du Merry – *4 r. Crété, 89440 Joux-la-Ville. 9km/6mi NE of Voutenay-sur-Cure on D 32. ☎03 86 33 65 54. Closed Oct–Easter (except weekends by reservation). 5 rooms.* This working grain-growing farm has strictly non-smoking rooms (some well-suited to families) spread around the vast breakfast room. Large garden with children's games, and hikes can be organised here.

Chambre d'hôte Le Moulinot – *D 606, 89270 Vermenton. 24km/15mi SE on D 965 and N 6. ☎03 86 81 60 42. www.moulinot.com. Closed 25 Dec–2 Jan. 6 rooms.* You cross a skinny bridge over the River Cure to reach this 18C mill bracketed by the river and a pond. The dreamily idyllic setting oozes charm and relaxation. A wooden staircase leads to lovely spacious bedrooms. The lounge-dining room looks over the water, and there's a swimming pool too.

⊝⊜ **Chambre d'hôte Les Vieilles Fontaines** – 89270 Sacy. 6km/4mi E of Vermenton on D 11. ℘03 86 81 51 62. http://lesvieillesfontaines.free.fr. Closed Nov–Mar. 🅿️ 🛏 3 rooms. 🍽 Half board available. ✕. Set lunch menu 21 €. Three simple but very comfy rooms in a stone house that was once home to a wine producer. The lounge in the vaulted former wine cellar is a sight to see. When weather permits, meals are served on a covered terrace. Four-person gîte available.

⊝⊜ **Chambre d'hôte Place Voltaire** – 15 pl. Voltaire, 89270 Vermenton. 24km/15mi SE on D 965 and N 6. ℘03 86 81 59 63. www.15place voltaire.com. Closed Nov–Mar. 🛏 4 rooms. 🍽. This stone-built village house has four rooms done out with old furniture. The King's Room is named in honour of Louis-Philippe, who, legend has it, stayed here for the inauguration of the canal. English breakfast served in the large dining room; pretty veranda looking into the garden.

⊝⊜ **Hôtel Mas des Lilas** – Hameau de la Cour Barrée, 89290 Champs-sur-Yonne. 9.5km/6mi SE on D 965 and D 606. ℘03 86 53 60 55. www.lemasdeslilas.com. Closed 23 Oct–4 Nov. 🅿️ Wi-Fi. 16 rooms. 🍽 8 €. These villas nestling in a lovely flower-filled gardens offer well-kept little ground-floor rooms with terraces opening onto the greenery.

⊝⊜ **Hôtel Normandie** – 41 bd Vauban. ℘03 86 52 57 80. www.hotel normandie.fr. Closed 18 Dec–2 Jan. Wi-Fi. 47 rooms. 🍽 9 €. This smart residence ticks all the boxes: a tranquil courtyard terrace, comfy rooms (go for those in the main house), an Art Deco bar-lounge, billiard room and gym.

⊝⊜ **Hôtel Le Maxime** – 2 quai de la Marine. ℘03 86 52 14 19. www.lemaxime.com. Wi-Fi. 26 rooms. 🍽 11 €. This former salt warehouse on the banks of the River Yonne was converted into a family-run hotel in the 19C. Nicely-refurbished with period-style furniture, the rooms have views over the river or the quiet courtyard.

⊝⊜ **Chambre d'hôte Château de Ribourdin** – 89240 Chevannes. 7 km/4.5mi SW on N 151 then D 1. ℘03 86 41 23 16. www.chateauderibourdin.com. ♿ 🅿️ 🛏 5 rooms. 🍽. This magnificent 16C château and dovecote rise proudly from the wheat fields beneath the village. Named after local châteaux, the bedrooms are in a converted 18C barn, where the breakfast room has a fine fireplace.

⊝⊜ **Chambre d'hôte Le Puits d'Athie** – 1 r. de l'Abreuvoir, 89380 Appoigny. 11km/7mi NW on N 6. ℘03 86 53 10 59. www.puitsdathie.com. Closed Jan–Feb. 🛏 4 rooms. 🍽. ✕ 45 €. The individually-decorated rooms of this Burgundian residence look wonderful: Mykonos, kitted out in blue and white, and Porte d'Orient (Door to the East), with its authentic Rajasthani door stand out. The lady of the house cooks up regional and Mediterranean dishes.

⊝⊜ **Chambre d'hôte abbaye de Reigny** – 89270 Vermenton. 24km/15mi SE on D 965 and N 6. ℘03 86 81 59 30. www.abbayedereigny.com. 🅿️ 🛏 5 rooms. 🍽. Peace and quiet guaranteed in the verdant fringes of the abbey, shaded by linden trees. Made-over rooms are both comfy and full of charm with their old-fashioned style. Coco Chanel works really well, with its period grey and blue wallpaper. Book ahead for *table d'hôte* meals.

⊝⊜ **Le Petit Manoir des Bruyères** – Les Bruyères, 89240 Villefargeau. 7km/4.3mi W on D 965. ℘03 86 41 32 82. www.petit-manoir-bruyeres.com. 5 rooms. 🍽. ✕. 46 €. This manor house with a glazed tile roof is a peaceful hideaway on the edge of a forest. Classy 18C rooms and a truly royal Montespan suite. Mushroom foraging in season. *Table d'hôte* Burgundian dishes fit for a king are served by the Louis XIII fireplace.

🍴/ EAT

⊝⊜ **La P'tite Beursaude** – 55 r. Joubert. ℘03 86 51 10 21. Closed 28 Jun–6 Jul, 28 Dec–11 Jan, Tue and Wed. Set lunch menu 19 €. Enter the doors of this charming eatery to find the essence of the Burgundian countryside. Dining room with exposed beams, heavy stone walls and an open kitchen.

⊜⊜ **Auberge Les Tilleuls** – *12 quai de l'Yonne, 89290 Vincelottes. 16km/10mi S on D 606 and D 38. ℘03 86 42 22 13. www.auberge-les-tilleuls.com. Closed 20 Dec–24 Feb, Tue and Wed. Set lunch menu 15 €. 5 rooms. ⫘ Half board available.* This small village inn will delight you with its setting, its summer terrace along the banks of the Yonne and succulent cuisine.

⊜⊜ **Auberge Le Voutenay** – *N 6, 89270 Voutenay-sur-Cure. ℘03 86 33 51 92. www.aubergelevoutenay.com. Closed 16–24 Jun, 1–21 Jan, Sun eve, Mon and Tue. ▣ 7 rooms. ⫘ 9 €.* Roadside 18C residence in pleasant grounds. Smart rustic dining room, a bistro area, and a little shop selling local produce. Retro-style rooms.

⊜⊜ **La Chamaille** – *4 rte Boiloup, 89240 Chevannes. 8km/5mi SW on N 151 then D 1. ℘03 86 41 24 80. www.lachamaille.fr. Closed 25 Oct–3 Nov, 21 Feb–8 Mar, Sun eve and Mon. ▣ 3 rooms. ⫘ 10 €, half board available.* Chamaille is surrounded by a delightful garden with a small stream meandering through fields stretching as far as the eye can see. The tastefully restored farmhouse has a pretty veranda.

⊜⊜⊜ **Le Bourgogne** – *15 r. Preuilly. ℘03 86 51 57 50. www.lebourgogne.fr. Closed 25 Apr–3 May, 8–23 Aug, 19 Dec–3 Jan, Thu eve, Sun and Mon ♿▣.* Agreeably rustic setting, nice summery terrace, and a market menu that reads as appetisingly on the chalkboard menus as it looks on the plate. A triumphant conversion, then, for this former garage.

⇗TAKING A BREAK

Le Galion – *2 r. Étienne-Dolet. ℘03 86 46 96 58. Summer open daily 10am–2am; rest of the year noon–1am. Closed 25 Dec–1 Jan.* This small galleon lulled by the Yonne waters offers splendid views of Auxerre and the surrounding countryside. A lively ambience and the odd improvised concert make this a popular café with locals.

Pullman Bar – *20 r. d'Egleny. ℘03 86 52 09 32. Open Mon–Fri 4pm–1am, Sat 4pm–2am. Closed 3 weeks in Aug.* This unassuming bar has more than 110 special beers from 18 different countries and over 40 cocktails, with or without alcohol. Ask to see the cigar box.

⇖SHOPPING

Au Fin Palais – *3 pl. St-Nicolas. ℘03 86 51 14 03. aufinpalais@9online.fr. Open daily 9.30am–7.30pm. Closed 15–30 Mar.* This shop offers a mouthwatering selection of the best regional produce, including liqueurs, brandies, beer from Sens, wines and the famous *nonnette* sweetmeats (iced gingerbread filled with jam). Also on sale is the pretty sapphire-blue stoneware pottery from Puisaye. Charming welcome.

Domaine Anita, Jean-Pierre and Stéphanie Colinot – *1 r. des Chariats, 89290 Irancy. ℘03 86 42 33 25. Open Mon–Sat 8.30am–6.30pm, Sun 9.30am–noon.* The wines from the Colinot estate are matured in accordance with long-standing Burgundy tradition. Tastings are organised in the storehouse. The vaulted cellars date back to the 17C.

Roy – *89-91 r. du Pont. ℘03 86 52 35 93. Open 5am–7.30pm.* A warm welcome awaits in this bakery and chocolate shop, where the delicacies of the house are introduced and explained with care. Confections created by the owner have won a wide audience, so sample a few!

P. Soufflard – *23 r. Joubert. ℘03 86 52 07 07. Open Tue–Sat 8am–12.30pm and 3–7pm.* You'll find an enormous array of local cheeses, all carefully selected by Monsieur Soufflard from a close group of suppliers. Try such specialties as *plaisir au chablis, brillat-savarin, pouligny-saint-pierre, vézelay or crottin de Chavignol.*

Tonnerre

Tonnerre is a pleasant little town, terraced on one of the hills that form the west bank of the Armançon and surrounded by vineyards and greenery. Its old hospital and the beautiful sepulchre it contains are among the treasures of Burgundy.

A BIT OF HISTORY

The Knight of Éon – It was at Tonnerre that Charles-Geneviève-Louise-Auguste-Andrée-Timothée Éon de Beaumont, known as the knight or the lady-knight of Éon, was born in 1728. After a brilliant military and diplomatic career, during which he sometimes had to wear women's clothes, he met with reversals of fortune and was forced to flee to London. He was refused permission to return to France except dressed as a woman. Returning to England, he died there in 1810. To the end of his life, there was widespread speculation as to his gender. The news of his death gave rise to a wave of curiosity ended only by an autopsy. Charles d'Éon was unquestionably a man.

WALKING TOUR
Start from place de la Gare.

Promenade du Pâtis
This is a pleasant shady walk.

▷ *Walk across place de la République to rue de la Fosse-Dionne.*

Fosse Dionne★
This circular basin, filled with blue-green water, was used as a wash-house. It is fed by an underground river that flows through a steeply inclined rock gallery (45m/148yd long) to emerge in the centre of the pool; its flow varies considerably according to season and rainfall. The pool overflows into the Armançon by way of a small stream.

▷ *Follow chemin des Roches.*

▸ **Population:** 5 274
⊙ **Michelin Map:** 319: G-4.
▯ **Info:** pl Marguerite-de-Bourgogne, 89700 Tonnerre. ℘03 86 55 14 48. www.tonnerre.fr.
▷ **Location:** The old town and the newer districts are dominated by the tower of Notre-Dame and church of St-Pierre, from whose terrace there is a good view of the town and its surroundings.

Église St-Pierre
⊶ *Closed for restoration.*
With the exception of the 14C chancel and the 15C square tower, the church was rebuilt in 1556 after the fire that ravaged the town. There is a handsome doorway on the south side with a statue of St Peter on the pier.

▷ *Walk along rue St-Pierre to see the unusual west front of Notre-Dame then follow rue de l'Hôpital leading to the former hospital; however, before you reach it, turn right onto rue des Fontenilles.*

Hôtel d'Uzès
A savings bank occupies this Renaissance dwelling, birthplace of the Knight of Éon; note the design on the doors.

Hôtel-Dieu (Old Hospital)
⊙*Open mid-Apr–mid-Oct 9.30am–noon, 1.30–6pm, Sun 10am-12.30, 2–6pm; rest of year daily except Wed 9.30am–noon, 1.30–5.30pm.* ⊙*Closed 25 Dec, 1 Jan.* ⊜*4.50€.* ℘*03 86 55 14 48. www.tonnerre.fr.*
This beautiful old hospital, erected between 1293 and 1295 by Margaret of Burgundy, widow of Charles d'Anjou, King of Naples and Sicily and brother of St Louis, has survived intact, apart from minor modifications. From the outside, the walls of the hall, despite

Fosse Dionne

S. Sauvignier/MICHELIN

their buttresses, seem to be crushed by the tall roof which covers an area of 4 500sq m/5 382sq yd. The west front was changed in the 18C.

Interior – Although shortened in the 18C, the great hall is of an impressive size (90m/295ft long and 18.2m/60ft wide). The broken-barrel vaulting and the oak timbering are remarkable. The 40 beds for the sick were set in wooden alcoves built in lines along the walls as at Beaune, which was built 150 years later. The walls themselves were pierced by high semicircular bays, divided by pointed arches. From 1650, the hall was put to many different uses and often served as the parish church. Many citizens of Tonnerre were buried

there, which explains the numerous tombstones. Note the gnomon (sundial) on the paving, designed in the 18C by a Benedictine monk and the astronomer Lalande (1732–1807).

The chapel opens off the end of the hall. The tomb of Margaret of Burgundy, rebuilt in 1826, is in the centre of the choir. Above the altar is a 14C stone statue of the Virgin Mary. To the right of the high altar, a little door leads to the sacristy which contains a carved **Entombment**★, presented to the church in the 15C by a rich merchant of the town. The figures of this Holy Sepulchre make up a scene of dramatic intensity reminiscent of Claus Sluter's style. In the north side chapel is the monumental

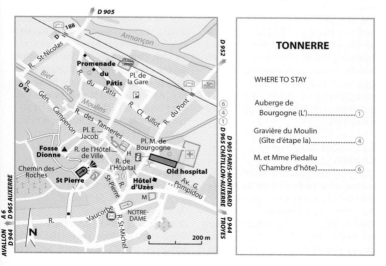

TONNERRE

WHERE TO STAY

Auberge de
 Bourgogne (L')...........................①

Gravière du Moulin
 (Gîte d'étape la)......................④

M. et Mme Piedallu
 (Chambre d'hôte)......................⑥

White Wines of Chablis

Chablis has been made in Burgundy since the 12C, when the vineyards stretched as far as the eye could see. Tending them was the population's sole occupation, and the source of an enviable prosperity. Today, the land is used more selectively, and the soil is the determining factor in the appellation on the bottle, which is a reference to the silica, limestone and clay content of the soil (as in Champagne), rather than to domaines, or specific vineyards (as in Bordeaux, for example).

The best vintages are the Grands Crus, mostly grown on the steep hillsides of the east bank: Vaudésir, Valmur, Grenouilles, Les Clos, Les Preuses, Bougros and Blanchots. Rich in aroma yet dry and delicately flavoured, distinguished by their golden hue, these generally bloom after three years in the bottle, but are rarely kept more than eight. Premier Cru wines are grown on both banks of the river; lighter in colour and less full-bodied, they are best aged three years, never more than six. More than half of the production, bearing the Appellation Chablis Contrôlée label, is very dry and pale, to be aged one to three years before reaching its best.

Often described as crisp or fresh, a good Chablis made exclusively from Chardonnay grapes is delightful with oysters, freshwater fish, ham or chicken dishes with creamy sauce. Lesser vintages, including hearty Bourgogne Aligoté or fruity Petit Chablis, are best enjoyed young with local country fare (grilled sausage, crayfish) or regional cheese (Chaource, St-Florentin) and fresh bread.

tomb of the French statesman Louvois, who acquired the county of Tonnerre in 1684 and served as Minister of War under Louis XIV.

Among the objects on view in the Salle du Conseil (consultation room) of the hospital is a great golden cross in which is mounted a piece of wood reputed to be part of the True Cross.

Museum – In the 18C hospital buildings, the collection includes several objects and manuscripts linked to its history: an 18C silver reliquary; the hospital's founding Charter (1293); the Last Will and Testament of Marguerite de Bourgogne, dated 1305. From the more recent past, a ward (1850) and operating theatre (1908) have been re-created for visitors.

EXCURSIONS
Chablis

This small town, with the feel of a big village, is tucked away in the valley of the River Serein, between Auxerre and Tonnerre. www.chablis.net.

Chablis is the capital of the prestigious wine-growing region of lower Burgundy. Thanks to its many old buildings,

harking back to its heyday in the 16C, it still has a medieval feel. The annual wine fair and the village fairs of November and late January, held in honour of St Vincent, patron of wine-growers (*see Calendar of Events*), recall the town's lively commercial past.

The **Église St-Martin** (*open Jul and Aug Mon–Fri 11am–1pm, 3–6pm; Fri–Sat 11am–1pm, 2.30–6pm; Sun 2.30–6pm; 03 86 42 80 80*) dates from the late 12C. It was founded by monks from St-Martines-Tours, who carried their saint's relics with them as they fled the Normans. On the door leaves of the Romanesque south doorway, known as the Porte aux Fers, note the early-13C strap hinges and the horseshoes, offerings made by pilgrims to St Martin. The interior is reminiscent of St-Étienne in Sens.

Château de Tanlay★★

Open Apr to mid-Nov. Guided tours (1hr) daily 10am, 11.30am, 2.15pm, 3.15pm, 4.15pm, 5.15pm. 9€. 03 86 75 70 61.

Approaching Tanlay from the east by D 965, there is a good view of this handsome residence and its park, which is

Ph. Gajic/MICHELIN

Château de Tanlay

particularly attractive in the evening light. The château of Tanlay, built about 1550, is a magnificent architectural composition and an unexpected surprise in this small village on the banks of the Canal de Bourgogne. The château is a fine monument to French Renaissance architecture at a time when it had broken away from the Italian influence.

Exterior – The small château (the Portal), an elegant building of Louis XIII style, leads into the Cour Verte (Green Courtyard), which is surrounded by arches except on the left where a bridge crosses the moat and leads to the great doorway opening onto the main courtyard of the large château.

The architect Pierre Le Muet, who oversaw work on the château between 1642 and 1648, designed the pyramidal obelisks at the entrance to the bridge.

The main living quarters are joined by two staircase towers to two lower wings at right angles to the main building. Each wing ends in a round domed tower.

Interior – On the ground floor, the hallway *(Vestibule des Césars)* is closed off by a handsome 16C wrought-iron doorway leading to the gardens. Go through the great hall and the antechamber.

The dining room features an eye-catching monumental white-stone Renaissance chimney-piece. Interesting items of furniture include a French Renaissance cabinet and a Burgundian chest.

The 17C woodwork in the drawing room bears the mark of sculptor Michel Porticelli d'Hémery. The pair of sphinxes with

women's faces on the chimney-piece are supposed to be Catherine de' Medici.

In the Bedchamber of the Marquis de Tanlay note the late-16C German School painting on copper.

Great Gallery★ – The old ballroom on the first floor is decorated with trompel'œil frescoes.

Tour de la Ligue★ – The circular room on the top floor of this turret was used for Huguenot meetings during the Wars of Religion. Like his brother Gaspard de Châtillon, François d'Andelot had embraced the Reformation, after which Tanlay became one of the country's two main centres of Protestantism.

The domed ceiling is decorated with a painting (Fontainebleau School) depicting major 16C Roman Catholic and Protestant protagonists in the somewhat frivolous guise of gods and goddesses.

Gardens – *Only partly open to visitors.* These lie either side of the long canal (526m/1726ft) built by Particelli, which is lined with ancient trees.

Château de Maulnes★

▶ *In the Cruzy-le-Châtel commune, 24km/15mi E of Tonnerre. Take D 952 to Villon and go right onto D 162. The access road climbs through the Maulnes forest.* ⌖ *Guided tour (1h) from end Apr to mid-Nov: wekends 2.30pm– 5.30pm. ⌖2 € (under 12s free). Request mobility scooter on intercom if required.* ℘*03 86 72 92 00. www.maulnes.com.* This Renaissance château (under restoration) is a true one-off: firstly, it is built

Château de Maulnes

Conseil Général de l'Yonne - Direction de la Communication

on a pentagonal plan buttressed by five towers, following a geometric design; be aware that it is built on springs that rise from a hilltop.

These springs are audible when you visit the château because they pass by the foot of the staircase.

ADDRESSES

🛏️STAY

🍽️ **Gîte d'étape La Gravière du Moulin** – *7 rte de Frangey, 89150 Lézinnes. 11 km/7mi SE ofTonnerre on D 905. ℘03 86 75 68 67. http://lagraviere dumoulin.lezinnes.fr. 4 rooms.* This former 19C mill astride the Armançon is now a hostel. Simple pine-furnished rooms have 2, 6 or 12 beds, with a maximum capacity of 32.

🍽️ **Chambre d'hôte M. et Mme Piedallu** – *5 av. de la Gare, 89150 Lézinnes. 11 km/7mi SE of Tonnerre on D 905. ℘03 86 75 68 23. 4 rooms. 45 €.* This charming house newly-built with respect for local traditions, offers attic rooms kitted out with old furniture. The veranda is a pleasant setting for breakfast, and the tranquil lounge is set aside for reading and rest.

🍽️🍽️ **L'Auberge de Bourgogne** – *89700 Tonnerre. 2km/1.25mi on rte de Dijon (D 905). ℘03 86 54 41 41. www. aubergedebourgogne.com. Closed 18 Dec–*

We can thank Antoine de Crussol, Duke of Uzès (1528–1573), and his wife, Louise de Clermont, the Countess of Tonnerre, for this daring commission. The main work (1566–70) follows Philibert de l'Orme's designs. It was unfinished when the Duke died.

18 Jan. Wi-Fi. 40 rooms. 9 €, half board available. 17–24 €. Revamped, functional rooms in a building next to the Épineuil vineyards. Those at the rear have lovely views over the countryside.

🍴EAT

🍽️ **Le Syracuse** – *19 av. du Mar.-de-Lattre-de-Tassigny, 89800 Chablis. ℘03 86 42 19 45. Closed Sun eve and Mon set lunch menu.* Seductive restaurant in the heart of the village with a pleasantly rustic dining room. Polished traditional cooking, a nice selection of Chablis wine, and service is spot on.

🛍️SHOPPING

Caveau de Fontenilles – *pl. Marguerite-de-Bourgogne. ℘03 86 55 06 33. Open Tue–Sat 9.30am–noon, 2.30–7pm; Sun 10am–12.30pm.* This winery has won several medals: recent prizewinners include the Pinot Noir and Chardonnay. Another star is the Cuvée Marguerite-des-Fontenilles, aged in oak and dedicated to the founder of the local hospital.

Noyers

Upriver from Chablis, this charming medieval town has kept its interesting architectural heritage: timber-framed houses or those of gabled stone with quaint outside stairs, and cellar doors opening onto pictur-esque streets and tiny squares, form an attractive setting enhanced at night by discreet lighting. Between June and September, the **Rencontres musicales de Noyers** provides entertainment for music lovers.

TOWN

Stroll through the town, admiring the 14C and 15C timber-framed houses in **place de l'Hôtel-de-Ville**, the arcaded stone house and Renaissance mansion in **place du Marché-au-Blé**, the Renais-sance façade and square tower of the **Église Notre-Dame**, and follow **rue du Poids-du-Roy** to the tiny **place de la Petite-Étape-aux-Vins**. From place du Grenier-à-Sel, a passageway leads to the river bank: here, a **promenade** planted with plane trees offers a pleasant walk and the opportunity to see the seven defensive towers still standing (out of

▶ **Population:** 734
◔ **Michelin Map:** 319 G5.
🮚 **Info:** 22 pl. de l'Hôtel-de-Ville, 89310 Noyers-sur-Serein. ℰ03 86 82 66 06. www.noyers-et-tourisme.com.
▶ **Location:** Noyers lies 30km/19mi N of Avallon.
👥 **Kids:** Enjoy the Naïve art in the museum, then climb on board the little Yonne train.
🕐 **Timing:** Summer brings musical events during the Festival des Grands Crus de Bourgogne.
🅿 **Parking:** The town is pedestrianised on Sundays in summer, so park near the salle polyvalente.
◉ **Don't Miss:** The medieval old town is a magical place to stroll when lit up at dusk.

a total of 23), which used to protect the town. Walk through the **Porte Peinte**, a square fortified gate, to return to the town centre.

ADDRESSES

🛌 STAY

◒ **Chambre d'hôte de la Vallée du Serein** – 35 Grande-Rue, 89310 Annay-sur-Serein. 5.5km/3.5mi NW on D 86 and D 45. ℰ03 86 82 63 98. http://valleeduserein.free.fr. Closed mid-Nov-end Mar. 🅿🛏 4 rooms. ⊠ ✕. There's plenty to savour here: the colour of the stone village, the tranquil courtyard, the restrained décor, exotic jam, and the stories of the globe-trotting owners. *Table d'hôte* meals by advance reservation.

◒◒ **Chambre d'hôte Château d'Archambault** – Cours. 2 km/1.2mi S of Noyers on D 86. ℰ03 86 82 67 55. www.chateau-archambault.com. 🅿 5 rooms. ⊠. This grand 19C country house once belonged to Napoleon III's chef. Tastefully restored in a sober

modern vein, rooms look over the grounds or kitchen garden. A gîte is also available.

◒◒ **Auberge La Beursaudière** – 9 chemin de Ronde, 89310 Nitry. 10km/6mi W on D 49. ℰ03 86 33 69 69. www.beursaudiere.com. Closed 3–29 Jan. ♿. Wi-Fi. 11 rooms. ⊠ 10 €. ✕ Set lunch menu 11 €. Priory outbuilding converted into characterful rooms and vaulted breakfast rooms; food-wise, expect staff in regional costume serving cuisine du terroir.

♈/EAT

◒◒ **Maison Paillot - Les Millésimes** – 8 r. du Poids-du-Roy. ℰ03 86 82 82 16. www.maison-paillot.com. Closed Sun eve and Mon. ♿🅿. Friendly deli-restaurant with great value lunch menu and regional produce with a twist.

Château d'Ancy-le-Franc★★

This château on the banks of the River Armançon is one of the most beautiful Renaissance mansions in Burgundy. Built in 1546 for Antoine III de Clermont, husband of Anne-Françoise de Poitiers (sister of François I's mistress Diane), using plans by influential architect Sebastiano Serlio, it was later sold to Louvois, Minister of War under Louis XIV, in 1684. In the mid-19C, the Clermont-Tonnerre family recovered it. In 1980, the estate and contents were sold; from 1985 to 1999 the castle was largely abandoned.

CHÂTEAU

Regional artists contributed to the sumptuous interior decoration, along with students of Primaticcio and Nicolo dell'Abbate. Some of the Renaissance murals are more intact than others, but as a whole they are remarkable.

Ground floor – Don't miss the fabulous Salle de Diane, whose Italian-style vaulted ceiling dates from 1578.

First floor – Beginning in the south wing, admire the **Chapelle Ste-Cécilea**, which, restored in 1860, is covered with barrel vaulting. The trompe-l'œil paintings (1596) depicting the Fathers of the

- **Michelin Map:** 319: H-5.
- **Info:** ⏱Open Mar–Nov. 🚶Guided tours (1hr) 10.30am, 11.30am, 2pm, 3pm and 4pm (Apr–Sept extra tour 5pm, Jul–Aug extra tour 9.30am). ⏱Closed Mon except public holidays. 🎫9€ (under 11s 6€). 📞03 86 75 14 63. www.chateau-ancy.com.
- **Location:** 18km/11mi SE of Tonnerre. Start outside in the Le Nôtre gardens. The château, with four identical wings linked by corner pavilions, is a perfect square.
- **Don't Miss:** For a special experience, book tickets for the monthly Concert Visits, where the tour is rounded off by a classical music performance. See www. musicancy.org for details.

Château d'Ancy-le-Franc

© Château d'Ancy-le-Franc

Desert are the work of André Meynassier, a Burgundian artist.

The **Salle des Gardes** was decorated for Henri III, although he never lived here. Facing the monumental fireplace is a full-length portrait of Marshall Gaspard de Clermont-Tonnerre (1759) by Aved. Horses pose along the walls of the **Galerie Pharsale**. The **Chambre des Arts**★ contains a rare 16C Italian cabinet with decorative inlay work. In the **Chambre de Judith** are nine high-quality paintings from the late 16C depicting the story of Judith. Judith and Holopherne are seen as likenesses of Diane de Poitiers and François I.

The **Cabinet du Pasteur Fido**★ has carved oak panelling and a magnificent Renaissance coffered ceiling. The scenes on the upper part of the walls are based on an Arcadian oracle about a faithful shepherd, hence the room's name.

The library, and the **Galerie des Sacrifices** lead to the **Salon Louvois**★ (the king's chamber where Louis XIV slept on 21 June 1674).

The Auxois region lies to the east of the wild Morvan, a green and fertile landscape where fortified towns jut from rocky outcrops, with cows grazing below. It is an area best explored at an unhurried pace to get under its skin and winkle out the attractions. There may not be the A-list sights of Dijon and Beaune, or the neatly combed millionaire's vineyards of the Côte d'Or further south, but a tightly knit cluster of medieval towns and fine châteaux is ample reward. The Romans didn't turn their noses up at this region either: their oppidums perch on rolling hills above the network of rivers. And let's not forget the region's real gem – the sublime 12C Cistercian abbey of Fontenay.

A place of exile and retreat

The fact that the scandalous libertine Roger de Rabutin was exiled by Louis XIV from Versailles to the château de Bussy-Rabutin speaks volumes about the Auxois region. This was the back of beyond as far as Parisians were concerned. The witty but tactless 17C count consoled himself in his gilded cage with an amazing portrait gallery of his lovers and other ladies in his life.

There were no such orgiastic shenanigans for the Cistercian monks at the Abbaye de Fontenay to mull over in their cells. A wooded vale in this backwater was the ideal spot for St Bernard to found the great monastery in 1118. Even after a spell when it served as a paper factory belonging to the ballooning Montgolfier family, it survives as the most perfect example of a Cistercian monastery. Try to coincide your visit with the dreamy atmosphere during the summer concerts.

Another ecclesiastical building that has been put to good use is the ancient Benedictine abbey at Flavigny-sur-Ozerain, a delicious fortified medieval village with an equally tasty surprise: confectionery fiends may already be fans of the pea-sized sugar-coated aniseed sweets in dainty little boxes that have been made here since the 9C. Setting off from Flavigny, the driving tour to the source of the River Seine takes you through splendid scenery.

But long before the Flavigny sweets were being made, there was a final showdown nearby between the Romans and the Gaulish army led by chieftain Vercingétorix at Alesia, now Alise-Ste-Reine. Or maybe not! The experts are still fighting it out to decide if this really was the site of the Caesar's final victory.

Highlights

1 Restored in all its glory, the **Abbaye de Fontenay** (p252)

2 Old Town strolling in **Semur-en-Auxois** (p256)

3 Romans vs Gauls at **Alise-Ste-Reine** (p259)

4 A rake's palace at the **Château de Bussy-Rabutin** (p260)

5 Aniseed sweets in medieval **Flavigny-sur-Ozerain** (p262)

You can learn all about it at the excellent museum on the site.

Classic France

If you want a town that sums up why rural France is so seductive, try picturesque old Semur-en-Auxois. The round towers of its 14C castle suddenly appear above a bend in the River Armançon, drawing you in to amble the streets of the old town and marvel at its Gothic Notre-Dame church.

And when you want to let off steam, jump on a bike at Montbard and cycle off alongside the Burgundy Canal once you've visited the great naturalist Buffon's château gardens and iron smelting forges. Hikers could explore the wild tracts of the Châtillon forest near Châtillon-sur-Seine, a modest little town with a museum housing the spectacular treasure from the tomb of a 6C BC Gaulish princess. Château hounds should also check out the grand pile at Époisses, and savour the village's pungently saggy cheese – after all, Napoleon was a fan, and the great gastronome Brillat-Savarin named it the King of Cheeses.

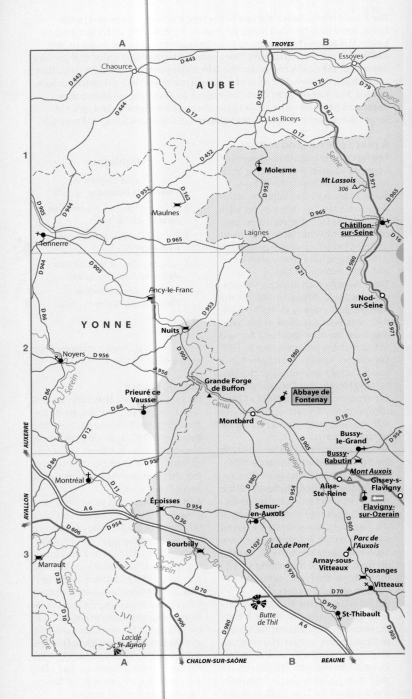

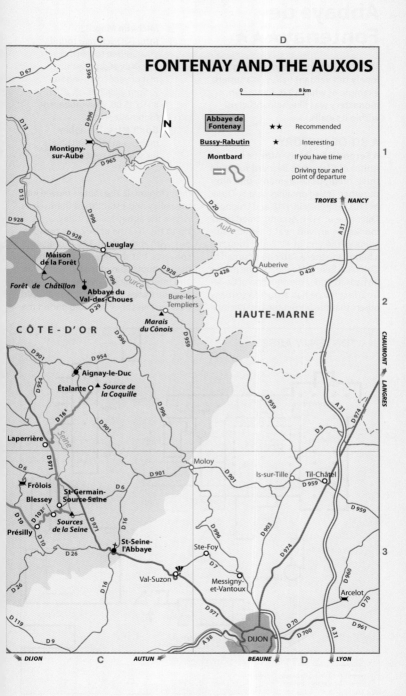

FONTENAY AND THE AUXOIS

0   8 km

Abbaye de Fontenay	★★	Recommended
Bussy-Rabutin	★	Interesting
Montbard		If you have time
		Driving tour and point of departure

N

TROYES   *NANCY*

D 67
D 396
D 966
D 13
D 965
Montigny-sur-Aube
D 13
D 928
D 20
Aube
A 31
D 928
D 996
D 928
Leuglay
Ource
D 928
Auberive
D 428
D 428
Máison de la Forêt
Forêt de Châtillon
Abbaye du Val-des-Choues
D 996
D 29
Bure-les-Templiers
HAUTE-MARNE
CHAUMONT
LANGRES
Marais du Cônois
C Ô T E - D ' O R
D 901
D 954
D 996
D 959
Seine
D 954
Aignay-le-Duc
Étalante
Source de la Coquille
D 16ᵉ
D 901
D 959
A 31
D 3
D 974
Laperrière
D 6
D 971
Moloy
D 901
Is-sur-Tille
Til-Châtel
Frôlois
Blessey
St-Germain-Source-Seine
D 6
D 16
D 959
D 959
D 10
D 102ᶜ
Sources de la Seine
D 971
D 996
D 903
D 974
Présilly
D 10
D 26
St-Seine-l'Abbaye
Ste-Foy
D 7
D 26
D 16
Val-Suzon
Messigny-et-Vantoux
D 960
Arcelot
D 70
D 119
D 971
D 70
D 961
D 9
A 38
DIJON
D 700
A 31
DIJON
C
AUTUN
BEAUNE
D
LYON

Abbaye de Fontenay★★★

The abbey of Fontenay, nestling in a lonely but verdant valley, is a superb example of what a 12C Cistercian monastery was like, self-sufficient within its walls.

A BIT OF HISTORY

A Second Daughter – After he became Abbot of Clairvaux, Bernard founded three religious settlements one after the other: Trois-Fontaines near St-Dizier in 1115, Fontenay in 1118 and Foigny in Thiérache in 1121. Accompanied by 12 monks, he arrived near Châtillon-sur-Seine at the end of 1118 and founded a hermitage there. After he returned to Clairvaux, Bernard found that the monks he had left under the direction of Godefroy de la Roche had attracted so many others that the hermitage had become

- **Michelin Map:** 320: G-4.
- **Info:** ◯ Open year round. ◝ Guided tours (1hr) Apr–Nov 10am–6pm, rest of year 10am–noon, 2–5pm. ∞9.20€. ♿ 𝄆03 80 92 15 00. www.abbayede fontenay.com.
- **Don't Miss:** The abbey makes a magical setting for summer concerts.

much too small. The monks moved into the valley and established themselves where the abbey stands today.

Up to the 16C the abbey was prosperous with more than 300 monks and converts, but the regime of Commendam – abbots nominated by royal favour and interested only in revenues – and religious wars brought about a rapid decline. The abbey was sold during the

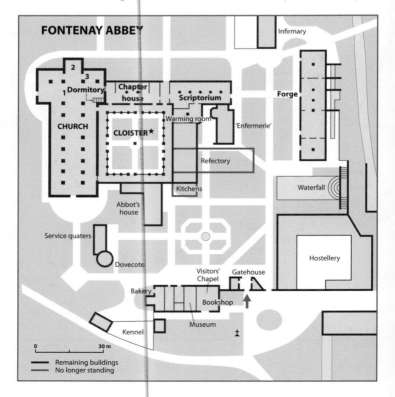

FONTENAY ABBEY

Infirmary
Dormitory
Chapter house
Scriptorium
Forge
CHURCH
Warming room
'Enfermerie'
CLOISTER★
Refectory
Kitchens
Waterfall
Abbot's house
Service quaters
Hostellery
Dovecote
Visitors' Chapel
Gatehouse
Bakery
Bookshop
Kennel
Museum

0 ——— 30 m
▬▬ Remaining buildings
▬▬ No longer standing

Cloisters

Alain Doire/Bourgogne Tourisme

French Revolution and became a paper mill. In 1906 new owners undertook to restore Fontenay to its original appearance. They tore down the parts which had been added for the paper mill and rebuilt the abbey just as it was in the 12C. The many fountains from which the abbey takes its name are today the most beautiful ornaments of the gardens surrounding the buildings; these were added in 1981 to UNESCO's World Heritage List.

VISIT

The main doorway of the porter's lodge is surmounted by the coat of arms of the abbey; the upper floor dates from the 15C. Under the archway, note the niche below the staircase: the opening at the bottom allowed the guard dog to keep an eye on the hostel, the long building on the right of the inner courtyard, where pilgrims and travellers were lodged.

After the porch, walk along beside a large 13C building, which used to house the visitors' chapel and the monks' bakehouse, remarkable for its round chimney. Today this houses the reception area and a small lapidary museum. Further on to the right is a magnificent circular dovecote.

Abbey Church

Built during the lifetime of St Bernard, the church was erected from 1139 to 1147, owing to the generosity of Ebrard,

Bishop of Norwich, who took refuge at Fontenay. The church was consecrated by Pope Eugenius III in 1147. It is one of the most ancient Cistercian churches preserved in France.

The façade, stripped of all ornament, is marked by two buttresses and seven round-headed windows, symbolising the seven Sacraments of the church. The porch has disappeared but the original corbels are still in place. The leaves and hinges of the doorway are exact reproductions of the original folding doors.

The Cistercian rules and plans of design have been scrupulously observed and despite the relatively small dimensions of the building (length: 66m/217ft, width of transept: 30m/98ft), the general effect is one of striking grandeur.

The nave, of broken-barrel vaulting, has eight bays; it is supported by aisles of transverse barrel vaulting, forming a series of communicating chapels, lit by small semicircular bays. The blind nave receives its light from openings in the façade and from those set above the chancel arch.

In the huge transept, the arrangement of the barrel vaulting and the chapels in the transept arms is similar to that in the aisles. In the north transept arm, note the statue (**1**) of Notre-Dame de Fontenay (end of the 13C); her smile and ease of pose recall the Champagne School.

The square chancel (**2**) with its flat chevet, is lit by a double row of windows in triplets (symbol of the Trinity).

Tombstones and the remains of the 13C paving of small squares of glazed stone, which once covered the floor of the choir and a great part of the church, have been assembled here. On the right, there is the tomb (**3**) of the nobleman Mello d'Époisses and his wife (14C). The stone retable of the former Gothic high altar (13C) is damaged.

The night stair to the monks' dormitory is in the south transept.

Dormitory

The monks slept on straw mattresses on the floor and each compartment was screened by a low partition. The superb oak timberwork roof is late 15C.

Cloisters

The cloisters, on the south side of the church, are a superb example of Cistercian architecture, both elegant and robust. Each gallery has eight bays marked by fine buttresses.

The **chapter-house**, with quadripartite vaulting and water-leaf capitals, connects with the eastern cloister via a splendid doorway. The monks' workroom or scriptorium lies at the end of the east range, from where a doorway leads to the warming room. The two fireplaces were the only ones allowed in the abbey apart from those in the kitchen.

The prison is open to view, as is the forge which was built by the river to drive its water-powered hammers and bellows. The monks cultivated medicinal plants in the gardens next to the infirmary, which is set apart from the other buildings. The new gardens laid out by an English landscape gardener were designed to soften the austere look of the buildings and to ease the flow of visitors around the abbey.

Montbard

Montbard rises up the slope of a hill that impedes the course of the River Brenne. Its most famous former resident is the great 18C naturalist Buffon, who has left his mark on the town of his birth.

A BIT OF HISTORY

Georges-Louis Leclerc de Buffon – Born at Montbard in 1707, Buffon showed a passionate interest in science and nature from an early age. In 1733, he entered the Académie des Sciences, where he succeeded the botanist Jussieu. Six years later he became Administrator of the King's Garden (Jardin du Roi) and museum, now the Jardin des Plantes.

Helped by the naturalist Daubenton (1716–1799), Buffon reorganised the Jardin du Roi, extending it as far as the Seine, adding avenues of lime trees, a maze, and considerably augmenting the collections of the Natural History Museum. He also began the gigantic task of writing the history of nature.

▶ **Population:** 5 582
⚅ **Michelin Map:** 320: G-4.
🯅 **Info:** pl. Henri-Vincenot, 21501 Montbard. ✆ 03 80 92 53 81. www.ot-montbard.fr.
◐ **Location:** Montbard lies on the river Brenne and the Burgunday canal in the Côte-d'Or department. It is 1hr from Paris' Gare de Lyon railway station by TGV train.

The first three volumes of his *Histoire naturelle (Natural History)*, written mostly in Montbard, were published in 1749 and the other 33 volumes followed over the next 40 years.

SIGHTS

Parc Buffon★

◷ *Open year round daily (garden).*
🞲 *Guided tours (1hr 30min; ⚏ 2.50€) of Tour de l'Aubespin and Cabinet, daily (except Mon) 7 Apr–30 Sept 10am– noon, 2–6pm.* ◷*Closed 1 Jan, 1 May,*

25 Dec. ☎*03 80 92 50 42.*
www.montbard.com.
In 1735 Buffon bought the Château de Montbard, which dates from before the 10C and was by then in ruins; he demolished all but two towers and the fortified wall of enclosure.

The gardens which he laid out, slightly altered over the years, now form the Parc Buffon. The paths and alleys provide a number of pleasant walks.

Tour de l'Aubespin – Buffon used the height of this tower (40m/131ft) to conduct experiments on the wind. From the top there is a fine view of the town.

Tour St-Louis – Buffon used the ancient tower as his library.

Cabinet de travail de Buffon – It was in this small pavilion with the walls covered with 18C coloured engravings of various bird species that Buffon wrote most of his *Natural History*.

L'Ancienne Orangerie (Musée Buffon)

🕐*Open daily except Mon 10am–noon, 2–6pm (Nov–Apr 5pm).* 🕐*Closed 1 Jan, 1 May, 25 Dec.* ☎*03 80 92 50 42. www.montbard.com.*
Buffon's stables now house a museum devoted to the great naturalist and his place in the history of Montbard and of 18C science.

Musée des Beaux-Arts

🕐*Open Jul–Aug daily except Tue 10am–noon, 2–6pm.* ☎*03 80 92 50 42. www.montbard.com.*
The fine arts museum contains a magnificent wooden triptych *(Adoration of the Shepherds)* by André Ménassier (1599) and 19C and 20C art. Three of the artists represented are natives of Montbard: the sculptor Eugène Guillaume and the painters Chantal Queneville and Ernest Boguet.

EXCURSIONS

👥🚶 Grande Forge de Buffon

▶*7km/5mi NW.* ♿🕐*Open Jul–Aug daily 10am–noon, 2–6pm; Apr, Jun, Sept 10am–noon, 2.30–6pm daily except Tue.* 💶*6€.* ☎*03 80 92 10 35.*

In 1768, when Buffon was 60 years old, he built a forge for the commercial exploitation of his discoveries about iron and steel and to continue his experiments with minerals on a large scale.

His industrial complex was on two levels: on the lower level were the production shops beside a channel containing water diverted from the River Armançon; on the upper level above the flood line were the houses and other facilities.

The **workshops** consist of three buildings separated by water channels which supplied hydraulic energy to the bellows and trip hammers.

The blast-furnace was reached from the upper level by a huge internal staircase; next came the refinery, the forge itself, where the iron was recast and beaten with the trip hammer into bars, and the slitting mill where the bars could be reworked. Further on is the basin where the raw mineral was washed before being smelted.

Château de Nuits

▶*18km/11mi NW.* 🕐*Open Apr–Nov.* 🚶*Guided tours (1hr) 11am, 2.15pm, 3.15pm, 4.15pm, 5.15pm.* 💶*7€.* ☎*01 47 63 82 78. www.chateaudenuits.fr.*
The castle was built in 1560 during the Wars of Religion. The attractive Renaissance façade of pediments and pilasters was formerly screened by a fortified wall. The east façade, facing the Armançon (the old border between Burgundy and Champagne), has retained its austere defensive appearance. The vaulted cellars leading to the east terrace contain a kitchen with an indoor well which enabled the castle to hold out against a siege.

A large stone stairway leads to the living quarters above, with its high fireplace in pure Renaissance style and 18C wood panelling. Visitors should also see the buildings occupied by the influential Order of St-Mark **(Commanderie de St-Marc)**, overlooking the River Armaçon, especially the late-12C chapel.

ADDRESSES

🛏 STAY

🍽 **Camping municipal** – r. Michel Servet, D 980 NW of town. ☎03 80 92 69 50. www.montbard.com. Open Mar-end Oct. ♿ **80 sites.** 80 places on a flat, grassy site, as well as mobile homes and mini-chalets ideal for families, plus children's games, ping-pong and tennis.

🍴 EAT

🍽🍽 **L'Écu** – 7 r. A. Carré. ☎03 80 92 11 66. www.hotel-de-l-ecu.fr. **3 rooms.** ☎ 12 €. Family-run place with three dining rooms: one vaulted, one with huge beams, and one with a modern touch. Traditional cuisine. A few renovated rooms.

🍽🍽 **Le Marronnier** – 6 rte des Forges, 21500 Buffon. 6km/4mi N on D 905. ☎03 80 92 33 65. http://perso. wanadoo.fr/lemarronnier. Closed 25 Dec –18 Jan. ♿📶 **5 rooms.** ☎ 7.50 €. Lovely place by the Burgundy Canal serving traditional fare in a pretty room with stone walls and a fine fireplace.

🍽🍽 **La Mirabelle** – 1 r. de la Brenne. 21500 St-Rémy 5km/3mi W on D 905. ☎03 80 92 40 69. lamirabelle2@free.fr. Closed 23 Dec–3 Jan, Sun and Mon eve and Wed. Former salt house by the canal with vaulted stone dining room. Tasty, skilfully cooked traditional cuisine served in a snug ambience.

Semur-en-Auxois★

Semur is the main centre of the Auxois agricultural and stock-raising region. The town marries with its setting in a picturesque scene: a tightly packed mass of small light-coloured houses, with the great towers of the castle and the slender spire of the church of Notre-Dame rising above, stands on top of a rose-tinted granite cliff, overlooking a deep ravine with the River Armançon at the bottom.

A BIT OF HISTORY

A stronghold – Semur became the stronghold of the duchy in the 14C when the citadel was reinforced by ramparts and 18 towers. The town was divided into three parts each with a perimeter wall.

🚶WALKING TOUR
Porte Sauvigny

This 15C gateway, preceded by a postern, marked the main entrance to the district known as the Bourg Notre-Dame.

▷ *Follow rue Buffon.*

▶ **Population:** 4 195
🗺 **Michelin Map:** 320: G-5. Local map see Le Morvan.
ℹ **Info:** 2 pl. Gaveau, 21140 Semur-En-Auxois. ☎03 80 97 05 96. www.ville-semur -en-auxois.fr.
😊 **Don't Miss:** Try to arrive along the Paris road, from where there is a good view of the ramparts and the town during the downhill run to the Joly Bridge.

Collégiale Notre-Dame

The church is in place Notre-Dame, flanked by old houses. It was founded in the 11C, rebuilt in the 13C and 14C, altered in the 15C and 16C, extended by the addition of chapels to the north aisle and restored by Viollet-le-Duc.

Exterior – The 14C façade, dominated by two square towers, is preceded by a vast porch. In rue Notre-Dame, the 13C door in the north transept (Porte des Bleds) has a beautiful tympanum depicting Doubting Thomas and the bringing of the Gospel to the West Indies.

Interior – There are several interesting chapels opening off the north aisle. In the second chapel, Mise au Tombeau, is a polychrome Entombment from the late 15C with monumental figures typical of Claus Sluter. The third chapel (**2**) vaulting has 16C stained glass illustrating the legend of St Barbara.

The last two chapels contain panels of stained glass given in the 15C by local guilds – the butchers (**3**) and eight panels from the **drapers**⋆.

Behind the pulpit is a 15C stone canopy (**5**), remarkably carved with a 5m/16ft-high pinnacle.

In the last chapel of the outer north aisle is a painted retable (**6**) dating from 1554, representing the Tree of Jesse. The retable is surmounted by a Gothic canopy of carved wood. The Lady Chapel (**7**) is lit by very beautiful stained-glass windows of the 13C restored by Viollet-le-Duc. In the south aisle there is a late-15C polychrome statue (**8**) of Christ bearing the Five Wounds.

▷ *Continue along rue Fevret.*

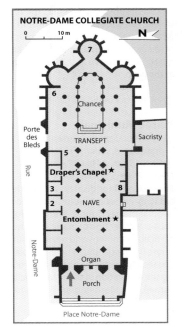

NOTRE-DAME COLLEGIATE CHURCH

Place Notre-Dame

Tour de l'Orle-d'Or and Musée
⊶ Closed to the public. This tower was part of the keep (razed in 1602).

Pont Joly
From the Joly Bridge there is an overall **view**⋆ of the medieval city. The bridge crosses the Armançon at the foot of the castle keep which once guarded the narrow isthmus joining the rose-coloured cliff, where the city started, to the granite plateau onto which it has spread.

Promenade des Remparts
The former ramparts along the edge of the granite spur have been converted into a promenade shaded by lime trees overlooking the valley of the Armançon. To reach the promenade, go past the hospital, a pleasant 18C building.

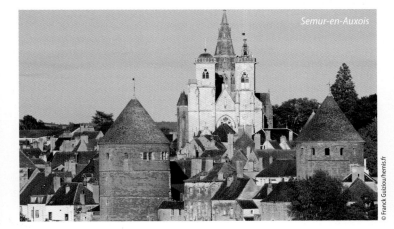

Semur-en-Auxois

© Franck Guiziou/hemis.fr

Rue Basse-du-Rempart skirts the foot of the ramparts. Their grandeur is emphasised by the enormous blocks of red granite, sparkling with mica and quartz, which serve as the foundations of the keep.

◐ *Walk back along rue Collenot.*

Musée Municipal

◷ *Open Apr–Sept daily except Tue 2–6pm; Oct–Apr Mon–Fri 2–5pm.*
◷ *Closed 1 Jan, 1 May, 15 Aug, 1 and 11 Nov, 25 Dec.* ✆ *03 80 97 24 25.*
The ground floor displays a collection of 13C to 19C sculpture, including many original plaster figures. The first floor houses a collection on natural science, particularly zoology and geology (such as rare fish fossils and mineral samples). The second floor has articles found during the excavation of prehistoric, Gallo-Roman and Merovingian sites and a small gallery of paintings.

EXCURSION

Époisses

◐ *12km/7.5mi west.*
This pleasant village, on the plateau of Auxois, is known for its castle and its soft, strong-flavoured cheese.

Château d'Époisses★

◷ *Open Jul–Aug daily except Tue 10am–noon, 3–6pm. Park year round daily 9am–7pm.* ✍*7€.* ✆ *01 42 27 73 11.*
www.chateaudepoisses.com.
The château is enclosed by two fortified precincts ringed by dry moats. The buildings in the outer courtyard form a small village clustered round the church, once part of a 12C abbey, and a robust 16C dovecot. The château was remodelled in the 16C and 17C and partly demolished during the Revolution. The Guitaut family, owners of the château since the 17C, have preserved many mementoes of famous people who have stayed here. In the entrance hall, Renaissance portraits are set into the panelled walls. The small room beyond has a richly painted ceiling. The salon's Louis XIV furniture includes chairs covered with Gobelins tapestries.

On the first floor the portrait gallery is hung with paintings of 17C and 18C personalities.

ADDRESSES

⌂ STAY

⊜⊜ **Chambre d'hôte La Maison du Canal** – *Pont-Royal, 21390 Clamerey. 16km/10mi SE on D 970 then D 70 (dir. Vitteaux).* ✆ *03 80 84 28 27.* 🅿 ⊟ *5 rooms.* ⊠. This early 19C building, on the quays of the Burgundy Canal opposite a marina, has carefully kept rooms looking out onto peaceful Auxois countryside. Information on boating available.

⊜⊜⊜ **Hôtel Les Cymaises** – *7 r. Renaudot.* ✆ *03 80 97 21 44. www.hotel cymaises.com. Closed 4–30 Nov and 7 Feb –1 Mar. Wi-Fi. 18 rooms.* ⊠ *8 €.* In the heart of the medieval city, this lovely auberge has renovated, soundproofed rooms. Take breakfast on the veranda. The garden is a riot of flowers.

⊜⊜⊜⊜ **Hostellerie d'Aussois** – *Rte de Saulieu.* ✆ *03 80 97 28 28. www.hostellerie.fr.* ♿🅿 *Wi-Fi. 42 rooms.* ⊠ *13 €, half-board available.* ✕ *26–57 €.* Basic, peaceful rooms made over with a designer look. Pleasant lobby lounge-bar. The contemporary restaurant serves traditional fare and opens onto the pool terrace with the town walls of Semur as a backdrop.

⊠ EAT

⊜ **Vieille Auberge** – *19 r. Verdun, 21350 Vitteaux. 23 km/14mi SE on D 970 then D 70.* ✆ *03 80 49 60 88. Closed 21–30 Jun 9–22 Jan and Mon. Set lunch menu 12 €.* A rustic-feeling bar leads into two country-style dining rooms in this family-run village inn serving traditional cuisine. Small terrace and boules area.

⊟ SHOPPING

Pellé – *1 r. de la Liberté.* ✆ *03 80 97 08 94. Open Tue–Sun 7am–7pm.* This famed chocolatier, open for 30 years, is full of temptations. Specialities not to miss are the Granité Rose de l'Auxois, made of chocolate, almonds and orange. Also on offer: some 25 types of cake.

Alise-Ste-Reine

*16km/10mi north-east
of Semur-en-Auxois*

Alise-Ste-Reine is on the slopes
of Mont Auxois (407m/1 335ft)
between the Oze and Ozerain valleys
overlooking the Les Laumes plain.
The first part of its name comes from
Alésia, a Gaulish, then Gallo-Roman
settlement on the plateau. The
second recalls a Christian woman,
Reina, who was martyred in the 3C.

A BIT OF HISTORY

Siege of Alésia – After his defeat at
Gergovie in the spring of 52 BC, Caesar
retreated northwards to join forces with
his lieutenant near Sens. Once united
they made for the Roman base camps,
but on route they were attacked near
Alésia by the Gauls under Vercingétorix.
Despite the surprise of their attack and
superior numbers, the Gauls suffered
a crushing defeat, and Vercingétorix
retreated to the camp at Alésia.

Caesar's legions surrounded the camp
with a double line of fortified earth-
works, such as trenches, walls, palisades
of stakes and towers. For six weeks, Vercingétorix tried and failed to break out.
A rescue army of Gauls, 250 000 strong,
could not relieve the besieged force and
withdrew. Vercingétorix was forced to
surrender to Caesar.

A battle of experts – During the 19C,
some historians hotly disputed the site
of Alésia as the scene of the siege. To
end the controversy, Napoleon III had
excavations carried out at Alise-Ste-
Reine from 1861 to 1865. These revealed
extensive military works, as well as the
bones of men and horses and a mass
of objects left behind during the siege,
from silver coins to weaponry.

More recently, excavations at Chaux-des-
Crotenay to the south-east of Champagnole in the Jura have revealed another
site which also claims to be Alésia.

The latest excavation work (1991–98)
in the area could not reconcile Caesar's
account of the battle with what was
found on location and, in November
1998, it was officially stated that Alise
was no longer considered the site of the
battle of Alésia. However, the discussions are definitely not over yet.

- **Population:** 660
- **Michelin Map:** 320: G-4.
- **Info:** pl. Bingerbrück, 21150
  Venarey-Les-Laumes.
  03 80 96 89 13.
  www.alesia-tourisme.net.
- **Don't Miss:** There is an
  excellent overview of the
  site from the panorama
  on Mont Auxois.

MONT AUXOIS★
Panorama★
From the bronze statue of Vercingétorix,
the view sweeps over the plain of Les
Laumes and the site of the Roman out-
works to the outskirts of Saulieu.

MuséoParc Alésia
*Open Jul–Aug 9am–7pm; Apr–Jun,
Sept 9am–6pm; Feb, Mar, Oct Nov 10am
–5pm. 9€, (children 6€). 03 80 96
85 90. www.alesia.com.*

The summit of the fortified settlement
(oppidum) was occupied by a Gallo-
Roman town. Signs and numbered sites
show the different districts grouped
round the forum. The western district
contained the theatre, religious buildings and a civilian basilica. The northern
district had shops, the bronze-workers'
guild house and a mansion, heated by a
hypocaust (underfloor heating); a statue
of the mother goddess was found in the
cellar, hence the name *Cave à la Mater.*
The craftsmen's district to the southeast
is composed of small houses.

To the southwest are the ruins of a
Merovingian basilica dedicated to St
Reina, which was the last building
erected on the plateau.

The museum contains objects excavated
from the Gallo-Roman town: statues
and statuettes, building fragments, the
reconstructed façade of a Gallo-Roman
chapel, coins, pottery etc.

Château de Bussy-Rabutin ★

Halfway up a hill a few miles north of Alise-Ste-Reine is the château of Bussy-Rabutin. Its highly original interior décor provides a fascinating insight into the mind of a scandalous former owner.

A BIT OF HISTORY
The misfortunes of Roger de Bussy-Rabutin

While his cousin, Mme de Sérigné, was very successful with her pen, Roger de Rabutin, Count of Bussy, caused nothing but trouble with his. Having compromised himself, in company with other young libertines, in a famous orgy in which he improvised and sang couplets ridiculing the love affair of young Louis XIV and Marie de Mancini, Bussy-Rabutin was exiled to Burgundy on the orders of the king.

Accompanied into Burgundy by his mistress, the Marquise de Montglat, he passed his time writing his *Histoire Amoureuse des Gaules*, a satirical chronicle of the love affairs of the court. This libellous work earned its author a stay in the Bastille, where he languished for over a year. Then he was sent home to Bussy, where he lived in exile – alone this time, as the beautiful marquise had forgotten all about him.

Michelin Map: 320: H-4.

Info: Château de Bussy-Rabutin, 21150 Bussy le Grand. Open Tue–Sun 9.15am–noon, 2–5pm (6pm May–Sept). Closed 1 Jan, 1 May, 1 and 11 Nov, 25 Dec. 7€. 03 80 96 00 03. www.bussy-rabutin. monuments-nationaux.fr.

Don't Miss: Take time to explore the park (34ha/84 acres), shaped like an amphitheatre with beautiful stone steps linking the levels, which makes a fine backdrop to the gardens with their statues, fountains and pools, apparently designed by Le Nôtre, Louis XIV's own gardener.

VISIT

This 15C fortified castle was bought during the Renaissance by the Comtes de Rochefort, who knocked down the wall enclosing the courtyard and transformed the defensive towers into elegant living quarters. The façade is 17C. Roger de Rabutin's grandfather began works on the ground floor during the reign of Louis XIII; the upper floors,

Château de Bussy-Rabutin

© Manfred Mehlig/Mauritius/Photononstop

completed in 1649, show the naissant Louis XIV style.

Interior – It was Bussy-Rabutin himself who designed the interior decoration of the apartments, a gilded cage in which he spent his exile, indulging in nostalgia for army and court life and giving vent to his rancour against Louis XIV and his unfaithful mistress.

Cabinet des Devises – Numerous portraits and allegorical paintings along with pithy maxims (devises) by Roger de Rabutin are framed in the woodwork panels of this room. The upper panels show views of châteaux and monuments, some of which no longer exist. Over the fireplace is a portrait of Bussy-Rabutin by Lefèvre, a student of Lebrun. The furniture is Louis XIII.

Antichambre des Grands Hommes de Guerre – Portraits of 65 great warriors, from Du Guesclin down to the master of the house, Maistre de Camp, Général de la Cavalerie Légère de France, are hung in two rows around the room. Some of the portraits are very good originals, but most of them are only copies. The woodwork and ceilings are decorated with fleurs-de-lis, trophies, standards and the interlaced emblems of Bussy and the Marquise de Montglat.

Chambre de Bussy – Bussy's bedchamber is adorned with the portraits of 25 women. That of Louise de Rouville, second wife of Bussy-Rabutin, is included in a triptych with those of Mme de Sévigné and her daughter, Mme de Grignan. Other personalities portrayed include Gabrielle d'Estrées, Henri IV's mistress, Mme de la Sablière, Ninon de Lenclos, the famous courtesan, and Mme de Maintenon.

Tour Dorée★ – Bussy-Rabutin surpassed himself in the decoration of the circular room where he worked on the first floor of the west tower. The walls are entirely covered with paintings, on subjects taken from mythology and the gallantry of the age, accompanied by quatrains and couplets. Bussy-Rabutin is depicted as a Roman emperor. Portraits of the personalities of the courts of Louis XIII and Louis XIV complete the collection.

Chapelle – The Galerie des Rois de France leads to the south tower, which houses a small, elegantly furnished oratory.

Flavigny-sur-Ozerain★

Flavigny's narrow streets flanked by old mansions, its fortified gateways and the remains of its medieval ramparts and abbey recall its past grandeur, and make it a favoured movie location (such as for *Chocolat*). Its setting, too, is picturesque: a rocky perch surrounded by streams.

SIGHTS

Old Houses★

Many houses have been restored; they date from the late Middle Ages and the Renaissance and are decorated with turrets, spiral stairs or delicate sculptures. Note, in particular, the Maison du Donataire (15C–16C) in rue de l'Église.

▶ **Population:** 341

⏱ **Michelin Map:** 320: H-4.

ℹ **Info:** pl. Bingerbrück, 21150 Venarey-les-Laumes. ℘03 80 96 89 13. www.alesia-tourisme.net.

▷ **Location:** 16km/10mi east of Semur, Flavigny-sur-Ozerain is just off the D 905 road.

◉ **Don't Miss:** Flavigny's famous aniseed sweets. This local confection, aniseed coated in snow-white sugar, has been made in the old abbey since the 9C. The pretty tins and boxes they come in are as attractive as the tiny sweets inside.

Ancienne Abbaye

Guided tours (10min) by appointment daily except Sat–Sun 9–11am. *Closed in Aug, 25 Dec–1 Jan and public holidays. 03 80 96 20 88.*

The Benedictine abbey, founded in the 8C, once consisted of a great church, the basilica of St-Pierre and the usual conventual buildings. The latter were rebuilt in the 18C and now house the aniseed sweet factory. There are interesting remains from the Carolingian period of St-Pierre.

Crypte Ste-Reine (*open Feb–Nov, Mon–Fri 9am–6pm; 03 80 96 20 88*) – The upper level of the double-decker Carolingian apse, reached by steps from the nave, contains the high altar. The lower chamber, built c. 758, contains the tomb of St Reina (*see ALISE-STE-REINE*). Following her martyrdom, her remains were buried here around 866. The finely carved pillar is a good example of Carolingian decorative work.

Chapelle Notre-Dame-des-Piliers – In 1960 excavations revealed the existence of a hexagonal chapel with ambulatory beyond the crypt. The style recalls the pre-Romanesque rotundas of St-Bénigne in Dijon and Saulieu.

Église St-Genest (*open May–Oct daily except Fri 1.30–5.15pm, (Sun 6.15pm); 03 80 96 22 77*) – This 13C church, built on the site of an even earlier religious building, was altered in the 15C and 16C. It has a stone central gallery dating from the beginning of the 16C. Other galleries run along the top of the aisles and the first two bays of the nave, something that is very rare in Gothic architecture. They are enclosed by 15C wooden screens. The stalls are early 16C.

Among the many interesting statues, note the Angel of the Annunciation, a masterpiece of the Burgundian School, in the last chapel on the right in the nave, and a 12C Virgin nursing the Infant Jesus, in the south transept.

Tour of the ramparts – Starting from the 15C gateway, Porte du Bourg with its impressive machicolations, take chemin des Fossés and chemin des Perrières to reach the Porte du Val flanked by two round towers. Nearby is the Maison Lacordaire, a former Dominican monastery founded by **Father Lacordaire**.

EXCURSION

Château de Frôlois

17km/10.2mi NW. Open Jun and Aug. Guided tours (1hr) 2–6.30pm. 4.50€. 03 80 96 22 92.

The Frolois family established its residence on this site in the 10C; the medieval fortress was often remodelled, leaving only the main building (14C–15C).

On the first floor, the family heir, Antoine de Vergy, has a room with a French-style ceiling decorated with the family coat of arms and initials. The ground floor was remodelled in the 17C and 18C, and is hung with attractive late-17C Bergamo tapestries.

DRIVING TOUR

SOURCE OF THE SEINE

50km/31mi circuit. Allow 1hr.
See Region map.

At St-Germain-Source-Seine on the Langres plateau, the River Seine bubbles up inside an artificial grotto at the feet of a copy of Jouffroy's Nymph of the Seine statue. The water trickles down the valley past the site of a Gallo-Roman temple, where excavations have found bronze and wooden artefacts now housed in Dijon's archaeological museum.

Continue to Étalante to find the Source of the Coquille. An excellent leaflet available from local Tourism Offices (*or download it at www.sitesnaturelsbourgogne. asso.fr*) is a great help here. A 1km/0.6mi circular walk leads to the source of this modest river through a splendid glaciated arena which is home to rare Alpine-type flora, including orchids. After taking in the view over the Châtillonais region, a steep trail leads to the crystal waters at the resurgence of the Coquille. Rambling across the Langres Plateau, you will come across other river sources, the Ignon, for example, which flows towards the Saône.

Châtillon-sur-Seine★

The trim little town of Châtillon is set on the banks of the young Seine, which is joined here by the River Douix. For several centuries, sheep breeding has been the main source of wealth on the dry plateaux of the Châtillon region (Châtillonnais), and up to the 18C Châtillon was the centre of a flourishing wool industry.

A BIT OF HISTORY

Talking peace with Bonaparte – In February 1814, while Napoleon I was defending the approaches to Paris, a peace congress was held in Châtillon between France and the countries allied against her (Austria, Russia, England and Prussia). Napoleon rejected the conditions laid down and fighting resumed, but his Empire soon fell.

The tide turns – In September 1914 French troops retreated in the face of a violent German attack. **Général Joffre**, Commander-in-Chief of the French armies, set up his headquarters at Châtillon-sur-Seine, where he issued his famous order of 6 September: "We are about to engage in a battle on which the fate of our country depends, and it is important to remind all ranks that the moment has passed for looking back..." The German advance was halted and the French counter-attack on the Marne was a victory.

SIGHTS

Musée du Pays Châtillonnais★

○Open Jul–Aug 10am–7pm. Rest of the year daily except Tue 9.30am–noon, 2–6pm. ○Closed 1 Jan, 1 May and 25 Dec. ◉6€. ℘03 80 91 24 67.
This museum is in the attractive Renaissance Maison Philandrier, but scheduled to move to the old Notre-Dame abbey. It houses interesting Gallo-Roman finds from 19C and early 20C excavations, particularly at Vertault (20km/12mi W of Châtillon). The pride of the museum is the extraordinary archaeological find of January 1953 at Mont Lassois near Vix.

▶ **Population:** 5 801
⊙ **Michelin Map:** 320: H-2.
▣ **Info:** 4 pl. Marmont, 21400 Châtillon-Sur-Seine. ℘03 80 91 13 19. www.mairie-chatillon-sur-seine.fr.

The Treasure of Vix★★ – *A reconstitution of the tomb is displayed behind glass.* The treasures were found in a 6C BC grave containing the remains of a woman: priceless jewellery, parts of a state chariot, countless gold and bronze items and a huge, richly-decorated bronze vase with a sculpted frieze made of applied panels portraying a row of helmeted warriors and chariots, and Gorgon's heads on the handles. Other items found in the tomb of the Gaulish princess include a massive golden diadem, bronze and silver goblets, wine jugs and jewellery.

Source de la Douix★

The source of the River Douix is in a stunningly beautiful spot at the foot of a rocky escarpment (*over 30m/98ft high*). The normal flow is 600l/132gal a second but it can reach 3 000l/660gal in flood periods. The promenade, laid out on a rocky platform, looks over the town and valley.

EXCURSIONS

Forêt de Châtillon

This vast forest, extending over 9 000ha/22 240 acres to the south-east of Châtillon-sur-Seine, offers walkers an unspoilt natural environment to enjoy.

Abbaye du Val-des-Choues

○Open Jul–Aug 10am–6pm Apr–Jun and Sept daily except Tue 1–5pm. Rest of the year weekends only 1–5pm. Hunting dog feedings Jul–Aug 4pm. ◉4€. ℘03 80 81 01 09. www.abbayeduvaldeschoues.com.
In the heart of the forest, surrounded by lovely gardens, this small museum houses collections relating to forests, hunting and gypsum. Sound and light (*son et lumière*) shows in summer.

Cascades du Hérisson
© Philippe Roy/hemis.fr

The capital and largest city by far in the Franche-Comté – as well as capital of the Doubs department – Besançon is lively all year round, offering everything from fascinating historical sites to rich museum collections, and from fine local cuisine and wines to an excellent cultural programme. The city continues to progress, and an ambitious project is under way to construct a contemporary centre for arts and culture, designed by the Japanese architect, Kengo Kumo, due to open in 2012. By contrast, the very green countryside outside the city, with forests on its doorstep, is a reminder that the traditional rural character of Franche-Comté is never far away.

Highlights

Dole – Former Capital

For many, the gateway to the Franche-Comté is the fine old town of Dole, which basks in its history as the regions former capital. Proud of having its own parliament, university and even being able to mint its own money, it fought hard in 1678 to hold onto its status. Once these symbols of power were relinquished to Besançon, Dole had nothing left to do except extend the town and create pretty squares and fountains.

The streets of the old town, the canals and the Doubs riverside are charming to wander around. One feature to look out for, also common to Besançon, is the use of distinctive, rounded iron bar grills protecting many windows. Dating from the 18C development of forged ironwork in the locality, they are called *rejas* meaning grills in Castilian Spanish, and thought to be a legacy of the Spanish occupation here.

Land of Forests and Rivers

Dole, Besançon and Baume-les-Dames all lie on the Doubs river; Ornans is on the Loue; and Pesmes is on the pretty Ognon river. Apart from during times of flooding – the Loue flooded the town of Ornans badly in 1953 and 1998 – these rivers have always been the life blood of the settlements that built up along their banks, as well as a source of inspiration and pleasure.

Gustave Courbet, the Realism painter born in Ornans, was much inspired by the landscape around his home, and he painted the Source of the Loue in 1864 when it was already becoming a tourist attraction. Today the pretty and fascinating environment around the sources of the Loue and the Lison are still much visited, with river caves to explore.

Salins-les-Bains lies on the tempestuous Furieuse river, a tributary of the Loue. The many forests and rivers in the region have been exploited as a great resource for its development. At one time, the Furieuse river provided water power to support 12 large sawmills , with rivers also being used for the transportation of logs.

East of Dole between the Doubs and Loue rivers, the extensive Chaux forest used to be home to more than 600 people who made their livelihoods as wood-cutters and blacksmiths, potters and glassmakers. The forest was considered so important in the industrial period of the 19C that the National department for Waters and Forests commissioned the architect Guidon to build seven Doric columns to mark the important corners of the forest. They can still be viewed today.

Today the forest is protected by the National Forest Offices. Popular with walkers and horse riders, it is widely used as a hunting ground both for animals and for mushrooms.

Land of White Gold

Today we take salt for granted, even when freely seasoning our food or driving along a treated road in winter. Demand for this precious commodity has always been high, since in the past it was essential for food preservation. Until the industrial revolution – when improved extraction methods, better transport infrastructure and more effective storage techniques brought down costs – salt was a hugely valuable, taxed commodity. France was notorious for its very high salt tax, the *gabelle*, levied from the 13C onwards and considered a factor leading to the French Revolution.

Inside Saline Royale d'Arc-et-Senans

Franche-Comté and nearby Lorraine had a salt production industry as far back as Roman times, with both regions benefiting from their proximity to the rock salt deposits in the Jura mountains and the underground water channels issuing from them. Constructed over salt-water springs and close to forests that provided wood for use as fuel in the manufacturing process, Salins-les-Bains was the most important production centre in the Jura during the Middle Ages. The prosperous Grande Saunerie, the town's huge saltworks, was like a fortress with its own walls, tower, prison and even its own coat of arms. However, by the time the Jura became part of France in 1674, the salt water had been over-exploited and local stocks of wood were severely depleted.

Such was the importance of the saltworks, and the dilapidation of the Salins buildings, that in the 18C the government commissioned the Royal Saltworks to be constructed 21km/13mi away at Arc-et-Senans, on the edge of the huge Chaux forest. Today we recognize the fine architectural work of Claude-Nicolas Ledoux in his designs for the "ideal town" of the Royal Saltworks, yet his engineering skills were considerable, too: a brine duct had to be created to transport the salt water the distance from Salins to the new factory at Arc-et-Senans, crossing hills and following two river courses downstream. The pipeline originally consisted of 15 000 hollowed-out pine tree trunks.

With the fashion for water cures, Salins was able to re-invent itself as a spa town in the 19C, but the spa eventually closed in 1962.

Saline Royale d'Arc-et-Senans

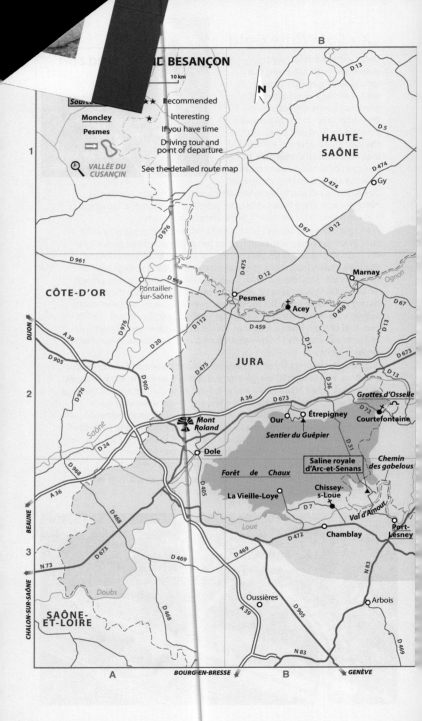

ND BESANÇON

10 km

Source   ★★ ★ Recommended

Moncley   ★   Interesting

Pesmes   If you have time

⇨   Driving tour and point of departure

🔍 VALLÉE DU CUSANÇIN   See the detailed route map

N

HAUTE-SAÔNE

D 13

D 5

D 474

Gy

CÔTE-D'OR

D 961

D 976

Pontailler-sur-Saône

D 59

D 475

D 12

D 67

Marnay

Ognon

D 976

D 20

D 112

Pesmes

Acey

D 459

D 67

D 459

D 13

DIJON

A 39

D 905

D 475

JURA

D 12

D 673

D 976

D 905

A 36

D 673

D 36

D 13

Grottes d'Osselle

Saône

Mont Roland

Our

Étrepigney

D 73

Courtefontaine

D 24

Dole

Sentier du Guêpier

D 31

Chemin des gabelous

D 968

Saline royale d'Arc-et-Senans

A 36

BEAUNE

D 468

Forêt de Chaux

D 405

La Vieille-Loye

Chissey-s-Loue

D 7

Val d'Amour

Port-Lesney

Loue

D 673

D 469

D 469

Chamblay

D 472

N 73

CHALON-SUR-SAÔNE

SAÔNE-ET-LOIRE

Doubs

D 468

Oussières

A 39

D 905

N 83

Arbois

D 469

A   *BOURG-EN-BRESSE*   **B**   *GENÈVE*

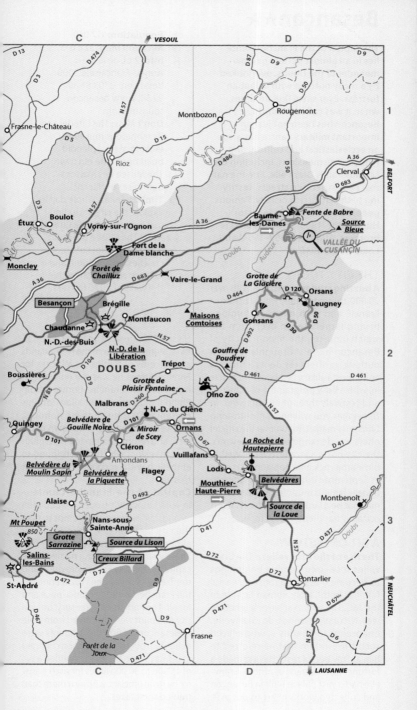

D 13

D 3

D 474

C

D 87

D 9

D

D 9

N 57

D 50

Montbozon

Rougemont

1

Frasne-le-Château

D 5

D 15

D 486

A 36

D 50

Clerval

A 36

D 683

BELFORT

Rioz

D 3

N 57

Baume-les-Dames

▲ Fente de Babre

Source Bleue

Étuz

Boulot

Voray-sur-l'Ognon

D 1

A 36

Moncley

N 57

Forêt de Chailluz

Fort de la Dame blanche

D 683

Vaire-le-Grand

Doubs

Audeux

VALLÉE DU CUSANÇIN

Besançon

Brégille

Montfaucon

Grotte de La Glacière

D 464

D 120

Orsans

Leugney

Chaudanne

N.-D.-des-Buis

Maisons Comtoises

Gonsans

D 50

D 492

D 30

N.-D. de la Libération

N 57

DOUBS

D 104

D 9

Trépot

Gouffre de Poudrey

D 461

D 461

2

Boussières

N 83

Grotte de Plaisir Fontaine

Dino Zoo

N 57

Malbrans

D 260

N.-D. du Chêne

Belvédère de Gouille Noire

D 101

Miroir de Scey

Ornans

La Roche de Hautepierre

Quingey

D 101

Cléron

Amondans

Vuillafans

Loue

D 67

D 41

Belvédère du Moulin Sapin

Belvédère de la Piquette

Flagey

D 492

Lods

Belvédères

Alaise

Lison

Mouthier-Haute-Pierre

Montbenoît

3

Mt Poupet

850

Nans-sous-Sainte-Anne

D 41

Source de la Loue

D 437

Doubs

Grotte Sarrazine

Source du Lison

N 57

Salins-les-Bains

Creux Billard

D 72

D 72

Pontarlier

D 72

St-André

D 472

D 9

D 471

D 467

D 9

D 471

Frasne

N 57

D 6

NEUCHÂTEL

Forêt de la Joux

C

D

LAUSANNE

269

Besançon★★

The capital of the Franche-Comté lies in an almost perfect ox-bow meander of the Doubs, overlooked by a rocky outcrop with a Vauban fortress. Ever since Roman times, when it was called Vesontio, Besançon has been not just an important military centre but also an ecclesiastical and cultural one. Fine private mansions, including the famous Palais Granvelle, line the narrow pedestrianised streets, testifying to the city's rich history. Famous people born here include Victor Hugo (1802–1885) and the Lumière brothers, Auguste (1862–1954) and Louis (1864–1948).

▶ **Population:** 117 080
◉ **Michelin Map:** 321: G-3.
🛈 **Info:** 2 pl. de la 1re-Armée-Française, 25000 Besançon. ℘03 81 80 92 55. www.besancon-tourisme.com.
◉ **Don't Miss:** The Citadel and its numerous museums; looking at the splendid buildings in the old town; The Musée des Maisons Comtoises in Nacray.
◕ **Timing:** Take a whole day to explore the city, including half a day to visit the Citadel.
👪 **Kids:** The Musée d'Histoire Naturelle has lots of creepy-crawlies, an aquarium and a full-size zoo, and all within the walls of a 17C fortress.

THE CITY TODAY

A buzzing student centre – With over 20 000 students, many from outside of France, and with micro-technology having largely taken over from the watch industry, the historical city of Besançon has a thoroughly modern outlook. It offers residents, students and tourists alike a bright centre to live in, with a busy programme of activities and festivals throughout the year. In December you will find a month-long Christmas market; in summer the citadel offers a wide range of cultural events; the city hosts a jazz festival as well as big-name rock and pop concerts, and in September it holds its now internationally famous music festival. Besançon may not be a large city, but for its size it certainly has plenty going for it.

A BIT OF HISTORY

The rise of the Granvelles – The Granvelles rose from humble beginnings to become one of the most powerful families in the Holy Roman Empire in the 16C. The first to achieve high office was Nicolas Perrenot de Granvelle, Chancellor to Charles V, who placed such trust in him that he referred to him as "my bed of rest". Having made a fortune from his various offices, Granvelle had a vast palace built in Besançon and collected works of art to put in it.

His son Antoine went on to become Cardinal, Prime Minister of the Netherlands and Viceroy of Naples. As Minister for Foreign Affairs he was the only nobleman from the Franche-Comté whom Philip II of Spain would allow into his presence. Despite all these honours, Granvelle never forgot the town of his birth and returned often to his magnificent mansion, which he continued to embellish with works of art and other treasures.

Capital of the Franche-Comté – In 1674 Louis XIV's troops, 20 000 men strong, laid siege in an attempt to take the city for France. After resisting for almost a month, Besançon finally fell. Three years later, the King named it the capital of the new French province, and the Treaty of Nijmegen (1678) annexed the Franche-Comté to France once and for all. The Parliament, treasury, university and mint were all moved from Dole to Besançon. At first the residents were delighted, but their pride soon changed to dismay when they were handed a bill of 15 000 to 30 000 livres for each transfer by royal officials, who also more than trebled their taxes.

Aerial view of the citadel

© CRT Franche-Comté/Eric Chatelain

CITADEL★★

Take the steep, winding rue des Fusillés-de-la-Résistance up behind the cathedral. ☉*Open Jul–Aug daily 9am–7pm; Apr–Jun and Sept–Oct daily 9am–6pm. Rest of the year daily except Tue 10am–5pm.* ⌖*8.20€ (children 4.60-6.50€; combined ticket for all citadel museums).* ☎*03 81 87 83 33. www.citadelle.com.*

During Roman times this high ground was crowned with a temple, the columns of which now feature on the town's coat of arms. Later, a church dedicated to St Stephen stood on this spot. After the French conquest in 1674, Vauban had most of the earlier buildings demolished to make way for the fortress which now overlooks the River Doubs from a height of 118m/387ft.

The citadel of Besançon has played a variety of roles – barracks, military cadet academy under Louis XIV, state prison and fortress besieged in 1814 – and both its natural setting and historical interest have much to offer. The fortress was built on a gentle ridge and has a more or less rectangular ground plan.

Three bastions (or *enceintes* or *fronts*) with large esplanades in between them stretch across its width one after the other on one side: Front St-Étienne towards the town, Front Royal in the centre and Front de Secours nearest the fortress. The whole site is surrounded by fortified ramparts, along which a watch-path runs. Several watchtowers (**Tour du Roi** to the east and **Tour de la Reine** to the west) and bartizans remain. The citadel of Besançon and the Vauban fortifications were listed by UNESCO as a World Heritage Site in 2008.

Chemins de Ronde (Watch-paths)

The watch-path to the west, which begins at the Tour de la Reine *(on the right in the first esplanade)*, reveals a wonderful **view**★★ of Besançon, the valley of the Doubs and the Chaudanne and Les Buis hills. The watch-path which leads off towards the Bregille gives a good view of Besançon and the Doubs meander. On the side of the fortress away from the town the **Échauguette sur Tarragnoz**, reached via the **Parc Zoologique**, overlooks the valley of the Doubs.

Musée Comtois★

This museum houses a large collection of exhibits of traditional local arts, crafts and folklore from the Franche-Comté.

Espace Vauban

The Cadet's building now houses an exhibit and film which trace the history of the citadel, reviewing the civil and military context of Louis XIV's reign, in particular the brilliant engineering accomplishments of Vauban.

♣♣ Muséum de Besançon★

The Natural History Museum is in two wings of the old arsenal and contains clear, up-to-date exhibitions on exotic fauna, with stuffed animals and birds, skulls and skeletons, and insects, including a large butterfly collection.

The **Aquarium Georges-Bresse** is in a large room on the ground floor of the Petit Arsenal. A succession of tanks (50 000l/11 000gal) imitates the course of the River Doubs, complete with trout, perch, carp, pike and catfish. There are also ponds outside.

The **Jardin Zoologique** (2.5ha/6 acres) is at the far end on the fortress on the slope known as the Glacis du Front St-Étienne and the Front de Secours moat. About 350 animals live there, including a growing number of felines and primates. The **Noctarium**, in a former powder magazine, houses creatures that are mainly active at night.

Musée de la Résistance et de la Déportation★

This museum on the French Resistance and deportation occupies 22 rooms and comprises a huge collection of photographs, objects, posters and documents on the birth and rise of Nazism, the Second World War, the invasion of France in 1940, the Vichy régime, the French Resistance, deportation and the liberation of France. Pictures, paintings and sculptures by inmates of German prison camps are also on display, along with contemporary works on this theme. An audio-visual room completes the visit.

✎ WALKING TOURS
1 OLD TOWN★★

The old town should be visited on foot (much of it is pedestrian zone). Park your car either in the car park on the Promenade Chamars, or on the north-west bank of the Doubs. Cross the Battant bridge.

Bound by the meander of the River Doubs, this part of town was once walled. Before going down the Grande-Rue, take a few steps back along the bridge to get a better view of the 17C

residences with beautiful grey-blue stone **façades**★ which line the banks of the Doubs.

◗ Head N along quai (or promenade) Vauban to passage Vauban leading to place de la Révolution; when the river is in spate, follow the road running parallel to the quai Vauban.

Place de la Révolution

This lively square, better known as place du Marché, is at a junction with the Musée des Beaux-Arts et d'Archéologie on one side and old buildings along rue des Boucheries.

Musée des Beaux-Arts et d'Archéologie★★

⏱ *Open daily except Tue 9.30am–noon, 2–6pm.* ⏱ *Closed 1 Jan, 1 May, 1 Nov, 25 Dec.* ✆5€ *except Sun; children free.* ♿ ✆03 81 87 80 49. www.musee-arts-besancon.org.

The Museum of Fine Arts and Archaeology is in the old grain hall, which dates from 1835. It was been extended in 1971 by a follower of Le Corbusier, Louis Miquel, who built an original construction of concrete in the courtyard consisting of a succession of gently sloping ramps with landings in between them. The museum contains some rich collections of works of art, some of which come from the Granvelle family, more particularly from Nicolas de Granvelle. At the heart of the building, the ground floor houses a collection of **Egyptian antiquities** (**Seramon's sarcophagus**★ still containing his mummy) and statues and objects from the Middle Ages and the Renaissance. In the side galleries, there is a chronological display of local archaeological finds (**Gallo-Roman mosaic** depicting a quadriga, a bronze bull with three horns, god with a hammer).

The section of **paintings**★ includes a wide variety of works by non-French schools, signed by some of the greatest names of the 14C to the 17C. Some of the most remarkable works include: The **Drunkenness of Noah** by Giovanni Bellini (1430–1516) in Venice; **Deposition**

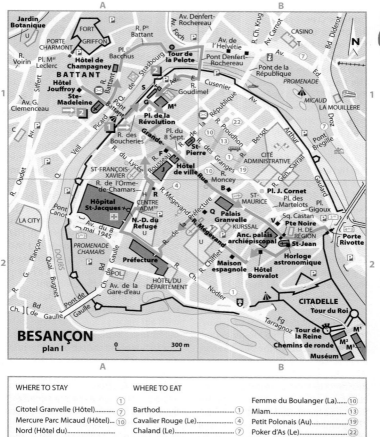

BESANÇON
plan I

0   300 m

WHERE TO STAY	WHERE TO EAT	
①		Femme du Boulanger (La)......⑩
Citotel Granvelle (Hôtel)....⑦	Barthod..............................①	Miam...................................⑬
Mercure Parc Micaud (Hôtel)..⑩	Cavalier Rouge (Le)..............④	Petit Polonais (Au)...............⑲
Nord (Hôtel du).......................	Chaland (Le).........................⑦	Poker d'As (Le)....................㉒

Ancien hôpital du St-Esprit.... **G**	Musée de la Résistance et de	Promenade Granvelle.............**S**
Bibliothèque municipale....... **B**	la Déportation....................**M³**	Promenade Vauban................**Q**
Espace Vauban..................... **M¹**	Musée des Beaux-Arts	Statue de Victor Hugo............**R**
Hôtel d'Emskerque................ **F**	et d'Archéolgie.................**M⁴**	Vestiges romains (Square
Musée Comtois..................... **M²**	Palais de Justice....................**J**	archéologique A.-Castan).....**V**

Musée des Beaux-Arts et d'Archéologie

© CRT Franche-Comté/Michel Joly

from the Cross by Bronzino (1503–1572) in Florence; the central panel of the **Triptych of Our Lady of Seven Sorrows** by Bernard Van Orley (1488–1541) in Brussels; **Ill-Assorted Pair** and **Nymph at the Fountain** by Lucas Cranach the Elder (1472–1553) in Germany. Flemish painting is also represented by fine portraits of animals and humans (**Portrait of a Woman** by Dirck Jacobs). In the gallery of 18C works, note the two panels illustrating **Scenes of Cannibalism** by Goya.

The French collection includes some 18C and 19C French masterpieces: tapestry cartoons on a Chinese theme by Boucher; works by Fragonard and Hubert Robert; sketches by David; and, best of all, landscapes by Courbet, The *Conche Hill* and the monumental painting **Death of a Stag**. Make a point of looking at some works by artists from the Franche-Comté (J Gigoux, T Chartran, JA Meunier).

A fine relief model of Besançon shows the triumphal arch, no longer extant, which once stood on the quai Vauban, and the old bell tower of the cathedral. The 20C has not been neglected: the Besson collection of paintings, watercolours and drawings includes some of Bonnard's best paintings, such as *Place Clichy* and *Café du Petit Poucet*, as well as the portrait of Madame Besson by Renoir, *The Seine at Grenelle* and *Two Friends* by Albert Marquet and *Yellow Sail* by Paul Signac.

The Cabinet des Dessins *(open by appointment only)* houses a comprehensive collection of over 5 000 drawings, including the famous red chalk sketches of the Villa d'Este by Fragonard. The drawings are exhibited in rotation, with only a selected few at a time on display.

> ◯ *Follow rue des Granges (behind the covered market) and turn immediately right onto rue R.-L.-Breton leading to place Pasteur and Grande-Rue.*

Grande-Rue

This street is an old Roman highway and is still the main road through the city. The part between the Pont Battant and

place du 8 Septembre is a pedestrian zone. Note the **Hôtel d'Emskerque** at no. 44, a late-16C mansion and one-time residence of Gaston d'Orléans, with elegant grilles on the ground floor.

Opposite, at no. 53, the interior courtyard has a remarkable stone and wrought-iron staircase. At no. 67, the **Hôtel Pourcheresse de Fraisans** also has a lovely courtyard staircase. No. 68, once the Hôtel Terrier de Santans, was built in 1770 and has a pretty interior courtyard. No. 86 used to be a **convent for Carmelite nuns**; it dates from the 17C and has an arcaded courtyard. At no. 88 stands the old entrance doorway to the **convent of the Great Carmelites** with a 16C fountain to the left of it. The sculptor Claude Lullier depicted the Duke of Alva, Philip II of Spain's military chief, as Neptune. No. 103 has a lovely timber staircase in the courtyard.

Hôtel de Ville – The town hall dates from the 16C. Its façade is decorated with alternately blue- and ochre-coloured rustic work. Opposite, the unusual façade of the **church of St-Pierre** is the work of Besançon architect Bertrand (late 18C).

Palais de Justice – The law courts has a pretty **Renaissance façade**★ by Hugues Sambin. The wrought-iron gates in the entrance doorway are really beautiful. The Parliament of the Franche-Comté sat in session inside, on the first floor.

Palais Granvelle★

The mansion was built from 1534 to 1542 for Chancellor Nicolas Perrenot de Granvelle. It has an imposing Renaissance façade. There is a rectangular interior **courtyard**★ surrounded by porticoes with depressed basket-handle arches.

Musée du Temps

◯*Open Tue–Sat 9.15am–noon, 2–6pm, Sun 10am–6pm.* ◯*Closed 1 Jan, 1 May, 1 Nov, 25 Dec.* ≈*5€, half-price Sat afternoon; free (with guided tour at 3pm) Sun afternoon.* ⟁ *℘03 81 87 81 50.* The clockmaking industry, established in Besançon in 1793, remained the town's main activity until the 1920s. This

© CRT Franche-Comté/Eric Chatelain

Palais Granvelle

museum in the restored Palais Granvelle has all kinds of objects connected with time: a rich collection of clocks, watches, tools and engravings from the 16C. Behind the palace, the Promenade Granvelle is a pleasant shady walk through the old palace gardens. It leads past the Kursaal, a concert and meeting hall.

◔ *Continue along Grande-Rue.*

Victor Hugo was born at no. 140, and the Lumière brothers, inventors of the first moving-picture camera, were born at no. 1 place Victor-Hugo.

Vestiges Romains (Roman ruins)

Rue de la Convention, the extension of Grande-Rue, offers a good view of square archéologique A-Castan, a pretty park with a row of columns which were once part of the peristyle of a nymphaeum. The channels of the aqueduct which supplied it can still be seen.

Go through the **Porte Noire**, a Roman triumphal arch built in the 2C. It would once have stood in solitary splendour. The sculpture work on it has been badly eroded by the weather.

Cathédrale Saint-Jean★

The cathedral, most of which was built in the 12C, has two apses, one at either end of the central nave. The bell tower collapsed in 1729 and was rebuilt in the 18C, along with one of the apses (Saint-Suaire, *left of entrance*) which was damaged when the tower fell in. The Saint-Suaire apse is Baroque in style and contains paintings from the 18C (Van Loo, Natoire, de Troy). In the south aisle, left of the great organ loft, is the famous painting by Fra Bartolomeo, the **Virgin Mary with Saints**★, executed in 1512 in Rome for the cathedral's canon Ferry Carondelet, abbot of Montbenoît and counsellor to Charles V. The left apsidal chapel houses the marble tomb of Abbot Ferry Carondelet. The second chapel includes a circular altar made from white marble and known as the **Rose de Saint Jean**.

The astronomical clock, **Horloge Astronomique**★ (◔*open Feb–Dec;* ◔*guided tours (20–30min) daily except Tue and Wed (Apr–Sept except Tue) at 9.50am, 10.50am, 11.50am, 2.50pm, 3.50pm, 4.50pm and 5.50pm;* ◔*closed 1 May, 1 and 11 Nov, 25 Dec;* ◔*3€;* ☏*03 81 81 12 76; horloge-besancon.monuments-nationaux.fr*) is a marvel of mechanics comprising 30 000 parts. It was designed and made between 1857 and 1860 by A-L Vérité from Beauvais, and reset in 1900 by F Goudey from Besançon. It is connected to the clock faces on the bell tower. The 62 dials indicate among other things the days and seasons, the time in 16 different places all over the world, the tides in 8 ports, the length of daylight and darkness, the

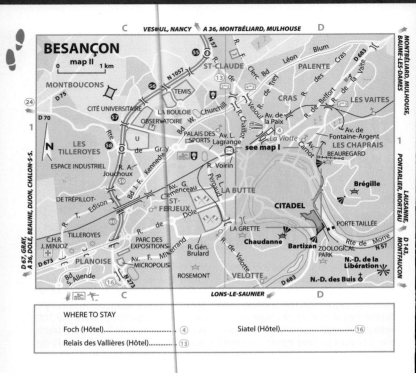

VESOUL, NANCY — A 36, MONTBÉLIARD, MULHOUSE

BESANÇON
map II
0   1 km

MONTBÉLIARD, MULHOUSE, BAUME-LES-DAMES

MONTBOUCONS

ST-CLAUDE   PALENTE

TEMIS   CRAS   LES VAITES

CITÉ UNIVERSITAIRE   LA BOULOIE   Churchill   Av. de la Paix

OBSERVATOIRE   La Viotte   Av. de Fontaine-Argent

PALAIS DES SPORTS   Lagrange   see map I   LES CHAPRAIS   BEAUREGARD

LES TILLEROYES   de Gray   Brégille

ESPACE INDUSTRIEL   R. A. Jouchoux   R. Voirin   LA BUTTE

DE TRÉPILLOT   ST-FERJEUX   CITADEL

C.H.R. J. MINJOZ   LA GRETTE   PORTE TAILLÉE

TILLEROYES   PARC DES EXPOSITIONS   Chaudanne   Bartizan   ZOOLOGICAL PARK

PLANOISE   Av. F. Mitterrand   R. Gén. Brulard   N.-D. de la Libération

MICROPOLIS   ROSEMONT   VELOTTE   N.-D. des Buis

PONTARLIER, MORTEAU   LAUSANNE

D 143, MONTFAUCON

D 67, GRAY, A 36, DOLE, BEAUNE, DIJON, CHALON-S.-S.

LONS-LE-SAUNIER

times at which the sun and the moon rise and set and, below the clock, the movement of the planets around the sun. Several automata are activated on the hour.

◉ *Take the pretty rue du Chambrier down to the Porte Rivotte.*

Porte Rivotte

This gate is the remains of 16C fortifications. After the French conquest, Louis XIV had the fronton decorated with a symbolic sun. The cliffs of the citadel tower above the gate. These cliffs once plunged straight into the river; the narrow strip of land along which the road passes was blasted out of the rock face. A 375m/1 230ft-long canal cuts through the cliffs in a tunnel, providing a shortcut past the Doubs meander.

◉ *Walk round the cathedral along rue du Chapitre and turn right onto rue du Palais. On the left is the fine Hôtel Bonvalot.*

Hôtel Bonvalot

Built between 1538 and 1544, this rather austere mansion is brightened up by its ogee-arched stained-glass windows.

◉ *Rue du Cingle leads to rue de la Vieille-Monnaie; turn right.*

Maison espagnole

10–12 rue de la Vieille-Monnaie.
Although built after the region was united to the kingdom of France, this house has clear Spanish features.

◉ *Rue de la Vieille-Monnaie is prolonged by rue Mégevand.*

Rue Mégevand

At the beginning of this street, at the junction with rue Ronchaux, there is a lovely 18C fountain representing the River Doubs.
A little further on to the right, place du Théâtre offers a very appropriate setting to the Classical-style theatre, the work of CN Ledoux (◉*see ARC-ET-SENANS*). On

the left side of the street, the university is flanked by the former St Vincent Abbey (now the Église Notre-Dame) which has retained the old bell tower and 16C doorway.

◗ *On reaching place de Granvelle, turn left onto rue de la Préfecture.*

Préfecture★
The erstwhile Palais des Intendants was built in the 18C after designs by the architect Louis.
Outside, on the corner of rue Ch.-Nodier, stands the pretty Fontaine des Dames (18C), or Ladies' Fountain, decorated with a mermaid (copy of a 16C bronze).

◗ *Return to the junction with rue de la Préfecture and follow rue Ch.-Nodier to place Saint-Jacques then turn right towards rue de l'Orme-de-Chamars.*

Hôpital Saint-Jacques
This hospital dates from the 17C. It has a splendid **wrought-iron gate**★ and a pretty 18C pharmacy. *(Contact the tourist office.)*

Chapelle Notre-Dame-du-Refuge
This chapel owes its name to an establishment founded in 1690 by the Marquis de Broissia to shelter young girls in danger of falling into vice. It was built by the architect Nicolas Nicole in 1739, and became part of the hospital in 1802. Even the building's architecture takes on a religious significance: the shape of the interior gradually changes from an oval to a circle, the symbol of perfection. Note the beautiful Louis XV woodwork.

◗ *Rue de l'Orme-de-Chamars is prolonged by rue Pasteur which leads back to the beginning of Grande-Rue.*

② QUARTIER BATTANT

This lively district on the north-west bank of the Doubs, once the vine-growers' area, is one of the oldest in the city.

Collégiale Sainte-Madeleine
This church was built in the 18C; the towers were added in 1830. The interior is vast, with elegant vaulting supported on fluted columns. The great organ (restored) is the work of Callinet.

◗ *Walk along rue de la Madeleine.*

On the corner of rue du Petit-Charmont and rue du Grand-Charmont stands the **Hôtel Jouffroy** which dates from the late 15C and early 16C.

◗ *Return to Église Ste-Madeleine and walk along the famous rue Battant.*

Hôtel de Champagney
This mansion was built in the 16C. Four gargoyles jut out over the pavement. Pass through the archway to admire the inner courtyard with its arcades. The passage leads through the Clos Barbusier, a garden of old roses, to Fort Griffon from where there is a good view of the rooftops of Besançon.

◗ *From the square containing the Bacchus fountain go down rue du Petit-Battant on the right.*

Tour de la Pelote
The rather curious late-15C tower was integrated into Vauban's defence system. It now houses a restaurant.

◗ *Walk across the Pont Denfert-Rochereau then turn right onto avenue E.-Cusenier to return to place de la Révolution.*

EXCURSIONS
Notre-Dame-de-la-Libération★
◗ *3.5km/2mi SE.*
On a vast platform, located 400m/437yd from the chapel, is a statue of the Virgin Mary erected as a gesture of gratitude for the liberation of Besançon. A large Romanesque crypt houses marble slabs bearing the names of the region's war dead. From the orientation table, the **view**★ extends over Besançon and the

surrounding area as far as the Vosges (*weather permitting*).

👥 Musée des Maisons Comtoises★

▶ *15km/9.5mi E on D 464 to Nancray. Allow half a day for your visit.* ○*Open Jul–Sept daily 10am–7.30pm; Apr–Jun and Oct–Nov times vary.* ○*Closed mid-Nov–Mar.* ▱*7.50€ (6–16 year olds 4€, children under 6 free).* ☏*03 81 55 29 77. www.maisons-comtoises.org.*

This open-air museum has reconstructed 30 typical Franche-Comté houses to demonstrate rural architecture and the country way of life as it was in the 17C to 19C. There are organic vegetable gardens, orchards and rare breeds of animals to encourage sustainability and biodiversity. Regular demonstrations and festivals are held on-site.

Boussières

▶ *17km/11mi SW along D 683 and D 104.* This village of the Doubs Valley downriver from Besançon boasts one of the few Romanesque churches in the region. **Église St-Pierre**★ – The massive porch built in 1574 opens onto the splendid four-storey Romanesque **bell tower**★ (11C), decorated with lombard bands with pilasters to the third storey.

ADDRESSES

🛏 STAY

▱▱ **Hôtel Siatel Chateaufarine Hôtel du Nord** – *8 r. Moncey.* ☏*03 81 81 34 56. www.hotel-du-nord-besancon.com. 44 rooms.* ▱ *7 €.* Situated in the historic quarter, this hotel dating from the 19C is a perfect base for venturing out into the old town. The rooms are practical and sound-proofed and the staff are welcoming.

▱▱ **Hôtel Foch** – *7 bis av. Foch.* ☏*03 81 80 30 41. www.hotel-foch-besancon.com. 27 rooms.* ▱ *7.20 €.* The rather severe façade of this large building on the corner reveals a well-run hotel. The entrance hall with a reception area and lounge lead through to the buffet breakfast room. Above, the 27 rooms are equipped with all comforts offering good value for money.

▱▱ **Citotel Granvelle** – *13 r. du Général-Lecourbe.* ☏*03 81 81 33 92. www.hotel-granvelle.fr.* ♿ *30 rooms.* ▱ *8 €.* This stone building has an ideal location just a few steps from the historic town centre. Most of the comfortable rooms lead onto a paved interior courtyard. Buffet breakfast.

▱▱ **Hôtel Siatel** – *3 Chemin des Founottes.* ☏*03 81 80 41 41. www.hotel siatel.com.* ♿ ▯ *40 rooms.* ▱ *6.20 €.* A functional hotel close to a busy main road, but the identical rooms are well sound-proofed. The dining rooms offers buffets, traditional meals and grills.

▱▱▱▱ **Mercure Parc Micaud** – *3 av. Ed.-Droz.* ☏*03 81 40 34 34. www. mercure.com.* ▯ *91 rooms.* ▱ *15 €.* Opposite the Doubs river, close to the old town where Victor Hugo was born in 1802. Rooms suit the demands of a business clientele; there is a decent bar and the modern-styled restaurant has a view to the gardens of the casino.

🍴 EAT

▱ **Le Cavalier Rouge** – *3 r. Mégevand.* ☏*03 81 83 41 02. www.cavalierrouge.com. Closed Sun.* A trendy urban atmosphere and speedy service attracts plenty of local regulars, who talk shop over the specialities of the day.

▱ **Au Petit Polonais** – *81 r. des Granges.* ☏*03 81 81 23 67. Open lunch Tue–Sun; evenings Thu–Sat. Closed Mon, 3 weeks end-Jul–mid-Aug and 2 weeks around Christmas.* A simple, unpretentious setting for traditional local cuisine. Warm, congenial atmosphere.

▱ **La Femme du Boulanger** – *8 r. Morand.* ☏*03 81 82 09 56. Closed Sun.* ♿. This friendly tea room and baker's café offers sandwiches made with Poilâne bread, salads and a dish of the day served both lunchtimes and evenings. The bright, sunny colour scheme, old tiles and wooden tables give a relaxed atmosphere in which to enjoy the good food.

🍽 **Miam** – *8 r. Morand.* ☎*03 81 82 09 56. Closed Sunday.* A very chic, designer restaurant which will whisk your palate far away from the banks of the Doubs river. International specialities include lamb tajine with apricots, lamb and mint chili con carne, and fresh pasta dishes prepared the Italian way.

🍽🍽 **Barthod** – *22 r. Bersot.* ☎*03 81 82 27 14. www.barthod.fr. Closed Sun and Mon.* ♿. Sit down on the terrace among the shrubs and potted plants and admire the view of the nearby waterfall. The owner is a wine buff who offers carefully planned menus (prices include wine) washed down by an interesting selection of wines. Don't forget to drop into the shop on your way out.

🍽🍽 **Le Poker d'As** – *14 sq. St-Amour.* ☎*03 81 81 42 49. Closed 12 Jul–11 Aug, Christmas holidays, Sun eve and Mon.* A 100 percent family affair: the young chef cooks up traditional and contemporary dishes in a rustic dining room decorated with wooden sculptures made by his grandfather.

🍽🍽 **Le Chaland** – *Promenade Micaud near the Bregille bridge.* ☎*03 81 80 61 61. www.chaland.com. Closed Sat lunch and Sun eve.* This charming old barge built in 1904 was converted into a restaurant in the 1960s. Moored along the Doubs, offering views of the old town and the Promenade Micaud. In fair weather, the meals are served on the upper deck, from where you can see the cormorants or watch the boats negotiating the river.

🍽🍽 **La Source** – *4 r. des Sources, 25170 Champvans-les-Moulins. 8km/ 5mi NW of Besançon.* ☎*03 81 59 90 57. www.lasource-besancon.com. Closed 31 Aug–9 Sept, 28 Dec–18 Jan, Wed eve except Jun–Aug, Sun eve and Mon.* 🅿. Big bay windows bathe the main room on the mezzanine with light, while the locals add a pleasant, lively atmosphere. Regional and traditional food is served.

🍴 TAKING A BREAK

Brasserie du Commerce – *31 r. des Granges.* ☎*03 81 81 33 11. Open daily 8am–1am.* This brasserie founded back in 1873 has kept its original décor and has become something of a Besançon institution. Its old-fashioned atmosphere is charming but its popularity is such that, on some evenings, it is almost impossible to find room to move, let alone a single seat.

Le Vin et l'Assiette – *97 r. Battant.* ☎*03 81 81 48 18. www.levin-et-lassiette. com. Open Tue–Sat 9am–9.30pm. Closed 1 Jan, 1–8 May, first 3 weeks in Aug, 1 Nov, 25 Dec, Sun and Mon.* This former wine-grower's cellar in the old quarter is in a 15C building which is an officially listed site. There are 300 French wines on the list including 30 from the Jura region. Wine buffs can taste wines by the glass in the vaulted cellar or in the restaurant, accompanied by small dishes such as a plate of *rosette* (dry pork sausage) or Comté cheese.

Baud – *4 Grande-Rue.* ☎*03 81 81 20 12. www.baud-traiteur.fr. Open Tue 2–7pm, Wed–Sat 7.30am–noon and 2–6.30pm.* This family business has literally become an institution in Besançon on account of the delicious food it provides: cakes and pastries, chocolates, ice cream, savoury and take-away dishes. The house speciality is *Frou-Frou* (milk chocolate mousse, caramelized crunchy hazelnuts and caramel mousse with crunchy chocolate pieces). If the terrace is crowded, just grin and bear it: it's definitely worth the wait.

🛍 SHOPPING

Marché des Beaux Arts – *6 r. Goudimel. Open every day except Sun 7am–7pm; Sun 8am–1pm.* You will find all the Franche-Comté local food specialities in this covered market, open daily. There are several butchers, fishmongers, greengrocers, Italian delicatessens and a baker, as well as purveyors of amazing local cheeses and cold meats. On Tuesday and Friday mornings, flower sellers, market gardeners and bric-a-brac vendors set up stands all around the market building.

Baume-les-Dames

Baume-les-Dames lies at the confluence of the Rivers Doubs and Cousancin. The relatively small historic town centre escaped destruction during the Second World War and has been extensively restored.

A BIT OF HISTORY

Caves, Abbeys and Boats – Baume-les-Dames owes its name partly to an old Celtic word meaning cave, and partly to an old abbey run by Benedictine nuns. In the 18C the canonesses of Baume-les-Dames were the cream of the aristocracy; to be admitted, they had to prove that they had 16 noble ancestors.
The physicist Jouffroy d'Abbans (1751–1832) first tested a steamboat at Baume-les-Dames in 1778; a monument near the bridge over the Doubs commemorates the event.

TOWN

Construction of the old abbey church was never really completed and it lies behind a large wall. After the revolution all the abbey artefacts of value were transferred to the **Eglise Saint-Martin**, whose interior gives an idea of the previous splendour of the abbey. Note the marble, bronze and iron **lectern**★ (1751) in the chancel and a superb wooden **crucifix**★ (1630) in the nave.

🚗 DRIVING TOURS

CUSANCIN VALLEY

25km/15.5mi round tour. Allow 3hrs 30min. Drive S out of Baume-les-Dames along D 50 to Pont-les-Moulins then turn left onto D 21.
The picturesque road runs through the green Cusancin Valley to the source of the river at Val de Cusance.

Source Bleue★

This is where the Cusancin springs up; to the left, the Source Bleue (Blue Spring), a

- ▶ **Population:** 5 349
- **Michelin Map:** 321: I-2.
- **Info:** 6 r. de Provence, 25110 Baume-les-Dames. ℘03 81 84 27 98. www.baumeslesdames.org.
- **Don't Miss:** The old town. The view from Fente de Barbre.
- 🕐 **Timing:** 2hrs to visit the old town.

pool of still waters in the woods; to the right, the Source Noire (Black Spring), which flows out of a cave at the foot of a limestone cliff.

◌ *Follow the narrow road up to Lomont-sur-Crête and turn left onto D 19E. Continue past the 2nd fork to Villers-St-Martin, turn right onto the forest road of Bois de Babre then onto the path to Fente de Babre and the cliff top.*

🔲 Fente de Babre

1hr 15min on foot there and back.
A pretty path running through a oak trees leads to the Fente de Babre, a joint in the rock which overlooks the south bank of the Doubs and offers an attractive **view**★ of Pont-les-Moulins and the Audeux Valley, Baume-les-Dames and the surrounding area.

◌ *Return to D 19E and turn right towards Baume-les-Dames.*

AROUND L'AUDEUX

🕐 *See Region map. Follow the D 50 south until Orsans. After the village take the first right.*

Église de Leugney

You can visit this church on request from Mr Chapuis. 1 r. des Jonquilles 25530 Bremondans. 🕐Open Jul–Aug 10am–6pm. ℘03 81 58 30 28.
Surrounded by a grassy cemetery, the church features a high bell tower porch (12C). Inside you will find an interesting, wooden **Statue of the Virgin Mary** (16C) that opens to reveal a represen-

tation of the Holy Trinity. Also notice the **Mirror with Virgin Mary** and an astonishing side door incorporating pieces of farm tools.

↪ *Return towards Orsans and take a left on D 120, then D 421 towards Gonsans.*

Grotte de la Glacière

⏱*Open Mar–Oct.* ↪*Guided tours (1hr) daily Jun–Aug 9am–7pm; Mar–May 10am–noon, 2–6pm; Sept–Oct 10am–noon, 2–5pm.* ⊜*6€.* ℘*03 81 60 44 26. www.grotteglaciere.com.* This 66m/217ft-deep glacial cave lets in daylight through a large opening. The **Maison des minéraux**, at the entrance, displays a rich collection of minerals from various countries.

ALONG THE DOUBS

52km/32mi circuit. 👁*See Region map. Allow 3hrs. Leave Baume-les-Dames east on the D 683 towards Montbéliard.* The road follows the Doubs valley. Tucked in the valley floor are little villages with red roofs that reflect in the river. On a nice day you can walk or picnic on the islets found towards Branne. At the foot of the Lormont mountains, the river veers to the right, and the valley runs below a limestone cliff.

The **church** at **Clerval** includes two interesting 16C statues each side of the crucifix and a 16C wooden Pietà in a side aisle.

The Doubs divides the town of **L'Isle-sur-le-Doubs** into three districts: the Ile (island) in the middle of the river; the Rue (street) on the north bank; and Le Magny on the south.

ADDRESSES

🛏 STAY

⊜ **Chambre d'hôte Chez Mizette** – *3 r. de l'Église, 25360 Vaudrivillers. 16km/10mi SE of Baume-les-Dames by D 50 until you reach Saint-Juan-les-Péquignots, then D 464. ℘03 81 60 45 70. www.mizette.com.* ⊟ *4 rooms. Meals* ⊜. Warm welcome, a peaceful atmosphere in the bright rooms and spacious lounge-library. Convivial *table d'hôte* meals.

⊜⊜ **Chambre d'hôte Chez Soi** – *R. du Rechandet, 25640 Ougney-Douvot. 11km/8mi SW of Baume-les-Dames by D 277. ℘03 81 55 57 05. www.chez-soi-france. com.* ⊟ *4 rooms. Meals* ⊜⊜. Follow the banks of the Doubs and you will reach this 18C farmhouse offering rooms by the river as well as a self-catering *gîte*. Wilma's Dutch-style breakfasts and meals are served under the trees at the water's edge.

🍴/EAT

⊜⊜ **Auberge des Moulins** – *2 r. de Pontarlier, 25110 Pont-les-Moulins. ℘03 81 84 09 99. www.aubergedes moulins.com. Closed 20 Dec–28 Jan, Sun and Fri Sept–Jun.* This comfortable and friendly country inn in the Cusancin Valley offers regional dishes with trout as a speciality. Rooms are both refined and rustic. The garden includes a stretch for private fishing.

⊜⊜ **Hostellerie du Château d'As** – *26 r. Château-Gaillard. ℘03 81 84 00 66. www.chateau-das.fr. Closed 26 Jan–9 Feb, 15 Nov–6 Dec, Sun eve and Mon.* This 1930s house exudes old-fashioned charm. Meals are served on the terrace in fine weather. If you stay the night, choose the upstairs rooms.

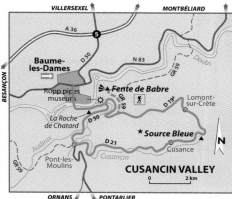

CUSANCIN VALLEY

Château de Moncley★

This rare example of neo-Classical architecture in the Franche-Comté region has an unusual concave façade and a wealth of interior decoration.

VISIT

By request with advance reservation at Besançon tourist office. ⊛6€. ℘03 81 80 92 55. http://moncley.jimdo.com.

The château was built in the 18C by Bertrand, on the site of an ancient feudal fortress, in a pleasant spot overlooking the Ognon Valley. The C-shaped façade is decorated with a group of four Ionic columns supporting a triangular pediment at its centre. The side facing the garden is embellished with a rotunda topped with a dome.

Inside, the vestibule is interesting. A dozen Corinthian columns elegantly support a balustraded tribune, reached by taking the majestic double staircase. On the first floor admire the family portraits and Louis XVI furniture, as well as hunting trophies and stuffed animals.

- **Michelin Map:** 321: F-3.
- **Info:** ℘03 81 80 92 55. www.besancon-tourisme.com.
- **Location:** 14km/9mi NW of Besançon.
- **Don't Miss:** The Louis XVI furniture in the château; the pretty village of Marnay.

EXCURSIONS

The little village of **Etuz** (*NE 6km/3.7mi by D 15*) is worth visiting not only for the 16C **chapelle Sainte-Anne** but for a neo-Antique double **"wash-house temple"** (1845) where the basins are supported by ionic columns. The village of **Marnay** (*SE 11km/6.8mi by D 15*) is dominated by the ruined château that was lived in by Louis XIV in 1674. Near the main square, the elegant Renaissance **Hôtel Terrier de Santans** (now the town hall) is one of several elegant 15C and 16C buildings.

ADDRESSES

🛏STAY / 🍴EAT

⊜⊜ **La Vieille Auberge** – *pl. de l'Église, 25870 Cussey-sur-l'Ognon. 7km/4.3mi NE of Moncley by D 14 then D 230.* ℘03 81 48 51 70. www.hotel-restaurant-25.fr. *Closed 23 Aug–6 Sept, 27 Dec–3 Jan, Mon, Fri evenings out of season and Sun evenings. Restaurant* ⊜⊜. You will receive a fine welcome at this stone-brick house covered with Virginia creeper. Enjoy home-made specialities in the wood-panelled rustic dining room.

⊜⊜ **Château de la Dame Blanche** – *1 chemin de la Goulotte, 25870 Geneuille.* ℘03 81 57 64 64. www.chateau-de-la-dame-blanche.fr. *Closed Sun eve and Mon.* 🅿 *24 rooms and 2 suites.* ⊠ *10€. Meals* ⊜⊜. A large mansion in the middle of an English-style park. Elegant rooms, all individual and non-smoking. The classic cuisine is served in a most elegant dining room complete with crystal chandeliers.

Château de Moncley

© A.J.Cassaigne/Photononstop

Pesmes

Perched above the river Ognon, Pesmes is considered one of the most beautiful villages in France. From the Middle Ages, the village and its château were fought over due to their strategic position: before it became French under Louis XIV it was Franc, Germanic, Burgundian and even Spanish. Walk along the labyrinth of pretty lanes and you will still see some vestiges of fortifications among the façades with alcoves, statues and mullioned windows.

▶ **Population:** 1 107
- **Michelin Map:** 314: B-9.
- **Info:** 19 r. Jacques-Prévost, La Tourelle, 70140 Pesmes. ℘06 87 73 13 05.
- **Location:** 19km/11.8mi S of Gray and 22km/13.7mi N of Dole, by D 475.
- **Don't Miss:** A visit to the Eglise Saint-Hilaire and a tour around the village to visit the châteaux.
- **Timing:** Allow 2hrs to visit the village on foot.

✎⚫WALKING TOUR

To explore this characterful Franche-Comté village, climb up the rue du Donjon to admire the old houses.
Turn left alongside the Trésor public.
The **Château de Pesmes** (10C) was built on the edges of the cliffs above the Ognon. Destroyed and re-built many times over the centuries, today all that remains is the guard room from the 14C and 15C and the 18C stables. Continue along the charming rue des Châteaux to admire the various grand houses that were once the pride of the village.
At the end of the road take a right on the rue de Granvelle.
The 12C **Eglise Saint-Hilaire** is quite well preserved. Highlights include the majestic **chapelle d'Andelot**⋆, built around 1560 by Pierre d'Andelot, the abbot of Bellevaux and made with black and red marble along with red stone from Sampans. In the **Grande Chapelle** are two statues from the Burgundy School, notably a marble 15C Virgin with Child. In the choir, a triptych painted on wood is by Jacques Prévost, a pupil of Raphaël.
Walk down rue Sainte-Catherine to see the charming row of little houses leading to the 16C **porte Loigerot**, one of the two remaining town gates.
*Go back up rue de Granvelle, then left on rue des Châteaux. Cross the terrace of the château to admire the **view** and go down by the escaliers de la Roche (stairs). Turn left on rue des Tanneurs, and left again on rue Vanoise.*

EXCURSION
Abbaye d'Acey

▶ *10km/6mi east of Pesmes, via Malans and Brésilley. Take the pretty D 459 via Vitreux. A place of prayer and silence, only the church is open for visitors.*
⏰*Mon–Sat 8.30am–noon, 2.30–6pm, Sun 2.30–4.30pm. ℘03 84 81 04 11. http://acey.eglisejura.com.*
Founded in 1136 and today home to 22 Trappist monks, Notre-Dame d'Acey is the only Cistercian monastery in Franche-Comté still inhabited by monks. The **church** ⋆ is the last remaining of the 13 churches built in Franche-Comté by the Cistercian order. The building that takes the place of the vestibule, the nave of the original church, has strong pillars that used to divide it from the aisles. A small door on the right is the entrance to the hugely proportioned church, notable for its plain architectural style and overall brightness. The structure forms roughly the design of a Greek cross with three short naves in front of a large transept, from which opens up an apse and four radiating chapels, in Cistercian style.
The church has been endued with a simple and harmonious look by the addition of **verrières monobloc** (a single piece of stained glass per pane) in which the range of colours is limited to black, grey, blue and white. They were created by local, contemporary artists: the painter Jean Ricardon and the master glass-maker Pierre Alain Parrot.

Dole★

The brown-tiled roofs of Dole's old houses cluster around the church and its imposing bell tower. The citizens of Dole are proud of their city; it was the capital of the free province of Burgundy (the Franche-Comté) for many centuries. The present city is adorned with many splendid monuments to its illustrious past.

▶ **Population:** 24 606
- **Michelin Map:** 321: C-4.
- **Info:** pl. Grévy, 39100 Dole. ℘03 84 72 11 22. www.tourisme-paysde dole.org.
- **Don't Miss:** Exploring the old town; the museum in Maison Natale de Pasteur. The Collégiale Notre-Dame.

A BIT OF HISTORY
The arrival of the French
By the 15C, Dole was already playing the role of a capital city, and it was not long before the flourishing town was noticed – and coveted – by Louis XI and the French. In 1479 the king laid siege to the town; Dole eventually fell and was burned to the ground. However, Louis' son Charles VIII returned the Comté to the Hapsburgs in 1493. French attempts to annexe the Comté were renewed under **Louis XIII**. In 1636 the Prince of Condé laid siege to Dole, but after a three-month bombardment was forced to withdraw.

In 1668 and 1674 Louis XIV's troops renewed the attack on Dole, which finally succumbed, and in 1678 the town and province were officially annexed to France.

The Sun King did not forgive Dole for having put up such strong resistance; he made Besançon the capital of the Franche-Comté instead, stripping Dole of its Parliament, university and ramparts.

WALKING TOUR
OLD TOWN★★
The old town is clustered around the church of Notre-Dame. Its narrow, winding streets are closely packed with houses dating from the 15C to the 18C, many of which have interesting details: coats of arms above doorways, turrets, arcaded inner courtyards and so on. Start your walk at place Nationale.

Place Nationale
This charming square in the centre of the old town has been restored and is once more a busy market square.

Collégiale Notre-Dame★
For access to the top of the bell tower, contact the tourist office: ℘03 84 72 11 22. The size of the 16C church's interior is striking. Its sober lines are a resolute departure from the excessive ornamentation of the Late Gothic style. It contains some of the first Renaissance works of art to manifest themselves in Dole, such as the beautiful **works in polychrome marble**★. These are characterised by motifs typical of the Dole workshops (foliage, tracery and birds) as, for example, on the façade of the Sainte-Chapelle, the organ case and the pulpit (Denis Le Rupt) and the holy-water stoup.

The marvellous carved wooden **great organ** dating from the 18C is one of the very rare examples of its type in France to have survived virtually intact. The organ builder was Karl Joseph Riepp.

▶ *To the right of the old town hall, take rue d'Enfer, rue de Besançon, place du 8-Mai-1945 and rue des Arènes.*

Place aux Fleurs
There is a pretty **view** of old Dole, dominated by Notre-Dame's bell tower.

Rue Mont-Roland
Note the polychrome marble and stone doorway of the old **Carmelite convent** (17C) and the façades of some of the private mansions, for example, the **Maison Odon de la Tour** (16C) and the **Hôtel de Froissard** (early 17C), where you should pass through the gate to admire the double horseshoe staircase and the courtyard's loggia.

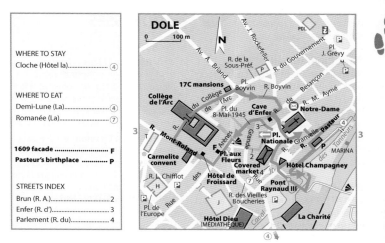

◐ *Right on rue du Collège-de-l'Arc.*

Collège de l'Arc

The Jesuits founded this school in 1582. Go under the arch; the deconsecrated chapel is distinguished by its richly decorated Renaissance **porch**, surmounted by a loggia with arches supported by the figures of angels in flight. Notice the two 17C mansions on the left that still have their small inner courtyards and beautiful balustrades.

◐ *Continue to Place Boyvin; rue Boyvin, rue de la Sous-Préfecture; and right on rue de Besançon.*

Cave d'Enfer

A plaque recalls the heroic resistance of a few Dole citizens during the attack on the town in 1479.

◐ *Turn back to reach place Nationale, then take rue Pasteur.*

Rue Pasteur

This street used to be called rue des Tanneurs, as all the houses of the hemp and leather craftsmen were here along the banks of the canal.

At no. 43 is the **Maison Natale de Pasteur** (◐ *open Jul–Aug Mon–Sat 10am–6pm, Sun 2–6pm; rest of the year times vary;* ☞ *4.50€;* ☎ *03 84 72 22 58; www.musee-pasteur.com*), the house where Louis Pasteur was born.

A museum to honour the scientist's life and work, it still contains the evidence of his father's trade as a tanner, with old tools and the tannery in the basement. In the living quarters, documents and souvenirs relating to Pasteur are displayed in several rooms. Portraits and personal mementoes recall his family and childhood; his laboratory equipment as well as notes and sketches of his work are displayed.

Among Pasteur's possessions on view are his university cape and cap, his desk, and two pastels executed in his youth.

◐ *Take the passage on the right of Pasteur's birthplace, follow the canal*

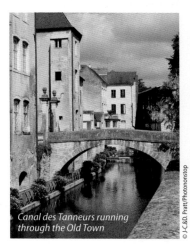

Canal des Tanneurs running through the Old Town

© J-C-&D. Pratt/Photononstop

*walk and take the footbridges to get to
the Pont Raynaud-III.*

Pont Raynaud-III

View of a handsome architectural group:
the Charité (18C hospital), the Hôtel-
Dieu (17C hospice) and an 18C convent.
The Grande Fontaine, an underground
spring and wash-house, can be seen
under the last arch of the bridge (to get
to it, go down passage Raynaud-III off
rue Pasteur).

Hôtel Champagney

An 17C portal surmounted by a crest
leads into a courtyard where two interesting staircases and a beautiful balcony
on corbels can be seen.

ADDITIONAL SIGHTS
Hôtel-Dieu

Construction of this huge hospital building started in 1613 and was interrupted
several times by sieges or wars. Built as
a hospice for the poor and sick, it was
the last major construction of prestige
built by the city before it lost its status as
capital when it was annexed by France.
Today it has been superbly restored and
since 2000 has housed a media library.
The initial impression of rather a severe
building is tempered by the imagina-
tiveness of the decoration, such as the
superb balcony which runs around part
of the building, supported by carved
modillons (brackets). Inside, the courtyard is arranged like a cloister with two
levels of galleries, linked by a staircase in
a tower; to avoid tiring the sick, the steps
become lower as you ascend.

Musée des Beaux-Arts★

85 r. des Arènes. ◷*Open daily except
Mon 10am–noon and 2–6pm.*
◷*Closed 24 Dec–2 Jan, 1 May, 1 Nov;*
⛭ ℘*03 84 79 25 85. www.musees-
franchecomte.com.*
The Museum of Fine Art's collections
include Gallo-Roman finds, Burgundian
sculpture and mainly French paintings
from the 15C to the 20C: Simon Vouet
(Death of Dido), Mignard *(Portrait of a
Woman and Her Son)* and several landscapes by Courbet and Pointelin.

ADDRESSES

☞STAY

⊜⊜ **Hôtel La Cloche** – *1 pl. Grévy.*
℘*03 84 82 06 06. www.la-cloche.fr.
Closed 24 Dec–2 Jan. 30 rooms.* ⇌ *9.50 €.*
Stendhal stayed in this old hose next
to the St Mauris square. Its rooms are
being updated in stages. Sauna.

⊜⊜ **Hôtel La Chaumière** – *346 av.
du Mar.-Juin.* ℘*03 84 70 72 40. www.la-
chaumiere.info. Closed 20 Dec–10 Jan,
last week Aug, Sun except evenings 15 Jun
–15 Sept, Sat and Mon lunchtimes.* ▣
⇌ *11 €. Restaurant* ⊜⊜. In a large
building on the road to Lons-le-Saunier,
the functional and well-maintained
rooms lead out to the peaceful garden.
Outdoor pool. Contemporary food
is served in the comfortable dining
room that has stone walls and exposed
beams. Summer terrace.

ⴼ/EAT

⊜⊜ **La Demi-Lune** – *39 r. Pasteur.*
℘*03 84 72 82 82. Closed 7–27 Jan,
Mon, Tue.* Enjoy regional delicacies,
buckwheat pancakes and grilled
meat on the terrace by the Canal des
Tanneurs or in the vaulted dining room.
Playing area for children.

⊜⊜ **La Romanée** – *11-13 r. des Vieilles-
Boucheries.* ℘*03 84 79 19 05. www.la
romanee.fr. Closed 1–8 Jul, 30 Aug–5 Sept,
Tue eve and Wed Oct–Jun.* This old
butcher shop, its meat hooks still on
the wall, serves hearty traditional meals.

ⵥSHOPPING

Marché des Halles – *pl. Charles-de-
Gaulle. Open Tue, Thu and Sat 8am–1pm.*
On market days the indoor market
explodes to life as shoppers and
merchants meet to trade wares. You'll
find fish, meat, poultry, cheese and dairy
and other high-quality products: the
best the region has to offer. Outside the
market hall, there are local second-hand
clothes traders and an Asian grocery.

Marché Bio – *Cours St Mauris, pla. Grévy.*
℘*06 08 83 88 32. Open Thu eve from 5pm
in summer.* A selection of excellent local
organic producers sell their goods here
on Thursday evenings in summer.

Forêt de Chaux★

This forest lies just east of Dole between the Rivers Doubs and Loue and with an area of more than 20 000ha/49 420 acres is the second largest in France. It originally belonged to the sovereigns, who hunted here; the nearby population also enjoyed extensive rights to the use of the land. These rights disappeared in the 19C, when the areas at the edge of the forest were given to the community (forêts communales), whereas the central part (13 000ha/32 123 acres) remained State property (forêt domaniale).

A BIT OF HISTORY

From industry to leisure – For centuries the forest, dominated by oak trees, has been a vital resource for the factories at its edge: saltworks at **Salins** and **Arc-et-Senans**, forges at Fraisans, glassworks at La Vieille Loye and so on.

⚒ **Michelin Map:** 321: D-4 to E-4.

ℹ **Info:** Dole Tourist Office, 6 pl. de Grévy, 39100 Dole. ℘03 84 72 11 22. www. tourisme-paysdedole.fr.

▶ **Location:** Extending almost to the edge of Dole, there are various entrances and parking areas all around the forest.

☺ **Don't Miss:** The Grottes d'Osselle (caves) and the village of Vieille-Loye.

◔ **Timing:** Allow at least half a day to visit the caves and the forest.

A leisure area has been established on the western edge of the forest to protect the woodlands elsewhere. Facilities include a bridle path, footpaths, a fitness trail, car parks and part of the long-distance footpath GR 59A from Dole to Arc-et-Senans, three game enclosures with various types of deer and wild boar, and

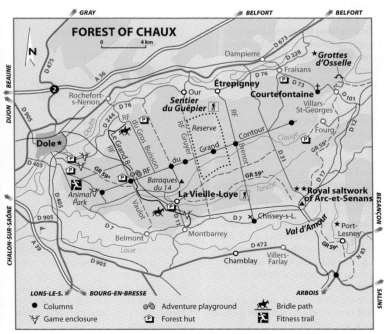

a nature reserve (88ha/217 acres) where deer and wild boar roam at liberty. You can observe these from two raised observation posts, or by strolling around the forest.

FOREST
La Vieille-Loye
This is the only village within the forest. It used to be inhabited by woodcutters, who lived in huts, or baraques. Exhibitions of their daily life are put on at the restored **Baraques du 14** (& ⓄOpen Jul–Aug daily except Fri 2.30–5.30pm; ⊗2.50€; ℘03 84 71 72 07).

Le sentier du Guêpier
This 4km/2.5mi-long trail offers an insight into the history of the forest. In **Etrepigney**, the starting point, a baccu – small woodcutter's cottage – has been

reconstructed, and in **Our** a 19C bread oven has been restored.

EXCURSIONS
Grottes d'Osselle★
ⓄOpen Jun–Aug 9am–7pm (Jun 6pm). Rest of the year times vary. ⓄClosed Nov–Mar. ⊗7€. ℘03 81 63 62 09. grottes.osselle.free.fr.
These caves are set in a cliff overlooking a meander in the Doubs. They were discovered in the 13C and have been visited since 1504. In the Revolution, the galleries were used as refuges and chapels by the priests; a clay altar can still be seen. A bear's skeleton has been assembled from bones found among the debris. Out of 8km/5mi of long, regularly shaped galleries, 1.3km/0.8mi have been adapted and opened for guided tours.

Saline Royale d'Arc-et-Senans★★

Not far from the River Loue is the old royal saltworks of Arc-et-Senans, a rare example of 18C industrial architecture, now on UNESCO's World Heritage List.

A BIT OF HISTORY
An ideal town in the 18C – In 1773, the King's Counsel decreed that a royal saltworks should be founded at Arc-et-Senans, using the salt waters of Salins and timber from the nearby forest of Chaux for fuel. **Claude-Nicolas Ledoux** (1736–1806), inspector general of the saltworks in the Lorraine and Franche-Comté regions and already a visionary architect, was commissioned to design it. Only part completed, it was an ambitious design: a whole town laid out in concentric circles with the director's residence at the centre, flanked by storehouses, offices and workshops, and extending out to include a church, a market, and other public facilities.

- ▸ **Population:** 1 428
- ⓒ **Michelin Map:** 321: E-4.
- ▯ **Info:** ⓄOpen daily Jul–Aug 9am–7pm, Apr–Jun and Sept–Oct 9am–noon, 2–6pm. Rest of the year times vary. ⊗7.50€. ℘03 81 54 45 45. www.salineroyale.com.
- ▸ **Location:** The Saline Royale dominates the little village of Arc-et-Senans S of Dole.
- ▸ **Don't Miss:** The musée Ledoux, with its fascinating collection of architectural models.
- ⓒ **Timing:** Allow 3hrs for the Saline Royale and spend the rest of the day in the Val d'Amour.

Unfortunately, the saltworks never produced as much salt as had been forecast and were eventually closed in 1895. Part of the buildings now houses a cultural centre for concerts and events. The gardens are replanted each year with a new contemporary theme.

VISIT

Gatehouse

The road to Salins leads to the gatehouse with its peristyle of Doric columns. Artificial grottoes recall the origins of salt. The building now houses the reception, bookshop, cafeteria and gift shop.

Director's Residence

The director's residence is much restored, having been badly damaged by fire in 1918 and a late dynamite attack which wrecked the façade. The salt warehouse was in the basement, with offices above and the landing of the main staircase was fitted out as a chapel.

A permanent exhibition arranged in 12 rooms called In Search of the Ideal City shows images of contrasting utopian social ideas including a project from Le Corbusier for a new French capital. The centrepiece of the exhibition is the **Grand Horloge des villes du monde** where the life of citizens in 12 cities around the world is shown in a small theatre fitted with webcams. In the basement, a display explains why this place was chosen for the royal saltworks and how the saltworks operated.

Courtyard

The semicircular courtyard, now a lawn, gives a good impression of the beauty and originality of the design of this complex. All the buildings around it face the director's residence, which is symbolically placed at the centre.

They are decorated with carved motifs: petrified water flowing out of the necks of urns, evoking the source of the salt-working industry. This stylistically unified complex is all the more striking for the beauty and solidity of its masonry. The influence of Palladio, the 16C Italian architect, is revealed in the Antique-style columns and pediments, whereas the roofs are constructed in a typical regional style.

Coopers' Building

The cooper's building houses the **musée Ledoux**, a collection of about 60 architectural scale models which reveal his ideas about the ideal society.

The right wing contains those buildings which were actually built: the theatre at Besançon, of which only the façade remains; the saltworks at Arc-et-Senans; and the Château de Maupertuis. In the left wing, the ideal city of Chaux, the gun forge and the guardians' house at the source of the Loue are all projects that Ledoux never realised.

WALK

Chemin des Gabelous

As you leave the saltworks, turn left then right at the roundabout along rue des Graduations. The signposted trail begins from the camp site; 5hrs 30min on foot, 2hrs 30min by bike.

The 24km/15mi waymarked path follows the historic trail from the salt-extraction site in Salins to Arc-et-Senans.

EXCURSIONS

Val d'Amour

This is the delightful name of part of the Loue Valley, best-known for its romantic legends and attractive river. The timber industry played an important role in the valley until the early 20C and before the railways, the Loue river was used for transporting the logs. The **Confrérie St-Nicolas des radeliers de la Loue** revives this traditional craft annually through a series of events.

Chamblay

Downriver from Chissey, and not far from the Chaux forest, this village had a long-standing tradition of timber-floating. The activity developed during the 18C in order to supply timber to the navy; later on timber was used by factories and for heating.

Port-Lesney★

This pretty village on the River Loue is popular in summer for a country holiday. On Sundays, fishermen, boating enthusiasts and lovers of trout and whitebait flock to the village.

There is a footpath *(1hr round trip)* from the Chapelle de Lorette which leads through the undergrowth to the Belvédère Edgar-Faure overlooking the village and the entire valley.

ADDRESSES

🏠 STAY

🛏️🍽️🛏️ **La Saline Royale** – ☎03 81 54 45 45. www.salineroyale.com. Closed Nov–Feb. 30 rooms. ☐ 10 €. A great way to appreciate this site with few people around, is to actually stay there in these splendid surroundings.

🛏️🍽️🛏️🛏️ **Château de Germigney** – 39600 Port-Lesney. 7.5km/4.8mi SE of Arc-et-Senans by D 17E and D 48E. ☎03 84 73 85 85. www.chateaudegermigney.com. Closed Jan. 20 rooms. ☐ 15 €. Restaurant 🍽️🛏️🛏️🛏️. You will find peace and calm in this old house surrounded by a park. Cossetted rooms are nicely furnished with cedar parquet floors. Some excellent cooking is offered in the two dining rooms.

🍽️ EAT

🍽️ **Le Relais** – pl. de l'Église. ☎03 81 57 40 60. Closed 15 Dec–15 Jan, Sun evenings and Mon. Close to la Saline Royale you will find good-value, local cooking served on the terrace or in one of the three rustic dining rooms.

🍽️ **Le Bistrot Pontarlier** – pl. du 8-Mai-1945, 39600 Port-Lesney. ☎03 84 37 83 27. Closed 2 Jan–2 Feb, Mon–Thu mid-Sept–1 May. On the banks of the Loue, eat perfect, bistro food outside under the Virginia creeper or in the attractive dining room.

🛍️ SHOPPING

Institut Claude-Nicolas-Ledoux – Saline Royale. ☎03 81 54 45 44. www.salineroyale.com. Bookstore specializing in architecture, utopian concepts, as well as the Franche-Comté region.

Salins-les-Bains ⚓★

The rather faded spa town of Salins lies at the bottom of the deep valley of the Furieuse, in the shadow of the fortresses of Belin and St-André. However, the real treasures of the town are hidden far beneath the ground, in the former salt mines.

▶ **Population:** 3 082
⏱️ **Michelin Map:** 321: F-5.
🏠 **Info:** pl. des Salines, 39110 Salins-les-Bains. ☎03 84 73 01 34. www.salins-les-bains.com.
👁️ **Don't Miss:** The guided tour of the Salines, a good introduction to a visit to nearby Arc-et-Senans.

A BIT OF HISTORY

White gold – In the past, salt was indispensable for preserving food. However, primitive mining methods made it so scarce and so costly that a salt mine was a real gold mine. Jean l'Antique, the most famous member of the Chalon family, seized the salt mine at Salins early in the 13C. The sale of the salt brought him huge sums of cash, which he was able to put to astute use, buying fiefs, vassals and the goodwill of bishops, monks, soldiers and wealthy merchants. Delighted with his increased power, he bestowed a charter on the home town of the salt mine, source of his wealth, in 1249, according it a fair degree of autonomy.

The timber trade – Huge quantities of wood were needed to heat the cauldrons used to evaporate water in the salt extraction process, with the result that the timber trade became almost as important for Salins as its salt mine. As many as 60 000 horse-drawn carts loaded with wood came into the town each year. The waters of the Furieuse were harnessed to drive 12 great sawmills. Salins soon developed a reputation for producing the best masts on the market, and became supplier to the French Navy. By the 17C Salins, with 5 700 inhabitants, was the second largest community in the Franche-Comté after Besançon, which had 11 500.

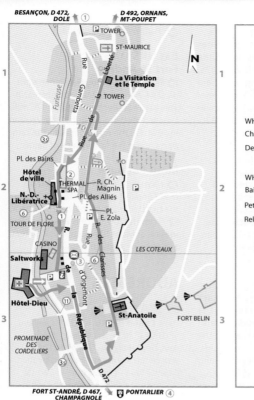

BESANÇON, D 472, DOLE ① D 492, ORNANS, MT-POUPET

TOWER
ST-MAURICE
La Visitation et le Temple
TOWER
N

Rue Liberté
Rue Gambetta
Furieuse

Pl. des Bains
Hôtel de ville
THERMAL SPA
R. Ch. Magnin
N.-D.-Libératrice
Pl. des Alliés
TOUR DE FLORE
Pl. E. Zola
CASINO
Saltworks
LES COTEAUX
Rue des Clarisses
Rue d'Orgemont
Hôtel-Dieu
St-Anatoile
FORT BELIN
PROMENADE DES CORDELIERS
Rue de la République
D 472

FORT ST-ANDRÉ, D 467, CHAMPAGNOLE   PONTARLIER ④

SALINS-LES-BAINS

0 _____ 200 m

WHERE TO STAY
Chalet Bel'Air...........................①
Deux Forts (Hôtel Les)................③

WHERE TO EAT
Bains (Les)...............................①
Petit Blanc (Le)........................②
Relais de Pont d'Héry (Le)...........④

🐾 WALKING TOUR
Start at the tourist office.

👥 Salines★ (Saltworks)
🕐*Open year round.* 🐾*Guided tour (1hr) Jul–Aug 10am–noon, 2.30–5pm. Rest of the year times vary.* 👕*Dress warmly.* 👁*5€ (under 12s free).* ☎*03 84 73 01 34. www.salinesdesalins.com.*
At this museum, you can learn about the complete process of making salt from the extraction from the salt waters to the preparation of the salt. The visit begins with the huge underground galleries, 200m/656ft long, with dramatic medieval archways overhead. The salt water was pumped up from the salt seams, using two wells fitted with a pumping system that still works today. Using a long beam, a hydraulic wheel activated the pump which drew up the water, which had a saturated salt content of 33kg/71lb of salt per 100l/22gal.

Enormous cauldrons of 45 000l/ 9 900 gal (one of which is on display) were heated over coal fires to evaporate the water and obtain the salt.

▷ *Cross the car park to the left toward the Hôtel-Dieu.*

Hôtel-Dieu
🕐*Open year round.* 🐾*Guided tours (30min) Jul–Aug 9am–12.30pm, 1.30–6pm (Sun 5.30pm). Rest of the year times vary. Book at the tourist office.* 👁*4.40€.* ☎*03 84 73 01 34.*
This hospice dates from the 17C. The pharmacy has some beautiful woodwork as well as a collection of pots in Moustiers faïence.

▷ *Turn left on rue du Dr-Germain, then right on Rue de la République (be careful, this is a busy thoroughfare). Go past the pretty fontaine des Cygnes.*

Rue de la République

At no. 79, the Maison des Carmélites (13C), with half-timbers, is one of the few to have survived the fire of 1825. A Carmelite convent was housed here from the 17C–18C. At no. 105 the Hotel Moreau displays a grey stone facade (18C). Continue to the Tour Oudin (13C-15C), at the entrance to the city.

▶ *Retrace your steps and turn right up the Escalier St-Anatoile. Alternatively, return to the swan fountain on rue de la République and climb via rue d'Orgemont and rue des Clarisses.*

The charming **St-Anatoile staircase** twists between stone walls. Fort Belin (19C) is visible in the distance.

Église St-Anatoile

This is the most interesting church in Salins, and one of the best examples of 13C Cistercian architecture in the Franche-Comté. Two protruding Flamboyant Gothic style chapels frame the beautiful Romanesque doorway. Inside, pretty round-arched arcades run along above the pointed Gothic arches separating the nave from the side aisles. Note the 17C pulpit, the 16C choir stalls with striking medallions and woodwork and the carved wooden organ case (1737).

▶ *Go down rue des Clarisses, cross place Émile-Zola and along rue Charles-Magnin. Right on rue de la Liberté.*

La Visitation et le Temple

Go through the archways of the former Visitandines convent (1710), now apartments, climb rue du Temple to view the handsome **portal**★ of marble and alabaster. The Temple (15C) is behind.

▶ *Return along rue de la Liberté.*

The monumental **doorway**★ of no. 13 is attributed to Claude-Nicolas Ledoux.

Hôtel de Ville

The town hall dates from the 18C. The 17C **chapel of Notre-Dame-de-la-Libératrice**, crowned by a dome, is in the town hall complex.

▶ *Return to the tourist office.*

EXCURSIONS
Fort St-André

▶ *4km/2.5mi S along D 472 then right on D 94, right on D 271 and right again.*

This is an excellent example of 17C military architecture, designed by Vauban in 1674. On the right, beneath the ramparts, there is a fine **view**★ of Salins.

Mont Poupet★

▶ *10km/6mi N on D 492 then left on D 273 and left again (parking area near the cross). 15min on foot there and back.*

From the top there is an impressive **view**★ of Mont Blanc, the Jura plateau and the Bresse plain.

ADDRESSES

STAY

☺☺ **Chalet Bel'Air** – 39330 Mouchard. ℰ03 84 37 80 34. www.chalet-belair.com. *Open daily Jul–15 Sept; rest of the year closed Sun eve except by reservation. Closed 27 Jun–4 Jul, 22 Nov–13 Dec.* 🅿 *9 rooms.* ☕ *8.90 €. Restaurant* ☺☺. Comfortable and quiet rooms in the heart of the region. The grill restaurant in a nearby building serves meat cooked on the large open fireplace.

EAT

☺☺ **Les Bains** – pl. des Alliés. ℰ03 84 73 07 54. *Closed 1–16 Jan, Tue lunch, Sun evening and Mon.* 🍴. The *morillette* and the *comtine* are just two of the imaginative creations from chef Maurice Marchand. Classical French cuisine served in the dining room; regional specialities in the brasserie below.

☺☺ **Le Relais de Pont d'Héry** – *rte de Champagnole, 39110 Chaux-Champagny, 5km/3mi south of Salins-les-Bains by D 467. ℰ03 84 73 06 54. www.relaispondhery.com. Closed 18 Oct–4 Nov, 15 Feb–3 Mar, Tue Sept–May and Mon.* Behind the unassuming entrance of this small house, you'll find two attractive dining rooms serving appetising traditional and French cuisine.

Nans-Sous-Sainte-Anne

This charming and tiny village near the source of the Lison is surrounded by plenty of natural sights.

A BIT OF GEOGRAPHY

Underground, overground – The River Lison, a tributary of the Loue, actually rises on the slopes of the forest of Scay. Its course on its upper reaches, the Lison-du-Haut, is quite irregular. It will vanish underground for a short distance, only to reappear for a little while, then disappear once more into a gully or crevice. The underground course of the river is marked over-ground by a largely dry, at times strangely shaped valley. The valley becomes deeper and deeper, forming a gorge which is spanned by the **Pont du Diable** (devil's bridge) over which D 229 from Crouzet-Migette to Sainte-Anne runs. After heavy rainfall, the river becomes a gushing torrent, filling the valley, before it cascades into the pool known as the **Creux Billard**★★.

👤👥 TAILLANDERIE★

🕐 *Open Mar–Nov.* 👁️ *Guided tour (45min) Jul–Aug daily 10am–7pm; rest of the year varies.* 💶 *5.20€ (children 2.50€).* 📞*03 81 86 64 18. www.musees-des-techniques.org.*
Just outside the village (follow the signposts) is the 19C tool workshop which forged agricultural tools until 1969. Working to capacity, it employed 25 workers, most of whom lived on the premises. Hydraulic power was provided by the Arcange, a tributary of the Lison. During the visit, the process of making a scythe is explained and you can see in operation the impressive **hydraulic wheel** (1891) which is 5m/16ft in diameter and activated the hammers, as well as an astonishing bellow machine.

HIKES

Source du Lison★★

10min there and back on foot.
🚶The abundant green foliage which surrounds this relatively large pool,

▶ **Population:** 141
🔧 **Michelin Map:** 321: G-5.
ℹ️ **Info:** 7 r. Pierre Vernier, 25290 Ornans.
📞03 81 62 21 50.
www.valleedelaloue.com.
🕐 **Timing:** A day to explore the village and environs. There are some excellent walks close by.

going right down to the water's edge, makes a pretty scene. This is the second largest river source in the Jura after the Loue, and even when the water level is low, it flows at 600l/132gal per second. Enter the cave through a small tunnel in the rock *(take a torch; slippery underfoot)* which ends at a pulpit-shaped rocky platform *(chaire à prêcher)*.
There are designated picnic areas.

▷ *Retrace your steps along the path and turn right onto a signposted, steep footpath up through the woods.*

Creux Billard★★

20min there and back on foot.
🚶 This deep rocky cirque (over 50m/164ft) is characterised by its strange light. The water in the pool is part of the Lison's underwater course, although the river's "true" source is the next cave along. The discovery that the Creux Billard is linked with the Lison's source was made after a tragic accident: in 1899 a young girl drowned in the depths of the pool and three months later her body was found downstream of the river's source.

Grotte Sarrazine★★

30min there and back on foot.
A gigantic natural cavity in the steep wooded rock face marks the opening to this vast cave (90m/295ft high). Its sheer size is best appreciated in summer when the spring is dry.
During rainy periods the resurgent spring, fed by an underground stretch of the Lison, flows out of the cave as a swollen torrent.

Ornans★

Ornans' history, number of inhabitants and industrial activity justifiably make it the small capital of the Loue Valley that inspired the town's most famous native, the painter Gustave Courbet.

A BIT OF HISTORY

Gustave Courbet– The great painter Gustave Courbet, master of French Realism, was born in Ornans in 1819. His parents were wine-growers and wanted their son to become a notary, but he abandoned his law books for the painter's easel, teaching himself by studying the paintings in the Louvre. His work provoked a storm of both praise and criticism. He was strongly attached to Ornans and found most of his subjects in and around his birthplace. Landscapes such as *Château d'Ornans* and *Source de la Loue* capture the essence of nature in the Jura. The subjects of his portraits were friends or members of his family; *L'Après-Dînée à Ornans* and *Un enterrement à Ornans* are particularly interesting as historical documents. He excelled at psychological portraits, especially of women, such as *L'Exilée polonaise*.

SIGHTS
Grand Pont

This great bridge is the most famous spot in Ornans, with its picturesque **view**★ of the town's old houses reflected in the clear waters of the River Loue.

▶ **Population:** 4 098

Michelin Map: 321: G-4.

Info: 7 r. P.-Vernier, 25290 Ornans. ℰ03 81 62 21 50. www.valleedelaloue.com.

Don't Miss: The stretch of river flowing between a double row of old houses on piles. See it from the Grand Pont, the bridge just downstream of the old town.

Timing: 2 days to explore the town and the local area.

Church

The church was rebuilt in the 16C, retaining only the lower part of the 12C bell tower from the original Romanesque building. The dome and the lantern turret date from the 17C.

The church was funded by the Chancellor and the Cardinal of Granvelle, who furthermore ensured that it received a regular contribution for 30 years from the sovereign, in the form of revenue from the sale of 10 loads of salt shipped from Salins every week.

Miroir de la Loue

The pretty stretch of water seen from the bridge downstream of the old town is known as the Loue Mirror. Church, town and cliffs are reflected in the water's silvery surface.

Grand Pont over the Loue

© CRT Franche-Comté/Barbara Gris Pichot

Musée Gustave-Courbet

⚬━ *Currently closed for substantial renovations and will re-open in 2011. Check for times and prices.* ✆ *03 81 25 81 25. http://musee-courbet.doubs.fr.*

The museum is in the old Hôtel Hébert, the beautiful 18C house where Courbet was born, as well as two other adjoining buildings, the maison Borel and l'Hôtel Champereux. You can follow the life of Courbet from Ornans to Paris, the work of the artist in his promotion of the new realism, as well as his political and social activities that forced him to go into exile. Previously various significant paintings were displayed, so expect these to feature in the new museum.

Muséee du Costume Comtois

⏱ *Open Jul–Aug 10am–noon, 2pm–6pm; May–Jun and Sept–Oct daily except Tue 2–6pm.* ⬠*3€ (children 2€).* ♿
Located in the former Chapel of the Visitation, this regional costume museum features an exceptional collection.

EXCURSIONS
Point de vue du Château★

▷ *2km/1.2mi N up a steep narrow road.*
There are fine **views** of Ornans and the Loue Valley from this viewpoint.

Fromagerie de Trépot

⏱ *Open Jun–Aug.* ⬟ *Guided tours (45min) Jul–Aug 10.30am–noon, 2–6pm, Sun and public holidays 2–6pm; Jun Sun and public holidays 2–6pm.* ⬠*3.50€.* ♿ *✆ 03 81 86 71 06.*
Founded in 1818, this cheesemaking facility used to make four Comté cheese wheels per day from milk supplied by eight or nine local farmers. Production stopped in 1977, but the tools and facility are now a small museum, with an interesting audiovisual presentation.

⬚⬚ Dino-Zoo★

At Charbonnières-les-Sapins. ⏱*Open May–Aug 10am–7pm (May–Jun 6pm). Rest of the year times vary.* ⏱*Closed Nov–Feb.* ⬠*9.50€ (children 7.50€). ✆ 03 81 59 27 05. www.dino-zoo.com.*
Learn all about life for prehistoric man, enter the world of the dinosaurs through life-size plastic models or just enjoy a picnic in the grounds.

🚗 DRIVING TOUR

ORNANS TO QUINGEY
⬥ *See Region map. 65km/42mi – allow 5hrs.*

▷ *Leave Ornans on D 67 W; after 2.5km/1.5mi take D 101 left.*

This route follows charming little roads along the banks of the Loue for the most part. The trip is at its most picturesque between Cléron and the confluence of the Loue and the Lison.

Chapelle de Notre-Dame-du-Chêne
The chapel can be seen from D 101. It was built to celebrate a miraculous revelation in 1803, when a young local girl claimed that there was a statue of the Virgin Mary in the trunk of a certain oak tree. Once it was opened up, an old terra-cotta Madonna was indeed found inside, the tree bark having grown over it.

The statuette, kept in the chapel, has drawn pilgrims ever since. A bronze Virgin stands where the oak once grew.

Miroir de Scey
This is the name (*miroir* means mirror) given to a beautiful meander in the Loue, where the trees on the river banks, and the ruins of a fortress, Châtel-St-Denis, are reflected in the river's waters.

▷ *After Scey-Maisières, turn left on D 9 towards Cléron.*

Cléron
From the bridge over the Loue a well-preserved 14C–16C **château**★ (⏱*open Jul–Aug daily except Mon, tour of the outside 2.30–6pm;* ⬠*3€; ✆ 03 81 62 19 03)* comes into sight downstream. The reflection of the château towers in the river, and the surrounding park make a beautiful picture. There is a pretty view of the valley upstream.

Cross the Loue at Cléron and follow S on D 103 towards Amondans, then Lizine where you take a right to D 135.

There are three viewpoints (car parks) all at the edge of cliffs overlooking the narrow and deserted river valley.

Belvédère de Gouille-Noire
Here is a fine view deep below of the Amondans stream as the small Loue tributary flows between two rocky spurs.

Belvédère de la Piquette★
15min round trip on foot from D 135.
Follow a wide path for about 100m/ 110yd, then take the path on the right; turn right at the edge of the cliff. There is a **view** of a meander in the Loue, around a wooded spur.

Belvédère du Moulin-Sapin★
Beside D 135.
There is a beautiful **view** of the peaceful Lison Valley. The bridge crosses the Lison just after it flows into the Loue, in a lovely calm **setting**★. The old Châtillon forge can be viewed from the road. Upstream of the dam, there is a pretty view of some little wooded islands.

Quingey
A path, bordered with plane trees, runs along the south bank of the Loue; the view of the little market town on the opposite bank reflected in the water is especially enchanting in the early morning.

ADDRESSES

STAY
Hôtel de France – *R. Pierre-Vernier. 03 81 62 24 44. www.hoteldefrance-ornans.com. Closed 8–21 Nov and 20 Dec –11 Jan. 25 rooms. 8 €. Restaurant.* Handsome country residence on the slope of a hill, opposite the bridge spanning the River Loue. Rooms on the garden side are quieter. The wood-panelled dining room has exposed beams and a fireplace.

EAT
Le Courbet – *34 r. Pierre-Vernier. 03 81 62 10 15. Closed 16 Feb–11 Mar, Sun eve Nov–Mar, Mon eve except Jul–Aug and Mar.* Located near the Courbet museum, this restaurant is decorated with numerous reproductions of the artist's work. A pretty terrace borders the Loue River. Contemporary cuisine incorporates fresh, market ingredients.

Ferme-auberge La Faye – *25620 Foucherans. 4km/3mi E of Foucherans, reach it by r. de Bonnevaux. 03 81 59 27 34. www.fermeauberge-lafaye.com. Open Fri eve, Sun lunch and all day Sat; barbecues every day. Reservation essential.* At this 19C working farm you can eat meat from the farm or seasonal vegetables from the garden in the very pretty panelled dining room or by the individual barbecue chalets in the garden (min. 6 people). Fondue, raclette and other local specialities may be ordered in advance.

Château de Cléron

G. Magnin-MICHELIN

Mouthier-Haute-Pierre★

and Gorge de la Loue

This charming village set in a rocky amphitheatre is, along with Ornans, one of the prettiest spots in the Loue Valley. The village is also the starting point to explore the dramatic Gorges de la Loue, an area often painted by Courbet.

▶ **Population:** 318
⛰ **Michelin Map:** 321: H-4.
🗊 **Info:** 7 r. Pierre Vernier, 25290 Ornans. ☎03 81 62 21 50. www.valleede laloue.com.
👁 **Don't Miss:** The viewpoints over the Gorges de la Loue, especially that of Moine de la Vallée. The splendid source of the Loue.
🕑 **Timing:** A day to explore the area including around 5hrs for the driving tour of the Gorges de la Loue.

🚗 DRIVING TOUR

40km/25mi – about 4hrs 30min.

GORGES DE LA LOUE

From Mouthier-Haute-Pierre, the Loue winds along the bottom of a deep and wooded gorge to its confluence with the Doubs, a popular trip with canoeists. In May the banks of the river are brightened by the cherry blossoms, and in summer the best light is at the end of the day.

◔ *Head SE on D 67 towards Pontarlier.*

Cascade de Syratu

On the edge of Mouthier-Haute-Pierre, you will see the Syratu waterfall, tumbling from a high cliff.

Source du Pontet and Grotte des Faux-Monnayeurs

45min there and back on foot from D 67.

🚶 The walk is mostly through woods, climbing up slopes that are sometimes quite steep. Iron ladders lead to two caves; that of the Faux-Monnayeurs is not recommended to visitors with no head for heights. The source of the Le Pontet is a resurgent spring welling up in a cave at the bottom of a wooded hollow. The Faux-Monnayeurs Cave (Counterfeiters' Cave, so named as it is said that counterfeit money was made here in the 17C) is about 30m/98ft higher up; this was the river's original source.

Belvédères★★ – Two viewpoints appear one after the other along D 67, from which one of the most beautiful meanders in the river can be seen, from a height of 150m/492ft.

Another viewpoint, known as the **Belvédère de Mouthier**, is found 300m/330yd further on. The **view★★** is remarkable, taking in not only Mouthier but also the upper Loue Valley at the end of the Nouailles gorge.

Gorges de Nouailles★

There is a walk (1hr 30min there and back on foot) from the Café La Creuse to the

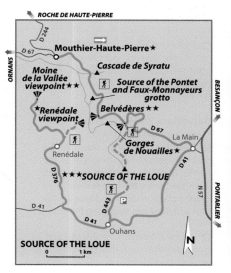

SOURCE OF THE LOUE

source of the Loue; take the path along the gorge which branches off from D 67. This path twists along the steep cliff.

🚶 The path gives beautiful **glimpses**★ of the gorge, which is over 200m/656ft deep. It goes to the bottom of the cirque in which the Loue rises. A footbridge leads to the cave from which the river springs.

◐ *After leaving Ouhans, head for the river's source along D 443, which climbs steeply uphill.*

Source de la Loue★★★
Park the car next to the little refreshment stall, Chalet de la Loue, and go down the path (30min there and back on foot) to the valley bottom.

🚶 This spot is one of the most beautiful in the Jura. A bend in the path suddenly reveals the Loue rising up from a steep-walled basin. It has been proved that the Loue draws its waters from the Doubs. It is also fed by infiltrations from the Drugeon and by rainwater draining off the plateau, with the result that the river's flow never falls very low. As a general rule the water is very clear, except after heavy rains.

The river rises from a vast cave at the bottom of a tall cliff about 100m/328ft high. From the cave entrance, there is a good view of the sheer power and size of the Loue's source.

◐ *Return to Ouhans and take D 41 on the right towards Levier, then right again on D 376. On leaving Renédale, park the car near the entrance gate of the path leading to the viewpoint.*

Belvédère de Renédale★
15min there and back on foot.

🚶 This pleasant path overlooks the Nouailles gorge from a height of 350m/1 148ft. It leads to a platform from which there is virtually a **bird's-eye view** down into the gorge; directly opposite are the cliffs with D 67 winding along them.

◐ *Take D 376 north; after 2.5km/1.5mi the road ends at the foot of a television mast, at a viewpoint.*

Belvédère du Moine-de-la-Vallée★★
There is a superb **panorama** of the Loue Valley north-west to Vuillafans, Roche mountain and the village of Mouthier-Haute-Pierre.

◐ *Take the road back to Ouhans and return to Mouthier.*

ADDRESSES

🏠 STAY

🛏 **Hôtel de France** – *1 pl. Pezard, 25930 Lods.* ℘*03 81 60 95 29. Closed 2 weeks in Feb and 25 Dec–1 Jan. 8 rooms.* ⊑*6 €.* Three nice surprises in this village restaurant: the terrace, the serene room at the back and the simple, carefully prepared dishes. Pleasant rooms.

🛏 **Hôtel des Sources de la Loue** – *25520 Ouhans. 10km/7mi S of Mouthier-Haute-Pierre by D 67 and D 41.* ℘*03 81 69 90 06. Closed 20 Dec–31 Jan, Sat lunch and Fri Oct–Apr. 15 rooms.* ⊑ *7.50 €. Restaurant* 🍽🍽. This unpretentious hotel is in a building typical of the region. The bar is a popular meeting place for locals. Simple guest rooms with wood panelling. Regional food.

🛏🛏 **Hôtel de la Cascade** – *2 rte des Gorges-de-Nouailles.* ℘*03 81 60 95 30. Closed 3 Nov–2 Mar.* 🅿 *17 rooms.* ⊑ *8.50 €. Restaurant* 🍽🍽. The Loue Valley is on the doorstep. The rooms are equipped with all modern amenities and some have balconies. The restaurant serves regional cuisine.

🍴 EAT

🍽🍽 **Ferme-auberge du Rondeau** – *25580 Lavans-Vuillafans. 15 km N of Mouthier-Haute-Pierre by D 67 towards Vuillafans, then D 27.* ℘*03 81 59 25 84. Closed Dec–mid-Jan and Mon out of season.* 🍴 *Reservation essential. 8 rooms.* 🍽🍽. This typical Franche-Comté chalet is in the middle of the fields of an organic farm. Meals include home-made bread, garden vegetables and fruit, and goat and boar reared on the property. There are eight comfortable, pretty rooms.

The Saône river rises in the Vosges and meanders down quite gently through the Franche-Comté to Burgundy and on to meet the Rhône, making one of the most pleasant ways to explore the valley by canal boat or bicycle. The department of Haute-Saône, whose capital is Vesoul, is criss-crossed not only by the Saône and its tributaries, but also by the pretty Ognon river, meandering through Villersexel. The rivers and nearby lakes give pleasure to locals and tourists alike, with fishing and kayaking popular pastimes. The pleasant town of Gray marks the end of the navigable part of the Saône.

The Wealth of the Churches

At the end of the 17C when Franche-Comté became part of France, the region enjoyed considerably increased prosperity. The region's huge resources of wood allowed prestigious, new buildings to be constructed in towns and villages. The new projects usually included fine churches, erected to prove the virtue of the citizens.

Special attention was lavished on the interior of these churches and in particular to the altar-pieces. Today, many of these have been meticulously restored along with other treasures in the churches, and the region of Haute-Saône has established the Route des Retables *(brochures available in local tourist offices)* which allows you to discover some of the region's valuable ecclesiastical heritage.

Around 30 churches in the region are listed including those at Gray-la-Ville, Vy-les-Rupt, Lavoncourt and Jussey, and an itinerary along the route can form the basis for further exploration of the pretty Saône Valley. Look out too for the fine stucco used in several churches, such as that on the pulpit in the St-Symphorien church at Gy. This was the work of the highly creative Marca family of Besançon, who originally came to Franche-Comté from Italy.

A Revival of Old Traditions

The museums in the castle at Champlitte faithfully display recreations of village life and work as it used to be in the Saône Valley. There is a revival in the area of popular festivals, many celebrating the best of the region's natural products, from honey and blueberries, to cherries and potatoes. To remind us that this was once a great wine-producing area, at Champlitte each January there

Highlights

1 Discover the hidden "traiges" in the old town of **Vesoul** (p302)

2 The recreated rooms and cellars inside the **Château de Gy** (p306)

3 Wander around the tastefully restored village of **Fondremand** and visit 13C oil and nut mill (p307)

4 La Rochère glass and crystal workshops at **Passavent** (p311)

5 The castle at **Villasexel** (p312)

is a wine festival. Fondremand hosts a festival of the arts every July, with street musicians, dancers, demonstrations of activities such as fencing and acrobatics, and fireworks. The same village holds a day of events each May called Terroir en Fête around the rather disparate activities of scale model-making and beef-rearing, a day which also features many local food products.

Source de la Romaine and the wash house, Fondremand

© Hervé Hughes/hemis.fr

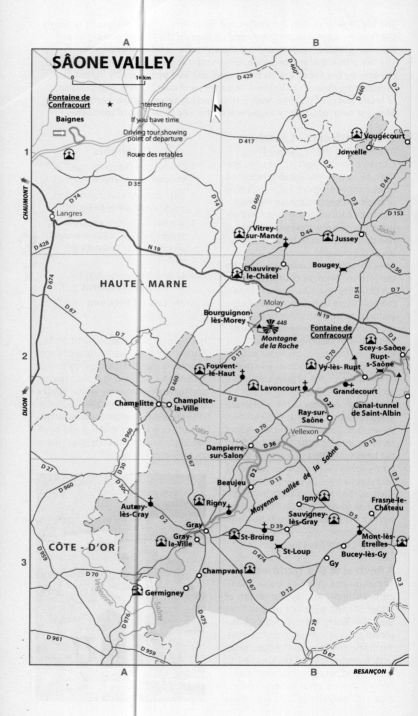

SAÔNE VALLEY

0   1 km

<u>Fontaine de</u>
<u>Confracourt</u>   ★   Interesting

Baignes   If you have time

                              Driving tour showing
                              point of departure

                              Route des retables

N

CHAUMONT

Langres

D 74

D 35

D 14

D 428

N 19

D 674

HAUTE - MARNE

D 67

D 7

DIJON

Vitrey-
sur-Mance

Chauvirey-
le-Châtel

Bourguignon-
lès-Morey

Montagne
de la Roche   448

Molay

D 460

D 17

Fouvent-
lé-Haut

Lavoncourt

Champlitte   Champlitte-
la-Ville

D 460

D 5

Ray-sur-
Saône

Salon

Dampierre-
sur-Salon

Beaujeu

D 70

D 36

Vellexon

Jonvelle

Vougécourt

D 429

D 460

D 1

D 417

D 51

D 460

D 44

Sâone

D 44   Jussey

Bougey

D 54

D 7

N 19

<u>Fontaine de</u>
<u>Confracourt</u>

Scey-s-Saône
Rupt-
s-Saône

Vy-lès- Rupt

Grandecourt

Canal-tunnel
de Saint-Albin

D 70

D 27

D 13

D 2

D 153

D 56

D 3

D 3

Moyenne vallée de la Saône

Igny

Sauvigney-
lès-Gray

Frasne-le-
Château

D 5

D 27

D 30

D 30C

D 960

D 67

Autrey-
lès-Cray

Rigny

Gray

Gray-
la-Ville

St-Broing

D 39

St-Loup

D 2

CÔTE - D'OR

D 959

D 70

Champvans

Germigney

Vingeanne

Saône

D 976

D 961

D 959

D 475

D 67

D 474

Gy

Bucey-lès-Gy

Mont-lès-
Étrelles

D 12

D 29

D 67

D 3

BESANÇON

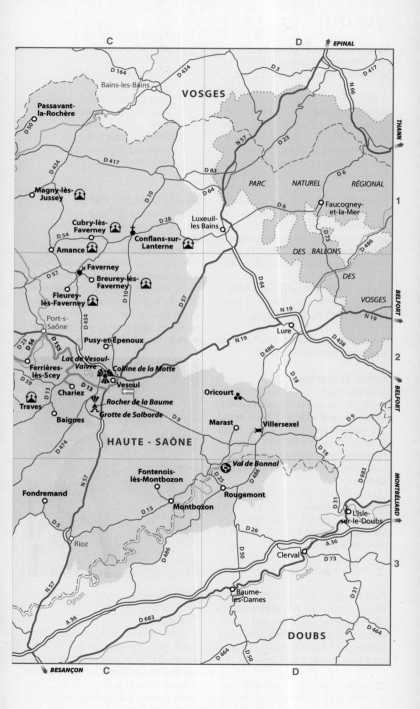

Vesoul

Sung about with affection by Jacques Brel, the town of Vesoul has an interesting and lively old town.

A BIT OF HISTORY

Birth of a capital – Prehistoric man first settled on the La Motte outcrop overlooking the town to the north. This settlement was replaced by a Roman military camp intended to guard the road between Luxeuil and Besançon. A small market town grew up in the 13C under the sheltering walls of the fort on the plateau. Then the inhabitants moved down into the plain, and Vesoul became an active commercial, religious and military centre. The fort was attacked several times and was finally razed in 1595.

OLD TOWN WALKING TOUR

See town plan. Allow 2hrs. Start from the car park on rue des Tanneurs.

Rue d'Alsace-Lorraine boasts several fine structures, particularly no. 22.

Église St-Georges

After two years of restoration the originality of this beautiful 18C Classical church has been reclaimed. The nave and aisles are at the same height, reminiscent of Gothic style with Rhenish influence. Note especially a splendid marble sculpture by the Italian Conova, **Vénus and Cupidon**★.

On the square outside, note at no. 2 **l'hôtel Baressois** (13–16C), with its mullioned windows. The contemporary fountain, by Aline Bienfait, is titled La Rencontre (the meeting).

▷ *Turn left to look down rue Salengro.*

Rue Roger-Salengro

At no. 11 note the **Hôtel Thomassin** (15C), its doors, windows and gutters graced with twist moulding. A few steps farther, peek to the right to see a flowered courtyard and a 15C tower.

▷ *Retrace your steps, take rue des Ursulines to Musée Georges-Garret.*

▷ **Population:** 16 370
◐ **Michelin Map:** 314: E-7.
◰ **Info:** 2 r. Gevrey, 70002 Vesoul. ℘03 84 97 10 85. www.ot-vesoul.fr.
◈ **Don't Miss:** The fine mansions of the old town and the "traiges".
◷ **Timing:** 1 day in the old town; 1-2 days to explore the Saône valley.

Musée Georges-Garret

◷*Open daily except Tue 2–6pm.* ◷*Closed 1 Jan, 1 May, 14 Jul, 1 and 25 Nov, 25 Dec.* ℘*03 84 76 51 54. www.museesfranchecomte.com.*
The lower floor houses temporary exhibitions and an archaeological department with an interesting collection of Gallo-Roman **funerary steles**. The upper floor is devoted to painting and sculpture, including a large collection of work by local artist **Gérome**.

Musée Georges-Garret

G. Magnin-MICHELIN

▷ *Turn right on rue des Annonciades.*

Traiges★

Possibly from Spanish influence , here you'll get a glimpse into the "hidden" corner of old Vesoul, with secret courtyards and gardens tucked between houses from the 16C and 17C. The word "traiges" may come from the Cas-

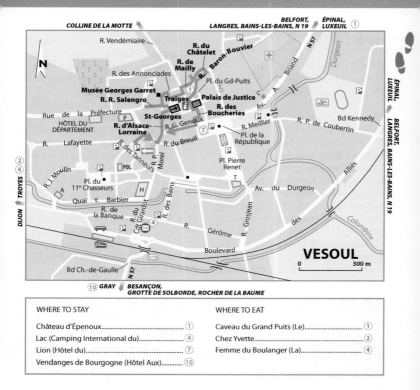

WHERE TO STAY		WHERE TO EAT	
Château d'Épenoux..................................... ①		Caveau du Grand Puits (Le)................................. ①
Lac (Camping International du)........................ ④		Chez Yvette.. ②
Lion (Hôtel du)... ⑦		Femme du Boulanger (La)............................. ④
Vendanges de Bourgogne (Hôtel Aux)............. ⑩		

tilian word "trajes" meaning path. The path ends at rue Paul-Petitclerc *(turn right)*. Note the fine ironwork along rue Vendémiaire.

Rue de Mailly
The **Hôtel de Magnoncourt**★ (1530) maintains its handsome staircase. Further on, you'll see two more buildings from the same period.

Rues du Châtelet et Baron-Bouvier
The path leads to the former site of the gate into the old city. *(Turn right.)* The rue du Baron-Bouvier here is lined with market stalls. Note at no. 2 the elegant **Hôtel de Montgenet** (1549), and opposite, the **Maison Cariage** (15C).

◗ *Turn left.*

18C buildings
The 18C was a time of prolific construction in Vesoul, particularly in this area, as seen by the many buildings with har-

monious and symmetrical lines: **Hôtel Lyautey de Colombe**★, **Hôtel Raillard de Granvelle** (place du Grand-Puits) and **Palais de Justice** (place du Palais).

◗ *Walk along the right side of the palais, and turn onto rue des Boucheries.*

Note, at no. 14, a handsome structure (1525), with tower, gargoyles and Gothic doorway.

WALK
Colline de la Motte
30min there and back on foot.
This isolated outcrop (378m/1 240ft) rises 160m/525ft above the Durgeon plain. A zig-zag path leads up to a terreplein, revealing a little chapel.
Next, you arrive at a terrace with a statue of the Virgin Mary: there is a beautiful **panorama**★ over the Langres plateau to the west, the Jura mountains to the south and sometimes even the summits of the Alps. A bronze orientation table reproduces the shape of the valley.

🚗 DRIVING TOUR

Heart of the Saône Valley
136km/84.5mi – allow 1 day.
▶ *Drive west out of Vesoul by D 13.*

This tour takes you along the Saône river to Gray (👁 *see page 305*).

The two villages of **Scey-sur-Saone-et-Saint-Albin** have been linked since 1807 and are dominated by the Comtois bell tower of the church. Both the distinctive **Hall church** of Saint-Martin and the town hall are listed buildings. The church includes some beautiful paintings, ironworks and sumptuous stained-glass windows above the altar. When you look around the centre of the town notice the sculptures on the façade of the old forge on the shopping street. At **Rupt-sur-Saône**, go up the 33m/108ft-**tower** of the old 12C château on one of the three hills of the village for a fine **view** over the valley.

The Roman 12C church Sainte-Marie-Madeleine at **Grandecourt** is moving in its simplicity, and the nearby church at **Lavoncourt**, rebuilt in 1670, is worth going in for its paintings and furniture. Make a stop at **Ray-sur-Saône** to visit the château and its beautifully maintained park. Reconstructed in 17C–18C it still retains a Medieval character thanks to its Roman tower. The **view** stretches to the Vosges and the Jura mountains. The origins of **Dampierre-sur-Salon** go far back, and the town boasts a beautiful **town hall-wash house**.

ADDRESSES

🛏 STAY

😑 **Les Vendanges de Bourgogne** – *56 bd Charles-de-Gaulle.* ✆*03 84 75 81 21. www.hotellesvendangesdebourgogne. com.* ▣ *18 rooms.* ☕ *6.50 €.* Near the old town and recently refurbished, this hotel offers comfortable, cosy rooms. The breakfast room is bright and there is a guest lounge with a fireplace.

😑 **Hôtel du Lion** – *4 pl. de la République.* ✆*03 84 76 54 44 . Closed 4–20 Aug and 26 Dec–7 Jan.* ▣ *18 rooms.* ☕ *6 €.* This inexpensive hotel has simple rooms and is conveniently close to the shopping streets. Breakfast is offered on the terrace in summer.

😑 **Camping International du Lac** – *70000 Vaivre-et-Montoille. 2.5km.1.5mi W of Vesoul.* ✆*03 84 76 22 86. Open Mar–Oct. 160 places.* Spread out over a huge recreational area on the edge of a lake, this campsite offers facilities for swimming, sailing, fishing, archery, tennis, table-tennis and basketball, and there are hiking trails and cycling paths.

😑😑 **Château d'Épenoux** – *5 r. Ruffier-d'Épenoux, 70000 Pusy-et-Épenoux.* ✆*03 84 75 19 60. www.chateau-epenoux.com.* ▣ *4 rooms.* In the midst of a park with 100-year-old trees, this little 18C château offers rooms furnished with antique furniture and lighting. Fine meals are offered in an elegant dining room, decorated in yellow.

🍴 EAT

😑 **La Femme du Boulanger** – *1 r. du Cdt-Girardot.* ✆*03 84 76 38 11. Closed Sat eve, Sun and Mon lunch.* ♿. *Booking advised especially at lunch.* From the outside there is quite a retro feel at this baker-cum-salon-de-thé-cum-restaurant. Inside it's more modern and you have a choice of huge salads, sandwiches, crêpes and a selection of hot meals and desserts. You can also eat on the pretty terrace by the river.

😑 **Chez Yvette** – *In the centre, by the pontoon (boat stops), 70130 Ray-sur-Saône.* ✆*03 84 78 41 07. Closed 24 Dec evening–5 Jan.* You will simply fall in love with this little café restaurant on the main street of Ray-sur-Saône. Regional offerings might include pike-perch or even bison fondue served with garden vegetables. All is served beautifully in a room decorated with pictures by a local artist, or on a small terrace. They sell local food specialities.

😑😑 **Le Caveau du Grand Puits** – *R. Mailly.* ✆*03 84 76 66 12. Closed 15 Aug–1 Sept, 24 Dec–3 Jan, Wed and Sat lunch, Sun and public holidays.* Walk down a few steps to a lovely vaulted cellar in this traditional family-run restaurant, popular with the locals.

Gray

This handsome town rises up like an amphitheatre from the banks of the Saône. While it played a major role in commercial river navigation in the 19C, Gray has now found favour with recreational boaters.

SIGHTS
Hôtel de Ville★

The town hall is an elegant building, with arcades in the Renaissance style (1572), embellished by pink marble columns and a beautiful varnished-tile roof.

Musée Baron-Martin★

Open May–Sept daily except Tue 10am –noon, 2–6pm. Rest of the year daily except Tue 2–5pm. Closed 1 Jan, 1 May, 1 Nov, 22 Dec–2 Jan. 3.60€. 03 84 65 69 10. www.museebaron martin.fr.

This art museum is in the 18C château of the Count of Provence, brother of Louis XVI. The first galleries contain works by Primitive western artists, then there are rooms for the Italian (16C–18C), Flemish (17C) and Dutch (17C) schools – including some **engravings by Rembrandt** – and French schools (16C–19C). The galleries continue with contemporary art from late-19C and early-20C including works by Albert Besnard and Aman Jean, Fantin-Latour's lithographic stones, and paintings by Tissot and Steinlen.

The 13C vaulted cellars include a small collection of antique items of all sorts, and the upper rooms are set aside for temporary exhibitions. Don't leave without seeing the **collection of pastels and drawings** from P. Prud'hon (1758–1823) including three portraits painted at the château itself.

Grande-Rue

Go into the courtyard of no. 71 and step back to look at the **Hôtel de Conflans** (16C) and its handsome "viorbe" (staircase in a tower). Leaving there, notice the Louis XIV gate at no. 54 and go into no. 32 for a quick look at the **hôtel-Dieu** (1747), today a care home. Follow the corridor opposite you to see the chapel

with 18C alter and tabernacle. For a look at a collection of rare ceramics (17–19C) you can visit the **apothecary** of the hôtel-Dieu by appointment with the tourist office. *Go back up la Grande-Rue to walk down the rue du Marché.*

Rue du Marché

You will see a statue of Saint Pierre Fourier by Grandgirard, and then at no. 10, the old communal grain store (16C), and at no. 4 the prestigious **hôtel Gauthiot-d'Ancier** where Saint Pierre Fourier lived in a cell room. Originally part of the building there is a unique example here of a **wooden pivotal staircase** (1550). *Visit through the tourist office.*
Turn right on rue des Casernes.

Originally a school, you'll find here the old **hôtel des Gouverneurs**, with its ornate doors and windows. Opposite the Carmelite chapel has been converted into a museum of religious art including a miraculous statue of the Virgin and Child brought to Gray by pilgrims. It is only open for visits occasionally.

EXCURSIONS

Gray-la-Ville *(1.5km/1mi W by D 39)* was the original town before Gray was established towards the end of 10C. The church here has a gilded **altarpiece★** (1697) that came from Gray's Notre-Dame church. *(Visits can be arranged through the town hall; 03 84 65 05 69).* In the church at **St-Broing** *(9.5km/6mi E by D 39)* the unusual **altarpiece★** by the stucco decorators, the Marca brothers of Gy, was restored in 2004.

In summer you can visit the interesting, family-owned 19C **Château de Saint-Loup** *(15km/8mi E by D 474).*

▶ **Population:** 6 262
◔ **Michelin Map:** 314: B-8.
▤ **Info:** Île Sauzay, 70100 Gray.
   03 84 65 14 24.
   www.ville-gray.fr.
◉ **Don't Miss:**
   The Renaissance Hôtel
   de Ville and the Musée
   Baron-Martin.

Gy

and Bucey-lès-Gy

Overlooking the road from Gray to Vesoul, on the edge of wooded hillsides, the city of Gy was once owned by the archbishops of Besançon, who resided in the château that dominates the town. The upper part of the town, built in the 12C on a rocky spur, blends in well with the commercial part of town, built lower down from 14C.

- ▶ **Population:** 1 034
- **Michelin Map:** 314 C8.
- **Info:** 11 Grande-Rue, 70700 Gy. ℰ 03 84 32 93 93. www.ot-montsdegy.com.
- **Don't Miss:** The impressive château with its unusual lathe; the old winegrowers' houses and tiny lanes in the upper town.
- **Timing:** Allow half a day to visit the town and the surrounding area.

A BIT OF HISTORY

The Archibishops' city – The land around Gy was sold by the Count of Burgundy to his brother, the Archbishop of Besançon in the 11C. From that time onwards Gy found itself in a strategic position defending itself against the powerful counts of Chalon Oiselay. In 1250 the archbishop **Guillaume de la Tour** ordered the first keep to be built and the fortifications were used later to defend the city from attacks from Montfaucon, Rougemont and the Duke of Burgundy.

In 1348 **Hugues de Vienne** granted the residents of Gy a Charter of Franchise, which allowed commerce, crafts and the vineyards to be developed. The archbishops were sometimes safer in Gy than in Besançon and would bring over their coinage workshops or their official courts. Right up to the Revolution, Gy remained the archbishops' safe haven.

TOWN

From the west the town is dominated by the 16–18C **Château**★ (◷open 1 Jul–15 Sept every day except Tue; ⚬guided tours 2–3pm and 4–5pm; Easter–1 Nov weekends and public holidays; ⚬4.80€), whose Flamboyant octagonal tower (15C) gives it great style. Note a rare steel and ebony **château lathe**★ with ivory handles, used for carpentry as well as clock-making.

There is much to see in other rooms including lavish sets of tableware and hunting trophies. The current owner was able to recreate several rooms accurately thanks to the meticulous inventories kept by each successive archbishop. A **wine museum** in the cellar is a reminder that this was once an important wine-growing area with 450ha/1 000acre of vineyards.

The winding lanes of the **Bourg-dessus** (upper town) make it seem like a medieval hamlet, with its pretty houses from the 16–18C. The rather grand Eglise Saint-Symphorien was reconstructed (1754–74) by the cardinal of Choiseul-Beaupré in Versailles-style.

Developed from the 14C, but at its most dynamic in the mid-19C, the **Ville basse** (lower town) includes the pharaonic **hôtel de ville** with Doric columns along its 40m/45yd façade, and by the same architect the **Grande Fontaine** (fountain) in antique portico.

EXCURSIONS

In the nearby village of **Bucey-lès-Gy** (3.5km/2.5mi to NE by D 12) you will discover the 1828 **wash house and town hall** combined together with three arches. Another interesting vast **wash house with fountain** (1833) is found in the centre of the pretty village of **Frasne-le-Château** (11km/6.8mi NE by D 474). Formed from two buildings with a cockerel on top, it uses the source of the Jouanne River.

The nearby church at **Mont-lès-Etrelles** includes an altarpiece (1730) from the famous, local stucco decorators the Marca brothers.

Fondremand
and the source of the Romain

For a very small village, Fondremand has lots going for it. Its delights range from the grand 11C keep, to numerous, tastefully restored 15–16C houses, and a source re-created in the Vaucluse style, in the 19C. Each July, the village draws an ever-growing crowd of people to enjoy its unique arts and cultural festival.

VILLAGE

Encouraged by the success of their annual festival, over the past few years the residents have worked together to restore many of the village houses and small mansions in a truly tasteful way. The festival has taken place annually since 1974 – today, there are three days in mid-July of concerts, plays, dances, street musicians, art shows and more. (see www.fondremand.com).

Church

Open weekends 9am–6pm.
In the 13C this building was part of the château. Outside you'll see an attractive Romanesque rose window, and inside a fine, early Gothic chancel with a tomb stone sculpted in Haut-Relief (16C). The two arcaded choir stalls are delightful.

Château

Guided tour Jul, 5pm; 1–22 Sept, 7pm; rest of the year by appointment. Closed 14 Jul. 3.30 € (children free). 03 84 78 20 03. http://chateau.fondremand.pagespro-orange.fr.
The visit focuses on the 11C keep: a staircase built into the walls leads to the guard room and the dungeon. You take a spiral staircase (15C) to see the main halls and the oak rafters. On the 3rd floor is a small museum of everyday objects, as well agricultural implements from 1850–1950. You can also visit the kitchen (15–16C) and the 19C stables.

Source de la Romaine

In 1831 the source of the Romaine, a small tributary of the Saône, was harnessed to create a most unusual wash

- ▶ **Population:** 196
- **Michelin Map:** 314 E8.
- **Location**: Fondremand is about 22km/14mi SW of Vesoul by D 474, then left on D 33 via Grandvelle-et-le-Perrenot and Maizières.
- **Don't Miss:** The lovingly restored town houses, mansions and wine-growers' houses; the mill near the source, showing a revival of a Medieval past.
- **Timing:** Allow half a day to visit the village and the mill. Allow more time if you go in July, when the arts and cultural festival takes place.
- **Kids:** The old 13C mill; and for the brave, the adventure trail that has been created in the nearby forest.

house at the base of the keep. The Neo-classical façade reveals an intriguing and pretty series of interlinking ponds, arches and walkways.

Huilerie-moulin

Follow the stream for 100m/105yd from the source de la Romaine. Open daily except Mon 2–6.30pm. Closed 16–19 Aug. 2 € (children 1 €). Shop with local food products (jams, teas etc.) 03 84 78 25 67. www.artisans-comtois.com.
Constructed in 1201 on the edge of the Romaine stream, this mill was used in turn for oil production to mill wheat and corn; over the years it was modified several times. Finally its use was abandoned just at the time when a dedicated miller decided to bring it back to life. Today it's been completely restored to how it would have been in the 18C, complete with wooden gears, a press and the millstone. Depending on the season it is used to make walnut oil, flour or simply apple juice.

Champlitte

Champlitte's border-town location has given it a particularly agitated history. However, its fortifications gave way long ago to wine-growers' houses, others known as "Spanish" houses and the elegant décor of the Renaissance château.

A BIT OF HISTORY

The vineyards – Not far from the Burgundy wine region, Champlitte once boasted over 600ha/1 483 acres of vineyards until a combination of diseases, weather conditions (frosts, hailstorms) and wars meant they were abandoned. In the mid-18C around 400 wine-growers left the town and emigrated to Mexico.

In recent times, instigated by local man **Albert Demard**, who also helped create the museums below, a small number of vineyards have been revived. Over 34ha/84 acres of vines produce decent country wines of all colours. To honour their history and the revival, the town celebrates with a **festival of Saint-Vincent** (patron saint of wine-growers) each year in January.

TOWN
Church

Rebuilt in the 19C, this church of Classical style retained its Gothic façade, as well as a 15C chapel. On the side is a Gothic tower (1437) which, it is said, was once 80m/262ft high. Inside you will see a 12C font and some very beautiful statues, showing the importance of religious art to a town that once had at least six monasteries.

Château

Only the façade with its elegant Ionic and Corinthian columns (16C) remains from the original Renaissance building. Rebuilt by the architect Bertrand (*see also CHÂTEAU DE MONCLEY*) in the 18C, today the building houses the Town Hall and the **Musée départemental des Arts et Traditions Populaires★**. This museum (*open Apr–Sept 9.30am–noon, 2–6pm, weekends 2–5pm; Oct–Mar*

▶ **Population:** 1 864
☉ **Michelin Map:** 314 B7.
▣ **Location:** Almost touching Burgundy's Côte d'Or, Champlitte is just 64km/103mi NE of Dijon by D 960 and Fontaine-Française; or from Gray, by D 67 (21km/34mi NW).
⊛ **Don't Miss:** The elegant Renaissance château and the two interesting museums of local collections.
☉ **Timing:** Allow half a day to explore the town.

2–5pm; ☉ closed Tue except Jul–Aug, 1 May, 1 and 11 Nov, Christmas holidays; ☞6€; ☎03 84 67 82 00; www.musees-franchecomte.com) displays a large collection of everyday and characteristic furniture, souvenirs and objects of all sorts from the Haute-Saône department and the nearby sub-Vosgien hillsides. Many are meticulously presented to re-create original rooms such as a school classroom, a grocer or a workshop. Of particular interest is the collection of medical and pharmaceutical items.

The nearby **Musée départemental des Arts et Techniques** (*R. des Lavières; ☉ same opening hours as above; ☎03 84 67 62 90*) houses a collection showing industrial developments from the first half of the 20C. It includes vintage cars, various machinery and steam-engines.

EXCURSIONS

The church at **Champlitte-la-Ville** (*1km/0.6mi E by D 103*) has a most elegant entrance door, as well as a 11C monolithic baptism font, decorated with symbolic carvings.

Continue on D 103 for 15km/9.5mi to visit the 18C **Eglise de Fouvent-le-Haut**. An early work of the architect Claude-Nicolas Ledoux (*see SALINE ROYALE*), who restored the whole church, it is notable in particular for the beautiful roof of its bell tower.

Chauvirey-le-Châtel

Surrounded by woodlands, this modest village enjoyed its hour of glory when it was a seigneury in the times of the Chauvirey family, one of the most powerful of the region. Of the two original fortified châteaux, all that remains is a chapel built in the 15C to keep safe an important hunting horn belonging to Saint Hubert, patron Saint of hunters.

▶ **Population:** 127
🜚 **Michelin Map:** 314 C6.
🛈 **Info:** Pl. de la République. 70500 Vitrey-sur-Mance. ☎03 84 68 53 89
◗ **Location:** 42km/26mi NW of Vesoul by N 19, then D 1 N to Cintrey.
🜊 **Don't Miss:** The richly decorated chapel of Saint-Hubert; the church of the Nativité-de-Notre-Dame with its multi-coloured wooden altar; the superb gilded altar of the church of Saint-Pierre in Jussey.
🕒 **Timing:** Allow half a day to visit the village and its surroundings.

VILLAGE

The flamboyant **Chapelle Saint-Hubert**, built in Gothic style, dates back to 1484. The richly decorated interior includes an interesting stone **retable of Saint Hubert**. The Rockefeller family tried to purchase the chapel in 1934 for the Metropolitan Museum of Art in New York, but local pressure prevented this. However, the enamelled gold hunting horn, encrusted with ivory and amber, that apparently belonged to Saint Hubert, was purchased by Richard Wallace in 1879 and is today in the Wallace Collection in London.

The **Eglise de la Nativité-de-Notre-Dame** is notable for its square bell tower

Chapelle Saint-Hubert

G. Magnin/MICHELIN

and the 17C carved wooden altar, as well as the impressive altar-piece.

EXCURSIONS

The architecture of the attractive 15C–17C **Château de Bougey** (9km/5.5mi W, ☎03 84 68 04 01; ➤guided tours 10am–noon, 2–6pm; 🕒closed last Tuesday each month) combines several different styles. Note, for example, the unusual steeple above the watch tower. Situated in a tiny village, this jewel of a little château has been undergoing extensive restoration projects for several years.

There's plenty of activity in the small town of **Jussey** (10km/7mi E by D 46). The old grain market today houses the tourist office and has a Classical arched façade. The **Eglise Saint-Pierre**, was re-built in the 18C, but retained its 16C chancel. There is much of interest inside, especially the gilded wooden **altar**★.

🚶 You can walk from Molay (8km/5mi S by D 1 then D 17) on a path up to the summit of the **Montagne de la Roche** for a beautiful **panorama** over the plain and the Vosges. On your return to Molay, you will see the wall of the ramparts of the **Néolithic site of Bourgignon-lès-Morey**, over 6 000 years old. A museum in the village presents further vestiges from this era.

Faverney
and around

A famous miracle occurred in 1608 when two Eucharists in the abbey at Faverney were rescued from a fire. Known for its 8C abbey, the town became a much-visited place of pilgrimage, and the most important dignitaries of the kingdom would come to prostrate themselves in front of the two miraculously saved hosts. One was transferred to Dole where a chapel at the Collegiale was consecrated especially for it. Today, time has moved on for Faverney, but the town never forgets its history.

- ▶ **Population:** 1 052
- **Michelin Map:** 314 E6.
- **Location:** Faverney is 19km/ 11.5mi N of Vesoul, by N 19, then D 434 N via Bougnon.
- **Don't Miss:** The abbey church, home to the divine host of the miracle.
- **Timing:** Allow 1hr to explore the village, longer to visit the surroundings.

A BIT OF HISTORY
The miracle of the hosts – In 1608, there were only a few monks that remained in Faverney, but as always they organised their annual celebration of the Eucharist for Pentecost. The evening before, the monks closed the church leaving the Monstrance, containing two hosts and relics of Saint Agathe, as well as two lit oil lamps, on a small altar. The next day, they discovered that a fire had destroyed the altar, but miraculously, the Monstrance remained suspended in mid-air. While the congregation participated in the Mass, they watched astonished as the Monstrance descended onto the altar of its own accord. The episcopal inquest that followed concluded that such a thing could not have happened "without intervention of a great power and the Will of God". The miracle of the hosts was authenticated by the pope in 1864 and has been venerated by the local faithful ever since.

ÉGLISE ABBATIALE
You can see the huge roof and two bell towers of the 11C abbey from far away. A victim of wars, fires and even, it seems, an earthquake in 1682, it has been rebuilt often: the porch dates to the 13C, the chancel and transept to the 14C and 15C. As at Baume-les-Messieurs, inside there are 11C pillars that are alter-nately round, octagonal or square. The divine host of the miracle is kept in the chapel on the left of the chancel. In the chapel on the right, a 15C statue, with a 17C gilded coat, represents Notre-Dame-la-Blanche, venerated since the 8C. Near the main altar is a 16C painting on wood of the **entombment** (influence from the Champagne region), with the figures dressed from that era.

EXCURSIONS
Fleurey-lès-Faverney
🕑 *4.5km/3mi S.*
Sadly repainted, the **retable** (1758) in the church is by the Deschamps brothers. However, notice the fine detail and movement in the superb wood carvings.

Amance
🕑 *6km/4mi NW by D 434.*
There are some particularly beautiful Renaissance houses in the main street of this village, especially the **Maison Bûcheron** (the wood-cutter's house).

Conflans-sur-Lanterne
🕑 *11km/6.5mi NE by D 28.*
Once attached to Lorraine, Conflans has benefited from its border position. The 14–18C **Église Saint-Maurice** (🕑*open Easter–1 Nov 9am–6pm by request from M. Gradnemange or the town hall; ☎03 84 49 80 03)* has an altarpiece in the chancel that is decorated with double cabled columns. The inverted columns, some with garlands of flowers or fruits, symbolize a prayer request that rises to God and the granting of that request returning back down.

Passavant-la-Rochère

and Jonvelle

This small village is best known for its centuries-old glassworks, which continues to pass down the know-how of the master glassblowers. On the edge of huge forests stretching northwards, Passavant is at the extreme north of the Haute-Saône.

EXPLORE

Verrerie et cristallerie de La Rochère★

Open for workshop visits 2 Apr–20 Jul and 20 Aug–29 Sept 10am–noon and 2.30–5.30pm; Oct afternoons only, daily except Sun. Exhibition shop open 31 Mar–30 Sept 10am–noon and 2.30–6pm; Sun and Oct 2.30–6pm; 24 Nov–31 Dec daily except 25–26 Dec 2–5.30pm. ℘03 84 78 61 13. www.larochere.com.

The La Rochère glass and crystal factory in Passavant was founded in 1475, making it the oldest glassworks still in operation in France. Glassblowing developed in this area in the 15C, because all the necessary raw materials were available here: silica as the main vitrifying substance, potassium from the ash of the local ferns as the melting agent, and wood to provide the heat.

Run by the same family since 1858, the factory diversified into making a speciality of glass tiles, at the same time as producing machine-blown glass and crystal objects made using traditional methods.

You can visit the **master glassblowers' workshops** and watch the production stages of hand-made and blown glass. An exhibition and video retraces the history of the technique of glass making and explains how it is made today at the La Rochère factory.

Behind the workshops, visit the **caveau Saint-Valbert**, which has a magnificent 17C vaulted room with a fine collection of old furniture and tapestries from Aubusson. In the same building, don't miss the **contemporary art gallery**

- **Population:** 725
- **Michelin Map:** 314 G5.
- **Location:** Ideally situated close to forests and waterways, Passavent is 42km/26mi NW of Luxeuil-les-Bains by N57, then D 64 towards Magnoncourt, D 417 west and D7 north towards Demangeville.
- **Don't Miss:** The amazing work of the master glassblowers of La Rochère; Gallo-Roman thermal baths in Jonvelle and the remains of its mosaic paving.
- **Timing:** Allow 2–3hrs to visit the glassblowers' workshops, have a look at the shop and the contemporary art gallery, and to explore the Japanese garden.
- **Kids:** The magic of traditional glassblowing.

that includes a collection of engraved glass lamps made at La Rochère. Afterwards you can relax in the very pleasant **Japonese Gardens** nearby.

EXCURSION

Jonvelle

12km/7.5mi SW. From Passavant, take D 417 and follow right for 7km/4.5mi.

The interesting church in this old country town has been restored repeatedly. The late 13C chancel has shimmering stained glass windows made in 1868 and an elegant gilded altar from 17C.

You can visit the **thermal baths** (*open Jul–Aug daily except Tue 2–6pm; Apr–Jun and Sept–Oct Sun 2–6pm; 2.50 €; ℘03 84 92 54 37*) west of the town (*1 300m/1 422 yd*) by taking the road in front of the cemetery. Renovated in 1968, a 2C Gallo-Roman villa houses the baths that have brick foundations one of them retains its original, elegant **mosaic paving**. Next door in a barn is a **museum** of old agricultural machinery and tools.

Villersexel
and around

Situated between the plateau and the confluence of the rivers Ognon and Scey, Villersexel was originally known for its dramatic castle. Today the village has made the most of its geographic position in the heart of the Ognon river valley to offer a wide range of tourist activities.

CHÂTEAU DE VILLERSEXEL

Guided tours with 2 days advanced notice mid-Apr–mid-Oct daily except Mon 3.30pm. 7 € (free for under 10s). 03 84 20 51 53. www.villersexel.com.

The current castle (1890) was built on the site of the ruins of a previous building that was destroyed in the battle of Villersexel in 1871. It used contemporary techniques (metallic framework by **Gustave Eiffel** in the dining room), in the style of Louis XIII (southern façade by **Garnier**).

The interior includes 19C furniture and various antiques. Especially notable are the 18C **Gobelins tapestries** and the beautiful caisson ceiling in the main sitting room. There is also an exceptional library containing more than 20 000 books. Finally, the stables were designed by **Claude-Nicolas Ledoux** (*see ARC-ET-SENANS*).

EXCURSIONS
Oricort

▶ *9km/5.5mi NW by D 486, then D 123.*

This **medieval castle**★ (*open Mar–mid-Nov daily except Tue 10am–noon, 2–7pm; 03 84 78 74 35; www.oricourt.com*) is a rare, authentic example of 12C military construction, still showing its high walls that have resisted countless battles. A double-walled fortress, you can still see the two courtyards, one of which includes a 22m/72ft-deep well, a large dining room, a baker and cellars. These, as well as the large pigeon house, illustrate the importance of Oricourt, whose owner was the chancellor of Burgundy, **Nicolas Rolin**, painted by Van Eyck.

▶ **Population:** 1 423
Michelin Map: 314 G7.
Location: Villersexel is 40km/25mi W of Montbéliard and 26km/16mi SE of Vesoul.
Don't Miss: The castle of Villersexel, including the Gobelins tapestries and its amazing library; the white stone buildings of Rougemont.
Timing: To make the most of the village and the area, allow at least a day.
Kids: The Rougement paleontology museum including the collections of fossils (mammoths, lions and bears).

Val de Bonnal

▶ *11km/7mi to SW.*

A leisure area where the lakes have been created on former sand quarries and are restricted to swimming and fishing. Walking paths and picnic places are marked, and there is a bird sanctuary.

Rougemont

▶ *12km/7.5mi SW by D 486.*

Today, the 15C **Cordeliers monastery** dominates this former fortified town. Note the white stone buildings in the lower town (town hall, wash house etc.) built 1830–50. The Musée de Paléontologie (*carrefour des Halles; visits on demand; 03 81 86 98 84*) includes prehistoric relics discovered locally including a vast collection of ammonites and bones and the largest "**septaria**"★ (cracks in rocks, formed from fossils on the sea floor) ever found in France.

Montbozon

▶ *20km/12mi SW by D 486, D 9 and D 49.*

This village is known for its sponge biscuits, made since the time of Louis XVI. You will discover some fine houses from 16–18C here as well as a semi-circular **fountain** from Louis Moreau, attached to the wall of the 18C castle's park.

Between Burgundy and Alsace, in the northernmost part of the Franche-Comté, this region includes parts of four departments: Doubs, Haut-Rhin, Haute-Saône, Vosges and all of the small Territoire de Belfort. From the top of the southern Vosges peaks of Ballon d'Alsace and Ballon de Servance, you can see as far as Germany's Black Forest, and even, on a clear day, to Mont Blanc in the Alps. It should come as no surprise that settlements in this region have been fought over bitterly through the centuries. The citadel at Belfort bears witness to the struggles, but a visit to the city and its environs shows a cultural legacy that has benefited greatly from often competing influences.

The Territoire de Belfort

France's 90th department, created in 1922 and the smallest after the Paris departments, the Territoire de Belfort was originally designated in 1871 after the Franco-Prussian war as a unique independent territory that was politically part of France. Colonel Denfert-Rochereau had held on to the fortified town of Belfort so spectacularly in the face of the German invasion that, even though the French had to give up Alsace and most of Lorraine to the Germans, they were allowed to retain French-speaking Belfort and its surroundings. The French badly wanted the Belfort citadel as their military stronghold, standing in line with the Vosges mountains. When France finally regained Alsace after World War I, it was discussed whether to incorporate Belfort into the Haut-Rhin department, but an agreement was reached that it remain separate, retaining the name of the old territory. In the modern era, when the French political regions were created, it might have been more logical to include the Territoire de Belfort in the Alsace region, but it ended up as part of Franche-Comté.

Grand designs: industrial and cultural

In the 18C–20C this region became home to a large and varied number of daring designs. Bartholdi, creator of the Statue of Liberty, conceived the huge Belfort lion sculpture, inspired by his travels in Egypt as a young man. Coincidentally, a lion was chosen by the Peugeot family, who hailed from near Montbéliard, as a symbol for their manufacturing company in the mid-19C. At the time they made a variety of products, most

Highlights

1 One hundred years of car-making at the **Peugeot museum** (p319)

2 Bartholdi's magnificent **Belfort lion** below the Citadel (p322)

3 Panorama from the Vosges summit **Ballon d'Alsace** (p326)

4 Le Corbusier's contemporary chapel at **Ronchamp** (p330)

5 A sip of **Fougerolles kirsch** or a taste of cherry jam (p332)

successfully coffee and pepper mills, but within fifty years they had built one of the first cars in France, having already become a leading name in bicycle manufacturing. Today, as Peugeot Citroën SA, the company is the second biggest European car manufacturer. Its largest factory is at Sochaux on the edge of Montbéliard, home also to its fascinating museum. Peugeot is just one of several firms that have made the region of Montbéliard, Belfort and their surroundings the principal industrial area of Franche-Comté, whose geographic position and the innovative ideas of its residents have made it an important centre of manufacturing and research and development.

Notable architecture ranges from the Belfort citadel, originally designed by Vauban, to the breathtaking modern chapel Notre-Dame-du-Haut by Le Corbusier. Built in the 1950s on the edge of a mining town in the Vosges foothills, the chapel's design and location has made Le Corbusier's concrete creation into a place of pilgrimage and spirituality that attracts visitors from around the world.

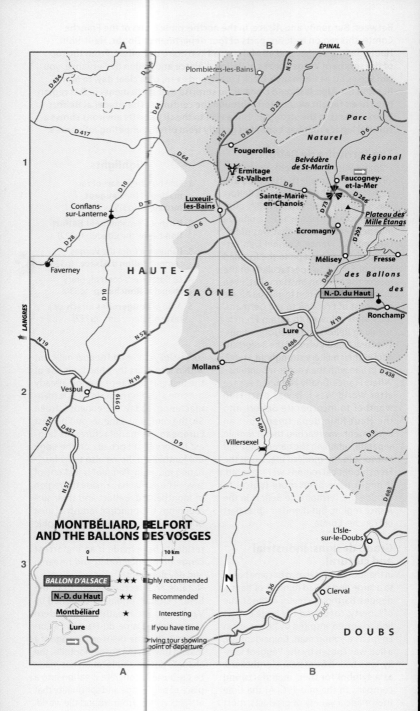

ÉPINAL

Plombières-les-Bains

Parc

Naturel

1

Fougerolles

Régional

Belvédère
de St-Martin

Ermitage
St-Valbert

Faucogney-
et-la-Mer

Conflans-
sur-Lanterne

Luxeuil-
les-Bains

Sainte-Marie-
en-Chanois

Plateau des
Mille Étangs

Écromagny

Faverney

Mélisey

Fresse

HAUTE-

SAÔNE

des Ballons

N.-D. du Haut

des

LANGRES

Ronchamp

Lure

Mollans

Vesoul

Villersexel

L'Isle-
sur-le-Doubs

MONTBÉLIARD, BELFORT
AND THE BALLONS DES VOSGES

0   10 km

N

Clerval

Doubs

D O U B S

BALLON D'ALSACE	★★★	Highly recommended
N.-D. du Haut	★★	Recommended
Montbéliard	★	Interesting
Lure		If you have time
		Driving tour showing point of departure

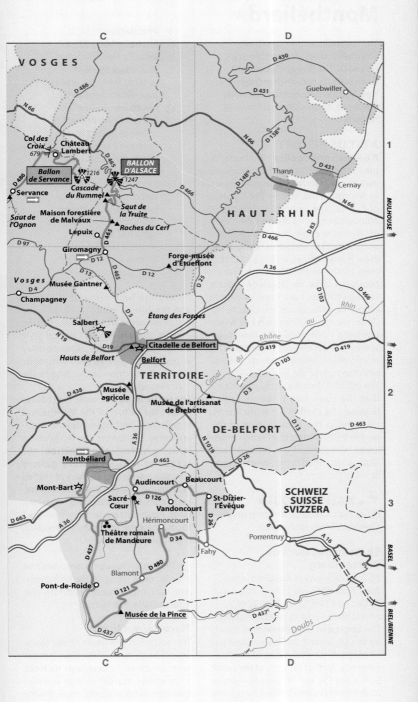

VOSGES

Guebwiller

D 430

D 431

D 486

N 66

Col des
Croix
679

Château-
Lambert

BALLON
D'ALSACE
1247

Ballon
de Servance

1216

Servance

Cascade
du Rummel

Saut de
la Truite

Saut de
l'Ognon

Maison forestière
de Malvaux

Roches du Cerf

Lépuix

Giromagny

Forge-musée
d'Étueffont

Vosges

D 4

Musée Gantner

Champagney

Salbert

Étang des Forges

N 19

D 19

Citadelle de Belfort

Hauts de Belfort

Belfort

TERRITOIRE-

D 438

Musée
agricole

Musée de l'artisanat
de Brebotte

DE-BELFORT

Montbéliard

D 463

Mont-Bart

Audincourt

Beaucourt

Sacré-
Cœur

D 126

St-Dizier-
l'Évêque

D 663

A 36

Vandoncourt

Hérimoncourt

Théâtre romain
de Mandeure

D 437

D 34

Fahy

Blamont

D 480

Pont-de-Roide

D 121

Musée de la Pince

D 437

HAUT-RHIN

Thann

Cernay

N 66

D 431

D 83

D 466

D 466

D 148bis

D 466

D 25

D 12

D 5

D 13

D 12

D 465

D 486

D 97

D 466

D 103

Rhin

du

Rhône

du

D 466

D 419

D 419

D 419

D 103

Canal

du

D 3

D 13

D 463

N 1019

D 26

SCHWEIZ
SUISSE
SVIZZERA

Porrentruy

A 16

D 437

Doubs

MULHOUSE

BASEL

BASEL

BIEL/BIENNE

N 66

D 138bis

C

D

1

2

3

315

Montbéliard★

The majestic castle high above Montbéliard testifies to this city's rich past. The flower-decked old town with its colourful architecture betrays a distinctly Germanic influence, the result of its unusual history.

A BIT OF HISTORY

A German principality – For four centuries the principality of Montbéliard was a small German enclave, known as Mömpelgard, within the borders of France. The princes and dukes of Württemberg, who divided their time between the castle here and their palaces at Stuttgart and later Ludwigsburg, drew many German artists and craftsmen to the town. Although French continued to be the language spoken, German influence was soon evident in economic, cultural and religious fields. Under the rule of **Friedrich I of Württemberg** (1581–1608), the town blossomed into an elegant Protestant city worthy of its princely residents, imbued with the style of the Renaissance.

The influx of Huguenot refugees meant that the town had to be extended beyond the medieval fortifications, resulting in the construction of the Neuve Ville. During the French Revolution, Montbéliard was besieged and finally succumbed to the French Republic on 10 October 1793.

✿ WALKING TOUR★

✿ See Plan II. Walk up the steep rue du Château leading to the castle.

Château des Ducs de Wurtemberg

🕐Open daily except Tue 10am–noon, 2pm–6pm. 🕐Closed 1 Jan, 1 May, 1 Nov, 25 Dec. ☞4.50€. ✆03 81 99 22 61. www.chateau-montbeliard.net/musee.

The **Logis des Gentilhommes** stands on the Esplanade du Château and has an elegant scrolled gable of Swabian influence. All that remains of the castle built in the 15C and 16C are two massive round towers surmounted by lantern turrets, the Tour Henriette (1422–24) and the Tour Frédéric (1575–95). The rest of the castle was demolished in the mid-18C to make way for Classical-style buildings. A beautiful contemporary wrought-iron gate by Jean Messagier closes off the doorway leading to the Tour Henriette.

The **castle museum** inside the château relates the history of the Montbéliard region from prehistoric days to modern times. The former vaulted kitchens house a **historical exhibition**; the ♟♟**Cuvier natural history gallery** contains interesting displays of stuffed local fauna; you can even listen to animals' cries such as lynx and numerous birds. An important section is devoted to paleontology, presented in a modern, and educational manner.

▶ Walk down rue du Château and turn left onto rue A.-Thomas, then left again onto rue Cuvier to rue de l'Hôtel-de-Ville leading to place St-Martin.

Place Saint-Martin

This square at the heart of old Montbéliard hosts most of the town's major events, such as the **Lumières de Noël**, a Christmas market in true German tradition (with pretzels, mulled wine

---

▶ **Population:** 113 059
🕐 **Michelin Map:** 321: K-1.
🛈 **Info:** 1 r. Henri-Mouhot, 25200 Montbéliard.
  ✆03 81 94 45 60. www.ot-pays-de-montbeliard.fr.
◐ **Location:** Montbeliard lies just north of the A36 between Belfort and Besançon, along the northernmost curve of the Doubs River. The historic town, where many shops and restaurants may be found, is mostly closed to vehicles. The industrial suburb of Sochaux, home to the Peugeot factory, is to the east.

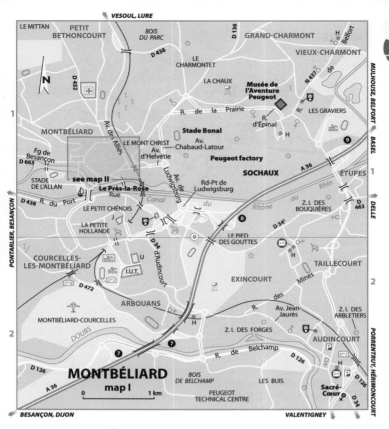

and Christmas trees (🕭see *Calendar of Events*). Many of the city's most important monuments are to be found on this square.

Musée d'Art et d'Histoire
🕭*Same opening times as château.*
👛*2€.* ✆*03 81 99 24 93.*
Built by the architect Philippe de la Guépière, the Hôtel Beurnier-Rossel is a typical 18C town mansion. Beurnier-Rossel's private rooms are especially characteristic of the era. Family portraits and period furnishings give them warmth: note the wood inlays by local craftsman Couleru, the ceramic stove by Jacob Frey and the encyclopaedic library.

The two upper floors are devoted to the history of the town and the region. The collections are varied: popular illustrations by the Deckherr brothers, religious items from Lutheran churches, old toys and music boxes.

Temple Saint-Martin★
🕭*Open 25 Nov–24 Dec 4.30–7pm, weekends 2–7pm.*

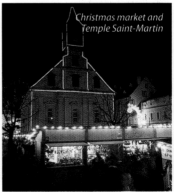

Christmas market and Temple Saint-Martin

M. Paygnard/MICHELIN

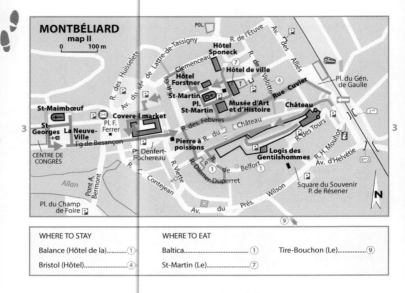

This is the oldest Protestant church in France (built between 1601 and 1607). The architecture of the façade draws its inspiration from the Tuscan Renaissance. The inside would be quite plain were it not for the original polychrome decoration, only rediscovered recently, on the mid-18C **organ** and the gallery.

Hôtel de Ville

The elegant pink-sandstone town hall was built from 1776 to 1778. In front stands a commemorative **statue of Cuvier** by David d'Angers.

Hôtel Sponeck

Located near the town hall, this 18C mansion is now the home of **L'Allan**, the national theatre of Montbéliard.

Georges Cuvier

Born in Montbéliard on 23 August 1769 Baron Georges Cuvier is honoured with a statue and a museum bearing his name. A gifted student, from 1794 he taught anatomy to college students. He was elected to the Académie Française in 1818, and is considered to be the inventor of comparative anatomy and of palaeontology.

Hôtel Forstner

This town house (probably from the late 16C) now houses the Banque de France. The building is named after its former occupant, the Chancellor of Friedrich I of Württemberg. The stately Renaissance façade features four storeys of superposed columns.

◗ *Walk around the right-hand side of the Temple and turn right into the Passage des Fleur. Turn left onto rue Georges-Clemenceau and follow to the left. Turn right to reach the covered market.*

Covered Market

The 16C–17C **halles** has a distinctive roof and long façades with large windows with double mullions. The enormous building was the meeting hall for the town council prior to 1793; it was then used as a store for the town's grain, as a market and as a customs post.

In place Denfert-Rochereau, a 15C flagstone can be seen, known here as the **pierre à poissons**; the stone was used by fishmongers on market day. In 1524, Swiss reformer Guillaume Farel is said to have used it as a pulpit.

◐ *Walk to place F.-Ferrer and continue along faubourg de Besançon to the Temple St-Georges.*

You are now in the suburb known as the **Neuve Ville**. Friedrich I commissioned Schickhardt to build this suburb in 1598, to accommodate the waves of Huguenot refugees fleeing France.

Temple Saint-Georges
The church was built between 1674 and 1676 when the Temple Saint-Martin was no longer deemed large enough; it is now a conference centre.

Église St-Maimbœuf
The lofty mid-19C church with its exaggerated ornamentation offers a physical reminder of the Roman Catholic church's reconquest of this bastion of Lutheranism after Montbéliard was reclaimed by France. The interior of St-Maimbœuf is lavish: monumental tribune with Corinthian columns, extravagant wooden stucco ornamentation, Baroque style altarpieces and so on.

◐ *Instead of returning to the town centre, return to place Ferrer, follow rue Ch.-Lalance, walk across the Pont A.-Bermont and follow the Allan to a flight of steps leading down.*

▲▲ Pavillon des Sciences
◷*Open Jul–Aug Mon–Fri 10am–7pm, Sat–Sun 2–7pm. Rest of the year times vary.* ◷*Closed Sept, 25 Dec, 1 May.* ◉*4.50€ (children 3€).* ⌨ ℘*03 81 97 18 21. www.pavillon-sciences.com.*
This centre offers the young and not so young a good introduction to scientific and technical culture by means of various activities and demonstrations.

SOCHAUX
The first Peugeot car – In the 18C, Jean-Pierre Peugeot was a weaver in Hérimoncourt. When his two oldest sons, Jean-Pierre and Jean-Frédéric, founded a steelworks in the mill at Sous-Cratet in 1810, no one dreamed that this small enterprise would be a huge international industrial concern by the 20C. Soon more factories were founded at Terre-Blanche, in the Gland Valley, Valentigney and Pont-de-Roide, producing laminated steel, saw blades, tools, domestic appliances and so on, while a factory in the old mill at Beaulieu turned out various types of velocipede and later bicycles. Finally, in 1891, Peugeot produced its first automobile with a combustion engine, called the Vis-à-Vis (face-to-face) because its passengers had to sit facing one another. Since then more than 600 different models of cars have been produced.

▲▲ Musée de l'Aventure Peugeot★★
◷*Open year round daily 10am–6pm.* ◷*Closed 1 Jan and 25 Dec.* ◉*7€ (children 10–18, 3.50€, under 10s free).* ⌨ ℘*03 81 99 42 03. www.musee-peugeot.com.*
The museum inaugurated a large extension in 2010 to celebrate the 200 years of the Peugeot company. Presented in a theatrical manner, there are displays of the output of the Peugeot company over the years through tools, coffee grinders, bicycles, and of course, cars. The latter are exhibited in an area made to look like an old *brasserie*, where you can start by admiring the Double Phaéton Type 81B 1906, the Bébé designed in 1911 by Ettore Bugatti and so on through the ages. Before you reach the gift shop, you will see the 406 from the film *Taxi*, next to the 206 model and its famous advertisement filmed in India. You can even try out the race simulator to see what it's like to be a racing driver.

Tour of the Peugeot factories
◌*Guided tours (2hrs 30min) Mon–Fri 8.30am by appointment.* ◷*Closed in Aug and the last week of Dec.* ℘*03 81 33 27 46.*
Sochaux is the largest Peugeot car production centre making the Peugeot 308, 3008 and 5008 models. The diversion of the Allan river has allowed the factory to expand greatly, and to adopt optimal, modern time-saving processes.

ADDRESSES

🛏️ STAY

⊜⊜ **Hôtel Bristol** – *2 r. Velotte.* *℘03 81 94 43 17. www.hotel-bristol-montbeliard.com. Closed 31 Jul–22 Aug.* 🅿 *48 rooms.* ⌑ *7.50 €.* This 1930s hotel is located near the château. The guest rooms facing the rear are relatively quiet, and there's a nice wine bar.

⊜⊜⊜ **Hôtel de la Balance** – *40 r. de Belfort. ℘03 81 96 77 41. www.hotel-la-balance.fr.* 🅿 ♿ *45 rooms.* ⌑ *9. Restaurant* ⊜⊜. This former 16C residence at the foot of the château has been converted into a charming hotel. The comfortable bedrooms are at the top of a splendid staircase carved in wood. The dining room, with its parquet flooring and wood panelling, is warm and inviting.

🍴 EAT

⊜⊜ **Le Tire-Bouchon** – *Le Pied des Gouttes. www.hotelrelaisvert.net. Closed 23 Dec–3 Jan. 42 rooms* ⊜⊜. Located in the middle of a shopping centre, this hotel has some small rooms around the patio, and larger ones in a new wing. The dining room is brightened up by greenery and paintings.

⊜⊜ **Baltica** – *8 r. de Belfort. ℘03 81 91 43 75. Closed Sun, Mon and Aug.* Voyage to the Baltic fjords without ever leaving Montbéliard via the Scandinavian specialities served here. Try the Baltica (marinated herring with potatoes) or the Royal Stockholm (three types of salmon with potatoes), and don't forget to stop in the shop for salmon or sturgeon to take home.

⊜⊜⊜ **Le St-Martin** – *1 r. du Gén. -Leclerc. ℘03 81 91 18 37. www.le-saint-martin.fr. Closed 13–20 Feb, 1–23 Aug, weekends.* This lovely old house with stone walls has three intimate, cosy dining rooms. The meals are traditional, based on what's in season with an emphasis on fish.

☕ TAKING A BREAK

La Paix – *12 r. des Febvres. ℘03 81 91 03 62. Open 7.30am–11pm. Closed Sun afternoon and Mon morning.* This small, unpretentious café offers regular Saturday evening events: from philosophical discussions to jazz concerts.

Belfort★

Belfort is in a strategic position on the River Savoureuse and by the 30km/19mi Belfort Gap which provides a natural passage between the two great valleys of the Rhine and the Rhône. Its main attraction is the imposing citadel built by Vauban on the east bank of the Savoureuse.

A BIT OF HISTORY

An invasion route – The Belfort Gap has drawn successive waves of invaders: Celts, Germanic tribes and soldiers of the Holy Roman Empire among them. The French finally conquered it in 1638, and Louis XIV ordered Vauban to make Belfort impregnable. The resulting fortified town is the great military engineer's masterpiece.

▶ **Population:** 50 863
🔵 **Michelin Map:** 314: J-7.
📄 **Info:** 2 bis r. Clemenceau, 90000 Belfort. ℘03 84 55 90 90. www.ot-belfort.fr.
⊙ **Location:** Treat yourself to an intriguing view of Belfort and its citadel by arriving via the Porte de Brisach. The historic town, boutiques, restaurants and cafés are east of the river, between it and the citadel.

The battles continue – During the 1870 Franco-Prussian War, 40 000 German troops besieged the town for several months without success. The

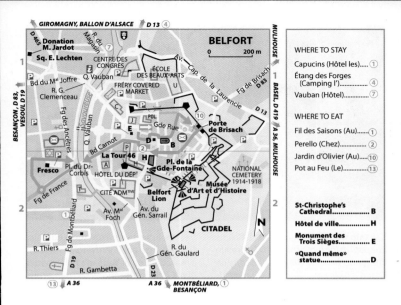

BELFORT

0   200 m

WHERE TO STAY

Capucins (Hôtel les).....	①
Étang des Forges (Camping l')................	④
Vauban (Hôtel)...............	⑦

WHERE TO EAT

Fil des Saisons (Au)........	①
Perello (Chez)................	②
Jardin d'Olivier (Au).....	⑩
Pot au Feu (Le)..............	⑬

St-Christophe's Cathedral...................	B
Hôtel de ville...............	H
Monument des Trois Sièges................	E
«Quand même» statue........................	D

town saw more action in November 1944, as the French army advanced towards the Rhine. Belfort was finally liberated from the Germans on 22 November after fierce street fighting.

Records – The years 1926 and 1990 are dates that reflect the main thrust of Belfort's industrial activity in the 20C. In 1926, the first electric train was produced in the Belfort workshops of the Société Alsacienne de Constructions Mécaniques; in 1990, the high-speed train TGV-Atlantique, built in Belfort (GEC-Alsthom), broke the world rail speed record reaching 515.3kph/320mph.

CITADEL★★

Open Apr–Jun and Sept 10am–6pm daily except Tue; July-Aug daily 10am–8pm. 7 € (children 4 €) inclusive ticket. 03 84 22 84 22. www.citadelle-belfort.fr.
A Key Position – Vauban began his masterpiece in 1687, surrounding the existing fortress and town with several pentagonal fortified walls anchored to the rocky cliff on which the buildings stood.

The work took about 20 years, but the fortifications would play their part in the town's history for several centuries. Modifications in the 19C improved the defence system even more.

Follow the circuit, **La Citadelle de la liberté** to explore the moats and bastions with illustrated information panels and an audioguide. A little train (departs pl. d'Armes) can take you up the Citadel.
Fort terrace – This public terrace gives an excellent view point, from which you will be able to understand the geographical situation of the fortress as well as its system of defence.

The **panorama**★★ reveals far away to the south, the Jura mountains; to the west the old town and the Fort du Salbert; to the north the southern Vosges with several peaks including the Ballon d'Alsace visible; to the east the fortress' curtain walls and the Belfort Gap.

You can make out the outline of the **Large basement**, a covered moat from the reign of Louis XV, which was used to provide shelter during attacks. Further east is the moat known as the **Grand Couronné**, with its bastions, the moat round the intermediate curtain wall (3rd moat) and that round the outer curtain wall (4th moat).

At the foot of the barracks to the east, the **cour d'honneur** (main courtyard) is surrounded by the Haxo casemates, which have been converted into art galleries. One of them houses the 1 000-year-old **well** with a depth of 67m/220ft.

Belfort Lion

© CRT Franche-Comté/Maison du Tourisme de Belfort

Curtain walls (*audioguide 1hr;* follow *the path at the foot of the fortress through the tunnel beneath the Lion and carry on along it until you get to the 4th moat*) – Note the impressive proportions of the moats and the **glacis**, a vast area of bare land which slopes gently away. Walking along the 4th or 3rd moats is a good way to see the defences in detail. The walk ends at the **Tour des Bourgeois**, the old tower from the medieval curtain wall demolished by Vauban.

The varied exhibits at the **Musée d'Art et d'Histoire** (*open July–Aug 10am–6pm; Apr–Jun and Sept 10am–noon, 2–6pm; rest of the year daily except Tue 10am–noon, 2–5pm; closed 1 Jan, 1 Nov, 25 Dec; 2.95€ (children* free) include items from the Neolithic, Gallo-Roman and Merovingian periods, a reproduction of Vauban's relief model of his 1987 fortifications and numerous military artefacts. A separate wing contains a collection of paintings, engravings, sculptures and photographs.

Belfort Lion★★

The great beast (22m/72ft long and 11m/36ft high), inspired by statues of the Egyptian Pharos and carved from red Vosges sandstone, symbolises the spirit and strength of Belfort's defenders in 1870. The work of **Frédéric Bartholdi**, it was erected piece by piece and completed in 1880. A path leads from the **viewing platform** (*open Jun–Sept 9am–7pm; Apr–May 10am–noon, 2–7pm; Oct–Mar 10am–noon, 2–5pm; closed 1 Jan, 1 Nov, 25 Dec; 0.90€; 03 84 55 90 30*) at the base of the Lion to the memorial. The Lion is even more awe-inspiring when it is floodlit at night.

WALKING TOUR

Old Town★

Follow the route marked on the map.
Following extensive restoration, it is only in the past decade that the once austere garrison town has come to life. The colourful façades of the houses, with pale stone decorations, lend a friendly atmosphere to the streets and squares. Particularly charming examples are to be found in place de l'Arsenal, place de la Grande-Fontaine, Grande Rue and place de la Petite-Fontaine.

Frédéric Auguste Bartholdi (1834–1904)

This sculptor was born in Colmar and showed his artistic prowess from an early age. He won a competition held by his home town in 1856 to find someone to execute a memorial statue of General Rapp. His travels in Egypt and the Far East affected his later work. After the Franco-Prussian war in 1870, Bartholdi sculpted a lot of patriotic monuments, the most famous of which are the **Belfort Lion** and the **Statue of Liberty** (1886) at the entrance to the port of New York.

St-Christophe's Cathedral
The church, built of red sandstone, has an 18C Classical façade. A frieze of angels' heads in relief runs all around the nave. The beautiful **gilded wrought-iron grille** enclosing the choir is similar to the railings by Jean Lamour in place Stanislas in Nancy. Note in the transept paintings by the Belfort painter G Dauphin; an *Entombment of Christ (on the right)* and *The Ecstasy of St François-Xavier (on the left)*. The 18C **organ**★, by Valtrin, has a beautifully carved and gilded wooden case.

Porte de Brisach★
This gateway, constructed in 1687, has been preserved in its original style. It features a pilastered façade decorated with the Bourbon coat of arms and, on the pediment, those of Louis XIV: the sun surmounted by the famous motto *Nec pluribus impar* ("not unequal to many"). Cross the road to admire it properly.

Porte de Brisach

G. Magnin-MICHELIN

Place de la Grande-Fontaine
The square owes its name to the successive fountains which have decorated it; the current one dates from 1860.

Hôtel de Ville
🕐*Open Mon–Fri 8.30am–6pm, Sat 8.30am–noon.* ℘*03 84 54 24 24. www.mairie-belfort.fr.*
The town hall was built in the Classical style. The beautiful Salle Kléber on the ground floor is a good example of late-18C French art (Rococo style).
There are paintings of Belfort's history in the main hall *(Salle d'honneur)* on the first floor.

Monument des Trois Sièges
This work by Bartholdi shows France and the city of Belfort with three defenders (Legrand in 1814, Lecourbe in 1815 and Denfert-Rochereau in 1870).

ADDITIONAL SIGHT
Donation Maurice Jardot★
🕐*Open July-Aug 10am–6pm; Apr–May and Sept 10am–noon, 2–6pm. Rest of the year 10am–noon, 2–5pm.* 🕐*Closed Tue, 1 Jan, 1 Nov, 25 Dec.* ⬤*3.95€ (children free).* ♿ ℘*03 84 55 90 90.*
In 1997, Maurice Jardot bequeathed 110 paintings by modern artists to the city. The exceptionally fine collection includes little-known works by Picasso, Braque and, above all, Léger.

EXCURSIONS
Fort du Salbert
▷ *8km/5mi NW on D 4.*
A winding forest road leads to the fort, at an altitude of 647m/2 123ft.
The vast terrace (200m/220yd to the left – viewing table) gives a marvellous **panorama**★★ over Belfort, the Swiss Alps, Ballon d'Alsace and surrounding mountains.

Étang des Forges
Park near the marina.
🏃 There is a nature trail round the lake. Information boards describe the flora and fauna found in this area (the little bittern, the smallest heron in Europe, the crested grebe and the coot).

Forge-Musée d'Etueffont
▷ *15km/9.3mi NE on N 83; then D 12.*
🕐*Open Easter to 1 Nov.* ☞*Guided tours (1hr 30min–2hrs) daily except Tue 2–6pm.* ⬤*4€ (under 13s free).* ℘*03 84 54 60 41.*
This small museum offers a glimpse at the way of life and the work of four generations of blacksmiths from 1844 and 1975. Working tools are on display.

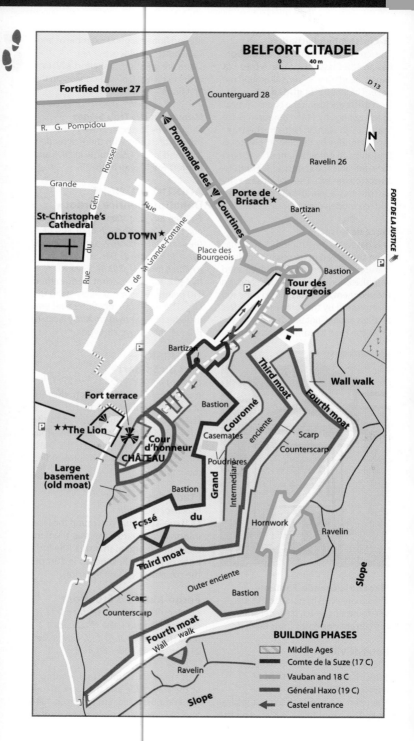

BELFORT CITADEL

0 — 40 m

Fortified tower 27

Counterguard 28

D 13

N

R. G. Pompidou

Ravelin 26

Roussel

Rue

du

Gén.

Grande

St-Christophe's Cathedral

Porte de Brisach ★

Bartizan

OLD TOWN ★

R. de la Grande-Fontaine

Place des Bourgeois

Bastion

Tour des Bourgeois

FORT DE LA JUSTICE

P

Bartizan

Wall walk

Third moat

Fourth moat

Fort terrace

Bastion

Couronné

★★ The Lion

Cour d'honneur
CHÂTEAU

Casemates

enciente

Scarp

Counterscarp

P

Large basement (old moat)

Poudrières

Bastion

Grand

Intermediary

du

Hornwork

Ravelin

Fossé

Third moat

Outer enciente

Bastion

Slope

Scarp

Counterscarp

Fourth moat

Wall walk

Ravelin

Slope

BUILDING PHASES

- Middle Ages
- Comte de la Suze (17 C)
- Vauban and 18 C
- Général Haxo (19 C)
- ← Castel entrance

ADDRESSES

🛏 STAY

🛏 **Camping L'Étang des Forges** – *1.5km/1mi N of Belfort by D 13, rte d'Offremont and R on r. Béthouart. ℘03 84 22 54 92. www.camping-belfort.com. Open Apr–Sept. 90 sites. Reservations recommended.* Ideally situated close to the town centre and by a lake and nature reserve, this campsite offers good facilities including a shop, a bar and games for children. Well-placed too for hiking, climbing, sailing and so on.

🛏 **Hôtel Les Capucins** – *20 fg Montbéliard. ℘03 84 28 04 60. www.capucins-hotel.com. 35 rooms. ⊐ 8 €. Restaurant 🛏.* The small but welcoming rooms are decorated with quilts and bright colours; rooms on the top floor are in the eves. Traditional food is offered in the two dining rooms.

🛏 **Hôtel Vauban** – *4 r. Magasin. ℘03 84 21 59 37. www.hotel-vauban.com. Closed Christmas holidays, 2 weeks in Feb and Sun eve. 14 rooms. ⊐ 8.50 €.* You will feel at home staying in this small family hotel, where the rooms have pictures painted by local artists. Relax in the pretty garden by the Savoureuse.

🍴 EAT

🍴 **Food tips** – The Belfort area offers numerous local specialities including: **L'Épaule du Ballon**: a lamb dish served with blueberries; **Le Belflore**: raspberry gâteau topped with almond-flavoured meringue; **Les Crottes du Lion**: flavoured chocolate truffles (hazelnuts, orange rind, nougat etc.).

🍴 **Au Jardin d'Olivier** – *54 r. du Gén.-Leclerc, 90600 Grandvillars. ℘03 84 27 76 03. Closed Sat lunch, Sun eve and Mon.* This auberge has recently been given a lick of paint with white walls and exposed beams in mauve. The young chef serves well-presented, contemporary cuisine.

🍴 **Au Fil des Saisons** – *3 r. de la Libération, 25600 Étupes. 18km/11mi S of Belfort by A 36 and D 61. ℘03 81 94 17 12. www.aufildessaisons.eu. Closed 4–24 Aug, 22 Dec–4 Jan, Sat lunch, Sun, Mon.* The food in this family restaurant is very much focused on seasonal produce, and the menu includes a good range of fish dishes. The dining room has been nicely modernised.

🍴 **Le Pot au Feu** – *27 bis Grand'rue. ℘03 84 28 57 84. Closed 1–20 Aug, 1–12 Jan, Sat and Sun lunch and Sun.* The chef in this bistro in a stone-walled cellar likes to prepare dishes from his childhood and regional cuisine. The blackboard shows daily specials from the market.

🍴 **Le Pot d'Étain** – *4 av. de la République, 90400 Danjoutin. 3km/1.8mi S of Belfort. ℘03 84 28 31 95. www.lepot detain90.fr. Closed 28 Jun–12 Jul, 1–9 Nov, 22 Feb–2 Mar, Sat lunch, Sun eve and Mon.* 🖸. New ownership and a new chef are providing confident cooking here. There are two rooms, the first offering *table d'hôtes* and the second is a more conventional dining area.

🍴 **Chez Perello** – *4 r. Porte-de-France. ℘03 84 21 37 34. www.bouchon-lyonnais-chez-perello.fr. Closed Sun, Mon.* This restaurant opened in 2008 in the oldest grocer's shop in France and is named in homage to the original grocer, Michel Perello, a local character. It's a superb setting for simple Lyonnais bistro food. There is a wine bar upstairs on Friday and Saturday evenings.

🚃 TAKING A BREAK

Le Piano-Bar – *23 fg de France. ℘03 84 28 93 35. Open Thu–Sun 8.30pm–1am.* This is undoubtedly the trendiest bar in town. Customers of all ages flock to this vaulted cellar in the town centre. Themed evenings offer anything from karaoke to jazz.

🛍 SHOPPING

Marché aux Puces – *Mar–Dec 1st Sun of the month 7am–noon.* Monthly flea market in the historic centre.

Le Grain de Café – *6 pl. Armes. ℘03 84 21 31 95. Open 9am–noon, 2–7pm (tea-room 8am–6pm). Closed Sun and Mon except when the flea market is on.* The son of Michel Perello keeps the tradition going in this delicatessen, which is also a tea room and serves light meals.

Ballon d'Alsace

and Ballon de Servance★★★

The Ballon d'Alsace is the southern peak of the rounded granite summits (ballons) of the Vosges range. It has beautiful forests of pines and larches, spectacular gorges and mountain pastures covered in colourful alpine flowers.

🚗 DRIVING TOURS

BALLON D'ALSACE
See Region map. 17km/10.5mi circuit. Allow 5hrs.

Giromagny

Fort Dorsner at Giromagny, built between 1875 and 1879, was the link in the line of defensive fortifications between the upper Moselle Valley and the fortress at Belfort. You can visit the summit and the restored building is occasionally open to the public.

Having passed Lepuix, a small town, the road follows a narrow gorge.

Roches du Cerf

These rocks line the end of an old glacial valley. They have deep horizontal stripes scoured out by the lateral moraine of the glacier. A rock-climbing school uses the site.

Cascade du Rummel
15min there and back on foot.
A signposted footpath leads to a bridge and then the waterfall, not far from D 465.

Continue along D 465 (ignore the route de Masevaux on your right).

The road leads upwards through pretty countryside. In the distance, you should be able to see Sewen and Alfeld lakes.

Ballon d'Alsace★★★
30min there and back on foot.
The footpath to the summit leads off D 465, from the monument to the mine-

- 🐾 **Michelin Map:** 315: E-9/10 and 314: I to J-6.
- 📷 **Info:** Parc du Paradis des Loups, Grande Rue, 90200 Giromagny. ☏ 03 84 29 09 00. www.ot-belfort.fr.
- 👁 **Don't Miss:** The magnificent panoramas from the Ballon d'Alsace and the Ballon de Servance; the route du Col des Coix.
- ⏱ **Timing:** Half a day for the Ballon d'Alsace, or you can spend several days exploring the area.

clearing experts. It leads to a statue of the Virgin Mary **Notre-Dame-du-Ballon**, which marked the frontier before Alsace was returned to France. The Ballon d'Alsace (1 248m/4 095ft high) is the most southerly peak of the Vosges range. From the orientation table the **panorama**★★ offers views north to the Donon, east over the Alsace plain and Black Forest, and south to Mont Blanc.

BALLON DE SERVANCE★★
See Region map. 37km/23mi circuit. Allow 4hrs.

West of the Ballon d'Alsace, the Ballon de Servance reaches 1 216m/3 990ft and is the source of the Ognon river. This tour follows the **Route du Col**★★.

Servance
On the way out of the village to the right, a path (15min there and back) leads to the Saut de l'Ognon, a picturesque waterfall gushing out of a narrow gorge. Take D 486 N towards Col des Croix.

Col des Croix
Alt 678m/2 225ft.
The Château-Lambert fort overlooks the border between the regions of Lorraine and Franche-Comté. It is also the watershed between waters which flow to the North Sea and those which flow to the Mediterranean.

Château-Lambert

Located 1km/0.6mi beyond the Col des Croix, this charming mountain village is home to the **Musée départemental de la Montagne** (⏱ *open Apr–Sept daily except Tue 9.30am–noon, 2–6pm, Sat–Sun 2–6pm (last admission 30min before closing); Oct–Mar daily except Tue 2–5pm; closed 1 Jan, 1 May, 1 Nov, 11 Nov and Christmas holidays;* 🚗 *4€ (under 16s free);* 📞*03 84 20 43 09; www.cg70.fr).* Among the displays, you will find a reconstruction of peasant life at the start of the 20C. Exhibits include a mill, a forge, a winepress and a sawmill. Nearby, visit the 17C **chapel** and the **St-Antoine Oratory**.

🚗 *Continue on D 16 E for 10km/6.5mi; this old strategic roadway runs along a ridge with pretty views of the Ognon Valley below, before entering the forest.*

Panorama: Ballon de Servance★★

🚗*Leave your car at the car park.*
🚶 *Follow the marked trail leading to the top (15min there and back on foot).*

Paragliding over Ballon d'Alsace
© CRT Franche-Comté/Jacques Jeanpierre

A fabulous prospect stretches out all around; to the west, the Ognon Valley, the glacier plateau studded with ponds (known as the **Plateau des Mille Étangs**), to the north-west, the Faucilles mountains and on the right, the Moselle Valley. North-east, you will see from the Vosges mountain range and eastward looms the rounded contour of the Ballon d'Alsace and on clear days, the Alps; to the south and south-east lie the foothills of the Vosges. You can follow a nature path from the auberge.

ADDRESSES

🏨 STAY

🏨 **Grand Hôtel du Sommet** – *At the summit of the Ballon d'Alsace, 90200 Lepuix-Gy.* 📞*03 84 29 30 60 . www.hotelrestaurantdusommet.com. Closed Mon except in school holidays, 23 Nov–26 Dec.* 🅿 *25 rooms.* 🍽 *6.50 €. Restaurant* 🍴. Waking up in the mountains and breathing in bracing country air, surrounded peaceful meadows of cows is what awaits you in this comfortable hotel and traditional restaurant. Pretty views of Belfort Valley or, on a fine day, the Swiss Alps.

🏨🏨 **Auberge des Mille Étangs et chambre d'hôtes du Monthury** – *Goutte Géhant, Monthury, 70440 Servance. 4.5km/3mi N of Servance by D 263 towards Beulotte-St-Laurent.* 📞*03 84 63 82 26 or 03 84 20 48 55. www.aubergedesmilleetangs.fr.* 🍽 *6 rooms. Restaurant* 🍴🍴. This bed and breakfast in an 18C farm opposite the Ballon de Servance in the valley of Ognon, allows you to lose yourself in nature. Bedrooms are simple, and meals of local produce are taken in the converted barn, which has pretty woodwork and a tiled floor. Fishing allowed in the private lakes.

🤾 SPORTS AND RECREATION

Skiing – *90200 Vescemont.* 📞*03 84 29 06 65. Enquire at the ski school chalet ESF at la Gentiane.* In winter the Ballon offers a range of snow sports. Downhill and cross-country trails attract novices and experts alike.

👨‍👧 **Acropark** – *90200 Lepuix-Gy. Open July–Aug 10am–7pm; rest of year times vary.* 📧 📞*03 84 23 20 40. www.acropark.fr.* This outdoor adventure playground has been established in the forest on the Ballon d'Alsace. Plenty of activities are available, which will appeal to all the family.

Plateau des Mille-Étangs★

The Plateau of a Thousand Ponds takes its name from the multitude of small lakes of glacial origin dotted about the area. Isolated and all but forgotten, it is popular with those looking to get back to nature.

🚗 DRIVING TOUR

See Region map. 28km/16.8mi – about 1hr. This route takes you over part of the Route des Étangs (70km/35mi), departure from Lure. Brochure available from tourist offices.

Faucogney-et-la-Mer

This ancient fortified village on the Breuchin river was the last place in Franche-Comté to fall to the French in 1674. Afterwards, on the orders of Louis XIV, the château and fortifications were razed. Mont St-Martin rises above the town at the edge of the plateau. The **église Saint-Georges** has a bell tower dating back to the 15C.

▷ *Leave Faucogney on D 266, towards the chapel and viewpoint of St-Martin.*

Belvédère de St-Martin

Follow the signs on a small road which leads upwards to the right.

⌖ **Michelin Map:**
314: G-6 to H-6.

▤ **Info:** 23 r. Jeannot Lamboley, 70280 Faucogney-et-La-Mer. ℘03 84 49 32 97. www.les1000etangs.com.

▷ **Location:** This magical spot is bordered by the regions of the Vosges and the Haute-Saône and hemmed in by the Ognon and Breuchin valleys.

The road meanders through a magnificent landscape; the dark woods open at times to reveal birch trees bending over lily-covered ponds. Stop near the chapel. 🚶 A trail goes around it and leads to the panoramic viewpoint; beneath it the valley spreads open all around.

▷ *Go back to D 266 towards La Mer. At La Mer, continue right towards Melay or Ternuay. You can take D 315 towards Servance to see the Saut de l'Ognon falls. From Melay, continue on D 239 towards Mélisey.*

Mélisey

Situated on the right bank of the River Ognon, the village is overlooked by the church with its 12C chevet. The village has a canal network and the **Bégeot**

Plateau des Mille-Étangs in autumn

© Brigitte Merle/Photononstop

Legends of the Plateau of a Thousand Ponds

With the mist swirling around the lakes, marshes and forests, it's not surprising that this is the perfect setting for numerous stories! In Fessey, for example, lies the Mourey stone, underneath which a magician's treasure trove is hidden; every year on Christmas Eve a giant submerges the stone in the nearby pond, giving enough time for the money to be counted, before he returns it to its rightful place. The waterfall at Brigandoux, owes its name to a Burgundy lord who became a brigand, and who fell into the abyss trying to cross it …

mill, which worked until recently, can be visited at weekends.

 ○ *Take two right turns to head towards Écromagny on D 73.*

Écromagny
This little village is centred around a pink-sandstone church, its belfry typical of the region. The **Pellevin Pond**, one of many surrounding the village, and one of the largest on the plateau, has been developed for water sports.

 ○ *Take a left towards la Lanterne-et-les-Armonts (D 137), then right on D 72. After Annegray, turn left on D 139 that leads to La Voivre, then Sainte-Marie-en-Chanois.*

Sainte-Marie-en-Chanois
Dedicated to Sainte Marie-Madeleine, the 18C interior of this church offers much to see. The altarpiece is by the Deschamps brothers, who came from Faucogney and were known for their altar pieces. The pulpit is decorated with beautiful paintings representing the evangelists. One of the stained glass windows shows Saint Colomban chasing out a bear from the cave above Sainte-Marie where he stayed alone to pray. At the time a chapel was built near the cave, but it was washed away. The water from a spring in the same place is considered miraculous and became a place of pilgrimage up until the Revolution. Since 2008, the site of the spring has been made accessible to visitors a path leads from Saint-Marie.

 ○ *Turn around and take D 72 which will take you back to Faucogney.*

ADDRESSES

🛏 STAY
🍽🍽 **Chambre d'hôte du Tréchoux** – Es-Vouhey, 70310 Faucogney-et-La-Mer. ℘03 84 49 35 59. www.trechoux.com. Closed 2 Nov–30 Apr. ♿⛽ 3 rooms. 🍴. Deep in the countryside, this 200-year-old restored farm has three ground-floor bedrooms with pine furniture. There's home-made bread and jam for breakfast, and packed lunches and meals available for walkers.

🍽🍽 **Auberge La Champagne** – 70270 Écromagny. 1.5km/1mi E of Écromagny by rte de Melay. ℘03 84 20 04 72. www.auberge-lachampagne.com. 🅿♿ 5 rooms. 🍴. Restaurant 🍽🍽. A peaceful place to stay in the middle of the forest, this 1761 farm has been nicely restored by the French-Swiss owners. The comfortable rooms are in a recently added annexe and there's also a dormitory (20 people). Breakfasts are copious, and Swiss and German specialities are offered for dinner, which may be taken in the garden. The owners breed dogs.

🍴 EAT
🍽🍽 **Auberge Les Noies Parrons** – 1 Noies-Parrons, 70270 Mélisey, 2km/1.5mi NW of Mélisey by D 72 dir. Faucogney. ℘03 84 63 23 34. Closed Mon and Tue except public holidays. A paradise for fishermen, this sweet 19C farm is surrounded by trees and lakes. So, it's no surprise to find traditional trout in a cream sauce on the menu. The chef used to be a butcher and makes his own terrines, foie gras, sausages, pork knuckle and pastry. The terrace is on the waterside.

Ronchamp

Until 1958, when the last colliery was closed down, Ronchamp was a mining town. Since the 1950s, however, it has been better known for its chapel of Notre-Dame-du-Haut, designed by Swiss architect Le Corbusier in 1955 to replace one destroyed during World War II.

- ▶ **Population:** 2 924
- ⏱ **Michelin Map:** 314: H-6.
- ℹ **Info:** 14 pl. du 14 Juillet, 70250 Ronchamp. ℘03 84 63 50 82. www.ot-ronchamp.fr.
- ▶ **Location:** Ronchamp is 19km/12mi W of Belfort.
- 🕐 **Timing:** Allow a day here.

SIGHTS

Notre-Dame-du-Haut★★

1.5km/1mi N of town via a steep uphill road. 🕐*Open Apr–Sept daily 9.30am–6.30pm. Rest of the year 10am–5pm (Nov–Feb 4pm). ℘03 84 20 65 13. www.chapellederonchamp.fr.*

Le Corbusier's comment on this chapel, which is one of the most important works of contemporary religious architecture, was that he had intended his design to create a place of silence, prayer, peace and inner joy. Overlooking the industrial town of Ronchamp, the chapel was constructed on a hill (472m/1 548ft), which had been dedicated to the worship of the Virgin Mary since the Middle Ages. It was built in 1955, the third on this site, constructed entirely of concrete; the brightness of its whitewashed walls looks dazzling against the dark grey untreated concrete of the roof. The rigid geometric lines of the walls contrast strikingly with the softer curves of the roof, which sweeps upwards in a graceful motion, and the rounded towers. In his conception of this chapel, **Le Corbusier** broke with the Rationalist movement and its inflexible designs, creating a work which has been described as architectural sculpture.

Inside, despite sloping walls and its relatively small size, the chapel seems spacious. The nave widens out towards the altar of white Burgundy stone, and the floor of the chapel follows the slope of the hill it is built on. The image of the Virgin Mary stands bathed in light in a niche in the wall. Light in the church filters through numerous different tiny windows randomly cut in the walls, allowing for a subtle interplay of light and shadow in the half darkness which softens the effect of the bare concrete walls. The three small chapels in the three outer towers contribute to this subdued lighting effect.

Musée de la Mine

🕐*Open Jun–Aug daily except Tue 10am–noon, 2–7pm. Rest of year 2–6pm.* 🕐*Closed 1 Jan, 1 and 8 May, 14 Jul. ⊜3.05€. ℘03 84 20 70 50.*

This museum retraces two centuries of mining in the region. The first gallery contains a display on coal mining – equipment, mining lamps, collections of fossils – and reproductions of mine disasters. The second gallery is given over to the life of the miners themselves, both pleasant aspects such as festivals, sports and musical activities, and the threat of illnesses such as miners' silicosis.

ADDRESSES

⍦/EAT

⊜ **Restaurant Marchal** – *26 r. des Mineurs. ℘03 84 63 18 15.* 🚬 ♿ *Closed Tue and Wed eve, 20 Jun–1 Jul, 3–9 Jan.* Recently rebuilt after a fire, and now with a bright interior, this restaurant is known for its light, but copious cuisine, especially its fried carp.

⊜⊜ **Hostellerie des Sources** – *4 r. Grand-Bois, 70200 Froideterre. 14km/8.5mi W of Ronchamp by N 19 and D 72. ℘03 84 30 34 72. Closed 5–24 Jan, Sun eve, Mon and Tue. Reservations essential.* The owner of this old farmhouse restaurant is a dedicated wine lover who enjoys sharing his passion. The well-presented cuisine, cooked by his son, will not disappoint.

Luxeuil-les-Bains ✝

This well-known spa town, with its historic red sandstone mansions, was home to a famous abbey founded by the Irish monk St-Columban in the 6C. These days visitors come to enjoy the abbey remains, the spa facilities and the local decorative lace, "Bâtarde de Luxeuil".

▸ **Population:** 7 575
⊙ **Michelin Map:** 314: G-6.
🄸 **Info:** r. Victor-Genoux, 70300 Luxeuil-les-Bains. ℘03 84 40 06 41. www.luxeuil.fr.
◖ **Location:** A 4km/2.5mi walk known as the" Sentier des Gaulois" leads from the baths past all the historical monuments of the town.

QUARTIER THERMAL

👥 Thermal Baths

3 r. des Thermes. ⊙*Open Mar–Nov.* ⊙*Closed Sun. Visits only by request.* ℘*03 84 40 44 22. www.chainethermale.fr/cures/stations-thermales/luxeuil-les-bains.html.*

Surrounded by a shady park, this imposing building, in the distinctive red sandstone of the Vosges, dates from the 18C (steeple 19C). It was built to replace the old Gallo-Roman spa by J. Querret, a disciple of Claude-Nicolas Ledoux. In the hallway are paintings by Jules Adler.

OLD TOWN

Maison du Cardinal Jouffroy★

The house in which Cardinal Jouffroy, Abbot of Luxeuil lived (15C) is the town's most beautiful. In addition to its Flamboyant Gothic windows and arcade, it has Renaissance features, including an unusual corbelled turret (16C) topped by a lantern. Famous figures such as Madame de Sévigné, Lamartine and André Theuriet all stayed in this house.

Beneath the balcony, the third keystone from the left shows three rabbits, sculpted in such a way that each appears to have two ears, although only three in total have been carved.

Musée de la Tour des Échevins

⊙*Open Apr–Oct Wed, Fri–Sun 2–6pm.* 👓*2.10€.* ℘*03 84 40 00 07.*

The Tour des Échevins dates from the 15C, and has a splendid Flamboyant Gothic loggia. The museum inside houses on the ground and first floors some remarkable stone funerary monuments from the Gallo-Roman

town (Luxovium), votive **steles★**, inscriptions, Gallic ex-votos, a reconstruction of a potter's kiln and so on. The second and third floors are occupied by the **Musée Adler** containing paintings by Adler, Vuillard and Pointelin. From the top of the tower (146 steps) there is a good **view** of the town and, in the distance, the Vosges, the Jura and the Alps.

Maison François-Ier

This Renaissance mansion is named not after the king of France, but an abbot of Luxeuil. Splendid carved faces decorate the Renaissance arcades.

Ancienne abbaye Saint-Colomban★

☙*For guided tours (45min), ask at the tourist office.* ℘*03 84 40 13 38.*

The eponymous St Colomban was chased out of the country, having criticised the king of Burgundy. He sought shelter in Bubbio, Italy.

Basilica – The present building, which replaced the original 11C church of which only traces are left, dates from the 13C and 14C. Of the three original towers, only the west bell tower remains. This was rebuilt in 1527 and the top of it dates from the 18C. The apse was rebuilt by Vauban in 1860. The north façade of the church can be seen from place St-Pierre. A Classical doorway with a pediment leads into the interior, which is in the Burgundian Gothic style. The **organ case★** is supported by an atlas and decorated with magnificent sculpted medallions. The south transept houses the shrine of St Columban.

Cloisters – Three of the four pink-sand-stone galleries remain. One arcade with three bays surmounted by an oculus dates from the 13C; the others were rebuilt in the 15C and 16C. The cloister houses the **Conservatoire de la dentelle**, a lacemaking workshop and school, with displays of the finest examples of the lacemakers' work (*open Tue and Fri 2–5pm; 03 84 93 61 11; www.dentelledeluxeuil.com*).

Conventual buildings – These include, to the south of the church, the 17C–18C *Bâtiment des Moines* (monks' building) and, on place St-Pierre, the 16C–18C abbot's residence, now the town hall.

EXCURSION
LURE
▶ *21km/13mi SE by D 64.*

On the edge of the sandstone Vosges mountains and on the border of Franche-Comté, this little town long maintained its independence, whilst at the same time being influenced by several cultures, from Irish evangelists in the 7C to Protestants from Montbéliard in the 18C.

Take a look in particular at the elegant 15C–18C Sub-Prefecture, which includes remains of the 7C abbey, and at 7 rue Pasteur at the interesting 15C sculptures on the façades.

Fougerolles

The little town of Fougerolles, was regularly fought over by the dukes of Lorraine and of Burgundy, until becoming French in 1704. Today, it is best known as the cherry capital and famous for its kirsch.

▶ **Population:** 3 874
- **Michelin Map:** 314:G-5.
- **Info:** 1 r. de la Gare, 70220 Fougerolles. 03 84 49 12 91 www.otsi-fougerolles.net.
- **Location:** Fougerolles is 10km/6.5mi N of Luxeuil-les-Bains by N 57.

SIGHT
Écomusée du Pays de la Cerise★
2km/1mi N on C 201. Open mid-Feb–mid-Nov. Guided tours (1hr 15min) Jul–Aug 11am–7pm, Sun 2–7pm. Rest of the year varies. 5€. 03 84 49 52 50. www.musees-des-techniques.org.

This interesting museum, in the hamlet of Petit-Fahys on the premises of one of the region's first industrial distiller-ies (1831), shows visitors an authentic kirsch distillery. Recently renovated, it relates the history of an activity that was essentially agricultural in the 17C and which became industrial in the 19C. Several rooms have been re-created to show the distiller's house, the servants' quarters, the maturing loft, and the workshops. You can see the huge shining stills worked by boilers or steam and follow the complete process of producing the kirsch. Other local agricultural activities are displayed too. Next to the buildings is an **orchard-conservatory** where the local varieties of cherry are cultivated.

EXCURSION
Ermitage St-Valbert
▶ *5km/3mi S. 03 84 49 54 97.*

A hermitage developed in the 17C near the cave where St Valbert lived as a hermit in the 7C. Note the statue of the saint carved in the rock.

Cherry Topped

Thanks to its famous kirsch, Fougerolles has been designated as a "Site remarquable du goût" ("special place of taste") since 1994. The local orchards have around 40 000 cherry trees, all varieties of the **guignes** family. The cherries are harvested by machine in early July. The town has its own Confederation of Tasters who promote the local spirit and other products.

PONTARLIER AND THE HAUT-DOUBS

You might think you are in Switzerland here, with a history of watchmaking, pastures grazed by cows with bells around their necks producing creamy cheeses, and mountain peaks with gorgeous views. Indeed, there is much in common between the Upper Doubs near Pontarlier and the Swiss Jura regions. In this border country, where smugglers often sneaked their contraband across the mountains, you can compare watchmaking museums on each side of the frontier, experience the famous Saut du Doubs waterfalls from the French and Swiss point of view, or simply take in a stunning panorama to the other side from a mountain-top.

A head for heights

It helps if you don't suffer from vertigo when you visit many of the spectacular natural sights around Pontarlier. Whether you are driving above the narrow Doubs gorge, viewing the gorge by tackling the Échelles du Mort (Ladders of Death), taking in the spectacular panoramas from the thousand-meter (3 300ft) peaks on the Franco-Swiss border, or marvelling at the water power of the Saut du Doubs waterfalls, having a head for heights will give you a definite advantage.

However, there are gentler offerings too in the lovely landscape of the Upper Doubs, in the foothills of the Jura mountains. Close to the resort of Malbuisson, the deep blue lakes of Saint-Point and nearby Remorey offer some easy walking options and a chance to observe an interesting protected nature reserve, the habitat of a large variety of birds. Water is an important feature all over the area with numerous lakes, waterfalls, springs and even caves with reputedly healing waters: the cave of Notre-Dame de Remonot is said by pilgrims to contain waters that heal eye afflictions.

If you are a fan of snow and winter sports, then in winter head up the mountains to the ski resort of Métabief-Mont d'Or which links six villages in a paradise for cross-country as well as downhill skiers.

Time for lunch

The Swiss may be famous for their timekeeping, but just over the border in Morteau, you will discover that a great tradition of watchmaking exists here too. You can spend a morning comparing the industries on both sides of the border with a visit to Morteau's watchmaking

Highlights

1 La Roche du Prêtre viewpoint of the **Cirque de Consolation** (p339)

2 A boat trip to see the **Saut du Doubs** waterfalls (p341)

3 The watchmaking museums in and around **Morteau** (p342)

4 A prison visit at the eagle's nest **Château de Joux** (p348)

5 A walk up to le Mont d'Or viewpoint at **Métabief** (p352)

Mont d'Or

© CRT Franche-Comté/Hervé Hughes

museum in Château Pertusier and those at La Chaud-de-Fonds and Le Locle in Switzerland.

Make time in Morteau or perhaps in a nearby mountain chalet to taste the famous Morteau smoked sausage, perhaps followed by some creamy Mont d'Or cheese and an aniseed liqueur from Pontarlier.

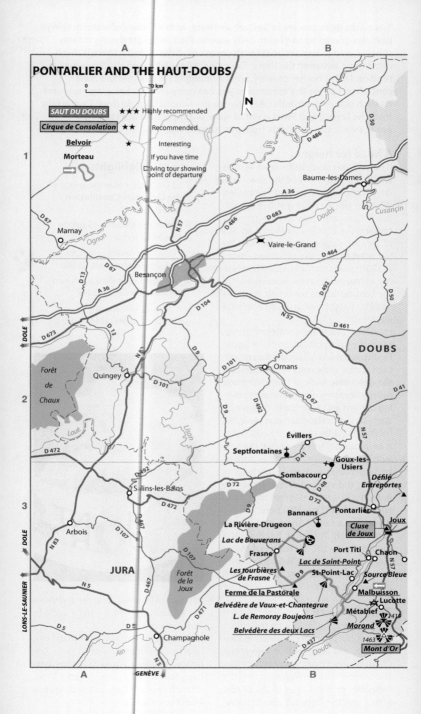

PONTARLIER AND THE HAUT-DOUBS

0 ——— 10 km

SAUT DU DOUBS	★★★ Highly recommended
Cirque de Consolation	★★ Recommended
Belvoir	★ Interesting
Morteau	If you have time
	Driving tour showing point of departure

DOLE

LONS-LE-SAUNIER

GENÈVE

DOUBS

JURA

Baume-les-Dames
Marnay
Besançon
Vaire-le-Grand
Ornans
Quingey
Forêt de Chaux
Salins-les-Bains
Arbois
Champagnole
Évillers
Septfontaines
Goux-les-Usiers
Sombacour
Défilé Entreportes
Bannans
La Rivière-Drugeon
Pontarlier
Cluse de Joux
Joux
Lac de Bouverans
Port Titi
Chaon
Frasne
Lac de Saint-Point
Les tourbières de Frasne
St-Point-Lac
Source Bleue
Ferme de la Pastorale
Malbuisson
Belvédère de Vaux-et-Chantegrue
Lucotte
L. de Remoray Boujeons
Métabief
Belvédère des deux Lacs
Morond
Mont d'Or

Forêt de la Joux

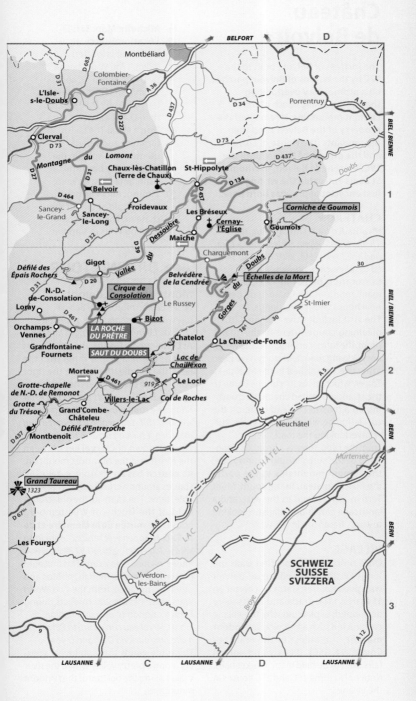

Château de Belvoir★

The fortress of Belvoir, built in the 12C by the barons of Belvoir, perches on a promontory overlooking the Sancey Valley south of the Lomont mountains. It remained the property of the Belvoirs and their descendants (the House of Lorraine and the princes of Rohan) until the 19C. Vincent de Belvoir, to whom St Louis entrusted the writing of the first encyclopaedia, was born here.

CHÂTEAU★

Guided tours (1hr) Jul–Aug 10–11.30am, 2–5.30pm, Easter–end Oct Sun and holidays. 5€. 03 81 86 30 34/91 06 02. www.chateau-belvoir.com.
Restoration began in 1955, and the many rooms of the Château de Belvoir now house lavish furnishings.

The visit includes the kitchen with its gleaming copper utensils, the guard-room, the former arsenal, and the weaponry. A living room and study have been attractively furnished in the Madge-Fà Tower, which owes its curious name to the strange bearded character crouching on a monster's head beneath the cul-de-lampe which supports the turret overlooking the road.

From the keep, there is a beautiful panorama of the surrounding countryside: the Lomont mountains to the north; the Maîche plateau to the south; Mont Terri in Switzerland to the east, and a landscape of hills and plateaux looking towards Besançon in the west.

VILLAGE

Once protected by fortified walls (no longer visible), the village of Belvoir was given tax-free status by charter on 11 March 1314. Trade and crafts were developed, explaining why the village constructed such a fine, wooden **indoor market**, the oldest in the Franche-Comté (14–15C). Weekly and annual fairs used to be held in the market halls. Notice also some 16C and 17C houses in the village.

- **Michelin Map**: 321: J3
- **Location:** The château de Belvoir is located 28km/17mi W of Maîche by D 464 and D 31, and 37km/23mi from Baume-les-Dames by D 50 south, then D 464 eastwards.
- **Don't Miss:** The lavish furniture and varied utensils on display in the château; the beautiful panorama from its keep.
- **Timing:** Allow an hour for the guided visit of the château. There are some evening visits in summer.

🚗 DRIVING TOUR

Montagnes du Lomont

See Region map. Leave Belvoir towards the west and take a right on D 31 for 15km/9.5mi. Turn right on D 683.
At **L'Isle-sur-le-Doubs**, the river Doubs divides the village into three with the Ile in the middle, the Rue on the right bank and the Magny on the left bank.
Take D 683 towards Besançon. After Rang, the road winds along between a wooded cliff and gentle valleys; leaving and then returning close to the river.
The little town of **Clerval** lies between the forest and the Montfort mountain. Its **church** has an altarpiece, two 16C statues around a crucifix and other valuable items. The château, the old stronghold of the Duchy of Württemberg houses the **musée de la Mémoire et de la Paix** (open weekends 2–6pm (also Wed in July–Aug); 03 81 93 84 29; www.musee-memoire-paix.org). This museum presents uniforms, medals, photos and other memorabilia from the two World Wars as well as the 20C conflicts during France's period of de-colonization.
From Clerval you can return to Belvoir on a circular route via D 27 and D 464.
The route winds through lovely scenery along a pretty valley where the river snakes along the bottom of the Lormont mountains.

Maîche

Welcome to Franche-Montagne border country, long known by smugglers of contraband. Be warned, some of the extensive plateaux here in the northern Jura mountains might give a few scary moments to hikers prone to vertigo. Close to the Dessoubre and Doubs valleys, Maîche occupies a pleasant site overlooked by the Mont Miroir (alt 986m/3 235ft).

▸ **Population:** 3 959
◔ **Michelin Map:** 321 K3.
▯ **Info:** Pl. de la Mairie, 25120 Maîche. ℘03 81 64 11 88. http://maiche.free.fr.
▻ **Location**: South of Montbéliard, by A 36, then D 437.
◈ **Don't Miss:** The splendid sculpted pulpit at the church of Saint-Pierre; the drive above the spectacular gorges du Doubs.
◔ **Timing:** Allow a good day to explore both the town of Maîche and the gorges.

🚗 DRIVING TOUR

La Franche Montagne
◔ *See Region map. 79km/49mi circuit. Allow 5hrs 30min.*
The River Doubs cuts through a deep, narrow gorge en-route to Goumois.

Maîche
Re-built in the 18C, the **church of Saint-Pierre** has a fine interior, in particular the baroque tabernacle, the organ and the superb **sculpted pulpit**. Left of the church, you will see the **castle of Charles de Montalembert** (1810–70), a well-known liberal Catholic polemicist. Churchill and de Gaulle met here in November 1944 to discuss the liberation of Alsace and Lorraine.

The **maîchard** or Comtois horse, a famous breed of draught horses, originates from Maîche. Every September the village stages a competition and a festival to ensure the survival of the breed.

▻ *Leave Maîche heading east on the D 437A; left on the D 237.*

Cernay-l'Église★
In this village, you will find the charming **church of Saint-Antoine**, which is interesting to visit. Inside you will find a superb Renaissance altar in coloured stone; a 19C pulpit watched over by a dragon; and beautiful statues including an unusual 16C representation of Sainte-Sophie with her three daughters: Faith, Hope and Charity.

▻ *Turn back on yourself and on the edge of Maîche take D 464 left towards Charquemont. Follow past La Cheminée border post (tell the official you are not going to Switzerland).*

View over the Doubs from the Corniche de Goumois

G. Magnin/MICHELIN

Les Échelles de la Mort★★ (The Ladders of Death)

Take the road on the left to the Le Refrain hydroelectric plant. This leads downhill to the bottom of the gorge, where there is an impressive **landscape**★ of tall cliffs crowned by firs and spruces.

🚶 *Leave the car in the plant car park and take the signposted path on the left (30min there and back on foot) to the foot of the Échelles de la Mort (☺steep climb through undergrowth).*

To reach the **viewpoint** requires climbing three steel ladders fixed into a rocky wall, which have solid reinforced steps and are equipped with hand rails (☺best avoided in wet weather). The climb leads up to a viewpoint about 100m/330ft high, overlooking the Doubs gorges.

▷ *Return to Charquemont and take D 10E to la Cendrée (car park).*

Belvédères de la Cendrée

🚶 Two paths 200m/220yd further on lead to the viewpoints, from which there are beautiful views of the Doubs gorge and Switzerland. The first path *(30min there and back on foot)* comes to a rocky spur which rises sheer 450m/1 476ft above the Doubs Valley. The viewpoint at the end of the second path *(45min there and back on foot; marked with arrows)* is at the top of the la Cendrée rocks.

▷ *Return to Charquemont and take D 201 right. At Damprichard, turn right on D 437A, to reach the Col de la Vierge (pass at alt. 964m/3 163ft) and the start of the famous Corniche de Goumois.*

Corniche de Goumois★★

This very picturesque road runs along the steep west side of the Doubs Valley. For 3km/2mi the route overlooks the depths of the gorge from a height of about 100m/330ft (*best viewpoints have protective railings*). The steep slopes are wooded or rocky, or carpeted with meadows. The landscape exudes a calm grandeur rather than wild ruggedness. The Swiss Franches Montagnes range are on the other bank of the Doubs.

▷ *Leave Goumois on the Swiss-French border by D 437B towards Montbéliard. At Trévillers, take D 201 right, then left on D 134 to Courtefontaine and Soulce. Continue on D 437C to Saint-Hippolyte.*

Saint-Hippolyte

This little town is surrounded by pretty **countryside**★, where the Dessoubre flows into the Doubs.

▷ *Leave on D 437 towards Maîche.*

Les Bréseux

The church of this modest village boasts a remarkable set of seven **stained-glass windows** (1948) made by the famous glassblower Alfred Manessier.

ADDRESSES

🛏 STAY

☺☺ **Moulin du Plain** – *25470 Goumois. 5km/3mi N of Goumois up a track.* ✆03 81 44 41 99. www.moulinduplain.com. Closed 3 Nov–21 Feb. 🚪 22 rooms. ⌾ 6.60 €. Restaurant ☺☺. On the banks of the Doubs, in the heart of a forest, this family inn is a favourite haunt of anglers. The simple, well-kept rooms all give onto the river. Regional specialities and trout dishes.

☺☺☺ **Taillard** – *3 rte de la Corniche, 25470 Goumois.* ✆03 81 44 20 75. Closed early Nov–early Mar. 17 rooms. Restaurant ☺☺☺. Overlooking the village and the Doubs, this hotel has been in the same family since 1874. Annexe rooms are nicer. Garden, pool and fitness room. Well presented classic cuisine.

🍽 EAT

☺☺ **Au Bois de la Biche** – *Belvédères de la Cendrée, 25140 Charquemont. 4.5km/3mi SE of Goumois by D 10e and a track.* ✆03 81 44 01 82. www.boisdela biche.com. Closed 2 Jan–2 Feb, Tue Oct–Mar and Mon. 3 rooms ☺☺ ⌾ 7 €. This old farm over the Doubs gorges serves regional cooking, and large bay windows offer a view of the Swiss Jura mountains. There are three simple, well-kept rooms.

Cirque de Consolation★★

The natural amphitheatre, from which the Dessoubre and its tributary the Lançot spring, takes the shape of a double semicircle against an awe-inspiring background of partly wooded rocky crags towering majestically to over 300m/984ft.

Michelin Map: 321: J-4.

Info: pl. de l'Hôtel-de-Ville, 25190 Saint-Hipplyte. &03 81 96 58 00.

Location: 13km/8mi N of Morteau. The drive from St-Hippolyte passes through the placid Dessoubre River valley before ascending to the craggy cirque.

Don't Miss: The breathtaking view from La Roche du Prêtre.

🚗 DRIVING TOUR

1 VALLÉE DU DESSOUBRE AND 2 CIRQUE DE CONSOLATION
47km/29mi circuit. Allow 6hrs.

Leave St-Hippolyte (&see MAÎCHE) on D 39 heading SW. Take some good walking shoes with you.

D 39 follows the course of the Dessoubre quite closely, going through the villages of Pont-Neuf and Rosureux. Stretching from Saint-Hippolyte, where the Dessboure flows into the Doubs to the cirque de Consolation, the peaceful valley runs between wooded slopes (fir, oak and ash) topped by limestone cliffs.

Gigot
The Dessoubre is joined here by a small tributary, the Reverotte, which twists its way west upstream of the village along a steep-sided valley known as the **Défilé des Épais Rochers**.

After Gigot, D 39 carries on along the banks of the Dessoubre, past woods and meadows with the river bubbling alongside.

Notre-Dame-de-Consolation
See Cirque de Consolation map.
This former convent designed by a Minimalist architect was a small seminary until 1981, and now serves as a spiritual centre. The Jesuit chapel contains

a beautiful **marble mausoleum**. The **park** *(allow 1hr minimum)* is a pretty place for a walk through fields, among trees, rocks, waterfalls, springs (Source du Lançot, Source Noire and Source du Tabouret) and the Val Noir (black valley).

Take D 39 towards Fuans, then several left turns on D 351, D 461, D 41 then immediately to Roche du Prêtre.

La Roche du Prêtre★★★
See Cirque de Consolation map.
This famous viewpoint offers unforgettable views of the Cirque de Consolation and its surroundings. The summit towers 350m/1 148ft above the wooded amphitheatre, punctuated by rocky outcrops, in which the Dessoubre rises.

Take D 41/D 46 towards the west.

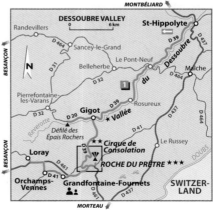

339

View from La Roche du Prêtre

©René Mattès/hemis.fr

Grandfontaine-Fournets

This hamlet at the heart of the Haut-Doubs is in typical Comtois style. It is home to the **Ferme du Montagnon** (& ⊙ open Apr–mid-Nov 9am–noon, 2–6pm; ℘03 81 43 57 86; www.montagnon.com), dating from the 17C and 18C. It still has its **loft**★ smokery (tuyé) where meat, hams, bacon and sausages are cured (locally cured products on sale).

Orchamps-Vennes

This sizeable mountain village occupies a high plateau set back from the D 461 between Besançon and Morteau. Its low-roofed houses adorn a charming setting of green meadows and trees. The 16C **church of Saint-Pierre and Saint Paul** is worth a visit.

▶ Take D 461 left, then after 2km/1.5mi turn right on D 19.

Loray

This village has houses typical of the region and a neo-Romanesque church with 18C furnishings. Not far off stands a 12C **Calvary**, which features a life-size statue of a figure holding a human head in its hand. Higher up are the Virgin Mary, Christ and St Michael overcoming the dragon. At the village square's centre is a 19C fountain wash-house with fluted columns topped by Doric capitals.

ADDRESSES

⌂ STAY

⊖ **Hôtel du Moulin** – 25380 Cour-Saint-Maurice. 1km/0.6mi SW of Pont-Neuf on D 39. ℘ 03 81 44 35 18. Closed Oct–Feb. 🅿 6 rooms. ☲ 6.50 €. Restaurant ⊖⊖. This charming 1930s residence has a scrupulously preserved part-retro, part-arty décor. Some rooms have terraces and there is a riverside garden bursting with flowers. Peace guaranteed.

⚲ EAT

⊖ **Ferme-auberge de Frémondans** – Frémondans, 25380 Vaucluse. 7km/4.5mi NE of Gigot by D 39, then track on left. ℘03 81 44 35 66. Closed Oct. Open Jul–Aug every lunchtime, Sat and Sun eves, rest of year open Fri eve–Sun lunch. 🅿 ⇄ Reservations essential. Tuck into specialities such as terrine, fondue, kid, stuffed cabbage, goat's cheese and homemade pastries at this family-owned farmhouse overlooking the Dessoubre Valley.

⊖⊖ **La Truite du Moulin** – Moulin-du-Bas, 25380 Cour-St-Maurice. 0.5km/0.3mi SE of Pont-Neuf on D 39. ℘03 81 44 30 59. Closed Dec, Tue eve and Wed. This former mill on the Dessoubre offers regional fare, with a speciality of trout from the river, served in a rustic, but warm dining room.

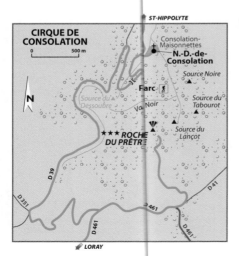

Saut du Doubs★★★

Bursting out of the Chaillexon lake, the waters of the Doubs plunge down in a magnificent drop, known as "le Saut du Doubs", one of the most famous natural phenomenons you can admire in the Franche-Comté. You can choose whether to see these falls from the Swiss or French side.

- **Michelin Map:** 321: K-4.
- **Info:** R. Berçot, 25130 Villers-le-Lac. ℘03 81 68 00 98. www.villers-le-lac-info.org.
- **Location:** On the border 10km/6mi E of Morteau.
- **Timing:** Allow at least an hour at the falls.

VILLERS-LE-LAC★

This small town in the Doubs Valley, where the river spreads to form the **Lac de Chaillexon**★, is the starting point of boat excursions to the **Saut du Doubs**★★★ waterfall.

Two slopes on either side of the River Doubs crumbled in and blocked a part of the valley, creating a natural dam which in turn formed the lake. There are two principal parts to it: in the first, the water is a single open stretch between the gentle slopes of the valley; in the second, it lies between abrupt limestone cliffs which divide this part of the lake into a number of basins. The serpentine lake is 3.5km/2.1mi long, and on average about 200m/220yd wide.

In the town, the interesting **Musée de la Montre**★ *(&Øopen school holidays daily except Tue 10am–noon, 2–6pm; ⚏5.50€; ℘03 81 68 44 53)* celebrates the history of watchmaking, a long-standing tradition of the Jura region on both sides of the Franco-Swiss border.

SAUT DU DOUBS★★★

The waterfall is at its best viewed in autumn after heavy rain, as it is less spectacular in summer.

From the raised level of the lake, the Doubs tumbles 27m/89ft to its natural level in a noisy and turbulent cascade of spume. There is a **boat service** *(Øopen daily Apr–Oct, limited departures in Mar and Nov; ⚏11.90€; ℘03 81 68 13 25; www.sautdudoubs.fr)* from Villers-le-Lac. The boats follow the river's meanders as they gradually open up to form the Chaillexon Lake; then they take their passengers through a gorge, the most picturesque part of the trip. From the landing-stage, take the path *(👣30min round trip on foot),* which leads to the two viewpoints overlooking the Saut du Doubs.

Saut du Doubs

G. Magnin/MICHELIN

Morteau

The tasty Morteau sausage is not the only thing that makes this little town famous. Morteau, located in the Doubs Valley, is particularly well-known for its high quality clock- and watchmaking skills, whose history is related in the town's fine museum.

CHÂTEAU PERTUSIER★

At the exit of town towards Pontarlier.
An elegant Renaissance town house built in 1576 by the Cuche family. Attacked by the Swedes in the 17C, seized in the Revolution, and damaged by a fire in 1938, the castle has been restored to house the watchmaking museum as well as temporary exhibitions.
Musée de l'Horlogerie du Haut-Doubs – ⓞ*Open daily May–Sept 10am–noon, 2–6pm; rest of the year daily except weekends, 10am–noon, 2–6pm.* ⓞ*Closed 1 Jan and 25 Dec.* ⚹6€. ℘03 81 67 40 88. www.musee-horlogerie.com.
This museum is a homage to the exceptional talents of the local watchmakers. Displays include the precision tools made by local craftsmen and a wonderful collection of clocks and watches through the ages. Note the highly unusual **astronomic clock**★ (1855).

GRAND'COMBE-CHÂTELEU

4 km/3mi SW by D 437, then left on D 47.
The hamlet of Les Cordiers has some lovely **old farms**★ with traditional *tuyés*.
👥 **Fermes-musée du Pays horloger** – 📷*Guided tour (1hr 30min) mid-Jun–mid-Sept 10am–noon, 2–6pm; rest of the year by request.* ⓞ*Closed 1 Jan, 1 and 8 May, 1 and 11 Nov, 25 Dec.* ⚹1.50€ (children free). ℘03 81 68 86 90. http://pages perso-orange.fr/fermes-musee.
In this museum, the 17C farm includes recreations of workshops for a blacksmith and a wheelwright, as they would have been around 1920.
The barn shows a collection of tools and the main rural activities of the region in the 20C. The visit also explores a typical local farm, known as *à tuyé* and the room used for smoking Morteau sausages.

▶ **Population**: 6 293
👤 **Michelin Map**: 321: J4.
🅰 **Don't Miss:** The watch-making museums at Château Pertusier in Morteau, and on the Swiss side at La Chaux-de-Fonds; the picturesque farms for smoking Morteau sausages, don't forget to try them.
🕐 **Timing**: Allow two days to include the driving tour.

🚗 DRIVING TOUR

5 ROUTE HORLOGÈRE FRANCO-SUISSE

80km/50mi circuit on Region map. Allow one day. ▷ *Leave Morteau by D 461 towards Villers-le-Lac.*
This Franco-Swiss drive takes you to traditional watchmaking towns on both sides of the border. Follow D 461 through Villers-le-Lac to cross the border at **Col des Roches**. Here, at the **underground mills** (ⓞ*open May–Oct;* ℘032 931 89 89; www.lesmoulis.ch) you can visit the deep caves where mills were built in the 17C and see a museum of the caves' unusual industrial history. Nearby **Le Locle** has a **Watchmaking Museum**★ (℘032 931 16 80; www.mhl-monts.ch) in the elegant 18C **Château des Monts**, which complements the one at La Chaux-de-Fonds. Perching at 1 000m/3 281ft, the Swiss town of **La Chaux-de-Fonds**, is the birthplace of **Le Corbusier**. As the cradle of watchmaking, and today at the cutting edge of micro-electronics, the town's **International Museum of Watchmaking**★★ (℘032 967 68 61; www.milh.ch) is very comprehensive. If you have time, return by the lovely wooded route above the **Gorges du Doubs**★ (👤*see p337*) leaving La Chaux-de-Fonds north towards Belfort. Then, follow D 461 towards Maîche. Leaving Charquemont, take a left on D 201, then D 436 towards Morteaux. After Russey, turn right towards Le Bizot. The 16C **Bizot church**★, with a superb **pulpit**, is well worth a look.

Montbenoît★

This village, in a picturesque setting on a hillside overlooking the Doubs, is the tiny capital of the so-called Saugeais Republic, dating back to the 12C. Montbenoît's old abbey is among the Jura's most beautiful architectural monuments and draws many visitors.

- ▶ **Population:** 329
- **Michelin Map:** 321: I-5.
- **Info:** 8 r. du Val-Saugeais, 25650 Montbenoît. ℘03 81 38 10 32. www.tourisme-loue-saugeais.fr.
- **Location:** The Saugeais Republic includes 11 villages including Monbenoît.
- **Timing:** Allow two hours to explore the abbey.

A BIT OF HISTORY

The rise and fall of the abbey – Montbenoît Abbey was founded in the 12C after the hermit Benedict (Br Benoît) came to live here, drawing crowds of followers with him. It was held in *commendam* from 1508 onwards; the abbots drew on the abbey's profits without having to either oversee the general administration of the abbey or even take part in its religious life.

The two most famous abbots were the Cardinal of Granvelle and Ferry Carondelet. The latter joined the order after being widowed, and became counsellor to Emperor Charles V. He was a luxury loving patron who had the church chancel rebuilt and filled it with the most beautiful works of art. He also made generous donations to the cathedral of St-Jean in Besançon, of which he was canon and where he was finally buried. During the Revolution, the abbey of Montbenoît was declared the property of the French state and its lands sold.

ANCIENNE ABBAYE★

Open year round. Guided tours Jul–Aug 10am, 11.15am, 2.15pm, 3.30pm and 4.30pm; rest of the year unaccompanied visit with guide sheet (ask at the tourist office). 3€. ℘03 81 38 10 32.

Ancienne Église Abbatiale

The nave of the abbey church dates from the 12C and the chancel from the 16C. The bell tower was rebuilt in 1903.

Nave – Against the first pillar on the south side is a monument (1522) to a local girl, Parnette Mesnier, who met her death while attempting to resist the unwelcome advances of a young man. Pretty Parnette fled him by clambering up the scaffolding above the chancel, which was under construction at the time. Just as the young man reached her Parnette threw herself to the ground below. Kind-hearted Ferry Carondelet

Cloisters, Ancienne Abbaye

G. Magnin/MICHELIN

donated the monument in memory of the young girl's defence of her virtue.

In the Chapelle Ferrée left of the chancel there is a 16C statue of St Jerome and a stone Pietà on the altar. The sculpted doors at the entrance to the Chapelle des Trois-Rois right of the chancel were part of the original 16C rood screen.

Chancel – Abbot Ferry Carondelet had travelled all over Italy as ambassador to the court of Rome for the government of the Netherlands and Flanders, and sought to re-create at Montbenoît some of the magnificence and refinement of the Italian Renaissance. He personally chose the craftsmen who took just two years to create this harmonious group of sculpture and stained glass, one of the great successes of the early Renaissance in the Franche-Comté. The brilliant colours of the ornamental foliage and arabesques are still visible on the pendentive vaulting, which is decorated with a delicate network of ribs.

The decoration on the magnificent **stalls**★★ (1525–27) is clearly the result of both a lively wit and great artistic talent; unfortunately, very few motifs have survived intact. Note the delicacy and variety of the ornamentation on the upper part between the pinnacles.

One or two cleverly sculpted scenes contribute to the richness of the whole (such as *Women Fighting*, symbolising the triumph of Truth over Error) and illustrate ideas taken from the Middle Ages (*Lay of Aristotle*, representing Science being punished by Truth).

There is a beautiful marble **abbatial recess**★★ to the right of the altar; a 1526 piscina, also in marble, is next to it.

Above the sacristy door is a low relief commissioned by Ferry Carondelet in memory of the Joux landlords. The sculpted man's head sticking out of the socle represents Ferry Carondelet.

Cloisters

The architectural indecisiveness of the Franche-Comté is in evidence in the 15C cloisters. Round arches are still used, whereas the corner doors are surmounted by Flamboyant Gothic ogee arches and sculpted tympanums: the twin colonettes have archaic style capitals.

Chapter-house

This chapter-house, which opens onto the cloisters, has diagonal groined arches springing from the door.

Note the 16C painted and gilt wood statuettes of the Virgin holding Jesus as well as of the Three Kings.

Kitchen

Admire the Louis XIV clock with one hand, a beautiful Louis XIII armoire and an enormous mantelpiece.

EXCURSION

Défilé d'Entre-Roche

◗ *2km/1.5mi N all along D 437.*

Downstream of Montbenoît, the charming Saugeais Valley becomes a twisting gorge extending almost all the way to Morteau (*see p342*). At the Défilé d'Entre-Roche, the road cuts between breathtaking limestone cliffs, in which there are two caves. The **Grotte du Trésor** (*8km/5mi north of Montbenoît*) cave has an incredibly high entrance arch which you will find along a signposted path (*5min from D 437, a little above road level*). The cave of **Notre-Dame de Remonot** (*9km/5.5mi from Montbenoît*) is a place of pilgrimage, in which the water is said to heal eye afflictions. The opening is at road level; a barrier protects the entrance.

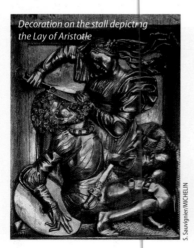

Decoration on the stall depicting the Lay of Aristotle

S. Sauvignier/MICHELIN

Pontarlier

The capital of Haut-Doubs, Pontarlier is located on a major crossroad between Franche-Comté and Switzerland, and has prospered over the centuries from its position. It makes a good base for summer excursions and is close to winter sports resorts.

▶ **Population:** 18 778
🚗 **Michelin Map:** 321: I-5.
🛈 **Info:** 14 bis r. de la Gare, 25300 Pontarlier.
    ℘03 81 46 48 33.
    www.pontarlier.org.
👁 **Don't Miss**: The amazing panorama from the Grand Taureau.
🕐 **Timing**: Allow a day to visit the town and surroundings.

A BIT OF HISTORY

The terrors of 1639 and 1736 – During the Ten Years War, French mercenaries spread fear and destruction throughout the Franche-Comté. On 26 January 1639, Pontarlier surrendered after a four-day siege led by Swedish forces. The town was pillaged, burned, and over 400 people died. However, it didn't become part of France until 1678, when Franche-Comté was officially annexed under the Nijmegen Treaty.

During the 18C, Pontarlier was damaged several times by fire, the worst being on 31 August 1736, destroying half the town largely built in wood. Pontarlier was reconstructed to plans by Querret. **The green fairy** – Pontarlier became the world capital for absinthe, known as *la fée verte* or green fairy, producing over 10 million bottles by the early 20C. However, the highly alcoholic herbal spirit was made illegal in France in 1915, as it apparently caused insanity. Finally legalised again in 2000, but at a lower strength, it is produced here once again.

SIGHTS

Église Saint-Bénigne

Rebuilt in the 17C and then restored, the church retained a 15C Flamboyant side doorway. This curious building has a blind façade on its right side, built after the 1736 fire to make the church blend in with the new square. The **belfry-porch** is in the style of mountain churches designed to withstand heavy snowfall. Inside there are two particularly interesting paintings either side of the chancel. Note also the 1754 pulpit and 1758 organ case, skillfully carved by the Guyon brothers of Pontarlier. With an Easter theme, the brightly coloured stained-glass windows (1975) are by G. Manessier.

Ancienne chapelle des Annonciades

This chapel, all that remains of the Annunciade convent, was built in 1612. The **doorway**★ dates from the beginning of the 18C. The chapel, now deconsecrated, has been turned into an exhibition centre.

Musée Municipal

🕐*Open daily except Tue 10am–noon, 2–6pm, Sat–Sun and public holidays 2–6pm.* 🕐*Closed 1 Jan, 1 May, 1 Nov, 25 Dec.* ♿*3.30€.* ♿ ℘*03 81 38 82 14. www.ville-pontarlier.fr.*
The museum, housed in what was a bourgeois home, built in the 16C and later modified several times, is devoted to local history, 19C and 20C Comtois paintings (including *Autoportrait au chien* by Courbet), 18C faïence, and objects related to the history of absinthe such as posters, engravings, decorated jars and so on.

Porte Saint-Pierre

This triumphal arch was erected in 1771, based on plans by Arçon, to celebrate the reconstruction of the city; the upper section, topped with a small bell tower, was added in the 19C. It resembles the Porte St-Martin in Paris.

EXCURSIONS

Grand Taureau★★

▶*11km/7mi E. Leave Pontarlier S along N 57 and turn left onto a minor road climbing the ski resort of Montagne du Larmont.* This is the highest point (1 323m/4 340ft) of the Larmont mountains, less than

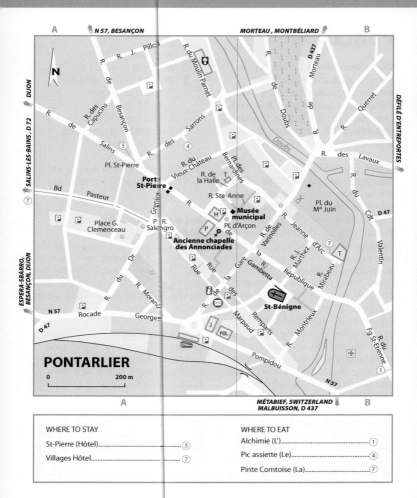

PONTARLIER

0   200 m

WHERE TO STAY	
St-Pierre (Hôtel)	⑤
Villages Hôtel	⑦

WHERE TO EAT	
Alchimie (L')	①
Pic assiette (Le)	④
Pinte Comtoise (La)	⑦

1km/0.5mi from the Franco-Swiss border. The **view**★ from here stretches over Pontarlier and the Jura plateaux to the west. For a full panorama, continue to the very top. Leave the car in front of the little chalet at the end of the road.

Panorama★★ (⚠ Climb up the slope that borders the chalet to the right and walk a little way along the ridge overlooking the Morte Valley, a continuation of the Val de Travers) – The all-round view takes in the parallel mountain ridges of the Jura, as far as the last line of mountains looming on the other side of the Swiss border, from the Chasseral to Mont Tendre. On a clear day the snowy Bernese Alps can be seen in the distance.

ADDRESSES

🛏 STAY

◯◯ **Hôtel St-Pierre** – 3 pl. St-Pierre. ℘ 03 81 46 50 80. www.hotel-st-pierre-pontarlier.fr. Restaurant closed Mon except holidays. ⅙. 12 rooms. ⚏7.20 €. Restaurant ◯. A newly renovated, centrally-located hotel, the rooms come in a variety of sizes and prices, all tastefully decorated and with double glazing.

◯◯ **Villages Hôtel** – 68 r. Salins. ℘ 03 81 46 71 78. 🅿. 53 rooms. ⚏7.50 €. Restaurant ◯◯. A convenient base for cross-country skiers, this hotel has been completely renovated and offers chic rooms in chalet style. The restaurant offers Swiss and Jura specialities.

ⵏ/EAT

🍴 **La Pinte Comtoise** – *4 r. Jeanne-d'Arc* 📞 *03 81 39 07 35. www.lapintecomtoise.fr* ♿. *Closed 1 week Feb, 2 weeks end Jul, 1 week end Aug, Wed eve and Sun (open Sun eves in summer). Reservations recommended.* Despite being a little away from the town centre, lovers of good food still seek out this restaurant with its distinctive red and gold sign. Good value food from local produce is served in a simple dining room with a décor of pastel colours.

🍴 **L'Alchimie** – *1 Av. de l'Armée-de-l'Est.* 📞 *03 81 46 65 89. www.lalchimie.fr. Closed 19–25 Apr, 1–15 Jul and Wed.* This welcoming restaurant is on a main road opposite the Nestlé factory. You will find inventive cuisine prepared with local produce, seasoned with spices and exotic flavourings. The décor is somewhat dark, but with a few Asian influences.

🍴 **Le Pic Assiette** – *11 r. St-Paul.* 📞 *03 81 39 06 42. Closed Aug, one week in Feb, Sat lunch, Sun eve and Mon.* An unusual restaurant in that the owners lived for some time in the Pacific: shades of the tropics flavour both menu and décor. They also serve regional cuisine, including a very tasty fondue with seasonal wild mushrooms.

ⵏ TAKING A BREAK

Pfaadt – *23 pl. St-Pierre.* 📞 *03 81 39 01 83. Open Tue–Sat 7am–12.30pm, 2.15–7pm, Sun 7.30am–12.30pm. Closed 2 weeks in Sept.* Pfaadt has been a dessert fixture in Pontarlier since 1953. Especially popular are the three-chocolate mousse, the absinthe ganache (shaped like the breasts of the "green fairy") and nine sorts of macaroons. Take a seat in the pleasant tearoom and indulge...

REGIONAL SPECIALITIES

Distillerie Pierre-Guy – *49 r. des Lavaux.* 📞 *03 81 39 04 70. www.pontarlier-anis.com. Open Tue–Fri 8am–noon, 2–6pm, Sat 8am–noon; visit 9–11am, 2.30–5pm. Closed 1 week mid-Oct and 1 week beginning of Jan.* This is one of the last two non-industrial distilleries remaining in Pontarlier. See how aniseed and herb-based apéritifs and liqueurs, including absinthe, are made. Fascinating.

Fromagerie de Doubs – *1 r. de la Fruitière, 25300 Doubs.* 📞 *03 81 39 05 21. Open Mon–Sat 8.30am–noon, 3.30–7pm, Sun and public holidays 5–7pm.* This cheese-making factory will show you how local cheeses like Comté, Morbier and Mont d'Or are prepared and matured in the traditional way. Tastings available, as well as an irresistible shop.

Château de Joux★

In a strategic position and with a superb view over the Joux cluse, this castle has been a fort, a prison and now a museum. A formidable eagle's nest, it has born more than 10 centuries of resistance, thanks to numerous structural changes.

- **Michelin Map:** 321: I-5.
- **Info:** 📞03 81 69 47 95. www.chateaudejoux.com.
- **Location:** 4km/2.5mi S of Pontarlier.
- **Don't Miss:** A renowned theatre festival, Les Nuits de Joux, takes place in the castle in summer.

A BIT OF HISTORY

The château was built by the lords of Joux in the 11C, enlarged under Charles Quint, and then Emperor Charles V. Vauban fortified it in 1678 to protect its vulnerable position near the border, after France annexed the Franche-Comté. The last modernisations were carried out between 1879 and 1881, by the future field marshal, Joffre.

Château de Joux

© Mathieu Guy/Fotolia.com

The stronghold has seen many prisoners. Mirabeau was locked inside after his father obtained an order for his arrest, hoping to cool down his hot-headed son and protect him from his creditors. In 1802, two insurgents against the Revolution escaped by sawing bars and climbing down curtains. By the time **Toussaint Louverture**, hero of Haitian independence, arrived soon after, security had been reinforced; the freedom fighter died here on 7 April 1803. In 2002 the Haitians erected a statue in his memory

VISIT

Open daily Apr–15 Nov. Guided tour (1hr15min) Jul–Aug 9am–6pm. Rest of the year 10–11.30am, 2–4.30pm. 6€, children 3.40€. Free audioguide. The tour of the five successive curtain walls covering 2ha/5 acres, each separated by deep moats crossed by three drawbridges, unfolds 10 centuries' of fortification. There is a beautiful view of the Doubs Valley and the Pontarlier cluse from the terrace of the gun tower. A **Musée d'Armes Anciennes**★, comprising 650 antique weapons, is in five rooms of the old keep. The collection ranges from the first regulation flint-lock rifle (1717 model) to repeating firearms from the Third Republic (1873). There is also an exhibition of military headgear – including a beautiful collection of shakos – and uniforms.

It is possible to visit the cells of **Mirabeau**, with a beautiful dowelled timber roof frame; that of **Toussaint Louverture**; and the tiny dark cell of the legendary Berthe de Joux.

EXCURSION
Cluse de Joux★★

This is one of the most beautiful examples of a Jura cluse. From the platform of the monument to the fallen of WW I at **Le Frambourg** there is an excellent **view**★★. The transverse valley through the Larmont Mountain cuts a passage just wide enough for the road and the railway line running from Pontarlier to Neuchâtel and Berne. Two strongholds command the cliffs: that of Le Larmont Inférieur to the north and the Château de Joux to the south.

ADDRESSES

STAY / EAT

Auberge Le Tillau – *Le Mont-des-Verrières, 25300 Les Verrières-de-Joux, 7km/4.3mi E of La Cluse-et-Mijoux by D 67bis and a minor road. 03 81 69 46 72. www.letillau.com. Closed 1 week around May and 15 Nov–15 Dec. Restaurant closed Sun eve and Mon. 11 rooms. 7.50€. Restaurant.* You can breathe in the mountain air at this delightful inn perched at an altitude of 1 200m/ 3 937ft amid pastures and pine trees. The peaceful rooms are comfortable, and the good traditional cuisine is made with fresh seasonal produce.

Malbuisson★

This small, scenic resort is on the east bank of the blue Lac de Saint-Point in the Upper Doubs Valley, enclosed at both ends by mountains.

RESORT

A path runs all around the **Lac de Saint-Point**★ *(23km/16mi; allow 6hrs; map available at tourist office)*. This lake was once linked with the Remoray Lake to form one expanse of water. Completely iced over in winter, it is the fourth largest natural lake in France at 6.3km/4.1mi long and 800m/875yd wide. The lake's very blue colour is explained by the waters being both pure and deep. **Chaon** on the northeast bank has the best view of the whole lake, and there is also a view from **Saint-Point-Lac** a little above Malbuisson.

The old **Fort Lucotte** at Saint-Antoine *(3km/2mi east; guided tours by appointment; ✆03 81 69 31 21)* has been used as an ageing cellar for Comté cheese since 1966. At any one time 65 000 cheeses will remain there for 10–20 months.

🚗 DRIVING TOURS

Vallée des Deux Lacs

See Region map. 16km/10mi circuit. Allow 2hrs. Leave Malbuisson to the southeast on the D 437 towards Mouthe.

▶ **Population:** 498
Michelin Map: 321: H-6.
Info: 69 Grande Rue, 25160 Malbuisson.
✆03 81 69 31 21.
www.malbuisson.fr.
Don't Miss: A walk around Lac de St-Pont; the Fort Lucotte cheese caves; the nature reserve and bird sanctuary at Lac de Remory.
🕐 **Timing:** Allow one to two days to explore the area.

Réserve Naturelle du Lac de Remoray

At an altitude of almost 1 000m/3 281ft, this nature reserve offers nature lovers a wealth of different ecosystems (lake, marshland, peat bog, meadow, forest) inhabited by numerous species of birds including a rare type of crake. The flora is equally rich with some 400 species.

Maison de la Réserve★ *(open daily year round 2–6pm, Jul–Aug 2–7pm; closed 20 Nov–3 Dec, 25 Dec and 1 Jan; 5.50€, 5–14 years 3€); ✆03 81 69 35 99; www.maisondelareserve.fr)* – Located on the way out of Labergement-Ste-Marie 3km/2mi south of Malbuisson, this centre offers information about the protection of the environment as well as the flora and fauna of the Haut-Doubs region. There are displays of stuffed animals in their natural habitat

Lac de St-Point

M. Paygnard/MICHELIN

(reconstituted), aquariums and collections of fossils.

Belvédère des Deux Lacs★
As you reach the end of the Remoray-Boujeons Lake on your way to Mouthe, turn right onto a minor road towards Boujeons. The small car park past the crossroad is the start of the path to the viewpoint, from which there is a beautiful panoramic **view** of the whole valley and the two lakes.

Lac de Remoray-Boujeons
Follow the road to Remoray-Boujeons and turn right on the D 46.
This picturesque lake is separated from St-Point Lake by a strip of marshland.

The Drugeon Valley
See Region map. 15km/9.5mi circuit. Allow 2hrs. Leave Malbuisson on the D 437 heading south. Turn right on the D 9.

▲▲ Ferme de la Pastorale★
At Bonnevaux, 18km/11mi northwest. ☎03 81 89 70 99. www.frasne.net/ pastorale/pastorale.htm. Guided visit (50min) Jul–Aug 3.30pm, 4.30pm and Wed eves; rest of the year daily except Sat 3.30pm, 4.30pm. 5€.
This huge farm based around a wooden structure from 1826, shows a reconstruction of the pastoral life on a farm in a golden age for farming. Just press the buttons in each room and learn...

▷ *Follow D 9 towards Frasne. Once you reach the forest of Frasne look out for the little grassy car park on the right.*

Les tourbières de Frasne
In this ecosystem of peat bogs, the increase in peat moss has reduced the humidity of the soil and allowed a gradual, if difficult, planting of pine trees and silver birch. Today this site is classified as a regional natural reserve, including in places up to 6m/20ft of peat, representing 6 000–12 000 years of growth.
Raised walkway (1.4km/1mi, 30min), or you can follow a walk around the peat bogs (5.8km/3.6mi, 2hrs 30min). The starting point is in the undergrowth

below the spruce trees. Panels at intervals give information about the peat as well as the flora and fauna. Note the slightly concave topography of the area due to it being a mature peat bog. The route continues through an area of living peat bog.

▷ *Return to Bonnevaux and turn left on D 47 towards Bouverans.*

Belvédère du lac de Bouverans
Car park is off the D 47. The viewpoint is reached by a steep path (150m/164yd).
From this viewpoint you will see a fine panorama over the lake, the marshes and the surrounding fields. You can watch the birds, especially the birds of prey that nest in the nearby cliffs.

▷ *Follow D 47 to La Rivière-Drugeon.*

▲▲ La Rivière-Drugeon
The village has created a **bird observatory** *(free access)* from which all the family can settle down quietly to spy on the birds of the marshland. There are explanatory information boards to help with the birds' identification.
In the old vicarage, an **environmental and historical centre** for the Drugeon Valley and the Upper Ain Valley holds temporary free exhibitions. A centre with documents on biodiversity and sustainable living is also open to the public (*open Mon, Tue, Thu, Fri 9am–noon; ☎03 81 49 82 99, ☎03 81 89 70 50 (town hall); www.cpiehautdoubs.org*). You can also visit the vicar's garden, enclosed by the old village ramparts, in which you will find medicinal plants, herbs, flowers and fruit trees, all used in the past by the church and its vicar.

▷ *Follow D 47 to Bonnevaux, then turn left on D 9.*

Belvédère de Vaux-et-Chantegrue
This viewpoint overlooks the winding Drugeon River surrounded by its fascinating flora. In autumn you will see a glistening array of colours, and in springtime, carpets of flowers.

This is another perfect place for bird-watching or simply to listen to the frogs croaking.

ADDRESSES

🏠 STAY

⊖ **Annexe Beau Site** – 65 Grande-Rue. ℘ 03 81 69 70 70. www.lelac-hotel.com. Closed 15 Nov–19 Dec except weekends. 🚻 🅿. 17 rooms. Functional rooms in an early 19C building, with columns adorning the entrance hall. You can eat cheese specialities or traditional cuisine at the Hôtel du Lac restaurant.

⊖ **Camping Les Fuvettes** – ℘ 03 81 69 31 50. Open 2 Apr–25 Sept. Reservations advised. 320 sites. Large campground with cabins and mobile homes for rent. In addition to aquatic facilities overlooking the lake, there is crazy golf, a playground, bar, store and restaurant.

⊖ **Hôtel de La Poste** – 61 Grande-Rue. ℘03 81 69 79 34. www.lelac-hotel.com. Closed 3–15 Jan, Sun eve and Mon. 10 rooms. 🍽 9 €. Restaurant ⊖. Pleasant, brightly coloured rooms; those facing the lake are quieter. Traditional cuisine and local specialities like meat *pierrade* served in the light-filled dining room.

🍴 EAT

⊖ **Auberge du Coude** – 25160 Labergement-Ste-Marie. ℘ 03 81 69 31 57. www.aubergeducoude.com. Closed 12 Nov–18 Dec, Sun eve and Wed out of season. This old house (1826) in between two lakes has modern guest rooms and a pretty garden with a pond. Try regional cuisine in the rustic dining room.

⊖ **Le Restaurant du Fromage** – 65 Grande-Rue. ℘ 03 81 69 34 80. www.lelac-hotel.com. Closed 13 Nov–21 Dec except weekends. With its sculpted wooden décor, this place looks just like a gingerbread house. It is a warm, convivial setting to sample local cheese specialities and other regional food.

⊖⊖⊖ **Le Bon Accueil** – 32 Grande-Rue. ℘ 03 81 69 30 58. Closed 17 Dec–16 Jan, Sun eve mid-Sept to mid-May, Tue lunch and Mon. Popular with locals and tourists, this family restaurant offers fine, contemporary cuisine. The chalet also has recently renovated, comfortable bedrooms.

🛍 SHOPPING

Atelier Bernardet – 12 r. Clos-du-Château, 25370 Touillon-et-Loutelet. ℘03 81 49 11 50. Open school holidays daily 2–7pm; rest of the year by appointment. Closed 1–15 Jul and Sun. Monsieur and Madame Bernardet share their passion for fine craftsmanship at their shop, full of traditional Franche-Comté clocks.

SARL Fonderie de Cloches Obertino Charles – 15 rte. de Mouthe, 25160 Labergement-Ste-Marie. ℘03 81 69 30 72. Shop open Mon–Sat 9am–noon, 2–6.30pm; tour of workshop Jul–Aug Sat 10am–noon. This foundry, set up in 1834, is one of the last of its kind in France and still casting bells (view by appointment only). The shop offers a wide range of items made on the premises: bronze and steel bells, small spherical bells, chimes, key rings and clocks.

Métabief-Mont d'Or ✳

With both downhill and cross-country ski facilities, Métabief-Mont d'Or is a winter sports resort encompassing six villages: Jougne, Les Hôpitaux-Neufs, Les Hôpitaux-Vieux, Métabief, Les Longevilles-Mont d'Or and Rochejean. In summer, mountain biking is the main activity.

▶ **Population:** 691
⏱ **Michelin Map:** 321: I-6.
ℹ **Info:** 1 pl. de la Mairie, 25370 Les Hôpitaux-Neufs. ℘03 81 49 13 81. www.metabief-tourisme.com.
◉ **Location:** The Swiss border is just 5km/3mi away, so be adventurous.

SIGHT
Église Sainte-Catherine

The unassuming church in the village of Les Hôpitaux-Neufs contains a real treasure, one of the finest **Baroque interiors**★ in the whole region (central altarpiece, side chapels, carved furniture).

ACTIVITIES
🎿 Alpine skiing

Downhill ski runs cover 40km/25mi and include a red run lit for night-time skiing; 7 chair-lifts and 15 drag-lifts take skiers to the long runs suitable for all levels. Main access points are: Métabief (X Authier car park), Jougne (Piquemiettes-les-Tavins) and Superlongevilles. The Morond chair-lift links to almost all the Métabief runs.

🎿 Cross-country skiing

Cross-country fans can glide over 210km/130mi of tracks, as well as 12.5km/8mi of cross-Jura trails; double tracks are provided to suit both styles of cross-country skiing.

Snowshoeing

The area also offers marked snowshoeing trails, with guiding recommended.

Summer sports

The village is popular in the summer, particularly for its mountain biking facilities, with multilevel permanent tracks for downhill, cross-country and trial practice. Other activities include two 600m/1 968ft summer toboggan tracks, a climbing wall, devil-karts, paragliding, biathlon training or simply hiking.

EXCURSIONS
Le Mont d'Or★★

About 10km/6mi, then 30min road trip on foot. ▷ Leave Métabief on D 45. At Longevilles-Mont d'Or, 200m/220yd before D 45 goes over the railway tunnel, turn left at the sign indicating Le Mont d'Or-sommet. At the end of the road, there is a big parking area.

🚶 From the car park, climb up to the Belvédère des Chamois, where a wide **panorama** opens up over the Joux Valley, the Swiss lakes and the Alps. In summer, look out for the Montbéliard and Simmental cows, whose milk is used for the famous Mont d'Or cheese, sold only from mid-September to mid-May.

Morond★

At the church in Métabief, turn left to reach the lower station of the chairlift (🕐 open weekends May–June, daily Jul–Aug; ☞3.50€; Dec–Mar (skiers and snow-shoers) 9am–5pm; ☞5€; 𝄐03 81 49 20 00).

🚶 From the top at Morond (*alt. 1 463m/4 800ft*) is a spectacular view over the Jura mountains, the Remoray lakes, Lake Geneva and the Alps.

🚂 Le Coni'fer

🕐*Open Jun–Sept. Departure days and times vary. ☞8€, 6–16 years 4€. 𝄐03 81 49 10 10. www.coni-fer.org.*
This tourist train has brought back to life the old Pontarlier-Vallorbe railway line, disused since 1971. The steam-powered train runs along 7.5km/5mi of track from Les Hôpitaux-Neufs to a natural sight known as Fontaine ronde.

ADDRESSES

🍴 EAT

☺☺ **Auberge La Boissaude** – *25370 Rochejean, 6km/3.7mi SW of Métabief by D 45. 𝄐03 81 49 90 72. http://laboissaude.free.fr. Closed last week Jun, 1–15 Dec, Tue and Wed. Reservation recommended.* This handsome Franche-Comté farmhouse perched atop the Mont d'Or has a typical mountain wooden interior. Delicious local hams, cheeses and tarts.

🛒 SHOPPING FOR CHEESE

Fromagerie du Mont d'Or – La Grange aux Fromages – *2 r. du Moulin, 25370 Métabief. 𝄐03 81 49 02 36. www.fromageriedumontdor.com. Open Mon–Sat 9am–noon, 3–7pm, Sun 9am–noon.* Visit this cheese factory and its maturing cellar to see how Comté, Morbier and Mont d'Or are made according to local tradition, and sample the end products. Then stop at the shop to stock up on cheese for friends at home.

LONS, ARBOIS AND THE LAKES

The capital of the Jura department, Lons-le-Saunier is worth exploring, but remains a modest town, perhaps out of deference to the grandeur of its surrounding landscape. The pull of the nearby countryside will lead you straight to the pretty vineyards that cloak the south-facing Jura foothills; or you might be drawn to spend all your time enjoying the extensive lakes and waterfalls. Whatever you choose to visit, do not miss the viewpoints from which you can admire the unusual and rather magical geological features here, the *réculées* or blind valleys near Baume-les-Messieurs and Arbois.

The natural partners of Jura: wine and cheese

It is partly the geography of lakes and mountains that makes Jura the smallest designated wine region in France. However, with huge areas ideal for grazing dairy cows, the other great gastronomic delight of Franche-Comté is Comté cheese, and more Comté is made than any other Appellation Contrôllée cheese in France. The main centre for Comté production is Poligny in the heart of the wine region, and both industries have created their own official, sign-posted tourist routes that are a delight to follow. Comté is a large wheel of cheese that is aged for an average of eight months before sale. Most Comté is made by cooperative cheese producers, where a group of farmers deliver the milk to a central place, known as a *fruitière*. Les routes du Comté (www.lesroutesducomte.com) provides details of guided tours, plus a useful list of farms, *fruitières* and cheese-ageing cellars that can be visited to understand more about the production, as well as to taste and buy the cheese at its source.

Similarly, the routes des vins du Jura (www.routesdesvinsdujura.com) lists family wine producers and cooperatives *(fruitières du vin)* that are open for tastings and cellar tours, though with the smaller ones it is best to call ahead for an appointment. The booklet and website list places to stay and eat along the route; many of the restaurants recommend selected local wines to match the foods. Tasting mature, nutty Comté cheese, a handful of walnuts and glass of the legendary aged vin jaune, a white wine unique to the Jura, is one of the great gastronomic experiences to be enjoyed in France.

Highlights

1 The viewpoints on the amazing circuit around **Baume-les-Messiers** (p360)

2 Discover the delightful town of **Arbois**, home to Pasteur (p363)

3 Find the amazing 200-year old **Président de la Joux** fir tree (p374)

4 A hike to see the **Hérissons waterfalls** (p378)

5 Explore **Château-Chalon** (p380)

The largest Jura wine festival, the Percée du Vin Jaune, is a glorious winter celebration held each year in a different town or village along the wine route, over the first weekend of February. The processions and stands bring together not only the winegrowers, but Comté and other cheese makers, and Morteau and Montbéliard sausage producers, too. In summer, many villages host their own smaller wine-tasting festivals at weekends, offering a delightful family experience in a rural setting.

Aire du Jura

This unusual service station is accessible from the motorway itself, and from the D 120 near Arlay, between Lons-le-Saunier and Poligny. If you do not have time to visit the famous Royal saltworks at Arc-et-Senans, in the grounds of the service station you can see various impressive sculptures based on sketches by architect Claude-Nicolas Ledoux. Regular, informative temporary exhibitions are held to highlight local gastronomy and other industries, and there is a permanent, excellent shop selling Jura wines, food and even a range of wooden toys.

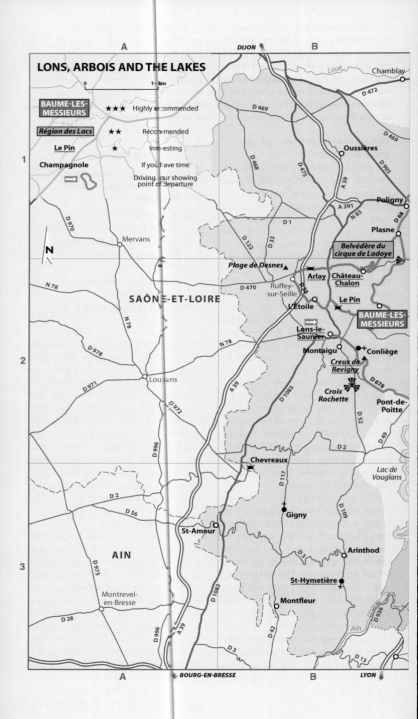

LONS, ARBOIS AND THE LAKES

BAUME-LES-MESSIEURS	★★★ Highly recommended
Région des Lacs	★★ Recommended
Le Pin	★ Interesting
Champagnole	If you have time
	Driving tour showing point of departure

DIJON

Loue

Chamblay

D 472

D 469

D 469

Oussières

D 905

D 468

D 475

A 39

Poligny

D 68

A 391

N 83

Plasne

D 970

D 1

Mervans

D 122

D 33

Belvédère du cirque de Ladoye

N

Plage de Desnes

Arlay

Château-Chalon

SAÔNE-ET-LOIRE

D 470

Ruffey-sur-Seille

D 68

Le Pin

L'Étoile

BAUME-LES-MESSIEURS

N 78

Lons-le-Saunier

N 78

D 978

Montaigu

Conliège

Creux de Revigny

D 678

Louhans

A 39

D 1083

Croix Rochette

D 971

D 972

Pont-de-Poitte

D 52

D 49

D 996

D 2

Lac de Vouglans

Chevreaux

D 117

D 2

D 56

Gigny

D 109

St-Amour

Arinthod

AIN

D 975

D 3

St-Hymetière

Montrevel-en-Bresse

D 1083

Montfleur

D 936

D 28

D 996

A 39

D 42

Ain

D 3

D 13

BOURG-EN-BRESSE

LYON

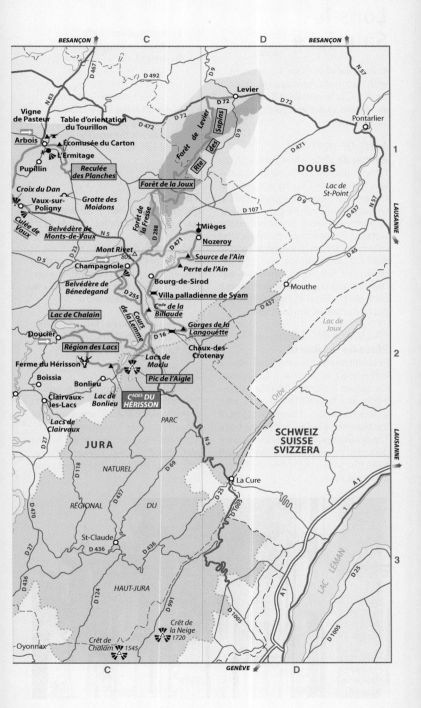

Lons-le-Saunier★

The capital of the Jura department, with its cultural heritage and spa facilities, is an excellent base for excursions to the vineyards or the Jura plateaux.

A BIT OF HISTORY

Rouget de Lisle – The author of the French national anthem, the *Marseillaise*, was born here in 1760. He enlisted with the army and became a captain of the Engineers, although his tastes ran more to poetry and music. He composed the war song for the Army of the Rhine, later to become known as the *Marseillaise*, in April 1792 at Strasbourg, where he was garrisoned. But the poet-musician was then imprudent enough to write a hymn dedicated to Henri IV, for which he was put into prison as a monarchist.

WALKING TOUR

Place de la Liberté

Recently nicely renovated, this square is the heart of the town. To the east the square is closed off by the imposing Rococo façade of the theatre, with a clock which runs through two bars of the *Marseillaise* before ringing the hour. The clock tower (Tour de l'Horloge) once defended the entrance into the fortified town (the square is located on the site of the old moat).

▶ **Population:** 17 879

Michelin Map: 321: D-6.

Info: pl. du 11–Novembre, 39000 Lons-Le-Saunier. ℘03 84 24 65 01. www.ot-lons-le-saunier.com.

Don't Miss: The arcades of Rue du Commerce and the majestic theatre. The caves at Le Creux de Revigny.

Theatre★

Open Jul–mid-Sept. Guided tours, ask at tourist office. ℘03 84 24 65 01.

Damaged by fire in 1901, the theatre, dating from 1847, had to be partially rebuilt. The architects drew their inspiration from the Opéra Garnier in Paris. The building was restored in 1997.

If you wish, you can first walk along rue St-Désiré to the Église St-Désiré which is slightly off this route.

Église St-Désiré

A beautiful 15C Burgundian School Entombment or Pietà is to the right of the chancel. The 11C **crypt** is one of the oldest in the Franche-Comté. The triple nave has six bays and is roofed with ribbed vaulting. The sarcophagus of St Désiré is in one of the three apsidal chapels.

Houses along Place de la Comédie

M. Paygnard/MICHELIN

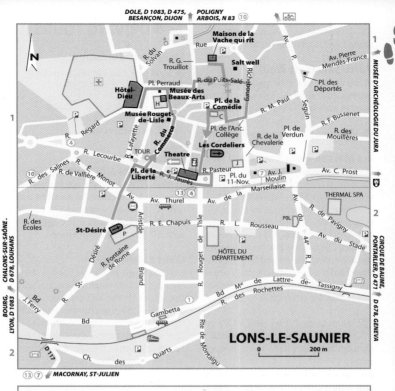

▶ *Return to the clock tower.*

Rue du Commerce★

The arcaded houses along this street (146 archways onto the street and under cover) make it very picturesque indeed. The houses were built in the second half of the 17C, after a terrible fire had literally cleared the space. Yet, in spite of the symmetrical balance dictated by the arcades, the people of Lons managed to manifest their taste for beauty as well as the independent spirit common to all Comtois people by varying the dimensions, curve and decoration on the arches.

Note the large roofs, with dormer windows to let in the light and tall chimneys.

The house in which Rouget de Lisle was born (no 24) is now a museum.

Musée Rouget-de-Lisle

◷*Open mid-Jun–mid Sept Mon–Fri 10am–noon, 2–6pm; weekends 2–5pm.* ⊚*1€. ℘03 84 47 29 16.*
Rouget de Lisle's birthplace has been turned into a small museum in which mementoes, documents and a video film relate the story of the French national anthem and its composer.

▶ *Continue to place de l'Hôtel-de-Ville and walk around it.*

The **Musée des Beaux-Arts** and the **Hôtel-Dieu**, are both 18C.

▷ *Walk across place Perraud and along rue du Puits-Salé to the spring.*

Puits-Salé (Salt Well)

In the centre of a little park, the town developed around this saltwater spring, used as early as the Roman period.

▷ *Take rue de l'Aubépine along the park.*

👥 Maison de la Vache qui rit

25 r. de Richebourg. ○*Open Jun–Aug daily 10am–7pm; rest of year varies.* 👓*7€ (6–18yrs 5€).* 📞*03 84 43 54 10. www.lamaisondelavachequirit.com.* Museum dedicated to the famous cubes of the Laughing Cow soft cheese, beloved by children, and first made in a factory on this site owned by the Lons-based Bel cheese company. Interactive educational visit and display of over 600 Laughing Cow artefacts.

▷ *Return to rue du Puits-Salé and turn left, then right into rue Richebourg and right again to place de l'Ancien-Collège.*

Rue de Balerne leads to **place de la Comédie** and its wine-growers' houses.

▷ *Follow rue du Four to rue des Cordeliers.*

Église des Cordeliers

Hidden at the end of a courtyard, this 13C church, restored in the 18C is the burial place of the Chalon-Arlays, who were Lons' feudal lords in the Middle Ages. Besides the Louis XVI **woodwork** in the chancel, note the 1728 pulpit executed by the Lamberthoz brothers of Lons.

▷ *Continue to place du 11–Novembre.*

The square is prolonged by the **promenade de la Chevalerie**, adorned with a statue of Rouget de Lisle by Bartholdi.

🚗 DRIVING TOURS

Le Plateau Jurassien

👆*See Region map. 19km/12mi circuit. Allow 4hrs.*

▷ *Leave Lons-le-Saunier heading southeast on the D 678. A drive along the Jura plateau above Lons.*

Conliège

Église (📞*03 84 24 04 93;* 👥*guided visits Mon–Fri on request from M. Broutet).* The church has beautiful wrought iron grilles, a lavishly sculpted 17C pulpit, pews from 1525, and a 16C reliquary with the relics of Saint Fortuné.

Creux de Revigny★

Limestone escarpments form a spectacular amphitheatre at Revigny, with the source of the Vallière river at the bottom. There are countless caves in the cliffs concealed by the vegetation. The locals hid in these caves during the Ten Year Warm in the 17C, making permanent homes there until it was safe to leave.

▷ *The road follows down to the Ain valley, which it joins at Pont-de-Poitte.*

ADDRESSES

🛏STAY

◲ **Nouvel Hôtel** – *50 r. Lecourbe.* 📞*03 84 47 20 67. www.nouvel-hotel-lons.fr. Closed 16 Dec–10 Jan. 25 rooms.* ☕ *7.50€.* This hotel is decorated with beautiful models of warships and boats. The rooms are simple and functional, but the welcome is warm.

◲ **Hôtel Gambetta** – *4 bd Gambetta.* 📞*03 84 24 41 18. www.hotel-gambetta-lons.com. Closed 23 Dec–4 Jan.* 🅿. *20 rooms.* ☕ *7.50 €.* Very close to the station and the main ring-road, rooms are well soundproofed, with some air-conditioned. Colourful, contemporary and comfortable rooms.

◲ **Hôtel Le Parc** – *9 av. J. Moulin.* 📞*03 84 86 10 20. www.hotel-parc.fr. 16 rooms.* ☕ *8 €. Restaurant* ◲*.* Well situated close to the centre of town, the rooms are simple and practical. A rather dark dining room serves regional food.

🍴🍴 **Chambre d'hôte Le Jardin de Misette** – *R. Honoré-Chapuis, 39140 Arlay. 12 km/7.5mi E of Château-Chalon by D 5 to Voiteur, then D 120. ℘03 84 85 15 72. http://sites.google.com/site/lejardin demisette.* 🍴. *4 rooms.* Country charm is offered at this winegrower's house on the banks of the Seille. Relaxed atmosphere with quiet rooms (there's a family room in a separate cottage) and evening meals provided with the family.

🍴🍴🍴 **Hôtel La Parenthèse** – *186 chemin du Pin, 39570 Chille. ℘03 84 47 55 44. www.hotelparenthese.com. Closed 20–30 Dec.* 🅿. *34 rooms.* 🛏 *11 €. Restaurant*🍴🍴🍴. Modern hotel close to the Jura vineyards offering three levels of comfortable rooms, many of which have a balcony overlooking wooded parkland. The contemporary restaurant has a focus on Jura food and wine.

🍴🍴🍴 **Domaine du Val de Sorne** – *39570 Vernatois. ℘03 84 43 04 80. www.valdesorne.com. Closed 20 Dec–5 Jan.* 🅿. *35 rooms.* 🛏 *12 €. Restaurant* 🍴🍴. This modern hotel is at the Val de Sorne golf course, and offers full leisure facilities. The rooms are being gradually refurbished. The restaurant overlooking the green offers barbecues in summer.

🍴/EAT

🍴 **Grand Café du Théâtre** – *2 r. Jean-Jaurès. ℘03 84 24 49 30. Closed 1 Nov–15 Nov, Sun.* Classified as a historic monument, this famous café offers decent, quality fare. With a terrace overlooking the square near the shops, it makes an ideal lunch stop.

🍴 **Le Relais des Salines** – *26 r. des Salines. ℘03 84 43 01 57. Closed 3 weeks in Jul or Aug, Sun, Mon and Tue eve. Reservations recommended.* The interior of this restaurant is decorated like an old coaching inn with tables in the stalls, plenty of wood and fine Jura furniture. It serves regional food and wine.

🍴🍴 **Le Strasbourg** – *4 r. Jean-Jaurès. ℘03 84 24 36 92.* Popular with locals and tourists alike, and another classified

monument, you can enjoy a drink at this grand 18C café inside or on the terrace. Brassierie-style food is served.

🍴🍴 **Ferme-auberge La Grange Rouge** – *39570 Geruge. ℘03 84 47 00 44. www.la-grange-rouge.com. Open Wed eve to Sun lunch, reservations essential.* ♿🅿🍴. *6 rooms* 🍴. In the hills south of Lons-le-Saunier, this inn is popular among locals. Phone ahead to ask about the day's menu. The cosy and quiet rooms exude country-style charm.

🍴🍴🍴 **Hostellerie St-Germain** – *Grande-Rue, 39210 St-Germain-lès-Arlay. ℘03 84 44 60 91. www.hostellerie saintgermain.com. 6 rooms* 🍴🍴. In the heart of the vineyards, fine local food is offered in two vaulted dining rooms. Try the home-made foie gras with morels and choose from their fine list of vin jaune. Recently renovated rooms are quiet.

🍴 TAKING A BREAK

Au Prince d'Orange – *1 pl. de la Liberté. ℘03 84 24 31 39. www.pelen.fr. Open (shop) Mon–Sat 8.30am–7pm, Sun 8.30am –12.30pm; (tearoom) 2.30–7pm.* The Pelen family has been making delicious pastries and sweetmeats such as *galets de Chalain* (chocolate-coated nougatine with praline) since 1899. The upstairs tearoom is cosy and elegant.

Pâtisserie Rouget-de-l'Isle – *22 r. du Commerce. ℘03 84 24 51 80. Open Mon– Sat 8am–7pm (Wed closed 12.30–1.30pm); Sun 8am–6pm. Closed 15–30 Jul.* This pastry shop occupies the birthplace of Rouget de Lisle and sells the famed macaroon named after him, plus 40 different kinds of chocolates. The tearoom opens onto the terrace in summer.

La Maison du Vigneron – *23 r. du Commerce. ℘03 84 24 44 60. Open Tue–Sat 10am–noon, 2–6.30pm.* Learn all about Jura wine at this shop with tastings and sales of the main regional wines.

Domaine viticole du Château d'Arlay – *r. de St-Germain, 39140 Arlay. Open mid-Jun–mid-Sept Mon–Sat 9am–noon, 2–6pm; Sun 2–6pm. Rest of year by appointment. ℘03 84 85 04 22. www. arlay.com.* At the tasting room in the château you can try the range of wines produced here including its vin jaune.

Baume-les-Messieurs★★★

Baume-les-Messieurs stands in a grandiose setting at the convergence of three valleys, one of which is the magnificent blind valley (reculée) of the Baume amph theatre. Particularly known for the picturesque abbey dating back to the 9C, the village itself is on the banks of the Seille.

▶ **Population:** 196
🚹 **Michelin Map:** 321: D-6.
🚩 **Info:** 10, pl. de la Mairie. 𝒫 03 84 44 95 45 www.baumeles-messieurs.fr.
🔵 **Location:** Try to arrive in Baume-les-Messieurs by the D 4 via Crançot; the approach into the village is particularly lovely.
🕐 **Timing:** A good day to explore this amazing place.

A BIT OF HISTORY

Monks and Gentlemen – The abbey at Baume was founded c. 870 and adopted the Benedictine Rule. One of its claims to glory is that in 909 six of its monks were among the founders of the illustrious abbey at Cluny. Monastic life, however, grew increasingly lax, as it did at St-Claude (🔵 see ST-CLAUDE); from the 16C onwards, the humble monks of the abbey's beginnings were replaced by canons of noble birth. These high and mighty Messieurs lost no time in modifying the name of their home, thus Baume-les-Moines became Baume-les-Messieurs. This lasted until the Revolution; in 1793 all the abbey's possessions were seized and auctioned off.

The adventurous life and times of Jean de Watteville – Jean de Watteville was one of the abbots of Baume in the 17C, as well as one of the most extraor-

dinary characters of his age, if one is to believe the Memoirs of St Simon. His many adventures have almost certainly been embellished.

Soldier, Franciscan friar, Carthusian monk, Turkish Pasha – Watteville initially followed a military career. While a minor officer in the Burgundy regiment during the Milan campaign he fought a duel with a Spanish nobleman in the service of the Queen of Spain and killed him. He fled to Paris. While there, he heard a sermon on the dangers of hell and, overcome with remorse, converted to Christianity. The ex-soldier became a Franciscan friar, then entered the abbey of Bonlieu as a Carthusian monk. Watteville soon tired of monastic life. He was caught climbing the wall in his bid for freedom by the prior himself.

Baume-les-Messieurs village and the Cirque de Baume

R. Mattes/MICHELIN

Watteville shot the man and escaped, crossing the Pyrenees into Spain. Leaving behind a second noble Spanish corpse, Watteville fled to Constantinople. The ex-monk converted to Islam and put his military talents to the service of the Sultan, who was so impressed that he promoted him first to Pasha, then to Governor of the province of Morea.

Abbot of Baume – After several years of living the high life surrounded by a sizeable harem, Watteville made an offer to the Venetians, whom he had been engaged by the Sultan to fight: if they could promise him papal absolution for his past crimes as well as the abbey of Baume as a reward, he would surrender his troops. This outrageous deal was struck, and our opportunist ex-Pasha shaved his head for the second time and took charge of the abbey of Baume.

The abbot remained as impetuous as ever, as several anecdotes illustrate. For example, Watteville had the series of ladders, previously the only way of getting to the bottom of the valley from Crançot, replaced by steps cut into the rock (the Échelles de Crançot). Seeing his monks taking infinite pains not to break their necks on the steep, slippery steps, the abbot flew into a rage, leapt onto his long-suffering mule's back and drove it down the steps, berating the monks as he went for their cowardice.

Parliamentary Intermediary – When Louis XIV invaded Franche-Comté, Watteville, after weighing up the French chances of winning, offered his services to the French king. Thanks to his skilful use of language, he won over the last centres of resistance (Gray, Ornans, Nozeroy) to the French king's cause without a single shot being fired.

After the Nijmegen peace treaty of 1678, Watteville returned to his abbey and a life of luxury. He died in 1702, aged 84.

ABBAYE

🕐 *Open all year for free visits.*
📷 *Certain parts only by guided tours (45mins) mid-May to Sept 10am–noon, 2–6pm.* ⊚*4.50€.* ✆*03 84 44 95 45.*

A vaulted passageway leads into the first courtyard, round which are the guest-house, abbot's house, keep, tower used as a court *(tour de justice)* and church.

Church – The 15C façade has an interesting **doorway**: God the Father giving Blessing is depicted on the central pillar and angels enthusiastically playing musical instruments in the side niches. The nave was once paved with tombstones, of which about 40 remain; the most interesting are leaning against the wall of the north side aisle. Close by is the modest tomb of Abbot Jean de Watteville. The Chapelle de Chalon, the mausoleum of the aristocratic Chalon family, is to the north of the chancel. There is a beautiful painted and sculpted 16C Flemish **altarpiece**★★ (📷*guided tour).*

Cour du cloître – A door in the middle of the nave on the south side leads to what used to be the cloisters. The monks' dormitory and refectory overlooked this courtyard.

Abbey buildings – An arch on the left leads into another courtyard surrounded by buildings which once contained the apartments of the aristocratic canons.

🚗 DRIVING TOUR

Cirque de Baume ★★★
21km/13mi round tour.

▶ *Leave Baume-les-Messieurs on D 70E3; left on D 70E1, to the bottom of the amphitheatre along the banks of the Dard.*

The tall rocky cliffs of this amphitheatre are an awe-inspiring sight. *Park near the Chalet des Grottes de Baume.*

Grottes de Baume★
🕐*Open Apr–Sept.* 📷*Guided tour (45min) Jul–Aug 10am–6pm, Apr–Jun and Sept 10am–noon, 2–5pm.* ⊚*5.50€ (children 3€). Dress warmly.* ✆*03 84 48 23 02.*

After the entrance gallery, visitors are taken through tall, narrow chambers to the **great hall**. The visit continues round a lake containing small, white blind shrimp. The **Catafalque gallery** is 80m/262ft high.

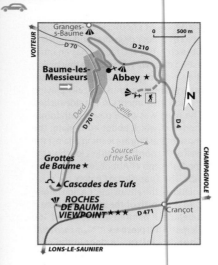

> Return to D 70 then right to Crançot. View of Baume after the second hairpin.

La Croix viewpoint

Stop at the D 70/ D 210 crossroads.
Take the path on the right into the forest, following the blue trail markers *(20min there and back on foot).* At the end of the path, near the cross, there is a **view**★ over Baume-les-Messieurs.

> Turn back, and if you like, head for the village of Granges-sur-Baume. *As you enter the village, a belvedere (follow the signs) offers another remarkable* **view**★. *Go back to the crossroads. Further ahead turn right on D 4, then right again at Crançot on D 471, then right once more towards the Belvédère des Roches-de-Baume.*

Belvédère des Roches-de-Baume★★★

Walk along the edge of the cliff which forms the famous viewpoint. At the last minute an astounding view of the entire amphitheatre unfolds though a gap in the rocks.
Near the viewpoint furthest to the right there are steps cut into the rock.
These steps, the **Échelles de Crançot**, lead down to the amphitheatre's floor and the caves.

> Return to D 471 and follow it to Crançot then take D 4 back to Baume-les-Messieurs.

ADDRESSES

🛏 STAY

⊝ **Camping municipal La Toupe** – *By the river on the road out of Baume on D 70 (dir. Lons-le-Saunier).* ℘*03 84 44 63 16. Open mid-Apr–Sept.* 🛏. *52 sites.* There are basic facilities at this shady, verdant campsite by the riverside in a gorgeous location: a reception chalet and two well-kept, but simple bathroom blocks surrounded by green.

🍽 EAT

⊝ **Le Grand Jardin** – *Pl. de l'Abbaye.* ℘*03 84 44 68 37. www.legrandjardin.fr. Closed mid-Dec–end Jan, Tue and Wed except Jul–Aug.* 📶 ♿ ⛵. *3 rooms.* ⊝⊝. In a charming little village house close to the abbey, the country dining room here has a fireplace. A menu of traditional dishes with regional touches is offered with delightful service. Under the eves upstairs are three guest rooms with wooden flooring.

⊝⊝ **Les Grottes** – *at the Grottes de Baume.* ℘*03 84 48 23 15. www.restaurant desgrottes.com. Open Easter–end Oct. Closed Mon except Jul–Aug.* 📶 ♿. *Reservations recommended.* The pretty 1900 pavilion lies just down from the caves, opposite the breathtaking Cascades des Tufs waterfalls, which you can enjoy from the shady terrace. In winter you can take refuge in the old-fashioned dining-room, reminiscent of a Scottish fishing lodge. Tasty local food might include Morteau sausage, chicken fillet in Macvin or local trout.

🛍 SHOPPING

Fromagerie artisanale d'Hervé Poulet et Fils – *39210 Granges-sur-Beaume.* ℘*03 84 48 28 32. Open Jul–Aug Mon–Sat 9am–noon, 3–7pm (Wed 9am–noon). Rest of year, same hours but closed Tue, Wed and Thu afternoon.* This family cheese-maker sells delicious Comté, Morbier and butter in their farm shop, next to a viewpoint of the Baume amphitheatre.

Arbois★

Arbois is at the entrance of one of the beautiful dead-end valleys known as *reculées* in the Jura, on either bank of the Cuisance. This picturesque town is surrounded by vineyards and considered the heart of the Jura wine region.

A BIT OF HISTORY

The varied wines of Arbois – Even if the Arbois vineyards received one of the first wine AOCs in France 1936, it was the charismatic wine producer and entrepreneur Henri Maire who pulled the wine region out of the doldrums after World War II. Henri Maire's small family vineyard grew greatly, and the winery became a listed company, but it has lately declined. The wine region in general, though, goes from strength to strength.

With three local grapes – Savagnin, Poulsard and Trousseau – grown alongside Chardonnay and Pinot Noir, a myriad of wine styles is made: from sparkling to very individual dry whites; light, but highly perfumed reds; the famous long-lived vin jaune; sweet vin de paille from dried grapes, and finally Macvin, made by adding spirit to grape juice.

On the first Sunday in September is a harvest festival in Arbois called the **Fête de Biou**. The wine-growers parade with an enormous bunch of grapes weighing up to 100kg/220lb, which is made of many smaller bunches of grapes bound together. After the procession, the Biou is hung in the nave of the church as an offering to St Just, the patron saint of Arbois.

Pasteur In Arbois – Although Louis Pasteur was born in Dole, his true home in Jura was Arbois. His father was a tanner who in 1827 moved the family to an old tannery in Arbois that later the scientist enlarged into a fine town house.

At the local school he was a conscientious pupil but never considered more than slightly above average. His greatest interest was drawing portraits in pastels and pencil of his parents and friends. To fund study for his baccalaureate at the Besançon lycée, he became a tutor. With his admission to the École Normale in Paris in 1843, Pasteur embarked on his distinguished career. Every year he

- ▶ **Population:** 3 509
- 🕭 **Michelin Map:** 321: E-5.
- 🖪 **Info:** 10 r. de l'Hôtel de Ville, 39600 Arbois. ℘03 84 66 55 50. www.arbois.com.
- ◖ **Location:** Arbois is on the Jura wine trail, with plenty of chances for wine-tasting.
- ◓ **Don't Miss:** The superb amphitheatre of the reculée des Planches, the caves and the many viewpoints.

Arbois and its vineyards

© CRT Franche-Comté/Sandrine Baverel

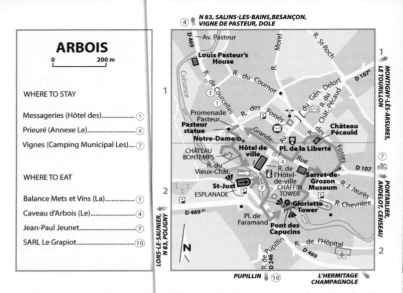

ARBOIS

0   200 m

WHERE TO STAY

Messageries (Hôtel des)...................... ①

Prieuré (Annexe Le)............................... ④

Vignes (Camping Municipal Les).....⑦

WHERE TO EAT

Balance Mets et Vins (La)..................... ①

Caveau d'Arbois (Le)............................ ④

Jean-Paul Jeunet................................... ⑦

SARL Le Grapiot.................................... ⑩

would return to Arbois, and in 1863 Napoleon III asked him to use his experience to help the wine-growers of Arbois improve their wine quality. In order to remain independent he purchased a small vineyard in Montigny-lès-Arsures, and in 1878 he studied the process of alcoholic fermentation. In proving that yeast existed in the air, rather than being integral to the grape berry, as previously thought, he was able to complete his studies on the importance of the process of pasteurisation. His work, of course, not only improved wine-making techniques, it also had a major influence on the understanding of hygiene and infectious diseases and thus formed the basis for modern medicine. Of his powers of observation, Pasteur would say "Chance favours only the prepared mind".

The great scientist would rarely miss the annual Fête du Biou. In 1895, illness prevented him from coming to Arbois and he died on 28 September.

☞WALKING TOUR

Allow 2h30. Start at the foot of the Église Saint-Just on the edge of the Cuisance.
In a warm ochre colour, the 60m/197ft-high **belfry** (16C) of the **Église St Just**★, dominates the town.

The large 12C–13C priory church includes a 1717 wooden pulpit and a chancel with

a Flamboyant window featuring the 12 apostles.

Cross the bridge on the left and turn immediately right into rue Mercière to Place Faramond. Here you will see several typical **wine-growers houses** (nos. 48–52) with trap doors at ground level to get the wine barrels in and out. Walk over the pretty **pont des Capucins** for a view over the Cuisance to the hills and the **Gloriette tower**. Continue and turn left on rue de Bourgogne, then right on rue du Vieil-Hôpital to the **Sarret-de-Grozon Museum** (✆ *open Jun–Sept 3–6.30pm except Tue*), an 18C mansion with original furniture and décor. Follow rue Maupré and rue des Fossés. Cross the garden on the left to **Château Pécauld** and the Jura wine museum. Follow the arcades of la Grande-Rue past Place de la Liberté and note a **statue of Pasteur** at the end of a garden on the left. Return to the church via rue du Vieux-Château.

MAISON DE LOUIS PASTEUR★

✆*Open Apr–Oct.* ☞*Guided tours (45min) Jun–Sept 9.45am, 10.45am, 11.45am and 2pm–6pm; Apr, May and Oct 2.15pm, 3.15pm, 4.15pm and 5.15pm.* ✆*5.80€.* ✆*03 84 66 11 72.*
Sensitively restored, Pasteur's house on the banks of the Cuisance looks much as it did when the family lived there.

There are numerous personal mementoes on display in the billiard room. On the first floor, two early drawings show his hidden talent as an artist.

The laboratory where Pasteur worked on his visits to Arbois includes the instruments and equipment that he used for some of his famous experiments.

EXCURSIONS
L'Ermitage
2.5km/1.5mi by D 469; after 1.5km/ 0.9mi turn right onto a road climbing in a series of hairpin bends to an esplanade.

From the edge of the plateau, near the chapel, there is a fine view of Arbois and the Cuisance Valley.

Pupillin
3km/1.9mi S along D 246.

This pretty vineyard village on the plateau above Arbois, is particularly known for one grape variety, Ploussard. At the **viewpoint** over the vineyards a sign declares Pupillin to be World Capital of Ploussard.

The village's wines are made from all Jura varieties and use the appellation **Arbois-Pupillin.** There are several good producers in the vicinity where offer tasting opportunities.

Grottes des Moidons
In Molain, 12km/7.5mi S by D 469 and D 4. Open Apr–Sept. Guided tours (45min) Jul–Aug daily 9.30am– 5.30pm. Rest of the year varies. 6€ (children 3.20€). 03 84 51 74 94. www.grottesdesmoidons.com.

Deep in the forest, these caves contain a wealth of **concretions**. The visit ends with a son et lumière show.

DRIVING TOURS

Reculée des Planches ★★
21km/13mi – allow one day.

Leave Arbois on D 107, then take D 247 to the right near the church in Mesnay.

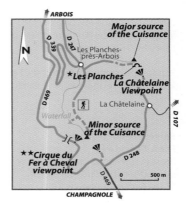

This road soon enters the Reculée des Planches. Go past the church on coming to Planches-près-Arbois, head past the stone bridge and take the narrow surfaced road sharply to the left, along the foot of the cliffs. Leave the car 600m/660yd further on.

Major source of the Cuisance
This is the more interesting of the two sources of the Cuisance, a tributary of the Loue. In rainy seasons the water cascades from a cave, which is also the entrance to the cave of Les Planches.

Grotte des Planches★
Open Apr–Sept. Guided tours (1hr) 10 Jul–20 Aug daily 1pm. Rest of the year daily 10am–noon and 2–5pm. 6€ (children 3€). 03 84 66 13 74. www.grottes-des-planches.net.

This cave was formed by water running between rock strata. Two of the galleries have been set aside for tourists, who can trace the underground path of the water as it flows through the rock.

Minor source of the Cuisance
500m/550yd from leaving Les Planches, then 1hr there and back on foot. On reaching Arbois head for Auberge du Moulin; park the car next to the river.

Follow the path uphill. This waterfall is formed by the young river and the spring itself in periods of heavy rain.

Retrace your steps. Straight after the bridge over the Cuisance, turn left on D 339, a narrow surfaced road leading uphill. Then take D 469, cut into the rock face, on the left. Leave the car in the car park 30m/33yd further on.

Retrace your steps for a view of the Fer-à-Cheval (horse-shoe) amphitheatre.

◯ *Return to the car and take D 469.*

Belvédère du cirque du Fer-à-Cheval★★
Leave the car near an inn and take the signposted path (10min) on the left.
⬜ The path goes through a little wood, at the edge of which the amphitheatre opens out *(protective barrier)*. There is a superb **view** of the reculée from the viewpoint overlooking the valley floor from nearly 200m/656ft up.

◯ *Return to Arbois on D 469.*

The Vineyards★
90km/56mi round tour – allow one day.
The region is divided into four AOC areas *(Appellation d'Origine Contrôlée)*: Arbois, Château-Chalon, Côtes-du-Jura and l'Étoile. 🕯 *For more information, see the chapter on Wine in the INTRODUCTION.*

◯ *Leave Arbois on D 1083 towards Lons-le-Saunier.*

Poligny
This little medieval town, surrounded by rich farmland and vineyards, has also earned itself a reputation as the capital of Comté cheese. Learn more about how it is made at the **Maison du Comté** (◯ open Jul–Aug 10–11.30am, 2–5.30pm; May–Jun and Sept 2–6pm; rest of the year times vary; ◉4€; ✆03 84 37 78 40; www.comte.com); then pick up some to take home at one of the shops in town. It is worth exploring the back streets of Poligny for some of its fine buildings, especially the **Collégiale Saint-Hippolyte**★ and its 15C statues.

◯ *Take N 5 towards Champagnole.*

Vaux-sur-Poligny
See the Cluniac church with an unusual roof of multicoloured varnished tiles.

Belvédère de Monts-de-Vaux★
This viewpoint *(car park)* offers a beautiful **view** all along the *reculée*.

◯ *Rejoin N 5 towards Poligny: after about 3.5km/2mi D 257 towards Chamole leads off to the right.*

The road climbs with extended **views**★ of the Culée de Vaux, Poligny and the Bresse region.

◯ *Return to Poligny. Leave on D 68 S.*

Plasne
A stroll around this hilltop village offers pretty **views**★ of the Bresse region.

◯ *Now take D 96, a narrow, bumpy road.*

Belvédère du Cirque de Ladoye★★
Car park above the reculée, right of the road, 40m/44yd after the D 96-D 5 junction.
The **view** is impressive.

◯ *Take D 204 at Granges-de-Ladoye. This road heads down to Ladoye-sur-Seille, before following the Seille Valley. Turn left at the junction with D 70, towards Baume-les-Messieurs.*

Baume-les-Messieurs★★★
🕯 *See BAUME-LES-MESSIEURS.*

◯ *Continue to D 471 and turn right towards Lons-le-Saunier. Shortly beyond a deep bend with a wonderful vineyard view, turn right onto a minor road towards Panessières. Follow the signposts to the Château du Pin.*

Château du Pin★
◯ *Open Jul–Sept 1–7pm.* ◉4€.
Built in the 13C by Jean de Chalon, Count of Burgundy and Lord of Arlay, it was destroyed by Louis XI, rebuilt in the 15C and restored in the 20C.

◯ *Continue to D 1083 and turn left towards Lons-le-Saunier; 1km/0.6mi further on, turn right onto D 38 towards St-Didier and L'Étoile.*

L'Étoile

In spite of its small size, L'Étoile has no fewer than five châteaux and several wine-growing estates where you can enjoy tasting their white wines.

Château d'Arlay★

🕐 *Open mid-Jun to mid-Sept.*
🐾 *Guided tours (30min) of the château, unaccompanied tours of the park and Jurafaune daily 2–6pm.* ✆*9€ (children 6.50€).* ✆*03 84 44 41 94. www.arlay.com.*
The imposing 18C château is surrounded by a superb park. The apartments of the Prince of Arenberg, who resided here around 1830, are open to visitors. Note the library and the doll's bedroom. The 👫**park**★ extends uphill to the medieval ruins of the original fortress, often used for demonstration flights of birds of prey (**Jurafaune**).

▷ *Follow D 120 to Voiteur, then take the D 5 winding up to Château-Chalon.*

Château-Chalon★

🕐 *See CHÂTEAU-CHALON.*

ADDRESSES

🛏STAY

ARBOIS

🛏 **Camping Municipal Les Vignes** – *Près du stade et de la piscine.* ✆*03 84 66 14 12. Open May–Sept. Reservations advised. 139 sites.* At this pleasant camping ground, shaded sites are arranged in terraces, offering views of the surrounding hillsides.

🛏🛏 **Hôtel des Messageries** – *R. de Courcelles.* ✆*03 84 66 15 45. www.hotel lesmessageries.com. Closed Jan and Dec. 26 rooms.* This former coaching inn in the town centre offers basic comfort at low prices: some rooms have no bathrooms. Rooms at the back are quietest.

🛏🛏🛏 **Annexe Le Prieuré** – *R. de l'Hôtel-de-Ville.* ✆*03 84 66 05 67. www.jeanpauljeunet.com. Closed Dec, Jan, Wed from Sept–Jun and Tue.* 🍴*. 7 rooms.* The quiet, carefully kept rooms in this fine 17C town house are furnished in charming old-fashioned style. It is the annexe for the hotel-restaurant Jean-Paul Jeunet, about 200m/210yd away where breakfast is taken.

POLIGNY

🛏🛏 **Domaine du Revermont** – *39230 Passenans. 11km/5.5mi SW of Poligny by D 1083 et D 57.* ✆*03 84 44 61 02. www. domaine-du-revermont.fr. Closed 22 Dec– 1 Mar.* 🅿️*.* 🛏 *10.50 €. Restaurant* 🍽🍽*.* Built in 1970 in the midst of pastures and vineyards, the large bedrooms in this hotel have views over the park. A pleasant dining room, in tones of yellow and orange with stone cladding and a fireplace, serves local cuisine.

🛏🛏 **La Ferme du Château** – *R. de la Poste, 39800 Bersaillin. 9km/5.5mi W of Poligny by D 1083, then D 22.* ✆*03 84 25 91 31. www.ferme-du-chateau.fr.* 🍴♿*. 5 rooms.* 🛏*. Restaurant* 🍽🍽*.* Extremely nicely restored, this 18C farmhouse has retained many original features such as the magnificent vaulted ceiling and columns in the large room used for receptions. The guest rooms are dark but elegant, looking out to the countryside. Meals are served in the evening on reservation.

🍴EAT

ARBOIS

🍽 **SARL Le Grapiot** – *R. Bagier, 39600 Pupillin. 3km/2mi S of Arbois by D 246.* ✆*03 84 37 49 44. Closed Thu and Sun eve, and Mon. Reservations advised.* This charming auberge, known for franc-comtoise dishes, is in the pretty village of Pupillin known for Ploussard wines.

🍽🍽 **Le Caveau d'Arbois** – *3 rte de Besançon.* ✆*03 84 66 10 70. Closed Sun eve and Mon.* Traditional cuisine featuring a few regional dishes accompanied by local wines is served in a bright, uncluttered dining-room.

🍽🍽 **La Balance Mets et Vins** – *47 r. de Courcelles.* ✆*03 84 37 45 00. Closed 30 Jun–7 Jul, 12 Dec–28 Jan, Sun and Tue eve, Wed.* Imaginative recipes to match the inspired wine list from local wine producers make for a memorable meal.

😑😑😑😑 **Jean-Paul Jeunet** – R. de l'Hôtel-de-Ville. ℘03 84 66 05 67. www.jeanpauljeunet.com. Closed Dec, Jan, Wed except eve in Jul–Aug and Tue. This prestigious establishment blends the traditional and modern in the heart of the little town of Arbois. The dining-room offers fine regional specialities and a superb wine list. Comfortable rooms feature contemporary décor.

CHÂTEAU CHALON

😑😑 **Les 16 Quartiers** – pl. de l'Église. ℘03 84 44 68 23. ♿. Closed end Nov–end Mar except weekends in Feb and Mar, Sun eve and Mon out of season, Thu eve in Jul–Aug. Time seems to stand still in this charming 16C village house with its pretty dining-room and shady terrace. Enjoy regional cooking or medieval specialities, with Jura wines by the glass.

POLIGNY

😑 **La Sergenterie** – 31 pl. des Déportés. ℘03 84 37 37 11. www.lasergenterie.com. This restaurant is in an old cellar with a vaulted, stone ceiling. Local, Jura specialities are served with local wines, as well as simple sandwiches, pizzas, hamburgers etc.

😑😑 **La Maison du Haut** – Les Bordes, 39230 Saint-Lothain. 6km/4mi SW of Poligny by D 259, then a track. ℘03 84 37 35 19 or 03 84 37 31 08. www.maison duhaut.com. Reservations essential. 5 rooms 😑. Hidden away in the countryside this quiet little 18C farm is the place to come to taste local, family-style cuisine. There are also 5 simple rooms and a dormitory (6 people) as well as the possibility of camping, renting a cabin or even stabling your horse!

🛒SHOPPING

ARBOIS

La Cave de comté – 44 Grande-Rue. ℘03 84 66 09 53. Open daily 9.45am–7pm. Closed 8–15 Jan and 28 Jun–4 Jul. Stock up on local cheeses including Comté, Morbier, Bleu de Gex, Mont d'Or, and other delicacies. Excellent café at the back.

Domaine Rolet Père et Fils – 11 r. de l'Hôtel-de-Ville. ℘03 84 66 08 89. www.rolet-arbois.com. Open daily 9am–noon, 2–6.30pm (Sun from 2.30pm). One of the largest family wine estates in Jura, it produces wines of all styles from Côtes-du-Jura, Étoile and Arbois appellations.

Fruitière vinicole Château Béthanie – 2 r. des Fossés. ℘03 84 66 11 67. www.chateau-bethanie.com. Cellar visits Tue–Sun (Jul–Aug) 11am, 2.30pm, 4.30pm. Closed 1 Jan, 25 Dec. This wine cooperative is one of France's oldest (est. in 1906). Free wine tasting in the summer. There are also two shops in the town.

Domaine André et Mireille Tissot – pl. de la Liberté. ℘03 84 66 29 78. www.stephane-tissot.com. Open 9am–12.30pm, 2.30–7pm. You will find an innovative range of modern-style Jura wines here along with classics like superb vin jaune.

Hirsinger – 38 pl. de la Liberté. ℘03 84 66 06 97. www.chocolat-hirsinger.com. Open 8am–7.30pm. Closed Wed and Thu except holidays. This renowned chocolatier sells an astonishing array of delicious home-made chocolates, including some unique to them.

NEAR POLIGNY

Fruitière de Plasne – 39800 Plasne. ℘03 84 37 14 03. www.comte.com. Open 10am–12.15pm, 5–7pm. Closed Sun aft except Jul–Aug. Comté, Morbier and Tomme de Jura are the cheeses made at this local cooperative. Visits to the ageing cellars are offered in season.

CHÂTEAU-CHALON

Domaine Berthet-Bondet – r. de la Tour. ℘03 84 44 60 48. www.berthet-bondet.net. Open by appointment daily except Sun 10am–noon, 2–7pm. Visit the 16C cellar beneath the house to taste superb Château-Chalon vin jaune amongst the barrels.

Champagnole

This leafy town in the heart of the Jura makes a relaxed base for explorations into the spectacular surrounding countryside.

🚗 DRIVING TOUR

Upper Valley Of The Ain
84km/52mi – allow 4hrs.
🕐 *See local map.*

▷ *Leave Champagnole heading west on D 471. At Ney, take D 253 to the left; after 2.5km/1.5mi take the road to the left for about 2.4km/1.4mi, until you reach a car park.*

Belvédère de Bénedegand
🚶 *15min there and back on foot.*
A pretty forest path leads to this viewpoint. There is a lovely view of the Ain Valley, Champagnole, Mont Rivel and, in the distance, the forest of Fresse.

▷ *Turn back to go through Loulle and Vaudioux and turn right on N 5. Take the first road on the left, D 279, and leave the car in the car park at the side of the road, near the Billaude waterfall.*

There is a good view of the waterfall and its setting from the platform below.

Cascade de la Billaude★
30min there and back on foot.
🚶 A new metal stairway leads down towards the waterfall with a signposted pathway leading right to the edge of the waterfall. Two viewing platforms have been created. At the top, the Lemme can be seen tumbling from a narrow crevice in a wooded setting between towering rock faces, dropping a total of 28m/92ft in two successive cascades. Delicately perfumed cyclamens grow near the waterfall in summer. For an easier walk *(15min there and back, reached from the car park)* there is also a pretty view from the **Belvédère de la Billaude**.

▷ *Return to N 5 and follow it to the left.*

▶ **Population:** 8 135
🕐 **Michelin Map:** 321: F-6.
🅘 **Info:** 28 rue Baronne-Delort, 39304 Champagnole. ✆03 84 52 43 67. www.jura-montsrivieres.com.
▷ **Location:** Head south or east of town for the Ain Valley, La Joux Forest and the lakes region.

River Lemme★
N 5 follows the valley of the River Lemme, a tributary of the Ain, as far as Pont-de-la-Chaux. The sight of this turbulent little river gushing between pines and rocky crags is fresh and exhilarating.

▷ *At Pont-de-la-Chaux, take D 16.*

Chaux-des-Croteney
This small town on the old salt route has vestiges of a château stronghold that was destroyed by Louis XIV. It has an interesting 15C church, but it is best known, linked with Syam, as one of the sites believed by archaeologists to be the ancient Alésia.

▷ *Take D 16 and D 127E1 to Les Planches-en-Montagne.*

Gorges de la Langouette★
🚶 *1hr round trip on foot. Leave the car in the shady car park after the bridge called La Langouette.*
There is a lovely view from this bridge of the Gorges de la Langouette, only 4m/13ft wide and 47m/154ft deep, cut into the limestone by the River Saine. The three **viewpoints**★ over the gorge can be reached by taking the path on the left before the bridge *(access also possible by car; follow the road indicated from the village of Les Planches)*. The steep footpath is signposted and leads to where the Saine cascades into a narrow crevice, the beginning of the gorge.

▷ *Return to Les Planches and turn right at the church; then just before*

Chaux-des-Crotenay, turn right again onto a forest road.

Vallée de la Saine

The route continues along a pretty road running through forest along the top of the cliffs which form the sides of the narrow valley of the Saine, a small tributary of the Lemme.

◐ *Turn right after coming out of the gorge and cross the village of Syam.*

Villa Palladienne de Syam★ (◐ open May–Sept daily except Mon and Tue 2–6pm; ◍6.50€; ℘03 84 51 64 45; www.chateaudesyam.fr)

is an amazing Palladian villa commissioned in 1825 by Emmanuel Jobez, a Forge Master who admired Italian architecture. The square plan underlined by long pilasters, the central rotunda and the Pompeiian-style decoration is reminiscent of Italian villas. The interior decoration

---

and period furniture are very attractive. Concerts are organised regularly, and there are even a few guestrooms.

The **Forges de Syam** (◐ *open Jul–Aug daily except Tue 10am–noon, 1.30–7pm; May–Jun and Sept Sat–Sun and public holidays 10am–noon, 1.30–7pm;* ◍*3€;* ℘*03 84 51 61 00; www.forgesyam.fr*) brought prosperity to the village under the First Empire when built in 1813 on the banks of the Ain.

Work here continued until recently, specialising in rolling processes on machinery nearly 100 years old. The story of the Smithies of Syam is detailed in an exhibit and short film.

◐ *North of Syam, turn right towards Bourg-de-Sirod.*

Bourg-de-Sirod

This village owes its pretty site to the many waterfalls and rapids formed by the Ain as it covers the 100m/328ft drop in altitude between the Nozeroy and Champagnole plateaux.

◐ *Leave the car in the car park near the Bourg-de-Sirod town hall (mairie). Follow the path marked Point de vue, Perte de l'Ain.*

Perte de l'Ain★

There is a superb **view** of the waterfall formed by the Ain as it disappears into a crevice between fallen rocks. Metal stairs and platforms allow you to take a superb walk along the river.

◐ *Carry on through Sirod and Conte.*

Source de l'Ain★

Leave the car at the end of the access road (through forest) which leads off D 283 after Conte.

🚶 Continue on foot *(15min there and back)* to the river's source, which is at the bottom of the thickly wooded, rocky amphitheatre. This is in fact a resurgent spring and has a very variable flow.

During the droughts of 1959 and 1964 the mouth was completely dry, and it was possible to climb up a part of the Ain's underground course.

Syam and the Battle of Alésia

Excavations in the Syam plain near the confluence of the Lemme and the Saine in the 1960s, led the eminent archaeologist André Berthier to believe the team had located the site of the Battle of Alésia. In 52BC having been besieged by Caesar's troops in the oppidum of Alésia for six weeks, the army of the Gauls is thought to have stormed down from the Gyts heights near Syam, where Vercingetorix had an observation post, in an attempt to join up with the Gallic relief forces which were attacking the Roman field camps defending the Crans threshold. In the ensuing battle, involving 400 000 men, the Gauls were unable to break through the Romans' double line of defence fortifications and suffered a crushing defeat. Today, debate continues as to the actual site of the battle.

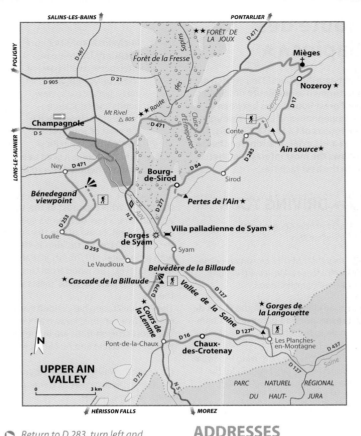

UPPER AIN VALLEY

0   3 km

◐ *Return to D 283, turn left and continue to Nozeroy.*

Nozeroy★

This picturesque market town is perched on a hilltop and has a certain old-style charm. The traces of its ancient ramparts and other defences remain, along with some old houses near its 15C church.

Mièges

This farming town grew up around a 16C priory. The **church** contains the late Gothic funerary chapel of the dukes of Chalon; note the ornate keystones on the ceiling.

◐ *Return to Champagnole by taking D 119, then D 471 to the left, which crosses the green Entreportes valley.*

ADDRESSES

🛏 STAY / 🍴 EAT

◒◒ **Hôtel Bois Dormant** – *Rte de Pontarlier.* ✆*03 84 52 66 66. www.bois-dormant.com.* ⊞. *40 rooms.* ⌷*10 €. Restaurant* ◒◒. Functional rooms with light, pine wood panelling, many of which open onto the forest. Spacious dining room extended by a verandah.

◒◒ **Auberge des Gourmets** – *Billaude-le-Haut, 39300 Le Vaudioux. 8km/5mi S of Champagnole (towards Geneva) by N 5.* ✆*03 84 51 60 60. Closed 20 Dec–31 Jan, Sun eve and Mon, lunch-times out of season.* This country inn on the edge of the road is popular among locals. The owner offers carefully prepared, succulent dishes at highly affordable prices. Meals are served in the traditional dining room or on the rustic-style verandah. A few rooms available. Swimming pool.

Route des Sapins★★

The beautiful 50km/31mi stretch of road known as the Route des Sapins (Fir Forest Route) runs between Champagnole and Levier, through the forests of La Fresse, Chapois, La Loux and Levier. The itinerary below follows the most interesting stretch with the best facilities.

🚗 DRIVING TOUR

55km/34mi from Champagnole to Levier– allow 3hrs .

▶ Take D 471 NE. At a crossroads on the outskirts of Equevillon, leave D 471 and follow the Route des Sapins.

The road climbs through the **Forêt de la Fresse**, offering glimpses of Champagnole to the left.

▶ Turn right on D 21, leaving the Route des Sapins to the left, heading for the D 288 junction, where you turn left

The road follows the line of the hillside, about halfway up, along the coombe through which the Angillon has cut its river bed. To the east of the road are the magnificent stands of the forest of La Joux, and to the west the 1 153ha/2 849 acres of conifers which make up the forest of La Fresse. Just before the village of Les Nans, turn left onto the forest road known as Larderet aux Nans, which gives a good view of Les Nans and the Angillon coombe. The road rejoins the Route des Sapins at the crossroads, Carrefour des Baumes, then passes through the northern part of the forest of La Fresse, through the village of Chapois and into the La Joux forest, climbing as it goes.

Forêt de la Joux★★

This is one of France's most beautiful evergreen forests. This area, covering 2 652ha/6 550 acres, is separated from the Fresse Forest by the Angillon rapids to the south; it borders Levier Forest to

Michelin Map: 321: F–G-6.

Location: The route is interspersed with parking spots, playgrounds, picnic areas, nature trails, viewpoints and education centres to help you make the most of your visit.

Don't Miss: Sapin Président de la Joux, a giant tree over two hundred years old.

the north. Whereas most of the trees are conifers, a few deciduous species can be found. Some of the firs are of exceptional size: up to 50m/164ft tall with a diameter of 1.2m/4ft just above ground level. The wood from this forest has been used for ships' masts since the 17C.

The Administration has divided the forest into five cantons, known as series. The most striking trees are in the cantons of La Glacière and Aux Sources.

▶ Leave the Route des Sapins to take the road to the Belvédère de Garde-Bois, which is near a chapel.

Belvédère de Garde-Bois

🚶 There is a pretty view of the deep Angillon Valley as well as the forest of La Fresse in the distance.

▶ Carry on east along the road that led to the viewpoint to rejoin the Route des Sapins.

The stretch of road from the Rond-du-Sauget crossroads is especially pretty.

Sapins de la Glacière

30min round trip on foot. Take the path which leads off right from the Route des Sapins coming from Champagnole.

🚶 This canton got its name from being the area where snow lies longest. Magnificent conifers, as straight as arrows, grow around a deep hollow in the canton's centre. There is a particularly tall, splendid tree next to the footpath. The quiet in the forest and subdued quality

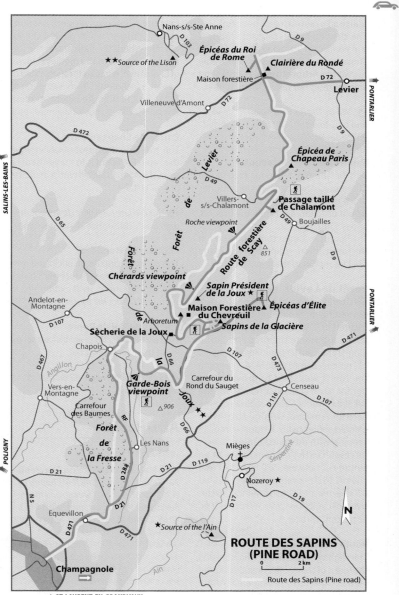

★★ *Source of the Lison*

Épicéas du Roi de Rome

Clairière du Rondé

Maison forestière

Nans-s/s-Ste Anne

Levier

PONTARLIER

Villeneuve d'Amont

Épicéa de Chapeau Paris

Levier

Forêt

de

Villers-s/s-Chalamont

Passage taillé de Chalamont

Boujailles

Roche viewpoint

Chérards viewpoint

Route forestière de Scay

851

Sapin Président de la Joux ★

Andelot-en-Montagne

Épicéas d'Élite

Maison Forestière du Chevreuil

Arboretum

Sapins de la Glacière

Sècherie de la Joux ■

Chapois

la

Joux

Carrefour du Rond du Sauget

Censeau

Garde-Bois viewpoint

906

Vers-en-Montagne

Carrefour des Baumes

★★

Forêt

de

la Fresse

Les Nans

Mièges

Serpentine

Equevillon

Nozeroy ★

★ *Source of the l'Ain*

Champagnole

ROUTE DES SAPINS (PINE ROAD)

0   2 km

Route des Sapins (Pine road)

N

SALINS-LES-BAINS

POLIGNY

PONTARLIER

ST-LAURENT-EN-GRANDVAUX

of the light filtered by the trees creates a soothing, meditative atmosphere.

Épicéas d'élite

The Route de la Marine leads to this stand of spruces. Alternatively, there is a signposted footpath leading off D 473;

the start is indicated about 1km/0.5mi S of the level crossing at Boujailles station (30min there and back on foot).

These are the most beautiful trees in the Esserval-Tartre spruce forest, hence their name.

Maison Forestière du Chevreuil

The clearing by this forester's lodge is a major tourist attraction in the region. Those interested in forestry will be able to visit the **Arboretum**, a test planting area for trees not native to the region.

▶ *Where the Route des Sapins divides into two, take the right fork, signposted Route des Sapins par les Crêtes.*

Sapin Président de la Joux★

This fir, the most famous tree in the Chérards canton, is over two centuries old. It has a diameter of 3.85m/13ft at a height of 1.30m/4.2ft from the ground, and is 45m/148ft tall.
The Route des Sapins carries on through the forest, offering a pretty view of the Chalamont dip to the left.

Forêt de Levier

This forest was once the possession of the Chalon family until it was confiscated in 1562 by Philippe II, King of Spain. It became the property of the King of France after Louis XIV's conquest of Franche-Comté in 1674. At that time the forest was used to provide timber for naval construction and for the Salins salt works. Local people also came here for firewood, so large areas were planted entirely with deciduous trees, in keeping with the forest's role as a useful resource. The modern forest, at an altitude of between 670m/2 198ft and 900m/2 953ft, covers an area of 2 725ha/6 733 acres and consists almost exclusively of coniferous trees (60 percent fir, 12 percent spruce).

Route forestière de Scay

This slightly uneven road, which crosses the forest of Levier offers some beautiful views of the surrounding area. At the **Belvédère de la Roche** the views over the Levier forest and the clearing with the village of Villers-sous-Chalamont.

Passage taillé de Chalamont

🚶 Shortly before D 49, a footpath leads off to the right (30min there and back on foot), along what was once a Celtic, then a Roman path. Note the steps cut into the sloping or slippery sections and the grooves which guided chariot wheels. Where the path leaves the forest, by the ruins of the medieval tower of Chalamont, it passes through a kind of trench, a technique which was imitated in the building of the nearby modern Boujailles/Villers-sous-Chalamont road.

Épicéa de Chapeau-Paris

This tree is to the forest of Levier what the Sapin Président is to the forest of La Joux. It is 45m/148ft tall with a diameter of 4m/13ft.

▶ *Take Route forestière de Ravonnet; then Route du Pont de la Marine (right).*

Clairière du Rondé

This clearing contains an enclosure containing Sika deer and a forester's lodge *(maison forestière, with exhibitions in summer; contact the tourist office).*

Épicéas du Roi de Rome

These trees are 200 years old; some are more than 50m/164ft tall.

▶ *Turn back to take D 72 on the left towards Levier.*

ADDRESSES

🏠 STAY / 🍴 EAT

🍽🍽 **Maison forestière du Chevreuil** – *39300 Supt. 3.5km/2.5mi N of Chapois by D 251, take D 107 dir. Censeau and the rte des Sapins, then follow signs. ℘03 84 51 40 85. Closed 16 Sept–15 Jun. Reservations advised.* Surrounded by pines, this unusual house offers simple, delicious meals and snacks. Play area for children. Food is served on the terrace until 8pm; best check the weather in advance.

🍽 **Chambre d'hôte Bourgeois-Bousson** – *15 Grande-Rue, 39110 Andelot-en-Montagne. 2.5km/1.5mi NW of Chapois by D 250. ℘03 84 51 43 77. Closed Nov–Easter. 🚭 🅿. 6 rooms. Meals 🍽.* This family house near the forest has a quaint, slightly old-fashioned atmosphere. Simple, comfortable rooms and traditional cuisine.

Région des Lacs du Jura★★

The Jura Lake District is the area between Champagnole, Clairvaux-les-Lacs and St-Laurent-en-Grandvaux, which boasts a string of delightful lakes – Chalain, Chambly, Le Val, Ilay, Narlay – set in peaceful, unspoilt countryside.

A BIT OF HISTORY

The peace shattered – In 1635, during the Thirty Years War, Richelieu attacked the Comté, and in the subsequent brutal campaign the lake district was overrun by Swedish troops, allies of the French. Homes were torched, crops cut down and vines uprooted. The resulting famine was so great that people even resorted to cannibalism. Terrible tortures forced people to reveal the whereabouts of their life savings. Entire families, discovered hidden in caves or underground passages, were walled into their refuge to die lingering deaths. The whole province was subjected to this appalling treatment, and large numbers of Comtois fled to Savoy, Switzerland or Italy. Some 10 000 to 12 000 settled in a single district in Rome, where they had a church built, dedicated to St Claude.

EXCURSIONS
Lac de Bonlieu

4.5km/3mi SE of Bonlieu on the picturesque D 678, then D 75E to the right.
This pretty lake in the forest is overlooked by a rocky wooded ridge crisscrossed by numerous footpaths. Boat trips can be taken on the lake. A forest road runs above the east shore, leading to a viewpoint at the south end of the lake, with a beautiful **view** of the Pic de l'Aigle, the lakes of Ilay and Maclu, and of Mont Rivel in the distance.

Belvédère de la Dame-Blanche★

2km/1mi NW of Bonlieu, then 30min there and back on foot. Drive towards Saugeot from the D 678/D 67 crossroads,

Michelin Map: 321: E-17.

Info: 36 Grande-Rue, 39130 Clairvaux-les-Lacs. ℰ03 84 25 27 47. www.juralacs.com.

Location: The driving tour starting at Doucier passes seven lakes. Most lookout points are accessible via short footpaths, although the hike to Pic de l'Aigle is more rigorous. Small villages with historic churches dot the area.

Don't Miss: The view from Pic de l'Aigle, which covers the entire Jura region.

*and after about 800m/875yd take the unsurfaced road to the right on leaving the forest. At the first crossroads turn left and *P* park the car at the edge of the forest.*
A rocky bank overlooks the Dessus and Dessous valleys. There is a view of the lakes of Chambly and Le Val to the left and the Pic de l'Aigle to the right.

🚗 DRIVING TOUR

Lac de Chalain and Pic de l'Aigle★★

Round tour of 46km/29mi – allow 2hrs 30.

Leave Doucier E on D 39 towards Songeson and Menétrux-en-Joux; after Ilay turn left on D 678 and exit before Chaux-du-Dombief.

P *Park the car 250m/275yd further on the Boissière road.*

Pic de l'Aigle★★
45min there and back on foot along a rather badly marked path; it climbs steeply to the right, towards the wooded outcrop of rock called Pic de l'Aigle.
The **view** from the top of the Pic de l'Aigle (993m/3 258ft) stretches across the entire Jura region, overlooking the Ilay cluse and the Chaux-du-Dombief

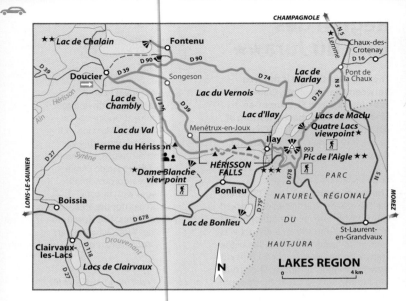

LAKES REGION

0   4 km

heights. The Jura mountain ranges tower on the left, behind which the summit of Mont Blanc can be seen in fine weather; the plateaux extend to the right, with their edge above the Saône plain.

▷ *Leave the road to Boissière on the right, and take a narrow road uphill.*

Belvédère des Quatre Lacs★
15min there and back on foot.
⚑ The lakes of Ilay, Narlay, the Grand Maclu and the Petit Maclu can be seen from this viewpoint.

▷ *Take N 5 left to Pont-de-la-Chaux, D 75 to Le Frasnois and right on D 74.*

Lac de Narlay
The triangular-shaped lake is overlooked by wooded slopes. At a depth of 48m/157ft, it is the deepest lake in the area. Its waters drain into several gullies at the west end, and flow underground for 10km/6mi, then re-emerge to feed into the Lac de Chalain.

Lac du Vernois
This little lake, surrounded by woods, comes into view suddenly at a bend in the road. There is not a house in sight;

the atmosphere is one of absolute peace and seclusion.

▷ *Continue along D 74 and take D 90 towards Fontenu.*

Fontenu
The church in this village is surrounded by century-old lime trees. About 800m/880yd beyond Fontenu is the north shore of the Lac de Chalain, from which there is an excellent **view★★**.

Lac de Chalain★★
This vast stretch of water, with three beaches, has become an important centre for water sports. It is also prized by fishermen for its pike and perch.
The lake has been categorised as an archeological site of national interest since 1995 and there have been numerous finds after an ancient city was discovered here in 1904.
The **Maisons néolithiques sur pilotis** *(accessible from La Pergola campsite at Marigny)*, were Neolithic houses on stilts, reconstructed on lake shore by archeologists, but left to degrade after the searches finished.

▷ *Turn back and keep right, taking D 90 towards Doucier.*

There is a second **view**★★ of the lake 500m/547yd after rejoining the road.

◯ *Return to Doucier on D 90 and D 39.*

ADDRESSES

🛏 STAY

◯ **Chambre d'Hôte Chez Mme Devenat** – *17 r. du Vieux-Lavoir, 39130 Charezier, 13km/8.1mi SW of Lac de Chalain by D 27. ℰ03 84 48 35 79. 🛏 4 rooms. Meals🍽.* Quiet, comfortable family house in a pretty village between Clairvaux-les-Lacs and Chalain Lake. There are more rooms in the cottage near the little wood. *Table d'hôte* meals with new regional specialities every day.

◯ **Camping Domaine de Chalain** – *39130 Doucier, 3km/1.9mi S of Lac de Chalain by D 27. ℰ03 84 25 78 78. www.chalain.com. Open May–21 Sept. 472 sites. Reservation recommended. Meals available.* This campsite on the lake shore is ideal for family holidays, with plenty of organised activities.

◯ **Camping La Pergola** – *39130 Marigny. ℰ03 84 25 70 03. Open 30 Apr–17 Sept. 350 sites. Reservation recommended. Meals available.* This site on the hill above the lake has heated pools and water sports facilities. Camping trailers available.

◯ **Camping Yelloh-Village Fayolan** – *39130 Clairvaux-les-Lacs, 1.2km/0.8mi SE of Clairvaux-les-Lacs by D 118. ℰ03 84 25 26 19. Open 14 May–11 Sept. 516 sites. Reservations recommended. Meals available.* This high-quality campground has widely spaced plots by a lake with a beach. Activities for children and a fitness trail for adults.

◯ **Chambre d'Hôte Les Cinq Lacs** – *66 rte des Lacs, 39130 Le Frasnois, 3.5km/2.3mi N of Ilay by D 75. ℰ03 84 25 51 www.5lacs.fr. 🛏 Reservations required. 5 rooms. Meals🍽.* The comfortable rooms are named after local lakes. The half-board formula will give you a chance to enjoy the succulent regional specialities.

◯ **Hôtel La Chaumière du Lac** – *21 r. du Sauveur, 39130 Clairvaux-les-Lacs. ℰ03 84 25 81 52. www.juralacs.com/adherents/lachaumiere.htm. Open Easter–Sept. 12 rooms. �board8€. Restaurant🍽🍽.*

With its own beach just a few paces away, this peaceful lakeside hotel has pleasing bedrooms that look out onto the lake or the trees. Jura specialities are included on the menu. Lovely terrace.

◯🍽 **Chambre et table d'hôtes L'Escapade** – *12 r. de la Maison-Blanche, 39130 Bonlieu. ℰ03 84 25 26 60. www.escapadebonlieu.weebly.com. 🛏 5 rooms. Restaurant🍽.* A painstakingly restored old farmhouse from 1815 with comfortable bedrooms. Breakfast and meals are served in a dining room with beams and arched windows.

◯🍽 **Hôtel Les Alpages** – *1 chemin de la Madone, 39130 Bonlieu. ℰ03 84 25 57 53. www.hotel-lesalpages.com. Closed 15 Nov–12 Feb, various restaurant closures. 9 rooms. ⊟9€. Restaurant🍽🍽.* The cosy rooms in this chalet have lake views. Franche-Comté specialities are served in the panoramic dining room or on the sheltered terrace.

🍴 EAT

◯ **La Sarrazine** – *39130 Doucier, 3km/1.9mi S of Lac de Chalain by D 27. ℰ03 84 25 70 60. www.restaurant-la-sarrazine.com. Closed end Nov–Feb and Wed out of season.* The new owners here have retained the specialities of grilled meat and pig trotters, as well as keeping the huge frescoes on the wall.

◯🍽 **La Poutre** – *25 Grande-Rue, 39130 Bonlieu. ℰ03 84 25 57 77. Open 6 May–31 Oct. Closed Mon except eves in season, Tue.* This handsome 18C building features rustic décor, with its large fireplace, Comtoise clock and Louis XIII chairs. Fine regional cuisine with regional accents.

◯🍽 **Au chalet** – *rte du Lac, 39130 Bonlieu, 1.5km/0.9mi E of Bonlieu by N 78, rte. de St-Laurent-en-Grandvaux. ℰ03 84 25 57 04. www.restaurant-au-chalet.com. Closed Jan, Tue, Wed evenings out of season.* Lovely chalet along the road to Bonlieu. Wooded interior. The chef makes good use of local products, and all regions of France are represented on the wine list.

◯🍽 **Le Comtois** – *Le Bourg, 39130 Doucier. ℰ03 84 25 71 21. Closed 28 Nov–11 Feb, Sun evening, Tue evening and Wed except 15 Jun–15 Sept.* This restaurant has a rustic décor and is known for its good local food and wine.

Cascades du Hérisson★★★

The Hérisson is a magnificent spectacle after rainy periods, with water tumbling down in a lengthy series of cascades. Although the falls are not quite so interesting after dry spells, the riverbed, especially between the Gour Bleu and the Grand Saut, features some fascinating evidence of erosion: natural stone steps, giants' cauldrons and multi-storeyed systems of caves.

A BIT OF GEOLOGY

From the beginning – The source of the Hérisson is at an altitude of 805m/2 641ft. The river forces a course down to the Doucier plateau dropping 255m/837ft in only 3km/2mi, by cutting through narrow gorges, forming spectacular waterfalls.

The Hérisson owes its picturesque stepped course to the differing textures of the horizontal limestone strata through which it flows. Each shelf is formed by strata of more resistant rock. The flow of small rivers in the Jura, a terrain of mostly porous limestone, is very dependent on the weather.

🚶 HIKE

From Doucier drive 8km/5mi SE along D 326; leave the car at the end of the road.

Lac de Chambly and Lac du Val

The D 326 road climbs the Hérisson Valley downstream of the waterfalls, giving the occasional glimpse of these two lovely lakes through the trees. The valley floor is flat and green, the slopes steep and wooded. Once it has passed through the lakes of Chambly and Le Val, the river flows into the Ain.

▷ *Continue on D 326 to the car park (fee charged).*

Maison des Cascades

Open Apr–Sept; Jul–Aug 10.30am–6pm, rest of year 11am–5pm. Closed Thu

🚹 **Michelin Map:** 321: F-7. Local map below or see Région des Lacs du Jura.

📋 **Info:** 36 Grande-Rue, 39130 Clairvaux-les-Lacs. ✆03 84 25 27 47. www.juralacs.com.

▷ **Location:** There are several possible departure points, but the most logical is Doucier. Most of this itinerary involves hiking through gorges (wear sturdy shoes). For those who don't wish a tough hike, there is a relatively easy walk from the Maison des Cascades to the foot of the Éventail waterfall.

👁 **Don't Miss:** The view over the falls from the Sentier des Cascades.

🕐 **Timing:** The hike described below will take a good three hours there and back.

Apr–May and Sept. ⬤4€. ✆03 84 25 77 35. www.cascades-du-herisson.fr. This centre offers a wealth of information not only about the Hérisson, but also about the local lakes and landscape.

Cascade de l'Éventail★★★

Allow 3hrs there and back on foot for this 7.4km/4.6mi hike. This is not a circuit, so retrace your steps for the return.
🚶 After about 200m/220yd the path brings you to the foot of this waterfall, where you will get the best view. The water tumbles a total of 65m/213ft in leaps and bounds, forming a vast pyramid of foaming water.

The path then leads very steeply uphill to the top of the Éventail waterfall.

Take the Sarrazine footbridge across the Hérisson, and then follow the path on the right to the Belvédère from where there is a beautiful view of the Hérisson gorge and the Éventail waterfall.

▷ *Return to the top of the waterfall and continue on the path.*

Grotte Lacuzon
Due to rockfalls, this cave is no longer open to the public.

◐ *Continue upstream along the south bank, to the Grand Saut.*

Cascade du Grand Saut★★
The best view of the Grand Saut is from the foot of the waterfall. The water falls from a height of 60m/200ft in a single cascade.

◐ *The footpath, now cut into the rock face, is very steep and quite narrow (but with handrails) in places as it leads to the Gour Bleu waterfall.*

Gour Bleu★
At the foot of this little waterfall lies a beautiful shallow basin *(gour)* in which the water is a clear blue colour.

◐ *The path carries on to the Saut Château Garnier and the Saut de la Forge waterfalls.*

Saut de la Forge★
The river, flinging itself from the top of a curving, rocky overhang, makes a very pretty spectacle.

Saut du Moulin and Saut Girard
1hr there and back from Saut de la Forge.
⬛ From the path, which runs through woods at some points and meadows at others, the Saut du Moulin can be

seen, near the ruins of the Jeunet mill, and, further on, the Saut Girard, falling from about 20m/66ft.

◐ *The path crosses the Hérisson at the foot of Saut Girard (café) and leads back to the Ilay crossroads, near the Auberge du Hérisson.*

EXCURSION
👥 Ferme du Hérisson - Les Phoebus d'Alenis
Val Dessous at Ménétrux-en-Joux.
🕐*Open Jun–Sept daily, rest of year weekends and public holidays only 10am–6pm.* ⊚*6€.* ☎*03 84 25 72 95. www.fermepedagogique-jura.com.*
A 2km/1.2mi trail along the Hérisson Valley offers the chance to encounter some of the ancestors of domestic cattle such as aurochs, bisons and other breeds of wild ox. There is also a mini-farm, appreciated especially by young children.

ADDRESSES

🛏STAY / 🍴EAT
⊜⊜ **Chambre d'Hôte et Restaurant L'Éolienne** – *Hameau la Fromagerie, 39130 Le Frasnois, 1km/0.6mi N of Ilay by D 39.* ☎*03 84 25 50 60. www.eolienne.net. Closed 12 Nov–21 Dec. 4 rooms. Meals*⊜⊜*.* A stone's throw from the Girard waterfall, this smart chalet offers extremely comfortable rooms and a restaurant offering Jura specialities.

Château-Chalon★

Perched on top of a solid rock escarpment, this old fortified village is also the kingdom of a legendary wine, vin jaune. Below the village fan out 50ha/125 acres of especially sunny and steep vineyard slopes, on a rare marl soil. The magic unfolds in the cellars, where the tradition of maturing this extraordinary wine over several years has defied the passing of time.

A BIT OF HISTORY

Jura gold– Many stories surround the origins of the pride of Jura wines, the famous vin jaune of Château-Chalon. However, it is certain that the abbey produced wine and that by the 13C the locally prized grape variety known today as Savagnin, was already grown here. The unusual technique of ageing the wine under a veil of yeast (*la voile*) is also very old, and studied by Louis Pasteur when he was in Arbois.
Once the Savagnin wine has fermented it is placed in oak barrels that are not completely filled. A veil of yeast forms preventing oxidation but giving its own particular flavour to the wine. Vin jaune may be bottled no sooner than 6 years and 3 months after harvest in a unique 62cl bottle called a *clavelin*. Very long-lived, it may age for decades or more.
The AOC Château-Chalon is only granted for wines made as a vin jaune (other wines made in these vineyards are labelled AOC Côtes du Jura). It is subject to stringent testing, firstly of the grapes in the vineyards and later of the wine.
Percée du vin jaune – This delightful, colourful festival takes place in a different Jura wine village each first weekend of February. It celebrates the release of vin jaune after its requisite period of ageing with a symbolic "piercing" of the first barrel.

WALK AROUND THE VILLAGE

Château-Chalon was fortified from the Gallo-Roman era, before the château was built and subsequently a Benedictine abbey established in the 7C.

▸ **Population:** 166
◉ **Michelin Map:** 321: D6.
▤ **Info:** pl. de la Mairie, 39210 Voiteur. ℘03 84 44 62 47. www.hauteseille.com.
◔ **Location:** From Voiteur, follow D 5 up a windy road to the village. The site is also mentioned in the Vineyard Tour in Arbois.
◈ **Don't Miss:** A wander around the pretty village, a tour of the vineyards and a taste of vin jaune.
◷ **Timing:** A visit in autumn rewards with exquisite colours in the vineyards.

Remains of a **fortified gate** and the **château ruins** testify to its powerful past. Lined with flowers, the village **streets** are full of character with wine-growers houses indicated by a large arched entrance and an exterior cellar trap door. Past the church is a lovely **view**★ over the Bresse plain and the Revermont.

Église Saint-Pierre
In the elegant 12C church, whereas the style is mostly Gothic, the chancel reveals Roman arcatures.

⚲⚲ Maison de la Haute Seille
Pl. de l'Église. ℘03 84 24 76 05. www.hauteseille.com. ◔*Open Apr–Oct. July-Aug 10am–1pm, 2–7pm, rest of year daily except Sun morning and Mon, 10.30–12.30pm, 2–6pm.* ⬯*4.50€.*
In a beautifully restored old abbey residence, this interactive exhibition relates the history of the village, the abbey and the Haute-Seille area. In the vaulted cellar is an explanation of the local Jura wines, along with an excellent film (14min) about vin jaune.

⚲⚲ L'école d'autrefois
℘*03 84 44 62 97.* ◔*Open Jul–Aug daily except Mon 10am–noon, 2–6pm; rest of the year by appointment.* ⬯*1€.*
This little museum re-creates a school classroom from the early 20C.

Église de St-Hymetière ★

The beautiful 11C Romanesque church west of St-Hymetière, a rural village on the borders of the Revermont, is miraculously intact.

Michelin Map: 321: D-8.
Info: Adapemont.
✆03 84 85 47 91.
www.adapement.assoc.fr.

CHURCH

Open 8am–6pm. For guided visits contact the Maison de la Petite Montagne. ✆03 84 85 47 91.

The church has several striking external features: old tombstones as flagstones on the floor of the porch; massive buttresses and narrow archaic windows on the south side of the church; tall pilaster strips; a protruding apse; and a tall octagonal tower.

Inside, the oven-vaulted chancel enclosed by plain arcading and the south aisle recall the original Romanesque building, whereas the main vault and north aisle bear signs of the 17C reworking of the masonry.

EXCURSIONS

La Caborne du bœuf

Follow signs to Sentier de la Caborne to a car park (1km/0.6mi from the church).

1.5km/1mi, 1hr there and back by a steep path that takes you across several gorges of the Valouse to view points, waterfalls and the cave. The Carbone du bœuf has the largest opening (20m/66ft high) of any cave in the Jura. The first "room" of the interior is lit, but the next 176m/192yd of cavern are not open to the public.

Arinthod

4km/3mi N by D 109.

The village lies on a fertile plain between two parallel chains of the Revermont mountains. The main square has a fountain from 1750, bordered by arcaded houses. A signposted walk (45min) around the village starts from the car park at the town hall (mairie).

Church – You cannot miss the impressive bell tower porch of this church, with a raised doorway. Inside, where the ribbed archways come down, you can make out the symbols of the four evangelists. Note the 17C pulpit and the large crucifix hung from the first span of the chancel, a work by Rosset (18C).

Montfleur

16km/10mi SW.

At the **Écomusée Vivant du Moulin de Pont des Vents** (*open mid-Feb–Dec except Sept and 1st week Jul, times vary; 3.60; ✆03 84 44 33 51; moulin. ecomusee.jura.free.fr*) you can tour a 19C watermill in working order and watch a demonstration of traditional bread and biscuit making.

Église de St-Hymetière

© CRT Franche-Comté

You might have to pack quite a large variety of clothes If you intend exploring the whole of the Gex area. Start with dinner dress and swimwear for the smart spa resort of Divonne, add casual beachwear for a break by the Lac de Vouglans, then hiking gear to see the finest mountain viewpoints, and don't forget plenty of layers to visit the source of the Doubs river at Mouthe, believed to be the coldest village in France. If you come in winter, just head with your ski gear straight to Monts Jura or Les Rousses, two of Jura's top winter sports resorts. The changes of clothes reflect the dramatically varied scenery in this area, stretching up and over the Jura mountains from Geneva.

Highlights

1. The contemporary art museum at the Abbaye, **St-Claude** (p388)

2. A hike up to see the dramatic panorama from the **Crêt de Chalam** above Pesse (p393)

3. Comté cheese tasting at the **Fort Les Rousses** ageing cellars (p395)

4. A stop at **Col de la Faucille** (p398)

5. A walk beside Lake Geneva at the pretty Swiss town of **Nyon** (p400)

Parc Naturel Régional du Haut-Jura

The Haut-Jura Regional Nature Park was inaugurated in 1986 and extended in 1998 to preserve the beautiful local forests and cultural heritage and create a new source of income for the region. The park's administration centre, **Maison du Parc du Haut-Jura** (www.parc-haut-jura.fr) is located in Lajoux, a small town east of St-Claude. It also serves as an information centre for those wishing to go on walking tours or enjoy other activities in the park.

The park covers 145 000ha/358 370 acres and encompasses 96 communities (communes), including St-Claude and Morez. The Crêt de la Neige (alt 1 720m/5 643ft), the highest summit in the Jura, offers plenty of opportunities for ski enthusiasts in winter, and for ramblers and mountain bikers in summer. Don't miss the museums which give an insight into the development of crafts and industry. The tourist offices in St-Claude and Les Rousses and the Maison du Haut-Jura in Lajoux give information on the park itself and its accommodation and leisure facilities.

More than green pastures

If you fly in to nearby Geneva airport over the Gex and Jura mountains in summer, you'll probably think the land is covered with green meadows, interspersed by forests, meandering rivers and glistening lakes. It's hard to imagine anything but the farming and cheese-making industries exist here. Yet the Franc-Comtois inhabitants have learnt how to make the best out of their rich natural resources.

Over the centuries the Jura craftsmen have developed numerous practical, imaginative and lucrative things to fashion out of wood from their abundant forests. The very old city of Saint-Claude is known as La Capitale de la Pipe, where pipe-smokers can admire an original collection of pipes from the 18C and 19C at a museum in the city, as well as visit specialist pipe shops. Learn about the traditional craft of woodwork at the Musée de la Boissellerie, a museum based in an old saw-mill in Bois d'Amont (part of the Les Rousses winter sports area). For children, a new treat is in store in 2012 when the original toy museum in Moirans-en-Montagne near the vast Vouglans lake re-opens as the Cité Culturelle de l'Enfant, boasting one of the largest collections of toys in Europe.

In the meantime, many delightful wooden toys made in Jura are widely available.

Wood has been used over the ages as fuel, especially here by blacksmiths and metalworkers, some of whom created

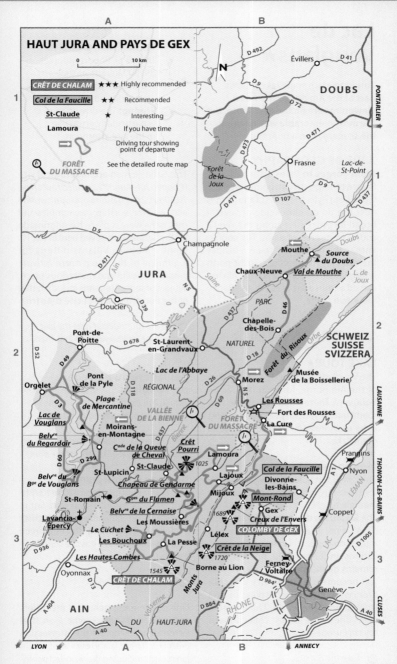

HAUT JURA AND PAYS DE GEX

0   10 km

CRÊT DE CHALAM ★★★ Highly recommended

Col de la Faucille ★★ Recommended

St-Claude ★ Interesting

Lamoura If you have time

Driving tour showing point of departure

FORÊT DU MASSACRE   See the detailed route map

DOUBS

PONTARLIER

Évillers

Frasne   Lac-de-St-Point

Forêt de la Joux

Champagnole

JURA

Doucier

Pont-de-Poitte

St-Laurent-en-Grandvaux

Mouthe   Source du Doubs   Val de Mouthe   L. de Joux

Chaux-Neuve

PARC

Chapelle-des-Bois

SCHWEIZ SUISSE SVIZZERA

Orgelet

Pont de la Pyle

Plage de Mercantine

Lac de l'Abbaye

NATUREL

Forêt du Risoux

LAUSANNE

Lac de Vouglans

Belvᵉ du Regardoir

RÉGIONAL

Moirans-en-Montagne

Morez   Musée de la Boissellerie

Les Rousses

Fort des Rousses

La Cure

VALLÉE DE LA BIENNE

Prangins

Belvᵉ du Bᵍᵉ de Vouglans

St-Lupicin

Cᵃᵈᵉ de la Queue de Cheval

Crêt Pourri

FORÊT DU MASSACRE

Nyon

THONON-LES-BAINS

St-Claude

Chapeau de Gendarme

Lamoura

Col de la Faucille

St-Romain

Gᵉˣ du Flumen

Lajoux

Divonne-les-Bains

Coppet

Lavancia-Épercy

Belvᵉ de la Cernaise

Mijoux

Mont-Rond

Gex

Creux de l'Envers

LÉMAN

Le Cuchet

Les Moussières

1689

COLOMBY DE GEX

Les Bouchoux

Lélex

Oyonnax

La Pesse

Crêt de la Neige

1720

LAC

Les Hautes Combes

1545

Borne au Lion

Ferney-Voltaire

CLUSES

AIN

CRÊT DE CHALAM

Monts Jura

Genève

DU   **HAUT-JURA**

RHÔNE

LYON

ANNECY

---

pioneering products. If you arrive in the area along the main N 5 road, you certainly don't need an eye test to see what the large factories on the dramatic approaches to the small town of Morez produce: after two centuries, the town still makes more than half of the spectacles sold in France.

Lac de Vouglans★

This long man-made lake follows part of the Ain gorge; the finest viewpoints are on the east shore, but the most memorable way to enjoy the scenery is on a boat trip.

A BIT OF GEOGRAPHY

From gorges to lakes – The Ain once flowed through striking gorges after the Cluse de la Pyle; the walls of the gorges now rise up on either side of several broad lakes created along the river's course by a series of dams. The confluence of the Bienne and the Ain divides the valley into two sections. To the north is the plateau through which the Ain has carved a course to the south, the Bugey mountain range.

🚗 DRIVING TOUR

LAKE TOUR★

The Vouglans dam flooded 35km/22mi of the Ain gorge, forming the Lac de Vouglans. There's no road all the way round but the itinerary below often gets close to shore and offers superb views of the lake.

Moirans-en-Montagne

This small town, lost in a wooded valley, is a centre for crafts and wooden toy manufacture.
The ♿ **Musée du Jouet**★ (Toy Museum; 5 r. Mugnin; ♿ ℘03 84 42 38 64; www. musee-du-jouet.fr) is closed for renovations until April 2012, but the shop remains open, and once it re-opens it will become a cultural "city" for children, with interactive displays of toys from around the world. The museum owns one of the largest collections of toys in Europe.

▶ *Take the D 470 S.*

Villards d'Héria

On the left, a small, steep road leads to the excavations.

- 🚻 **Michelin Map:** 321: D-8.
- 🛈 **Info:** 2 pl. Robert-Monnier, 39260 Moirans-en-Montagne. ℘03 84 42 31 57. www.jurasud.net.
- 🕐 **Timing:** The driving tour is particularly attractive in the late afternoon.

This Gallo-Roman **archaeological site** (🕐*open Jul–Aug;* 👣*guided tours (1hr) 10.30am, 2pm, 3.30pm and 5pm;* 💶*3€.*) was used for worship; two temples and the baths were a place for pilgrimage for the Sequani who lived here in the 1C. Climb up above Villards-d'Héria for a glimpse of the Lac d'Antré *(private property)*, a wild and mysterious place, subject of several legends including that of the flooded village of **cité d'Antré**.

▶ *At the roundabout take the exit for barrage de Vouglans (D 289, then D 299).*

Belvédère du Barrage de Vouglans
2km/1.2mi from D 299.
Good view of the Vouglans dam.

▶ *At Menouille take D 60 right, which leads to the level of the top of the dam.*

Barrage de Vouglans
The 103m/338ft-high and 420m/1 378ft-long arch dam, which was first put in service in 1968, is only 6m/20ft thick at the top. Containing 600 million cu m/2 119 million cu ft, it is the third largest reservoir in France.

▶ *Drive N along D 60.*

One of the most beautiful meanders of the flooded valley can be seen after Cernon, shortly before the intersection with D 3. There is a **view**★★ of a wild landscape, including the wooded peninsula which extends to the middle of the lake *(car park right of the road)*. Vaucluse Forest (named after the Carthusian monastery flooded when the lake was built)

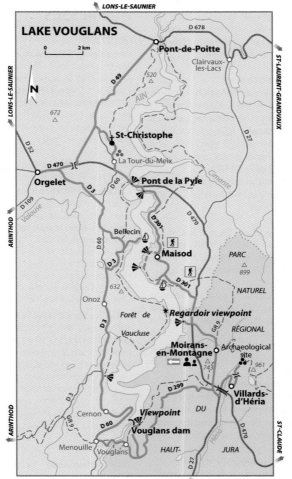

LAKE VOUGLANS

stretches a little further to the right. On the way to Orgelet, the road runs past the Bellecin water sports centre which includes a beach with facilities.

◗ *Left to Orgelet at the D 3 intersection.*

The road climbs, with views towards the wooded heights of Haut-Jura.

Orgelet

The interior of the **church** in this little town is surprisingly spacious, with a tall Gothic vault and wide galleries across the west end of the nave and above the

first arches of the aisles on either side of the nave. In the church is also an exceptional portion of 13C **coloured tiling** recently recovered from the ruins of the château that dominated the town.

◗ *From Orgelet, continue to Point-de-Poitte along D 470 and D 49.*

Pont-de-Poitte

There is a view of the River Ain from the bridge. When the water is low the giants' cauldrons are very much visible. When it is high, the rocky bed disappears under an impressive foaming torrent.

▶ *Leave Pont-de-Poitte S on D 49. 6km/4mi further on, take D 60 to the left, then turn left again towards the little village of St-Christophe.*

Saint-Christophe

Set against a high cliff, St-Christophe is overlooked by the remaining walls of a château and the pilgrimage **church of St-Christophe** (🕐*open mid-Jun to mid-Sept 9am–noon, 3–6pm; spring and autumn by appointment, ask M. Marcel Buffet;* 📞*03 84 25 42 58).*

This was built in the 12C and 15C and contains interesting works of art and wooden statues.

▶ *Go down to the village of Tour-du-Meix and take D 470 to the left. From the elegant Pyle Bridge, follow D 301 to the right (200m/220yd beyond the bridge).*

As you turn, there is a lovely **view**★ of the whole stretch of water contained by the dam. More **glimpses**★ of the reservoir appear between the oaks and evergreens which line the twisting road.

Maisod

1hr there and back on foot.

🚶 There is a signposted footpath in Maisod by the château entrance, which leads to the cliff overlooking the reservoir, and then continues along its edge.

▶ *Carry on along D 301. A road leading to the edge of the lake leads off 1.5km/1mi beyond Maisod. Turn right on D 470 towards Moirans.*

Belvédère du Regardoir★

15min round trip on foot.

🚶 There is a superb view from the platform overlooking the crescent-shaped section of reservoir.

▶ *Continue on D 470 S.*

ADDRESSES

🛏STAY

🛌 **Camping Trelachaume** – *39260 Maisod, 2km/1.2mi S of Maisod by D 301.* 📞*03 84 42 03 26. www.trelachaume. com. Open 17 Apr–4 Sept. Reservations recommended. 180 sites.* Pleasant campground with outstanding views over Vouglans Lake, the mountains and the leafy forests. You can rent chalets, mobile-homes or tents. Many sporting facilities including sailing, volley ball and a paddling pool.

🛌 **Camping Surchauffant** – *At Pont de la Pyle, 39270 La Tour-du-Meix.* 📞*03 84 25 41 08. www.camping-surchauffant. com. Open May–14 Sept. Reservations recommended. 135 sites.* Those keen on bathing, water-skiing and fishing will be able to indulge in their favourite sport in Vouglans Lake, a few steps away from the camp site. Chalets and mobile homes available.

🛌🛌 **Chambre d'Hôte La Baratte** – *39270 Présilly, 5km/3.1mi N of Orgelet by D 52 then D 175.* 📞*03 84 35 55 18. www.labaratte.fr.* 🍽 *4 rooms. Meals*🛌🛌*.* The former barn and stables of this old farmhouse have been converted into impeccably kept rooms with all modern conveniences. Local Franche-Comté specialities are served with their own walnut and hazelnut oils.

🍴EAT

🛌🛌 **Le Maurianna** – *23 r. Roussin, 39260 Moirans-en-Montagne.* 📞*03 84 42 60 78. www.maurianna.com. Closed Sat lunch and Sun, Ascension week, last week Aug–15 Sept, Christmas holidays.* Maurianna was the old Gaul name for the town that became Moirans. This restaurant has a focus on Franc-Comtois specialities, but prepared in an innovative way.

🛌🛌 **Le Regardoir** – *At the Moirans-en-Montagne Belvedere.* 📞*03 84 42 01 15. www.leregardoir.com. Closed mid-Dec to mid-Jan; Mon and eves except Fri and Sat outside Jul–Aug. Reservations recommended.* High up above the lake on the cliff-side, this is the perfect place for lunch with a superb view over the emerald lake and the surrounding green hills.

Saint-Claude★

The town of St-Claude, tucked amid delightful countryside between the River Bienne and River Tacon, is the most important tourist centre in the Haut-Jura. The heyday of its very famous abbey was in the 11C, but by the 16C it was in decline and all that remains from this period is the cathedral. Surrounded by forests, wood has always been important for the prosperity of the town and the surrounding region.

A BIT OF HISTORY

The Jura pioneers – As early as 430 the future **Saint Romain** and his brother **Lupicin** became religious hermits in the forests of the Haut-Jura. After their deaths, a monastery named **Condat**, was founded in the same place. Numerous priories were established by clearing the forest and eventually more than 500 monks lived in the area. From the boxwood, they would carve little statues, crucifixes and chapels to sell to visiting pilgrims. It was the start of the wood industry, that would later be so important for the region.

Saint Claude, originally archbishop of Besançon, came to govern an austere Benedictine abbey here in the 7C and remained for 55 years. Responsible for raising moral standards, his name was adopted in the 12C for the monastery and surrounding region.

The end of Serfdom – By the 18C the lordly canons, distinctly lacking the moral tone of their saintly predecessors, were regarded by the 14 000 inhabitants of the abbey lands as a handful of utterly shameless layabouts. In 1770, six Haut-Jura villages took out a lawsuit against the chapter to win their freedom. Their case made a tremendous impact; even **Voltaire**, living at Ferney at the time, came to the aid of the villagers by writing pamphlets. After a court case lasting five years, the canons, who refused point-blank to give any ground, emerged victorious. The bishop suggested that, as their rights had been officially recognised, they might like to

- ▶ **Population:** 11 9505
- **Michelin Map:** 321: F-8.
- **Info:** 1 av. de Belfort, 39203 St-Claude. ℘03 84 45 34 24. www.ot-saint-claude.com.
- ▶ **Location:** The town is in the middle of the Parc Naturel Régional du Haut-Jura not far from the Franco-Swiss border.
- ▶ **Don't Miss:** The new Musée de l'Abbaye and its amazing collection of contemporary art.

Saint-Claude pipes

S. Sauvignier/MICHELIN

make the generous gesture of liberating their serfs on their own initiative. The monks refused. The bishop appealed to King Louis XVI, but even he did not dare intervene. Finally, the problem was settled by the outbreak of the Revolution: the religious principality of St-Claude was abolished, its goods and lands confiscated and its serfs freed.

The capital of pipemaking – in 1854, a Corsican supplied local pipemaker, Daniel David with some briar, alleged to be superior to boxwood for making pipes. David had such a success with the new product that he established a highly successful business in Saint Claude. The town retained a monopoly on this type of pipe manufacture until 1885.

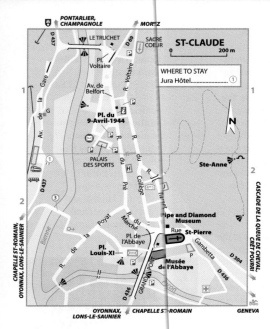

ST-CLAUDE

0   200 m

WHERE TO STAY
Jura Hôtel...................... ①

SIGHTS

Setting★★

From **place Louis-XI**, there is a beautiful
view★ above the old ramparts. Cross
the Grand Pont bridge to reach the stairway to the escaliers le faubourg. From
the bottom of the steep, picturesque
rue de la Poyat is a view over the Tacon
valley. This street was once an important
link between the upper district (around
the abbey) and the suburb inhabited by
workers and craftsmen.

Before the modern bridges were built,
it was also one of the routes taken by
pilgrims on their way to revere the relics
of St Claudius.

Cathédrale Saint-Pierre★

This cathedral church was once the heart
of the abbey community. The present
building, originally built in the Gothic
style in the 14C and 15C, was finished
in the 18C with the addition of a Classical façade. The 15C tower was extended
higher in the 18C. The most interesting
part of the exterior is the east end, with
its watch-turrets topped with spires.
The beautiful rectangular interior is
plain, even austere, and is supported
by 14 massive octagonal pillars.

Left of the entrance, a
restored Italian **altar
piece**★★ was donated
in 1533 by Pierre de la
Baume, the last bishop
of the Franche-Comté,
who lived in Geneva, in
gratitude to St Peter for
protecting him through all
the political and religious
disturbances.

The chancel is lit by
stained-glass windows★
restored in 1999 and con-
tains magnificent sculpted
wooden stalls★★ which
were begun before 1449
and finished in 1465 by the
Geneva craftsman Jehan
de Vitry. The Apostles and
the Prophets are depicted
alternately on the back-
rests, then the former
abbots of the monastery;
scenes from the abbey's
history with the founders St Romanus
and St Lupicinus, are represented on
the large and small cheekpieces; the 19C
restorers added scenes of everyday life
to the elbow rests and misericords.

St Claudius' tomb drew crowds of pilgrims until 1794. Emperors, kings and
lords all came to venerate him. **Anne of
Brittany** had been unable to conceive
until her pilgrimage to the Jura, after
which she bore a daughter to Louis XII
and named her Claude (the future wife
of François I and Queen of France). The
shrine was burned during the Revolution, and the remaining relics of the
saint are kept in a reliquary in the chapel
south of the chancel.

Musée de l'Abbaye/Donations Guy Bardone - René Genis★★

3 pl. de l'Abbaye. ○Sept–Apr 10am–
noon, 2–6pm except Mon and Tue; May
–Aug 10am–noon, 2–6.30pm except
Tue. Closed 1 May, 1 Nov, 25 Dec and
1 Jan. ≈5 € (children 2.50 €). ℘03 84
38 12 60. www.saint-claude.fr.

Opened in 2008 in the old Abbey palace (15–18C), this excellent museum is
divided into two parts. Cross the ground

floor dedicated to temporary art exhibitions to go down to visit the **archeological relics of the abbey from the 12C**. Superbly laid out, you will see part of the old monastery onto which are superimposed the tombs and cloisters from the 11C, chapels from the 13C and 15C, and improvements from the 18C. The history and live of the monks are explained with interactive exhibits and information panels. The archway of the chapel of Claude Venet (1478) is decorated with **a mural painting of Christ enthroned**★.

Look out for the inscription with the call to prayer at the entrance of the chapel. As you come back up, take a look at the garden with the sculptures of **l'Homme qui marche sur colonne** by Rodin and **le Coureur Grand** by Germaine Richier. The second part of the museum shows the superb **collection**★★ of more than 330 works *(more than two-thirds drawings)* donated to the town of Saint-Claude by the painter-collectors **Guy Bardone** (born in 1927 in St-Claude) and **René Genis** (1922–2004). According to what they came across and what appealed to them, these artists have brought together a collection of pieces, mainly figurative, that date from the end of the 19C to the 1990s. Works from the schools of Poetic Realism, Cubism, Impressionism and the Nabis all rub shoulders together.

The museum owns 32 drawings from **Bonnard**, works of **Baudin**, **Brianchon**, **Lesieur**, **Marquet**, not to mention **Picasso**, **Buffet**, **Braque**, **Chagall**, **Giacometti**, **Goya**, **Villon**, **Rebeyrolle**, **Dufy**, **Vuillard**, **Roussel** and more. A room is devoted to the two donors and a film presents their works and the history of their legacy.

Exposition de Pipes, de Diamants et de Pierres Fines (Pipe and Diamond Museum)

1 pl. J-Faizant. ⏰*Open May–Sept 9.30am–noon, 2–6.30pm; rest of year daily except Sun 2–6pm* ⏰*Closed Nov 1–20 Dec.* ◉*5€.* ⚹. ☎*03 84 45 17 00. www.musee-pipe-diamant.com.*

This collection of 18C and 19C pipes, some artistically decorated, is very varied, as you would expect in the town that remains an important centre for pipe-making.

The Chancellerie displays a collection of pipes marked with the names of those admitted into the famous pipe makers' guild of St-Claude including, in 2007, Patrick Louis Vuitton.

ADDRESSES

🛏STAY

🛏 **Jura** – *40 av. de la Gare.* ☎*03 84 45 24 04. www.jurahotel.com. 35 rooms.* ☐*7.50€. Restaurant*☐☐. This hotel is located opposite the station and overlooks the Bienne river. Choose one of the larger, recently renovated bedrooms (some with a terrace) with a view over the mountains. The large bay windows in the restaurant give a nice panorama over the town and the river; food is traditional and well served.

🛍SHOPPING

Marché – *pl. du 9-Avril. Thu morning.* The weekly market is the place to find regional specialities, such as cheeses, as well as other tempting food stalls. *In July–Aug there is also a craft market on Tuesdays at the Grenette.*

Genot Maitre Pipier – *13 fbg Marcel.* ☎*03 84 45 00 47. Open Mon–Fri 9–11.30am, 2–6pm, and Sat in Jul–Aug.* ◉*1.80€ to visit the workshops.* A young master-pipe maker has taken over this workshop and will share with you his passion for the craft of turning a lump of wood into a pipe. The shop is in pl. de l'Abbaye.

Crémerie Clément – *5 and 7 r. du Pré.* ☎*03 84 45 09 70. Open Mon–Sat 8am–12.30pm 2.30–7.30pm, and in summer only Sun 8am–12.30pm.* You will find all sorts of local Jura food and drink at this crémerie, which has been here since 1920. Cheese, charcuterie, terrine, honey and chocolates are side by side with Jura wines, beers and spirits.

Morez

Until 1860 Morez was the centre of France's watch-making industry, but for the past two centuries, it has been at the forefront of the manufacture of spectacles, producing over half of France's spectacles today. Linked to the outside by two impressive viaducts, the town extends over 3km/2mi at the bottom of the valley of the river Bienne, an important energy source to the town.

A BIT OF HISTORY

The capital of spectacles – The banks of the Bienne river attracted watchmakers, blacksmiths, enamellers and more, but the town of Morez ended up specialising in the making of spectacles. Although glasses had existed since the 13C, the big breakthrough came in the 18C when **Pierre-Hyacinthe Caseaux**, who made nails near Morez, developed the wire frame to replace the nails previously used.

The first glasses workshop was established near Morez in 1796, and from 1830 the glasses produced were being sold beyond the local area, and eventually to the whole of France. New factories sprung up and in 1860, Morez launched the **pince-nez**, took on making optical glasses and became the metropolis of glasses-making, producing up to 12 millions of pairs per year.

Today, the area around Morez has 60 glasses factories providing for 54 percent of the French market, but competition from China is taking its toll. The local firms specialise increasingly at the top end of the market, with innovative new designs and materials.

Musée de la Lunette

pl. Jean-Jaurès. ◷*Open 10am–noon (1pm in Jul–Aug), 2–6pm.* ◷*Closed Tue, public holidays and 1–25 Dec.* ᕦ. ⌐3€. ℘*03 84 33 39 30. www.musee-lunette.fr.*

The history of the manufacture of spectacles from the 13C up to the modern day is shown through a film and exhibits, including glasses used by 13C monks.

▶ **Population:** 5 462
⌖ **Michelin Map:** 321: G7.
▤ **Info:** pl. Jean-Jaurès, 39400 Morez. ℘03 84 33 08 73. www.haut-jura.com.
▣ **Location:** Morez lies on the N 5 highway that links Champagnole with the col de Saint-Cergue. From this main road you can look down on the town and at the zig-zag roads that serve it. You can also admire the grandeur of the viaducts that carry the railway.
⊜ **Don't Miss:** The Spectacles museum; a drive in the Bienne valley making the most of the many view points.
◷ **Timing:** Allow a day for the town and surroundings, not forgetting some time to try the famous Morbier cheese.
♟ **Kids:** The Spectacles museum offers excellent educational displays.

An interactive area explores the workings of the eye.

🚗 DRIVING TOUR

Vallée de la Bienne
Tour of 82km/51mi shown on the map of the valley (above). Allow 3hrs.

▷ *Leave Morez on N 5. 2km/1.4mi N you reach Morbier.*

Morbier

This little town above Morez, also involved in the spectacles industry, is better known for the soft cow cheese that bears its name.

A cheese-maker has opened a charming little museum *(open daily 8am–noon)* to explain the different production stages of this cheese. Morbier, an AOC cheese, is recognisable by the fine, horizontal lines of black, tasteless ash that run through it.

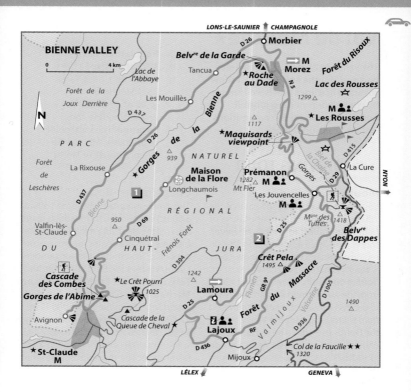

Maison de la Flore de Longchaumois

Longchaumois. Open 15 Jun–30 Sept 2–6pm. 4 €. www.longchaumois.eu.
Stop at this little museum to enjoy the displays of flowers and butterflies, as well as displays describing the work of the spectacle-makers and other local trades. Adjoining is a pretty wooded park with a marked botanical path.
The road continues to the **Belvédère de la Garde** with a superb view over Morez and its amazing viaducts.
Cross Morez and take D 25, parallel to N 5. On a very tight bend in the road is the spectacular **Belvédère des Maquisards**★ overlooking the gorges on the other bank below Fort des Rousses. Continue on the very windy D 25 through the woods and on to the D 29 for more glimpses of the bottom of the **gorges de la Haute-Bienne**.

Return to Morez by N 5.

*Take D 26 towards La Rixouse following the **gorges**★ de la Bienne. At La Rixouse, take D 437 towards Saint-Claude with good views on the left-hand side.*

Just before Saint-Claude, take the steep little road right up to Avignon *(D 303)*, where you will find a fine **view** over Saint-Claude after 1.5km/1mi.

Return to D 437 in Saint-Claude and take D 69 towards Morez. There is a car park on the first big bend on the right.

On the other side of the road, steps go down to the pretty, shady path towards the spectacular **cascade des Combes** waterfall and the **gorges** of the tumultuous Abîme river.

*Drive towards Cinquétral, where a belvedere gives a fantastic **view**★★ over Saint-Claude nearly 400m/1 300 ft below.*

Val de Mouthe★

The valley between La Chapelle-des-Bois and Mouthe enjoys regular snow coverage in winter, and is well known by cross-country skiers. It often hosts International ski competitions like the Transjurassienne.

▸ **Population:** 958.
⚲ **Michelin Map:** 321: H-6.
ℹ **Info:** 3 biz r. de la Varée, 25240 Mouthe.
  ℘03 81 69 22 78.
  www.otmouthe.com.
◗ **Location:** The focal point of the valley, Mouthe lies 32km/20mi NE of Morez.

🚗 DRIVING TOUR

Mouthe
You might shiver a little to hear that the village of Mouthe has a reputation of being the coldest in France. However, this is a positive advantage in the ski region of the Jura where the snow-cover is somewhat irregular elsewhere.
Source du Doubs – The road that leaves from the war memorial in Mouthe leads to the river's source (car park 100m/110yd from source). The Mouthe Valley where the Doubs rises, has a mixed landscape of meadows and fir trees. At an altitude of 937m/3 074ft, the clear spring gurgles from a cave at the foot of a steep slope in the forest of Noirmont. There is a marked **path**.

Chaux-Neuve
6.5km/4mi SW by D 437.
This resort is famous for its ski jumps that are accessible all year round – in summer the jumps have a synthetic covering. Chaux-Neuve is also used as a training ground for Nordic Combined skiing as well as for dog-sledging.
Parc Polaire★ (left on D 46 towards Chapelle-des-Bois; open all year, times vary; 7€ (4-11 years 5.40€); ℘03 81 69 20 20; www.parcpolaire. com) – Here you can observe a pack of Samoyeds, huskies and Greenland dogs living together in the wilds. Recently, the park has also brought over reindeer from Sweden and Finland, now forming the largest herd in western Europe. Tarpan (Eurasian) wild horses and yaks are among the other wild animals you will find here.

◗ Continue along D 46 which runs through the Combe des Cives.

Chapelle-des-Bois
This simple mountain village (alt 1 100m/3 609ft) surrounded by meadows in the heart of the Haut-Jura national park, has become a major centre for cross-country skiing. In summer, the surrounding countryside is ideal for long rambles. Take D 46 to the **Écomusée Maison Michaud** (open Jul–Aug daily except Sat 2–6pm (Tue and Fri also 10am–12.30pm); rest of the year times vary; 5€, children 2.60€; ℘03 81 69 27 42; www.ecomusee-jura.fr), based in a 17C farmhouse. The museum shows what life in such an isolated dwelling would have been like and the importance of the fire-place, which occupies virtually a room of its own, where the family would have cooked bread, cured meats and made cheese. Bread and cakes on sale.

ADDRESSES

🛏 STAY
Auberge du Grand Gît – 25240 Chaux-Neuve. ℘03 81 69 25 75. www.d-klik.com/auberge. Closed Apr, 16 Oct–20 Dec. 8 rooms. 9€. Restaurant. Near the ski jumps, this recently built chalet offers a family atmosphere and quiet rooms with wood-panelled walls. Country-style cooking.

🍴 EAT
Auberge de la Distillerie – chez Michel, 25240 Chappelle-des-Bois. ℘03 81 69 21 64. www.auberge-distillerie.fr. Closed 2nd week of June; check out of season. 8 rooms. Enjoy regional specialities around the fireplace in this basic mountain farm. Simple rooms.

Lajoux

A small village on the road to the Col de la Faucille, Lajoux is at the centre of the Parc Naturel Régional du Haut-Jura and at the gateway of the high valleys, the Hautes-Combes. The village is notable for the large Maison du Parc, which has an educational exhibition about the Jura environment. A winter and summer family resort, Lajoux lies on the route of the Grande Traversée du Jura itinerary for skiers, cyclists and walkers.

🚗 DRIVING TOUR

See Region map. Allow 6hrs.

▶ *Leave Lajoux on the D 292, pass Molunes and arrive at Les Moussières.*

At the **Maison des Fromages** in the little mountain resort of Les Moussières (🕐*open 8am–noon, 2.30–7pm; ✆03 84 41 60 96*), the speciality is Bleu de Gex cheese, though other the other Jura AOC cheeses, Comté and Morbier, are also made. You can watch the making of the cheese through a plate-glass window, and buy some to take home, too.

Take D 25 S to L'Emboissieux, then left to the mountain village La Pesse at the heart of dog-sledging activities. From Pesse, take the road opposite the church towards La Borne au Lion. After 4km/2.4mi you come to a crossroads (car park nearby).

From here continue on foot *(10min there and back)* to the Borne au Lion, a strategic Franche-Comté border post, also the site of Resistance activity in 1944. There is a good view from here over the Jura mountains.

Cret de Chalam★★★

This is the highest peak (1 545m/5 069ft) in the range overlooking the Valserine from the west, in the south of the Haut-Jura regional park. It is easily accessible to serious ramblers.

For a dramatic **Panorama**★★, take the right-hand path from the Borne au Lion car park; 1hr 30min on foot round trip.

ℹ **Info:** 27 le Village, 39310 Lajoux. ✆03 84 41 28 52. www.tourisme-hautes-combes.com.

▶ **Location:** 19km/12mi E of Saint-Claude by D 436.

🕐 **Timing:** Allow a day for the driving tour, or several days to make the most of the rich landscape of the Haut-Jura regional park.

🥾 The entire length of the Valserine Valley can be seen from the summit. The view to the east stretches as far as the **Jura range**, before the land drops down to the Swiss plain. The gullied slopes of **Roche Franche** can be seen right in front of you; to your left are the Reculet and the **Crêt de la Neige** (1 720m/ 5 643ft); to your right is the Grand Crêt d'Eau, beyond the Sac pass. In clear weather, even **Mont Blanc** is visible. There is an extensive **view** to the west of the Jura mountains and plateaux. Return to La Pesse and turn left on D 25 for 7.5km/4.8mi, then right on D 124. Turn right to **Les Bouchoux**★ an unusual, peaceful village high up above the Tacon valley. Leave the village by D 25E1 to L'Emboussieux and on to the region of Bellecombe.

There are dramatic view points arranged along the D 25; particularly worth seeing is the promontory of the **Belvédère de la Cernaise**★ with a bird's-eye **view** of the Flumen Valley, of Saint-Claude and the Septmoncel plateau. Follow the D 25, then take a left at l'Évalide on D 436 towards Saint-Claude. The Flumen mountain stream, a tributary of the Tacon, can be seen cascading through a wild **gorge**★.

The curious natural site of **Chapeau de Gendarme**★ consists of once horizontal layers of rock, which were compressed and lifted during the Tertiary Era and became twisted without breaking.

At the edge of Saint-Claude, take two right turns on D 304 towards Lamoura. Drive through Lamoura, then turn left to return to Lajoux by D 436.

Les Rousses ♨ ❄

This resort, on a plateau a stone's throw from Switzerland, is renowned for its skiing, high-quality leisure activities and convivial atmosphere. In summer, it is popular with ramblers and mountain bikers, while water-sports enthusiasts head for the nearby lake. The resort includes four villages: Les Rousses, Prémanon, Lamoura and Bois d'Amont.

SKI AREA
Alpine skiing 🎿

There are four linked ski areas, including one in Switzerland, offering 40km/25mi of runs of various levels of difficulty: 16 green runs, 7 blue, 16 red and 4 black runs accessible via 40 ski lifts. There is a choice of ski passes combining several ski areas or the complete area, with free ski shuttle buses linking the villages.

Les Tuffes 🎿 – This is mainly a nursery area, ideal for beginners and families. There are long green runs, some blues and two red runs. Thanks to a chairlift, beginner snowboarders also enjoy this area. Be warned, it does get busy here.

La Serra 🎿 – The ski standard here is higher: one beautiful green, run but mostly blue and red runs.

Le Noirmont 🎿 – Beginners should avoid this area, as even the long green run accessible by chairlift requires self-confidence. The red and black runs are the favourite haunt of snowboarders who speed down the often icy slopes.

La Dôle 🎿 – The highest point of the massif is in Switzerland. In fair weather,

- ▶ **Population:** 3 018
- ⏱ **Michelin Map:** 321: G-8.
- 🔖 **Info:** 795 r. Pasteur, 39220 Les Rousses. ✆03 84 60 02 55. www.lesrousses.com.
- ◖ **Location:** The resort area lies on the Franco-Swiss border. The highest point of the ski areas varies from 1 420m/4 659ft and 1 680m/5 512ft at La Dôle, which is in Switzerland, so keep your passport handy.
- 👥 **Kids:** In addition to the slopes, children will love the glimpse of Inuit and Sami life at the Centre Polaire in Prémanon.

the view of Lake Geneva and of the Alps is unforgettable. Competent skiers will appreciate the blue, red and black runs; there are also a few short green runs.

Cross-country skiing ⛷

There are 250km/155mi of double tracks suitable for both styles of cross-country skiing; 35 trails varying in difficulty (from green to black). The 76km/47mi Trans-Jurassienne race starts at Lamoura.

Luge

There are official sledging slopes at the Port des Jouvencelles (Les Tuffes) and at the base of the Serra and Noirmont areas, as well as in the villages of Lamoura and Prémanon.

Snowshoeing

Accessible to all, this activity still requires a minimum of fitness, so practice on the few waymarked trails around the resort before embarking on long excursions. There are guided tours with a member of the École du Ski Français (ESF).

SIGHTS
Les Rousses

The village developed round its church during the 18C. The former wooden houses were replaced by apartment

Cross-country skiing in Les Rousses

A. Cassaigne/MICHELIN

blocks, chalets and hotels. From the terrace in front of the church, there is a fine view of the Lac des Rousses and the Risoux mountain range.

Fort des Rousses

This fort, built in the 19C, is one of the largest in France; there is a vast network of underground galleries which could house up to 3 000 men. No longer used by the military, one part is now the **Caves Juraflore** (👓⚬guided tours (1hr 30min) with film and cheese tasting; by reservation through the tourist office; ⚬5€; ℘03 84 60 02 55), where there are huge Comté cheese-ageing cellars. The longest measures 214m/234yd.

In another part is ⚬⚬ **Fort des Rousses Aventure** (🕐opening times vary; ℘03 84 60 02 55; www.lesrousses.com), with three supervised adventure trails for children graded according to their level of difficulty and including suspended footbridges, via ferrata and so on.

Lac des Rousses

2km/1.2mi N.

Covering almost 100ha/247 acres, this lake is very lively in summer, its swimming and watersports facilities attracting many holidaymakers.

EXCURSIONS

Bois d'Amont

The village has a long woodworking tradition; learn more about it at the **Musée de la Boissellerie** (🕐open daily mid-Jul to Aug 10am–noon, 2–6pm; rest of year Wed–Sun 2.30–6pm; 🕐closed Oct–Nov; ⚬6€; ℘03 84 60 98 79; www.museedelaboissellerie.com), in a former saw-mill. Demonstrations and audio-visual presentations illustrate local wood crafts, such as making boxes for cheese.

Prémanon

Overlooked by Mont Fier (1 282m/4 206ft), this village and the nearby hamlets rise in terraces from the banks of the Bienne to the small Dappes Valley which marks the border with Switzerland. In an unusual building the ⚬⚬ **Centre Polaire Paul-Émile-Victor** (🕐open daily except Tue 10am–noon, 2–6pm;

🕐 closed 15 Nov–15 Dec and 1 Jan; ⚬5.20€ (children 2.60€); ℘03 84 60 77 71; www.centrepev.com), is a museum all about the world of polar expeditions, as well as the life of the Inuit and Sami peoples.

👁Don't miss the magnificent 3.10m/10ft-high stuffed white bear.

Lamoura

In the town hall of this mountain village the **Musée du Lapidaire** (🕐open 20 Dec–10 Apr, Jun–Sept; 👓⚬guided tours (45min) daily except Sat 2.30pm–6pm; Jun and Sept Sun 2.30–6pm; ⚬3.50€. ♿ ℘03 84 41 22 17) is devoted to the traditional craft of gem-cutting, once widely practised here. The museum contains a collection of gems and tools, and offers a demonstration on this dying art.

🚗 DRIVING TOUR

Forêt du Massacre

34 km/21mi circuit. ♿ See Region map. Allow 45min.

▷ *Leave Lamoura to the northeast on the D 25.*

Much enjoyed by cross-country skiers, this forest is one of the highest on the French side of the Jura, reaching 1 495m/4 900ft at **Crêt Pela**, from where there is a **view** that extends to the Alps. The forest boasts several rare mountain plant species and spruce, some of which you will drive past on the pretty **route de la combe du Lac** (D 25).

▷ *At Jouvencelles, turn right towards the ski lift car park, then take the track to Les Tuffes. After the last buildings, turn left onto a road which veers off onto the forest road. Leave your car 750m/800yd after.*

Walk to the **Belvédère des Dappes** *(15min there and back)* at 1 310m/4 300ft altitude for a view over Les Rousses and its lake, La Cure, Le Noirmont, la Dôle and on a clear day, the Swiss Alps. *Return to Lamoura via Lajoux.*

ADDRESSES

🏠STAY

🛏 Stay anywhere in the four villages and your hotelier should provide you with a Carte d'Hôte, which gives you discounts off several activities in the resort.

🍴🍴 **Hôtel La Redoute** – 357 rte Blanche. ☎03 84 60 00 40. www.hotel laredoute.com. Closed 6 Apr–7 May, 5 Nov–5 Dec. 🅿. 25 rooms. ⊆ € . Restaurant 🍴🍴. This family hotel stands at the entrance to the skiing resort. The accommodation consists of simply decorated but carefully kept bedrooms. Meals are served in a large rustic-style dining room. Good selection of affordable menus, including one for children.

🍴🍴🍴 **Le Lodge** – 309 r. Pasteur. ☎03 84 60 50 64. www.hotellelodge.com. 11 rooms. ⊆ 9.50 €. This old house has been decorated in Alpine style with lovely soft furnishings. Spacious and elegant rooms make this a comfortable place to stay.

🍽EAT

🍴🍴 **L'Atelier** – 1867 r. de Franche-Comté, 39220 Bois-d'Amont. 8km/5mi N of Les Rousses along D 415. ☎03 84 60 94 15. www.restaurant-latelier.fr. Closed spring holiday, All Saints holiday, Sun eve, Mon and Tue. Attractive, contemporary décor, with paintings on

the walls, provides the backdrop for this restaurant, but it is their good classical cuisine that counts. The menu changes with the seasons, and has an emphasis on lake fish.

🍴🍴🍴 **Arbez Franco-Suisse** – 601 r. de la Frontière, 39220 La Cure . 2.5km/ 1.5mi SE of les Rousses by N 5. ☎03 84 60 02 20. www.arbezie-hotel.com. Closed Nov, Mon and Tue out of season. This bilingual hotel is located on the border between France and Switzerland. As regards meals, you can choose between the informal brasserie on the French side, and the dining room on the Swiss side with its wooden décor.

🛍SHOPPING

Boissellerie du Hérisson – 101 r. Pasteur. ☎03 84 60 30 84. Open daily 9am–noon, 2–7pm; out of season Tue–Sun 9.30am–noon, 2–7pm. This shop offers an incredible range of fine, beautifully crafted wooden objects (old-fashioned toys, board games, chests) made for the most part by local artisans.

Fromagerie des Rousses – 137 r. Pasteur. ☎03 84 60 02 62. Delicious cheeses for sampling and for sale here include Comté, Tomme de Jura and Morbier. Visit at 9am to see the cheese-making. You'll also find fine dairy products (butter, crème fraiche, fromage blanc) as well as preserves, mushrooms, honey, and wines and liqueurs of the region.

Monts Jura✳

The villages of Mijoux and Lélex in the upper Valserine Valley are linked with the Col de la Faucille and most recently to Menthières, near Bellegarde. Together they form the Jura's most southerly and its highest winter sports resort, Monts Jura. It lies within the boundaries of both the Réserve Naturelle de la Haute Chaîne de la Jura and the Parc Naturel Régional du Haut-Jura, an area known for its abundance and diversity of flowering plants.

🕭 **Michelin Map:** 328: I-3.
🏢 **Info:** 01410 Lélex-Mijoux. ☎04 50 20 91 43. www.monts-jura.com.
▶ **Location:** The village of Mijoux is linked to the Col de la Faucille and to Mont-Rond by ski lifts.

ACTIVITIES
Ascent of Crêt de la Neige★★
Alt 1 720m/5 643ft. 🕙Open 10 Jul–29 Aug Sat, Sun and public hols 9am–1pm, 2.15–5.30pm. 🎫6€. ☎08 36 68 39 01.

⛷ In Lélex, take the Catheline cable car (10min one way). On arrival, start walking right towards the Crêt de la Neige along a safe but slippery path *(allow 3hrs there and back; hiking boots recommended)*.

Beyond the Grand Crêt, to the east, are views of the Jura mountains, Lake Geneva, and the famous Geneva fountain. The summit reveals a panoramic view of the Alps. Between Lélex and Mijoux is the restful Valmijoux countryside with the River Valserine flowing through the green pastures.

Alpine skiing

The three Alpine ski areas comprise 49 runs (60km/37mi) for all levels of proficiency, and with the best height drop in the Jura resorts (800m/ 2 625ft). Much of the area has artificial snow-making facilities.

Lélex-Crozet *(900m to 1 700m/2 953ft to 5 577ft)* – The village has a kindergarden where the youngest can enjoy the pleasures of sliding on the snow. The Lélex cable car leads to Catheline giving access to various runs and the resort's highest point, Monthoisey (1 680m/5 315ft).

Mijoux-La Faucille *(1 000–1 50m/3 281–5 085ft)* – A chairlift links Mijoux and the Col de la Faucille. From there, a hybrid gondola and chairlift *(télécombi)* runs to the top of Mont-Rond (1 534m/5 033ft).

There are wide, easy runs for beginners and two red runs for the more advanced. Very long blue and green runs go back down to Mijoux.

Menthières *(1 000-1 530m/3 281-5 020ft)* – A chair lift links with tow lifts to take you up to the Crêt de Frasses from where there are two reds and a long blue run.

Cross-country skiing

La Vattay *(1 300–1 500m/4 264–4 920ft)* – The area's international renown is fully justified by its extensive facilities (restaurant, bar, equipment hire service, Nordic-skiing school…) and by the quality of its 100km/62mi of pisted double tracks and competition tracks.

La Valserine *(900–1 080m/2 953–3 543ft)* – Less popular, less challenging but pleasant even so, this area reveals the charm of this yet unspoilt valley. The 40km/25mi of tracks are also pisted for both styles of cross-country skiing.

JURA MOUNTAINS

Snowshoeing

There are marked paths from the Col de la Faucille, Menthières, La Vattay and from the villages of Mijoux and Lélex.

Summer activities

When the snow goes, there is still plenty to do in these mountains. Walking and mountain biking are made easier in peak season when the cable cars operate.

EXCURSIONS
Mont-Rond★★

▶ Take the D 1005 from the col de la Faucille to reach the Mont-Rond télécombi station (⏱ open daily 3 Jul –29 Aug and the two weekends before and after 10.30am–5.30pm; ◉6€), where you can park the car.
Alternatively, at Mijoux you can take the chairlift that leads to the lower station of the col de la Faucille cable car.

🚶 From the top of the cable car, follow the Mont-Rond path to reach one of the most famous viewpoints in the Jura. Of the Grand and Petit Mont-Rond, the latter is more interesting.

Belvédère du Petit Mont-Rond – The dramatic view from the viewing table is breathtaking. At one sweep, you can take in a huge panorama running from the rift valley with Lake Geneva, the majestic Alps extending over an area 250km/155mi wide and 150km/93mi deep, as well as the whole Jura mountain chain and the Dôle (in Switzerland).

Colomby de Gex★★★

The same access as Mont-Rond. Take the télécombi (gondola/chairlift) to the belvédère Petit-Mont-Rond, then follow the GR 9 footpath (signposted) along the ridge. You can also walk from the bottom of the télécombi (4hrs return).

🚶 At 1 689m/5 545ft, the Colomby de Gex is one of the highest points in the highest chain of the Jura range. The summit offers an extensive **view**★ of the valley of Lake Geneva, and beyond it the Alps stretching 250km/155mi.

🚗 DRIVING TOUR

FROM LA CURE TO GEX

27km/17mi. Allow 30min.

▶ Leave La Cure on D 1005.

The road leaves the forest of Massacre to the right, beyond the dip where the Valserine flows; on the left is the Dôle (1 677m/5 510ft) on the Swiss side.

View of the Mont Blanc range from Col de la Faucille

© TTL Images/Alamy

Col de la Faucille★★

At an altitude of 1 323m/4 341ft, the pass cuts a passage through the great mountainous Jura spine separating the Rhône Valley and Lake Geneva to the east from the Valserine Valley to the west.

The pass is one of the main routes through the Jura mountains. The descent to Gex offers unforgettable **views**★ of Mont Blanc directly ahead and, from the end of the pass road, down into the Valserine Valley from over 300m/984ft.

Descent to Gex★★

Having crossed the pass, the road leads through pine forest. It opens up after the La Mainaz hotel, making a great hairpin meander round the green fields and houses of Le Pailly. Leave the car on the roadside where it widens to enjoy the splendid **panorama**★★. Lake Geneva appears often in a haze, sometimes even disappearing entirely under a sea of clouds, whereas the peaks of the Alps stand out quite sharply.

The Napoleon fountain (1805), built at the same time as this amazing road, comes into sight further down, on the side of the road as it makes a tight hairpin bend around a house.

The countryside around Gex appears shortly afterwards, spread out at the bottom of the slopes, with its checkerboard landscape of fields.

Divonne-les-Bains ✦

Divonne is a well-known spa town half way between Lake Geneva and the great Jura mountain range, on the Franco-Swiss border, and has plenty of luxury hotels, a golf course, a racecourse and a 45ha/111-acre lake.

▶ **Population:** 7 400
👍 **Michelin Map:** 328: J-2.
🈯 **Info:** r. des Bains, 01220 Divonne-Les-Bains.
 𝒫04 50 20 01 22.
 www.divonnelesbains.fr.
🔘 **Location:** Divonne is on the border and can be reached from the col de la Faucille or from Geneva (19km/12mi).

A BIT OF HISTORY

The Romans enjoyed the waters at Divonne, building an 11km/6.6mi aqueduct to carry them to their colonial capital Noviodunum (Nyon). In later years, the springs ran on forgotten until 1848, when Dr Paul Vidart founded a spa. It soon became famous, attracting clients like Prince Jérôme Bonaparte and Guy de Maupassant.

SIGHTS

Thermal Baths

🕐*Open Mon–Fri 9am–8.30pm (9.30pm Mon and Wed), Sat 9am–6pm, Sun 9am –2pm.* 🚫*Closed 14 Nov–21 Mar.* ⊜*18€.* 𝒫*04 50 20 05 70. www.valvital.fr.*
The spa specialises in the treatment of ailments associated with modern living, such as stress and insomnia. However, they also organise wellness packages for those who just want to pamper themselves a little.

Lake

This vast artificial lake has a **beach**, and is popular for windsurfing and sailing. Located near the lake, the **racecourse** is used in summer for flat racing and also for trotting races.

PAYS DE GEX

Very close to the city of Geneva, the pretty village of **Gex** *(8km/5mi SW of Divonne)* is a good starting point for walks. There are magnificent views of Mont Blanc from the place Gambetta.
Creux de l'Envers *(2hrs on foot there and back, starting from the bottom of rue du Commerce, then along rue Léone-de-Joinville, and returning via rue de Rogeland on D 1005 N of Gex)* – 🚶 This pleasant walk takes you to a wooded gash in the mountainside through which flows the River Journans.
The narrowest place is known as the **Portes Sarrasines**; the mountain stream rushes through a small gap in the rock flanked on both sides by limestone escarpments looking like a door frame.
Ferney-Voltaire *(15km/10mi SE of Gex by D 1005)* – On the border with Switzerland, Ferney, as it's known locally, was home to the famous author Voltaire from 1759–78. A visit to the house where he held court will please both his fans and those less acquainted with his work. Built by Voltaire to replace a fortress too austere for his tastes, the **château** *(guided tours only, 3 Apr–4 Nov, reservation at 𝒫04 50 40 53 21)* is in the Doric style and surrounded by a landscaped park. Voltaire took his role as landlord very seriously; he had sanitation installed in the village, part of his estate, and endowed it with a hospital, school and clockmaking workshops. The house contains many mementoes of the philosopher's life, including his portrait by Quentin de La Tour.
Very close to Ferney, across the border in Switzerland, is the important international organisation **CERN/The European Centre for Nuclear Research** *(𝒫+41 22 767 76 76; http://outreach. web.cern.ch/outreach)* with permanent exhibitions allowing the public to get some understanding of its complicated work. There are also guided tours *(half a day)* including a presentation of current research projects, a film and visit to one of the experimental activities or to one of the **nuclear accelerators**.

🚗 DRIVING TOUR

SWISS EXCURSION INTO VAUD CANTON

35km/22mi. Allow 5hrs.

▷ *Leave Divonne towards the motorway (E 25-E 62) marked Lausanne-Genève.*

Continue underneath the motorway in the direction of Coppet. (Full details of sites in the Swiss Green Guide.)

Coppet

On the banks of Lake Geneva, the little town of Coppet has a main street lined with arcaded houses, built in the 16C after the invasion of the Bernese army. Overlooking the lake is the **Coppet castle**★ that still belongs to the family of the famous Madame de Staël, a woman of letters, whose turbulent life lead to her to initiate "the salon of Europe" where celebrities of the time debated important issues.

▷ *Go down to the road along the lakeside and follow towards Lausanne.*

Nyon★

This town has been inhabited since the time of Julius Caesar, who founded a Roman colony there. Wander around the charming upper quarter, overlooked by the **feudal castle**, with its little streets, acarded houses and fine old squares. The **lakeside quarter** of Nyon is also what makes the town so attractive. By the banks of **Lake Geneva** you will find a park with floral walkways, a nicely laid-out pleasure port and a view over to the French side of the lake (4km/3mi). Near the port, in an 18C hospital. the **musée du Léman** is devoted to the story of Lake Geneva. Exhibits in the museum include aquariums, scale models of boats and paintings of the lake.

▷ *Follow the road for 2km/1.5mi in the direction of Lausanne.*

Prangins

Overlooking Lake Geneva and surrounded by an English-style park, the **château de Prangins**★★ was built in the French style of the 1730s. By turn it has been the domain of a lord, the home of a prince, a school and a family home. Today it houses the **Swiss National Museum** which complements perfectly its counterpart in Zurich, devoting itself to the 18C and 19C history of the country. The basement is dedicated to Swiss life in the pre-industrial era.

Don't forget to take a look outside at the vegetable garden, where 18C fruit and vegetable species are grown; in the background is a view to the Dôle mountain and the Jura range of mountains.

▷ *Return to Nyon and turn right to Divonne-les-Bains.*

ADDRESSES

🛏 STAY

🍽🍽 **Jura** – 43 *rte Arbère.* 📞*04 50 20 05 95. www.hotel-divonne.com. 29 rooms.* ⊊*9.90€.* This family-run hotel in the centre of town offers functional, well-kept rooms. New rooms in the annexe have a terrace.

🍽🍽🍽 **Auberge des Chasseurs** – *01170 Échenevex, 11km/6.8mi SW of Divonne by D 984C.* 📞*04 50 41 54 07. Closed 12 Nov–28 Feb, Sun evenings and Mon except Jul–Aug, Tue and Fri lunchtime. 15 rooms.* ⊊*12€. Restaurant* 🍽🍽. Peaceful inn offering cosy bedrooms and views over Mont Blanc.

🍴 EAT

🍽 **Les Quatre-Vents** – *pl. des Quatre-Vents.* 📞*04 50 20 00 08. Open Tue–Sat 6.30am–7pm, Sun 6.30am–2pm. Closed Oct and 2 weeks in Feb.* Tuck into delicious home-made pastries in this tea shop and art gallery.

🌙 NIGHT OUT

Casino de Divonne-les-Bains – *av. des Thermes.* 📞*04 50 40 34 34. www. domainedivonne.com. Open noon–4am (from 8pm for the traditional games).* 259 slot machines, with some of the highest jackpots in Europe, roulette, blackjack, and poker are all available. 4 restaurants.

The Bugey district nestles in a deep bend in the upper Rhône in the southern part of the Ain *département,* easily accessible from either Lyon to the west, or Geneva in Switzerland to the east. Its highest point is Le Grand Colombier (alt 1 534m/5 032ft) at the southern end of the Jura range. The imposing mountain can be viewed from many directions, looming up above the Rhône river and the Bugey vineyards scattered along the valley. To the north, the power of the Rhône is harnessed by the impressive Génissiat dam, one of many hydro-electric plants to exploit the force of the river.

The Highway of the Titans

Due to its many lateral valleys and gentle mountains, the Bugey region has been used as a thoroughfare for many centuries. Fortified towers and castles, built to protect the routes, are scattered throughout the region; while it's very isolation attracted monks looking for a peaceful, solitary refuge, hence many monasteries and abbeys were established.

In the 18C Spanish troops marched through the Bugey in the war of the Spanish Succession, and in the 19C coalition forces banded together against Napoleon here. During World War II, the region was the scene of many battles. It paid a particularly heavy price, losing a large number of both civilians and local Resistance fighters, and having many residents deported and executed by the occupation forces.

The railway from Lyon to Geneva was completed in 1855, bringing development to the Bugey. Soon after, the towns of Bellegarde and Ambérieu both did well from the arrival of the railway. However, in recent times it has been the construction of the spectacular section of the A 40 motorway between Bourg-en-Bresse and Bellegarde that has helped bring tourists and business into the region. In 1986 when the French president, François Miterrand, visited the construction site of the Bugey section, he dubbed it the Autoroute des Titans (highway of the Titans).

This part of the highway includes three long tunnels and 12 vertiginous viaducts up to 100m/330ft high. There is even a little museum at the Lac de Sylvans rest stop which presents displays of the construction process and how it transformed the landscape and local economy.

Highlights

1 Take a dip or just walk around lovely **Lake Nantua** (p403)

2 Visit the copper factory and explore the village of **Cerdon** (p405)

3 Climb up the 1 165 steps to the **Fort de l'Écluse** (p407)

4 Learn about the power of water at the **Génissiat dam** (p408)

5 Drive up to **Le Grand Colombier** and admire the view (p410)

Culinary Heritage

The original capital of the Bugey, the town of Belley was the birthplace of Jean-Anthelme Brillat-Savarin, author of the witty compendium of culinary anecdotes *La Physiologie du goût* (*The Physiology of Taste*). Belley also houses the administrative offices for the little Bugey wine region, which rejoiced in 2009 when it was finally awarded the coveted AOC (Appellation d'Origine Controllée) for its wines. The vineyards are scattered in valleys around the *communes* of Belley and Ambérieu in particular, producing light reds and fresh dry whites from a range of grapes. Quality is improving and the wines are gaining a greater following. To the north, the vineyards of Cerdon (*see p404)* grow grapes to make highly unusual semi-sweet rosé sparkling wines, made in a traditional way called the Méthode Ancestrale.

The Bugey produces typical mountain cheeses similar to those produced all over Franche-Comté. However, the most famous Bugey speciality is freshwater crayfish from Nantua, often used in a sauce (immortalised as Sauce Nantua), served locally with delicate pike dumplings (*quenelles de brochet*).

BUGEY

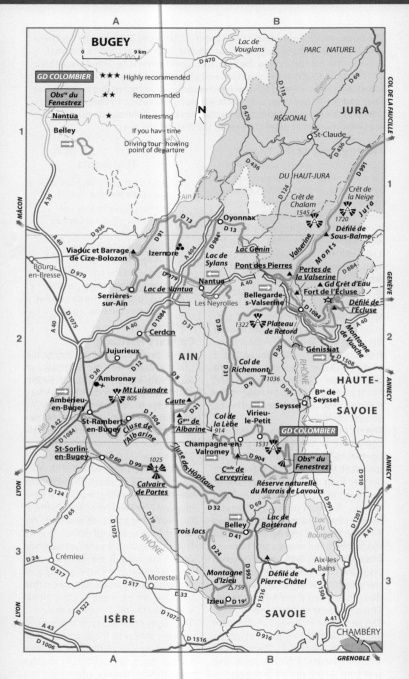

BUGEY

| 0 | 9 km |

GD COLOMBIER ★★★ Highly recommended

Obsᵉ du
Fenestrez ★★ Recommended

Nantua ★ Interesting

If you have time

Driving tour showing
point of departure

N

Belley

Lac de
Vouglans

PARC NATUREL

D 470

RÉGIONAL

JURA

St-Claude

DU HAUT-JURA

Crêt de
la Neige

Crêt de
Chalam
1545

1720

Défilé de
Sous-Balme

Oyonnax

D 13

Izernore

Lac Génin

Viaduc et Barrage
de Cize-Bolozon

Pont des Pierres

Pertes de
la Valserine

Gd Crêt d'Eau
Fort de l'Écluse

Serrières-
sur-Ain

Lac de Nantua

Nantua

Les Neyrolles

Bellegarde-
s-Valserine

Défilé de
l'Écluse

Cerdon

AIN

1322

Plateau
de Retord

Montagne
de Vuache

Génissiat

Jujurieux

Col de
Richemont

1036

HAUTE-

Ambronay

Mt Luisandre
805

Caute

Col de
la Lèbe
914

Virieu-
le-Petit

Bᵍᵉ de
Seyssel

Seyssel

SAVOIE

Ambérieu-
en-Bugey

St-Rambert-
en-Bugey

Cluse de
l'Albarine

Gᵍᵉ de
l'Albarine

Champagne-en-
Valromey

GD COLOMBIER

1531

Obsᵉ du
Fenestrez

St-Sorlin-
en-Bugey

1025

Cluse des Hôpitaux

Cᵃᵈᵉ de
Cerveyrieu

D 904

Réserve naturelle
du Marais de Lavours

Calvaire
de Portes

Trois lacs

Belley

Lac de
Barterand

Lac
du
Bourget

Crémieu

Moreste

Montagne
d'Izieu
759

Izieu

Défilé de
Pierre-Châtel

Aix-les-
Bains

ISÈRE

SAVOIE

CHAMBÉRY

GRENOBLE

Nantua★

*Haut Bugey, Gorges de L'Ain,
Plastics Vallée*

Nantua, tucked in a steep-sided, evergreen-forested **cluse**★★ on the shores of a glacial lake, is a charming resort known for its freshwater crayfish *(écrevisses)* and a type of very light dumpling *(quenelles à la Nantua)*.

▶ **Population:** 3 693
⚑ **Michelin Map:** 328: G-4.
🗊 **Info:** pl. de la Déportation, 01130 Nantua. ℘04 74 75 00 05. www.nantua-tourisme.com.
◖ **Location:** Nantua is a good base from which to explore both the Ain Valley and the Haut-Bugey.

A BIT OF HISTORY

Within these walls – Nantua grew up around a Benedictine abbey founded in the 8C. In the Middle Ages it was a free town surrounded by solid ramparts, which it needed, as it was continually caught up in the turbulent religious and political disputes between the Bugey, the Franche-Comté, Savoy and Geneva, not to mention between France and the Germanic Empire. Henri IV annexed Nantua to the kingdom of France in 1601.

RESORT
Lake★

Formed from a deep valley created by an old glacier moraine, the Nantua lake is 2.5km/1.5mi long and 650m/2 132ft wide. It is fed by numerous streams and springs including the Neyrolles. The water flows out of the lake via the "Arms of the lake" and into the Oignin, a tributary of the Ain river.

The whole lake is surrounded by the mountains of the Haut-Bugey, with the steep slopes on the northern side ending in rock-strewn wooded banks. There are attractive views both from the esplanade, shaded by beautiful plane trees, and from the Avenue du Lac.

The lake has been turned into a watersports area, and during high season there are plenty of leisure and sporting activities available including supervised swimming, pedalos, canoeing, sailing, water-skiing and fishing.

Abbatiale Saint-Michel★

This church is the last trace of a 12C abbey destroyed during the Revolution. The beautiful Romanesque portal is badly damaged, but the Last Supper can nonetheless be discerned on the lintel.

The chancel contains some beautiful carved woodwork and kneeling angels either side of the altar (17C and 18C). Note the **Martyrdom of St Sebastian**★★ (1836) by Delacroix on the north wall.

Musée d'Histoire de la Résistance et de la Déportation de l'Ain et du Haut-Jura★

⏱*Open May–Sept daily except Mon 10am–1pm, 2–6pm.* ✆4 €. ℘04 74 75 07 50. www.musees.ain.fr.

Housed in a building where resistance fighters were interned, this is a very moving museum. Through an excellent audioguide including the voices of former French maquisards and a British soldier, the museum traces the rise of Fascism and recalls France's Vichy administration, the Occupation, the Resistance, the Maquis and deportation. Numerous documents, mostly collected locally, and an educational film testify to the struggle between the Nazis and the Maquis in the Bugey region.

🚗 DRIVING TOURS

1 HAUT BUGEY
130km/81mi circuit. Allow one day.

◖ *Leave Nantua to the N on the picturesque D 1084, which runs alongside the Lac de Nantua. Turn left at Montréal-la-Cluse; 2km/ 1.2mi after Ceignes, turn right on a road leading off D 2084 and follow it for about 300m/328yd.*

As well as spectacular scenery, the tour includes an important resistance memorial near Cerdon and the village's fascinating copper factory museum.

Grottes du Cerdon

🕐 *Open Apr–Sept.* 🚶 *Guided tours (1hr 30min) Jul–Aug 10am–6pm; Apr–Jun; rest of the year times vary.* 💶 *6€. ℰ04 74 37 36 79. www.grotte-cerdon.com.*

This cave was hollowed out by a subterranean river which has now dried up. The tour takes you past beautiful stalactites and stalagmites into an immense cavern in which a 30m/98ft-high arch is open to the sky. In the past, cheese was left to mature in the cave.

Cave used for maturing cheese, Cerdon

© Hervé Hughes/hemis.fr

Belvédère de Cerdon

Driving towards Cerdon, a viewpoint has been created on the right-hand side of the road near the restaurant. It provides a magnificent panoramic **view**★★ of the Cerdon vineyards and of the Haut-Bugey landscape.

Val d'Enfer

Approaching the village of Cerdon the road continues into a hairpin bend at the Pont de l'Enfer bridge. The village suffered from cruel Nazi reprisals and this bleak site, where significant numbers of Maquis forces would gather, was chosen to build the **Mémorial des maquis de l'Ain et de la résistance** in memory of the 700 forces who died. The imposing monument (by Charles Machet) houses the tomb of the unknown Maquis ard and dominates the cemetery in which lie 88 resistance fighters.

Cerdon★

The pretty village of Cerdon is renowned for its semi-sweet sparkling rosé wines that became AOC in 2009. The picturesque, narrow village streets are decorated with fountains and stone bridges spanning the waterways.

Time has stood still at the copper factory **La Cuivrerie**★ (♿🕐 *open year round;* 🚶 *guided tours (1hr) Jul–Aug daily 9.30am–noon, 2–6.30pm; rest of the year times vary;* 🕐 *closed 1 Jan, 25 Dec;* 💶 *5€;* ℰ*04 74 39 96 44; www.cuivreriedecerdon.com)* that has been in operation in the village since 1854. The museum and tour explain the stages of copper production and include a rare collection of copper pieces. There is a factory shop on-site.

▶ *Continue along D 9084 towards Pont-d'Ain; 6km/3.7mi further on, turn left onto D 36 towards Ambronay.*

Jujurieux

This village, boasting 13 castles, enjoyed an extraordinary boom in the 19C on account of its weaving industry.

In 1835, CJ Bonnet, a silk manufacturer from Lyon, set up the **Soieries Bonnet** (🕐 *open mid-Jun–mid-Sept;* 🚶 *Guided tours (1hr15) daily except Tue 10am–noon, 2–6pm;* 💶 *4.50 €;* ℰ*04 74 37 23 14). Production ended in 2001, and today the site is the heart of a huge conservation project to preserve and document everything to do with the production of fine silks.*

▶ *Follow D 12 towards Corlier and turn right on D 8 to Hauteville-Lompnès.*

Hauteville-Lompnès

The town, on a high plateau (850– 1 200m/2 789–3 937ft), is a popular holiday and sporting resort, known for the quality of its air.

▶ *Take D 21 on the right.*

Gorges de l'Albarine★

As the River Albarine flows southwest, it has cut many impressive gorges along its course. As the road leaves the gorge, you can see the **Cascade de Charabotte**★, formed as the Albarine

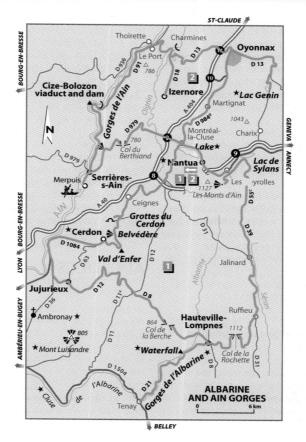

cascades down a 150m/492ft drop on the edge of the Hauteville plateau.

◯ *Return to Hauteville-Lompnès and take D 9 over the Col de la Rochette, altitude 1 112m/3 648ft, as far as Ruffieu; take D 31 N, D 31F at the Jalinard junction, D 39 on the left and D 55C on the right. Then take D 55D through Granges-du-Poizat to reach Les Neyrolles. From here, take D 39 on the left.*

After a few hairpin bends in the road there is a remarkable **view**★★ of the steep slopes of the Nantua cluse and of the lake; this is a magnificent sight at sunset.

◯ *Return to the village of Neyrolles, from where D 39 leads to D 1084, which turns off to the left back to Nantua.*

2 GORGES DE L'AIN AND PLASTICS VALLÉE
ⓘ *See Region map. Allow one day.*

◯ *Leave Nantua along D 1084 to Cluse then drive straight on along D 979 towards Bourg-en-Bresse. Turn right before the bridge onto D 91C to Serrières.*

This tour takes you to the centre of the European plastics industry as well as to some fascinating Gallo-Roman ruins.

Serrières-sur-Ain
Superb scenery round a one-arch bridge spanning the River Ain.

◯ *Follow D 91 towards Merpuis and turn right towards the Merpuis site 2km/1.2mi beyond the bridge then take the road down to the Allement reservoir.*

Boat trips on the River Ain

🕐 *Open May–Sept Mon–Sat. Trips (1hr15) at 3pm and 5pm.* 🚶8€. ⚓ 𝒫*04 74 37 24 35. www.ile-chambod.com.* Take a trip aboard a flat-bottomed boat; hydroelectric installations have considerably modified the landscape.

▶ *Return to Serrières and continue along D 91 which follows the gorge north to Thoirette, past the Viaduc de Cize-Bolozon, with splendid river views.*

Barrage de Cize-Bolozon

Built between 1928 and 1931, the 156m/170yd-long "mobile" dam has an overhead crane. The valley progressively opens up, yet remains impressive due to the majestic mountains on each side.

▶ *At Le Port, do not cross the bridge, but follow D 18 towards Oyonnax. Then take a right to Izernore.*

Izernore, la gallo-romaine

Izarnodurum was a village of the powerful Séquanes tribe of ancient Gaul. On an important trade route, the village reached its apogee in the 2C with the building of a new temple and spa. Along with a few villas and the Quartier des Amphores, these are all the ruins that remain following the barbarian invasions of 4C, 8C and 10C.

Some historians believe that Izarncdorum may have been the famous Alésia but there is no proof. A **museum** presents selected items from the vast Izernore collection.

Oyonnax

Once famous for its wooden combs, Oyonnax is today the heart of the European plastics industry. The name Plastics Vallée was coined in 1986, to group together specialist plastics manufacturers within a 50km/31mi radius.

The collection of the **Musée du Peigne et de la Plasturgie** (♿ 🕐 *open Jul–Sept Mon–Sat 2–6pm; Oct–Jun Tue–Sat 2–6pm;* 🕐 *closed public holidays;* 🚶*3.80 €;* 𝒫*04 74 81 96 82 www.tourisme-oyonnax.com*) gives a good overview of the evolution and variety

of products manufactured in Oyonnax. Exhibits include combs made of boxwood, horn and Celluloid, and the machines that made them.

▶ *From the town centre the Lac Genin is sign-posted. Take the D 13 and after 7km turn right to the lake.*

Lac Genin★

Much frequented by the residents of Oyonnax, this small lake is in an attractive **position**★ surrounded by meadows and wooded hills. Its shady banks offer pleasant walking. The lake offers skating in winter and supervised swimming in summer.

ADDRESSES

🛏 STAY

🛏 **Lac Hôtel** – *22 av. de Bresse, 01460 Montréal-la-Cluse.* 𝒫*04 74 76 29 68. www.lac-hotel.com. Closed 26 Dec–1 Jan. 28 rooms.* 🍽*6 €.* Reasonably priced, clean, basic rooms soundproofed against nearby traffic noise, and internet access.

🛏🛏 **L'Embarcadère** – *av. du Lac.* 𝒫*04 74 75 22 88. www.hotelembarcadere.com. Closed 20 Dec–5 Jan. 49 rooms.* 🍽*9 €. Restaurant*🛏🛏. Pleasant menus and comfortable rooms a stone's throw from pretty Nantua Lake.

🍴 EAT

🍴 **Auberge du Lac Genin** – *01130 Charix, 16km/9.9mi NE of Nantua by D 74 until you reach Molet then D 95 up to the lake.* 𝒫*04 74 75 52 50. Closed 17 Oct–3 Dec, Sun evenings and Mon.* Enjoy the blissful quiet of this lakeside mountain inn in the heart of woodland. Bedrooms are decorated in the rustic style. Grilled meat is the speciality of the house.

🍴🍴 **Auberge Les Gentianes** – *01130 Lalleyriat, 12km/7.5mi E of Nantua by N 84 and D 55B.* 𝒫*04 74 75 31 80. Closed 5–31 Jan, Sun evenings, Mon and Tue.* Charming house with a terrace serving deliciously fresh produce.

Bellegarde-sur-Valserine

Défilé de l'Écluse

Situated close to the Swiss border and the Jura mountains, this small industrial town is named for the gushing mountain stream La Valserine which meets the Rhône here. Well placed on the route from Lyon to the Mont Blanc tunnel, the town only developed in the 19C after the arrival of the railways and the introduction of electricity. Bellegarde-sur-Valserine is at the heart of a region that offers visitors a wealth of fine excursions.

▶ **Population:** 10 846
♿ **Michelin Map:** 328: H-4.
🅸 **Info:** 24 pl. Victor Bérard, 01202 Bellegarde-Sur-Valserine. ℘04 50 48 48 68. www.ot-bellegarde01.fr.
◗ **Location:** To the north lies the scenic Valserine Valley, best explored from south to north in the afternoon. There are more areas to explore by car to the south and southwest.

LA VALSERINE

The River Valserine is 50km/31mi long and drops 1 000m/3 280ft from its source to its junction with the Rhône at Bellegarde-sur-Valserine. This mountain stream runs through a charming valley known as Valmijoux bounded on both sides by mountain ranges with two high peaks almost facing each other. The **Crêt de la Neige** (1 717m/5 633ft), the highest summit of the Jura mountains, is so called because it retains a few patches of snow on its north face all year. Its "twin" on the other side of the valley is the **Crêt de Chalam** (1 545m/4 069ft).

To see the **Berges de la Valserine**★, from the town centre (tourist office), follow D 1084 towards Lyon. Park just behind the railway viaduct (rue Louis-Dumont). 🚶 The Valserine skirts the town but, because of its steep banks, it was difficult to reach in the past. A path from the viaduct now enables visitors to walk all the way to the Pertes de la Valserine *(allow 2hrs there and back)*.

For the **Pertes de la Valserine**★ head north out of Bellegarde along N 84, pass beneath the railway line and continue for 2km/1.2mi. There is parking on the right-hand side of the road. Follow the path *(45min there and back)* down through the undergrowth, with steps cut out. It leads to a curious spot where the Valserine disappears from view amid a setting of rocky crevices and

great cauldrons *(oulles)* scoured out in the rocks by the river. The waterfall is a little further upstream.

🚗 DRIVING TOURS

DÉFILÉ DE L'ÉCLUSE★
32km/20mi circuit. ♿ See Region map.

◗ *Leave Bellegarde E along N 206.*

This picturesque transverse valley separates the Grand Crêt d'Eau and Montagne de Vuache ranges. The river, the D 1206 Franco-Swiss highway and the scenic D 908A all run through the valley.

◗ *Beyond Longeray, just before the entrance to the tunnel, turn right towards Fort de l'Écluse.*

Fort l'Écluse★
🕐*Open mid-Jun–mid-Sept daily 10am–6.30pm. (Guided tours 2hrs Sat–Sun 4pm).* ≈*5 €.* ℘*04 50 56 73 63. www.fortlecluse.fr.*
This remarkable fort was built high above the Rhône between 1820 and 1840. Its strategic position meant it was bitterly fought over in 1944. It is a hard climb (1 165 steps, 1hr up and down) to the top, but the view is worth it.

◗ *Go through the tunnel and continue along D 1206 to the right; in Chevrier, turn right onto D 908A and return to Bellegarde via D 1508.*

FROM BELLEGARDE TO THE COL DE LA FAUCILLE

See Region map. Allow a half day.
Leave Bellegarde-sur-Valserine on the D 1084. 4 km/2.5mi after Châtillon-de-Michaille, turn right on the D 14, then at Montanges, take a right on the D 14A.

Pont des Pierres★

This elegant and daring bridge crosses the river between Montanges and La Mulaz. The single arch straddles the gorge and presents an impressive spectacle in rainy weather: the Valserine, covered with foam and squeezed by steep vertical walls, is joined by noisy cascades of water hurtling down from both sides, dragging stone and earth behind them.

Défilé de Sous-Balme

The road climbs back up the valley alongside the wooded cliff faces. Between Chézery-Forens and Lélex, the Valserine crosses the wild Sous-Balme gorge, which stretches for 5 km/3 mi between the crêt de Chalam and le Reculet.

Barrage de Génissiat★

Until the Génissiat dam was opened in January 1948, the waters from the Rhône river, flowing from Bellegarde, would disappear into a 60m/197ft-deep cleft. It was known as the "loss" of the Rhône. The site has been transformed into a reservoir-lake, 23km/14mi long, complete with pleasure boats in the summer season. The lake lies in the bottom of the valley, and below Bellegarde it fills the gorges that have been cut out by the river, which at its narrowest point runs between two cliffs just 1.70m/5.6ft apart.

SOME BACKGROUND

Le Rhône jurassien – From its source in Switzerland at 2 200m/7 218ft altitude in the glacial cirques of the

Monts Jura (*see p396*)

Follow D 991 to the village of Mijoux. Then take D 936 up through hairpin bends to the **col de la Faucille★★** (*see p398*), known for its spectacular view over the Jura. Visit the **Petit Mont-Rond** for another fine panorama from the Jura to the banks of Lake Geneva.

ADDRESSES

STAY

Hotel Hermance – *19 r. Bertola. ℘04 50 56 28 04. 17 rooms. ⌑7 €.* Modest hotel in the centre of town that is currently being renovated and will soon have 25 rooms. Choose a quieter room on the 4th floor (elevator). Owners live on-site.

Hôtel Le Sorgia – *01200 Lancrans, 2km/1.2mi N of Bellegarde by D 16. ℘04 50 48 15 81. Closed 22 Aug–16 Sept, 20 Dec–6 Jan, Sat lunchtime, Sun evenings and Mon. 17 rooms. ⌑6.50 €. Restaurant.* Simple, carefully kept rooms in a pretty family house. Country cooking is offered in the rustic dining room or on the terrace.

- **Michelin Map:** 328: H4.
- **Location:** The dam is 13km/8mi south of Bellegarde-sur-Valserine, following D 25, D 991 to Billiat, then D 72A. Attractive views from the top of the installation.
- **Don't Miss:** The impressive structure at a height of 104m/340ft and the evacuation channels from the Rhône at a high water period.
- **Timing:** The dam is most impressive in early summer when the evacuation channels are working at full flow.
- **Kids:** They will be enchanted by the "ski jump" which gives rise to a huge spray of foam.

Oberland, between the Furka and Grimsel passes, until it arrives at Lake Geneva (alt 309m/1 014ft), the Rhône rushes along like a torrent. Muddy and stony when it enters the lake, it re-emerges remarkably clear. The French Rhône is almost like a new river that has just formed. Crossing through the Jura its drop is seven times less than that in Switzerland. However, its passage remains uneven, and depending on the season, its height varies between 0.3m/1ft and 5m/16.4ft.

On leaving Geneva, the Rhône is joined by the full and fast-flowing Arve, bringing glacial waters from Mont Blanc. 30km/18.6mi on it collides with the steep, high barrier of the Jura that forces it to cross the parallel mountain chains by a succession of transverse valleys. The first of these valleys is the défilé de l'Écluse (⌖ see Bellegarde-sur-Valserine). At Geneva the Rhône is 350m/1 148ft wide, but here it shrinks to 20m/65ft in order to force through a passage.

Power stations – In France the development of the river is in the hands of the Compagnie Nationale du Rhône. Between Geneva and Lyon, nine power stations use the Rhône: Verbois and Chancy-Pougny in Switzerland and a further seven in France: Génissiat, Seyssel, Chautagne, Belley, Brégnier, Sault-Brenaz and Cusset-Villeurbanne.

VISIT

Once nicknamed "the angry bull", today the Rhône is harnessed by a series of dams. The Génissiat dam is 104m/341ft high, 140m/459ft long and 100m/328ft thick at the bottom and is a gravity dam, meaning that its own weight resists the force of the water.

It retains 53 million cu m/ 1 480 million cu ft of water and extends 23km/14.3mi to the Swiss border.

The water flow of the Rhône can increase from 140 to 2 800 cu m/4 945 to 98 900 cu ft, so to protect against

the dangerous water level rises, two evacuation channels have been built. The right-hand channel is in the open air and known as the "saut à ski" or ski jump; the one on the left bank is underground. When it's working (usually in early summer) the "saut à ski" emits a dramatic spray of foam. A walking circuit is signposted between the "saut à ski", the château and the dam, with picnic places and view points.

🚗 DRIVING TOUR

Le Tour de Retord
73km/45mi circuit. Allow 3hrs.

From the Génissiat dam, drive south over the Col de Richemont, through the undulating, densely wooded area of la Michaille, with occasional glimpses of the Rhône valley and the mountains. After the pass, the Haut-Volromey presents a pleasant pastoral contrast. Once you reach Hotonnes, head towards le Grand-Abergement and onto the Plateau de Retord. To reach the highest part take a right at La Manche and you will find a **panorama**★★ over the Alps (Mont Blanc to the southeast), la Valserine, le défilé de l'Ecluse and the Bourget lake. The green landscape gives a sense of isolation, and if you visit at the end of May you will find a vast area of daffodils. Continue on to Bellegarde to return to the Génissiat dam.

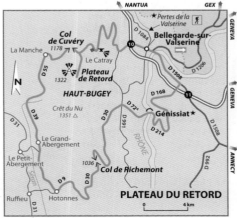

Grand Colombier★★★

This is the highest peak (1 531km/ 5 023ft) in the Bugey region, at the tip of the long mountain chain separating the Rhône from the Valromey. The arduous climb offers exceptional panoramic views.

⌚ **Michelin Map:** 328: H-5.

🏠 **Info:** 6 r. de la Mairie, 01350 Culoz. ℘04 79 87 00 30.

📍 **Location:** The road climbs from Virieu to a parking area, from which the mountain is accessible on foot. From there you can drive along a ridge up to another viewpoint. After that, there is a steep descent into Culoz.

👁 **Don't Miss:** The panoramas from the summit and from the Observatoir du Fenestrez are well worth the arduous climbs.

🚗 DRIVING TOURS

FROM VIRIEU-LE-PETIT TO CULOZ
29km/18mi. Allow 2hrs.

After leaving Virieu, the road climbs the slopes of the Grand Colombier along a series of hairpin bends. Once it reaches the forest, the road passes through stands of fir trees. The gradient becomes 12 percent (1:8), then 14 percent (1:7) and finally even 19 percent (1:5). After passing the Lochieu road on the left, it comes to beautiful mountain pastures at La Grange de Fromentel, from which there is a good view of the Champagne-en-Valromey valley.

Climbing about 1km/0.5mi further up through the forest, the road branches off to the left towards the Colombier service station and hotel; the last bend up the mountain leads to the pass.

Grand Colombier★★★ – From the car park, there are easy footpaths up to both Grand Colombier peaks. On the rounded northern peak there is a cross and a viewing table *(30min round trip on foot)*; the south peak ends in a steep crest on the west face of the mountain *(45min round trip on foot)*.

There are vast panoramas of the Jura, the Dombes, the Rhône Valley, the Massif Central and the Alps; in fine weather three lakes can be seen twinkling in the sun – Geneva, Bourget and Annecy.

Back in the car, on the east face of the mountain, the road runs through pastures before entering the forest. At a hairpin bend 5km/3mi from the Grand Colombier summit, take the right turn for the **Observatoire du Fenestrez★★**.

A footpath leads to the edge of the cliff from where you can see the Culoz plain

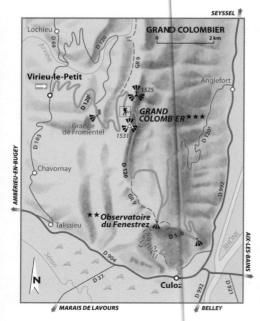

about 900m/2 950ft below. The Lac de Bourget and the city of Chambéry can be seen to the southeast, Lake Annecy to the east, and beyond, the view stretches as far as the Alps. Return to the main road and turn right (15 percent/1:7 gradient downhill).

After 4km/2.5mi keep right towards Culoz when the road forks left to Anglefort. There are impressive views of the Bugey region, the Rhône Valley and the Culoz plain on the way (13 hairpin bends).

LE VALROMEY
72km/45mi – allow 6hrs.

This drive extends the tour of le Grand Colombier to include the valley of Valromey, part of the Haut-Bugey. At Lochieu, the **Musée du Bugey-Valromey** presents scenes of everyday local and religious life, as well as evoking the early pioneers of hiking and other sports. From here, take the steep road over **Le Grand Colombier** to Culoz, and on to the **Réserve Naturelle du Marais de Lavours**, where you can explore the marsh on foot, or at the visitor centre.

EXCURSION
Seyssel
Once a major port on the River Rhône, Seyssel is now better known for its excellent white and sparkling wines. The **Barrage de Seyssel** *(1.5km/0.9mi upstream)* was built to regulate the Rhône downstream of Génissiat. Above its lake is the spur on which stands **Bassy Church**.

ADDRESSES

⌂ STAY
⊜ **Au Vieux Tilleul** – *01260 Belmont-Luthézieu, 10.5km/6.5mi W of Virieu-le-Petit by D 69F then D 54C. ℘04 79 87 64 51. Closed Tue lunch, Sun evening and Mon Oct–Apr.* ▣. *16 rooms.* ⊜8 €. *Restaurant*⊜⊜. Elegant décor, comfortable, well-kept rooms and kind hospitality will ensure that your stay here is a most pleasant one. Superb views of the forest and the Grand Colombier. The kitchen offers inspired cooking.

Belley

This peaceful town lies in a little valley watered by the Furan in the heart of the beautiful Bugey region. One of Belley's claims to fame is being birthplace of France's great epicure Jean-Anthelme Brillat-Savarin.

A BIT OF HISTORY
The Physiology of Taste – When Jean-Anthelme Brillat-Savarin was born in Belley in 1755, at 62 Grande Rue *(courtyard open to the public)*, he was destined be a lawyer like his father. In 1789, he was elected deputy of the States General, but five years later he was forced to flee, first to Switzerland, then to the US. He returned to France in 1796. In his free time he wrote, initially legal or political works, then the little masterpiece which earned him his fame: *The Physiology of Taste*. In 30 essays he examines the various aspects of and issues associ-

▸ **Population:** 8 466
⦿ **Michelin Map:** 328: H-6.
▤ **Info:** 34 Grande Rue, 01300 Belley. ℘04 79 81 29 06. www.cc-belley-bas-bugey.com.
◗ **Location:** An appealing base from which to explore the surrounding attractions of the scenic Bas Bugey.

ated with good living and good food; philosophical principles appear side by side with reflections on gluttony, sleep and dreams.

TOWN
Cathédrale St-Jean-Baptiste
◷*Open daily 9am–noon and 2–6pm.* Although the cathedral was almost entirely rebuilt in the 19C, it still has its original north portal, dating probably

from the 14C: a door beneath a pointed arch, between two blind arcades.
Inside, the six-bayed **chancel** (1473) and the triforium with its pretty open-work balustrades are also original.

Palais épiscopal
A bishop was in residence in Belley from 555. The 18C palace is thought to have been built to designs by Soufflot. It now houses the library, a music school and a concert and exhibition hall.

WALK
Take D 992 on the left which runs along-side the canal, then take D 37 on the right. After Nattages, follow the direction to Chemillieu. The view opens up to the Yenne basin, the Dent du Chat, Mont Revard (glimpsed through the gap of the Col du Chat), and the Chartreuse mountain range (the Grand-Som and Grande Sure summits).
Leave the car near the wash-house in the hamlet of Nant. Take the tarmac path on the immediate left, which soon becomes a stone track along the rock face to the top of the gorge.

Défilé de Pierre-Châtel
 1hr 30min there and back on foot
There is a **view**★ of the ravine from the top of a rocky outcrop left of the path. The Rhône has found a crack in the Jura mountains' armour; it cuts into the mountain range at the Col de Pierre-Châtel, forming a gorge, then flows on into a valley which it follows as far as its confluence with the Guiers. The build-ings of an old Carthusian monastery tower above the ravine. The **Chartreuse de Pierre-Châtel** *(founded 1383)* soon had fortifications added to it, before being fully converted into a fortress in the 17C, when it found itself situated on the frontier, as Bresse and Bugey regions were handed over to France.

DRIVING TOUR

LA MONTAGNE D'IZIEU
45km/28mi circuit.
Allow 2hrs 30min.

 Leave Belley on the D 992 (south).

Bypassing the Izieu mountain, the road follows the Rhône, that changes direction again. Joined by the Guiers, it heads northwest in a gap in the plateau.

Izieu
This peaceful village was the setting for a tragic event of the Second World War. Forty-four Jewish children who had found refuge there, and the adults with them, were betrayed and sent to Ausch-witz. The **Musée-Mémorial** *(open mid-Jun–mid-Sept 10am–6.30pm every day. Rest of the year 9am–5pm except Sat 2pm–6pm and Sun 10am–6pm; closed weekends in Dec and Jan; 7 €; 04 79 87 21 05. www.memorialalizieu.eu)* brings to life the daily routine in this short-lived safe haven and the trials of Nazi occupation.

 Return to La Bruyère and turn right onto the old D 19 through the villages of Brégnier-Cordon and Glandieu.

Cascade de Glandieu
The water from this waterfall is used on weekdays by two hydroelectric plants.

 Turn right on the D 10, then take a left on D 24 to Ambléon.

Trois lacs
On a clear day, stop at a bend in the road to the **Ambléon** lake, for a **view** over the Grand Colombier and Mont Blanc. Narrow bendy lanes lead to the lakes **Arborias** and **Armaille** where you will find good picnic places.

ADDRESSES

STAY
 Chambre d'Hôte Les Charmettes – *La Vellaz, St-Martin-de-Bavel, 01510 Virieu-le-Grand, 11km/6.8mi N of Belley by N 504 until you reach Chazey-Bons, then D 31C. 04 79 87 32 18. 3 rooms.* This charming Bugey farmhouse has converted its stables into pretty, comfortable bedrooms. Cooking facilities are available for residents.

🛏🛏 **Chambre d'Hôte Ferme des Grands Hutains** – *Le Petit Brens, 01300 Brens, 3km/1.9mi S of Belley by D 31A.* ☎*04 79 81 90 95. Closed Nov–20 Dec and Sun.* 🛏 *4 rooms. Meals* 🍽. A haven of peace with a wonderful mountain view. Enjoy meals under the oak tree in summer or by the fire-place in winter, with home-grown vegetables to accompany local farm meats. The cosy rooms beneath the eaves are for non-smokers only.

🍴/ EAT

🛏🛏 **Auberge La Fine Fourchette** – *D 1504 towards Virignin.* ☎*04 79 81 59 33. Closed 22–31 Aug, Sun evenings and Mon.* Hearty and classic cuisine is offered in a hunting lodge-type setting. From the large bay windows you can see the Rhône canal and the town of Belley, but opt for the terrace if weather permits as the dining room is rather dark.

Ambérieu-en-Bugey

As the home of the famous airman Antoine de Saint-Exupéry and the contemporary Olympic swimmer Laure Manaudou, it is the worlds of sport and transport that lie at the heart of Ambérieu. Its location on a crossroads makes it easy to explore the valleys of the Bas Bugey to find out about the history and industrial heritage of this busy thoroughfare.

EXCURSIONS

Mont Luisandre★

🚶 *1hr 15min there and back on foot.*
Take the steep, stone track between two houses in the village, to the left of the wash-house. A 15min walk brings you to a steep bank, where you take the path to the right which leads up through meadows to the summit.
There is a cross at the summit (alt 805m/ 2 641ft). Walk round the grove to obtain a sweeping **view**★ of the Château des Allymes on one of the spurs of the Bugey, the Dombes plateau, the confluence of the Ain and the Rhône and the wooded summits of the Bugey region, slashed by the deep gorges of the Albarine.

Château des Allymes

🚶 *30min there and back on foot from Bréy-de-Vent.*
🕐*Open Jul–Aug daily 10am–12.30pm, 1.30–7pm. Rest of the year times vary.*

- 🗺 **Michelin Map:** 328: G4.
- ℹ **Info:** R. Alexandre-Bérard, 01500 Ambérieu-en-Bugey. ☎04 74 38 18 17. www.ville-amberieuenbugey.fr.
- ▶ **Location:** West of A 42 the D 1084, D 1075 et D 1504 meet at Ambérieu.
- 🕐 **Timing:** Explore the surroundings rather than the centre of Ambérieu. Allow half a day.
- 👁 **Don't Miss:** The walk to Mont Luisandre, the *Cluses* (Gorges) and the little lanes in Saint-Sorlin.
- 👪 **Kids:** The museum of traditional activities in Saint-Rambert-en-Bugey.

🎫*4€.* ☎*04 74 38 06 07. www.allymes.net.*
This fortified château was laid out as a square. The courtyard in its centre is protected by a solid, square keep in one corner, and a round tower with a lovely **timber roof**★ in the other.

🚗 DRIVING TOUR

BAS-BUGEY

St-Rambert-en-Bugey
This little industrial town in a green valley on the banks of the Albarine houses a **Musée des Traditions bugistes** (🕐*open Tue–Sat 9am–noon, 2–5pm,*

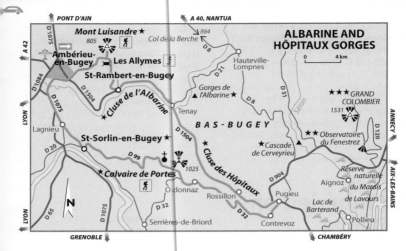

*Sun 10am–noon, Mon 2–5pm; ⊖3€;
𝒞04 74 36 32 86)* in which traditional
industries are on display along with a
reconstruction of the inside of a house
from days gone by.

The road between Argis and Tenay, at
the bottom of the cluse, passes one factory after another. These used to specialise in silk by-products, but now produce
nylon and its derivatives.

Cluse de l'Albarine★

This gorge cuts across from Ambérieu
to Tenay. The Albarine, the railway line
and the road wind along together between the steep slopes on either side.
The wooded upper slopes culminate in

limestone ridges in which the rock strata
run diagonally and at times almost verti-
cally between crumbling boulders.

Cluse des Hôpitaux★

This gorge opens up between Tenay and
Pugieu. Its steep rocky sides, taller
and craggier than those of the Cluse de
l'Albarine, and its plunging gorge give
the landscape a bleak and rugged air,
accentuated by the almost complete
absence of houses.

Calvaire de Portes★

The summit on which this Calvary
stands (alt 1 025m/3 363ft) at the tip of
a rocky spur can be seen from a long

Fresco of St Christopher, St-Sorlin-en-Bugey

way off. From the viewing table, the view encompasses the small, pointed mountain called Dent du Chat (cat's tooth; alt 1 390m/ 4 203ft), to the left the towering form of the Grand Colombier (alt 1 531m/5 023ft) and to the right the plain through which the Ain flows on its way to the Rhône.

St-Sorlin-en-Bugey★

This village occupies a picturesque site at the foot of a cliff which overlooks a curve in the Rhône Valley. Wander through the narrow streets and admire the carefully restored houses on the way up to the church; at the intersection with the montée des Sœurs, note the fine 16C **fresco depicting St Christopher**. The church has seen several restoration projects and extensions. The most important improvement restored the interior structure by raising the archway and erecting tall Gothic pillars supporting a connecting archway.

Ambronay

Ambronay developed around a Benedictine abbey founded in the 9C by St Bernard, one of Charlemagne's knights (ruins of the Carolingian church have been found under the choir and chancel).

ANCIENNE ABBAYE

Open Apr–Sept 9am–6pm; Oct–Mar 9am–4pm. 04 74 34 52 72. www.ambronay.org.
The church, cloister and chapter-house, as well as most of the conventual buildings, remain of the **abbey**, which has been rebuilt several times.

Church★

This dates mainly from the 13C and 15C. Many figures on the façade were destroyed during the Revolution.
The lintel of the doorway on the left represents scenes from the Life of the Virgin. The Resurrection of the Dead can be seen on the lintel of the central doorway *(13C, extensively restored)*.
The **Chapelle Ste-Catherine**, north of the chancel, contains the 15C **tomb★** of Abbot Jacques de Mauvoisin, who had the church restored.

Cloisters

Access through a door in the south side aisle.
The cloisters, a 15C construction, consist of arcades with graceful tracery, surmounted by a gallery reached by the substantially restored Louis XIV corner staircase.

- ▶ **Population:** 2 241
- ⚙ **Michelin Map:** 328: F-4.
- 🛈 **Info:** 10 pl, Xavier Bichat, 01450 Poncin. 04 74 37 23 14. www.paysducerdin-valleedelain.fr.
- ◖ **Location**: 6km/3.7mi N of Ambérieu.
- ⌖ **Don't Miss:** The Ancienne Abbaye and in particular the renowned Baroque music festival that takes place in the abbey each year from mid-September to mid-October.

Cloisters, Ancienne Abbaye

G. Magnin/MICHELIN

INDEX

INDEX

INDEX

INDEX

INDEX

INDEX

♀/ EAT

INDEX

MAPS AND PLANS

MAP LEGEND

★★★ **Highly recommended**

★★ **Recommended**

★ **Interesting**

Tourism

Sightseeing route with departure point indicated	AZ B Map co-ordinates locating sights
Ecclesiastical building	Tourist information
Synagogue – Mosque	Historic house, castle – Ruins
Building (with main entrance)	Dam – Factory or power station
Statue, small building	Fort – Cave
Wayside cross	Prehistoric site
Fountain	Viewing table – View
Fortified walls – Tower – Gate	Miscellaneous sight

Recreation

Racecourse	Waymarked footpath
Skating rink	Outdoor leisure park/centre
Outdoor, indoor swimming pool	Theme/Amusement park
Marina, moorings	Wildlife/Safari park, zoo
Mountain refuge hut	Gardens, park, arboretum
Overhead cable-car	Aviary, bird sanctuary
Tourist or steam railway	

Additional symbols

Motorway (unclassified)	Post office – Telephone centre
Junction: complete, limited	Covered market
Pedestrian street	Barracks
Unsuitable for traffic, street subject to restrictions	Swing bridge
Steps – Footpath	Quarry – Mine
Railway – Coach station	Ferry (river and lake crossings)
Funicular – Rack-railway	Ferry services: Passengers and cars
Tram – Metro, underground	Foot passengers only
Bert (R.)... Main shopping street	③ Access route number common to MICHELIN maps and town plans

Abbreviations and special symbols

A	Agricultural office (Chambre d'agriculture)	P	Local authority offices (Préfecture, sous-préfecture)
C	Chamber of commerce (Chambre de commerce)	POL.	Police station (Police)
H	Town hall (Hôtel de ville)		Police station (Gendarmerie)
J	Law courts (Palais de justice)	T	Theatre (Théâtre)
M	Museum (Musée)	U	University (Université)
			Hotel
			Park and Ride

Some town plans are extracts from plans used in the Green Guides to the regions of France.

COMPANION PUBLICATIONS

REGIONAL AND LOCAL MAPS

✦ To make the most of your journey, travel with Michelin maps at a scale of 1:250 000 – 300 000: Regional maps nos. 519, 514, 515, 520 and 523 and the new local maps, which are illustrated on the map of France below. For each of the sites listed in this guide, map references are indicated to help you find your location on these maps.

✦ In addition to identifying the nature of the main and secondary roads, Michelin maps show castles, churches, scenic view points, megalithic monuments, swimming beaches, golf courses, race tracks and more.

MAPS OF FRANCE

✦ And remember to travel with the latest edition of the map of France no 721, which gives an overall view of the region of Burgundy-Jura, and the main access roads which connect it to the rest of France. The entire country is mapped at a 1:1 000 000 scale and clearly shows the main road network. Convenient Atlas formats (spiral, hard cover, "mini" and motorways) are also available.

INTERNET

✦ Michelin is pleased to offer a route-planning service on the Internet: **www.ViaMichelin.com.** Choose the shortest route, a route without tolls, or the Michelin recommended route to your destination; you can also access information about hotels and restaurants from The Red Guide, and tourist sites from The Green Guide.

✦ There are a number of useful maps and plans in the guide, listed in the table of contents.

You know
the Green Guide

...Do you really
know **MICHELIN**?

● Data 31/12/2009

The world No.1 in tires
with 16.3% of the market

A business presence in over **170 countries**

A manufacturing footprint
at the heart of markets

In 2009 **72** industrial sites in **19** countries produced:

- **150** million tires
- **10** million maps and guides

Highly international **teams**

Over **109 200** employees* from all cultures on all continents

including **6 000** people employed in R&D centers

in Europe, the US and Asia.

*102 692 full-time equivalent staff

The Michelin Group
at a glance

Michelin competes

At the end of 2009

Le Mans 24-hour race
12 consecutive years of victories

Endurance 2009
- 6 victories on 6 stages
in Le Mans Series
- 12 victories on 12 stages
in American Le Mans Series

Paris-Dakar
Since the beginning of the event,
the Michelin group has won
in all categories

Moto endurance
2009 World Champion

Trial
Every World Champion title
since 1981 (except 1992)

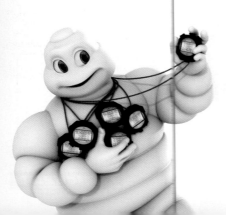

Michelin, established close to its customers

○ **72 plants in 19 countries**
- Algeria
- Brazil
- Canada
- China
- Colombia
- France
- Germany
- Hungary
- Italy
- Japan
- Mexico
- Poland
- Romania
- Russia
- Serbia
- Spain
- Thailand
- UK
- USA

● **A Technology Center spread over 3 continents**
- Asia
- Europe
- North America

◐ **Natural rubber plantations**
- Brazil

Our mission

To make a sustainable contribution to progress in the mobility of goods and people by enhancing freedom of movement, safety, efficiency and the pleasure of travelling.

Michelin committed to environmental-friendliness

Michelin, world leader in low rolling resistance tires, actively reduces fuel consumption and vehicle gas emission.

For its products, Michelin develops state-of-the-art technologies in order to:
- Reduce fuel consumption, while improving overall tire performance.
- Increase life cycle to reduce the number of tires to be processed at the end of their useful lives;
- Use raw materials which have a low impact on the environment.

Furthermore, at the end of 2008, 99.5% of tire production in volume was carried out in ISO 14001* certified plants.

Michelin is committed to implementing recycling channels for end-of-life tires.

*environmental certification

Passenger Car Light Truck

Truck

Michelin
a key mobility enabler

Earthmover

Aircraft

Agricultural

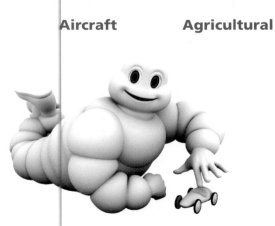

Two-wheel   **Distribution**

Partnered with vehicle manufacturers, in tune with users,
active in competition and in all the distribution channels,
Michelinis continually innovating to promote mobility today
and to invent that of tomorrow.

Maps and   **ViaMichelin,**   **Michelin**
Guides   travel   **Lifestyle,**
                      assistance   for your travel
                      services   accessories

MICHELIN
plays on balanced performance

● **Long tire life**

◉ **Fuel savings**

○ **Safety on the road**

... MICHELIN tires provide you with the best performance, without making a single sacrifice.

The MICHELIN tire pure technology

1 **Tread**
A thick layer of rubber
provides contact with the ground.
It has to channel water away
and last as long as possible.

2 **Crown plies**
This double or triple reinforced belt
has both vertical flexibility
and high lateral rigidity.
It provides the steering capacity.

3 **Sidewalls**
These cover and protect the textile casing
whose role is to attach the tire tread
to the wheel rim.

4 **Bead area for attachment to the rim**
Its internal bead wire
clamps the tire firmly
against the wheel rim.

5 **Inner liner**
This makes the tire
almost totally impermeable
and maintains the correct inflation pressure.

Heed
the MICHELIN Man's advice

To improve safety: I drive with the correct tire pressure

I check the tire pressure every month

I have my car regularly serviced

I regularly check the appearance

of my tires (wear, deformation)

I am responsive behind the wheel

I change my tires according to the season

www.michelin.com
www.michelin.(your country extension – e.g. .fr for France)

VIN DE BOURGOGNE

CHABLIS

APPELLATION CHABLIS CONTRÔLÉE

Jean-Pierre Alexandre Ellevin

MIS EN BOUTEILLE PAR JEAN-PIERRE ET ALEXANDRE ELLEVIN
À 89800 CHICHÉE (FRANCE) TEL. 03 86 42 44 24

12,5% vol. - 750 ml

PRODUCE OF FRANCE - CONTIENT DES SULFITES

Michelin Apa Publications Ltd

A joint venture between Michelin and Langenscheidt

58 Borough High Street, London SE1 1XF, United Kingdom

No part of this publication may be reproduced in any form
without the prior permission of the publisher.

© 2011 Michelin Apa Publications Ltd
ISBN 978-1-907099-09-0
Printed: March 2012
Printed and bound in France - N° 201203.0218

Although the information in this guide was believed by the authors and publisher to be accurate
and current at the time of publication, they cannot accept responsibility for any inconvenience,
loss, or injury sustained by any person relying on information or advice contained in this guide.
Things change over time and travellers should take steps to verify and confirm information,
especially time-sensitive information related to prices, hours of operation, and availability.